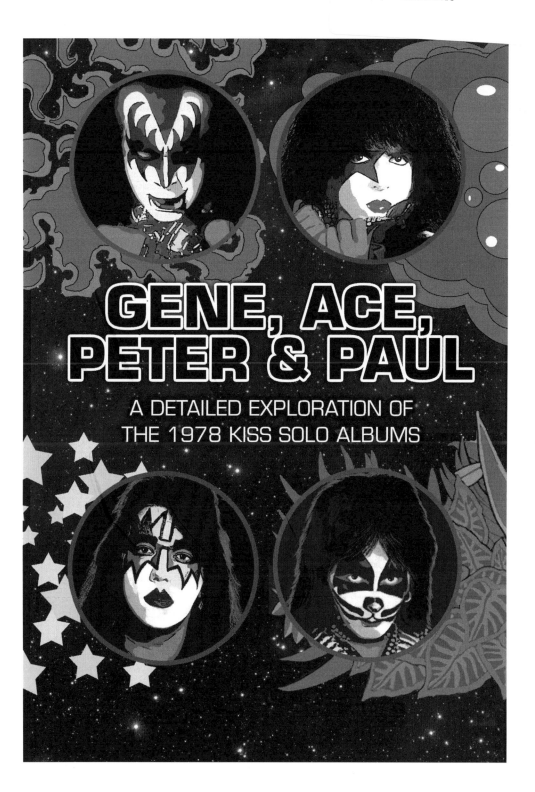

GENE, ACE, PETER & PAUL

A DETAILED EXPLORATION OF THE 1978 KISS SOLO ALBUMS

GENE, ACE, PETER & PAUL

A detailed exploration of the 1978 KISS solo albums

By Julian Gill

Second Printing
ISBN-10: 0-9822537-6-1
ISBN-13: 978-0-9822537-6-2

"Never have all the members of an ongoing rock 'n' roll band released their own albums simultaneously. Never have the members of a band taken a touring break specifically to grant each one the time to develop his own individual statement... KISS is more than a rock 'n' roll band. KISS is an institution, and to its fans, inspiration. The albums were done to prove that there is a place in a group for its members' unique temperaments to be expressed, without altering that group's inner harmony. When the KISS members decided to create their own albums, they contacted many friends and colleagues outside the band to play at the sessions" (PR).

In memory of Neil Bogart, William M. Aucoin and Sean Delaney: Visionaries, dreamers and believers in the impossible, without whom...

Editor's note: The editing of the interviews comprising this work has been approached with a desire to leave the original intent and "voice" of the interviewee intact, even at the cost of correct grammar. Except in the most egregious cases, a bare minimum of correction has been done, and in some cases the ubiquitous [sic] has been inserted, out of respect to what are in essence transcriptions of conversations converted into a more readable form. Hopefully, the unique character of each interviewee's "voice" is preserved, and won't cause too much reader discomfort! Please also consider that one person conducted and transcribed the vast majority of these interviews, and another is taking on the task of editing the work. Therefore, only the former would recall the nuances only present in the original tone of the conversation.

CONTENTS

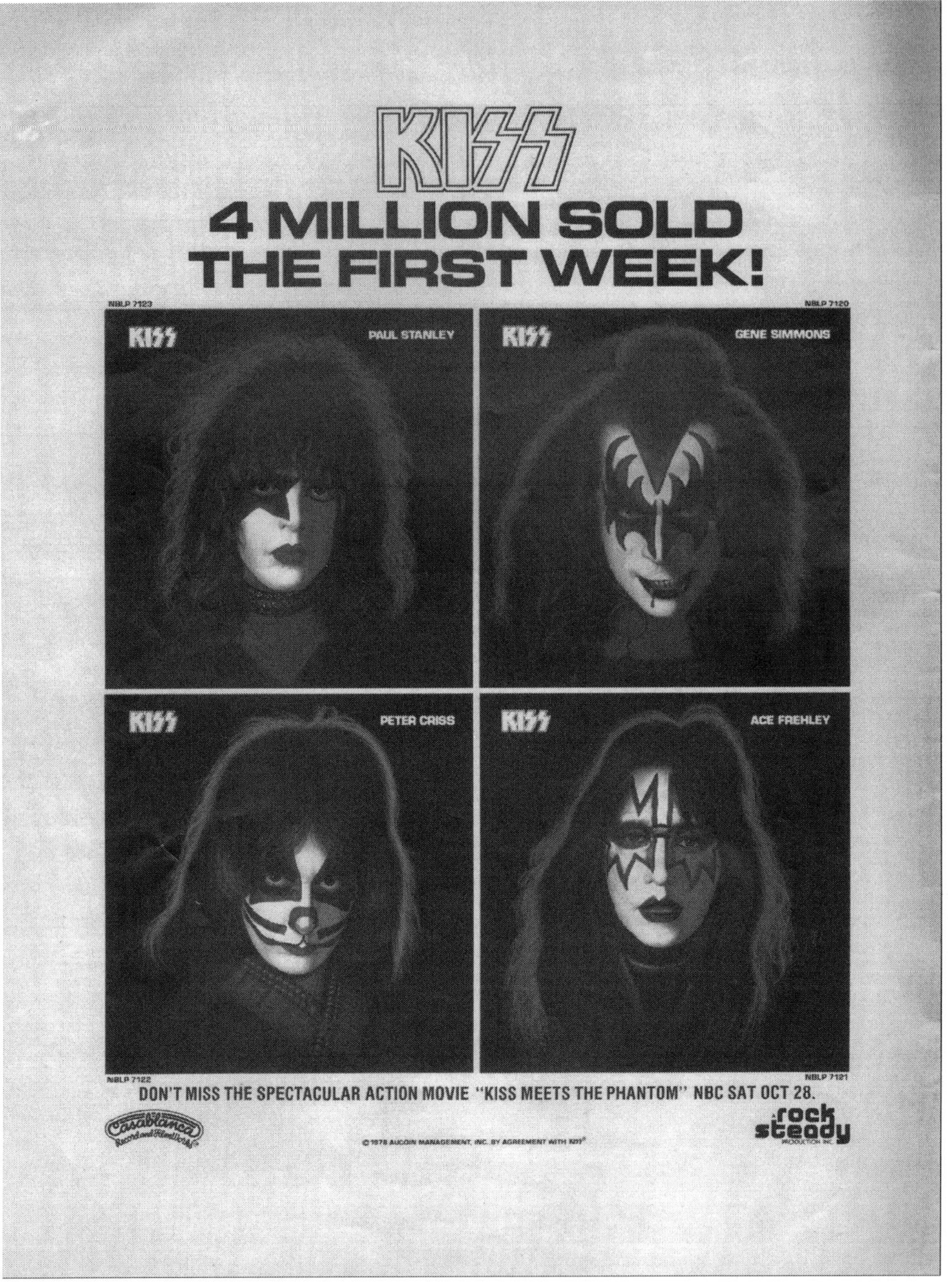

(Billboard Magazine ad, Sept. 9, 1978)

Introduction

September 18, 1978. KISS made music history when they simultaneously released the member's four solo albums. The albums were backed by an unprecedented, multimillion dollar marketing and publicity campaign, and a total of more than 5.3 million units were shipped to retailers, creating KISSteria and representing perhaps one of the last examples of record industry excess in the '70s. "Gene, Ace, Peter & Paul: A Detailed Exploration of the 1978 KISS Solo Albums" is based in large part on a 2013 KISSFAQ.com celebratory retrospective that commemorated the 35th anniversary of the solo albums. That "Back in the Solo Album Groove: The KISS Albums. 35 Years Later..." project was an ambitious multi-week retrospective dedicated to arguably one of the biggest milestones in KISStory.

"Everybody's grown tremendously with their albums. And the really nice thing about it is that when the albums [are] all done, [and] each of us hears the other, it's really a great way of saying, 'Hey, this is what I'm about. This is the way I've always heard things.' It's like really getting to know somebody even better than you do." — Paul Stanley, 1978

By 1978 KISS had transformed from simply a rock band into a cultural phenomenon. Gene Simmons, Ace Frehley, Peter Criss and Paul Stanley had just completed their busiest year to date in 1977: a 12-month cycle that yielded the "Love Gun" studio album, "Alive II" and an intensive touring itinerary — including the band's first tour of Japan. Under the direction of manager Bill Aucoin, what followed was a year that firmly established and took "Super KISS" over the top, cementing their status as an American cultural icon. Following the conclusion of the "Alive II" tour, Casablanca Records released the first proper KISS greatest hits package, "Double Platinum," in April 1978. The band then embarked on the filming of "KISS Meets the Phantom of the Park," a made-for-television movie that premiered on NBC television in October. Meanwhile, the flood of KISS merchandise — from belt buckles, sleeping bags, makeup kits, and dolls — became a tidal inundation of retail outlets nationwide. KISS was everywhere. The transformation into a brand was fully underway.

The solo albums presented the KISS members like fans had never heard them before. Simmons called on a cavalcade of stars to round out his LP, from artists such as Donna Summer and Helen Reddy to Aerosmith's Joe Perry and Cheap Trick's Rick Nielsen. Containing an impressive breadth of material, the album spanned Beatles-inspired tunes, lushly orchestrated ballads and electrifying rock tracks, with a touching cover of the Disney classic "When You Wish Upon A Star" thrown in for good measure. For his solo album, Frehley teamed with renowned producer/engineer Eddie Kramer, who was fresh from spearheading the band's last two studio albums and "Alive II." With only two lead vocals to his credit at that point, Frehley's album was arguably considered the wildcard of the bunch. But with an armory of guitars and amps, a bolt of confidence and drummer Anton Fig in tow, the Spaceman had an ace up his sleeve.

Meanwhile, Criss fulfilled his musical dreams by presenting a song cycle reflecting his diverse interests, from R&B and old-time rock and roll to delicate ballads and even a disco-flavored tune, which pre-dated the 1979 hit "I Was Made For Lovin' You." The Catman was aided by an A-list of studio musicians and the talents of KISS creative guru Sean Delaney and Grammy-winning producer/songwriter Vini Poncia. Stanley expanded his creative horizons, mixing straight-ahead KISS-inspired numbers with dynamic tracks that showcased his impressive vocal range, including his first-ever performed ballad. The Starchild tapped an able group of musicians, including guitarist Bob Kulick, who had ghosted guitar tracks on the studio side of "Alive II." In a sense, Stanley's album ultimately defined a model for his future output within KISS.

Nearly 4 decades later, "Gene, Ace, Peter & Paul: A Detailed Exploration of the 1978 KISS Solo Albums" puts the four KISS solo albums under the microscope like never before. More than 30 brand-new interviews were conducted with various individuals who either worked directly on the solo albums or have a strong connection with the projects. These interviews offer readers fresh first-hand perspectives straight from studio musicians, producers, engineers, and songwriters, and the creative professionals working in the KISS camp at the time.

A supporting series of topical features further illuminates KISS' activities in 1978 while dissecting the albums and offering in-depth analysis and biographical information on the albums' participants.

There is only one way to conclude any introduction to this work...

To: Gene, Ace, Peter & Paul

Solo Albums Overview

Gene Simmons

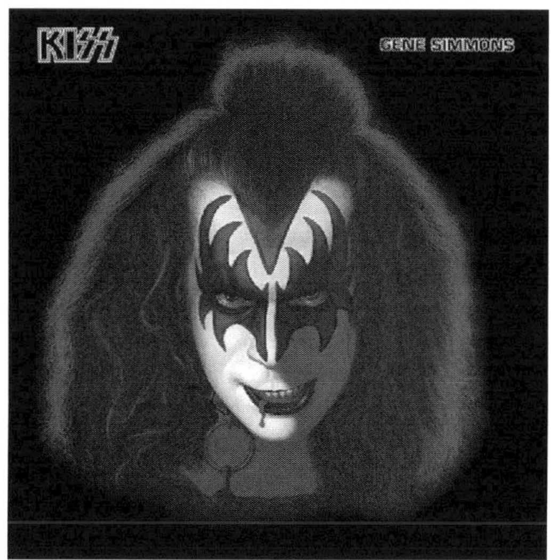

Release Details:
Casablanca NBLP-7120

Tracks:

A1. Radioactive
(3:50) - Gene Simmons
[● USA #47; CAN #66; UK #41]

A2. Burning Up With Fever
(4:19) - Gene Simmons

A3. See You Tonite
(2:30) - Gene Simmons

A4. Tunnel of Love
(3:49) - Gene Simmons

A5. True Confessions
(3:30) - Gene Simmons

B1. Living in Sin
(3:50) - Gene Simmons / Sean Delaney / Howard Marks

B2. Always Near You/Nowhere To Hide
(4:12) - Gene Simmons

B3. Man of 1,000 Faces
(3:16) - Gene Simmons

B4. Mr. Make Believe
(4:00) - Gene Simmons

B5. See You in Your Dreams
(2:48) - Gene Simmons

B6. When You Wish Upon a Star
(2:44) - Ned Washington / Leigh Harline

Album Details:
Produced by Sean Delaney and Gene Simmons. Recorded at The Manor, Shipton-on-Cherwell, Oxfordshire, England; Cherokee Studios, Los Angeles, CA; and Blue Rock Studio, New York City, NY, April – July 1978. Mixed at Trident Studios, London,

England, by Mike Stone, John Brand, Allen Douglass and Frank D'Amico. The album was originally intended to the titled "Man of 1,000 Faces," but the overall marketing plan for the four solo albums changed that. Early pressings include "Something seem larh" etched into the wax as part of an inside joke.

Chart Action:
Chart Peak (USA): #22 (1/6/79) with 22 weeks on charts. Other countries: AUZ #32; CAN #21; JAP #24.

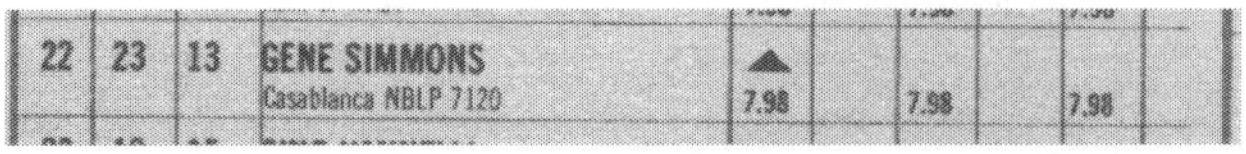

22	23	13	GENE SIMMONS Casablanca NBLP 7120	▲ 7.98	7.98	7.98

10/14/78	10/21/78	10/28/78	11/4/78	11/11/78	11/18/78	11/25/78	12/2/78	12/9/78
88	56	46	42	38	34	32	30	28
12/16/78	**12/23/78**	**12/30/78**	**1/6/79**	**1/13/79**	**1/20/79**	**1/27/79**	**2/3/79**	**2/10/79**
26	23	23	** 22 **	22	30	39	69	116
2/17/79	**2/24/79**	**3/4/79**	**3/11/79**	**3/18/79**				
151	167	170	179	X				

RIAA/Sales:
"Gene Simmons" was certified gold and platinum by the RIAA on 10/2/78. It has sold over 31,000 copies since the SoundScan® era commenced in 1991. The album was certified gold by the CRIA (Canada) for sales of 50,000 copies on 12/1/78. Contemporaneously, Casablanca had shipped 1,391,411 copies of Gene's album by the end of June 1979, the most of any of the solo albums.

Singles (USA):
Casablanca NB-951: Radioactive (Edit) / See You in Your Dreams

Billboard Hot-100 Chart:

12/2/78	12/9/78	12/16/78	12/23/78	12/30/78	1/6/79	1/13/79	1/20/79	1/27/79
84	73	61	50	50	50	** 47 **	47	X

Cashbox:

12/2/78	12/9/78	12/16/78	12/23/78	12/30/78	1/6/79	1/13/79	1/20/79	1/27/79
82	72	65	59	54	X	** 51 **	65	96
2/3/79								
X								

Performed Live:
"Radioactive" was performed by KISS during the 1979 "Return of KISS" tour. "See You Tonite" was a common song performed on the 1995 convention tour and appeared on the "MTV Unplugged" album. Parts of other songs were attempted on occasion.

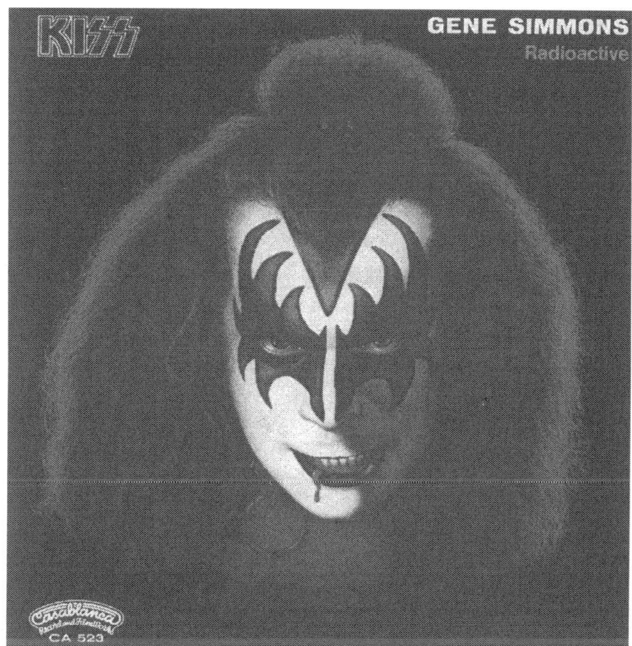

THE KISS SINGLES.

BULLET! BULLET! BULLET!

© 1978 AUCOIN MANAGEMENT INC. BY AGREEMENT WITH KISS ®

rock steady

(Billboard Magazine, 12/9/78)

Gene Simmons: In the Solo Album Spotlight

The "man of 1,000 faces" makes believers of those who don't just listen with their eyes.

The rejection of KISS' music has long been considered a matter of listeners hearing with their eyes, and ultimately failing to give the music a fair evaluation on the grounds that they neither like nor understand the band's image. For Gene Simmons, who had been judged by such parameters from the band's beginnings, the same could be said to be the case when fans picked up his 1978 solo album. In some ways, it was his (and each member's) own fault: He had allowed himself to generally be typecast growling out material more aligned with his onstage persona, with a couple of exceptions that hinted to a different side of his musical character. Offstage, the man behind the mask was quite a different creature creatively. Few had heard his softer side, asides perhaps on "Great Expectations," a song that lacked any of the subtle introspection or vulnerability present in his numerous acoustic works, or "Goin' Blind," for which little really needs to be said. There's a duality encompassed within the whole "Gene Simmons" package. Is it ego-maniacal or a psychological need that drives the man to thank just about everyone he's encountered since arriving in America in 1958 — except the kitchen sink? Is it a name-dropping narcissist who has a guest list that shouts "look here — look at me," or is it simply a matter of someone who's amazed at the success his work has brought that allows him to celebrate a solo-outing with such guests and wants to share that joy? It's probably a mix of both, and it is probably unwise to measure the 1978 version of Gene against the perception of him more than thirty years later.

If fans were expecting an album full of songs in the vein of "Almost Human" then they'd have had few reference points to consider what Gene might have had in mind. For Gene, the premise for the albums was simple, both for him and the other members of the band: "I've never done this kind of stuff before [on a KISS record]; it would have been too much of a departure. It's another thing to have 'God of Thunder' on and album with 'Mr. Make Believe' which I think will be out by the time the article is so everyone will know what it sounds like. I guess the big secret about all of us in the band is that we have all been writing different kinds of songs all along and because of all the self-imposed restrictions, you know, about how we are supposed to sound like. We've never done them. It's no one's fault, it's just the way we wanted to sound like" (Rock Magazine). In an interview with Steve Rosen, Gene explained the goals of his solo album: "I wanted to do the songs in a way that when people listened to them they wouldn't say, 'God, listen to all the guitars.'

What I wanted is to have people sit down and say the songs are good. The songs were given a nice kind of honest treatment, and the arrangements are such that you aren't constantly distracted by particular instruments... That's part of the sound; you can play with that because you're already comfortable with it. If you're [producer] Phil Spector, you can have a wall of sound that people understand — that's the style you're dealing with, that's the genre — and then the song works naturally and you're not stumbling over: 'Gee, that's a big sound.' If you're Pink Floyd and all of a sudden you sound like KISS, everybody will say, 'Whoa, wait a minute,' and then they don't pay attention to the song" (Guitar Player, 1978). In essence, he wanted to challenge the listener and make the song the focus while not being cornered by his role within KISS. He recalled the decision to play guitars on the album instead of bass: "A bass player in a band and he goes into a different kind of record is usually handicapped in a sense because if he's played bass on the record then everything's going to revolve around that. These were different kinds of songs" (Hit Parader, 2/79).

Of the four members of KISS, Gene was the only one to truly embrace the concept of going solo. That meant breaking away from the concept of KISS, and the boundaries the band imposed in order to remain within the confines of what the fans found acceptable. The band had discovered its niche, and while experimenting with "Destroyer," they had quickly retreated to their original premise for the albums that followed. For Gene, it wasn't just a matter of thinking outside of the box, but removing the boundaries the "box" represented completely — or in essence getting a new box! Ace and Paul rocked out, honing their material to represent the ultimate "fully realized" versions of themselves. With few exceptions neither digressed too far from their existing personal musical definitions within the band — their music was generally what one would have expected it to be. Peter too, while straying far from the bread and butter of KISS, remained honest to the sort of material he'd brought to KISS — were one to judge his solo album then it's second only to Gene's at breaking away from the "KISS" mould. Like a magician, he wanted to surprise the listener: "They're the kind of songs nobody has ever known that I'm capable of writing, number one; or that I could sing at least two octaves above the voice that I use on record, number two; and that in fact that I had a different voice at all, number three" (Hit Parader, 2/79). Gene, if nothing else provokes, teases and cajoles the listener. He presents the demon in the Ron Frangipane composed introduction to "Radioactive," and then goes 90 degrees sideways into a classic 50s rock 'n roll direction with full piano embellishments and touches of funky bass lines, along with sound-effects and female backing-vocals. In some ways it was pure Las Vegas, a precursor to what KISS became (visually at least) in 1979. According to Gene the introduction was, "Janis Ian... Singing in Latin... The Latin says something like, 'I see no evil, I hear no evil, it's not around me at all'" (Rock Magazine). In another interview Gene suggests that the Latin was similarly suppsed to mean "I am pure but I am surrounded by evil" (Hit Parader, 2/79).

And that introductory piece, straight ought of the Bob Ezrin playbook of audio storytelling, is the album's "I am not just the 'Demon'" declaration, something that the rest of the album lives up to. The discordant acoustic introduction to "Burning up with Fever" serves as to segue to the KISS cast-off track. Who would expect classical guitar on a Gene Simmons album? Well, he could and he did. With an almost Southern-revival chorus one can nearly see Gene preaching from the pulpit while a robe-clad choir sings the refrain. While these opening tracks may have been more of the up-tempo and familiar material on the album they couldn't be further away from the imagery generated by and for KISS. "See You Tonite" seals the deal with its beautiful and evocative acoustic arrangement. It is quite nearly impossible to be further removed from the music of KISS than with this song. The harmonies pay homage to the material of Lennon & McCartney, yet orchestral flourishes also take the material into the realm of Simon & Garfunkel. Taken from his past it offers the listener a glimpse into the young and developing Gene, circa 1970.

"Tunnel of Love" returns the listener to more comfortable rock territory with a song initially rejected from the "Love Gun" that dated from Gene's brief involvement with the then unknown Van Halen brothers (they performed on the original demo of the song with him in late-1976). In one sense it's almost inexplicable that they weren't brought in as guests for the studio version at the time given Gene's relationship with the band at the start of their career and their "You Really Got Me" single hitting #36 on the Billboard Hot 100 singles charts in early 1978. In fact Gene had considered having Ace guest for the guitar solo for the song! "True Confessions" continues in the same vein as "Radioactive" as good time rock 'n roll, powered by piano and strong backing vocals; in this case featuring Helen Reddy. According to Gene, "Helen Reddy was incredibly straight. She was like, 'I am woman, glorified.' She had a song called 'I Am Woman' and that was her big hit and I think she was offended by all this male 'cock rock' type of music, but she was willing to do it" (Special Delivery #13). And that must have made her a heck of a trophy for his cavalcade of guests. While the demon may have been celebrating a type of music closer to the 1950s he was also celebrating the lifestyle he had attained by 1978 and perhaps just slightly mocked himself with "Living in Sin." One that one track Gene's "Hello Baby" again harkens back to the 1950s and the "Big" Bopper's famed introduction on his hit "Chantilly Lace." For that matter, so too the hysterical Cher and Chastity Bono telephone conversation alludes to Bopper's phone call and the subject matter to what Gene was known to like!

Returning to material with a Beatle-esque feel is the hybrid "Always Near You/Nowhere To Hide." With a melody generally reused in 1981 as part of "Only You" the piece is more of a lounge music style that ambles in a somewhat directionless manner, building with acoustic guitars, harmonies, electric sections, orchestras, and backing vocals, until it transitions into the "Nowhere to Hide" section. If nothing else it is representative of the "kitchen-sink" or blender approach where everything is thrown into the mix, perhaps for the sake of art. "Man of 1,000 Faces" pays homage to the nickname of one of Gene's Hollywood horror film heroes, Lon Chaney, though it also serves as an obvious claim to the title for Gene himself — if the music on the album were not illustrative enough to make that point. The 1978 form of the song was more autobiographical in nature. Gene recalled, "Although nobody's going to see behind the mask, what I'm trying to tell everybody is that it really isn't a mask. It's just one of the different faces, and everybody's got many, many different faces. And people are not the same with any two people" (Grooves, 1978). The song had originally been intended for a KISS album, but was deemed unsuitable at the time. Gene recalled, "I've been meaning to do that for about four years now. Originally it was going to be on 'Dressed To Kill,' but we all decided that it would be too early and it would be showing too much" (Hit Parader, 2/79).

Like other material "Mr. Make Believe" alludes to an exploration of his character with powerful backing vocals and harmonies that had permeated his pre-Wicked Lester compositions. The song was one of Gene's first attempts to write a song about himself. "See You In Your Dreams" was an opportunity to allow Gene to right what he had felt had been a failure with the KISS version recorded for the "Rock And Roll Over" album. Unfortunately, Gene wasn't particularly happy with this version either: "In my head I heard much more a Humble Pie thing, but it came off sounding much poppier than that" (Firehouse #58). It did allow Gene to bring in Michael Des Barres to scream along with the girl backing vocals. Perhaps a result of this second attempt this is the sole song on the album to have a true KISS feel on it.

Gene opted to close the album with the unexpected, as if the other material on the album had been "expected" — a cover of "When You Wish Upon A Star," a sentimental tip of the hat to the Disney cartoons that helped Gene learn English soon after moving to America in 1958. Gene recalled the importance of the song: "When I first heard that song I could barely speak English but I knew the words were true. Anybody can have what they want; the world and life can give its rewards to anyone" (Kerrang #160). Additionally, Gene's belief in the subject matter of the song — that all things are possible — embodies the American dream, something that he has certainly accomplished: "The lyrics are the heaviest lyrics that have ever been written because they can apply to anybody. Anybody who's got a dream can relate to them... But I think it's universal at the same time. It can be personal to everybody. It doesn't have anything to do with age or sex or anything" (Grooves, 1978).

The primary recordings for the album were completed at The Manor in England following the conclusion of the Japanese tour in April 1978. Most of the guests recorded at Cherokee Studios in June and July following the conclusion of filming of the TV movie. Following mixing at Trident Studios in London, some last minute overdubs were recorded at Blue Rock Studios in New York in July. Putting the album under the spotlight simply illuminates the incredible amount of influences integrated and expressed by Gene's effort. It's too easy to dismiss the album as pompous and self-gratifying simply because of a perceived overload of guests or the excessive "thank you" messages which at times appears to simply be name-dropping for the sake of doing so. Ultimately, behind the mask the musical contents are far more representative of the man and artist than perhaps was obvious.

Ace Frehley

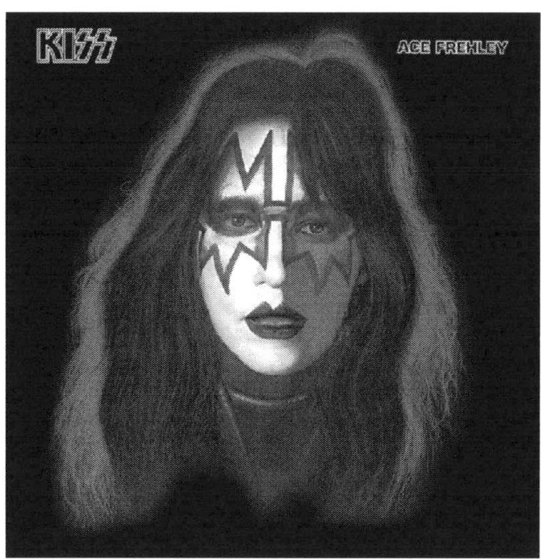

Release Details:
Casablanca NBLP-7121

Tracks:

A1. Rip It Out
(3:39) - Ace Frehley / Larry Kelly / Sue Kelly

A2. Speedin' Back To My Baby
(3:35) - Ace Frehley / Jeanette Frehley

A3. Snow Blind
(3:54) - Ace Frehley

A4. Ozone
(4:41) - Ace Frehley

A5. What's On Your Mind?
(3:26) - Ace Frehley

B1. New York Groove
(3:01) - Russ Ballard
[● USA #13; CAN #25; NZD #24]

B2. I'm In Need Of Love
(4:36) - Ace Frehley

B3. Wiped-Out
(4:10) - Ace Frehley / Anton Fig

B4. Fractured Mirror
(5:25) - Ace Frehley

Album Details:
Produced by Eddie Kramer and Ace Frehley. Recorded, mixed, and engineered by Eddie Kramer, Bob Freeman, Eric Block, and Don Hunerburg at "The Mansion," Sharon, CT, and Plaza Sound Studio, New York City, NY, June - July, 1978. Prior to recording the album Ace held at least two demo sessions for material for the album with Anton Fig, who had been put in contact with Ace by a bass player trying out for Anton's band, Spider. This early 1978 demo session was Anton's first connection with anyone from KISS putting to rest any suggestions that he had anything to do with the drumming on "KISS Alive II" in late-1977.

Chart Action:
Chart Peak (USA): #26 (1/13/79) with 23 weeks on charts. Other countries: CAN #34;

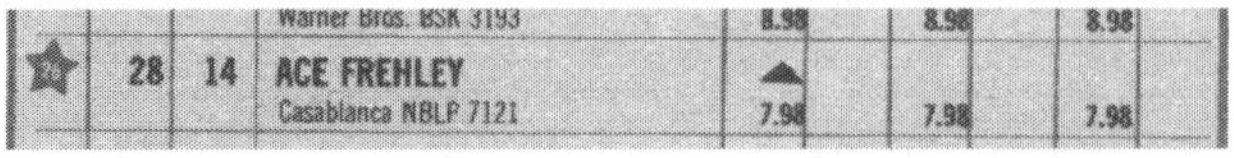

28	14	ACE FREHLEY Casablanca NBLP 7121	7.98	7.98	7.98

Billboard Top-200 Chart:

10/14/78	10/21/78	10/28/78	11/4/78	11/11/78	11/18/78	11/25/78	12/2/78	12/9/78
87	65	55	50	46	42	39	38	36
12/16/78	**12/23/78**	**12/30/78**	**1/6/79**	**1/13/79**	**1/20/79**	**1/27/79**	**2/3/79**	**2/10/79**
34	32	32	28	**** 26 ****	26	26	50	50
2/17/79	**2/24/79**	**3/4/79**	**3/11/79**	**3/18/79**	**3/25/79**			
69	77	97	114	176	X			

RIAA/Sales:
"Ace Frehley" was certified gold and platinum by the RIAA on 10/2/78. It has sold over 46,000 copies since the SoundScan® era commenced in 1991. The album was certified gold by the CRIA (Canada) for sales of 50,000 copies on 12/1/78. Contemporaneously, Casablanca had shipped 1,387,852 copies of Ace's album by the end of June 1979, including 18,739 picture disks (the most of the four band members).

Singles (USA):
Casablanca NB-941: New York Groove / Snow Blind

Billboard Hot-100 Chart:

10/14/78	10/21/78	10/28/78	11/4/78	11/11/78	11/18/78	11/25/78	12/2/78	12/9/78
87	81	70	60	50	46	42	34	30
12/16/78	**12/23/78**	**12/30/78**	**1/6/79**	**1/13/79**	**1/20/79**	**1/27/79**	**2/3/79**	**2/10/79**
25	23	23	19	17	16	14	**** 13 ****	13
2/17/79	**2/24/79**	**3/3/79**	**3/10/79**					
35	61	100	X					

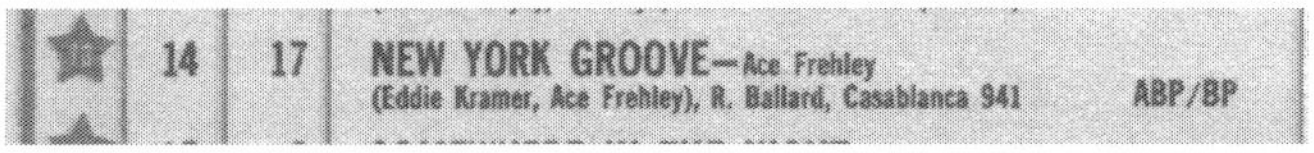

14	17	NEW YORK GROOVE—Ace Frehley (Eddie Kramer, Ace Frehley), R. Ballard, Casablanca 941	ABP/BP

Cashbox:

10/14/78	10/21/78	10/28/78	11/4/78	11/11/78	11/18/78	11/25/78	12/2/78	12/9/78
85	77	68	57	50	45	41	37	31
12/16/78	**12/23/78**	**12/30/78**	**1/6/79**	**1/13/79**	**1/20/79**	**1/27/79**	**2/3/79**	**2/10/79**
28	25	23	X	21	19	17	**** 16 ****	24
2/17/79	**2/24/79**	**3/3/79**	**3/10/79**					
42	79	90	X					

Performed Live:

"New York Groove" (along with another then new Ace vocal, "2,000 Man") was performed by KISS during the 1979 "Return of KISS" tour in support of "Dynasty." Ace has also performed more than half of the album throughout his solo career. "Rip it Out" was the very first song performed by a newly solo Frehley's Comet at their debut gig at S.I.R. Studios in New York City on November 30, 1984. During the early years of that band, Ace was careful to balance his sets in favor of his new solo material, rather than relying overly on KISS songs, or even those from the 1978 album. Part of this, most likely, was a result of the limited set times he had available as an opening act, though once he was essentially back in the clubs for the "Trouble Walkin'" tour more legacy material started to be added. In his second post-KISS career "Snow Blind," with a "I Want You" ending tag, has regularly been included (it had first been performed in 1990), and even the "Fractured Mirror" instrumental has made an appearance (other than being used as the intro to the show). "Speedin' Back To My Baby" has often been included as part of a medley in addition to being fully performed.

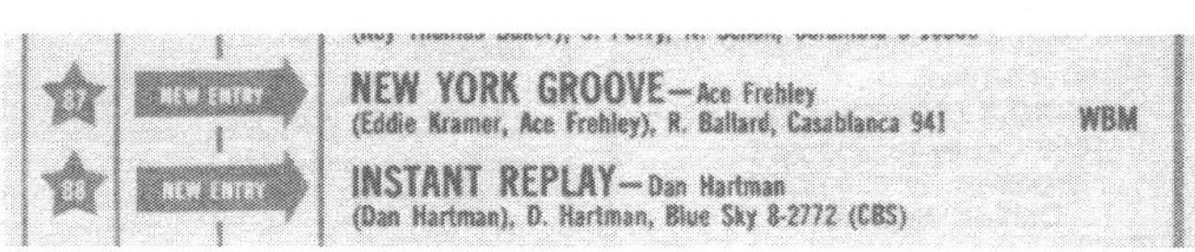

87 NEW ENTRY NEW YORK GROOVE—Ace Frehley (Eddie Kramer, Ace Frehley), R. Ballard, Casablanca 941 WBM

88 NEW ENTRY INSTANT REPLAY—Dan Hartman (Dan Hartman), D. Hartman, Blue Sky 8-2772 (CBS)

(Oh, look, who's that one spot behind the Spaceman, 10/14/78)

(Unloading excess U.S. album stock? NME, 3/3/79)

Ace Frehley: In the Solo Album Spotlight

Fractured reflections on "Ace Frehley," some 35 years later. Is it really that good? You bet it is.
By Tim McPhate

"There's no question in my mind that the competition between Ace, Gene, Paul, and Peter was going to be huge. And certainly, they denigrated the possibilities that he would come up with a good album. They all thought that they were going to have the top album. In fact, what happened was Ace trumped them all with a brilliant album." — Eddie Kramer

Going into the solo album project, it is no slight against Ace Frehley to say that his LP was going to be the wild card of the quartet. After all, Frehley had only written a handful of KISS tracks (mind you, some classics such as "Cold Gin" and "Parasite") and sang two lead vocals up until that point ("Shock Me" and "Rocket Ride"). And sure, he had displayed an uncanny ability to craft fiery, memorable solos that fit KISS' songs like a glove. But could Frehley come up with enough musical goods to carry an entire album? He readily admitted on WPIX FM's "Sunday Magazine" show in October 1978, "For the past few albums, prior to the solo album, I only wrote one or two songs off the albums. I guess I was kind of stagnant for a while, you know, was bogged down mentally with personal things... When you're constantly touring and recording, for me I couldn't find the time to write and be as creative as I wanted to be."

For all the talk about Frehley's laziness, he wasted little time in getting to work on his album. Right off the bat, he made a key decision to surround himself with talent who would help him shine. Ace was certainly excited about the project: "I'll be able to do things on the solo album I haven't been able to do with KISS. I've always wanted to do a blues song, a couple of songs with some weird, off-beat time changes which really isn't in the tradition of KISS, like 3/5 or 7/8 time. I should have my brother play some classical guitar. There'll probably be one or two instrumentals with a lot of guitar overdubs and a lot of different harmonies happening" (Circus, 4/27/78).

Bringing Eddie Kramer onboard was a brilliant, if obvious move. The statured producer/engineer had helmed KISS' previous two studio albums, "Rock And Roll Over" and "Love Gun," long players that showcase an Ace Frehley in his musical prime. There was a comfort zone for Frehley in working alongside Kramer, who seemed to bring out an intangible quality in the Spaceman. Having had Kramer coax the vocals out of him previously made Ace sure that Eddie would be able to work best with him, having developed a familiarity with one another.

In a more curious move, Frehley secured the services of a relative unknown to fill the drum chair: South African-born Anton Fig. It proved a stroke of genius. The classically trained and jazz-schooled Fig added a powerful depth and rhythmic dimension to the album that is still evident some 35 years later. In a twist of fate, Fig learned of the opportunity through one of Frehley's friends, Larry Russell, who was auditioning for Fig's then-band Siren.

"He was auditioning for us and he said to me, 'I've got a friend, Ace. He's doing a solo record and he's looking for a drummer. I think I can get you an audition,'" said Fig. "You know, I had heard of KISS. But to me, KISS was a band on the side of a bus basically. Anyway, I went up to play with Ace."

With his jamming partner in tow, Frehley penned some lethal hard-edged material, with lyrical themes centering on the darker side of sex, drugs and rock and roll. Outside of the KISS framework, Frehley enjoyed room to experiment musically with different sounds and textures. Appropriately, for his solo project the Spaceman took matters into his own hands by playing a majority of the instruments on the album.

"I played lead guitar, rhythm guitar, acoustic guitar, synthesizer, and bass," boasted Frehley. "The singing came out a little better than I thought [it would be]. I'd only sang twice prior to this album... I didn't consider myself a lead vocalist. I still don't, but somehow I pulled through singing lead on eight tracks... I was considering getting in some guest vocalists to do lead tracks; I didn't think I'd be able to handle them all" (WPIX FM "Sunday Magazine").

Harkening back to his days with Led Zeppelin, Kramer set up tracking sessions for the album at the Colgate Mansion in Connecticut. Sequestered away from the hustle and bustle of New York, recording in the spacious mansion afforded Kramer, Frehley and Fig the perfect fun, creative atmosphere to graft the album's basic tracks. For overdubs, sessions moved to Plaza Sound in New York, which was situated above Radio City Music Hall. Frehley and his team were able to take plenty of time to ensure the tracks were in tip-top shape.

"Whenever we did KISS albums, a lot of times we were on a very hectic schedule," said Frehley. "A lot of times we didn't have as much time as we wanted to to do records, especially guitar solos. In this case, I took two months to record [my album]. It was the kind of thing where I brought all my guitars and all my amplifiers to the studio and sometimes we just spent a whole day on a guitar solo to get the right sound. I think it shows."

Indeed, Frehley's six-string work is superlative throughout, and represents arguably the high-water mark of his career as a recording guitarist. With his battery of guitars and amps at the ready, Kramer and engineer Rob Freeman captured some sterling guitar tones. The combination of Frehley's guitar and Fig's drums made for a powerful hybrid, forming the framework for the heaviest, most sonically assured set of the four KISS albums.

"Rip It Out" gets the album off to a raucous start. Heavy power-chord riffing and a monstrous Fig groove set the right mood for Frehley who sends a kiss-off to some bitch who probably wasn't worth it in the first place. "I think it's better / If we just part and don't so goodbye," growls Frehley. Fig's drum break is arguably the song's high point. (Interestingly, Fig double-tracked his drum solo to add an extra layer of punch.) The drummer's boisterous fills finally give way to Frehley, who tears into a masterful solo ripe with Ace-isms — spaced-out bluesy licks, unison bends, dizzying vibrato, and pull-offs — that form a cohesive musical statement.

One of the more fun tracks on the album, "Speedin' Back To My Baby" is driven by Fig's sturdy shuffle beat. Centered around the key of G, Frehley's blues-based intro lick is doubled an octave above. The song had been written while KISS were on tour in Tokyo. Similar to situations on Paul Stanley and Peter Criss' albums, the presence of female background vocals — provided courtesy of Susan Collins — add an element of contrast to Frehley's vocals. (Check out Collins cutting loose at 3:06.) However, the cherry on top of this particular track is the Hendrix-inspired backward guitar solo. Today, one click of the mouse in Pro Tools will flip a guitar solo. In 1978, however, there was meticulous craftsmanship involved.

"Ace overdubbed his solo normally, doing any number of takes until he was satisfied with what he played," said Freeman. "After Eddie and I comped a track, I copied the solo onto a piece of ½" tape on another machine and marked the head and tail of the solo with paper leader tape. Then I flipped over the ½" tape and "flew" the solo back onto the multi-track, recording it forwards on the 24-track tape as it played backwards on the ½" machine."

"Snow Blind" gets off to subdued start with a sluggish power chord-based riff that descends in half steps from C5 to A5. After four bars, Frehley plays the rhythm part in a lower position to fatten the sound. (Also, check Fig's coy use of the cow bell.) One of the more deliciously weird tracks on the album, careful listeners will detect spaceship-style sound effects in the background and a nice bit of audio trickery with the delayed repeats when Frehley sings "Lost in space... Ace... Ace... Ace..." The tune kicks into double-time for the solo at 1:42. Underneath Frehley's solo is the ARP Avatar synthesizer, which provides an off-the-wall melodic counterpoint. The Spaceman's lead here is a clinic in how to utilize repetition in a musical manner.

With lyrics such as "I'm the kinda guy/Who likes getting high," the lyrical motif of "Ozone" is hardly confusing. Led by a simple lead guitar melody that is hard to shake, the lyrics take the backseat in this composition, which seems more of a musical showpiece. Tucked in the mix is acoustic guitar, which shimmers nicely alongside Frehley's Les Paul riffing. The solo section is based entirely on triplet-based lines, giving off an exercise-type feel that is atypical for a Frehley lead. "Ozone" is one of the three tunes to feature Will Lee on bass.

"What's On Your Mind?" is a fresh slice of power pop in the key of D, and perhaps a harbinger to such future Frehley gems as "Talk To Me." "You're breaking my heart/I'm falling apart," sings an almost vulnerable Frehley. The song's harmony changes modes between the verses and chorus. The presence of the natural C in the Cadd9 chord in the verse evokes D Mixolydian while the presence of C# natural in the descending chorus chord sequence spells D major. There are little guitar pyrotechnics here, just perfectly layered rhythm parts and a simple lyrical solo. Another fun harmonic tidbit: the song ends on the V chord: A major.

The lone cover on the album, "New York Groove" is the perfect storm of musical ensemble playing and expert production. According to Fig, there was a different approach to this particular song.

"I think that song was recorded more like you would approach a single," said Fig. "The drum part was really defined. I wasn't just jamming and playing."

In delivering one of his more comfortable vocals on the album, there's little doubt that the tone of the lyrics resonated with the Bronx-born Frehley. That feeling surely translated to Russ Ballard, the song's author.

"When Ace did his thing on it, it sounded a bit more mature," said Ballard. "He brought a hooligan, tough guy kind of attitude to it."

A little-known fact is that "New York Groove" was re-cut twice in the search for the perfect take.

"Eddie and Ace arrived at Plaza Sound with a version of 'New York Groove' recorded at the mansion. But there was something about the overall feel of it that wasn't sitting quite right with them," explains Freeman. "Ultimately a decision was made to re-cut the song from the ground up, starting with a new basic track consisting of drums and rhythm guitar. So one day we cleared the studio, set up Anton's drum kit, and recorded a second version of 'New York Groove' utilizing Plaza's nice open room for drum ambiance while Ace played along in the control room. But after careful analysis of Russ Ballard's original songwriting demo (a cassette tape they kept playing over and over for comparison to what we were doing), it was decided to re-record 'New York Groove' yet again with further subtle changes to the tempo and/or drum feel. So on another day we set up the drums again and recorded a third basic track for 'New York Groove.' The third one was the charm and became the final version of the song."

"New York Groove" ascended all the way to No. 13 on the Billboard Hot 100. The song's success not only caught his bandmates by surprise, but the interior of the KISS camp.

"It was unexpected, which is one of the reasons you do creative projects that hopefully stake out some new territory," said Christopher K. Lendt, who oversaw the business affairs for the solo albums. "I don't know who identified the Russ Ballard song for Ace Frehley but obviously that was a brilliant choice and the way it was produced was perfect for Ace."

The rhythm guitars in "I'm In Need Of Love" rely on a heavy use of delay. Another tune that breaks into double time, Fig and Lee hold down the rhythm section while Frehley's busts out his longest solo on the album. The 36-bar lead is a nice study in contrast and contains many of the hallmarks of Frehley's style. For the first eight bars, he brandishes a composed melody, which he doubles with a harmony part in bars 5-8. Frehley then lets loose into a series of improv-based flurries. (Check the rare Ace tap at 2:41). The Spaceman ends his solo with a line built from sixths, coming to rest on the sweet major third note (G#).

"Wiped-Out" is a head-spinning collaboration between Frehley and Fig. Frehley plays a Keith Richards inspired rhythm figure in the verses, revolving around C and D major chords. The drummer takes the spotlight on this track, twisting and turning rhythmic feels during the verses, pre-chorus and chorus, lending an unsettling and unpredictable undercurrent. Lee's slippery bass line and Frehley's wah-wah scratches add touches of funk. (Once again, Frehley ends his solo on the major third note.)

Closing the album is "Fractured Mirror," a hypnotizing instrumental that is both beautiful and ominous. The ringing of a bell in the intro adds an eerie sense of finality as Frehley enters with an arpeggiated guitar figure based on B and A major triads. An open-chord acoustic guitar figure utilizing the open B and E strings follows yields a strong ringing effect. Sparse percussion and thick power chords enter the fray. In the second verse, Frehley adds touches of melody on top with the ARP Avatar synthesizer. His sinister line at 2:34 would not sound out of character in a horror film. As the song fades, the reprise of the opening guitar figure provides a bookend of sorts. The journey is complete.

Certainly the stride Frehley found on his solo album would spill into "Dynasty" and "Unmasked," albums on which he would contribute three songs each. "I would say I'm more confident now as a singer and guitar player than I have ever been in my life," said Frehley in 1978.

Frehley's musical talents also caught the attention of his collaborators.

"No diss to the other guys in KISS, but Ace was the musician in the band, as far as I'm concerned," said Lee. "He's the real musical craftsman on his instrument kind of guy. What can you say? The guy's a mother-fucker man."

"Sometimes when he plays it's almost like you can hear that mental determination and grit where he'll just force his will through," said Fig. "It's just an inner strength I feel that he has."

Though unbeknownst to him at the time, Frehley set the bar for his career with his 1978 solo album. It's a creative standard he has unfortunately been unable to match. That said, "Ace Frehley" is an inspiring achievement to be proud of.

Peter Criss

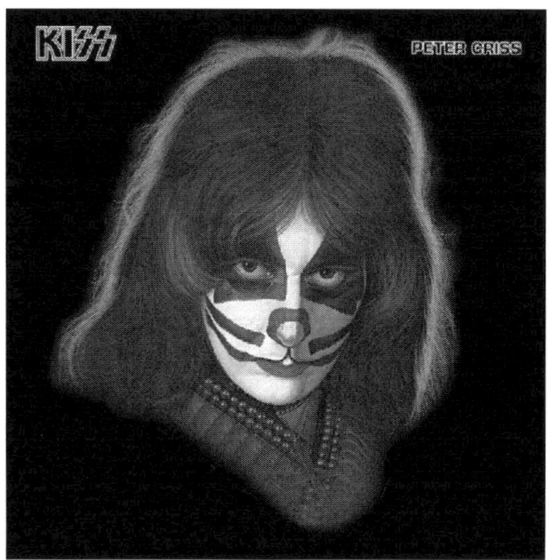

Release Details:
Casablanca NBLP-7122

Tracks:

A1. I'm Gonna Love You
(3:18) - Peter Criss / Stan Penridge

A2. You Matter to Me
(3:15) - John Vastano / Michael Morgan / Vini Poncia
[● USA 1/79, did not chart]

A3. Tossin' and Turnin'
(3:58) - Ritchie Adams / Malou Rene

A4. Don't You Let Me Down
(3:38) - Peter Criss / Stan Penridge
[● USA 10/78, did not chart]

A5. That's The Kind Of Sugar Papa Likes
(2:59) - Peter Criss / Stan Penridge

B1. Easy Thing
(3:53) - Peter Criss / Stan Penridge

B2. Rock Me, Baby
(2:50) - Sean Delaney

B3. KISS the Girl Goodbye
(2:46) - Peter Criss / Stan Penridge

B4. Hooked On Rock And Roll
(3:37) - Stan Penridge / Peter Criss / Vini Poncia

B5. I Can't Stop the Rain
(4:25) - Sean Delaney

Album Details:
Produced by Vini Poncia. Tracks A1, A2 & A5 produced by Vini Poncia, Peter Criss and Sean Delaney. Track A3 produced by Vini Poncia and Peter Criss. Recorded and engineered by Vini Poncia at Sunset Sound Studios, Hollywood, CA; and Electric Lady Studios, New York City, NY, spring 1978.

Chart Action:
Chart Peak (USA): #43 (11/25/78) with 20 weeks on charts. Other countries: CAN #52;

45 7 PETER CRISS
Casablanca NBLP 7122 7.98 7.98 7.98

10/14/78	10/21/78	10/28/78	11/4/78	11/11/78	11/18/78	11/25/78	12/2/78	12/9/78
85	77	59	53	49	45	**** 43 ****	47	47
12/16/78	**12/23/78**	**12/30/78**	**1/6/79**	**1/13/79**	**1/20/79**	**1/27/79**	**2/3/79**	**2/10/79**
46	46	46	66	66	74	73	85	95
2/17/79	**2/24/79**	**3/3/79**						
145	195	X						

RIAA/Sales:
"Peter Criss" was certified gold and platinum by the RIAA on 10/2/78. It has sold over 23,000 copies since the SoundScan® era commenced in 1991. Contemporaneously, Casablanca had shipped 1,317,664 copies of Peter's album by the end of June 1979.

Singles (USA):
Casablanca NB-952: Don't You Let Me Down / Hooked On Rock And Roll
Casablanca NB-961: You Still Matter To Me / Hooked On Rock And Roll

Performed Live:
"Tossin' And Turnin'" was performed by KISS during the 1979 "Return of KISS" tour. Peter also performed it live with Stan Penridge in 1984.

Peter Criss: In the Solo Album Spotlight

A fresh examination of the Catman's 1978 solo album and no, it's not that bad.
By Tim McPhate

Paul Stanley has admitted simply "not getting" Peter Criss' solo album. Gene Simmons was more critical: "Out of all the records that we've ever done solo or as a group, I think that one showed that the guy behind it didn't really have a clue" (Behind The Mask).

Those are some harsh words, Gene. But who said anything about your "A**hole" album?

In all seriousness, the answer is no. As in, no, Peter Criss' 1978 solo album is not the musical equivalent of horse manure. Gene and Paul — and some KISS fans, for that matter — have staked their claim to the contrary, but at a certain point one has to wonder if their words are really a reflection of the actual music or the person whose makeup adorns the album cover.

Some 35 years later, I'm quite comfortable with saying that "Peter Criss" is the most underrated of the four solo albums, and arguably the most musically mature. And while it will never replace "Hotter Than Hell" in the pantheon of KISS classics, it's a solid effort that can yield an enjoyable listening experience if you're so inclined and open-minded.

One of the main criticisms levied against "Peter Criss" is that it sounds nothing like KISS. Well, to state the fairly obvious, "Peter Criss" was not supposed to be a KISS album; it's a Peter Criss solo album. As such, and the difference is critical, this was an opportunity for Criss — who sang the lead vocal on KISS' highest-charting U.S. single — to make a personal statement outside of the constraints of the band.

"The songs I want to do I couldn't do with KISS. I'd like to use horns, strings, black chicks. I'm basically into R&B, country & western and rock" (Circus, 4/13/78). Fans had been pre-warned! The mission for the album was certainly clear to the album's co-producer, Vini Poncia.

"At the time we were making [the album], our focus was on Peter the singer," said Poncia. "It was designed around Peter doing songs that were emotional, songs that he could relate to" (Behind The Mask).

In 1978 Poncia was fresh from winning a Grammy for Best Rhythm & Blues Recording in 1977 for Leo Sayer's "You Make Me Feel Like Dancing," a song he co-wrote. A man with a strong ear for melody and a knack for sharp arrangements, Poncia had cut his musical teeth in the '60s as a songwriter with partner Peter Anders, placing songs with artists such as the Ronettes, Bobby Bloom and Darlene Love. Taking notes in the studio from producer Richard Perry, Poncia subsequently made his own foray into record production, taking the helm on albums for artists such as Melissa Manchester, Ringo Starr and Lynda Carter (yes, that Lynda Carter). Aside from his production work, Poncia — a fellow Italian — also played a key role on Criss' album by bringing in his own clique of session musicians, including bassist Bill Bodine, guitarist Art Munson, horn arranger Tom Saviano, and keyboardist/string arranger Bill Cuomo.

Poncia was perfect for Peter, but not the first choice. "I'm hoping to do the album with Jimmy Iovine. I really need someone who knows arrangements, someone who could take a song apart, knows how to write strings and horns" (Circus, 4/13/78). Another early choice was disco producer Giorgio Moroder. Later yet came the rejection from Tom Dowd.

Poncia came onboard to steer the album's final sessions in Los Angeles, longtime Criss cohort Stan Penridge recalled "normal eight-hour" days during which the producer ran a tight ship. For his part, Criss remembered an argument-free atmosphere in the studio with Poncia, allowing him to concentrate on his goals for the project.

"Music is a circle, clothing's a circle, everything's a circle, it comes back," said Criss. "I want to bring back that era when Sam & Dave and Motown was really big. And they had the Supremes and the Shangri-Las, and it was a really happening era."

When pondering Criss' words, one important thing to consider is that he was 32 in 1978. The lone KISS member over 30 at the time, Criss was also between 4 and 7 years older than the other band members. As such, he was exposed to a different group of artists in his formative years. Where the other member's musical epiphanies had the Beatles [in 1964] as their catalyst; Peter's musical experience had started a decade earlier.

"I love R&B. I grew up on that," said Criss. "I've always [listened to] James Brown and Wilson Pickett, Otis Redding. It's good stuff."

"What the album did foremost was give Peter a chance to get in touch with his roots," explained Poncia. "He was able to do some white R&B, and bluesy kind of things that he grew up with. He was able to show the world a different side to him" (Behind The Mask).

This "different side" would turn out to be autobiographical in many ways. The Brooklyn-born drummer was known for not only wearing his heart on his sleeve, but also a volatile temperamental side. In hindsight, the songs and performances comprising "Peter Criss" mirror a tumultuous period in his life — whether it was feelings of discontent with his standing in KISS, experiencing the disintegration of his first marriage to Lydia Criss, beginning a steamy love affair with a "Playboy" bombshell, or living out a care-free, fast-and-loose lifestyle in L.A. If anything, "Peter Criss" is certainly a close-to-the-bone journey, and one containing arguably some of the Catman's finest vocals of his career.

"Don't you tear my heart out/And lie it on your shelf," howls Criss in "I'm Gonna Love You," a tune that kicks off the album with some '70s-era Stones swagger. One of the few Penridge-co-written Lips-era remakes on the album, "I'm Gonna Love You" surely benefitted from a full-band arrangement compared to its original flat-lining folk-based form. Criss' unmistakable drum groove is complemented by a creative, bouncy bass line from Bodine. Horns arranged by Saviano add R&B/soul texture, while the lead guitar lines (primarily consisting of double-stops) bring some bluesy rock flare.

Though Criss delivers an energetic vocal and the arrangement is sturdy, "You Matter To Me" feels like the one song that is perhaps out of place. Brought to the table by Poncia, the tune's synthesized disco undertones clash with the album's more rootsy flavors. Interestingly, "You Matter..." is the first song on an album with a KISS logo to dabble in disco, pre-dating "I Was Made For Lovin' You" by one year. It also bears the lesser-known distinction of being recorded by John Travolta's little brother, Joey Travolta (the song is the opening track on his 1978 Millennium/Casablanca debut album).

The lone cover song on the album, "Tossin And Turnin'" was originally recorded by Bobby Lewis and spent seven weeks at No. 1 in 1961. "I always liked it because I have insomnia ... I related to it," said Criss regarding the decision to cover the song. (Aside from Criss, other artists who have covered the tune include Joan Jett and polka star Jimmy Sturr.)

The combination of Criss' vocal and Poncia's updated arrangement equates to one of the album's high points. Adding a slight personal touch, Criss altered the line "the clock downstairs is striking four" to "three" — his lucky number. While staying faithful to the original recording, Poncia adds enough of a unique spin — most notably, the tempo is brought down to let the song breathe a bit more. Background vocals are provided courtesy of Maxine Willard, Maxine Dixon and Julia Tillman, one of several instances on the album that finds Criss' gravelly growl complemented by female vocals. The horns are again tastefully arranged by Saviano, with some slightly different accents compared to the original recording.

The eight-bar sax solo is played by Michael Carnahan, who also takes some slight liberties with the original solo. "Tossin' And Turnin'" would be Criss' solo album representative in the set list on KISS' 1979 tour in support of "Dynasty."

Another song with Lips ties, "Don't You Let Me Down" could easily be mistaken for a Ben E. King outtake. With a strong harmony throughout — the verse particularly features an I-vi-ii-V cadence — Poncia had a good framework upon which to build his sterling arrangement. Firstly, the song's steady rhythm is formed by a subtle Bodine bass line and a sparse drum beat by Criss. Faint wah-wah guitar scratches, acoustic guitar strums and a breezy synthesizer patch fill the mix, providing the perfect atmosphere for Criss' sedate vocal. (The lush R&B-ish background vocal blend is courtesy of Criss, Penridge and Poncia, adding an effective element.) Compared to the original demo, the key of the song was raised one whole step from G major to A major to better suit Criss' range. Criss has identified the song as a love letter to Debra Jensen, the "Playboy" model whom he had met prior to the recording of the album and would latter marry.

The title for the closer on side one, "That's The Kind Of Sugar Papa Likes," was borrowed from a line by Humphrey Bogart in the 1948 film "The Treasure Of The Sierra Madre." Yet another Lips-era song, the Catman propels this sexually charged number with not only his spirited vocal, but his groovy drumming. Listen to how Criss rocks a simple straight-edged beat during the verse and proceeds to mix in some swing in the chorus. Criss erupts with a few "Baby Driver"-esque ad-libs as the chorus rides the song out, while upping the percussive energy accordingly with a pounding triplet cymbal pattern. The in-the-pocket guitar solo comes courtesy of Toto guitarist Steve Lukather.

Speaking of Lukather, the pool of musical talent assembled on "Peter Criss" is impressive. Also adding six-string textures throughout the album are the likes of seasoned jazz player John Tropea, Munson, Starz' Brendan Harkin, and the versatile Elliott Randall. Bodine and Neil Jason lay down the bottom end and drummer extraordinaire Allan Schwartzberg subs for Criss on three cuts. Bill Cuomo and Richard Gerstein (aka Richard T. Bear) add keyboards, while the aforementioned Saviano manages the horns. In 1978 many, if not all, of these musicians were not only top players on the session scene, but seasoned pros who understood how to effectively play for the song.

Moving on to side two, the momentum slides a bit with the presence of three ballads. (In hindsight, perhaps the track listing could have been altered to balance the album's dynamics.) "Easy Thing," a song in the key of D major, seems like a lyrical sentiment that hit Criss close to home. "Love is such an easy thing to lose," the Catman croons, as if he was pondering his own relationship troubles at the time. The song transforms into full-fledged "power ballad" territory, convening electric guitar, the rhythm section combo of Jason and Schwartzberg, and a saccharine-laced string arrangement by Cuomo.

With its Bob Seger-inspired stomp, "Rock Me Baby" is one of two songs penned by Sean Delaney and one of a handful of tracks with basics cut in New York at Electric Lady Studios prior to Poncia's involvement. "Baby, who you been lovin' since your man's gone?" ponders Criss. Saviano contributes another winning horn arrangement on top of Gerstein's rock and roll-flavored piano. Meanwhile, background vocals from Annie Sutton and Gordon Gordy answer Criss' rasp. The simple, melodic solo comes courtesy of Tropea.

The all-acoustic "KISS The Girl Goodbye" is the album's streamlined answer to "Beth." A quiet campfire-style tune in the key of A, Criss' vocal is supported by a simple chord structure and plaintive lead lines. With another set of lyrics that tugged at his heart strings, Criss has stated that the song doubled as a bittersweet love letter to his first wife Lydia. Of musical note, "KISS The Girl..." is the rare KISS-related song to contain a diminished chord within its harmonic framework. And how about the Catman's falsetto, something that was unexpected and surprising?

The last of the Lips-era remakes, the infectious "Hooked On Rock 'N' Roll" drops in one last attempt at a rock and roll/R&B hybrid, mixing in enough contributions from Poncia to earn him a songwriting credit. "Mama told me long ago / Ain't no future in that rock and roll / And I said, "Hey mama, it's burnin' hot inside my soul," shouts Criss against a Stax-inspired cocktail of guitar, piano and horns. In a subtle arrangement twist, for the restatement of the bridge, Poncia, Penridge and Criss pepper in some cool doo-wop-style background vocals. Lukather makes his second guitar solo cameo, navigating the I-IV-V-based progression flawlessly.

Criss saves his best for the album's final track, the stunning "I Can't Stop The Rain." An eloquent ballad in the key of F, Gerstein's piano, Tropea and Randall's guitars and a picture-perfect string arrangement from Cuomo help set the perfect mood for Criss, whose vocal positively drips with emotion. "It takes a witch to curse that goddamn sky," condemns Criss, succumbing to the flood. A proper tip of the cap to the late Delaney for penning this tremendous song is a necessity. And it would be remiss not to offer kudos to Criss for turning in one of the best recorded vocal performances of his career.

Within the context of this summary, it's only appropriate to note that Criss required the most assistance of the four KISS members with his solo album. Not only was he aided by Poncia, Delaney and an A-list group of musicians as mentioned, the album consists of a cover song, a song brought in by Poncia, Delaney's contributions, the leftover material from Lips, and a couple of other Criss/Penridge co-writes. Of course, as with all Criss/Penridge collaborations, it's not exactly clear as to the degree the Catman actually contributed.

On a related note, there seem to be a couple of lingering misconceptions about "Peter Criss." Some misinformed reviews of the album — by fans, critics or otherwise — have described it as containing jazz nuances. There are absolutely no jazz elements to be found anywhere on this album. There is R&B, soul and rock and roll elements, most certainly yes. But Jazz? No. Second, Peter Criss did, in fact, play drums on six tracks. As has been well documented, Criss was involved in a car accident on May 27, 1978, which badly injured not only himself but tour manager Fritz Postlethwaite. According to Criss, when sessions resumed in June he played drums with little casts on each finger. Truthfully, it's pretty easy to hear that Criss is playing on the majority of the album, as reflected in the album's credits. And besides, even if he didn't play drums on any of the tracks, as some are still apt to incorrectly claim, would it really matter? As Poncia stated, the goal of this album was to showcase Peter Criss "the singer."

Unfortunately, Peter Criss "the singer" failed to catch on with the record buying public and fans alike, peaking at only No. 43 on the Billboard 200. This was the lowest peak position of any of the solo albums. Along with Simmons' eclectic LP, "Peter Criss" proved to be a bit of a head-scratcher. And given the band's abrasive effect on the mainstream media, there was little hope of a single crossing over to a potential willing audience. (Ironically, Criss' album is the only KISS solo album to be backed by two singles — "Don't You Let Me Down" and "You Matter To Me.")

As for why this album didn't resonate with actual KISS fans in 1978, I believe the music confused them. Asking 8–16 year olds — an age group that made up the majority of KISS' fan base at the time — to get onboard with an album full of songs that had next to nothing to do with "Love Gun," "Deuce" and "Strutter" was, to borrow someone else's words, "highly improbable." It was almost a case of expecting younger fans to listen to their parent's music.

"The sad thing is I don't think [some of the songs] really got their just dues," said Criss. "Like 'I Can't Stop The Rain' and a few other songs that are my all-time favorites. They have so much meaning, you know, to me."

Discussing the four KISS solo albums has emerged as one of the favorite pastimes for KISS fans of all eras. And I've seen enough discussion and debates to know that If there is one KISS solo album that gets torn down the most, it's "Peter Criss." In the end, music — including songs performed by Criss — is purely subjective. However, regardless of your take or mine, "Peter Criss" is a snapshot of the Catman in 1978 and a window into his musical soul. But maybe KISS fans didn't really care to get to know Peter Criss on that level.

Paul Stanley

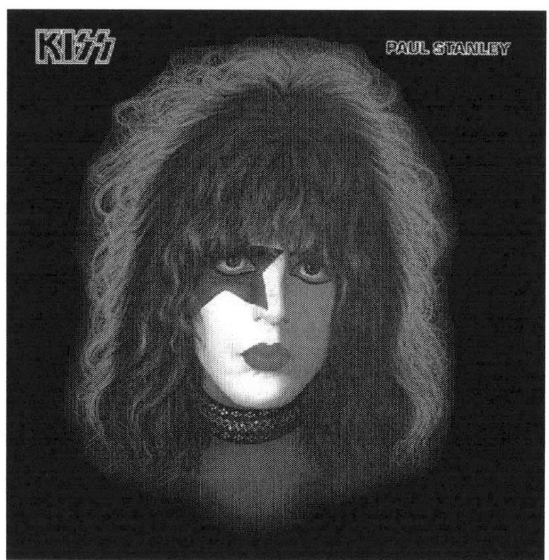

Release Details:
Casablanca NBLP-7123

Tracks:

A1. Tonight You Belong To Me
(4:39) - Paul Stanley

A2. Move On
(3:07) - Paul Stanley / Mikel Japp

A3. Ain't Quite Right
(3:34) - Paul Stanley / Mikel Japp

A4. Wouldn't You Like To Know Me
(3:16) - Paul Stanley

A5. Take Me Away (Together As One)
(5:26) - Paul Stanley / Mikel Japp

B1. It's Alright
(3:31) - Paul Stanley

B2. Hold Me, Touch Me (Think of Me When we're Apart)
(3:40) - Paul Stanley
[• USA #46; CAN #64; UK #48]

B3. Love in Chains
(3:34) - Paul Stanley

B4. Goodbye
(4:09) - Paul Stanley

Album Details:
Produced by Paul Stanley. Tracks A5, B1, B3 & B4 Produced by Paul Stanley and Jeff Glixman. Recorded and mixed at Electric Lady Studios, New York City, NY; The Record Plant and Village Recorders, Los Angeles, CA; and Trident Studios, London, England, February – July, 1978. Mixed at Trident Studios, London, England, by Mike Stone.

Chart Action:

Chart Peak (USA): #40 (12/16/78) with 18 weeks on charts. Other countries: CAN #43;

42	10	PAUL STANLEY Casablanca NBLP 7123	7.98	7.98	7.98

10/14/78	10/21/78	10/28/78	11/4/78	11/11/78	11/18/78	11/25/78	12/2/78	12/9/78
89	67	57	51	49	43	41	41	42
12/16/78	**12/23/78**	**12/30/78**	**1/6/79**	**1/13/79**	**1/20/79**	**1/27/79**	**2/3/79**	**2/10/79**
**** 40 ****	40	40	50	49	49	82	126	162

RIAA/Sales:

"Paul Stanley" was certified gold and platinum by the RIAA on 10/2/78. It has sold over 33,000 copies since the SoundScan® era commenced in 1991. The album was certified gold by the CRIA (Canada) for sales of 50,000 copies on 12/1/78. Contemporaneously, Casablanca had shipped 1,300,539 copies of Paul's album by the end of June 1979, which, surprisingly, was the fewest of the four solo albums.

Singles (USA):

Casablanca NB-940: Hold Me, Touch Me / Goodbye

Billboard Hot-100 Chart:

11/4/78	11/11/78	11/18/78	11/25/78	12/2/78	12/9/78	12/16/78	12/23/78	12/30/78
85	74	66	59	57	53	47	**** 46 ****	46
1/6/79	**1/13/79**	**1/20/79**	**1/27/79**					
71	97	98	X					

Cashbox:

11/4/78	11/11/78	11/18/78	11/25/78	12/2/78	12/9/78	12/16/78	12/23/78	12/30/78
84	74	65	59	54	47	45	42	**** 41 ****
1/6/79	**1/13/79**	**1/20/79**	**1/27/79**					
X	59	91	X					

Performed Live:

"Move On" was performed by KISS during the 1979 "Return of KISS" tour. Paul eventually performed "Tonight You Belong To Me," "Wouldn't You Like To Know Me," and "Goodbye" during his 1989 solo tour. All four songs were again performed during his 2006/7 "Live to Win" tours. "Goodbye" also made regular appearances on the 1995 convention tour and "Move On," "Take Me Away (Together As One)" and "Tonight You Belong To Me" were all attempted.

Paul Stanley: In the Solo Album Spotlight

A refocused examination of the Star Child's 1978 solo album and, it's alright.

"I feel that I've really come out on my own. I think my solo album is definitely as purely me as can be expected. I mean, nobody is going to sound totally original" (Guitar Player Magazine, 1978).

Of the four members, Paul Stanley's solo album probably presented the greatest challenge in its creation. Where Gene may have been the "face" of KISS, Paul was the front-man, the heart and soul of the band and its primary songwriter. Paul's album was always going to "sound" like a KISS album since his was also the primary voice for the band, and if nothing else that provided Paul with a delicate balancing act to attempt. Yet, for all of that pigeon-holing, Paul's body of work prior to 1978 had run a gamut of styles, from soft acoustic ("Hard Luck Woman") to straight-forward rockers ("Hotter Than Hell") through tongue-in-cheek songs with thinly veiled sexual innuendo ("Love Gun"). From such a menagerie one might expect Paul to provide a similar range of material when unleashed in the studio without any of the restrictions of working within the framework of KISS. Ultimately, though, Paul stretched his boundaries for his album, without over-reaching or heading into any uncomfortable directions. Instead, he relied on subtle touches or lush embellishments to present a highly focused atmosphere. In some ways he played it safe.

Paul's second choice producer, Jeff Glixman, may have seemed odd — his first, Ron Nevison was unable to be scheduled (he was busy taking UFO to the next level). By 1978 Jeff had really only worked with one band, Kansas, having producing four of their albums. It had been a successful pairing that included their hit song "Carry on Wayward Son." His services were only utilized as a co-producer on four of Paul's album's tracks ("Take Me Away (Together as One)," "It's Alright," "Love in Chains," and "Goodbye"), with Paul handling the rest of the production duties himself. There has been some suggestion that the partnership with Glixman was not working out for Paul and that he decided to finish the production of the album himself. However, the reality of the situation is actually reversed. Paul had enjoyed a guiding role in the production of KISS albums, so the requirement for him to use a producer was somewhat moot. His project started out with him simply hitting the studio with a band, and his material, and working the arrangements out with repeated takes while each musician found their groove. The need for a "name" producer was likely foisted on him by the label, and it is clear the neither of the parties had defined their roles when they started working with one another.

The other core player in the project was guitarist Bob Kulick, who finally received a credit for his performance on a KISS-related project. Bob was not a surprising choice for lead guitar duties. While Paul certainly had the chops to play just about every instrument himself he was more than comfortable and secure to use the services of a guitarist he had often cut demos with. Bob recalled that Gene also wanted him to play on his album, but once he'd recorded with Paul he wasn't "allowed" to (Sherman, Dale – "Black Diamond 3" [DS-BD3]). This is somewhat illustrative of the inherent competition that existed between certain band members on their solo projects, though it wouldn't be too surprising considering either of their roles and the state of interpersonal relationships within the band by 1978. Ironically, even with this sense of competition, there was a guitarist who would appear on both Gene and Paul's solo albums in the form of Steve Lacey. It seems that certain session players were "shareable," while others were not...

One might be able to suggest that Paul's completed album was somewhat formulaic. Songs starting acoustically before heading into full-throttle rock territory, as had been done with "Black Diamond" or "I Want You" are present: The epic "Tonight (You Belong to Me)" is strong evidence of that, though it takes that building style to a whole new level with the lush layering of the guitars and vocals (along with the further prominent use of the e-bow that had emerged on "Love Gun"). In discussions in Guitar Player magazine, Paul commented about some of the technical experimentation during the creation of the album: "I used the E Bow on quite a few [tracks]. I really found it incredibly useful. I don't know how practical it is for live performing, because you can only utilize it on one string at a time, which really makes it a little difficult. Most of the time on [the album] when there was an E Bow there was really between three and six of them over-dubbed. They were on 'Tonight You Belong To Me'; on the melodic line from the front of the heavy section, it's not a keyboard, it's the E Bows. On 'Move On,' the next song, they come in around halfway through the solo; there's about six of them there. And then on 'Ain't Quite Right,' they tend to give a certain kind of mood, like a haunting kind of sound. To me it's something like an oboe, or a synthesizer crossed with an oboe, and I've been fascinated with sounds like that ever since I can remember" (Guitar Player Magazine, 1978). If it isn't "new," then it was certainly a highly refined and focused presentation of that sort of style of song with the arrangement and execution demonstrating a high level of attention to detail. As an opening track it lays down a gauntlet of sorts.

More than an album of two sides, Paul's album was an album of two disparate major sessions: East Coast and West, or the "Jeff" versus "Paul" halves. Recording of the album started at Paul's favorite studio, Electric Lady, in New York City. In fact, the first half of the album really wasn't supposed to be the album recordings in the first place. Paul recalled, "I started the album about six months ago as what I thought were going to be demos. It's just a hobby of mine to go in the studio and see what happens. So I cut four things, figuring that when I did the album I would wind up re-cutting them, but I wound up using them... Before he [Jeff] came out, I again wanted to go in the studio and fool around so I cut 'Hold Me, Touch Me'" (Hit Parader). Bob also remembered the split in the recording sessions: "We did half the record in New York, and then there was a break and I had gone to Europe and Australia with Meat Loaf. We came back and the rest of the band went to Hawaii and we went to LA and worked on the rest with Paul. So Steve and I stayed actually at the Westwood Marquis and we were there for like six weeks" (DS-BD3). The break in recording can be dated to have occurred around May/June 1978 due to Meat Loaf's touring schedule at the time (The band's final show in Melbourne took place on June 28). Paul, too, would have been busy in May with obligations relating to the "KISS Meets the Phantom of the Park" movie filming in California. Bob has recalled that the first sessions in New York were conducted in a fast-paced businesslike manner, "It was amazing because the half that we did in New York took like 10 days. We went in there all business and just took care of it. The part in LA took like 10 times as long. Because it was LA, 'What time do you wanna start today'? 'Well, I want to go to the beach, and then...' We didn't get any work done, but we had fun" (DS-BD3)!

The material initially cut at Electric Lady, in late-February 1978 (Sharp, Ken – Behind The Mask) with Dave Wittman engineering (assisted by Michael Frondelli), included: "Tonight You Belong To Me," "Move On," "Ain't Quite Right," and "Wouldn't You Like To Know Me." This is likely due to the participation of both Richie Fontana (drums), Steve Buslowe (bass), and the "Rouge" girls (Maria Vidal, Diana Grasselli, and Miriam Naomi Valle) on backing vocals. Steve, like Bob, had been working with Meat Loaf on his "Bat out of Hell" tour, and was brought into the sessions by Bob when Paul requested a bass player. Bob remembered, "The bass player on the record was the bass player who worked with me at the time in Meat Loaf. And he was the bass player who had worked with me with Michael Bolotin who went on to become Michael Bolton" (DS-BD3). Steve also later made a guest appearance on Bruce Kulick's "Worlds Apart" Blackjack album released in 1980. Richie, who had been working with Billy Squier in the Bill Aucoin managed band Piper, was recruited through that connection, though Piper had toured also with KISS for a short run of dates prior to their split. As part of the AMI family Richie was a known quantity to Paul, who was probably more than aware of the demise of that band when he requested Richie's services. Richie went on to work with the Sean Delaney Skatt Brothers project in 1979. The "Rouge" girls were the vocalists in "Desmond Child & Rouge," a band that had been formed while the members was in college and were starting to build a following when they met Paul in New York. Their connection with Paul eventually led to the first Paul Stanley and Desmond Child co-written song, "The Fight" (appearing on their 1979 debut album). Desmond and Paul's song-writing partnership became more important in the years to follow.

These core songs provide the starting sequence for the first side of the album and were produced by Paul. "Move On," if nothing more than homage to Bad Company and straight-forward rock 'n' roll, allowed Paul the use of the prominent backing vocals of the "Rouge" girls, in a manner similar to how the "KISSettes" (Tasha Thomas, Ray Simpson, and Hilda Harris) had been used on "Love Gun." As a result the first songs are more of a band effort and there's a special synergy that carries through. Working in such a casual manner also seems to indicate that these sessions were more demo than fully-fledged album recording sessions. Of this batch of songs two had been co-written by Mikel Japp. Mikel would be the only co-writer credited on Paul's album, working on three songs with him ("Move On," "Ain't Quite Right," and "Take Me Away"). Mikel had been introduced to Paul via photographer Barry Levine, who suggested that the two get together to write and playing a demo of the melodic "A Piece of The Action" for Paul. The pop song had been placed with John Waite's The Babys for their Ron Nevison produced "Broken Heart" album in 1977. Paul and Mikel got together at a rehearsal studio in Los Angeles and worked out idea pieces that Mikel had into the resulting three songs. Other elements of Paul's influences come out on songs such as "Wouldn't You like to Know Me," which while following a straight-forward good time rock style allows Paul's Raspberries influences to come through.

The remaining song on Side-A of the album, "Take Me Away (Together as One)," the third Japp co-composition, is a transitional song in terms of the players involved. It's the sole song on which Carmine Appice drums, and the final contribution of Steve Buslowe on bass. It seems likely that it was the first song cut in L.A. at Village Recorders with Jeff Glixman engineering. With layers of acoustic and electric guitars with ebbs and flows the song is highly representative of the personal musical growth of Paul as an artist as he paints broad strokes musically. Carmine was one of the most notable guests on Paul's album, having by 1978 played with the likes of Vanilla Fudge, Cactus, and Rod Stewart. Cactus, naturally, was a band that Wicked Lester guitarist Ron Leejack had been doing session work (and limited live performances) prior to working with Gene and Paul. Carmine had several connections with the KISS camp, having been managed at the time by Aucoin Management, and later having another manager who had been part of Aucoin Management. Carmine's involvement on Paul's album was simply a result of he and Paul being friends, and Paul asking him to appear on a song. Carmine recalled, "I used to hang out with Paul. When they were doing the solo albums Paul asked me to play on his - so I did" (Metal-exiles.com).

The final four songs from the Los Angeles sessions (and album) feature a different rhythm section: Drummer Craig Kampf, who had worked with the Hudson Brothers and Nick Gilder (other Casablanca artists) and also went on to work with the Skatt Brothers project, and bassist Eric Nelson was in the Nick Gilder band. Of the four songs the stand-out remains "Hold Me, Touch Me (Think Of Me When We're

Apart)," the single released in support of the album and Paul's first fully-fledged ballad. Paul was ready for some limited experimentation outside the confines of the band structure. The project allowed him to write strictly for himself rather than trying to fit material into the image the band presented. It would be something of a cop out to suggest that any of the songs on Paul's solo album could have fit easily on a KISS album, but it really isn't too far from the truth with some of the songs having similarities with earlier compositions. The comparisons do more to strengthen Paul's musical vision as being a guiding factor in the sound KISS had developed. "Hold Me, Touch Me" was the only song on the album to be primarily Paul on guitar, including the solo. He recalled, "for a song like 'Hold Me, Touch Me' I wanted a very glassy sound, so I used an acoustic guitar strung with the high strings, and I capoed it at about the 9th fret. It's very, very tricky" (GPM, 1978). As a single the song missed the mark only reaching #46 on the US charts, perhaps not as rewarding as it should have been for the effort made to create the track and bravery of stepping outside of the comfort zone in relation to the type of material that may have been expected. Doug Katsaros played piano and arranged the strings on the piece while he and Peppy Castro contributed backing vocals. Peppy had known Ace Frehley prior to KISS and later worked with numerous KISS/Kulick brothers-related artists including Bob's Balance band project, Michael Bolton, and Ronnie Spector. Doug also later worked with Balance and Michael Bolton, plus Cher and Bon Jovi.

"It's Alright" was one of the tracks for which Paul used a Gallien-Krueger amp, rather than usual Marshall. Paul felt the amp change was better suited for "that gritty kind of Stonesy, ballsy rhythm sound" (GPM, 1978). And like the other "heavier" songs on the album Paul used the capo to allow him to use "open chords as opposed to bar chords" (GPM, 1978) which he felt sounded better - he use the capo on the majority of the songs on the album. When asked about the guitar tunings used, Paul responded, "I've been playing in open G, with only five strings, taking the low E off removing it completely. The high E string is tuned down to D. I think it's D, B, G, D, G [from high to low]" (GPM, 1978). While Paul didn't shirk experimentation, the underlying premise for the album seems to have been to keep it as organic as possible. There would be no 90 degree directional changes. He recalled the ethos, "It was very informal. Some people have asked, 'How long did you rehearse?' There was no rehearsal. I would call everybody up and bring them into the studio and we played on the spot, nobody knew the songs, I hardly knew the songs, I usually wrote them just before I got into the studio" (Hit Parader, 2/79).

With the E Bow only being utilized for its atmospheric enhancing effect on several tracks, the album remained quite basic and straight-forward in its construction. There was little over-playing, or showing off, and the structure of the material was kept very matter-of-fact rather than being excessive. In those terms the album was the least egotistical of the four. Closing numbers "Love in Chains" and "Goodbye" can easily compete with the most rollicking tracks on Ace's album. "Love in Chains" features contributions on guitar by Steve Lacey, who also performed on Gene's album. "Goodbye" was the last track recorded for the album, at the Record Plant, a somewhat quaint flourish of using a closing track with a message. Paul worked rapidly to complete his project, not only due to the time limitations imposed by the label. Paul, in some ways, was afraid to lose the spontaneity by over-thinking any aspect of his solo album: "I think part of what you lose if you spend too much time mixing is you lose emotions, spontaneity. So basically that's the same reason I didn't rehearse the band, because you give people too much time to learn a song and they come up with parts that may be musically much more interesting but what they're losing is all the heart in the thing" (Hit Parader, 2/79). The point that he and his participants didn't really have much time available to them is rather moot.

With recording completed the album was mixed at Trident Studios in London, England in August 1978. Paul used Mike Stone, having liked the work he'd done on Gene's album. Paul recalled, "Then I went over to England. A lot of people talk about going for that English sound. No obviously, the best way to get an English sound is to go over to England. So I went to work with Mike Stone who did Queen and did Gene's album... I knew what I was looking for — I wanted the heaviness at the bottom, but didn't want the bottom to detract from everything else. What happens in a lot of heavy records is that there's so much crunch in the bottom that it overpowers the whole track... there's so much boom and kick drum that it's irritating, almost obnoxious. So what I was going for was much more balance, full sound, with a really clear bottom" (Hit Parader, 2/79). When released in September, "Paul Stanley" only managed to reach a disappointing #40 on the charts, a mere three positions higher than "Peter Criss." The album was the shortest charting of the four solo albums, spending just 18 weeks on the charts. Apparently, Paul was able to live with a comment he made to Richard Robinson in Hit Parader Magazine: "I think everybody's prepared for whatever's going to happen with the albums. Which is not going to be that one album's going to bomb. So you're dealing with relative success in relationship to each other. There's not going to be one that's not going to do well. It's just a matter of which one's going to do better" (HP 4/79). Regardless of whatever level success the album did or did not attain, it was a representation of the musical maturity level Paul had reached as a writer, performer, and producer. Like Ace, the album would be a stepping stone to a new phase in his career as he explored different styles of music and embraced a softer side. He wasn't pandering to any particular style or audience.

From Paul's album three "alternate mix" versions of songs are available in collector's circles: "Tonight You Belong To Me," "Wouldn't You Like To Know Me," and "Take Me Away (Together as One)." While these songs are described as being "alternative mixes," take into consideration that Paul's demos often sounded nearly identical to the fully recorded versions, and that some material on Paul's album was essentially cleaned-up demos that sounded good enough to be released. In most cases the differences between these "alternative mixes" and the release versions are minor. There has also been the suggestion that he remixed some tracks at a late stage being dissatisfied with the original efforts. On "Tonight You Belong to Me" the acoustic guitar intro is more basic (rough) and lacks the variable speed overlay of the album version. "Wouldn't You Like To Know Me" is some 20 seconds longer than the album version, having a third repetition of the chorus at the end of the song during the fade out, versus the album version, which starts fading during the second chorus repetition. Finally, "Take Me Away (Together as One)" is some 16 seconds longer than the album version. Of the three "alternative mixes," the differences between this and the album version of the song are most noticeable. Immediately, in the 25-second introduction there are multiple cymbal fills, rather than the single fill prior to the lead guitar and vocals beginning on the album version. Instead of ending with a simple fade out, as does the album version, this song continues the instrumental section before ending with an amp feedback section culminating in a single struck chord. On none of the "alternative mixes" are there any lyrical or arrangement changes.

KISS

THANKS YOU

NBLP 7123

NBLP 7120

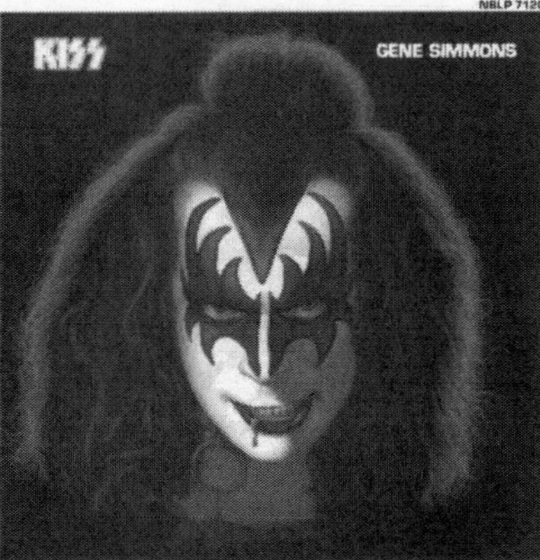

NBLP 7122

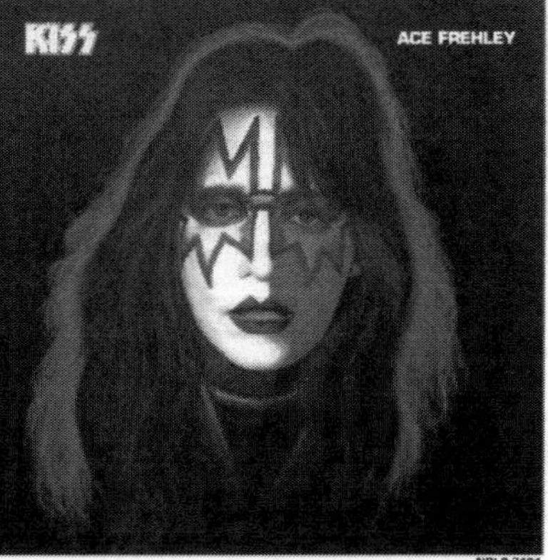

NBLP 7121

DON'T MISS THE SPECTACULAR ACTION MOVIE "KISS MEETS THE PHANTOM" NBC SAT OCT 28.

Casablanca

© 1978 AUCOIN MANAGEMENT, INC. BY AGREEMENT WITH KISS

A rock steady PRODUCTION INC.

(Billboard Magazine, 10/14/78)

Solo Album Fast Facts

Gene Simmons' had the largest number of guest performers on his solo album.

Ace Frehley used the fewest number of performers on his solo album.

Ace Frehley's solo album has sold the most copies in the post-1991 SoundScan era.

Peter Criss' solo album debuted highest on the Billboard Top-200 Album Charts at #85 (10/14/78), followed by Ace (#87), Gene (#88) and Paul (#89).

Gene Simmons' solo album surged the greatest number of places on the Billboard Top-200 Album Charts in its second week of charting moving up some 32 places. Peter's surged the fewest, just 8 places. And Paul and Ace's both moved up 22 spots.

Gene Simmons' solo album charted the highest on the Billboard Top-200 Album Charts eventually reaching #22 (1/6/79).

Peter Criss' solo album reached its highest placing on the Billboard Top-200 Album Charts (#43) in its seventh week.

Ace Frehley's solo album charted for the most number of weeks: 23, reaching #26. Gene's was right behind him with 22 weeks.

Paul Stanley's solo album charted for the fewest number of weeks: 18, only reaching #40.

Ace's "New York Groove" was the only legitimate hit single from the solo albums reaching #13 on the Billboard Hot-100 singles chart (2/3/79).

Peter Criss' was the only solo album supported by two singles releases. Neither charted.

Paul Stanley's "Hold Me, Touch Me" single didn't quite make top 40 in the US, but it did linger on the charts for 12 weeks.

Only Ace Frehley's and Gene Simmons' solo singles were performed live by KISS during the "Dynasty" tour.

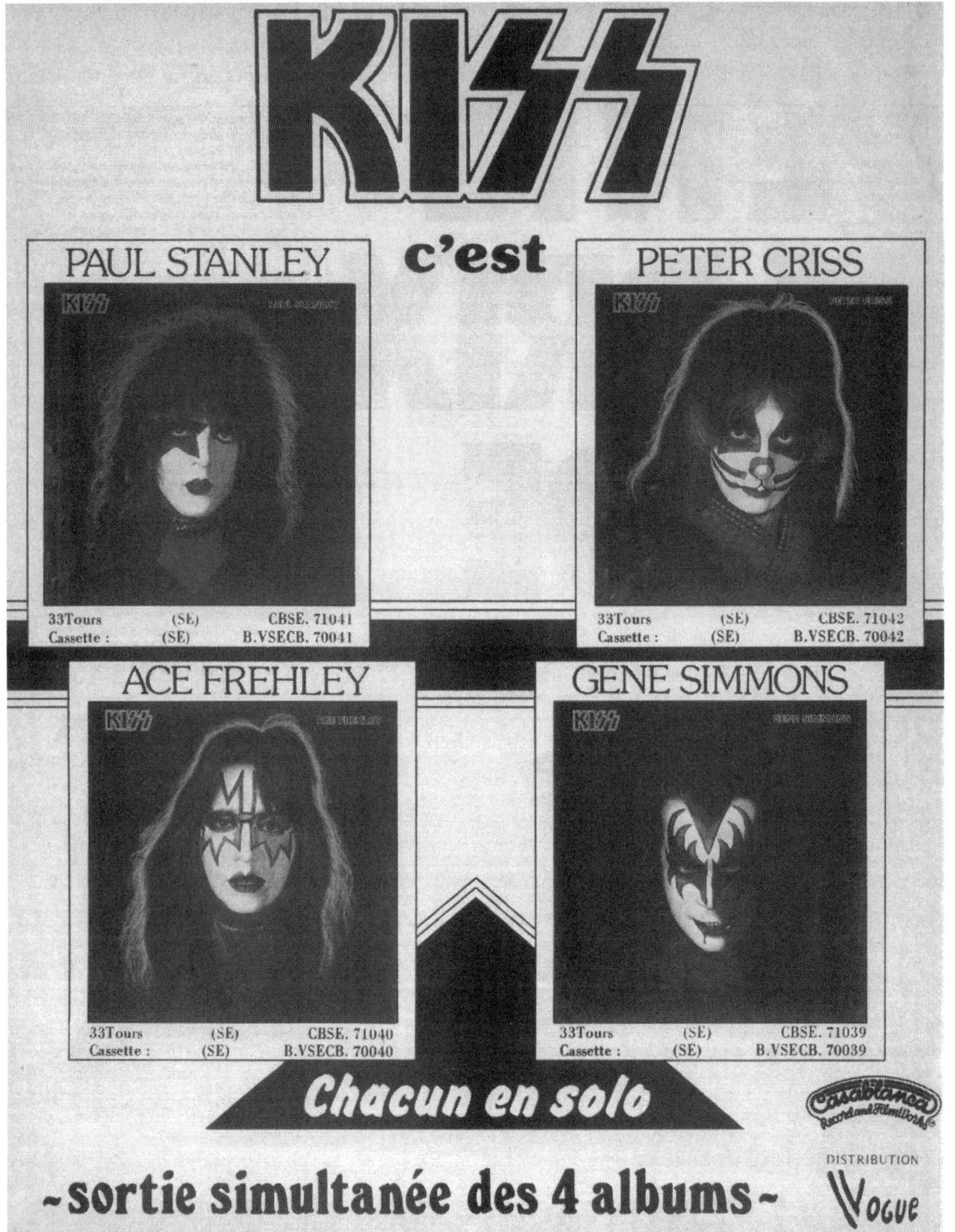

(French solo albums ad)

"Gene Simmons" Related Interviews

"I wanted to do the songs in a way that when people listened to them they wouldn't say, 'God, listen to all the guitars.' What I wanted is to have people sit down and say the songs are good" (Guitar Player, 1978).

Ben D. Bollinger

In an exclusive interview, founder of the Citrus College Singers details his involvement on Gene Simmons' 1978 album and recounts a "first-class" experience for his students.
Interview by Tim McPhate

Ben, you founded the Azusa Citrus College Singers in 1968. What was your purpose in founding the group?
Ben D. Bollinger: Well, when I started, I went to USC as an opera major and I left USC and went to Ramona High School in Riverside for six years. And then I came to Citrus. And you have to remember, I never ever ever touched a pop piece of music. I was all about classical music and opera. I transferred to Citrus and I realized in building the program that I couldn't build it purely on a classical base. In other words, if we wanted to travel around the world and compete internationally, I had to find a way to raise money with these young people. And so we started doing a tremendous amount of Christmas concerts in all of the major venues in L.A. If you check any of the major venues from the clubs to the finest country clubs, the Citrus Singers did their Christmas show. So, to answer your question, we set out, of course, to create a great music department at Citrus College and ended up realizing we had to take some side trips along the way in order to fund and support that program.

And moving ahead one decade later to 1978 and the natural question: How did you come to receive an invitation to participate on Gene Simmons' solo album?
Well, it's really interesting how this happened. I was doing a lot of television work and a lot of studio work and I had a dear friend in Cher. Gene ended up living with Cher for a period of time. And he asked me if I would bring my singers in 1978 to celebrate her birthday at the Beverly Hills Hotel on Sunset Boulevard. And I told him, "Sure, I'd be happy to." And she loved a song called "If." And I had a brilliant young singer by the name of John Cavazos, and the group was excellent at the time. And we went out and sang for Cher and got to meet her and spend some time with Gene. And I got a call that afternoon, "Look, would you be interested in doing my solo album?" And I said, "Gene, I don't know." I liked him — by the way, as you know, the image these guys portray is not normally who they are. For example, Alice Cooper married one of my Citrus singers, Sheryl Goddard. For the parents of these young people to see these singers around these kind of people — like Alice had snakes all around him — they didn't know what to think about it. And as you know, that group didn't let anybody see who they were. They wore outfits and [makeup].

That's right.
A lot of my parents were concerned that I was doing this. But I told them, "Believe me, Gene was an educator at one time and he's a really good guy." So anyway, I ended up telling Gene, "Okay, I'll go do it." Well, the thing to understand about background singing is nothing is written out. And when you go to the studio, you have to have extremely talented people that will listen carefully and will back up what Gene wanted done. And he just loved the first two numbers we did. He was just thrilled to death. So we came back the second day and did "When You Wish Upon A Star." And I don't think Gene has a great voice, but he probably sang on that as well as he can sing. And the track behind him was really quite excellent. And I'll also tell you that KISS hired really excellent people from the Los Angeles area, the instrumental people. They didn't spare a nickel on those albums. Cherokee Studios is where we did the work. Grace Slick and [the band] Queen were in the studio with us there. So the kids got to meet a lot of these professional groups. They learned tremendously during that three-day period, a lot about the recording studio and about the recording engineers.

It sounds like an amazing experience for a college choir.
If you go back and research Citrus, we were much more than a college choir. We won international competitions in Austria and around the world as a college choir. But also we did a string show that was all pop and we did a Christmas show that had performances sold-out, 1,500 [people] a performance. So this group was far beyond the average college group. You could not hire them three years out. That's how booked they were. So Gene recognized the fact that here's a group with some brilliantly talented people, people now that are in the industry making a living with music. So I think it's maybe the wrong approach to say choir. They were a choral program when they went to Europe. And they were a pop program when they went to Hawaii, Japan and other parts of the world.

I understand completely. [Editor's Note: Gene Simmons credited the group as the Azusa Citrus College Choir on his album.] Can you describe how the ensemble's vocal parts were formulated? Did Gene play the tracks and describe what he was looking for?
I think it's really important to understand the whole process of background singers. You know, it would take me two hours to explain to you that all of those pop guys from Britain and throughout the world were looking basically for the black choral response. They wanted something that was really a soul and spirit; they wanted something that "responded" and they wanted good voices behind them. And today, I'm sure you're aware, they can sing any note they want to sing and they can use the tuner and bring it into tune. That was not the case at all with us. Gene would sing a phrase and say, "Look, can you back this?" And we would stop for a minute and we'd say, "How about a three-part female sound Gene? Listen to this." And then he'd say, "No, I think I'd like to have..." And then we'd put tenors in the

high register in with it and mix it. And in those days, the sound was maybe not as quite as "forward." The recording technique was to somewhat bury the background. Certain groups actually brought it forward — you'd get a different sound. The mix is so very important. Now the guy that mixed for Queen was the guy who was mixing for Gene's material that night.

That would have been Mike Stone.
Yes. And he was wonderful to the kids. He explained everything he was doing. If you listen to the recording with Gene, there's not a lot of bass in it. In other words, he wanted that kind of gospel, high-tenor mix with the female voices. So you get that kind of response, except for "When You Wish Upon A Star." What we went back to was a pretty straight tone emulating the Disney quality. I have to tell you, in all honesty, the great thing about that group in '78 was you told them what you wanted and they gave it to you. If we wished, we could have done many, many, many [recordings]. We got many requests after Gene to do background work but we didn't because we knew we were taking jobs away from people.

Would you say this group in 1978 was the finest you had during your career?
That would be hard to say. They would be amongst the finest. I had some magnificent groups and brilliant voices so I would be afraid to say it was the best. But I would say that many of the young people in that group went out to Broadway and to New York and became major talents.

Ben, you are credited as the director of the ensemble on the album. You're there in the studio, with your students and with Gene. Can you give us an outline of your role in that setting?
My role is somewhat passive because when I went in, I was going to conduct "When You Wish Upon A Star," and I realized that with Gene and with Ace and with those guys, they're not a real disciplined [band]. These guys kind of operate on their own battery, you know what I mean? And they wouldn't be doing anything and we'd be sitting around doing nothing. And then they'd come down from upstairs and say, "Okay. Here's what we're going to do. Let's try this and let's try that." There's no question that Gene was the key to the whole thing. And he treated the kids first-class. Anything they wanted, it was there for them. So basically what I became was a surrogate to what Gene asked me to do. If the group was setting up an up-tempo set, I would just kind of roam back — not so much conduct — but roam back in and listen in and hear if the part singing was being done in a manner that was acceptable to me. And in every case it was. To be honest with you, and I'll be very frank, I think maybe a lot of those kids knew more about that genre, about that music, than I did. I used to tell them, "I know what I'm doing when it comes to Brahms and Shostakovich and instrumental or vocal, but when it comes to pop music a lot of you kids are way ahead of me so let's not play games."

(Laughs) Ben, I sent you the tracks that feature the ensemble. In listening to them some 35 years later, what are your thoughts?
I listened to all three of them. I haven't heard them for probably five years. But I listened to them and I'm still very pleased. In other words, what we got out of that recording was exactly what Gene wanted to get out of it.

You just described Gene treating the students "first class," so this was a positive educational experience and Gene interacted well with them?
Yes, he really did. And it's really interesting, they had read a lot of things about Gene [and KISS] — you know, maybe they were anti-Christian or anti-this or anti-that, and had sexual innuendos [in their songs]. And I said, "Listen, don't ever judge anybody in this industry until you meet them and see what you think." I used Alice Cooper as an example: Alice Cooper married a Baptist minister's daughter. Was he satanic because he had snakes crawling all around him? Well no, of course not. He was an extremely bright businessman. I met him and he's a very sharp guy. Well, with Gene Simmons, the kids got to meet him and evaluate for themselves what kind of man he was. And he treated them with respect. He was a class act. He was fun — all the guys were fun. The kids got to see them without their masks on. The biggest mistake I made in the whole thing was I put my name on the album. I should have never done that.

Yes, you are indeed credited on the album.
Yeah, I shouldn't have done it because then kids started calling me from all over the country and I had to change my phone number.

And here it is, all these years later and I'm calling you again (laughs).
Well, it's incredible. I did a lot of albums and never used my own name; I used a pseudonym. In this one, I just thought, "Well, with my friendship with Cher and knowing Gene at that time, I will go ahead and use it." And I shouldn't have.

So a bunch of KISS fans were calling you?
The kids would call at all times of the night, from all over the country — in New York, Philadelphia and Pittsburgh — saying, "What do they look like? What are they like? What kind of guys are they?" At first, I tried to be nice but then I had to change my number.

Ben, did you or the school get compensated for the work?
They made a contribution to the foundation. I refused to accept any money for it. The kids knew going in that they would not be paid for it. I did not want them paid for it. But he made a contribution to the foundation, which helped them in their travel. And we often did that because we didn't want to get the kids in a position where they were taking money from background singers that would have only gotten that wage. We worked at a lot of studios. It was an amazing time and I had

to kind of cut it off after this because we did this album and you can end up doing an awful lot of that work and it's one experience the kids should have in college, but it's not the only one they should have.

So there were some other pop/rock recordings that you were featured on?
I was, but I prefer to not go into that. If I did, some of them — I'm just not very proud of.

But you are proud of your involvement on Gene's album?
Yes. I was okay with this because I liked the fact that they were all doing solo albums. I liked the fact that Gene was really sharing his soul with people. There was no foolishness to this album. If you listen to "When You Wish Upon A Star," Gene was saying, "Here's who I am."

That's absolutely correct, Ben. Gene has stated that the song meant a lot to him growing up and he was adamant about interpreting it on his solo album.
He was. And I suggested to him at the time, "What a perfect example," because those Disney sweeteners, we did a lot of that kind of stuff. And it's so simple. You just straighten the tone and sing a four-part structure and bend the rhythm a little bit and that's all you had to do.

The KISS solo albums were hugely promoted when they were released in September 1978. Was the fact that the ensemble was featured on Gene's album heavily publicized around campus?
No. To be honest with you, if you're a chemistry teacher, an English teacher or a French teacher at a university, you don't get very much recognition. In '73 we were getting tremendous recognition all over the world. And if you said, "Citrus College," they said, "Citrus Singers." And I found it important not to flaunt it or not to say, "Look what we have done." Because we weren't doing this for the college, we were doing this for the students to expand their horizons. It was important for them to have this kind of an experience. When they sat in a classroom, everyday, it was Brahms and Mozart. And now they had to step out and do Gene Simmons. And they realized within the field of music, you have to have an extremely gifted person and be able to do many, many facets in order to make a living with music. And I think they realized that. They realized that in the studio; they realized that in the way they were treated. And by the way, young people recognize when they're being looked down on or whether being respected. And I had the feeling through that entire session that Gene and KISS treated the young people with the utmost respect. And when the students walked out they had a very fine experience.

Sometimes fans don't get to hear these types of stories so I think it's fantastic to learn this. Did you ever interact with Gene after the album was released?
I'll be honest with you, after that experience, I never had contact with Gene again.

Did you stay in contact with Cher?
No, I have not. I did meet her at the Hollywood Golden Apple Awards. We did the Hollywood Golden Apple Awards for many years. I did say hello to her but I haven't seen her for many, many years. I know that, [around] this time with Gene, her daughter was just a little beautiful little blonde girl and her mother was also there at the hotel. We had an airplane write "Happy Birthday Cher" in the sky. And on the hotel lawn the singers sang "If a picture paints a thousand words." Remember that piece?

Sure, the Bread song.
She loved that number and so John sang it to her. We had a nice arrangement. To be honest, it was like a friendship thing. "Would you do this?" "Yes, I'll be happy to do it for you." We met in the night and passed and that was it.

Switching gears, today your family operates the Ben D. Bollinger Candlelight Pavilion Dinner Theater. Can you tell us about this endeavor?
Sure. We've been here 28 years and we've had fascinating experiences and we've had tough times like any other business, but it could never exist without my son Mickey and my daughter Mindy. And they're doing better work now, in the last five years, since I retired, than I was ever capable of doing up until that point. So, if you don't mind, I'd like to turn it over to Mickey and let him explain what they're doing and how they're doing it.

Sure.
Michael "Mickey" Bollinger: Well, it's interesting, we've always been based around Broadway performances and this whole thing started because of dad's Christmas shows out at Citrus College and that whole concept is what created this. So we started out doing just basically Broadway productions and fine dining and over the years we've morphed into a lot more than that. We've got a summer concert series going on. We have groups that perform plays — so there's something going on here all the time, in music and theater. And it's been very successful.

And you are located in Claremont, California?
Correct.

Over a typical week, what type of entertainment does the pavilion feature?
Thursdays through Sunday is when we do our Broadway musicals. And Tuesdays and Wednesdays is when we do our tribute bands, our summer concert series. We also do children's workshops.

What are some of the Broadway shows you are featuring currently?
We do a little bit of everything. Right now, we're doing "The King And I." We just got through with "The Full Monty." We have "The Sound Of Motown" coming up, which is a show that we've written that showcases all of the great music of Motown. We've also got "Seven Brides For Seven Brothers" and our Christmas show, of course.

How many people does the facility hold?
299.

And this is a family-based business, correct?
Ben D. Bollinger: Yes, Mindy's the producer, she's taken my place. And Mickey is the general manager — he runs the entire facility.

Thanks, Mickey. Ben, one final question. I understand you retired from Citrus College in 2005. And I am aware that the music program has built quite a nice reputation, including cultivating positive relationships with industry organizations such as The Recording Academy. Are you proud of your legacy?
I am extremely proud. I'm also proud of this experience with Gene. I was dean of the division when Gunnar Eisel and Bob Slack walked into my office and said, "Ben, we want to build a recording arts studio." I almost threw them out physically because I only had two classrooms on that side of the building. And the more I thought about it, I called them in, went up to the president, and [we] decided to do it. Now when I did this, most of the financial support on that campus had to float into that facility. It was very expensive. Well when that happened, the faculty wasn't happy with Ben Bollinger. And we built the recording arts studio that brought some of the top [companies in] — Universal, Sony — I could tell you hours of what went on. But I have to say that Bob Slack has done a magnificent job there working with the Grammys. And I have a tremendous sense of pride knowing about the program that I built — but also the fact that we stepped away from just having just a choir. We built a first-class music program.

John Cavazos

In an exclusive interview, member of the Citrus College Singers recollects his "first taste being in the big time" in the studio with Gene Simmons and a nerve-wracking experience with Cher.
Interview by Tim McPhate

John, you are one of the singers from the Azusa Citrus College Choir on Gene Simmons' 1978 solo album. At that time, what year were you in at Citrus?
John Cavazos: I was in my last year there.

And your major was music?
It was music. It was a junior college and so I went on afterwards to Brooklyn College in New York after I moved there. And I'm actually now finishing up another degree. It's been a long journey for me because show business got in the way of my education.

How many years were you at Citrus?
I was there for three years. And the reason is because of the performing group, most of us who were in that group would stay for three years. There were lots of opportunities and doors that opened.

Were you in the choir for all three years?
Yeah. It was actually an ensemble. I know [Gene] listed it as a choir. It really wasn't. There were I think 30 of us and we did more than just sing classical music. We were all dancers as well so we performed pop music as well.

What was the exact name of the ensemble?
We were actually known as the Citrus College Singers. It was a very diverse group. To be in it you had to be able to sing classical repertoire as well as pop repertoire and you had to be able to dance. So it was all inclusive. And it was perfect for me because I went into musical theater in New York.

Before we get to Gene's album, let's chat about Cher. In his 2001 autobiography, Gene Simmons recounts the story of how the ensemble sang for Cher on her birthday in May 1978. Can you tell us about this experience?
Yeah, actually I was the guy that sang the solo to her. It was her 30th birthday and they obviously were dating at the time. And Gene invited us to come to [his] bungalow at the Beverly Hills Hotel. And he surprised her. I'm sure she wasn't too happy about it at first because, you know, she didn't have any makeup on or anything. But we sang *a cappella* the song "If" by the group Bread. And it happened

to be in the pop show that we did. It happened to be my solo with the group backing me up. So he brought her out and after a couple of seconds she warmed up and smiled, and we started singing. And I started walking toward her to sing the solo and, as I would normally do, I would take the lady by the hand. And so I took her [hand] and when I did she grabbed me and I was really nervous. You know, hello it's Cher! And she took her hand and put it on my heart and I'm sure it was bumping a mile a minute. And as I was singing, "And one by one, the stars will all go out," she looked at me and she goes, "Oh, you're nervous. How sweet." And I about pooped my pants because I thought, "Oh my gosh." (Laughs) She was actually very, very sweet about it and she knew we were just kids and we were in awe of who she was. And of course, KISS was very popular at the time and nobody had ever seen them without their makeup. It was really a super cool moment for all of us.

Did you sing any other songs, or was it just one tune that you performed?
We sang that one tune to her. And then she said, "Thank you." She was very gracious and then she kind of disappeared back into the bungalow. And then Gene was standing and talking to Ben [Bollinger] for a couple of minutes. And I think that's when he approached him and said, "Hey, I'd like for you guys to sing on the album." I think that's where that moment happened. And the rest of us, we were kind of over to the side taking pictures like geeky kids. It was fun.

As a college student at the time, what was your opinion of KISS?
Well, I was not a rock and roller although I appreciated what [KISS] did and they were certainly incredible musicians. I had great respect because I'm a musician as well; I play keyboards as well as perform. I was more of an Earth, Wind & Fire, Chicago type of guy. And of course disco, because it was the big thing at the time. There were some solo artists that I liked; I'm a big Billy Joel fan. So that was kind of the music that I listened to. Earth, Wind & Fire and Chicago — those were my two groups. I did listen to some rock and roll. I did listen to Three Dog Night and I listened to Led Zeppelin, as I think all teenagers did. You could experiment listening to different groups in trying to decide what you liked.

John, what do you remember about heading out to Cherokee Studios in Los Angeles for Gene's album?
The first couple of times, I think we went out in vans. But it was done in sections. There was this one part, I can't remember what song it is, it's where the turnaround goes [sings the ensemble's part from "True Confessions"]. And we were singing in octaves. I think that was really the only one where everybody was singing. They had us all in the studio and Gene was in the center. And he was in his glory; he loved it because he loved young people. And he was in the center kind of waving us on and making us smile and getting us all excited. And it was fun. It was just so incredibly cool. At the time, I had done some studio work, and I ended up in the business. Besides what I did in New York, I also did a lot of session work. So it was kind of my

first taste being in the big time. Even though he was jumping up and down and having a lot of fun, it was serious business. We had to get it done. And they broke us up into groups for the other two songs, depending on what they needed. I think for one group, I think there were six or eight of us. And we sang some "aahs" and some "oohs" and then we sang something where whatever Gene was singing, he was singing some kind of a line, and we were singing in unison with him in the same octave or up an octave, and trying to make it sound ethereal. They did a lot of experimenting with the sound. And of course, like I said, here's Gene and we're going, "Oh my gosh, he has no makeup on. We see him." (Laughs) I mean, everybody sees them now but at the time it was a big deal.

Yes it was. I believe it was a three-day period during which you recorded — is that what you remember?
Yeah, (pauses) I think the third day it was just a smaller group of us that were out there. I remember there was one particular day where everybody was crammed inside the studio, all 30 of us, singing at the top of our lungs. And then they broke us up into groups. And I think maybe the third day, it was a smaller group. But yeah, it was three days.

Ben described Gene as being wonderful with the students and really interacting well with all of you.
He really was. I mean, he even stuck out his tongue out for us.

That's Gene. (Laughs)
You know, if you've seen my website then you know I went to New York and had a career on Broadway. I worked with some of the biggest stars in the world and some of them were really nice. And some of them weren't very nice at all. Gene was absolutely just as nice as he could be. [He was] very friendly [and] very unassuming for a guy who had achieved so much. Onstage, he had a persona. But he really dug us and he really liked who we were and he admired what we could do and he let us know that. And that was very impressing, I think, to all of us. I know it was to me. He was very generous and very respectful of who and what we were. I think there were maybe some engineers [who said], "Who the heck are these kids?" But he didn't. He thought it was the coolest thing and he loved our sound and said, "You guys are so talented. I wish I could sing like you." He was great.

That's a nice snapshot. Ben also said there were a couple of artists around the studio. He specifically mentioned Grace Slick and members of Queen. What's your recollection?
There were a lot of people in those sessions. Cher was there for one of them, sitting in the booth. I don't know, she was kind of incognito. I do remember a couple of the session singers, some of them went on to do a lot of session work with people like Streisand. There was a guy, I can't remember his name. You know,

if you know anything about this industry, you know that people come in and out of those sessions all the time, to hang out and give their opinion. So there were people floating in and out. I don't know that I particularly paid attention to them. Even then, I was pretty focused on what I was doing.

What are your recollections of how Gene articulated what he was looking for in terms of the vocal parts on the three songs?
I think that was probably the biggest challenge because most of us were used to reading charts and reading music in front of us. We were all musicians and could all read music. So I think Gene just knew that he had a vision in his head and wanted a sound, but he couldn't really articulate it on paper. So we experimented a lot. We got in there and he said, "Okay, let's have you guys try this and let's have you try that." And we also interacted, as well as Ben. He would say, "Well, the girls could do this or the guys [could do that]." And we would say, "How about if we do this?" And he would listen to it and go, "That's really cool. I like that. Yeah, let's do that." It was very collaborative and he was pretty open. For the first one hour, maybe it was a little rough in terms of actually getting into it because we were trying to figure out what this was going to sound like. But once we did, we listened to the track over and over again, [and] he would explain to us, "This is what I'm looking for. This is what I want it to sound like." So, because he was collaborative, he was open to the suggestions. And sometimes we would sing something, and he'd go, "No, I don't like that." Or, "I want it more like this. Let's try this." And we finally got it and then we started the takes.

The ensemble is featured on three songs: "True Confessions," which also features Helen Reddy. Then there's "Always Near You/Nowhere To Hide," which was more of an experimental song for Gene. And then there's the Disney cover "When You Wish Upon A Star."
Yes, that's correct. I don't remember us singing "When You Wish..." And that could have been a smaller group. I know one of our girls had a really high voice and they wanted her to do something and that might have been "When You Wish..." So it may have just been her on that one particular song because I know she did something by herself. I don't remember what it was, but she was brought into to do some kind of an *obligado*. From what I remember, it was "True Confessions" and "Always Near You[/Nowhere To Hide]" — I think those are the ones that the ensemble was used on. Again, that was a long time ago. I don't remember exactly. But I know that one of our girls did something on her own and I think it might have been that one.

I'm asking you questions like this all just happened last week! (Laughs)
Yeah. I mean some of it is very clear to me. Of course, my friends that love KISS think it's the greatest thing every time I tell them about it or they ask me about it. They're like, "Oh my God! You sang with Gene Simmons!" And I will tell you this:

When I first began in the business, I used it on my resume. And there were people who would look at it and go, "You sang with Gene Simmons?" — Because I was in the theater. I was like, "Yeah." And they said, "That's really cool." So obviously it helped me.

In listening to these tracks some 35 years later, what are your thoughts, John?
I was really surprised. I think "True Confessions" is the one that I really have the most memory of. I really don't have memories of the others at all. I don't know why. I think because we probably spent the most time [on it]. "True Confessions" was the first one we did and it was the one that took the longest because we were trying to figure out what the heck we were doing. That one kind of stuck with me because there's a hook in the song that we sang. And so we all sang that wherever we went — we toured a lot all over the world and we'd be on tour singing it and humming it and talking about it. And we still have pictures — I've got a picture on Facebook, unfortunately not with Gene, but right after we came outside of the studio.

But I was surprised at how well it came together when we were recording just our part of it. To me, it sounded corny, like, "How's this going to go together with this guy who's really a rock and roller?" And when we all got a copy of the album and when I listened to it, I went, "That sounds pretty good!" Obviously it's very, very different, but I thought it got his desired effect. He was happy with it. He was a professional and he was not going to release something that he didn't think was good. It's actually a great album. Like I said, I'm not a big fan of super hard rock and roll but they're great musicians. And I admire and I respect what they do.

The interesting thing is that Gene's album is eclectic. There are straight-ahead rock tunes, but there are also Beatle-esque excursions, some songs with orchestration and the Disney tune. To be candid, his album kind of threw some KISS fans for a loop.
Well, I think it tells about what kind of a guy he is. I think at heart he's a musician and I think he appreciates all types of music. And he's obviously pulled from all of those for his inspiration. So why not?

You mentioned getting a copy of the album. Did you actually go out and purchase it?
(pauses) I lost the album — the album got accidentally thrown away or something during my move. I was moving from one apartment to another in New York and I lost it. But maybe about five years ago, I bought the CD because I wanted to have it because some of my friends were like, "Oh come on. You didn't ..." I was like, "Dude, I sang on it! Look." And I'd show them. Because it's so random, I mean it's so freaking random.

Ben intimated that this was a unique occurrence for the ensemble. But he also said that the ensemble got a lot of invitations to perform on other artists' albums afterward.
Correct. You know, we did a lot of stuff in Hollywood. We sang for a lot of star events, so we sang for a lot of celebrities. We were invited to sing for "The Mary Tyler Moore" show, I think back in 1976. We were actually on the set and we sang for her show. And Valerie Harper was still on the show and Cloris Leachman — so all these people were there. We did stuff like that. We constantly sang. We did private parties in Beverly Hills, Bel Air and Hollywood because they would hear us and then they would invite us to their home and say, "Can you come entertain during Christmas?" And we would come in and we were in the room with these huge stars, some of the biggest stars in Hollywood, and they would sit still and listen to us sing. So we were used to having that kind of an experience. That's why many of us were in that group, because it afforded us that. And for those of us that went into the industry and made it a profession, it was in some ways a door opener. Gene happened to be one that offered us this opportunity. And yeah, there were a lot of other things that came our way.

Ben was very careful. We were his kids. He was not going to expose us or subject us to anything that he felt was not [good for us]. Even though we were 18, our parents were entrusting him as we traveled, not just in California, but all over the country and all over the world. They were trusting that he was watching out [for us]. And there are things that younger people should not be exposed to. So I think Gene was obviously very respectful because Ben didn't care who anybody was. He was very respectful and very honorable and we never saw anything that was, you know, questionable. I think in that regard, hats off to Gene because he respected that, hey, we were college kids. Obviously, we weren't naive and we probably saw worse. But still, we were on company time, so to speak. And things have to be done in the right way. And there were a lot of other stars that were very much the same way. Cloris Leachman, in fact, I just ran into her not too long ago in Orlando, and she was just as sweet as she was then. We took a picture together. We worked with Carol Burnett and she was just as sweet as she could be as well. You know, there are people in this industry who are like that. And Gene was one. He was very, very nice to all of us. It was really great.

John, the KISS solo albums were widely promoted when they were released in September 1978. Was the sense among the ensemble that, "Hey, this is a pretty cool thing that we're being featured on a solo album by a member of KISS"?
Oh yeah. I mean, we had a lot of different people who were huge rock and roll fans and were big KISS fans. So yes, are you kidding? We were like instant celebrities in our neighborhoods and at school. We were running in the halls, "Oh my God. Look at this!"

Ben mentioned that he had to change his phone number. Since his name was listed on the album cover, apparently he got calls from a bunch of fans.
Oh I'm sure he did. You know, I left right after that. In fact, that was one of the last things that I did in the group because I moved to New York. Some of those kids were first or second year students and that was one of the last things I did before I left.

Ben described you as one of his top students. Can you speak about what he meant to your career and the importance of your experience at Citrus College?
Ben is one of my mentors. I had great mentors in high school; I went to an award-winning dramatic and music high school. I really didn't know that a group like this existed at a junior college because I had other plans. But Ben scouted me out and the girl that I was dating at the time — we were in the same school — and he brought us both into the group. He groomed us and gave us wonderful opportunities. He was a task master, but in a great way. He was very demanding. He gave me tons of opportunities — we did a local television program, it was a religious program, and he gave me the opportunity to go on there and sing. He challenged me in every way possible. He demanded a lot from me and put me in positions of leadership. And I think I took that and the other things that I learned from the other mentors in my life and I brought it into [my career]. Like I said, I spent about a decade in New York working in theater. I respect him and all that he did for me. It was invaluable.

John, can you outline the arc of your career and talk about what you are up to nowadays?
Well, like I said, I moved to New York in the late '70s and spent up until the late '80s doing Broadway shows and everything that actors do — commercials and national tours and all that kind of stuff. The church that I belonged to in New York, right in the city, was actually started backstage at "Dreamgirls." So it was a church full of actors, performers, dancers, musicians — people in our worship team were the bass guitarist and lead guitarist for Roberta Flack. It was pretty cool. I got married and I had two children. We decided to move to Florida in '99. I had no intention of working for Walt Disney World, but be that as it may, it turned out that way. And I've been there for 10 years and my daughters are grown. I sing with the group Seven — it's seven guys, it's kind of like Il Divo, but more religious and patriotic and kind of Americana-type music. And I do a lot of session work here in Orlando and in Nashville for commercials, background on people's albums. And for Disney, I do some session work for some of the stuff that you hear when you go to Disneyland or Disney World or in a commercial or something like that. And I sing with a group called the Voices Of Liberty at Epcot and that group's been there for about 30 years. So I keep myself pretty busy.

And here's this random Gene Simmons thing on your resume. I'm curious; do you get a lot of questions about this particular project?

Oh people talk about it all the time. One of the guys I work with is a huge KISS fan. And when I told him, he totally freaked out. He was like, "Oh my God dude. I can't believe it. Tell me everything about it! I want to know what it was like." Because it is, it's so random and it's so off the cuff. I'm basically a musical theater performer — how did I end up singing backgrounds for Gene Simmons?

Eric Troyer

Vocalist/pianist rewinds to the sessions for Gene Simmons' solo album, the days of Wicked Lester and an early KISS gig, and shares recollections of Cher, Sean Delaney, Lassie, and more.
Interview by Tim McPhate

Eric, can you give us a general overview of your musical career in 1978?
Eric Troyer: I guess I was probably pretty much a session singer at that point. I was doing a lot of sessions. And I had known Gene and Paul since the Wicked Lester days. We were produced by the same guy, Ron Johnsen, back at Electric Lady Studios when they were Wicked Lester. We used to hang out a lot together and Gene and I were pretty good friends. We spend a lot of time going out to eat and just sort of hanging out. He was very helpful in trying to direct me in some career moves, to do a solo career. He made some really great suggestions and it really helped me along in a lot of ways. But it [the solo career] didn't really turn into much, which was totally fine for me actually as it turned out. But we hung out a lot together and I was doing a lot of session singing. At that time, I was pretty much hanging out in New York. But for some reason as I look at [Gene's] album, I see that he must have cut a lot of those tracks in New York because they're all New York musicians. But he flew me out to L.A. and I hung out with him and Cher for probably about 10 days while we did a couple of things. I was at the studio when there was a lot of the other stuff going on too.

It's interesting that you have ties to Paul and Gene going back to Wicked Lester.
I was at one of their very first concerts at [the library]. Ron Johnsen, he said, "You got to come along and see Gene and Paul. It's a group called KISS and they're going to put on makeup and it's pretty wild and everything. They're just trying it out at this place." It was in New Jersey or somewhere, Englewood Cliffs or somewhere like that. [Ed: The "1973 Library Party," a benefit for the Palisades Free Library, took place in Palisades, N.Y., on May 26, 1973.] It's funny because I saw Paul recently. We did a show with them in Newfoundland about a year ago and we were just chatting about that. But yeah, I was pretty good friends [with them]. Paul came out to New Jersey with our manager and hung out at the sessions and stuff. We were all kind of in the same ballpark at Electric Lady Studios when Ron Johnsen was producing Wicked Lester and my band as well.

That's wild. Getting into Gene's album, it was recorded at a few places, at the Manor in England; Cherokee Studios in L.A.; and Blue Rock Studio in New York. So you were present at the Cherokee sessions?
Yep.

Do you recall any of the other musicians who were present while you were in the studio?

Yeah, I was there when Skunk Baxter did some guitar work. Rick Nielsen — it's funny because when Cheap Trick first burst out they came to New York and did a show at Max's Kansas City and Gene and I went to see them. Gene said, "You've got to come along and see this band. They're outrageous. We're thinking about bringing them along on tour with us." So we went and we sat right in front. Rick, of course, was throwing picks at us all night. And Gene was throwing hundred dollar bills at him (laughs). It was really cool. So I knew Rick from those days. And then he was there at the session and he did some guitar work and it was really nice to see him. I've seen him a few years since too — he's a great guy, a great guitar player. We were hanging around with Cher a lot because Gene and Cher were together at that time. So I was there [when] Cher did her vocal part on "Living In Sin at the Holiday Inn," which reminded me of that whole thing. I was just listening to it just a few minutes ago and I was like, "Oh my God. That was so awesome!" And Bob Seger and I did some vocals. I think I did some vocals separately too. I played piano — there's some banging piano that I put on both those tracks ["Living In Sin" and "Radioactive"]. I was also there when Helen Reddy did her vocal part — she was kind of a pain in the ass but...

She was featured on the track "True Confessions."

Yeah, that's it. She was just as you might imagine. I don't know if you're familiar with her persona or her career, but she's kind of proper, sort of a bit of an attitude kind of a girl.

She and Gene must have been quite the combo.

(Laughs) It was really funny. He's so outrageous — oh my God, the things out of his mouth, to women especially. He used to say the most outrageous things to women and I'd say, "Gene, come on man!" So I was there for that. Oh, interestingly enough, Lassie is on there. It's funny, but we drove up [to] Lassie's trainer's [place], this guy named Rudd Weatherwax. I think he trained all the Lassies. But we went up and recorded Lassie barking and it was pretty interesting.

The producer for Gene's album was Sean Delaney. What do you remember about working with Sean?

I remember Sean really well. He's a very wild guy, very fun-loving, very outrageous, [and] part of the whole thing with Gene and the management. Sean was a really great guy. He was really great in the studio because of his energy — you know Gene is pretty calm and more subtle and sarcastic, and that kind of thing. But Sean was really exuberant and just like this big puppy dog — really excited about everything and just full of ideas and good humor and good vibes.

You are credited as playing piano on a couple of tracks, one of which was "Radioactive," the single from the album. What do you remember about the piano part on this track?

I remember a little bit of it. They knew they wanted some real banging sort of rock and roll piano. So I'm playing like these high-up eighths, you know [sings melody and rhythm], "Gang, gang, gang, gang," that kind of stuff. I actually think I do that on both tracks, that sort of thing. And I think it helped because there are some gaps in some of the spacing in the arrangement. And when I listen to it now, I listen to the drums, the drums are so pre-'80s (laughs), it's pretty funny. But a lot of the parts sound really good. It was recorded really well. I think they probably said, "We'll hear the tracks and you play." You know, Gene was pretty loose with that. The background vocals he was very specific with, "I want this something here, something here, maybe a little higher." But the piano part, I think it was like, "We'll listen to this song, run it down and play some parts." I think what happened was I started to work out some parts and then they would listen and say, "Well, do more of *that* there and a little less of *that* there." And it just sort of shapes itself, which is pretty generally how I would work when I would do piano overdubs and stuff like that.

I assumed the piano would have been an overdub situation.

Oh yeah. They cut the basic tracks in New York, Neil Jason and all those guys are New York guys. I'm sure they must have done all the basics there. This was after the fact.

The interesting thing with "Radioactive" is there are technically two parts to the song — there is the ominous introduction with strings and some dissonant piano at the very beginning. Did you play that part?

I think that was all done in New York. I don't think I did. I'd have to listen to that again just to see. I was listening to it and it sounded pretty cool, I liked it. It sounded really, well Beatle-y. There was a lot of that going around, the sort of vibey pastiche.

This piece has always fascinated me, probably because it was my first exposure to KISS. I heard this track when I was 4 and was of course scared to death. You have this eerie string arrangement, Janis Ian singing in Latin, another voice — which I believe is Sean — singing through a harmonizer, and it all creates sort of a swirling effect. And then it just evaporates into this great rock tune.

Yeah. I actually really liked it. I had forgotten about that, you know because I haven't listened to [the album] for a long time. But I listened to it and said, "Oh, that's really cool. They really did a good job." It looks like they got some string players in, and I forget the arranger...

Ron Frangipane.
Ron Frangipane, absolutely. He was from Electric Lady, that's one of Gene's probably old friends from the same time that I met Gene. He did a lot of arranging and I know his name from Electric Lady.

Moving on to "Living In Sin," which you said featured some similar rock and roll-style piano parts. What do you remember about this track and Cher's cameo?
I remember thinking, "Oh my God, this is so hilarious. It was really awesome." Cher was there [and] in and out of the studio, I don't think she was working on anything at that particular time. She was around and hanging out occasionally. I remember her doing that. But when I listen to it now, I'm like, "Gee, I'm like all over that track." I can hear my voice singing and I think I might have even come up with — there's like an answer part at the end. I'm not sure of this but there was kind of like an answer part at the end and I did some of those vocals with Bob Seger, who was a real sweetheart too. A really nice guy. And we sang some on the same mic for some of the tracks, but I think I might have done some high bits [alone] because I can hear my voice sticking out pretty high and Bob didn't have a particularly high voice. He was more of a baritone.

Did you sing any backgrounds with Gene sharing the same mic?
Yeah. He and I did some tracks and I don't think he sang — it seems to me that we had three singers when Bob, me and somebody else (pauses) ... I guess it was probably Gene but it might have been... Is Rick listed as a singer?

Rick is only listed as a guitarist.
I just seem to remember that there were probably three singers. It was probably Gene. It's a little hazy.

Well, interestingly Mitch Weissman has stated that you may have sang background vocals on some of the Beatle-esque tunes on the album — "See You Tonite," "Always Near You/Nowhere To Hide," and "Mr. Make Believe." Might this be what you're remembering?
I think they did their [parts] in New York though.

Well, I did speak with Mitch and I know that he mentioned in the "Behind The Mask" book that it's he and Joe Pecorino from Beatlemania singing on those songs and he also mentions your name. So maybe you blended in a separate part in Los Angeles for those particular tracks?
Yes, I think I maybe did do that. I know Mitch well, he's a great guy. He was a New Yorker. But that's my impression too because I was there — I might have been there for a week to 10 days. And I know I was at the studio a lot and I remember just participating in quick things, "Can you go out there and do this and sing that?" And they were nearing the finish of it so that would have been the time where they

thought they needed something, some little bit. And that was kind of my specialty, singing high and adding little parts here, ghosting vocals and stuff like that. That is my memory, that I ran out there and did a bunch of vocals. It just wasn't on those two songs.

Interesting... Would you have made any contributions to any songs that might have been left off the album?
I don't know that they did more than they needed? I think they pretty much knew what they wanted to do and it was pretty well set. At the time I remember Gene was very secretive about "When You Wish Upon A Star." He was like, "Oh this is going to blow people's minds. I'm going to sing this song and you're not going to believe this." He wouldn't tell me what it was until the day that we walked in and he was singing it. There was some big moment when he sort of revealed it and we were like, "Holy shit, that's awesome." It was pretty funny. But I don't know that they did more tracks than they needed — they might have cut more in New York and then narrowed it down. That was pretty common, to do a couple of extra tracks. But at the time we were working out in L.A., I didn't know [of any] other tracks.

The thing about "When You Wish Upon A Star" is that no one would have expected Gene Simmons to cover that song.
Nope, absolutely not. That's why he did it.

That kind of leads into my next question. What do you remember about Gene's mental state during this time? Did you sense from him that he was very serious about this project? Or was it a lot of fun and games?
Well, you've got to say that it was a bit of both really. I mean, Gene is the most serious businessman — he's all focused, he's totally focused on one thing. He's monomaniacal. He really is a very focused guy. And you know, he's a straight guy. He's a teetotaler — no drugs, no alcohol ever. He's really anti all that stuff. He's got a very clear head and he's very organized [and] he knows where he's going. But, I wouldn't say he's a jokester, but he's a witty guy and he'd have a lot of funny things to say. Actually, that's not true. He is a jokester, what am I saying? (Laughs)

Gene definitely has a comedic side.
Totally. He's like Henny Youngman. That's right, I totally forgot that. He would always have a string of jokes, you know, "Did you hear the one about ...? Did you hear the one about...? Did you hear the one about...?"

Do you recall that Gene was trying to get the Beatles on his album?
Yeah. I remember that he was trying to do that. He spoke about that at the time and he said, "I got the next best thing. I got the Beatlemania guys."

And what was the story with Lassie? Why would Gene have wanted a dog on the album?
Oh yeah. I don't remember exactly what track it's on, but he was looking to do a "let's just get everybody on this album. Let's just load it up with interesting stuff." And I don't know what made him think of Lassie, but Lassie was more in the consciousness at that particular time. The TV show had probably ended for a bit, but it was still very popular. But I don't exactly know why.

And Lassie didn't come down to the studio, you guys went to Lassie?
Yeah, we went up to Lassie. We went up and did a field recording. We drove all the way up to wherever it was. I remember driving past the Knott's Berry Farm so it was way out... somewhere (laughs). And it was a beautiful area and we set up the mics and everything and recorded it.

Trying to get the dog to bark?
Yeah, they could get it to bark on command. Speaking of barking, my dogs are barking down stairs right now (laughs).

(Laughs) Obviously, Gene's album is quite eclectic. There's a range of material and there's "When You Wish Upon A Star" and there's the "special guest" cast. But some have criticized the album for having "too much sizzle and not enough steak," as Paul Stanley would say. What's your take, Eric?
Well, Gene used to say to me, he used to be very bold and clear-cut about, "[KISS is] just doing this one slice of music." I think he loved the Beatles and he was into lots of other music as well. And I think if you talked to Paul, he would be too. But they knew that KISS had to be very clear-cut [with] no ambiguity [to] what they were doing musically. And so they really honed it and towed the line with that. But this was an opportunity for Gene to stretch himself out a little bit. So he took that opportunity. And it might have been Sean's influence too, you know, "Why don't you get this? Why don't you get that?" Sean was that kind of guy, "Oh man, let's get Lassie!" So he would have prodded and pushed Gene in that direction, which I think was kind of a natural direction for Gene anyway because he really like the Beatles and he was definitely influenced by all that stuff. But I think [the album is] pretty cool. I like both of those tracks [I played on]. I think they're really good. There's more depth to them, it's not just slamming, in your face kind of rock and roll.

So did you ever meet Peter and Ace?
Oh yeah, sure. I knew them all really well. I sang on a Peter Criss album, the one that Vini Poncia did afterward.

"Let Me Rock You," which was released in 1982.
Yeah, that's the one. Yeah, he was a nice guy, Peter. I don't know what he's doing these days.

I know you were on John Lennon's "Double Fantasy" album. Peter actually does a cover of Lennon's "Jealous Guy" on that particular album.
That's right.

Eric, the KISS solo albums were released in September 1978, a time when KISS were surely at their peak. What do you recall about the publicity surrounding the albums' release?
It was a big deal. It definitely was a big deal. There was a lot of press and they released it with big fanfare. Bill Aucoin, I knew Bill pretty well and he was genius at all that stuff. Between him and Gene, I mean they were both top business minds. They knew how to do all this stuff. So yeah, there was a big hoopla. They had big press and everything. I wasn't a part of any of that but I just remember seeing it and reading about it. It was a pretty successful PR campaign that launched the whole thing. Everybody was talking about it, you know the musicians in the city. I lived in New York so everybody knew a lot of the guys that were on the albums. It was pretty impressive.

Getting a little into your career, Eric. Once again, you were featured on John Lennon's "Double Fantasy" album. What was that experience like?
Yes, I sang on the song "Woman." I did quite a few vocal parts on that. It was amazing. Of course, one of my boyhood idols was the Beatles. Just to work with one of the Beatles was just mind-blowing. It was an amazing couple of days. I spent a couple of days in the studio with them. It was a great experience. John, we came out in the room and played the guitar and sang "Woman" over and over again while we worked out parts. It was just like, "Oh my God, I'm sitting here with a Beatle and listening to him sing." (Laughs) You're used to hearing his voice in a speaker and he's there singing. It was pretty amazing.

And tragically, we lost John Lennon right after that album was released.
Yeah, a couple of days before he was killed — I was really good friends with [producer] Jack Douglas, and that's how I got the session — Jack said, "You know, we're wrapping up now. You want to come up and listen to some of the mixes? John's talking about putting a band together and maybe doing some live gigs. He wants you to come up and maybe you could do some vocals for him live." I said, "Okay, yeah I'll come up in the next couple of days." You know, when you're doing these sessions, you also stop and think, "Can I have a picture with you and me?" (Laughs) And you just can't do it, you feel so lame. I've worked with a lot of people and never asked them for a picture and autograph or any of that stuff. And now of course, I wish I had. But he's one of those guys, oh man, I would have loved an

autograph and a picture with him would have been incredible. But, it was not to be. I have the experiences and I have the memory and it was really amazing.

That album went on to win the Album of the Year Grammy.
Yes it did.

Pretty cool to be featured on that! Looking at some of your other work, did you sing on Billy Joel's "Uptown Girl"?
Yeah, "Uptown Girl." [I was] on the whole album, "An Innocent Man."

That's my favorite Billy Joel song.
Me and Rory Dodd are the first voices you hear on that, [sings melody] "Oh, oh, oh, oh, oh, oh."

The vocal arrangement is superb.
The arrangements, some of them, we had an arranger come in and kind of work on parts. But a lot of them didn't work so a lot of them we kind of made up on the spot. It was kind of sort of a partnership of the arranger and we kind of modified his parts. But yeah, that's a great vocal arrangement. I mean, I can claim to have modified it here and there, but that was a fun album. We did some great stuff on that album.

In your career, you've worked as a studio musician, you've been a member of ELO Part II, you've written jingles and children's music, and you run a recording studio, Wonderwerks/Charlestown Road Studios. That's quite the career resume — can you update fans on any current musical projects you're working on?
Well, I'm presently doing a soundtrack to a horror movie, which I'm having a lot of fun doing. I'm doing children's music. I'm working a lot with my band the Orchestra, I'm leaving for a tour tomorrow in Mexico and Texas and we've got dates all over the globe. TheOrchestra.net is our website. But I do a lot of different things. I'm actually working on a bunch of projects now. If I get things organized, I'd like to get some kind of social media things going. I wanted to try and put together a YouTube channel because there's a lot of cool tracks that I'm working on now which they don't have any purpose to them — so I'm not in any hurry to get them done — but it would be nice to get them released. People are always bugging me, "What are you working on now? What are you working on now?" It's like, "Well, I'll show you at some point." (Laughs)

And you mentioned you saw KISS fairly recently. Can you tell us about that?
Yeah, weirdly enough we opened for them at a festival up in Newfoundland. It was really nice to see Gene and Paul again because I had kind of lost track of them. I don't really have much contact with them anymore.

That would have been the Salmon Festival in 2011.
Yeah, that's right. It was great, it was really fun. It was nice to see them. It was a ridiculous travel nightmare to get there. We actually had to rent a plane; we had to charter a small plane for the last leg of the journey up there. We arrived after being up all night trying to get there because there were some weather problems and they cancelled our flight and stuff like that. We got there about 11 a.m., basically ran out onstage and did our set. I mean, we were so delirious. And as I'm walking offstage, I saw Paul. I was like, "I know that face, oh yeah!" Paul was standing over at the side and I went over and gave him a big hug. He was really nice and we had a long chat and walked backstage and Gene was there. He was like, "Eric Troyer..." You know he was complaining about something I had done. It was hilarious (laughs). It was like, 25 years pass and the first thing out of his mouth is, "Why didn't you do that?" Like I had just seen him two weeks ago! Because he was upset at me a long time ago because instead of pursuing me solo career I went out on tour with Meat Loaf. So you know, he always remembers those kinds of things where I didn't listen to him (laughs).

Eric, you have an interesting perspective in knowing Paul and Gene going back to their Wicked Lester days. Here it is in 2013 and KISS are celebrating 40 years. Paul and Gene have kept KISS together through various lineup changes over the years. Why have they been able to make it work for four decades?
Well, they kind of grew up together. They have a common background. I mean, I met Gene's mom. She used to make us breakfast at his place back in the day. She was wonderful; she would make these potato pancakes, these latkes. There's a cultural bond there. And then, they just have a harmonious relationship. I mean, I don't know whether they've ever had any major fights. It's interesting because they have a division of labor that works really well, and a partnership. Gene is kind of the mastermind of everything ... he's just really a smart businessman. And Paul was always like the front guy. He was the good-looking sort of front face. And Gene was kind of this evil counter force to that. And it just worked. And unfortunately Ace and Peter were kind of interchangeable and that's what happened too, because of the problems with them and all that down through the years. They became interchangeable. But it was always Gene and Paul — they were the original partners. And man, they've stuck together.

Michele Slater

Production coordinator for Gene Simmons' solo album details her responsibilities, an attempt to secure the Beatles and Lassie, and provides her perspective on why KISS fans didn't embrace the solo albums.
Interview by Tim McPhate

Michele, if we go back to 1978, what was your status in the music industry at that time?
Michele Slater: I was working for Bill Aucoin and Sean Delaney at Aucoin Management. I had my fingers in every pot that Sean Delaney was working on. He was the artist development and a producer for Aucoin Management, so he was handling all of the artists for Aucoin. That would have been KISS, New England, Billy Squier's band Piper, and so on. I was his production assistant.

When did you come onboard?
I would say the end of '77, beginning of '78.

Had you met all of the band members of the members of KISS by that point?
Oh sure, they were in the office all the time.

In looking at the credits on Gene's 1978 solo album, you are credited as a coordinator. Was the fact that you were working under Sean the reason why you landed this particular position?
Yes. Sean was producing the album with Gene. And they were doing it in L.A. at Cherokee. Sean had me come out; I lived at the Sunset Marquis and I handled everything that was going on in the studio because there were a lot of musicians going in and out. That included travel, booking, getting in touch with their managers and putting them in touch with Gene. Gene took a very active role in producing his own record. He made decisions with Sean as far as who was going to do what and then we'd find them and get in touch with them and see if they were available to come in and do a guest spot.

So those were your primary duties?
Yeah, it was contacting them, finding their managers and getting contact information that Gene didn't have. Gene had quite a bit of it.

Melanie Delaney is also credited as a coordinator. Did you know Melanie? And did she have any relation to Sean?
You know, I don't think so. I remember Melanie. She was not in L.A., she was doing some things in New York. I did not work with her on the day-to-day in L.A. In L.A. it

was just me in the studio with Sean and Gene and of course Mike Stone and the other engineers.

Of course, Gene's album is notable for the formidable list of guest talent — from Helen Reddy to Joe Perry to Bob Seger to Janis Ian. Are there any particular standout memories having to do with some of the celebrities that were secured?
No. What I can tell you is that they were all very involved in doing their part. There was very little partying going on — Gene is of course a very serious, non-partying person. He's extremely professional and very low key and the atmosphere was always very professional. The only anecdote I can really give you is when Cher came in to do the phone call on "Living In Sin." That was a lot of fun. I did that with her. We were supposed to be a bunch of teenage girls making that phone call. You can hear the screaming going on in the background and so on (laughs). Other than that, it was pretty straight ahead. They came in and did their part and it was a wrap.

In terms of location, Gene recorded his album at Cherokee Studios in Los Angeles, Blue Rock Studios in New York and The Manor in London. Did you make the trek to any of the other locations?
No. I only did the [sessions] in L.A. We were in L.A. for about eight weeks. Other than Janis Ian, everyone that is on the album came into the studio in L.A.

Were the special guests' travel expenses — airfare, hotel, etc. — part of the official recording budget?
That's right. It came out of the album budget.

That must have been quite expensive.
Well, Sean and Bill were handling the album budget. You have to remember, it was also 1978. The airlines weren't insane with prices the way they are now. It was pretty reasonable. And they all had hotel accommodations — they stayed at the Sunset Marquis or they stayed at the Riot House on Sunset or the hotel of their choice.

Gene has claimed that he tried to secure the Beatles for his album. Do you recall any talk about Gene trying to secure them for the project?
Yeah, Gene really wanted to make this special. He did reach out. And it wasn't a flat "no." It was a scheduling issue. So he thought it would be fun to bring those guys in.

So contact was definitely made with the Beatles' camp and the offer was being considered?
It was on the table for consideration, absolutely.

Interestingly, Paul and Linda McCartney are listed in Gene's "thank" you credits. He also thanked Donny & Marie and Stevie Nicks, among many others. Would you recall any particular reason why he thanked some of these artists?
I was not involved in doing those credits with Gene. I can tell you that he knows everybody that's named there. I wish I could tell you that they were involved in some way, but not when I was working on the album.

When we spoke with Eric Troyer, he recalled capturing a field recording with Lassie. What do you recall about Lassie?
Lassie, oh yeah (laughs). That was a real highlight. We traveled to Rudd Weatherwax's house to record Lassie with a remote recording device, which at the time was like the size of a gas tank. It was myself and Mike Stone and an assistant engineer, and it was a real treat. It really was. We had the existing Lassie and we had the puppy that was being trained to come up as the new Lassie. So we spent some time there so that Lassie could do her bit. Rudd was really sweet. He lived in a California mountain town — I don't recall which town that was. But it was a real highlight, for me anyway.

It's interesting that you captured a recording because I'm not sure if the dog made it onto the album.
You know what; I don't recall whether or not the dog made it on the album. She did bark on command. But I don't think she made it on the album. But I haven't listened to the whole thing all the way through in a long time.

I've listened to the album and if she's there, I don't hear her. It's funny because I've read that Gene wanted to have Lassie on the album but I was never aware that a field recording was actually captured. I wonder who has the Lassie outtakes!
I don't know. But we did record her. I have pictures of myself with Lassie. It was a thrill for all of us — everybody knows Lassie (laughs).

One of the criticisms levied against Gene's album is that he seemed to focus too much on the star power he was securing rather than the actual music. You recalled that he was very businesslike in the studio. From your vantage point, did he take this project seriously?
Yes. And I would not agree at all with that assessment. At all! Gene, from what I recall and being involved in the project as deeply as I was for that period of time, when he was bringing all those people in it wasn't about getting those people in and thinking about album sales. They were already really big stars. That was not something that Gene was focusing on. I think his motivation was to get the talent. We had great studio musicians, Eric being one of them — Eric was a very close friend of Gene's. Gene's motivation was to capture something special, not to use it as a selling point. He wanted to make [the album] something different. And he was

very serious about it. It wasn't like, "Hey, let's go throw an invitation to this one." It wasn't like that. He was very thoughtful about it, "Okay, I want Jeff Baxter to come in and do a guitar solo ... let me think about what song is right for him." He was very thoughtful about which musicians would work on what songs. And it was more about bringing in a sound, not a name. Do you know what I mean?

I remember with Bob Seger, he was also very, very serious as well. These were not "hey, let's get down and party" sessions. This was serious work. Bob Seger was very thoughtful about what he was going to do. You know, they all enjoyed it. The songs were fun and Gene's motivation was very clear. These artists did not feel like they were being taken advantage of or used in any way. And that's because of the way Gene approached it — that was not the motivation. That kind of hypothetical thinking is for people that weren't there. They don't know and they're making up their own story for whatever reason without finding out the truth. And the truth was Gene was looking for a sound, a sound he could bring to the songs. You get a Bob Seger, you get a Jeff Baxter — you got a specific sound. They bring in their own parts; they bring in the way they play.

Gene's album is certainly diverse. You have Beatle-esque excursions, songs with orchestras and choirs, a cover of "When You Wish Upon A Star," and some traditional rock-flavored tunes. I think the album's eclectic nature confused KISS fans.
Well, the four albums didn't get as much attention as they should have. I think the fans expected to get four KISS albums and that wasn't the point behind this. The point was you had four individual musicians who were extremely creative and they wanted to spread out and do something on their own. And what happens with a lot of bands is that when that happens, the band breaks up. But that's not what happened here, because they worked so closely together and they had Bill Aucoin managing them. Bill was a real visionary. That's why you have four album covers that look the same, but are not. You have four different faces and four different sets of music, and each one is unique to that musician. The fans expected four KISS albums and they didn't get it. Paul Stanley's album is a little more subdued, and Gene's album is more along the lines of what KISS was doing at the time. It was their individual creations. And each one was able to spread their wings and do what they wanted to do, not what the band needed to do.

That's the whole point of a solo project.
Exactly. But the beauty of it was that they all did the solo albums together and they all helped each other. That was the beauty behind doing it that way. Bill Aucoin was brilliant, he truly was — what a loss. I mean so many of the people who worked on these albums are gone. It's very sad. Sean is also gone. Sean was also brilliant. He was coined as the "fifth KISS" because he did all their staging and helped with all

their costumes. Between Sean and Bill, they were brilliant and they brought them up from nothing.

KISS were extremely fortunate to come into contact with people like Bill and Sean and Neil Bogart.
That's right. Casablanca was great to them and Casablanca loved them, and they were very close with the folks at Casablanca.

The KISS solo albums were released simultaneously in September 1978. From your perspective, just how much work was put into the entire project?
Well it was a big project. It went on for months and it all had to be coordinated so they were all released together. Casablanca was very involved. Think about what goes into the pre-production, the production, the post-production and mastering of one album and then the release, and what's going to happen around the release — the marketing budget, the publicity, the press, the travel. Think about doing that with four albums, all at the same time. It was a very, very big undertaking.

Of course, Casablanca pressed a lofty sum of more than 5.3 million albums. And while the albums all sold fairly well, there was a big pile of albums that were ultimately returned. What's your theory as to why the albums didn't meet the sales expectations?
I think that everyone expected these to explode. But I think it was a result of the fact that the fans were expecting four KISS albums and they didn't get them. And I'm not so sure the press was very kind with their reviews on the albums. I think everyone was looking at it with an extremely critical eye instead of looking at it as a fun, unique project, like, "Wow, look at how these four guys stretched out and did their own thing." Instead of reviewing them as individual creations, I think they looked at each one of them as a KISS album. And I think that's where the difficulty came in. I think the fans were absolutely expecting four KISS albums, and so were the press. And when they didn't get it, they cut it to pieces (laughs). That's my take on it. I recall that there was a lot of talk about the fact that they were getting bad press. And everyone was pretty disappointed. It wasn't what anyone expected, for sure.

I think that's a completely valid take, and I would agree. Speaking from a fan perspective, when KISS have tried to step outside the box, the majority of fans haven't seemed willing to embrace it. In other words, KISS fans want KISS to be KISS.
Correct. Because I was working with them and part of the company, I knew what was going on and I understood it. Of course, I had my favorite songs and there were some songs I didn't like at all — but I loved the albums. But I knew what they were trying to achieve. And the fans didn't.

Did you work on any of the other solo albums, by chance?
Not in an official capacity. I didn't do anything with Ace and Peter. I did some things for Paul, like contract things and little stuff here or there.

Given your close proximity, can you share some of your general impressions of the KISS members?
I didn't know Ace and Peter that well; they didn't come around as much as Paul and Gene. Gene was in the office pretty frequently and so was Paul. What I can tell you about both of them is that they're both very serious, and both clean. No drugs and alcohol. Never. Their whole thing was music and that's where all the energy was going. It was all about the music. And it would go from one album to another to another. They had a huge body of work. They would finish one and start the next. They were always working. And if they weren't writing, they were on tour. They were very busy guys. Paul is very laid back, very sweet and very down to earth. I had dinner with him once with a bunch of people. I was sitting next to him and we starting talking about furniture. He was telling me he was getting some new furniture and he was asking my opinion on a couch, which I found kind of shocking (laughs) — that he was that involved in his decorating. It was like, "Wow, I saw a whole different side to him." Where Gene is concerned, Gene is a very, very serious man. He has a very dry sense of humor. Between him and Mike Stone, they had me laughing quite a bit because Mike Stone was English and their humor is extremely dry. Have you watched Gene on his reality show?

Oh sure.
Okay, well you get Gene. He's very serious and very dry, but he has a great sense of humor but you wouldn't know it. You'd think, "Oh my God, this guy has got to be really strange." And he's not at all (laughs). He's a straight-ahead businessman and very serious about his music. I really enjoyed watching "Family Jewels" because when I was working with him he was going out with Cher. He and Cher were together for quite a while and it was much later that he ended up having his kids. I really enjoyed seeing him interacting with his kids, it was really quite funny (laughs).

Michele, how long did you end up working for Aucoin Management?
I was there a little over two years. I left and went to work for Phil Ramone.

He passed away this year, unfortunately.
Yeah, it was very, very sad. I went to a music memorial for him and his family was there. It was nice to see everybody and I hadn't seen Phil in probably about a year, but we were in touch. I'd call him when I just missed him. He was always so busy; it was hard to see him that often. He was constantly traveling. It was a real sudden and unexpected loss.

And as we mentioned previously, Bill passed away in 2010. Had you spoken to Bill at all prior to his passing?
No I hadn't. I had not kept in touch with Bill or Sean, unfortunately. I moved on and worked for Phil. It was kind of an extension of what I was doing with Gene. With Phil, I was his production assistant and I was in the studio with him all the time, for three years. So Phil and I stayed very close over the years. I'm also very good friends with his wife. They don't live far from me so I'd see them when I could. It was a different relationship, it was much closer.

Understood. How about Paul and Gene? Has it been a while since you've spoken with them?
I haven't spoken with Paul or Gene since I left Aucoin Management. No, I'm wrong about that. I spoke with Gene when he was with Diana Ross. Do you remember that?

Sure. That would have been in the early '80s.
Right. After I left Phil, I was independent for a while, before I went to work for "Saturday Night Live." And I was doing independent production assisting and contracting and so on, and Diana was looking for an assistant. She wanted someone to work only for her. Gene called me about that and I interviewed with Diana.

Your mentioning "Saturday Night Live" reminds me how KISS never played on the show.
I don't recall them ever being on it. I have no idea why. That's probably the next question (laughs). I don't know if they turned it down — you know, that's not really their venue. How could they pull that off on that stage?

That's a fair point. From what Paul and Gene have said over the years, there's a New York contingent — people such as Lorne Michaels, Jann Wenner and the like — who have turned their back on the band and as a result never gave them a fair opportunity. KISS did perform on the show "Fridays" in 1982. "Fridays" was kind of like ABC's version of SNL.
Did they do their whole stage show?

No, it was definitely a streamlined stage. They were promoting their concept album, "Music From The Elder," another album the fans didn't accept (laughs).
Right.

What are you up to in the music industry nowadays, Michele?
I'm doing marketing and public relations and I'm a social media specialist. I'm working primarily with Jana Mashonee, who is a brilliant singer and songwriter. Her voice is just spectacular, it's right up there with Mariah Carey and Alicia Keys. I

handle all of her social media, marketing plans and public relations. I'm also independent so I could be hired by any other artist to do the same. There's not a lot of money out there right now, as you know, and obviously with labels they have their own people inside. But there are several independent artists that I've worked with that have been pretty great. And it's usually short-term and I work within their budget. And what I like to do is teach them how to handle their own social media and marketing. I basically mentor them at the same time I take over their communications for a period. It's a lot of fun.

We're talking about a different era but, hypothetically speaking, do you feel the solo albums could have benefited from a tool such as social media?
I think it would have helped because it would have had the artists' voices. Gene, Paul, Ace, and Peter all could have had their own Facebook pages and Twitter pages. They could have been talking about it. I definitely think it would have been much more of a success had there been social media then.

Michael Des Barres

Renowned musician/actor recalls early experiences with KISS and working with Gene Simmons and provides his two cents on the direction of Simmons' solo album, details on his current projects and a window into his fascinating five-decade-plus entertainment career.
Interview by Tim McPhate

Before we get to Gene Simmons' 1978 solo album, I'd like to go back a few years. Your group Silverhead played a gig with KISS and Fleetwood Mac on Jan. 26, 1974, at the Academy of Music in New York City. Do you have any recollections of that gig?

Michael Des Barres: Yes, I remember standing in the wings with Johnny Thunders who had provided me with a joint of Angel dust. I saw Peter go up 15 feet and I thought, "Ah, so we're going on after these monsters." And you must remember that Silverhead at that time weighed 150 pounds collectively; so all of us would have gotten into one of Gene's boots. Being on Angel dust and looking around at this incredible theatrical presentation — I was raised in theater so I immediately loved specifically Gene and Paul for their chutzpah. The Dolls were the band that everyone was digging and [KISS] had the whole idea of creating this incredible comic-book thing and that's all Gene's sensibility, I think, and I'm sure Paul had a great part in it.

Clearly Gene is an aficionado of pop culture and that includes that whole world of fantasy. I was so fucking loaded when I saw him just creeping around that stage I really believed it. I think what he created is so significant and so interesting. As an actor I was trained in mime and we studied *kabuki mie*, which is a Japanese form of mime and it's very ritualistic. And what Gene gave to rock and roll was this tempo, this threatening pre-historic Japanese Godzilla with a bass guitar. It was phenomenal and I loved them from the minute I saw them. And obviously Thunders was in his own way completely rock and roll in the truest sense of the word. And we were both marveling at how interesting it was. This was very early in their career, Aucoin had them, but it was very early, obviously because they opened for Silverhead, who was a cult band. And Gene said, "Listen, I've got a Silverhead poster on my wall. You're the greatest." As a result of that meeting, he put Detective, my next band on Swan Song, on a tour, for which I was incredibly grateful. And I ended up singing on his solo album.

There's a song called "Ain't None Of Your Business," which was demoed by KISS for their 1976 "Destroyer" album and features Peter Criss on vocals. This song was later cut by your band Detective on your 1977 self-titled release. Can you give us the story of this song from your perspective?
Well, it was a great song. The whole thing about bands in those days was you wrote your own songs, and fuck everybody else. But that song came along and we loved it. The history of it was it was brought to me by one of our managers at the time, a major coke dealer whose name I cannot repeat. It's such a good song, "Ain't None Of Your Business," and it had such attitude and we played it, and everybody looked at each other and said, "We'd be fucking idiots not to do this." It suited us better than I thought it suited KISS, because KISS was more of a pop-rock band and we were a bluesy rock band.

Would you even have been aware that KISS previously cut a demo for that tune?
No, it was only brought to my attention years later. I did not know the history of the song, but then again I wasn't really aware of any history. I was living so much in the moment (laughs), which is a polite way of describing my lifestyle. For many years I didn't care about things like that. All I did was deal with what was in front of me. There was enough going on with Jimmy and Robert. Those days were so epochal that who cut what as a demo was not in my frame of reference.

In late 1977 Detective opened up some dates for KISS, including a gig at Madison Square Garden on Dec. 14, 1977. Take us back to that gig.
Sure. Put it this way, I was in Detective: There was nobody in that wonderful venue dressed as any member of Detective. I wore makeup at all times but it was a different band. But if you walked out there and you saw, I think, 19,000 people dressed as the headliner, I mean ... So what I did was, and I continued this through our career when we supported bands, in between songs there would be a couple of people fixing their hair, adding a little bit more mascara to make them really look like Gene, Paul, Ace, and Peter. And I would scream out a member of KISS' name. I would go, "Gene Simmons!" And they'd scream. And then the next time, I'd go, "Paul Stanley!" And they'd scream. So from where those boys were in their dressing room, all they could hear is us finishing a song and they'd hear the crowd go insane! It was so funny. When I supported Duran Duran later I did the same thing. I'd yell, "Simon Le Bon!" They'd go mad. And it was hilarious because my band was laughing hysterically at this absurd paradox. We were a pretty good fucking rock and roll band but we were greeted with complete silence because they had come to see their gods. And so I'd mention the gods' names in between songs and it sounded like we were going down as a storm.

(Laughs) Michael, KISS had two factions, if you will. There was Gene and Paul, who were very straight-laced and didn't drink or do drugs. And then there was Ace and Peter, who were known to get pretty wild on the road.

I was much more in the Gene and Paul camp. Even though I was loaded, I was much more into the intelligence and the awareness and the incredible insight they had into what the audience wanted. And I wanted to know about that because any idiot can take drugs and jump into the swimming pool and drive their Rolls-Royce into the ocean. Anybody can do that. But very few people can create a band as lasting and as incredible as KISS. And that is because of Gene and Paul's relationship and their relationship with their fans. That's what interests me. The only kind of hotel story I have is I was with Gene in his hotel suite and I remember he ordered some food. I didn't hear what he ordered. But the room service person came in and there was a trolley filled with desserts. And he ate every fucking dessert on that trolley.

Gene is known to have a sweet tooth.
Yeah, so that's way more interesting than saying how much coke Ace snorted.

(Laughs) Moving into 1978, the four KISS members were each doing solo albums. How did you receive the invitation to sing on Gene's album?
He called me. He didn't send an invitation dripping in blood (laughs). He picked up a phone, he said, "Hey MDB, you wanna sing on this thing?" I said, "Fucking-A!" I mean this guy was really good to me. It's hard to get a great tour like that and it's hard to play the Garden and he did it and he made it happen. I was delighted. I love him. He's a fantastic person.

You would have been at the L.A. sessions, correct?
I was at the L.A. sessions, yeah. My voice is pretty distinctive and the only story that I remember from that was how in control of the situation he was and how free he let the musicians be. One thing he asked me to do was sing a harmony part with two other chaps. Now, that is not my forte. My forte is screaming. So I said, "No, I can't do that Gene. Just give me a track." (Laughs) So he gave me a track and you can hear me wailing away in the background apparently. I mean I hadn't heard it in 30 odd years until somebody posted it the other day on Facebook.

There's a scream in the intro at about five seconds in.
That would be me. Rock and roll to me, for singers, is very much about how distinctive their ad-libs are. If you really look at the great singers, you know Rod, Mick and Robert; the most interesting thing about them is how they set up a solo with a scream, how they come back out of a solo into a chorus or a verse, or what they do in between the lines. Rock and roll is all between the notes, as you know, you must be a music aficionado otherwise you wouldn't be doing this. You know what I'm talking about? So if you want to have me on there, you want to have me making noises that sound authentic (laughs). I didn't particularly sing — I made authentic noises!

The tune also features background vocals from some females, one of which I believe is Katey Sagal of "Married With Children" fame. Do you remember singing with the females?
Oh no. I don't like singing around the mic with anybody. I stood at the microphone, put the fucking cans on and sang my ass off. I mean Katey Sagal, I'm sure smelled nice, but I didn't give a shit.

(Laughs) Did you know the song features a guitar solo by Rick Nielsen of Cheap Trick?
Yeah, Rick is brilliant. Cheap Trick is one of the all-time pop-rock bands.

So "See You In Your Dreams" was essentially a one-off? Was there any talk of you singing on any other tunes?
It was at the end of the recording process, as far as I remember. If he asked me to do another, I would have, at that point, and still would do anything. If he asked me to come [and] sing on an album, I would do it. I did what I asked to do as best I could.

Gene had a cavalcade of stars on this album. Aside from you, there was Cher, Rick Nielsen, Joe Perry, Donna Summer, and Helen Reddy, among others. What are your thoughts on the direction Gene took with his album?
What you've got to understand is Iggy Pop is my favorite recording artist. So Donna Summer, Cher, et cetera, mean nothing to me. I don't know them personally although I know Cher a little bit. But all of that I thought was a bit of an odd choice, to be honest. I think he should have sat down with Steve Marriott, Jeff Beck and Cozy Powell and done a rock and roll record. It's interesting man, if you want to go metaphysically deep into this, when you're on your own and you're in a huge band and you make a record, it will obviously go platinum. But for me, it's an opportunity to really express what you're really thinking. Gene has always gone for what he thought was the lowest common denominator, I think. He's so talented as a bass player and a pretty good singer that I think he could have gone another way. And if I had been him, I would have. But they were such a corporation by then, they had to emulate KISS records. But I believe in my heart of hearts, if he wanted to make an individual statement, that's what he should have done. All the other people you listed there, with the exception of Joe Perry, are mainstream show biz people. Rock and roll is not mainstream show biz.

Michael, to be candid, I think some fans would agree with you. In other words, what's the deal with Gene Simmons collaborating with Donna Summer or Helen Reddy?
I think it was a huge error, and you can quote me. But the caveat is, I had such faith in him as a musicologist and [his] great understanding of British blues rock and if he'd done that with participants who were capable of playing that kind of music

authentically, I think that record could have exploded. Of course, I've got a platinum album from it so obviously it did well. But at that stage, were numbers really necessary? Was more money needed? Because it was very, very critical how he made that record. I mean I went in there and sang and Gene was in the control room. (Pauses) He's very much like Louis B. Mayer or something, you know from the old days of MGM. He's a studio head — he's a catalyst — he's a businessman. And sometimes I think, even though now they are unbelievably popular and have so incredibly penetrated pop culture that would have been an opportunity to express himself as a musician and singer. That's just my two cents.

It's an interesting take, Michael. The KISS solo albums caused quite a stir upon their release in 1978. Casablanca Records shipped 5.3 million albums into stores and undertook a multimillion dollar media campaign to promote them. Legend has it that the campaign caused quite a stir with other labels and artists. Michael, as an artist yourself, what were your thoughts on the way the albums were promoted?
I could give a shit. I didn't think about that stuff. I do now with my current projects, think about marketing. But in those days, marketing was for businessmen. I was into rock and roll (laughs). I didn't think about what other people were doing. And if it was promoted like that, I'd probably run a mile away. I only did it because I love Gene; I didn't do it because I wanted to be on a hit album. I did it because he asked me to. I was never marketed so that's not my thing. But in terms of business changes, in retrospect, when Jim Carrey got $20 million to do "Cable Guy," movie stars felt the same way. It's business. They upped the ante in terms of promotion because their empire, the merchandising, was as important as the lyrics. So it's a whole different world when you're coming from the streets of London. There are no Michael Des Barres dolls that I'm aware of (laughs).

Getting into some other topics... The late musician Mikel Japp, who actually collaborated on songs with Paul Stanley, mentioned to us in an interview a few years back that you helped get him sober. He said, and I quote, "Not to get into that too much but I want to thank Michael Des Barres for well ... being there for me. I have been free of all substances for over 23 years!" What are your recollections of Mikel Japp and helping him?
You know, I'm really reticent to take credit for anything like that because you can only stop indulging in poison yourself. I loved Mikel and I respected him very much. I was very sad to hear what happened to him. I can just be an example. I've been sober 32 years so it's been quite a journey for me because when I did get sober I was a pariah in rock and roll. I was a leper. "What on earth are you doing? That isn't rock and roll." And of course those people, well the ones who are still alive, have gotten sober. I just happened to be blessed to get it a little quicker when I looked in the mirror and I saw Iggy Pop's grandmother looking back at me. So it was vanity that got me sober. But Mikel Japp, God bless him for saying that. But he did the

work and that's what has to be done. As an individual you've got to take responsibility for who you are. And one is inspired perhaps by people around them who can change their consciousness, and I'll take a "thank you" for that. I just don't drink. I don't use coke. I find it toxic. It's kid's stuff. I think Mikel sensed that. He was such a talented dude. He didn't need that. The whole myth about drugs being creative, maybe for a year or two, but then psychosis sets in and you're about as creative as a fucking ashtray.

I know Steven Tyler has expressed a similar sentiment.
Steven and Joe, of course, are friends that I knew. Then the big phenomenon in the last few years has been rock and roll sobriety, which is: "Vicodin is okay." And that's a shame because prescription drugs have played havoc with people's sobriety because they feel it's prescribed. But these doctors are drug dealers. They're no better than the guy on the corner with a bag of crack. In fact, I think they're probably worse. Dr. Conrad Murray is experiencing that and others should too.

Aside from music, you have quite the profile as an actor. In television, you've starred on shows such as "WKRP in Cincinnati," "Roseanne," "St. Elsewhere," "MacGyver," "Seinfeld," and "NCIS." Do you have a particular favorite show from your TV resume?
In a general sense, I am glad to work. I will say, "Yes," to anything in the beginning because one's business assumption of a rock and roll musician is that they're incapable and, like Ozzy, they are going to bite the heads off the casting director. So I had to do every fucking show to make them realize that I knew what I was doing, because I was trained as an actor as a kid. Most people don't know that. I had to prove myself so I said yes to anything. And I think an artist one does that in the beginning. Secondly, the favorite show I've ever done was playing Murdoc in "MacGyver." That was a character I could develop over the years and know what I was going to do. I learned how to use weapons, how to use disguises and various prosthetics [and] makeup. He was an assassin. I think I'm probably most known for that character. It was a joy to go up to cause havoc in Vancouver and play the notorious assassin Murdoc.

You were also on "Melrose Place," which was a bit of a guilty TV pleasure of mine back in the day. Did you get along well with Heather Locklear?
Yes, Heather is the greatest girl in the world. I adored her and still do. She loves rock and roll music, as evidenced by her legacy. And like all smart, beautiful women, she didn't take her sexuality seriously at all. In fact, she made fun of it, which was charming because it made her not be self-conscious as an actress. That's the worst thing you can be, when you're very aware of your own beauty and your own physical charisma that you rely on that and you don't do the work. There was never a day that that year we worked together on that show where she wasn't prepared, ready, knew everybody's name on the set. And was a true pro. If there's

one thing I've come to really value, it's being on time and know your fucking lines. And that applies to every crew member and I am the same. I will learn every crew member's name the first day I'm on the job and I will remember it. I just did "NCIS" with Mark Harmon and that show was a joy. It was in the middle of me doing my "Carnaby Street" album and they wanted to use a couple of songs from that album and I thought that would be a wonderful tie-in. And working with David McCallum — he was Illya Kuryakin [in "The Man from U.N.C.L.E"] for Christ's sake — it was a mind-blowing experience. I think shows like that are successful because they're professionals, they know what they're doing, [and] they've got a great rhythm together. It was a pleasure.

You released a new studio album in 2012, "Carnaby Street." The album was recorded and mixed in 10 days. I take it you believe in spontaneity, Michael?
Yep.

That's quite an anomaly, especially in today's music industry.
I believe in spontaneity in every area of my life. But I do believe before you go into the studio you know the fucking songs. Let me make an analogy, Detective — Led Zeppelin gave us a million dollars and we spent it. Because whatever you were given, you spent in those days, in 1977. And I spent three months getting a drum sound, okay? (Laughs) And that was in between getting in the Jacuzzi. It was absurd. Now, I'm paying for everything myself. No way is anybody going in the fucking Jacuzzi when we're here to be laying down tracks. We did some dates in Austin, Mobile, Alabama, Nashville, and L.A. — we played like crazy old blues musicians at all these clubs. And everybody went nuts because it's a great album. It's a real rockin', bluesy '60s record. You get into a room — which is my whole thing — with five guys, put the headphones on, look at each other, love each other, and rock the fuck out. And that's it. If somebody drops the damn tambourine, I could give a fuck.

More recently, you released a single, "The Key of Love," which is an exquisite ballad. I really like this tune.
Thank you.

It has a Faces vibe going on. How did this song come to be?
Well, I wrote it for my woman, who I've been with over four years, Britta. She's changed my whole view of many things. I wanted to write a song for her. And it was very early on in our relationship. Listen, there's nothing that makes a woman happier than sitting on the end of the bed while they're tucked up in bed and playing a song that you just wrote for them. It was the sacred, romantic sealing of our relationship when I wrote that song. "I wrote this song in the key of love" is the chorus. And she just flipped out and wept, and I wept. Then I went away to Texas and I cut it with Jesse Dayton who is a well-known, brilliant country artist and a

great writer. I actually wrote the song on my own but he produced it and did a great job. We put it out for Valentine's Day. I've been so lucky doing this stuff in the last couple of years. Because I run everything, it's all mine and I do it myself. I have a staff of two and we just kick ass. I did a live acoustic show [recently] in a packed club here [in Los Angeles] and I'm putting that out. I filmed it. I mean, you can do anything now. I'm free. We're free as a bird from the corporate fools who said there was no single. There is no such thing as a single, there's music. Music is free anyway.

The video is really nicely shot as well, Michael.
Yeah, we shot that in the Pacific Palisades across from the Pacific Ocean. I just wanted to show nature. I take a lot of photographs and I love nature. I wanted to be in a beautiful, romantic situation that did not involve a car, a girl, short skirts and Tawny Kitaen. I just wanted it to be a guy singing about somebody he loves, without seeing the girl. This is a realization he's in love and this is a realization he has on his own. And I wanted to show that wonderful feeling of joy that you don't have to diminish by some sexual connotation. I'm not into that shit. It's too obvious, it's too boring, [and] it's too dumb.

When is the last time you spoke with Gene?
You know, I played Shannon's husband on a TV series.

Yes, I've seen a picture of you two from the show.
So basically I married her before he did (laughs). I did a benefit for Jerry Shirley, who is the drummer with Humble Pie. And Steve Marriott was a friend of mine and I consider him the greatest rock and roll singer that ever lived. Jerry asked me to come and sing so I sang "I Don't Need No Doctor" and "C'mon Everybody." And his son Nick Simmons was there and he sang a song. Gene came to that and I saw him there. I was also at the wedding, and I go to birthdays and all that. But we both work a lot. You know what we did do, that was pretty funny? We played squash a couple of times. He was a demon on the squash court, an absolute demon. It was hilarious. Not that he wore the gear while we were playing (laughs). He won. I'm good and I'm in pretty good shape and he beat me every time.

That's quite a vision: Gene Simmons playing Squash.
(Laughs) Shannon, I keep in touch with and Gene, every now and then. I just love him. I have such a soft spot for him. There's only a few people in the last 40 years that I've been doing this that have stuck in my head with a picture of an honest, truthful man who was very good to me.

KISS are celebrating their 40th anniversary this year. You saw them in the very beginning and at the height of their popularity. From your perspective, how have Gene and Paul been able to make this work for four decades?

Well, it's a tribute to Gene and Paul, for one thing. The original band — the other two, nobody knows who they are, they're replaceable. In 10 years KISS will be playing, but it won't be the guys in KISS. It's almost like writing a play that any great actor could play that role. The KISS phenomenon is so perfect that anybody could do it, anybody that's good and talented. It would be like only one actor playing "Hamlet." "Hamlet" is 500 years old and it's played by every great young actor of a generation. And I see KISS as being absolutely as classic as one of the Bard's plays because it's a cultural moment. And no matter who is in KISS, it will be KISS, and young 'uns will always dig it. There will be a KISS spaceship in a couple of years.

(Laughs) Gene has probably trademarked that already.
Oh, no question about it (laughs). There's a whole chain of KISS restaurants on Venus. You know he's got that sussed out. But my point being, is it a credit to Gene and Paul? Of course it is. They created it — the other two went along with it. But the reason the band has stayed together is because Gene and Paul stayed together. They didn't fuck up. They didn't break it up [and] they didn't get angry at each other. They didn't let ego get in the way. Paul is quite happy to let Gene create this merchandising empire. And Paul's a very serious musician. He really is.

We've talked quite a bit about Gene, what are your thoughts about Paul's musical talents?
Well, listen to Paul sing, who does he really sound like? Steve Marriott. (Mimics high singing) Up there, he's way up there. It's all high, exactly where the British blues kids, like me and Terry Reid — that's where we'd sing, in that register. That's where he sang. He's very good. He's also got a great very light tenor, hence he did the musicals. Which I thought was a very brave thing to do, to branch out and do something completely different. Whether it was a success for him or not, I don't know? I'm sure he got a lot out of it. But he was brave enough to break the mold and try something new.

Michael, your entertainment career spans more than five decades, between music and acting. And you're still going. What's your secret?
Love, and being open to everything that happens around you. Connecting with the world, engaging with the world, [and] not hiding from the world. Some people become more withdrawn because they're getting older. What I've done is remain curious and enthusiastic. I have a very disciplined life in terms of what I eat and how I work out and it's given me the energy to be able to be of service to others. I care about people, I want them to be happy and I want them to love one another. And I put my money where my mouth is when necessary. I am there for all of my friends and family because the world as it is today has never been more challenged and never been more technologically proficient. But with all the connectivity has come great alienation. Many, many people are isolated and alone and yet we are capable of the greatest connection, with the Internet and with social media, than

ever before. But anxiety has risen in these last few years with this incredible phenomenon of social networking. Why is that? I believe it's because people are isolating because they're not looking out after their communities, and perhaps they're not loving their families the way that they could. Because we're all capable of everything, on a universal level. I don't want to get too sermonizing here, but to answer your question; this is how I do it. Because I care about other people. It's not about me anymore. I used to do all of this for me. Now I do it for you.

Mitch Weissman

Background vocalist/original "Beatlemania" cast member recalls his contributions to Gene Simmons' 1978 solo album and his work with Paul Stanley and Gene Simmons on albums such as "Animalize" and "Crazy Nights," plus a potpourri of KISS stories and tangents.
Interview by Tim McPhate

Mitch, when did you first meet Gene Simmons?
Mitch Weissman: I met Gene Simmons in 1976 when we were rehearsing for "Beatlemania" at S.I.R. Studios in New York City. We had these four hour a day lockouts, five days a week where we rehearsed. We rehearsed for that show until it opened in May 1977, from July of '76. It was a great job back then. Beer was two and a quarter in a green bottle, rent was $275 and I was getting paid $300 a week to rehearse. So you couldn't spend enough money. We were in studio A or B for the lockouts, two different casts — four guys for four hours, us for four hours. And whoever was across the hall — Foreigner, Roberta Flack — all these people, we met every one of them and they'd come in and watch us do Beatles songs. So one day, Gene and Paul come walking in. Big John [Harte] came in and said, "The guys want to come in." So they came in. And they sat with us for the whole day and said, "Sing some more songs." They said, "Sing this, sing that." We're sitting there and Ace was nowhere to be found. But Peter kept coming in, in a blue jogging suit. He comes through the door, "Are we rehearsing yet?" I go, "No Peter, not yet." We'd do some more songs and the door would open again, "How about now?" "Nope, not yet Peter." The very last time, in unison, the four of us and Paul and Gene without even turning around, we go, "Not yet Peter!" He goes, "Okay!"

The next day Big John came over and said, "You guys have to come across the hall. They want to play for you." So we went over to watch them play. They started the first song; it could have been "Strutter." It was just in a small rehearsal room. They were starting a tour. During the first few minutes of the first song, Gene pops a bass string and Ace's amp blows up and starts smoking. They're freaked. We barely got to say hello to Ace and Peter. Big John comes in and ushers us out the door. That's the end of that. A few nights later I was at this club. This woman comes up to me and goes, "Hi, you don't me, I'm Lydia Criss. My husband just wants you to know that the guys were so upset when the stuff blew up because they felt like they were playing for the Beatles. And they wanted to give you guys a show because you played for four hours for them." So we were friends from that day. Then in '78 I was down in L.A. and I got a phone call from the office in New York trying to find me and Joe Pecorino to sing on Gene's album.

What do you know about Gene's effort to get the actual Beatles on his album?
He did. He had always wanted to get Paul and John but their schedules were, as he said, too busy. But who knows if they would have sung on it? So the greatest thing he said in print was, "I got the next best thing." So Joey and I went down there to Cherokee Studios.

So you were at the L.A. sessions?
Yeah, they called us down. When I walked in Janis Ian was finishing up her part and Joe Perry had just done his guitar solo. And I remember playing ping-pong with Rick Nielsen. Then we started to sing the vocals for "Mr. Make Believe" and all that stuff. We worked the parts out but Joey's voice didn't blend. So it was me, Gene and Eric Troyer. Eric's voice didn't blend either. So it's just me and Gene on some of those backgrounds.

On "Mr. Make Believe"?
"Mr. Make Believe" and "Always Near You/Nowhere To Hide." "Mr. Make Believe," I think I arranged more of the backgrounds than Gene did. It was easy to do. We doubled each other's voices, or tripled them. I don't have a very strong falsetto, but combined with his it was fine. "See You Tonite" is the two of us also. When they did KISS Unplugged and they did that song, I felt like a proud father sitting there watching when those vocals came up. (Sings) "Ah, ah..." It was really cool.

How long did it take to arrange that part?
We did them on the spot. He had an idea and then we added the harmonies. It was great. We were down there at night. Joey was seeing Debralee Scott from "Welcome Back Kotter." She was there. Cher was ill. And Gene wanted us to have his moneybag T-shirts so she came down the hill from her house in a limousine. I remember, "Cher's outside." I ran out the door and the window went down like six inches and she handed me the shirts and I went back inside. (Laughs) Then at one point, we were all waiting around, and Debralee comes running in and said, "You've got to go next door because George Martin is recording America." I went in the room to say hello and said, "Thank you for recording the Beatles." He said, "Don't thank me, thank him..." And there was Geoff Emerick sitting there.

How was Gene approaching the project from your perspective? Did it seem like serious business for him?
I would say he was serious. Gene can be very goofy and nobody ever sees that side. But he's very very normal and he does have a professorial way of talking to you. But he'd go out and eat with my wife and me around Manhattan, and he'd always do this funny thing like a guy with his mouthful of food and he'd laugh. It was hysterical (laughs). Those sessions were loose but when we got together he had definite ideas of what he wanted to do. I think the basics were done, certainly enough for us to sing over. If Joe and Rick were in there, they must have been

doing overdubs on their parts too. Sometimes I'd walk in and see all these people and go, "What the fuck am I doing here?" (Laughs)

Some have the opinion that the cast of special guests might have been a little too far reaching.
You know the old analogies to the Beatles with all four of them having unique personalities? He made a big Beatles sort of pop record. That's what he wanted to do. "Radioactive" was not the same as "When You Wish Upon A Star."

Do you remember him saying anything to you about covering a Disney tune?
No, he didn't tell me. I just remember when I got the record and saying, "This is unbelievable. This is great."

The participant list reads like a Hollywood "Who's Who" at the time.
It's like a cast of thousands. Whoever he could get, they would come in and play. His albums got good reviews. Ace's album I think got better reviews than all of them because of "New York Groove." I remember they sent me all four copies.

How many days do you recall being in the studio?
I think I was there for two nights. We actually had two weeks off between the show continuing in Los Angeles and me and Joe Pecorino going to Chicago to open "Beatlemania" there. That's when the call came in. We went to do it and it was really fun. Here's a fun story. In September 1978, I got back to New York. Somewhere in that time period Peppy Castro had a party at his house on 24th Street. He had a top-floor townhouse and he'd have roof parties. One night, we're having the greatest time up on the roof and all these people are there. Paul was there and he and I start talking. We hadn't seen each other for a while. And he gives me his phone number and says to me, "Give me a call." I remember very vividly the next morning waking up and seeing the phone number written down and saying, "I can't call that guy." My wife goes, "Why?" I go, "That's Paul Stanley. I can't call him."

The next year, July Fourth of 1979, he actually comes up to me at another party and says, "How come you didn't call me?" (Laughs) We were just normal friends by that time. There was a time in the '80s where me and Gene and Paul were inseparable. And I actually was the one guy who was friends with both of them, even when they separated themselves. It was like, "When we go out, don't tell Gene what we did." Gene would say, "What'd you do last night?" I'd say, "I can't tell you." Not that we were doing anything bad, he just wanted a separate life. I was like the man in the middle. I wrote some stuff that didn't make it on "Creatures" and didn't make it on "Lick It Up." We were friends all that time and socializing. They were out there one day doing sessions at Wally Heider's, so it must have been for "Creatures," and they called me on the phone and said, "We're not going to use any of your tracks." I said, "Bummer. So when you come back next week, where are we going to eat?" They said, "Did you hear what we just said?" They were all on speaker phone.

This was stuff you wrote with Gene and Paul?
Yeah, demos and stuff. There are a whole lot of demos floating out there. The "It's Gonna Be Alright" demo is Gene over the click track. Mikel Japp had this riff, I did the passing chords, they were kind of Beatle-esque. I remember the first time we played "Thief in the Night" for Wendy O. Williams. She said, "You guys are really demonic."

I love that track. Back to Gene's album, did you make any contributions that weren't used?
No, I did not. It was strictly the backgrounds.

What's your favorite song of the three you're featured on?
"See You Tonite." It's one of my favorite tracks. I think it's a great pop song. I'm surprised no one has covered it. It's pretty straightforward. I remember we came back and I think we just wiped out the background vocals and Gene and I sang them again. I've got all these demos of us doing stuff. "What You See Is What You Get" is funny. On the last record, he's got that song on there. It's the same thing.

"Monster"?
It's "Eat Your Heart Out." He and I have a version of a song called "Eat Your Heart Out."

It's the same tune?
No. What was funny, I actually sent him an email; "It's about time you finally figured out what to do with that title." (Laughs) He just recycled the title. Our song, I thought, was one of the best pop tunes ever. Gene used to have a notebook, which would literally have song titles and lines from songs. One day, my wife just threw out, "No sooner said than done." That became the Keel track. It made more sense to say "Easier Said Than Done." She shouted it out and he wrote it down and ended up writing a song. When Gene and I would write, we'd throw anything against the wall and see what stuck. When Paul and I would write, we'd go to S.I.R. He'd play drums and I'd play guitar. Or I would play drums. That's where we wrote "Get All You Can Take."

I love that track.
There are about 12 verses to "Get All You Can Take." I wrote them all. I would sit there, I felt like I was writing "Taxi" by Harry Chapin. Eventually we just picked three and we finalized them. The comping of the solo on "Get All You Can Take" is Paul and Mark St. John. Paul is playing more lead on that track than Mark is. I also

remember Gene was at his apartment, we were in Paul's old apartment on 52nd Street where Bob Kulick used to rent from. I'm in the bathroom on the phone, he's in the living room, [and] Gene's at his place. We're trying to figure out, what is the line we can sing instead of "What fucking difference does it make?" on "Get All You Can Take."

You were writing on the phone?
In this one case we were stuck with the line. At one point in time, there was a whole bunch of ideas written for what it could be. We just couldn't come up with the line and then finally Paul said, "I'm just singing, 'What fucking difference does it make?'" I think that might have been the first time we came up with it because it made sense but it was around the time Tipper Gore's parental advisory shit was happening.

Paul reaches the stratosphere with his vocals on that song. But it fits the energy of the track.
He sings great on that song. On "Animalize" I'm actually playing rhythm guitar on a few of the tracks I wrote.

Did your parts make it to the album?
They made it on the album; I'm just not credited. The funny thing is "Murder In High Heels," I wrote that riff. It's me that wrote that stupid song (laughs). I wrote, just about the top off the top of my head, "You know she could / She's a get-rich bitch / You better get her while the gettin's good." We would do this sort of scat stuff, and it was phenomenal writing with him. With Paul, I just wrote tons of verses and we paired it down. When we were doing that song at Right Track, (sings pre-chorus riff to "Murder In High Heels"), that's me on the rhythm guitar. Paul was talking with his parents about something about one of his cousins. He said, "You record." And he gave me the biggest compliment at the time. He said, "You know, I consider myself one of the best rhythm guitar players in the world. I don't have anybody on these records. But go ahead and play." The other thing about "Murder In High Heels," when Gene left for "Runaway," I played the bass line. But I played the riff wrong, so Jean Beauvoir had to re-record it.

There's been a lot of speculation that Gene didn't play a lot of bass on "Animalize."
He played some. I know on that one, I was called in to play bass because he had already gone for the movie. So Jean played it again. It's my own riff and I got it fucking wrong! (Laughs)

What about "While The City Sleeps"?
That's me basically doing Free's "Wishing Well." When Gene and I wrote, almost 90 percent of the time the music would almost be all mine and the lyrics were a co-

write. "What You See Is What You Get" is a great song. I'm surprised no one has released it. There a demo around somewhere. It's Eric Carr's drum track from "Lick It Up," and me and Gene. We left Gene's apartment, and we said, "What a song!"

Gene's musical talents tend to get overlooked given his public persona. Having worked with him, what are your thoughts on Gene as a musician/songwriter?
As a musician and a songwriter, I think his talents are pretty damn good. He's good at pulling in ideas from everybody in the room, getting people to put out the best they can put out and managing to keep things loose when they should be loose.

Any good stories from the "Animalize" sessions?
The best story I can tell is when Paul and I went to record the vocals for "Heaven's On Fire." Cathy St. George was in the other room, his girlfriend at the time. We were running the tracks and he says, "I'm going to take a pass at it." He didn't feel he quite opened up enough. So the tape is rolling in the control room and he doesn't hear Eric's click track for whatever reason on this take and he's doing the yodeling. He doesn't realize it's running and he's yodeling. And the drums and first chord come in. We froze. And we go, "No one's ever going to believe that that wasn't an edit." It was just him warming up and serendipitously when the music started, it was at the end of that. It wasn't like he was trying to come up with that. He was just warming up. And on the best warm up he did, the tape was rolling. So we kept that on there. He had me in the control room listening to him and I guess in some sense I produced the vocal. He said, "How was that?" I said, "That's fine." I don't think I had to tell him to go back and do anything more than maybe 10 percent of anything. He'd come in, "Should I do that again?" "No." "I'm going to sing that again." "Fine." I think that vocal was done almost magically.

You have a unique perspective given you worked closely with Paul and Gene. How did you view their musical partnership in KISS?
I would say their partnership was based on the blend of the relationship. At times, I think one would drive while the other wouldn't. When Gene was doing the movies, Paul was driving. I remember Michael James Jackson coming to them and saying, "I don't need to be on this record."

He's credited as drum producer on "Animalize." It's not a formal producer credit.
They didn't force him off, he just said, "You're doing fine without me." On that album, Paul had to drive because Gene went off to do the movie. It's funny when they went back to the makeup and costumes and disassociating themselves from those records, a lot of my royalties disappeared. I also remember hearing that song "Reason To Live" and calling Gene on the phone, "Does anyone want to tell them this is 'I Want To Know What Love Is'?"

Some fans have made that parallel.

I said, "I'm not going to tell them." That was when everything was in turmoil. And you had the shrink running things.

Jesse Hilsen.

Yeah. Toward "Animalize," they were buying Ace out at the time. We almost got into a huge fight, corporate-wise, because they were going off to Europe to do the first tour after "Animalize." They had already sold like 1.7 million records and I hadn't signed any papers because I just figured, "I'll sign them when they come along." They were going to try and give me an advance before the signings. And I didn't think that the publishing papers and the advance were two separate things. Very naively they said, "We can't give you any money." I said, "Well, I guess I can't sign any papers." Gene thought my lawyer was holding them up. And then Howard Marks was calling me. And I was like, "Hold on." I got them on the phone on a conference call with their lawyers, my lawyer and me. And at one point, they said they couldn't give me money because they were going to give Ace a ton of money to leave. There would literally be times where they were floating in between "Lick It Up"'s comeback where I would pay for things. I had my "Beatlemania" money still saved. I know that at the end of that relationship, they found out that everything they already owned was being leased back to them like three or four times already. I called Gene and said, "I'm very sorry to hear you aren't working with Howard anymore. I'm sorry he left." He said, "He didn't leave." Gene didn't curse much at all but he said, "We fired his fucking ass."

A few more questions to take us out, Mitch. When was the last time you spoke with Joe Pecorino?

About a year or so ago. He's in New York. He still does casual gigs. He got married and I think he's got one kid. He's good. He just had his 60th birthday on May 13th. I was invited but I couldn't make it.

Did you get a gold or platinum album for your work on Gene's solo album?

Yeah. They're in storage in Long Island. What's funny, for the "Animalize" one they spelled my name wrong on the plaque. I sent it back to the RIAA guys to get it redone. The night they got presented with their four platinum albums for "Animalize" in New Jersey at the Meadowlands, I was there. They had no place to take them. So I took them back in the limo to my apartment. From there, me, Desmond Child and Paul went to see somebody play in Desmond's little Volkswagen Beetle. (Laughs) This was before Desmond became Desmond. I actually got asked to write for Bon Jovi's "Slippery When Wet," because Paul recommended me as a writer.

What do you remember about Paul introducing Desmond Child to Jon Bon Jovi?

He hooked them up because I got a phone call from Jon and Richie on a conference call saying, "Paul says you would be great to write with. Can you do this?" My eight-year marriage was coming to an end and I looked at my royalties and said, "I better take some time off and see if I can make this work." It makes for a great fucking story. All for love I went that way and it didn't work out. And "Slippery When Wet" goes "boom."

You mentioned you had a Vinnie Vincent story. How about it, Mitch?
What's funny is I remember when KISS were looking for guitarists after Ace, Grover Jackson had sent a bunch of cassettes and Paul and I sat in that apartment on 52nd Street and listened to all of the guitar players — Allan Holdsworth and all these different guys that were being submitted. And Vinnie's demo was in there. The song that sold Paul was "Tears." I don't remember any great guitar playing on it at all. That's when I first heard Vinnie. He was brought in on "Creatures" because Ace was starting to fall apart. And then he came in for "Lick It Up." I remember Gene calling me at my apartment on 74th Street on the West Side and saying, "Come over to the hotel." It was a hotel on the East Side. Vinnie was in the room for like five or six days. I went over and met him and it was great. He was a huge Beatles freak like them so the three of us spent the entire afternoon singing Beatles songs. I also remember at the end, when the tensions started, all the people around Vinnie were telling him, "You were the one that made these guys."

He co-wrote eight of the 10 songs on "Lick It Up."
Right, and "Lick It Up was a hit. So you could see how he would think that. At the end I remember Gene and I sitting at Radio City Music Hall at the end of their stint of gigs [in 1984]. Vinnie was in the band and backstage he was talking to a bunch of guys from Connecticut about where he was going next and how he was going to the next level. And he was then out of the band. He thought he was bigger than the band.

Richie Ranno

Starz guitarist recalls a last minute phone call requesting his participation on Gene Simmons' solo album and challenges being part of the AMI family.

Richie, if I may, let's set the stage for your career arc in 1978. Would it be correct to say that Sean Delaney discovered Starz in 1975 and brought you to the attention of KISS' manager Bill Aucoin following which you signed with AMI which resulted in a deal with Capitol Records?
Richie Ranno: Yes, that's exactly what happened. He [Sean] was friends with Pieter Sweval [Starz/Skatt Bros. drummer] and he went and heard the band before I was even in it. They were called the Fallen Angels. He said, "Wow, you guys are really great." KISS wasn't really big yet, it was the summer of 1975. He said, "You know, we're looking for another band," even though KISS hadn't broken big yet. He just wanted to have another band. I think they wanted a more normal kind of thing besides the hectic crazy thing that KISS was doing. So they liked the band and started managing them. Then they decided that the band could really use two guitar players, so I auditioned. I was the 75th guy to go down there, I think. They just couldn't find a hard-rock guitar player. In that day and age in New York City there were no hard-rock guitar players, which is kind of funny when you think about it. I went down there and played exactly what they wanted to hear because that's what I was at the time. And we fired the keyboard player a few weeks later because it really didn't make sense to have a keyboard player and changed the name to Starz, and there you go.

You shared guitar duties with Brendan Harkin, who we've also spoken with for his contributions to Peter Criss' solo album! Tell me how the guitar duo in Starz divided the guitar duties and worked together in their own band?
To be honest, Brendan is an incredible rhythm guitar player. I think he is one of the greatest I've ever heard at rock rhythm, just tight — he's got a great right hand. He's just phenomenal. And it just seemed to sound better when he played more rhythms and I played more single note stuff. I'm more of a bluesy style, rock style guitar player, so I ended up playing more guitar solos than he did. But we did do a lot of dual guitar solos and at that point, maybe on the record, there would be no rhythm guitar. Or we'd overdub with rhythm guitar, but you really didn't miss it live. So we did a lot of dual guitar solos that were really cool that we worked out. That's how it divvied up. I don't know if Brendan was really happy about the situation, because he did leave the band after the third album! But anyway, we're still friends at this point in time, so whatever it is it's over.

Richie, who would you cite as your guitar influences?
Going back to when I was a teenager there's no question that it was Eric Clapton, the Cream style Eric Clapton, Jimi Hendrix, Jeff Beck and Jimmy Page, all in one.

That's kind of the holy trinity of players from the time (laughs)...
(Laughs) There are four of them... That's what it is! But you have to understand I had already started playing guitar before any of them had a hit. So, I was already pretty good by the time I heard any of them — Jeff Beck was the first with "Over Under Sideways Down" and "Shapes of Things" — I'll never forget it and it changed my life. And my life kept getting changed musically as each of those guitar-players came to the forefront over the span of maybe two years. And I learned to play exactly like each one of them and then came up with my own style out of it.

Your raw and rockin' self-titled debut album followed in 1976, produced by Jack Douglas. In some ways you seem more connected with Aerosmith — you opened for them on tour too, right?
Yeah, we did one pretty major tour with them and then parts of other tours.

You guys were known for ripping it up in concert, combining catchy choruses and memorable riffs, along with in your face delivery. I've mentioned Aerosmith, but what target market was Starz most interested in breaking into?
I don't know — that wasn't my job. I just played the music!

(Laughs)
You know what I mean? We didn't think in those terms back then. Actually, the record company was horrible and management wasn't much better because what happened, and I don't blame them necessarily, was that KISS wasn't that big when we started with them [AMI]. And then all of a sudden, three or four months later "Alive!" comes out and they become the biggest band in the world for the next couple of years. And let me tell you, that is probably what killed our career. Because there was nobody standing over the top of the record company — Record companies were totally clueless back then. Absolutely clueless! Managers had to explain to them what to do. Unfortunately, our manager was busy counting his money and figuring out what was going on with KISS.

And of course that manager was Bill Aucoin...
Yes.

So he was very much distracted and you were playing second fiddle to KISS on Aucoin Management's radar of importance. Everything was dropped at AMI for KISS...
But no one could have possibly predicted after three albums — that whether you realize it or not that those three [KISS] albums flopped — no one could have

predicted that they were going to sell over 2 million albums on their next release and become the biggest band in the world. No one! It was as weird as that Peter Frampton thing that happened right afterwards. Frampton ["Comes Alive," January 1976; Note the eponymous "Frampton" album released in 1975 did hit #32, just as KISS' "Dressed To Kill" album had] comes after KISS.

Those two are great examples of live albums really breaking bands to a wider audience. Both had essentially bombed with their studio releases — live albums completely saved their careers, didn't they?
And Bob Seger was the next one by the way.

Absolutely, that's right, "Live Bullet [April 1976]..."
Yeah, it's really weird how that happened. And the Frampton thing — we toured with Frampton before our album came out. We were playing in the mid-South mostly and did something like 10 shows with him. It was in theaters, and we were unknown and didn't even have an album out. The theatres were half sold-out and to be honest, I wasn't impressed, even minutely, with Peter Frampton. Don't ask me why, but I wasn't impressed with the live act. Over the years I've realized what a great guitar player, and singer, and song-writer he was, but to just stand there as an unknown not knowing what he was doing really didn't hit us. All five of us thought that it sucked, to be quite honest with you, and I don't mean to put him down — I do think he's great, so don't get me wrong. But, the crowd, maybe a thousand people or so, were really into it and screaming and yelling. And I thought the talk-box thing was just a shitty gimmick. So it really shocked us when the live album came out sold like 20 million copies [Ed. currently 8x Platinum in the U.S.]. There's no predicting this shit is what I'm trying to get at. I'm not saying Frampton's bad. Frampton, over time, I came to appreciate and he is great. He's a great guitar player, he's great at everything, but I wasn't impressed by that act that really made it very big. I really wasn't.

So that goes back to my question of "who are you targeting," it's all luck or in the stars who actually makes it and who doesn't?
You throw the paint against the wall and what sticks, sticks. Capitol Records was completely incompetent. It was just a bunch of music executives who were hooked on cocaine. I really don't give a shit, they can sue me, but it's a fact. They were all, with the exception of a few hard working serious people, fucking drug addicts and 35 years later I don't give a shit. They were drug addicts and they didn't know what they were doing. They can deny it as much as they want. But every time they came up to us — we didn't do drugs — I'll just speak for myself and not anybody else, and they stopped doing this after the first time around. Around the band there would be executives and they'd be like, "Hey Richie, Richie, come here I got something for you." And they'd take me to the bathroom and open up an aluminum foil thing with cocaine and I'd be like, "Keep that for yourself, buddy." This happened

everywhere we went and it didn't matter how high (high up in the company, not 'high') the executive was. They were all a bunch a drug addicts.

Yeah, Larry Harris wrote a book about Casablanca Records and details some of the snow storm and pill-popping that seemed to go on at record labels in the 1970s...

Well, I knew Larry Harris. Not well, but I did know him from when I was in Stories because he had worked with Buddah and Stories was on Buddah. So I knew Larry and Neil [Bogart]. But I know Larry wrote the book, but I've never read it. But I'm telling you Capitol Records, what I can speak for; they can all go down a shitter for all I care. I don't want to ever speak to any of those guys again to be honest with you. But every now and then, one of them says "Hi" to me on Facebook and that's fine. It's not their fault individually. It doesn't matter anyway because here I am, it's 35 years later, and I'm alive, healthy and happy. So it really doesn't matter.

Absolutely!

But they definitely ruined what should have been a stellar career and wasn't. I'm not resentful or bitter. I might sound it, but I'm really not!

"Violation" and "Attention Shoppers" followed in 1977 and 1978 respectively. Wasn't "Violation" supposed to be titled "Red Hot?"

No, "Violation" was supposed to be called "Second Offense" because we got so much shit for the first album by the press because of "Pull The Plug," that we figured we'd offended so many people so let's offend more and call it "Second Offense." But management said, "There's no song called 'Second Offense,' so you can't call it that; you have to have a title track for the album." And "Violation" worked. It's fine.

Give us a snapshot of your career in early 1978? Third album's out, it came out in January 1978...

That album sucked. We didn't use Jack Douglas, I don't know why. I think we were being sabotaged by management, but no one has ever answered the question why. It doesn't really matter. Instead of recording at a top studio we recorded at a shit studio with no producers, us producing it ourselves and we didn't know what we were doing. The album kind of sucks, although a lot of Starz fans tell me they like it. Great. But it really didn't help our careers and then we switched a couple of member around and came back with a new album right away. That was a great rock album, but by then we got so fed up with everything that we just called it quits.

Do you recall how you were offered the opportunity to perform on Gene Simmons' solo album?

Well, Gene and I were pretty good friends back then. What happened was, I'd said to Sean, "I hope I can play on Gene's album you know I've always been such a big supporter of the guys in KISS and Gene." And he's like, "yeah, yeah, I'm producing it." Then I never heard from them and they went over to England. I guess they mixed it in England and I wasn't included, and I thought that kind of sucked — I would have liked to have been on it. But I didn't really give a shit, ultimately. Then they came back from England and I get this call one day and Sean says, "What are you doing tomorrow?" And I'm like, "Nothing." And he says, "Oh good, could you play on Gene's album?" And I said, "I guess" even thought I thought it was done.

So they went to mix "Tunnel of Love" which they originally had Joe Perry play on but wiped his track and had Jeff Baxter play on it. Then, for whatever the reason, they wiped his track. So they had the whole thing done except that single track. They were going to get Nils Lofgren in New York. But Nils wanted a limo from his house in the D.C. area to the airport, wanted like four limo rides — he had a lot of demands. So Sean was like, "Number one he's got a lot of demands. Number two he's not a hard-rock guitar player. Number three, Richie Ranno lives like eight miles away and can do this in a heartbeat." And Gene said, "You're right, call him." So I went in there and I played, and other than the very first guitar that you can hear, the rhythm guitar — Gene was playing that I believe — other than that I'm playing everything on there. Management didn't properly change the credits so it appears that there are three guys playing on "Tunnel of Love", but there aren't.

So that would have just been and overdub situation, go into the studio and punch the solo in. Do you recall how many takes you took to get the solo you wanted?
I'm pretty much a first take guy on everything I do, ever.

You're not into over-analyzing it or mapping a solo out — you just go in and do it?
There's no reason to. I know exactly what I want to do and I do it. But I'll say, "If you don't like it, I'll do it again." And they've always said, "No, that's perfect." You know, that's the way I've done Starz albums. That's the way I've done every album. It's just the way I like to work. I know what I want to do and have a real sense of how I play. If you make me play the same thing over and over, I always tell them, "I'm going to play it worse 'cause I'm going to lose interest. I got it right now. My heart's in it right now!" And that's the way I've been. I still record all the time and that's how I do it. It was great — it was a lot of fun. I think they asked me to play the solo four times and then they pieced it together a little bit taking parts of one and another which was fine...

That's the standard process of comping to get the best overall performance, right...
Yeah, they did that. It was fun; we all had a good time. We had a lot of laughs in the studio that day. Mike Stone was behind the board. He did Queen's stuff and I love

Queen. Gene and Sean gave me a hug and I left and then I eventually got a platinum award hanging on the wall for it, which was nice. It was that simple.

When we spoke with Brendan he mentioned that he didn't get an award for his work on Peter's album, so you're one up on him there.
(Laughs) I didn't know that. I don't think Peter's went platinum, I thought it only went Gold [Ed. It went platinum too]. But who knows, back then you could manipulate the market because they didn't have SoundScan. No one really knew... You know who reported sales? The label!

Absolutely, it was all a game. You ship enough, or say you did, and that's your numbers.
Exactly, and you don't tell them how many returns you got. We always suspected that we sold at least 500,000 on "Violation," but they never certified it Gold, but think about it. If they did they would have owed us the money for Gold sales.

There's no interest for the record labels, even today, to be audited.
No, well now the record companies got what they deserved, they're nearly all out of business.

Did you have much interaction with the members of KISS. I'd have thought being a part of AMI that you would have bumped into them?
Of course we did. We were very close with them. We went to parties all the time together.

Did you do any other recording work with Gene? He was known to pull in other musicians who were available to do demo recordings.
Well, he used to bring in Dubé [Joe X.] to play drums all the time. Dubé was the drummer from Starz. We'd be rehearsing and Gene and Paul would be standing over in the corner waiting for us to get done so that Dubé could go to some recording studio with them at midnight. And I believe they actually used some of those recordings, the drum parts of Dubé's, we don't really know, Dubé thinks so 'cause he knows what he played. But there's no proof...

It's entirely possible; JR Smalling discovered some of his drum tracks on some songs on KISS' 2001 box set...
There's a bunch of songs around that 1978 period in particular that Dubé was working out at night with Paul and Gene at night in a recording studio. And by that point we all know what Peter [Criss] was doing and I can't imagine that Peter was on a lot of that stuff to be honest with you.

There's always been a question by some as to whether Peter Criss was the drummer on the studio side of "Alive II" so I guess anything is possible. I think it

was once rumored that Cheap Trick's Bun E. Carlos had drummed on some KISS tracks. Perhaps the rumor had some truth and just got the actual band wrong.
Dubé says he remembers some of those songs. But we were in the midst of craziness. We didn't know what was going on either. We were on the road continuously or writing to make an album or recording an album. It was just complete chaos in our lives. It was fun, but it's hard to remember this and that and all that shit!

Were you given any other tracks to work on, on Gene's album, or was it just the one?
No, they just asked me to do that and I was happy to do it. I had a great time doing it. It was great working with Gene, Sean and Mike Stone. Sean was a great great guy. I can't say enough about him. He was a bit manic, a bit crazy, but incredible. I'll tell you what, if you watch the movie "School of Rock." I don't know if anyone knew Sean, but Jack Black's character is Sean Delaney.

That's a good one! He was certainly passionate and creative.
I'll tell you, I spent an unbelievable amount of time with Sean. He came to every single rehearsal and every single gig we did, from the time I joined the band (and probably a bit before then) through our first big tour and then he was off doing some other stuff. He was a great inspiration to us, a driving force. He did the same thing for KISS prior and those guys really don't fess up for that and give him the credit he deserves. I don't know why. I know they don't speak poorly of him anymore — I know they did for a while. Unfortunately, Sean was involved in drugs and they weren't, and I wasn't either, and it definitely affected his personality for a period of time. But he still was the great person he was.

He was a great personality and incredible music.
Sean was an absolute genius.

So, Starz puts out "Coliseum Rock" [late-1978] and then things kind of fall apart. What happened to Starz in the end?
Stupid management things... We didn't want to make a fifth album on Capitol because we hated their guts by that time. Beyond words! We didn't want to be in the same room with them. We didn't want to talk to them. We didn't want anything to do with them! And Bill said, "Well Ranno, they want you to do a fifth album." And we said, "Then we'll do a fifth album of shitty bubble-gum covers because we don't want to write and slave over our own music anymore where they have anything to do with it." So Bill said, "Okay, I'll tell them that you want to leave the label." We said, "Great!" What we didn't notice, and we felt that management should have noticed, was there was a new form of music starting, called new wave. Now I hate that shit, but it's called new wave. Sorry, that's maybe going to offend a lot of people when they hear that, but I hate that shit. Don't get me wrong, I love

the Police, I love Squeeze — there's always great bands in a genre that you may not like, and I didn't like the genre. What we didn't know was that there was this new thing really building up and the record companies were only signing bands from the new thing. So we shouldn't have left the old thing because we couldn't get another record contract. There were only maybe 12 labels at the time. Whatever it was it wasn't many. Our management should have known that only new wave bands were being signed and that we shouldn't have left that awful label. We would have been better making our fifth album that was already written, on that shitty label.

That would have been the smart thing to do, but that doesn't always happen, right?
So then, when we couldn't get a record contract. We said, "Fuck it." We did get back together a year later and we toured and then people dropped out and we wound up with just me and Michael, and two new guys, drummer Doug Madick and Peter Scance on bass, and we wrote some new stuff. We got a deal with an Atlantic subsidiary, called Radio Records, but we felt bad about keeping the name because so many guys had changed. So we didn't keep the name Starz — this time the mistake was ours. So we used the name Hellcats. As the album started getting really good national airplay the label went under. As a subsidiary of Atlantic we were hoping they would pick it up and take it from there, but contractually they weren't allowed to do that. And then I just said, "I don't like the music business anymore, I'm out." And I've been out of the music business ever since then, around 1983. I do other things and I play music. I just don't consider myself part of the music business. I don't like it. I just play music, there's a big difference.

There's a gigantic difference. You're out there because you want to perform and enjoy playing music, but not base your livelihood on it.
Right, and I don't live and die for it. When I wake up in the morning I just wake up in the morning. I don't wake up and go, "Where's my career today?" People who do that, I don't believe they're having fun. I've never enjoyed playing music more than I do right now, other than when I was a teenager. To say that at my age, I'm playing at a little club tonight with three other great musicians, and we're going to have a great time. There may be only two people there and it doesn't matter to me, that's not why I do it.

Didn't Starz get back together in the early 2000s and do some gigs.
Yes, we've been doing gigs every year since 2003, three to seven gigs a year. We went over to England in March and did the Hard Rock Hell Festival in Wales, and played a great club in London [Underworld]. We had a great time!

I read an article where Bill had shown up for a Starz gig in the early 2000s and Michael refused to talk to him. I don't want you to speak for him, but had you

had a relationship with Bill in the years since he managed the band, before he died?
There was at least 10 years or more that I didn't to speak to him and I was kind of angry with him at the time. And then we reconnected because I ran the New York KISS Expo for many years. We reconnected, and I was a little hesitant at first, but we got friendly. I'm so glad we did. I can't say a bad thing about Bill Aucoin. He was just a great, great person. He was brilliant and he and Sean were just two amazing people I was blessed to have been involved with. What happened when I explained that he should have done this, or should have done that, I don't fault him for that or blame him for that. Yes, he should have done those things, but he was distracted with KISS and I get it. I understand that — it's where the money was at. But he was just a great person and I'm glad we reconnected and stayed friendly right up until the time he died, which was a real tragedy. I really only have good things to say about him.

Once KISS became that big entity they were like a monster eating babies!
Right, none of the other groups made it and that's why. He did expand his business and that was the smart thing to do. He did try and add on more people, but somehow it just was never the same. KISS got too big, and that's the way it goes. You roll the dice. You look back at Starz music and it still sounds great today. And you wonder, it was just as good as Styx and Aerosmith and Rush, and all the bands that sold 2 million records apiece, and we didn't [make it]. And it bothers me to a certain extent that I'm not playing the big places, I'm playing the little places. I stopped playing music 100 percent, except for in my living room, for eight years. I just really, really got back to do it because I love it. And that's fine with me. If someone asked me to go on tour with them, who was really cool, and paid me well enough, I would probably do it but, until then I'll play every opportunity that I get!

The KISS solo albums were a major industry event in 1978. There was a huge marketing and publicity campaign surrounding the albums and they all shipped platinum. Did a sense of sensationalism trickle down to the musicians? As a working musician back then, what was your perception?
I thought it was big! I was a KISS supporter. I wasn't one of those people who hated KISS. Most musicians resented and hated those guys and I was not that way. I loved them and thought that what they did was great. Their show was phenomenal and it was exciting, and I was all for anything that made them bigger or made them better. But that success really ruined them at the same time. It ruins all groups, not just them. That kind of success is hard to handle. It gets competitive within the group. The big mistake probably, and Bill said this for years, when they did the four solo albums they didn't foresee the competition between the four of them and that really ripped the band apart.

That's going to going to happen with any egos. I can understand other bands not being impressed with KISS because they'll never claim they're virtuosos on their instruments, are they?

No. But you know what, if you saw them live, especially between '75 and '78, they were phenomenal. I'm telling you, and I don't care what anyone says. I'm an accomplished musician, and I know that those guys did, what they did... You know, if you play within yourself, that's greatness and if you know your limitations and play to them, that's all it takes. I saw them on big stages and was very, very impressed. They were great.

It goes back to that saying, do one thing very well rather than many mediocre things.

That's exactly right. They really nailed it.

"Ace Frehley" Related Interviews

"My idea of a solo album was to do as much as I could on my own. I'm sure everybody looked at it different ways. But me, just being the lead guitarist of the band, you know, the lead guitarist can play rhythm guitar. Any rhythm guitar can play bass. Anything I didn't feel proficient at I would hire someone to do. And that's what ended up happening. I played just about every track" (Grooves, 1978).

Susan Collins

Vocalist details her experience working on Ace Frehley's album, lending her "Brooklyn street" sound to the three tracks she sang on, her tie to Neil Bogart, a recent meeting with the Spaceman, and why "New York Groove" has "balls."
By Tim McPhate

Susan, how did you receive an invitation to sing vocals on Ace Frehley's solo album?
Susan Collins: I had worked with Eddie Kramer, going back to Jimi Hendrix. I worked with Eddie on a number of projects back in the day at Electric Lady. And David Lasley and I had done many, many projects together as background singers. I think what happened, Eddie had requested me and we had lost contact over the years. And I got a call from David and he said, "It's funny, I got a call to do this record and I was going to call you, and Eddie Kramer asked if I'm still in contact with you." And he told Eddie, "I was going to call her anyway." So it was really perfect.

You would have sung during the sessions at Plaza Sound in New York, correct?
Yes. Back in the day, I used to go from studio to studio. I could be doing three of four sessions in a day at places like Electric Lady, the Hit Factory or the Record Plant. I had actually never worked in this specific studio before. It was in the Radio City Music Hall building. It was quite interesting for me because it was a fantastic studio.

Was Ace around during your session?
At the session that I did, he was absolutely there.

Was that your first time meeting Ace?
Back in the day, I was singing with the Electric Light Orchestra so there were many, many different parties and people would come to see you and you would be introduced. But no, I never really had an opportunity to sit there and have any cohesive conversation with him at all. I had many more conversations prior to this with Paul, a couple with Gene, but nothing memorable. But Paul and I were friendlier.

So what were your first general impressions of Ace?
You know, I have to be honest and tell you he was the nicest and sweetest guy. He knew who I was by my reputation and he wanted, through Eddie Kramer, "my sound" on his record. That's why he hired me, for my sound. But he didn't know what he was going to be getting when I walked into the room. He was so respectful and so sweet. When I said, "Ace, what do you think about this?" He was like,

"Susan, just do whatever you want. I'll take whatever I like and I'll leave the rest." He really respected and allowed actual creative freedom.

I want to get into the process for your vocal parts in a minute. But regarding the album's credits, you are credited as singing background vocals on three tracks: "Speedin' Back To My Baby," "What's On Your Mind?" and "New York Groove." The credit actually reads "David Lasley and Susan Collins & Co." Can you shed some light?
Yes, I'll tell you why because this is what happened. Are you familiar with David's sound? David has one of the most gorgeous voices you've ever heard in your life. I happen to love the way he sings low, but he's a very high singer. He always sings higher parts. The reason "& Co." is listed is this — when we did "New York Groove," I did "New York Groove." I tripled myself. My voice is tripled.

Your voice is very prominent on the track.
Well, that's why. And what happened was, after that, they had called in Benny Diggs — they called in three guys, and they have all since passed away. One of the guys that they called in at the end of the session I did, they called in to do a low voice. They put his voice on and then they took it off. They never used it. So I guess, in all due respect, they said "& Co." because they didn't end up using a lot of the vocals that they recorded. I know that for a fact. And two of the three guys, I was trying to remember the other black guy's name, who was fabulous. Benny Diggs also sang with Luther [Vandross], who should rest in peace, and sang on both of my solo albums. Oh, Phillip Ballou was the other one. He also passed away.

So these guys came in, tried some vocal parts, but they got left on the cutting-room floor?
I know that they didn't make "New York Groove" and I know they didn't make "Speedin' Back To My Baby." But David Lasley did do some work on "New York Groove." We did the "oohs" together. That's just me and David and the "oohs" are actually mixed way back, if you notice. I didn't know about them calling the other guys. And I'll tell you how I found out. A couple of years ago, "New York Groove" was used as a jingle. I had called the union because I said, "You know, we should be getting T&R [talent & residual] royalty checks." I called David Lasley before I called the union and said, "David, have you heard the spot?" And he said, "Yeah, but I don't think it's us." And I said, "It sounds exactly like the track, what are you talking about?" And he said, "Susan, I don't think it's us." And we listened back together. And he told me back in the day, they had called Benny and Phillip to put in additional "oohs" to give it a more soulful sound, and that it was not what they wanted, so they mixed it way back. And P.S., it was not us on the track; I want to say it was some jingle company out of Detroit or Chicago that emulated exactly what we did, because they didn't want to pay for the buyout. Oh well.

Did Ace sing background vocals with you at all?
No, he was not part of the backgrounds. But he never left the session.

In terms of your vocal parts, Ace let you have free reign to try ideas?
I came up with a couple of things for "New York Groove." Where he gave me more free reign was "Speedin' Back To My Baby." He just let me go wild.

Your voice is very prominent on that song as well.
(Sings main chorus melody) That's me. I don't think that David worked on any of those lines.

Susan, near the end of the song, you're cutting loose with some improvisational lines.
Yes, I go (sings line) "Oh, Speedin' back..."

That's it! How did that part come to be?
They played the track and I just did my thing. As a matter of fact, I wanted to do something else and I came up with an idea as I was singing. I said, "No, no, I have another idea," because I was so excited. Ace and Eddie were like, "No, no this is perfect! Susan, don't overkill it."

Did you put any of the other ideas down on tape?
I tried a couple of things. You always try a couple of things. It's very rare that you keep the first thing that you do. I think I tried a couple of things and they put them down but they didn't make the record. And to Eddie and Ace's credit, of all the KISS solo records, Ace was the only one to have success. Ace was instrumental in choosing parts as well. And Eddie was a genius. I think on any record you put down a number of ideas on different tracks and you pick and choose.

Your voice provides a perfect complement to Ace's on "Speedin' Back To My Baby."
Thank you very much.

As you mentioned, "New York Groove" was a big hit. Were you specifically trying to add a "New York"-style personality to your part?
That's why they called me. I was always hired for my tough Brooklyn sound. And that's what Eddie wanted. He wanted that New York, street, Brooklyn sound. That's where I started singing, on the streets of Brooklyn. When I was about 12 or 13 years old, I was in a pizza place across the street from the projects where I grew up, and I heard a song called "Be My Baby" on the jukebox. Every day after school, my mother would give me a quarter to get a slice of pizza and a small coke, and I would have a nickel leftover. And I put the nickel in the jukebox and played "Be My Baby." Well I found out that for a quarter I could play it six times instead of five. So I would

play "Be My Baby" over and over again. These very tough guys from the projects who wore leather jackets — you know when you're 12 years old, and guys are 16 it's like they're 50 — well the guys in this group were *a cappella* singers and one of the guys came up to me, and he said, "You are really good. You wanna sing with us?" Of course, I said, "Yeah, I wanna sing with you." You know who was in that group? Neil Bogart.

Really?
Neil Bogart grew up in the same projects I grew up in. One of the guys was from Vito & The Salutations. All these guys are dead now, every one of them are gone. We used to sing *a cappella*, underneath the stairwell, to get the echo. They would sing "Duke Of Earl," "A Teenager In Love" and they would make me sing the lead on all these boy songs, because they never sang girl songs. And I only wanted to sing girl songs. So I now have a show "You Can Take The Girl Outta Brooklyn" that is all about how the song "Be My Baby" changed my life and how I was signed to Don Kirshner with my first publishing deal. Donnie said to me, "Sue, babe, if there is anyone you'd want to write with, who would it be?" And without missing a beat, I said, "Ellie Greenwich," because Neil Bogart bought me a 45 because he knew how much I loved "Be My Baby." By this point, I guess I was 14 and on the record it read, "Written by P. Spector, J. Barry and E. Greenwich." And he told me who the names were and when I heard Ellie, I knew Ellie was a girl and I wanted to write with her and that meant I could really be a songwriter. Ellie became one of my closest, dearest friends till the day she passed away. She was my son's godmother.

That's a neat story. Susan, were you familiar with the original version of "New York Groove"? A group named Hello had a hit with it in the UK in 1975.
You know, I have to tell you, I did not know that. I always thought that Ace's was the original.

"New York Groove" has been able to attain the rare status of being a song that has transcended generations. It's been used by the Yankees and it's been featured in television and commercials. Why do you think that song has made such an impression?
I love MOR [middle of the road] music. I love Karen Carpenter and schmaltzy, beautiful ballads. Every song about New York — from Frank Sinatra and Billy Joel to everybody — was always MOR and poppy. "New York Groove," to put it bluntly, had balls. It had New York balls. Even a doctor or a lawyer or a surgeon would say, "Boy, that song has balls!" That's why. "New York Groove" put it exactly the way it should have been put. "I'm back in the New York groove." It's timeless, it's ageless. You could sing it and refer to it as back in the '30s or you could sing it right now in 2013.

An interesting aside, the song was actually written by an Englishman, Russ Ballard. Susan, how would you describe the atmosphere for your session?
Well, I can only speak about the session that I did, and I worked my ass off at that one session. And that session was supposed to start earlier, but I was coming from another session. I was coming from the West Side — I think I was at the Record Plant. I was booked for a session with a possible hour, which meant they had the right to keep you an additional hour. Well, when that hour was over, I had a lot more work to do, they said, "Now we want you to sing on this." I don't remember who it was for. So I had to call and say, "I can't start until 7 p.m." And it was supposed to start at like 3 in the afternoon. They were totally cool. I felt so badly. David said, "Don't worry about it. Ace is very cool. He doesn't usually show up on time." When I was arrived, he was there, Eddie was there and the engineer — everybody was all set up. It was like, "Okay, put your stuff down, let's listen to the tracks and go in and do it." So it was professional from the minute we walked in. There were no drugs there. I have to be honest, and I know that Ace was notorious, there were no drugs. He was working and he was a pleasure to work with. He was respectful, nice and sweet. Anton Fig was also there.

I was going to ask if there were any other musicians hanging around.
While we were doing the session, two guys walked in. They stayed and they waved to me, I waved to them. For the life of me, I don't know who they were. When I did some part, they looked at me from the control room, [and] they were like, "That was fucking incredible!" And then they left. Anton Fig stayed for quite some time. Anton's a very soft-spoken, shy guy. And it was only when I started working on Letterman, that Anton reintroduced himself to me.

Aside from accolades for Ace, Anton has received much praise for his drum work on the album, and rightfully so.
Anton Fig is just incredible. His drum work is incredible. I know that they're still very, very good friends. I have to tell you that Anton Fig was such a good friend to Ace Frehley and really got him through a lot of stuff. He was the definition of a friend. I'm best friends with Paul Shaffer to this day. And we were both signed to Donnie Kirshner. Beside Paul Shaffer in the dictionary for friend, it says Anton Fig.

Would it be fair to say that your favorite track from the three you sang would be "New York Groove"?
It's "New York Groove," because I have a jukebox in my house. And every time I hear that song, it puts a smile on my face. Not because I'm on it, just because the song itself is like a no-brainer. It just makes you smile.

The KISS solo albums were a major event in the music industry in 1978. What do you recall the industry chatter being like?
On a scale of 1 to 10, among the musicians, don't forget [KISS] were in a certain genre, so within that genre, that was a very big deal. That was probably an 8 or a 9. Were they with the musicians that I was with? The studio cliques ... Hugh McCracken, Jimmy Maelen, John Tropea, David Spinozza [and] Will Lee — all of these guys. On a scale of 1 to 10 [for these guys], it was a 5.

When we spoke with John Tropea, he expressed a similar sentiment. He said it was a big session, but maybe not at the top of the heap.
Right.

Susan, you got to hang out with Ace at one of his book signings in 2011. What can you tell us about that?
A guy named Jimmy McElligott — who is also a fabulous guitar player — called me and said, "There's a book signing in New Jersey tonight at a store called Bookends. Why don't we go? It's Ace." And I said, "Come on, it's raining." And he said, "Come on, let's go. We'll go to dinner." We went and in the rain, mind you, there was a line out the door, around the store, in the parking lot to the back of the store. People were waiting in line. The line continues to go in the store and they're waiting. I walk in the store and Jimmy and [his wife] Joanne said, "Come on, we'll get in line." So I went into the store, they were like, "Susan, what are you doing?" And my husband said, "Just follow her into the store." There's this big burly guy up at the top of the stairs, obviously in Ace's camp, with the owner of the store. And I said, "Would you please go and tell Ace that Susan Collins is here." And the guy looks at me and says, "Who is Susan Collins?" And I said, "I'm Susan Collins." "Well, where does he know you from?" I said, "I'm the voice of 'New York Groove.'" This guy looks at me, he had to be 6-foot-4, [and] he became a 5-foot-2, 90-pound child.

The owner of Bookends went down and came right back up — now again, there was a line going down the stairs, all around the entire lower floor of the store, with these barricades. People were waiting in line to buy the book for him to sign it. She comes back up the stairs and says, "Please follow me. How many in your party?" I go down the stairs, there's a desk set up with a red-velvet drape underneath. There were two bodyguards with Ace sitting at a table, and this blonde bombshell sitting on the side — A totally voluptuous blonde. I walk straight up to him and he looks at me and I went, "Hi Ace." And he goes, "Susan!" He jumps up and comes from behind the desk, hugs and kisses me. It was so hysterical! In true Ace fashion he said to her, "Babe, this is Susan Collins. This is the voice of 'New York Groove.' This is the girl I told you about." She gets off her chair and I hug her. She was going to shake my hand. And I hugged her. And he introduces me, "This is my fiancé." I hug her and tell her what a sweet, lovely guy he is and how respectful he was. And Ace goes, "Susan, I can't tell you what a thrill it is. I've been sober five years." That's what he shared with me. I said, "Ace, I'm so proud of you. And I'm so proud that you've done this book and that you have such a beautiful and nice fiancé. I wish you only the best." The whole interaction was like five to seven minutes, because there were people waiting. I said, "Ace, get back to what you're doing. You have all these people waiting." He said, "Wait, wait, I've got to sign this book for you." I said, "Let me buy it first!" He looked at me and said, "This is my pleasure." And he signed the most beautiful thing in his book to me. Well, there were people in line who had already bought the book, and he looks at them, and they had already heard the whole exchange, and he announces to them, "This is the woman that sang 'New York Groove'!" So as I'm leaving, diehard KISS fans are saying, "Would you please sign my book?" By the time I got out of there, I signed so many books. And by this point, my poor friends were waiting for me.

Ace is really a nice guy. It was so great. He looked so good. The fact that he shared with me that he was sober and in the program and doing so well — I know that under the influence people do very stupid things. And it's not necessarily who they are. And I know that he's burned a lot of bridges. But you've got to forgive and forget because when people do things under the influence, that's not who they are. And thank God, his best friends were people who did not indulge so somewhere in his psyche, at least he chose a very quality group of people, especially Anton Fig.

That's a great story. Susan, you mentioned your acclaimed autobiographical musical revue, "You Can Take The Girl Outta Brooklyn (But You Can't Take The Brooklyn Outta The Girl)." Are more performances in the works?
I took the summer off because [my musical director] Bette Sussman was out with Cyndi Lauper for a while. I won't work with anyone else. But come the end of September, I will start doing it again at the Cutting Room and I'm doing different dates around town. The dates will be on my professional Facebook page.

You mentioned the great Paul Shaffer. He has said, "Susan Collins is my favorite singer ... period!" That's pretty high praise, Susan.
Yeah. I met Paul before "Saturday Night Live" was even a TV show. I got a call from Anne Beatts, who was married to Michael O'Donoghue, who was the head writer for "Saturday Night Live." He has since passed away. They got divorced and she became the producer/director for a TV show called "Square Pegs" that ran for a couple of seasons. I got a call from Anne and Martin Mull to write a song called "A Letter To Patty," which was about Patty Hearst, and do a demo for an up-and-coming possible show called "Saturday Night Live." So I went to Martin's apartment, this is way back in the day, and I wrote a song with them. I went in to do the demo and there was a kid on the drums, cutting the drum track. I said to this guy, "Who's that guy on the drums?" And he said, "Oh, it's this new kid in town from Canada." When he was done, I went in to put my vocal on. And he came up to me after and he said, "Do you know any Ronnie Spector songs?" I said, "Are you

kidding me? They call me Ronnie!" And he played the piano and I sang every possible '60s song there was. And they were all Ellie's songs. And that was Paul Shaffer. Paul played the drums because they didn't have a drummer. He was the best keyboard player I had ever heard in my life.

My musical director at the time was a guy named Kenny Ascher, who is incredible. Paul Griffin was a musical director and keyboard player for me, who has since passed away. He was incredible. Paul Schaffer was in another league. Paul said to me, "Susan, you're the reason I moved to New York. The reason was to hear a voice like yours." He lived two blocks from me and we became the best of friends. "Saturday Night Live" went on the air and I became the vocal contractor. Paul worked on the show for a very short time. He brought me up to Kirshner, he was signed to him, and they did the TV show "A Year At The Top," which was a Norman Lear show. It was about three guys who sold their souls to the devil to become rock stars. Paul was one of them. Donnie was the partner with Norman Lear and Josh Mostel was the devil. Greg Evigan was the other second guy in the rock group and Donnie Scardino, who is now an enormous director in L.A., [he was the other guy]. Jeff Barry was the producer of the theme song. Everything was going full-circle. Unfortunately, the sitcom didn't make it and Paul had to come back to New York. But the good news was he came back to "Saturday Night Live." He's my son's godfather and Ellie Greenwich was his godmother. My son Tucker Caploe, he's going to be 21, he's one of the most incredible singers you've ever heard. He's a quadruple threat — he's a dancer, singer, songwriter, and actor. And Paul said to him, "Tucker, whatever you do, you're going to make it because you've really got the goods."

Susan, are there any other projects or activities that you can update us on?
I'm producing a couple of very young artists. I'm mentoring them as songwriters and collaborating with them and teaching them how to write songs. I'm a voice teacher now. In September, I will be the in-house vocal coach at the Clive Davis Institute at NYU. Back in March I did a paid audition workshop for NYU. Paul came up and played two songs with me so I could perform for the kids and show them how to sell a vocal. The thing today about kids, and mind you all these kids at the Clive Davis Institute are enormously talented, but they're emulating vocal sounds that are all electronically created. So they end up sounding like they're whining. They're all whining and what they don't get is that when you go into a studio, you don't rely on Auto-Tune. You do it yourself. If you can't make the note, don't go in the studio. They all rely on Auto-Tune [because] they want a certain sound. They all try to sound like whomever it is that they're emulating. It's not real. I teach my kids how to be real.

So I have these two girls, one I wrote a song with, called "Won't Take It Anymore." It's by Alexa Natalie. She's only 14 years old, but the song really stands up. And it's a story about bullying. I've been working with a guy named Art Labriola, who has won Grammys. I've been working with him for 25 years, he's amazing. So I do projects with Art. When I auditioned for the Clive Davis Institute, I was very honest and said, "You have guys with Ph.D.s in music. You have people who can pull out a syllabus. I don't even know what this is. I quit school when I was 15. I learned how to read and write just by doing sessions. I faked my way at the beginning. I was self-taught." And when they called me, I have to tell you, I did not think I was remotely close, but they said, "You're exactly what we want and you're exactly what we need because you're the real deal." You know what, that's what it's about. It's not about emulating. It's about being true to who you are and knowing that what you have is something very special.

Will Lee

Grammy-winning musician/renowned studio bassist recalls throwing it down at the Plaza Sound sessions for "Ace Frehley," working with the Spaceman and details his new solo album, his Beatles side project and why it's good to be Will Lee.
By Tim McPhate

Will, before we get into Ace's solo album, you have ties to Gene and Paul's pre-KISS days. Please explain.
Will Lee: Yeah. They had this band Wicked Lester. I was working at Electric Lady in Studio A doing all kinds of projects there, different people's records, and they would be back in Studio B recording Wicked Lester stuff with Ron Johnsen, trying to get a record deal. I came to New York in 1971. I came from Florida where I lived for six years. My dad was a music educator; in fact he was the dean of the Miami University School of Music. So we moved from Texas in '64 and then I hit New York in '71. Electric Lady turned out to be a studio that was really near my first apartment [in New York]. So I'd go over there and see what was going on and so I got to know everybody. Back in the back room, there were these guys trying to get this record deal, this Wicked Lester. This guy named Ron Johnsen believed in them and was trying to make them sound as good as possible. Ron Johnsen was a great engineer and he was giving all of his time to these guys, trying to get them off the ground.

Wicked Lester is interesting. I remember getting a vinyl copy of those Wicked Lester songs when I was younger and being thrown for a total loop. There were a couple of songs that ended up on KISS albums. But ultimately Gene and Paul decided to abort that project and go in another direction. And that direction was KISS.
Well, they were trying anything. [Wicked Lester] was an eclectic mix — it was folksy, poppy, whatever the hell they were doing. They were just trying to get it happening.

Will, if we go back to 1978, what was your status as a musician at that point?
By then, I was really established as a studio player in New York, and I'd done probably 200-300 albums at that point. I was already known around town as a guy who could get it done. I don't know how I had known Eddie Kramer but we had a good relationship somehow. I think he just liked my playing. And I was just one of those kind of established guys who people knew you could count on to do anything.

So Eddie would have brought you into the fold?
Maybe. It might have been him or Ace. And Anton could have even had something to do with it. I'm not sure. I know that Anton was really itching to play and at that point.

You and Anton go way back. How well did you know Anton prior to Ace's album?
Really hardly at all — I kind of knew who he was, but we hadn't logged a lot of hours playing together. He was certainly the right man for the job on that gig.

Indeed. Will, you mentioned Gene and Paul, but do you recall meeting Ace for the first time?
You know, I think I remember meeting him at Record Plant during [some] KISS sessions. I could be wrong about the chronology of that but I do remember seeing him outside [the Record Plant]. The studios in New York — there was always more than one room in a studio — usually you have an "A" room and a "B" room, or three rooms or something. And then you run into all the other people doing sessions in the hall. And I think that's where I first met Ace in the hall at Record Plant — Ace in the hall (laughs).

That could be 1977. KISS recorded their "Love Gun" album there with Eddie.
Yeah, it could have been. I mean we were all a bit in a haze in those days, I don't know if you've ever heard of any of that type of stuff.

(Laughs) Well, judging by the lyrics on Ace's album — "Ozone," "Wiped-Out," etc. — I can sort of fill in the blanks.
(Laughs)

By the time you came onboard for the album several tracks had already been cut at the Colgate Mansion in Connecticut. So I believe the sessions you participated in would have been at Plaza Sound.
That's where we were. Plaza was really cool, it was right above Radio City Music Hall. It was in the same structure as that building. And I remember having this moment; I didn't have this reference point at the time [because] I hadn't really heard the story about the Beatles track "She Loves You." But when they were at Abbey Road recording that in the studio, they were surrounded by women. And you can hear the confidence and the excitement and the testosterone that's going on when you hear "She Loves You," you can just imagine that [and] you can really understand where all that incredible spirit came from. There was energy surrounding the building. On the Ace project, we had the Rockettes looking in the window at our session.

The Rockettes?
Yeah, Radio City Music Hall had these chicks called the Rockettes. They're like a bunch of chorus girls. They had heard what was going on upstairs, "Oh God, one of the guys from KISS is upstairs making an album!" So they'd come upstairs and you'd see them peering through the doors and it was like, "Yeah, this is our 'She Loves You' moment."

(Laughs) Right. I understand that you worked fairly quickly and that you may have completed your bass tracks as fast as two days. Does this sound accurate?
Yeah, I remember cutting live with Anton actually.

Really? By the time you came on board, I think Anton had cut a majority of his drums. So I thought it was an overdub situation.
What I remember is — I'm not even sure if we were tracking while Ace was playing — I'm pretty sure that Anton and I played together along with something that was already recorded. And I just want to say that when I hear those tracks, especially "Wiped-Out," I mean Anton's come a long way, but that was really a very mature, crafted, great part-playing, inspired Anton Fig at his best on that record. And he still sounds the same.

Musically, Anton works in some interesting twist and turns on that track.
Yeah, it's like an M.C. Escher painting, right?

(Laughs) There is a different feel for the verses, the pre-chorus and the chorus.
The time turns around; it goes from like 6/4 to 4/4. I have to say, you know I've logged an awful lot of hours playing with Anton, not only with Eric Johnson when we did a bunch of stuff with him in the last couple of years, but also almost every Monday morning we play together with a guy named Oz Noy.

Two fantastic guitarists.
It's crazy. I've gotten to have Anton play stump the band with his turning the groove upside-down many a times.

Your bass line on "Wiped-Out" is cool. Some of the lines almost have a funk feel, and you're getting creative with some slides.
Yeah, I tried to bring the funk (laughs).

There's also some wah-wah tucked in the mix. It's not Funkadelic but...
Well, you know it's New York, part of the New York groove.

Did you and Ace interact in terms of bass parts or did he pretty much leave you to do your business?
Well, it was almost obvious what to play. I mean Ace could have played bass on the tracks that I played on. He could have played his ass off on that shit. But I just remember that everything was so guitar-based and there really wasn't any need to stray too far from the established figures and grooves that the guitars had laid down. It was really strong, you know, you didn't want to pull away from it too much. As a bass player, there's this fine line between totally supporting the song and bringing something special into the song. You're always riding that line. I always think of Ringo Starr. People say, "Was Ringo a good drummer?" I'm like, "You're kidding me, right?" If you're a songwriter, that's exactly who you want to be playing drums on your song. Because he'll not only support the song and bring the beat and basic groove that you need, but he'll bring something so special to it that he'll shape it in a way that nobody else could touch what he does. For me, as a bass player, I'm always trying to be Ringo. I'm trying to bring something but I'm also trying to not fuck with the song so much that it turns into a different piece of material.

I think your bass parts on the songs definitely fit that profile. "Ozone" has more of a laid back, jam-type feel. The solo is based on triplets so Ace's rhythm is fairly regimented. And you and Anton are interjecting some interesting musical accents underneath.
We were just having some fun with it. And that's the same with the other song, "I'm In Need Of Love." I really felt like bringing the funk to that song. Because it was in a good key for it, it was laid nicely on the bass.

That solo section goes to the key of E, which is every guitar player's favorite key.
(Laughs) The key of life! Yeah, man.

From the first time you ever played with Anton, do you remember hitting a good groove with him?
Oh hell yeah, it was perfect. He has a way of laying it down, he's not only laying it down, he's listening the whole time too. He's not like a machine. He's like a human who's really in control of the groove.

Generally, do you recall what Ace was doing during these sessions? Was he playing along or in the control room?
He was doing a little bit of playing in the studio. But I think I remember there was a big bed of stuff to play to, because they had already down loads of loads of work before I came in.

Judging from the lyrical themes in these songs, it's obvious Ace that liked to have fun and was known to party back in the day. Was it a crazy environment in the studio or was it all about work?
It was kind of boringly work-like, environmentally speaking (laughs). Eddie Kramer wasn't going to settle for a whole lot of bullshit. He didn't want to fuck around; he wanted to get some music on tape. And I also think that a lot of it has to do with things that were established before I came in. I think that the fact that I was in there, there was a little bit of respect coming my way from everybody, knowing that I was really busy and that I wasn't going to fuck around either, and also that I had a pretty good track record. I think it was also probably known by everybody in there that I had been friends with the other KISS guys from way back when. Not that there was a competition, I think there was a little bit of respect coming my way in the kind of way, "This guy's family. Let's let him do his thing and not get in the way." I felt really free to throw down.

Will, would you recall your set up in terms of the bass you used and the amplification?
(Pauses) It was '78 so at that point I could have brought in a P-Bass. I had really gone from growing up playing through amps to gravitating towards going more direct in the studio because that way they could do whatever they wanted with compressors and shit. So I think I probably went direct but if I know Eddie Kramer he ran me through an amp in the big room, even though to the best of my knowledge and memory, I think I played in the control room. But I think [there was] an amp and the drums going on outside in the big room and I was behind the glass sitting there by the board with the guys, the producer, engineer, and probably Ace too.

You've worked with some amazing guitarists in your career. What's your take on Ace's guitar work in listening back to these tracks some 35 years later?
Well, no diss to the other guys in KISS, but Ace was the musician in the band, as far as I'm concerned. He's the real musical craftsman on his instrument kind of guy. What can you say? The guy's a mother-fucker man.

(Laughs) It seems Ace took people by surprise because everyone — from the band to the label — wasn't sure what he was going to bring to the table with his solo album. And Ace ended up turning in this great, guitar-heavy album with lots of attitude and some slamming tracks from the likes of yourself and Anton. And on top of that, he scored the lone hit from the solo albums with "New York Groove."
Yeah, I think he said, "Fuck everything. I'm going to just go for it." And he did.

At the time of their release in September 1978, the four KISS solo albums caused quite the stir. When you were participating, did you get the sense that you were part of such a big project?
Yeah, I remember that I was fully aware of what else was going on. Everything was taking place in New York. Guys were going in working on Gene's record; guys were working on Paul's record, et cetera. The buzz was around. And I don't know how Casablanca felt about it in the end, but they got a lot of platinum out of the concept.

Well, as you're likely aware, they shipped an insane amount of albums, more than 5.3 million. And while the albums sold reasonably well, they didn't sell out of the entire shipment, which ultimately led to a lot of returns. In terms of the project being a success or failure, I guess it depends upon the viewpoint.
Well, I bet a few heads rolled. You've got to hand it to them for taking a chance because it was a good idea. It was also a huge risk because they really didn't know when they were signing the guys up to do this what was really going to come out of them.

Getting into your career, Will, you've played with Anton in the "Late Show with David Letterman" band for years.
31 years so far.

Is that gig as cool as it seems to be?
Yeah, it's a good gig. Are you kidding, any gig's a good gig (laughs).

And you have a new solo album coming out, "Love, Gratitude and Other Distractions." What can you tell us about this project and who is featured on it?
Of course, what else would it be called? (Laughs) There are a lot of great guys on it: Billy Gibbons, Steve Lukather, Pat Metheny and Oz Noy, from the guitar world. Allen Touissant is playing, Paul Shaffer is playing. It's less of an album than it is just a collection of tunes. The album should probably be called "Sybil" or something like that because of the multiple personalities. But I like a lot of different shit so the album could also be called "Shit I Like."

(Laughs) When is the album dropping?
It came out in Japan in July. It's coming out in America [on] August 20, and Europe in September.

And fans can check out the album on your website and the usual retailers?
Yeah, we're taking orders at CD Baby, Amazon and iTunes.

Aside from the laundry list of artists you've worked with, you're in a Beatles tribute band the Fab Faux, which reflects your lifelong love of the Beatles. Can you tell us a little bit about this project?
I sure can. We play every weekend. The Beatles were the thing that really kicked my ass into being a musician — almost anybody would probably say the same thing. It's almost a cliché but it's true. Throughout my whole career, I've been thinking no matter what kind of song or track or flavor of music I'm working on, it's always been in my head like, "Okay, the Beatles are always informing me. What would they do here?" It always gives me really, really good guidance and it's been a thread running through my whole career. And not wanting to ever be the guy who is pigeon-holed into any one thing, I've always really loved when jazz guys thought I was a rock guy and when rock guys thought I was a jazz guy. But as far as the Beatles are concerned, if there's any one thing that I don't mind being associated with, it would probably be a guy who is way into the Beatles. That's something I don't mind being said about myself.

Throughout all this time, even though the Beatles have been sort of underscoring my whole life, I've never once dreamed of having a Beatles band because I thought, "There's enough of those — Who gives a shit?" But then I met our drummer back in 1998, I was on a little trio tour with the late Hiram Bullock through Europe — he was a great guitar player and one of my best friends. He always liked to have singing drummers in the band because he liked to have a trio with three-part harmony going on. And he found this guy named Rich Pagano to play drums on the gig. I had never heard of Rich Pagano, but when I got on the gig I heard something in his voice that was very John Lennon-y and I heard something in his playing that was extremely Ringo-y.

After the tour was over, I came back to New York and it dawned on me, "Wouldn't it be fun to go onstage with this guy and three other guys? Not two other guys — not to be a four-piece Beatles band because you can't bring their records to the stage with four guys. You really need that fifth guy to do the extra harmony part, the extra percussion part or the extra keyboard part." So I said to Rich, "Look, I want to put a Beatles band together. You want to go onstage? Not to have a career out of it, but to just go play some Beatles records onstage, bring it live to the stage." And he was up for it. And the only other guy I really had in mind for it was Jimmy Vivino, who is one of these guys with great ears, knows a lot about music and records, plays his ass off, and sings. He's kind of a historian in the way that Paul Shaffer is kind of an archivist/musician about music — he knows all the details. It took a little convincing but I finally got him to say yes. Then I was stuck because I didn't know who the other two guys were going to be, but I found the other two guys. And it's been the same five guys since 1998. And we're playing constantly.

What's your repertoire like? Do you guys mix and match songs and albums?
We do all kinds of shows. We have a four-piece horn section and a two-piece string section. My favorite kind of shows, that we do, are the unpredictable ones, like a potpourri of different songs from different eras, but way out of order. Just like blast the audience with a song they couldn't have expected was going to be next. And also we're known for doing whole albums, including "The White Album."

"Rubber Soul" is one of my favorite Beatles albums.
Oh yeah, that's a really good one to do. We're going to be doing that a few times in the future. We'll be doing some "Rubber Soul" shows, some "Revolver" shows, some more "White Album" and "Sgt. Pepper" shows, but my favorites are the roller-coaster rides of the unpredictable songs.

I was actually at the Rock and Roll Hall of Fame induction ceremony in March.
That was fun.

That's another great gig there, Will. Jamming on all of those classic songs and playing with an all-star cast of musicians. How long have you been doing the Rock Hall gigs?
Every year since they've started.

The more I've talked with you, the more I'm thinking it's good to be Will Lee.
It's not a bad thing. I work hard and love what I do.

Rob Freeman

Award-winning engineer details everything you want and need to know about Ace Frehley's solo album, including the sessions at Plaza Sound, capturing Frehley's guitar sounds and vocals, recording the hit single "New York Groove" and the nuances behind tracks such as "Fractured Mirror," working alongside the legendary Eddie Kramer, and more.
By Tim McPhate

Rob, what do you recall about getting the invitation to participate as the recording engineer on Ace Frehley's 1978 solo album?
Rob Freeman: I got the call to work on Ace's solo album sometime in June 1978. I'm not sure if it came directly from Eddie Kramer, with whom I had previously worked, or from someone in the KISS organization. Either way, I was thrilled to get that call because I had a sense that recording that album was going to be a big step forward both for me and for Plaza Sound, the studio I had been working so hard to advance. By the summer of '78, I had already recorded some noteworthy albums at Plaza Sound with a variety of artists — among them, The Ramones' first album, "Ramones"; Blondie's first two albums, "Blondie" and "Plastic Letters"; and Richard Hell and the Voidoid's "Blank Generation" — but these were mostly "downtown" New York artists, and, at least back then, my work with them hardly garnered the kind of worldwide recognition that a KISS album would.

Was this your first KISS-related project?
Yes, Ace's album was the first. I guess the other KISS band members and the rest of their organization liked what I did for Ace because after that they called me to work on the "Music from the Elder" and "Lick It Up" albums, as well as to put a number of radio and television commercial spots together for them. I also designed and installed a home recording system in Paul Stanley's uptown NYC condo.

You said you had worked with Eddie Kramer prior to Ace's solo album. What projects did you do with him?
I first worked with Eddie on some tracks by a great Brooklyn band called The Laughing Dogs. I think that was sometime in late '77 or early '78. Unfortunately, those recordings were never released, even though we put a lot of effort into them. After that, Eddie and I worked together on a singer-songwriter's project. Then sometime after doing Ace's solo album, I worked with Eddie again on some early Twisted Sister tracks.

Having worked in the trenches alongside him, what do you think are the strengths that Eddie Kramer brings to a project?
Eddie is a studio renaissance man. He could produce wonderful records, engineer innovative and exciting sounds, and even perform musically. He was comfortable on either side of the control room glass and, while cutting tracks, would often spend time out in the studio with his artists, leaving me to man the recording console on my own. I loved hearing this somewhat edgy veteran of rock 'n' roll sit down at a piano and begin tapping out sensitive, classical melodies. He played just beautifully. Eddie drove his sessions with a hard-nosed sense of purpose, but he was never too self-absorbed to not listen to someone else's suggestions or to handle a note of worthy criticism. When I first started working with him, I was well aware of his legendary career (The Beatles, Led Zeppelin, Jimi Hendrix... I mean, come on!!). So I considered myself very fortunate to be sitting next to someone with his level of experience and success. I kept my eyes and ears open and learned a lot from him.

Socializing with Eddie outside the studio I discovered him to be a very gracious host. He had a terrific sense of humor and could be hysterically funny. So between Eddie's joking around and Ace's twisted, relentless humor, there were always sources of comic relief if things ever started to get tense in the studio.

The album was recorded at the Colgate Mansion in Connecticut and Plaza Sound in New York. Were you present for all of the recording sessions?
The basic tracks for the bulk of Ace's album (Anton Fig's drums and Ace's first round of guitars) were recorded at the mansion in Sharon, Connecticut. Unfortunately, I wasn't there for that part of the project. Eddie recorded those tracks on his own using a remote truck. I wish I had been there though, because it sounded like it was an awesome experience and loads of fun. They placed Anton's drum kit on the top landing of a sweeping, wooden staircase and recorded its ambiance from several vantage points. There were plenty of ballroom-sized rooms in the mansion with wonderful-sounding wooden floors and walls in which to record Ace's guitar amps and acoustic guitars. And they all stayed right in the house so they must've had a blast, sonically and otherwise.

Although I wasn't at the mansion, I got to experience the majesty of those drum recordings every time I brought up the console faders. They were amazing and, needless to say, very well recorded by Eddie. After cutting basic tracks at the mansion, Eddie and Ace moved the project to Plaza Sound Studios in New York City. They didn't travel light as they brought with them some thirty reels of 2" master tapes weighting almost 400 pounds. So to answer the second part of your question, yes, I was present at all of the Plaza Sound recording sessions, which consisted of two to three weeks of overdubbing and about ten or so days of mixing.

What was Plaza Sound like, and why do you suppose Eddie chose it for overdubbing and mixing Ace's album?

To give you a sense of what Plaza Sound was like, I'll start off with some of Plaza's amazing history. The studio room, with its incredible dimensions — 65' wide by 100' long with 30' ceilings — was constructed in the 1930's by NBC at tremendous cost (I've heard as much as $2.5 million in equivalent dollars today). It was originally designed as an orchestral space for the Toscanini Orchestra to do live radio broadcasts. A legacy from those days was a wealth of classic orchestral instruments such as tympanis, tubular chimes, glockenspiel, harpsichord, and, most notably, an exquisite 9-foot Steinway concert grand piano. Amazingly, there was a fully functional Wurlitzer three-manual pipe organ installed right in the studio that had been used as a practice organ for the theater below. In the '50s and '60s, Plaza Sound was the busy hub for Riverside Records and many of the major jazz artists of the day; Wes Montgomery, Milt Jackson, Bill Evans, Cannonball Adderley, Art Blakey, Pharoah Sanders, and many more recorded there.

To get to Plaza Sound, you entered the Radio City Music Hall building through the 51st Street stage door entrance. Plaza Sound occupied a large portion of the seventh floor of the building. The rest of it was used for rehearsal spaces and storage rooms. In order to acoustically isolate it from the Music Hall below, the entire seventh floor was "floating," suspended on felt-covered steel springs and cork. Even the elevator shafts were isolated and only went up to the sixth floor. That meant there was always that last full flight of stairs to climb while carrying heavy amps and other things. Once you made it up the stairs, you still had a long walk ahead through a labyrinth of grey painted hallways before arriving at Plaza Sound's door, but it was always worth the trek!

One side note: Just down the hall from Plaza Sound were two enormous rehearsal rooms used by Radio City's famous Rockette dancers. Sometimes when they rehearsed, you could actually feel a gentle swaying sensation in the studio as the steel springs holding up the seventh floor of the building compressed and expanded with the dancers' movements. Whenever they took a break, a bevy of sweaty dancers headed straight for the water cooler stationed right outside Plaza's control room door. This would invariably lead to our taking a break so that Ace and others could spend a little time schmoozing with the ladies.

Plaza Sound's control room was fairly long and narrow — maybe 40' by 20' — but wide enough to set the main monitor speakers back from the console. The console, with a sofa right in front of it, occupied the bulk of the main area while the outboard rack, tape machines, and a large storage closet took up the space at the back end of the room. Compared with many studios of the day, Plaza had a relatively small control room, but with its effective acoustic treatment, you could definitely get the job done in there.

Why did Eddie choose Plaza? As I mentioned, Eddie had recorded other projects at Plaza Sound prior to doing Ace's album there so he was familiar with Plaza's wondrous eccentricities and spectacular acoustics. He knew that overdubs recorded in Plaza's room would nicely complement the basic tracks recorded at the mansion. Also, I'm sure all of Plaza's prized, classic microphones and other equipment added to the allure Eddie felt when he decided to book the studio. But it might only have been after spending time with Ace's tracks at Plaza Sound and hearing how great rough mixes were sounding outside the studio that Eddie decided to stay and mix the album there.

What console, tape machines, microphones, and other gear were used for the sessions at Plaza Sound?

By the time Eddie Kramer walked into Plaza Sound in late '77-early '78, the studio proudly sported a top-of-the-line Studer A-800 2" 24-track machine. That was the Rolls-Royce of multi-track tape machines, with a price tag to match. We had Studer and MCI ½" 2-track mixdown machines and a fabulous API 32-input recording console, one of the first APIs installed in NYC. Although API consoles like the one at Plaza Sound are no longer made, the heart of the board, its distinctive-sounding inboard modules — equalizers, compressors and gates — are still in high demand today and can be purchased as outboard "lunchboxes."

The control room had a pair of enormous URIE 813 Time-Aligned™ studio monitors sitting on custom-designed pedestals on either side of the studio-viewing window. I really wasn't a fan of large studio monitors; though they may have offered superior fidelity, they just weren't representative of what most people listened to in their home or in their car. Besides, extended listening with large speakers could cause ear fatigue. Still, it was always a kick to crank up the 813s and blast ourselves out every now and then. For more down to earth referencing of what we were doing, I preferred the popular Yamaha NS-10s (with the legendary Kimwipe over the tweeter, of course!) and the even smaller Auratones that sat atop the console.

Plaza Sound's outboard rack featured a museum's-worth of classic vacuum tube devices such as Pultec equalizers, Pultec filters, and Teletronix LA-2A compressors. There was also a nice assortment of solid-state gear including Eventide DDL (Digital Delay Line), Eventide harmonizer, Eventide flanger, URIE LA-3A and 1176 compressors, DBX compressors and noise gates, and more.

A lot of the top studios had this sort of high-quality gear in their control rooms. But one of Plaza's strongest and most unique assets remained hidden from sight... until you unlocked the doors of the studio microphone closet. Plaza possessed a treasure trove of vintage mics, many dating back to the '30s and '40s. There were warm-sounding vacuum tube condenser mics such as Neumann U47s (with original tubes), Neumann U67s, and Neumann KM-56s, and a pair of AKG C-12s, that rare and most precious breed of orchestral mic. There were plenty of Neumann U87s, the transistor condenser workhorses of the day; AKG 414s, another popular go-to mic; as well as a variety of dynamic mics such as Sennheiser 421s, AKG D-12s, and some Shure mics. There were also delicate vintage ribbon mics such as RCA 77s and RCA 44s. I spent many thoughtful moments staring into the abyss of the open mic closet deciding whether to reach for tried-and-true standards or to experiment with some new and exotic mic combination. There were always plenty of inviting options.

Befitting the studio's expansive size and ceiling height, Plaza Sound had enormous, old-style roll-around microphones boom stands as well as plenty of "gobos" ("go betweens" that were sound-deadening baffles) and sizable moveable walls. There was a huge movable vocal booth that could be placed anywhere in the room and a good-sized vocal/drum booth with a large window at the far end of the studio.

Plaza concealed even more hidden treasures. Down the hall from the studio, housed in a small storage room, Plaza had two vintage EMT reverb plates with vacuum tube electronics that were kept impeccably tuned. They were a joy to splash onto almost any kind of tracks. Their reverb decay times could be modified remotely in the control room using small antique-looking wheels. Further down the hall was a magnificent live echo chamber consisting of a large, highly reverberant chamber, an Altec Big Red speaker cabinet (to send sounds out into the chamber) sitting in one corner, and a microphone (to pick up the sound of the room's reverberations and return it to the control room) in another corner. These days, "reverb" is a plug-in found on a laptop. By any standards, Plaza's glorious analog reverbs were truly jewels.

Generally, it seems that basic tracks were cut at Colgate Mansion and guitar overdubs and vocals were recorded at Plaza Sound. Does this sound accurate?
Well, it's accurate with the exception of "New York Groove" which was re-cut from scratch, and then re-cut again, at Plaza Sound, and "Rip It Out" with its amazing double-tracked drum solo. There might have been one more basic track cut at Plaza, possibly "What's On Your Mind," but I'm not positive about that.

Eddie and Ace arrived at Plaza Sound with a version of "New York Groove" recorded at the mansion. But there was something about the overall feel of it that wasn't sitting quite right with them. Ultimately a decision was made to re-cut the song from the ground up, starting with a new basic track consisting of drums and rhythm guitar. So one day we cleared the studio, set up Anton's drum kit, and recorded a second version of "New York Groove" utilizing Plaza's nice open room for drum ambiance while Ace played along in the control room. We may have also cut drum tracks for "Rip It Out" on that same day. But after careful analysis of Russ Ballard's original songwriting demo (a cassette tape they kept playing over and over for comparison to what we were doing), it was decided to re-record "New York Groove" yet again with further subtle changes to the tempo and/or drum feel. So on another day we set up the drums again and recorded a third basic track for "New York Groove." The third one was the charm and became the final version of the song.

At the time I thought all this re-recording of "New York Groove" a bit nitpicky. I suggested a much easier approach to changing the tempo of the song utilizing the Studer 2" machine's VSO (variable speed oscillator). Varying tape speed was common practice back then even though it altered the sonic and pitch characteristics of already recorded tracks to one degree or another depending how much speed variation was applied. I think Ace and Anton were game for that approach as well. But Eddie had other thoughts on the matter. He insisted that the tempo and recorded sounds remain "pure," so we ended up re-recording the entire track... twice. They had the time, the budget, and the willingness to do it, so why not? Besides, in the end, whatever they did, and for whatever reasons, was certainly justified, as "New York Groove" became a big hit for Ace. It sounds as fresh and exciting today as it did when we recorded it in 1978.

Eddie has described a special technique for recording Ace's vocals that involved a bottle of beer and Ace lying on his back while singing. What do you remember about recording Ace's vocals and would you say Ace had a case of "vocal fright"?
I suppose it's true that Ace wasn't too keen on recording vocals, at least not at first. I remember being somewhat baffled (so to speak) by his vocal reluctance, blindly assuming that his vast experience recording and touring the world with KISS should have given him every confidence. I wasn't aware that Ace had sung only two lead vocals on KISS records prior to doing his solo album. Perhaps he viewed singing more as a chore than a chance at self-expression, just a part of the process he'd have to get through in order to realize his vision of the album. Ace knew he could make his guitars "sing," but now he also had to do it with his voice, and he had to carry an entire solo album in doing so. I suppose that kind of pressure could get to anyone, so it's not surprising that Ace may have developed a touch of "vocal fright," as you call it.

So, for whatever reasons, Ace wanted to sing while lying down on the studio floor. I figured, okay, he's the artist and that's how he wants to do it. I was all for doing whatever it took to get those vocals on tape. We dragged a large piece of carpet into the middle of the studio, dimmed the lights, and Ace began singing vocals lying on his back on the studio floor. I did what I could to help him get situated there and remember taking a bit of time to tweak his headphone monitoring balance so he would feel as comfortable as possible singing with "cans" on. The lying-on-the-floor method probably only lasted a couple of songs. Once Ace felt assured that his vocals were in good hands with Eddie and I caring for them, he stood up and sang confidently on mic.

From that point on, Ace's confidence grew by leaps and bounds. He began to approach his vocals in a positive way, always wanting to better himself. By the end of the project, Ace became as productive and enthusiastic about his vocals as he was about his guitar tracks. Although he may not have admitted it at the time, I suspect Ace really enjoyed the experience of singing out in the open space of Plaza's studio room. That room had character... it had history.

Now, as to Eddie's account of the lying-on-the-floor technique, I recall a couple of things slightly differently (not that it makes any real difference at this point in time). Eddie has stated that Ace held a bottle of beer in one hand, and that most surely did happen at some point. But what you may not have heard about is that Ace had arranged for a small refrigerator to be brought into the studio that he kept well stocked with bottles of champagne in addition to beer and other refreshments. So it's just as likely that Ace was holding a bottle of champagne as a bottle of beer when he sang. Eddie's and my recollections also differ regarding what Ace might have held in his other hand. Eddie has said that Ace held a Shure SM-57 (dynamic) mic in his hand while singing lying down. I'm sure we tried recording that way at least once or twice. But Ace relied on seeing his lyrics in front of him as he sang (not an unusual method) so he would have needed at least one free hand to hold a lyric sheet. I recall hanging a bulky, heavy Neumann U47 microphone right over Ace's face enabling him to lie down and sing without holding a mic. No matter whose details are correct, Ace's methods for recording vocals in the studio were truly unique and, for the most part, quite memorable.

Vocals were certainly not Ace's strong suit, though he does have a unique voice. Do you remember the general process in organizing his final vocal tracks? Were there multiple takes recorded, and were they compiled together?
Yeah, a unique voice, to be sure, but one that honestly expressed what Ace was about at the time. You hear pure Ace in those vocals — his earnest singing of his lyrics. You can even hear his great sense of humor in places.

Ace's lead vocal tracks were recorded pretty much the same way his guitar solos were. Ace would sing through a song or part of a song, laying down as many as eight or ten tracks in some cases. If needed, we might "punch in," re-recording a word or a phrase on a particular track, or we might decide to wait to look for "fixes" on alternate take tracks. When Ace was done singing, Eddie and I would painstakingly sift through all the tracks and create one solid "comp" (compiled) track while Ace took off for parts unknown. Sometimes we'd finish a comp session when, after playing the result for him, Ace would be duly inspired to go out on mic and sing some more in an effort to top his previous performances. Then we'd do some more comping, adding in whatever new and improved vocal sections Ace might have given us. We hopped from song to song, not always bothering to complete one before working on another. Working that way, Ace's vocals for any particular song could have been recorded over a span of several days.

Singing sections of a song one at a time, punching in words or phrases, and comping tracks were hardly unusual techniques; they were done all the time by all kinds of artists. Using any or all of those tricks didn't necessarily mean you couldn't sing well or that you couldn't make it all the way through a song. They were simply more weapons in the studio arsenal intended to help artists get their best performances down on tape (as it was at the time). Truthfully, and ironically, of the many, many singers I've worked with over the years, only one comes to mind as being truly capable of laying down a great lead vocal track in one uninterrupted pass of a song, and that was Ace's own band mate, Paul Stanley.

Anton Fig's drum work has been praised not only by KISS fans, but by Ace and Eddie as well. Though the album is guitar-heavy, Anton's drums are surely a key component. What do you think about Anton's drum work on the album? And do you recall the microphone set up to capture his drums?
Anton totally rocked Ace's album! But remember, I wasn't at the mansion when they recorded most of the drum tracks, so I couldn't tell you which mics were used. I did have the pleasure of working with Anton on a number of other projects, including Link Wray's awesome "Bullshot" album and some recordings with Robert Gordon, so I can tell you first hand that he was a recording engineer's dream. He was a studio-savvy drummer who delivered crisp, consistent drum hits with just the right ratio of cymbals to skins, had great feel and erupted with explosive, exciting fills.

Eddie had his favorite go-to mics for recording drums, and I had mine. Some of the microphone techniques used for recording tracks, including guitar tracks throughout Ace's album, were an amalgam of both of our favorites. As a result, it's really not possible for me to recount exactly which mics were placed on Anton's kit or anywhere else for that matter. Maybe Eddie knows, but I surely don't. For "New York Groove" and "Rip It Out," Anton's kit was set up in the middle of the open studio with no baffles or walls around it. I can only guess that there might have been an AKG D-12 in or near the bass drum, a Neumann KM-56 pencil mic on the top snare head, a Sennheiser 421 on the high hat, Neumann U87s on each tom, and a couple of AKG C-12s overhead, hung high above the kit. But don't quote me on that!

Ace played bass on a majority of the album's tracks. Would he have cut his bass tracks live with Anton or did he overdub the bass later?

Ace played mostly rhythm guitar parts while cutting basic tracks with Anton at the mansion. One of Ace's first tasks when he got to Plaza Sound was to lay down a round of bass tracks for all of the songs on the album. I remember being really impressed with Ace's bass playing. He nailed his bass parts with a strong, aggressive attack, playing in perfect sync to his rhythm guitar tracks. I was about to get even more impressed once Ace started burning guitar solos!

Will Lee was brought in to play bass on "Ozone," "Wiped-Out" and "Fractured Mirror." Do you remember Will coming in to play at Plaza Sound?
Do I remember Will coming in to Plaza Sound? Like it was yesterday! Will was such a trip — funny and outrageous — and the sessions I did with him (for Ace and other artists) were always memorable. I think he might have come in twice for Ace's album, possibly on consecutive days. As I said, Ace tried bass parts for each song on the album before he and Eddie decided which songs could benefit most from the Lee touch. Will was (and still is) the consummate professional. Despite having never heard Ace's songs prior to coming to the studio, he seemed to instinctively know every progression and nuance of the arrangements, even on his first run-through.

At one point Will asked if I wanted to hear his bass talk. I said, "Sure," and he proceeded to scrape the pick along the high end of the fret board in a way that somehow made the instrument clearly say, "Hel-lo!" He repeated this a couple of times and then made the bass deliver another two-syllable utterance that I won't repeat here. It was incredible! One time I saw Will casually reach over and partake of some "refreshment"... while the red (recording) light was on and he was in the middle of laying down a bass track. When he saw me observing him, he just smiled and continued his flawless playing without skipping so much as a beat. He was truly one with his instrument. What a guy!

Do you remember some of the specific guitars and amps Ace utilized on the album?
When it came to guitars and amps, Ace was king. He had arranged for his substantial collection of guitars and amps to be brought in for the project and had them all lined up along the studio wall. Ace would choose a guitar he thought best suited for the part about to be recorded. Then he'd walk the line, plugging from amp to amp looking for a particular sound. It never took him very long to find just the right combination. Once the right amp was chosen and set, we'd run a long guitar line so Ace could play the instrument in the control room while his amp spewed out in the studio where it would be mic'd and recorded.

With Ace knowing exactly what guitar sounds he wanted and how to get them, I didn't get as involved in setting instruments or amps as I normally might have. I was more concerned with the acoustic placement of the amps and with the choosing and placement of microphones. I remember being pleasantly surprised by Eddie's level of involvement in guitar and amp choices for Ace to use. I don't know why I was surprised, you know... the "Jimmys" (Hendrix and Page). On occasion, Ace would go for a particular combination and Eddie would suggest another one. But they always came to an easy agreement.

Among all the beautiful instruments, electric and acoustic, that Ace presented, I certainly remember his amazing double neck guitar. I don't think I had been up close and personal with one of those before working on Ace's album. It was the coolest thing, a six-string electric and a twelve-string electric together in the same body. For "Fractured Mirror," Ace re-tuned the 12-string neck so it would ring sympathetically while he played only on the 6-string neck, much like a sitar with its underlying sympathetic strings. The result was brilliant, a sound I had never heard before. When it came to guitars and amps, Ace sure knew his stuff.

Do you recall what recording techniques you used when recording Ace's guitar tracks?
Well, because of the vastness of Plaza's room and the uniqueness of its acoustic design, even "usual" recording techniques would often yield distinctive results. It was a pleasure to experiment there, and both Eddie and I played around with mic and amp placements quite a bit. It was common to place at least two mics on an amp setup, one fairly close to the amp, maybe one to two feet away, and another farther back, maybe eight to ten feet away, depending on the volume of the amp.

The type of sound that was desired for a particular part of a song would determine just how an amp would be set up acoustically and recorded. For example, rhythm parts tended to be more immediate, more in-your-face. So they would usually be recorded with the amp baffled around with gobos or the large moveable walls in order to contain the sound and minimize room ambiance leaking into the mics. On the other hand, guitar lines and solos might have been recorded with the amp left out in the open room, capturing its ambiance at a distance, giving it a more open, live concert sound.

On occasion, for something different, we'd haul Ace's amps down the hall into one of the Rockettes' rehearsal rooms. These were large, empty rooms with some type of composite flooring and room-length mirrors on the walls. They were not acoustically deadened in any way so when the dancers rehearsed with their tap shoes on in there, the sound was thunderous, almost deafening. Sonically, the rehearsal rooms were very bright and reverberant so any guitar amp recorded in there would tend to take on those characteristics as well. Vintage tube mics worked great in that environment as they colored the sound with their own warmth.

Ace is credited with playing a guitar synthesizer on the album. I believe he has mentioned it was an ARP Avatar that he used. What do you remember about this instrument and what track(s) was it featured on?
Ace brought an amazing array of pedals and effects boxes to the sessions at Plaza Sound. He had all the toys that produced effects most guitarists of the day might use (delay, fuzz, distortion, chorus, phasing, flanging, wah-wah, etc.). He'd bring them all into the control room and hook up whichever he needed when we were recording guitar lines, solos, or certain rhythm parts.

I should mention that many, though not all, of the guitar effects that can be heard throughout the album — long, swooping delays, flanging, and the like — were produced with pedals and committed to tape right along with Ace's performances. This was advantageous for a couple of reasons: Ace could play his parts using the feel and timing of "live" effects, and Eddie and I saved a lot of time and effort by not having to recreate those kinds of effects in the final mix.

At one point Ace brought out this large box and plunked it down on the producer's desk next to the console. I had never seen anything like it before, at least not for use with a guitar. It was the ARP Avatar and it resembled an oversized drum machine or a synthesizer module (without a keyboard) more than a guitar effects box. They were relatively rare and quite expensive, with a price tag around $3,000. Ace was one of the first musicians in the New York area to have one.

Basically, the Avatar took the guitar output signal and modified it in many of the same ways a regular synthesizer might; it had banks of oscillators, LFOs (low frequency oscillators), gates, triggers, filters, ADSR (attack, decay, sustain, release) envelope controllers, and more. The difference between the Avatar and other synths was that it was specifically designed to be responsive to the unique expressiveness of a guitar as a controller. It could track string bends, vibrato, harmonics, etc., making it capable of producing unique guitar-oriented sounds and effects. The Avatar added some really interesting colors to many of Ace's parts.

Considering the Avatar's "cool" factor, I thought Ace used it very tastefully throughout the album, maximizing its effectiveness when it was used. It was subtly peppered throughout tracks like "Ozone" but can be notably distinguished in a few key places on some of the other tracks. One example can be found behind the solo on "Snow Blind" where the Avatar sounds very much like a high organ part and then plays the rising line under the end of the solo starting at around 2:21. It can also be heard drifting in and out throughout "Fractured Mirror" before appearing very distinctly as the high arpeggio line that comes in at 2:34.

Ace has described some songs as having four guitar tracks, with all the parts blended together. Would you say there was a lot of thought put into layering guitar tracks?
If Ace said four guitar "tracks" he probably meant four guitar "parts," because there were way more than four tracks used for guitars on many of the songs. You should have seen the track layout sheets-some would have made a great addition to the album liner notes for those interested in that kind of thing. There were the usual eight or nine drum tracks (close mic'd tracks for each drum plus stereo room ambiance tracks), a few tracks for lead vocal, harmonies, and background vocals, and the remaining twelve or more tracks could have been filled up with all manner of guitar tracks. There were track sheet notations like "rhy git" (rhythm guitar), "git dbl" (double), "git lines," "git harm" (harmony), "intro git," "end git," "solo comp," "solo harm," "drone git," "bell git," "ac git" (acoustic guitar), "ARP lines" (ARP Avatar guitar synthesizer), "ARP chords," "git FX (effects), etc. Some of those sheets, like the one for "Fractured Mirror," read like a buried treasure map that only the select few — Eddie, Ace, and I — could possibly decipher.

I'm sure Ace put a lot of forethought into designing the layering of all those guitar parts. But each time he recorded a new track, the parts just flowed out through his fingers so naturally and effortlessly that it seemed like they were made up on the spot.

"Speedin' Back To My Baby" is a fun tune. The solo is actually backwards, a tip of the hat to Hendrix, if you will. Today, one punch in Pro Tools will flip a guitar solo. Who had the idea to flip this guitar solo and can you explain how that was accomplished with 1978 technology?
I couldn't tell you for sure whose idea that was... Ace's? Eddie's? Mine? It probably wasn't mine because Ace's solos were hallowed ground and that was such a drastic alteration of one of his performance. But you never know. In any case, it was a great idea and made for a fantastic backwards solo ala Hendrix's "Castles Made of Sand" or The Beatles' "I'm Only Sleeping," which, with all due respect, predates that.

There were two main ways of accomplishing backwards tracks back then. One was to take the multi-track master tape and flip it over on the 2" machine. This method was done often enough, but had a couple of potential pitfalls. For one thing, you really had to be careful about which tracks you arming for record and punching in on. Think about it: when you flip over a 24-track tape, what was on track twenty-four is now on track one, what was on track seven is now on track eighteen, and so on. So if you're not super careful, you could easily erase something you really intended to keep. Also, while you're recording that way, you're listening to all the other tracks playing backwards so it's not always easy to find the tempo of a song or where you are in the arrangement or even where the punch in and punch out points are supposed to be. It can be quite a challenge.

For "Speedin' Back," I employed a much easier and more controlled method. Ace overdubbed his solo normally, doing any number of takes until he was satisfied with what he played. After Eddie and I comped a track, I copied the solo onto a piece of ½" tape on another machine and marked the head and tail of the solo with paper leader tape. Then I flipped over the ½" tape and "flew" the solo back onto the multi-track, recording it forwards on the 24-track tape as it played backwards on the ½" machine. You may ask, "how can this be accomplished with any accuracy?" Well, with both tape machines running at 30ips (inches per second), it was simple enough to physically measure and mark a point on the ½" tape that was thirty inches (one second) from the beginning of the piece (which was actually the end of what Ace played forwards). Then all that remained to turn a bit of technical studio wizardry into a magical musical moment was to hit record on the 24-track and play back on the 2-track at precisely the right moment... and voila!

I read somewhere years later that Ace said I flew that backwards solo in on the very first attempt. It's certainly possible that it may have happened that way, but what's more likely is that it took a couple of warm up shots and compensating adjustments to drop the solo in at just the right spot to make it work musically. Still, Ace's words were most kind and I thank him for his vote of confidence.

The song also features some Ferrari motor sounds, which I have read were actual tapes. Is this true?

Oh, boy, the Ferrari tape! For weeks I had been hearing about some car recordings that Eddie had ordered from somewhere that would be delivered at some point. I don't know if they were recordings commissioned specifically for Ace's project or just pulled from a sound effects library. When I heard that they wanted to "fly" car effects in to "Speedin' Back to My Baby," I offered to find some in Plaza's extensive sound effects library. But Ace and Eddie wanted no part of that. They said the sound had to be that of a specific year Ferrari with a specific type of engine, a sound so specific, I imagined, that only the most discerning Ferrari connoisseurs could possibly recognize it. I remember how excited Eddie and Ace were when those tapes finally arrived and I "flew" the car effects in to the multi-track master tape at the end of the song. Then we all drove off into the sunset and broke for dinner.

"What's on Your Mind?" is a fan favorite on Ace's album. This song features an acoustic tucked neatly behind Ace's electric guitar. Do you remember what microphone was employed to capture Ace's acoustic?

It's always a joy to hear a musician who is known primarily as a hard-rockin' electric guitarist pick up an acoustic guitar and start playing it delicately and beautifully. So it was with Ace who had obvious mastery over all his instruments, electric guitars, acoustic guitars, and basses alike.

As to which particular mics may have been used to record Ace's acoustic guitar on that song, I can only tell you there was a plethora of vintage tube mics at Plaza Sound; there were also two extreme tube mic enthusiasts (Eddie and I) there to appreciate and use them. Eddie's mic preferences for acoustic guitar were probably different than my own "usual" choices. As a result, I have only vague recollections about which mics were used for which instruments throughout the project. I wish I could recall those particulars better for you. But I do know we had a choice of anything from a warm Neumann U47 to a wonderful AKG C-12 to a crisp Neumann KM-56 to place on Ace's acoustic guitar. It could have been any of those or even some combination that was used.

At first listen, the key single-note guitar part on "New York Groove" sounds like a wah-wah pedal, but Ace has revealed it was actually a talk box. What do you remember about capturing this signature sound on this song?
It was a talk box, another of Ace's toys. A talk box is an electronic box that splits the guitar output signal and sends it out through a long plastic tube that you stick in your mouth. Then you modulate the sound with mouth movements and it all gets sent out to an amp or through a DI (direct input) to the console. As far as I'm concerned, that talk box part made "New York Groove."

Interestingly, the recorded version does not contain a guitar solo, though when performed live, Ace did add a solo section. Do you remember if a guitar solo was discussed for "New York Groove"?
I never heard any discussions about putting a guitar solo on "New York Groove." I remember just expecting there would be one, but it never materialized. The guitar parts, sans solo, consisted of the talk box, the funky R&B style rhythm, the downward "shoots" and plucky lines between vocals (recorded, I believe, at the same time on one track), and the chorus power notes. That was pretty much it. In putting the production together, Ace and Eddie stuck faithfully to the arrangement on Russ Ballard's original demo, which sounded very much like the demo of a hit song, which it turned out to be, but which didn't include a solo.

"New York Groove" proved to be the lone big hit from the four KISS solo albums. The song climbed to No. 13 on the Billboard Hot 100. Do you recall listening back to the final version and thinking there was something special there?
Something special? You bet! It was simple... solid... catchy... well produced... it had everything it takes to be a hit. But hits aren't just made in the studio. They're made after the fact through promotions, airplay, fan response, and sales. Listening in the studio, it was too early to think about any of that. But it was an exciting track, and it really came to life once Ace put his vocals on it. Then it reached a whole other level

with the addition of those great background vocals. It was one of those rare tracks that sounded "finished" way before the final mix. I never tired of listening to it outside the studio, too, in my car — ah, cassettes, how quaint! — or on the train on my way into the city. That was always a good sign.

One fun recollection I have is going into the studio to help Ace sing those "oo-oo" vocals right before each chorus. They needed to be sung in a semi-falsetto and I guess Ace was a bit weak in that range of his voice. So I offered to go out and sing the part together with him. The height difference between us was so great that I had to stand on a box so I could reach the mic at the same level as Ace. Singing with Ace was a fond highlight of the project for me.

In guitar circles, Ace influenced many guitar players to pick up an instrument. Yet when, say Rolling Stone, runs a best-of guitar player list, Ace doesn't seem to make the grade alongside peers such as Angus Young and Joe Perry. What is your take on Ace Frehley's guitar style and his musical sensibilities?
Ace's level of talent blew me away. I don't know about Rolling Stone's list, but on my list, he'd be right up there with the great guitarists of rock 'n' roll. He was musically focused and technically capable throughout the entire project. He never wavered or had moments when he wasn't sure what to play or what to do. He'd just pick up one of those amazing instruments of his, plug into an amp, and off he went.

I thought Ace's rhythm playing was phenomenal. He had a great feel and he knew lots of studio tricks like double-tracking parts or breaking parts up onto different tracks with different sounds. But when it came to laying down solos, Ace was on fire. I'd watch him wailing a solo and sometimes his gaze would sort of drift off, as if he was playing by instinct with no conscious thought and he'd finish the pass with a shrug of his shoulders and an inquisitive look as if to say, "I wasn't quite here for that one... how was it?" I don't think there was ever really a "bad" solo on any of the tracks he recorded — everyone was amazing. Sure, there might have been a clam (bum note) here or there, but those were rare and could easily be fixed.

Here's how it went: Ace would play around until we got a great guitar sound for the solo. Then he'd start laying down a string of solos, each one recorded on a separate track of the multi-track tape. After he'd given his all, Ace would disappear for a while — maybe he'd walk outside or drift down into Radio City Music Hall to watch the show — while Eddie and I would go to work on the solo. The ultimate solo was somewhere on those tracks; we just had to find it by putting together all the right pieces. We'd begin the process by making a detailed "map" of each track's strengths and weaknesses throughout the solo. Like I said, there were plenty of great moments on each track to choose from, but decisions had to be made that would result in one incredible, coherent solo. We'd chip away at it, building phrase by phrase, measure by measure, even note by note sometimes until we had a totally smoking solo.

This process of comping tracks, using bits and pieces from various tracks and combining them onto one track, was common practice back then and is still used today for creating "best of" guitar, vocal, or other tracks. It was tedious work but it often resulted in amazing moments of studio magic. The greatest reward was seeing Ace's face light up when he listened to the fruits of our labors.

All signs point to Ace being extremely motivated during the making of his solo album. How would you describe his frame of mind during the sessions?
As I mentioned, Ace remained focused and on point throughout the project. He had a great mindset and was very personable and hysterically funny. His only shortcoming, if you consider it that, was that he often arrived to the Plaza Sound sessions quite late after the commute from his home in Connecticut to New York City. The distance... the traffic... it was understandable to a degree, but it did happen a lot. On the positive side, it gave Eddie and me a chance to listen to the previous day's work and to strategize a game plan and begin setting up for the day's session. When Ace finally arrived, usually with his pal Bobby McAdams in tow, it was with such a burst of laughter, good energy, and readiness to plug in and work that his tardiness was immediately forgotten.

Ace had a singular vision for his album and seemed hell-bent on achieving it. It took a lot of work to make that album, but as I saw it, Ace remained positive and fully motivated at all times. He exhibited necessary amounts of patience — things don't always zoom along in the studio and occasionally get bogged down — but he also knew how to keep the sessions moving forward at a good pace.

He and Eddie seemed to really hit it off as well. They joked around quite a bit, and we all laughed a lot. They had a type of shorthand between them that enabled quick, efficient communications sometimes with very few words. By the end of the project, I was right there with them, and no one was talking to anyone else... just kidding.

Sonically, Ace's album is arguably the most powerful of the four solo albums. In scanning the album with fresh ears, what is your opinion of it and is there anything you would change?
In preparing for this interview, I listened to the Ace Frehley album a lot. Simply put, I liked it back when I made it, and I still like it today. The songs are fun to listen to, and the album as a whole has great energy and sounds really good. Do I hear things I'd change? Sure. I could listen to almost any of the records I've made over the years and, now with fresh ears, invariably find things that might have been done a bit differently. But that's just me. I liken it to dressing up for a special occasion and

having your picture taken. Years later, you might look at that photograph and notice a button wasn't buttoned or your hair wasn't quite right. When others look at the same photo, most don't see those kinds of things as problems, if they notice them at all; only you do. It's kind of like that with records. You dress them up and take the "snapshot." People get familiar with them and, hopefully, like them the way they are; they're not looking for flaws.

What was it like mixing the album with Eddie?
Mixing Ace's album with Eddie was a great experience. I remember feeling elated at that point in the project, partly because we were about to finish a KISS album but also because I would be mixing alongside Eddie Kramer, who had recorded and mixed many great albums I'd revered over the years.

In 1978 recording console automation systems were still in their infancy. They were expensive and, in my opinion, rather cumbersome to operate. Some studios had installed automation systems by then, but the API console at Plaza Sound was not equipped with any automation. That meant final mixing of Ace's album had to be done the old-fashioned way, by hand, not computer. Maybe it's because we had no automation at Plaza Sound, but at the time, I preferred mixing by hand anyway. It offered one final opportunity to perform the record, playing the console and peripheral equipment almost like you would an instrument. Each pass of the song could be significantly different from the last as you took spontaneous chances, discovering new ways to add fresh excitement to a record you'd been living with so closely for weeks on end. Of course, you can always create excitement with automation, too, but mixing by hand yielded so many unexpected moments-explosions of too much reverb, overzealous panning, things popping out where not expected — all pleasant surprises that helped keep the creative juices flowing.

We started each mix by setting instrument and vocal balances, stereo placements, reverbs, delays, and other effects for the whole song before recording anything on the ½" mixdown machine. Once set, we may have tried to nail a complete mix from top to bottom in a single pass, but more often than not, mixing for each song was accomplished in sections. We'd mix just the intro, working on it over and over until what we committed to ½" tape sounded just right. Then we'd move on to the first verse, the first chorus, the solo, and so on, mixing and listening over and over until each section was just how we wanted it. We'd often go back and remix sections out of sequence as needed. And of course, special attention was always given to endings, especially if they incorporated a delicate, manually executed fadeout. We'd mix the endings again and again until we hit that ever-elusive, magical moment when a fade crests and slowly begins to ebb. Once all the mix pieces were committed to tape, I would sit down in front of the ½" tape machine and begin editing the "best of" pieces together, physically cutting the tape and splicing it back together using a white grease pencil (to mark the cut points), a splicing block (to hold the tape in place), a demagnetized single edge razor blade (to make the cuts), and special Scotch splicing tape (to put the edit pieces together). There was no slick cross-fade editing like in Pro Tools; there was no Pro Tools.

There were plenty of precision mix moves that needed to be executed throughout the various sections of each song. Many of Ace's songs were quite complex with lots of guitar tracks and effects to deal with. There were also some specific vocal effects that needed to be crafted during mixdown, like shaving the "sp" off the word space so that whenever Ace sang "lost in space" at the end of each "Snow Blind" chorus, the delay would echo back "Ace... Ace... Ace" — or at least that's what I was trying for. Certain mix moves required more than the four hands Eddie and I could provide. In those cases, Ace would be recruited to lend a hand (or two), punching a button, tweaking a knob, swishing a pan pot from one side to the other, or riding faders up or down an exact amount at precisely the right moment in a song. Mixing 24 tracks without automation could get really crazy at times but we got it done with a great sense of fun and, of course, lots of laughter. "Fractured Mirror," with its oozing, constantly evolving guitar parts was particularly challenging with lots of mix moves throughout. That one could easily have taken a couple of days to mix. Only after each song's mix was declared finished would we allow ourselves to take a deep breath, sit back, and take in what we had accomplished. Working long hours well into the night — night after night — mixing the album was an exhausting but satisfying part of the project.

Any funny stories come to mind from those sessions?
Lots of wacky stuff went on. Ace loved to laugh and would crack us (and himself) up telling funny stories and jokes at every opportunity. Champagne and other "refreshments" flowed throughout the project helping to keep spirits high. There were times when Ace arrived at the sessions — it didn't matter what hour of the day — having imbibed the better part of a bottle or two of champagne in the limo on the way into the city. Eddie and I would be quietly talking in the control room, when suddenly the door would burst open and Ace would stumble in, laughing and hitting the floor in hysterics. It was actually a pretty effective way to set the mood for the day's recording session.

There's one thing that always brings a smile when I think about those sessions. As I mentioned earlier, Plaza Sound was situated on the seventh floor of the Radio City building. Just down the hall from Plaza's control room was a "secret" access way that led to the executive elevator, which went down to a private viewing box overlooking the theater. That box was strictly reserved for Music Hall VIPs and was normally off limits to Plaza Sound's clients unless special arrangements were made. Not being one to bow to formalities, Ace would, from time to time, while Eddie and I were busy comping tracks or editing something, grab a bottle or two and stealthily make his way down to the private box to watch the show. We'd have no idea where he had gone. But invariably, after a while, the in-house phone would ring and a voice at the other end of the line would say something to the effect of, "Plaza? We think one of yours is down here sleeping in the executive box. Kindly come and retrieve him." You gotta love Ace!

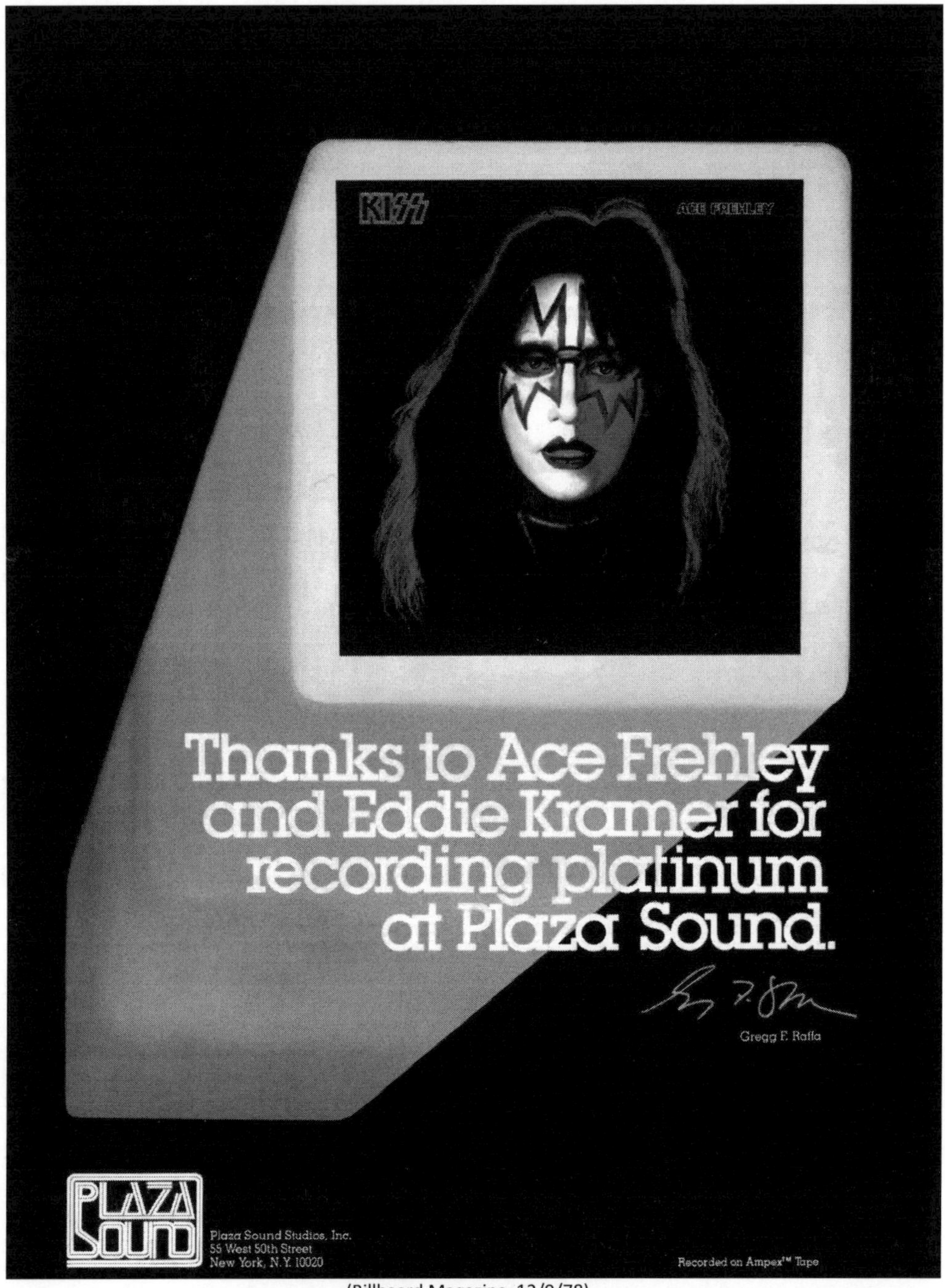

(Billboard Magazine, 12/9/78)

Russ Ballard

Award-winning songwriter details the creative process for his iconic song "New York Groove," the recording of the original version by Hello and his recollections of how the song came into the Ace Frehley fold. Russ also discusses additional KISS-related songs such as "Into The Night," "Let Me Rock You" and "God Gave Rock And Roll To You," and putting his life down in his music.
By Tim McPhate

Russ, for my first question, I'd like to go back to 1974. That year Argent actually headlined several concerts with KISS serving as the opening act. I know you left the band around this time, but did you perform with Argent on those dates?
Russ Ballard: I remember doing two shows with KISS. One was at the Academy of Music, I think when they were beginning. I remember them setting up the big logo behind the drums. I didn't know what to expect but there seemed to be a buzz. And then I saw the band take the stage with the makeup and stuff. I thought, "This is cool." (Laughs) Then I remember another show we did with them in St. Louis. It was a Sunday night, I think, at a beautiful theater. It held about 2,000. I had a good look at them that night from the side. I thought they were great.

According to the book "KISS Alive Forever," KISS and Argent were set to do a longer tour.
I just remember doing two shows. I don't remember talk of any more. When I left the band they kept going. They could have [talked about it].

Russ, you were born in Waltham Cross, Hertfordshire in England. That's quite the long way from New York. Am I correct in saying you came up with the song title for "New York Groove" while on a plane?
Yeah. I had just produced a solo album for Roger Daltrey. I played on his first album and he asked me if I'd like to produce his next album, "Ride A Rock Horse." It took about six months. This was 1975. After finishing, we both thought it would be a good idea to go to Sterling Sound in New York to get it mastered because everyone said that was the place where the cuts sounded louder and that they were a better mastering facility than the one in London. I went on a plane to New York. While on a plane, I always carried a little notepad and a pen around with me. I always found it very inspiring to be on a plane. As soon as you get away from home, ideas come to you. And I thought, "I'm back in the New York groove." That's what was in my head because I hadn't been there for a couple of years. And I told that story about "Many years since I was here." (Laughs)

Did you have a particular affinity for New York?
I loved going there. It's always so exciting. When you're with a bunch of guys in a band, it was always good to go there. There's so much to do there. I was looking forward to going there. I didn't write any more on that plane, just "New York Groove." It was later that I finished the song in the studio when I had to. It was that time in the studio and I had to come up with something. I just had this title and I had a Super Vamper harmonica with me. In my head, I always wanted to do a Bo Diddley beat. I wanted that Bo Diddley thing (sings the rhythm of the Bo Diddley beat). And the words, I just made them up in the studio. It was probably the first rap. You think about Ace shouting, "Here I am again in the city / With a fistful of dollars / And baby you better believe." It's like a rap in the '70s.

And the band you were in the studio with was Hello?
Yes. They were 16 years old. My brother saw the band and he said to me, "I've just seen this group. They're 16. They're an amazing little band." My friend, who was a good mate of mine, wanted to manage a band. So he got in touch with them. We went to the father's house of the guitar player. They set up in the house and they played. And I thought, "Yeah, they're great." He got them a deal with Bell Records, which became Arista. They did one song and then I took them in the studio and I got them to stamp on a table, you know, with these big platform boots. I got them to stamp on this table like (mimics stomping drum rhythm). I just made up the tune as we went. I said, "E, right. A, E, B." (Laughs) I was making things up as we went along. And it was pretty exciting to do that. It made it energetic, which I really liked.

Of course, Hello's version became a Top 10 hit in the UK in 1975. Did you sense there was something special after hearing the playback of the track?
I think it had quite a verse to it. The verse was melodic and it was going to places that you didn't expect to go. Yeah, I thought it was great. The main thing, Bell Records thought it was very radio friendly. And they got it out there. They did every kind of TV show for it. When I heard that Ace was doing it, that was great as well.

The song is just a perfect storm. You mentioned the catchy Bo Diddley rhythm. It has a sing-able melody and lyrics that paint an authentic atmosphere. In terms of the composition of the song, one of the things I've always loved is the modulation up a half-step before the second verse. As a songwriter, what was your thinking in deploying that device in that spot?
Well I always used to do it. I did it in so many tunes. It's a thing that is not done these days. You just don't hear those modulations. They usually go up a step, or sometimes a minor third or they go up more. I did it in a lot of tunes over the years (laughs), almost everything I wrote I wanted to do a modulation because it always seems to give a tune another energy. As soon as it goes up, "Ah, this is great." It makes you feel like it's going somewhere.

Getting into 1978, the four KISS members were each at work on solo albums. Ace Frehley teamed with producer/engineer Eddie Kramer for his album. How were you made aware that Ace wanted to cover "New York Groove" on his album?
I think my publisher from New York told me. I'm sure that's how it happened. But Eddie phoned me. Eddie Kramer phoned me two houses ago (laughs) and he was talking about it. I don't remember too much about the conversation. But I was aware of Eddie from his work with Jimi Hendrix. I was aware of him being a very, very good engineer. It was nice talking to the man because he had a good reputation.

I think the sentiment was that this song somehow was a great opportunity for Ace. Do you recall when you first heard Ace's recording of "New York Groove"?
I think I heard it on tape, I am sure it was a cassette tape. I think I heard it at the publisher's office. I know I went to CBS Records in 1978 to do something out there. I can't remember exactly, but I do remember hearing it out there. I'm sure it was in CBS' offices.

And how would you assess Ace's interpretation of the song?
He did a great version. It sounded like punk to me, it sounded like a guy just throwing it together. There was a little bit more attitude because Hello were kind of young and I think they sounded young — they hadn't been in the studio very much. And I was just throwing it out to them and they were sort of copying what I was doing initially. When Ace did his thing on it, it sounded a bit more mature. He brought a hooligan, tough guy kind of attitude to it.

Ace is from New York and I think the song hit home with him.
Yeah, it was a good version. I liked it.

"New York Groove" proved to be the big hit of the four KISS solo albums, rocketing to No. 13. Was it communicated to you that it was going to be released as a single? And was it a surprise to you that it became a hit again?
I was pleased when they said it was going to be a single. I was very pleased. I always had "Billboard" anyway, so I used to look at the charts. I knew what was going on in the charts and I saw it going up the charts. I was wondering if it was too "tough" to get into the 20s.

The song also became a bit of a staple for KISS live, as well as during Ace Frehley's solo concerts. In fact, some fans associate Ace with this song. If asked to choose, whose version do you like best: Hello's version or Ace's?
I think I go for the Ace version because it's more kind of street somehow. The other one was a little more manufactured. It had those filtered sounds, where I think Eddie Kramer went for more of the straight-ahead guitar sounds and straight-ahead drum sounds. It was like a band playing in front of you. Also Ace shouted it more

like a street kid. Hello sort of whispered it. I was whispering (whispers), "Many years since I was here." They were copying what I was doing. It wasn't their fault; it was mine (laughs).

In the grander scheme, the song has crossed over into popular culture. It's been featured in baseball stadiums, at football games, and in commercials and TV shows.
Well, it's a good thing it has New York in the title, you know what I mean? (Laughs) I wasn't thinking about that at the time. It was used as the theme for the tattoo series "N.Y. Ink" as well. It's great because the next generation becomes aware of it. I love that. If there's an avenue to promote the tune, I'm all up for that.

More recently, Sweet recorded "New York Groove." Have you heard that version?
Yeah, I heard that. It was sent to me strange enough.

For their arrangement, they mixed in elements of "Empire State Of Mind," which was a recent hit featuring Jay-Z and Alicia Keys.
That's right, they did. That was sent to me (laughs). A song can take on its own life after a time. That's what a publisher said to me. I said, "Does publishing turn you on?" He said, "What I love is following a song. They take on a life of their own." And it's true.

Russ, you have a few other ties to KISS that I'd like to touch upon. Staying with Ace, he recorded a song called "Into The Night" for his first post-KISS solo album in 1987. That song was originally featured on your 1984 self-titled album. What can you tell us about the origins of writing this one?
I loved that feel. I wanted to do something that went (sings main rhythm to "Into The Night"). I just love that feel. That feel always sounds good on an album (laughs). And I wanted to get a bit dark and talk about what's going on in the night. I guess something like the atmosphere of — although it was on the West Coast — "Pretty Woman." The girl is walking the streets and there are the drug dealers and the guy is sort of sleeping right on the street. That [kind of] feel. And then hopefully throwing in an element of surprise by saying, "You see that guy? Well that's me." That was the idea. I had Simon Phillips cut the drums on that and I had Mo Foster on the bass. They were a great rhythm section. They did a really good job [on my version].

I believe there was a three-year lapse between your version and Ace's. What do you recall about learning that Ace was covering another one of your tunes?
You know, I've never spoken to Ace.

No kidding?
I've never met him. And I've never spoken to any member of KISS. It's crazy.

I was going to ask about that. I have to say I'm surprised to learn this since you have multiple songs with KISS ties.
Yeah, it's mad. But it's one of those things. Part of the fact is that I came off the road. I mean, I do a few gigs in Europe. But I mainly sit at home and write. I do sometimes put a band together but I haven't [toured] America since 1976 so our paths really haven't crossed. The only time I saw Gene Simmons was at the Sunset Marquis in L.A. I was there doing some writing. I was having some breakfast with a guy by the pool in the morning. At the other end of the pool was Michael Bolton sitting with Gene Simmons. They were sitting together real quietly. This guy said to me, "That's Michael Bolton. He just did 'The Johnny Carson Show.'" And after I finished talking with him, they walked over the length of the pool and they stopped at the table. Gene Simmons didn't say anything to me. And I never said anything to him (laughs). Michael Bolton did the talking. He said, "Do you ever write with anybody?" I said, "Well I've just started to write with people." And he said, "Would you fancy writing with me?" And I told him I couldn't because I had to get home. Michael and I spent the evening in the bar — Gene wasn't there. I went home the next day or the day after. Michael contacted me actually last year so that was nice. But I never spoke to Gene. It's crazy. It was just one of those situations where we saw each other but it didn't go any further (laughs).

That is a bit odd. Gene is usually not at a loss for words. If you had to ballpark it, around what year would this have been?
I'll tell you when it was, it was the time when Michael Bolton's first big single got to number one, which was "How Am I Supposed To Live Without You," because he had just done that song on "The Johnny Carson Show." So it was either '89 or '91.

That would have been 1989 then. Around that time, KISS recorded a song that Paul Stanley co-wrote with Michael Bolton. It was a ballad titled "Forever," and it was actually a Top 10 hit in 1990. Who knows, perhaps that's why Gene and Michael were together.
That's probably why.

So back to "Into The Night."
Yeah, I wasn't aware of Ace doing that one. I don't think anybody told me about that until I heard it being played on radio stations. And I saw it in "Billboard," and I remember thinking, "Is that my song?" Because he called it "Into The Night."

That's right. There is the subtle difference in the titles.
Yeah, mine was called "In The Night." And he called it "Into The Night." I remember thinking, "I wonder if that's my tune? He already did 'New York Groove.'" (Laughs)

Logistically speaking, with a cover song, is someone just able to make a change to a song title even though it might be a small change like that?
Yeah, these days if people want to do your song and they want to change anything, they usually get in touch and say, "We intend to do a lyric change." I don't remember that going on with Ace but you know, it's one word.

Skipping back to 1982, original KISS drummer Peter Criss released his second solo album following his departure from the band. The album was actually titled after one of your songs, "Let Me Rock You." How about this song, Russ?
I did a demo. I remember doing that. It's strange that was the only version of that song. I did the demo at my friend's studio. I used to do 24-track demos. I was probably the only person in England who was doing 24-track demos (laughs). My friend had a 24-track studio. I used to pay to get in of course (laughs). I would have three tunes that I liked and I would go into the studio. But with that one, I wanted to make a rock-soul record. I went in and I actually paid a trumpet player, a tenor sax player and a trombone player. There was a brass section on the demo. This was a demo, so I thought a lot of the song; otherwise I wouldn't have done that. I'd like to hear my demo now, [but] I don't know where it would be. I think it was less rock and more soul. I would have liked to have done that more rocky than my demo. I think Peter Criss, with his version, he turned it into a rock song. It was meant to be a rock song. My version came out more as a soul song.

I'd love to hear your demo, Russ. I really like the tune. I think it's one of the more fun tracks on Peter's record. His version has a rock flavor but I can hear some of the soul elements you're referring to. There's accented guitar rhythms, piano and even some doo-wop style background vocals.
Yeah, yeah. I was doing a kind of retro thing with the chords as well. I was doing that kind of thing with the chords, that classic kind of sound — I'm trying to remember the rundown (laughs).

Peter also recorded another one of your songs for that album, "Some Kinda' Hurricane." What do you remember about this song?
Yeah, I recorded that myself. I did that at Utopia [Studios]. I did that as a single. I did a great demo of it. I put so many drums on this thing, because it went (sings rhythm of guitar riff). That was the feel of the demo. I played the drums on it. I was tracking toms and tracking toms and tracking toms again, over and over — so it sounded monstrous. And then everybody liked it and said, "Why don't you try this as a single?" And Phil Wainman, who was a good friend of mine and a drummer, strange enough — he used to produce Sweet at one time. He said to me, "Why don't you come into Utopia?" which was his studio. We did a version. It wasn't bad. I was pleased that it was at least heard, you know.

I did do some research and unfortunately I couldn't find any audio of your version [Ed. It was released as a non-album single in the U.K. (Epic S-EPC-49845) on Feb. 4, 1977 backed with "You Can Do Voodoo").
I know. I wouldn't know where to find it now either (laughs).

(Laughs) "Let Me Rock You" kind of came and went rather silently. It wasn't even released in the United States until years later. Would you have been cognizant of the fact that Peter did two of your tracks for this album?
It wasn't until later. It was a lot later when I heard it. And I was pleased.

Moving to 1991, KISS recorded a revamped version of the Argent song "God Gave Rock And Roll To You." Is it true you wrote that song after a bout with depression?
Yeah, I was coming out of it. If you've ever been depressed, it's one of those sort of things where I was overworked and I just didn't get any sleep and you sort of start feeling low. I never cancelled a gig. I always worked my way through it. But if you've ever suffered from that kind of depression, you think it never will go away. Day after day — though I haven't felt depressed for many, many years. But everyday seems to be gray. You wake up and it's gray again and it's gray again. And you think, "Is it every going to change?" I guess life is all about change. And suddenly you seem to slowly come out of it. I was taking some pills and the doctor said, "Stop taking everything you're taking, sleeping pills and whatever you're taking. Stop!" And I came out of it and it was like being reborn. I don't remember ever feeling so euphoric, but still stable. You can be euphoric and unstable but I was euphoric and stable and it's the most incredible feeling. And I wrote "God Gave Rock And Roll To You" and the words sort of conveyed it.

The first verse of my version was meant to be funny: "Love your friend and love your neighbor / Love your life and love your labor / No, it's never too late to change your mind / Don't step on snails, don't climb in trees / Love Cliff Richard but please don't tease," that wouldn't have happened in the States obviously, so they had to change that (laughs). And the second verse: "If you wanna be a singer or play guitar / Man, you gotta sweat or you won't get far / Because it's never too late to work 9 to 5 / And if you're young, you'll never be old / Music can make your dreams unfold / How good it feels to be alive." That was how I was feeling and I just conveyed that. And I did the same thing when I did a song for Santana called "Winning," although I wrote it for myself. But that was about coming out of my depression too. (Sings) "One day I was on the ground / When I needed a hand / And it couldn't be found ... Now I'm winning." I mean, I've actually put my life down in so many tunes when I look back. That's why depression can be good if you're trying to express oneself.

That's fascinating, Russ. There are a number of interesting musical twists and turns in this particular song, including the very quiet bridge featuring vocals and acoustic guitar. What was your inspiration for changing the song's dynamics at that point?
I don't know why (pauses). We were just kind of experimenting with going up and down. It was a progressive time. It was 1973. That was a time when you saw more progressive bands. That was the thing that everyone was doing. They were doing time signature changes, tempo changes and going up and down. I was trying to write two songs in one. I was doing things like "It's Only Money Part 1" and "It's Only Money Part 2" with different feels. And I developed that. I listened to a lot of Beach Boys and I quite liked the things like "Surf's Up" with those little voices they were using. I was heavily influenced by their style at the time. I did like KISS' version because it had a great feel and a great tempo. It was more up and sung out and I do prefer that. And it was much more thought about than ours, actually.

I remember first hearing the track via the video on MTV in summer 1991. And I went out and bought the soundtrack for the film it was featured in, "Bill And Ted's Bogus Journey." They re-released it on their 1992 studio album "Revenge." The song proved to be a big hit for KISS overseas.
It was a big hit. It got to number four here. I'll tell you how that happened. Do you know Nigel Harrison?

The musician?
Yeah, he was the bass player in Blondie. When I was out there in 1991, I think it was, I was at the record company at where he worked. I was waiting to go into an office to see an A&R man and Nigel Harrison walks through the door and said, "Russ, do you know we're making a movie? Have you heard of 'Bill & Ted's Excellent Adventure'?" And I said, "Yeah." He said, "We're making a follow-up and I've told everybody that 'God Gave Rock And Roll To You' would be a great song for the movie." And this is how it started. I said, "Oh, great. Fantastic." And he said, "We're looking for a group to perform it." And he mentioned three or four bands and luckily in the end they came up with KISS. That was the best band of them all actually.

Do you remember any of the other bands that were considered?
Believe it or not, I think one of them was the [London] Quireboys.

Interesting... The record label would have been Interscope Records.
Interscope, that's where I was. Nigel Harrison was there. Whether he's still there now, I don't know.

As you mentioned, KISS changed some of the lyrics.

They had to be changed. They were very good about the song splits and everything. It was great. It's great that songs do have a life and they can come back again in different guises (laughs).

Absolutely. I think it's an interesting "KISStorical" fact that your songs have ties to each of the original members of KISS.
I've always loved the band. They were the first band to try that kind of thing. They were innovators.

Russ, belated congratulations to you for being honored with the Classic Songwriter Award from "Classic Rock Magazine" in 2012. How did it feel to be recognized by an esteemed publication?
It's probably because I'm old (laughs). When you get to a certain age they say, "We better give him his turn." (Laughs)

(Laughs) Well, I also think it has something to do with your talent and your body of work. Russ, you released your most recent studio album, "Book Of Love," in 2006. You've mentioned you play some gigs from time to time. What can you us about what you are up to nowadays?
Yeah, I just did a gig with Argent recently. It was great. It was for charity. A friend of ours has had some bad luck so we did it for charity. It was so great to play again. It's a funny thing, when you play again after many years; you realize why you did it in the first place. I got into music to be in a group. I never got into music to write songs. I got into music to really be on the road and to be in a band. I just got sidetracked into writing. It was so great to play. I still make music. And I go out on the road with my own band, but it's mainly in places like Europe — Germany, Austria, and Switzerland. I'm doing a gig in Lisbon on the 28th of September [2013]. I've been asked to do a festival in Wales in March of next year. And I love it because it gets sweeter as you get older, Tim.

Anton Fig

"The Thunder from Down Under" revisits Ace Frehley's 1978 solo album and working on the album's demos, and offers insight regarding some of his favorite tracks such as "Rip It Out" and why "Ace Frehley" is not only an important part of the Spaceman's evolution, but one of the favorite albums he has ever played on.
By Tim McPhate

Anton what was going on with your musical career in 1978?
I was playing around New York in the rock scene. I had moved down from Boston where I had gone to music school and got a music degree. I studied classical percussion and jazz. So I was pretty much heavily into jazz all that time but when I moved down to New York I got back into rock, which is what I had grown up playing as a kid in South Africa. And I think around that time I had done a record with Link Wray called "Bull Shot." I was in a rock band called Topaz; some of the guys in the band had gone off to play with Bob Dylan. Through that I got to play with Robert Gordon and Link Wray. So I was kind of touring around and playing with Robert and Link and at the same time I had formed my own band with some fellow South Africans. At the time we were called Siren, but we became Spider. We were rehearsing and actually looking for musicians around that time. We had a loft downtown in New York.

I think that's where your connection to Ace comes in. I understand that you came to play with Ace through a bass player named Larry Russell, who was auditioning for Spider. How did Larry bring up the Ace opportunity?
Well, he was auditioning for us and he said to me, "I've got a friend, Ace. He's doing a solo record and he's looking for a drummer. I think I can get you an audition." You know, I had heard of KISS. But to me, KISS was a band on the side of a bus basically. It was a lot of advertising and marketing but I didn't know the material that well. Anyway, I went up to play with Ace. He did four demos up at a small studio in Queens or [maybe it was] the Bronx. And we did "Rip It Out" and three other songs I don't remember. We barely spoke. I just kind of played with him. I mean, I asked him if he was the rhythm guitarist [in KISS]. I didn't even know. He asked me to come up and do another four songs with him. And then there was also another connection through Siren. Eddie Kramer was interested in our band and he was also going to produce Ace's record. I knew Eddie. I had never really worked with him but I knew him. After the two demo [sessions], Ace asked me to do the record. I was about to go on a five-week tour of Europe with Robert Gordon and Link, so I went off and did that. And when I got back, I think the next day I went up to the Colgate Mansion in Connecticut and we recorded most of the album there.

If you think back to the demo sessions, did you feel an instant chemistry with Ace?
I felt like I could play his music really well. When we did "Rip It Out," when it came time to record it for real, he played me the demo and said, "I want you to do exactly the same fills that you did on the demo." Those fills I just did off the top of my head. I didn't really give it any thought. I sort of copied myself from the demo so obviously something was working right from the get-go. But I felt like we could just play well together.

Anton, do you remember thinking that Colgate Mansion was an odd locale to record the album?
Not really. Led Zeppelin had done something like that beforehand. To experience the world of real rock stardom firsthand was new to me. Of course, I had seen it in magazines and all that, but to actually go to a big mansion and play, this was a whole new world for me. The way we did it, I was set up on a stairwell. There were these stairs and then a landing and then another staircase. So I was set up there. Ace sat right next to me and his amps were in the dining room or one of the big ballrooms. And we recorded a lot of the songs, maybe three-quarters of the record, just with rhythm guitar and drums. You know it was in the old days — no Pro Tools, no clicks. There was a remote truck outside where the studio was. That's how we did most of the record.

In terms of the final takes, was there one magical take or were some tracks comped together?
They really didn't comp that much because you had to cut tape as opposed to what you can do in Pro Tools now. There was minimal comping compared to what people do these days. I think basically we had to get one good take. That's the old way of recording. I grew up recording like that so it was fun for me.

I think that's one of the reasons why the album sounds so alive. Anton, would you recall what kit you played on the album?
It was one of Ace's kits. It was different drums; I don't think it was all part of the same set. I don't actually remember, to be honest. It wasn't like a fancy kit or anything.

And one bass drum?
Yeah, one bass drum.

Your drums are incredible on the album. Were you happy with the drum sound that was ultimately captured?
Yeah, I thought it sounded really good. You know, you listen to it now and it doesn't sound as big as what you can do these days, but it's got a lot of personality. It still

sounds strong. I think that we captured the vitality in the actual playing. I'm quite happy with the sound.

Did you have freedom in terms of crafting your drum parts? Or did Ace or Eddie interject any specific ideas?
You know, I don't remember specifically. But I do remember thinking I could do whatever I wanted to do. I'm sure they had suggestions along the way. But it was never a restrictive environment. I just played however I heard it. And that seemed to work.

I'd say so. Eddie Kramer has said that you all stayed at the mansion and that, while there was work to be done, there was also a fair share of good fun. What do you recall about the atmosphere?
Well, we got everything done we had to do. I remember there were nights of having big meals and laughing a lot. It was totally fun. It wasn't like just work and work and work. It was a pretty relaxed pace. I can't remember exactly how many songs we did a day, two songs a day or something like that. We had a certain number of days to get them done, but it certainly didn't feel that pressurized.

Overdub sessions for the album took place in New York at Plaza Sound, which was located above Radio City Music Hall. I understand you've said that some basic tracks may have been re-cut there, specifically for "New York Groove," "Rip It Out" and another song — what's your memory of what was accomplished at Plaza Sound?
I think "Rip It Out" was recorded there. I know "Rip It Out," on the drum solo, I double-tracked it. And I definitely remember double-tracking the drums there. I doubt that we would have just gone and done that because Eddie would have wanted to have exactly the same sound. So I'm pretty sure that "Rip It Out" was recorded there. And "New York Groove," I'm pretty sure that was recorded there as well. It's funny, I don't remember playing "Rip It Out." I do remember double-tracking the drum solo there though. I just don't think they would have taken the drums and just double-tracked the solo and not have done the whole song at the same time.

Speaking of which, the album gets off to a raucous start with "Rip It Out." There's some heavy power-chord riffing and a classic, in the pocket Ace solo. But I think what also grabs the listener is your energetic drumming. You just mentioned that the solo part was improvised. What do you think inspired you to come up with that on the spot?
I don't know, it just seemed appropriate. It seemed to fit the song. It's aggressive and (pauses) I didn't think about it. I just played it. It was good fortune.

So here's a prime example of an instance when inspiration took over in the heat of the creative process.
I'm glad about it. I'm very happy with it. It holds up today so that's cool.

And you doubled the solo part. What was the thinking in doubling that?
Well, that was Eddie's idea. It was just to give it a slightly different sound. It's doubled pretty tight. It was just to make it jump out a little bit more, not to fix anything. One thing that you can tell, on the last fill I go around the toms. When I did it the first time, I went from the high tom down to the low tom, from left to right. When I doubled it, I went the other way around. I went from right to left. And the other fills, including the snare drum leading up to the fills; I think that's all doubled exactly the same.

You know, a lot of the songs I don't actually remember cutting. I sort of have a picture of myself sitting on the stairwell playing with Ace. With "Snow Blind," I think I came up with playing the cowbell. One thing I do remember was on "Wiped-Out," Ace was playing this riff and I started to play drums to it. The time doesn't really change, it's just the way the drums change that make it sound like it's in a different time. It implies that he's playing it a different way. We were jamming on it. It's cool — we sort of made it into a form where one way was the verse and one way was the chorus. It just changed on the chorus. The two different drum patterns changed over the guitar he was playing. We got a version down and he said to me, "Why don't you go and write some words and I'll give you a writing credit? Because you helped make the riff sound different." Then I went home and wrote the words and he gave me a writing credit on the song.

So you definitely wrote all the lyrics?
I was responsible for making the riff "weird" and I wrote the lyrics, yeah. He may have changed a sentence here or there, but I basically wrote it.

You've described that you were "turning around" the beat in "Wiped-Out." It's really cool how the drum feel changes underneath the guitar.
Yeah, well it's like he's playing the same riff over and over again. But the way that the drums are, it makes it sound like it's one way and then it makes it sound like another way.

Of course, "New York Groove" is the big hit from the album. The song is such a wonderful example of musical ensemble playing — everything seems to fit together like a glove.
I think that song was recorded more like you would approach a single. The drum part was really defined. I wasn't just jamming and playing. It was a little more worked out and deliberate and I was kind of playing the same thing over and over again, so the drums just kind of disappear into the song. I took a different approach

to the song. I remember we overdubbed handclaps and we had a sound effect box. There was gravel in it and you could stomp your feet in the thing to get that crunchy kind of sound on all the beats. I remember the background vocal session, overdubbing the vocals. It was a layered approach and there was a lot more care taken, as opposed to when it was me and Ace playing. This was a more crafted approach definitely.

Indeed. Did you sense anything special about the track after it was finished?
We were thinking how perfect it was for Ace. We thought it was a great song. I had no knowledge of what the other guys were doing with their solo records. I had absolutely no idea. I just remember thinking, "This is sounding really cool." I don't know if I knew that it was definitely going to be a hit. But I remember thinking it sounded great and really rounded out the whole record.

Are there any other standout tracks for you, Anton?
You know, I love the whole record. It opened the doors for quite a few other things for me. It was a very exciting time in my life, just being young and in New York. It's one of my absolute favorite records that I've played on. I just have a really good feeling of the whole thing. I'm so happy to be a part of it.

Rightfully so. Interestingly, there is one track you did not play drums on and that's the final song, the instrumental "Fractured Mirror." A drummer named Carl Tallarico played on that track. Do you recall why you didn't play on this tune?
He was a friend of Ace's. When I got to the Colgate Mansion, that song had already been recorded. I'm not sure why. I don't think there was any reason, maybe Ace wanted to have him on the record. Or maybe it just came out great and there was no point in redoing it.

Will Lee ended up playing bass on three tracks — "Ozone, "Wiped-Out" and "I'm In Need Of Love." Do you remember being around at Plaza Sound when Will tracked?
Yeah, just about the whole record is Ace playing everything and me on drums. And there are some songs where there are some background vocalists, like "New York Groove." And then there were a couple of songs I remember that Will played on. That was an overdub situation. I remember coming into Plaza Sound one day and Will was doing his bass overdubs. I sort of met him; I didn't really know him in those days. I think soon after we did Joan Armatrading's record together.

One known outtake exists from the Ace' 78 sessions in fan circles: "All For Nothing." Does that tune ring a bell as something you played on?
I don't remember that. It's quite possible that I played on it, but I don't know.

Eddie Kramer has intimated that Ace's 1978 solo album contains his best work. Anton, what's your take?
Well, I think there's other records that he did, the Frehley's Comet records, that really have some great songs on them. But you know, the thing was it was so unexpected. I don't think the other members of KISS expected Ace to have the breakout album. It was a huge leap for Ace. I don't think he'd done much singing and certainly not that much writing. It was a very important record in his evolution. It certainly contains his best stuff. I'm not saying that he didn't write to the same heights with some of his other work. But it was absolutely a fantastic record.

You hit on a great point. I don't think Paul and Gene, and perhaps Peter, expected Ace to come up with such a strong album. Do you remember Ace saying, "I'm going to show them..."?
I don't remember if there were discussions like that. I think at some point, we all said, "This is a great record. It's going to be competitive." I'm not sure that anybody knew what anyone else was doing. I certainly didn't know what anyone else was doing but that doesn't mean that Ace didn't. You know, he must have wanted to do really well and prove something. I don't know what the feeling was when he started but certainly I do feel that somewhere through the process, it was like, "Wow, I think we've really got something here."

Musically speaking, it seems all signs point to Ace being extremely focused on this project.
Yeah, the songs were really good. Everything just sort of gelled.

One quote from you that has stood out to me is that you once said that what makes Ace such a great musician is that "his will comes through in his playing." Can you elaborate on this thought?
I just feel that he's got a really strong mindset. And sometimes when he plays it's almost like you can hear that mental determination and grit where he'll just force his will through. I'm talking the mental coming through the music kind of thing. It's just an inner strength I feel that he has.

Anton, I would like to ask a couple questions about "Dynasty" and "Unmasked," if I may. Of course, it wasn't known for quite some time that you played on either of these albums. You have recounted that KISS asked you not to tell anyone and that's exactly what you did.
Yeah, they asked me not to say anything and I didn't. To be honest with you, I was fine with that because that was the deal. To this day, I still feel funny talking about. It came out in Gene's book and it came out on the remastered versions. So once they talked about it, I could. After I did Ace's thing, I was introduced to Bill Aucoin, their manager. Bill ended up managing Spider, so we were all kind of connected. It really wouldn't have been cool, especially because they asked me not to say

anything. And they had a reason for preserving that. Even when they took off the makeup, it still was part of the folklore. I wasn't going to be the one to say anything. I'm just not that kind of a person. It seems weird in this day and age where no one can keep a secret. But it was part of the deal and I was fine with it.

We just spoke about how you had free reign for Ace's album, but for "Dynasty" and "Unmasked" were there any general instructions to play any parts "like Peter" would have?
I had free rein on the KISS records too.

In hindsight, it obviously sounds nothing like what Peter would play. I was just curious if there were any discussions along those lines.
They never said anything to me. I just played it how I wanted to. Take "Hard Times," we did the demo up at North Lake Sound. I played it and the drum part was pretty well done on the demo. When it came time to do it live in the studio for real, I played what I had come up with. But I don't remember them ever telling me, "You've got it to do it like this because otherwise it's not going to sound right." They let me play however I wanted. It was actually great from that point of view.

Your drumming is stellar on those albums, which leads me into my next question. I understand that you and Ace had a discussion about you possibly joining KISS. But you weren't interested?
Spider had a song in the Top 40 at that stage...

"New Romance (It's A Mystery)."
Yeah. So it seemed, "Well, it would be great but I've got my own band and who knows what's going to happen there." (Pauses) It was a really difficult thought process for me, but I kind of felt like I should stay with my band. Then after that, I heard that Gene and Paul said that they weren't sure if they wanted me and Ace to be a unit, you know what I mean?

I think I do.
So that was it. When I look back on it, I'm happy with the way my musical life has gone. And I'm really happy for the time that I participated with Ace and KISS. I got kind of the best of both worlds.

You've been with the David Letterman band since 1987. How fortunate do you feel to have such a cool gig?
It's great. It's a life changer because it's a steady gig, you're in town and you're playing in a great band and playing with great guest musicians. And it doesn't take up that much time that you can't do other things as well.

Apparently, there are some nice fringe benefits as well. I saw you recently gave supermodel Chrissy Teigen a drum lesson.
Oh yeah (laughs).

Anton, who do you cite as your drum influences?
Well, I initially liked Earl Palmer, the English invasion — Ringo, Charlie, Mitch Mitchell, Keith Moon, Ginger Baker, and John Bonham. And then the jazz guys like Tony Williams, Jack DeJohnette, Elvin Jones, and on and on. There are so many great guys around now.

Your resume is incredible. In terms of guitarists, you've played with talented musicians such as Eric Johnson, Joe Satriani, Link Wray, Joe Bonamassa, Oz Noy, and the late Gary Moore. Who are some of the favorite guitarists you have played with?
All those guys that you mentioned, everyone has something different to offer. They're all fantastic in their own way. And they're all individual in their own way. Sometimes when I put mental pictures together of some of these fantastic guitar players I've played with, it feels mind-boggling. I feel super lucky to have been able to have played with them.

Are you still active in terms of gigging?
I am. I recently did two weeks at the Blue Note with Mike Stern and Eric Johnson. I just came back from a tour with Joe Bonamassa and the singer Beth Hart. That's going to be a DVD. A few months ago, I did another DVD with Joe, a power trio thing in London. There's a lot of stuff going on. I'm doing a bit of producing. I do drum tracks for people from my home studio. A few years ago, I released a solo record called "Figments." Ace is playing a solo on there, Oz is on it, Richie Havens is on it, Brian Wilson ... a lot of different people are on it.

Any plans for another solo album at some point?
Maybe. Not at the moment. I'm enjoying doing lots of different things.

Recently, some pictures surfaced of Ace in the recording studio. Apparently, he is at work on new music. When was the last time you spoke with Ace? And would you be open to collaborating with him again?
I would always play with Ace. He's got a road band now and he may want to record with the same band that he can take on the road. The "Anomaly" record was done to try and get close to the original Ace [solo] record. If he called me and wanted me to play, I definitely would. He was in town recently and texted me, and we were going to get together for dinner, but it just didn't work out. We're still in touch and we're still friends. We've been very close for many years.

Eddie Kramer

Legendary producer/engineer recalls a "big family gathering" at the Colgate Mansion and revisits how Ace Frehley stacked the deck and trumped his bandmates with a brilliant solo album and why it embodies the true essence of rock and roll.
Interview by Tim McPhate

Eddie, when Ace knew that the KISS members were going to do solo albums, I'm betting that you were the first call that he made. What do you recollect about the initial decision to work with Ace on his solo album?
Eddie Kramer: My recollection is that Ace and I were always pretty close because he loved what I did in terms of sounds. And I think recording Ace was going to be a wonderful challenge and very exciting because we just seemed to enjoy each other's company and I enjoyed getting him cool sounds. And this was a time when Ace was flying high, and I mean that figuratively speaking, in terms of his popularity. I always admired him as a guitar player. I thought he was much underrated, and I've said that before in the press. I think what we decided to do was to get into the studio and try and cut an album that really kicked ass!! And he had some great songs — thank goodness we were able to get that one song (laughs), which put his album way above any of the other guys.

"New York Groove," which was written by Russ Ballard.
Russ Ballard, right.

"New York Groove" had been recorded by a British group called Hello, and it was a hit circa 1975. As far as a general timeline, the recording sessions took place in June/July 1978 and the album was released in September.
Right, we rented the Colgate Mansion in Sharon, Connecticut, and used the Fedco mobile recording truck. Have you seen those pictures?

I think I've seen one or two on Ace's website, and I know you've said you have a bunch of pictures from the sessions.
Yeah, I do. They're great. So the decision was made, I think between Ace and myself, figuring out who the musicians were going to be. We knew that we wanted Anton and he was the key to getting the cool drum sound and feel, I mean he was just remarkable on this record. He just hit so bloody hard and did such fabulous stuff and Ace and he had worked together, if I'm not mistaken, on something prior. Maybe they jammed together.

Well, I have to be honest, Eddie, there are a lot of rumors that swirl around some KISS albums to this day. There's a longstanding rumor that Anton possibly played on a couple of the studio tracks on side four of "Alive II," but I don't that it has ever been confirmed if he played or not.
I think that is correct. I seem to remember that he did actually play on something that was recorded in a theater in New Jersey.

Interesting. The studio tracks on "Alive II" were recorded at Capital Theater in Passaic, New Jersey.
Yeah, I think there was a track that he did because shall we say that Peter Criss was unavailable that day (laughs). But I think that there was a history there of respect for Anton's ability. Obviously, he went on to David Letterman and all that. [He'd] seen him play in clubs and I know that there was a point where Ace and Anton got together and they really dug each other, so that was cool. And so the decision was made to get Anton.

I believe Ace played bass on a majority of the tracks. And then Will Lee, who also went on to play in the Letterman band, was brought in for a few tracks.
Yes, I've always been a huge admirer of Will Lee's bass playing. And he still rocks my world in terms of feel and technique. Now the mansion I'd known about through a friend of mine, but the guy who owned the mansion was (laughs) a little difficult to deal with. He owned a recording studio somewhere else in Connecticut, but he also owned this bloody great big Colgate Mansion. I called him up and said, "Hey, I want to bring a truck up and cut some tracks here." After some protracted negotiations ... (laughs), we managed to get in there. But the place was odd and definitely a bit haunted. However, it was so cool, with this massive staircase and huge paneled rooms, which gave us the ability to separate Ace's mountain of amps and the bass. After looking at my options, I decided to put the drums at the top of the staircase. They just sounded ridiculous!

The album has such a great drum sound.
Oh yeah, I've got pictures of Anton's kit at the top of the staircase. It just sounded ridiculous. The front living room was where we put all of Ace's amps.

What was the overall recording atmosphere like?
Cutting the tracks was hilarious. I mean we laughed our asses off so much. The place was pretty much haunted, as I said before. Everybody had a bedroom up there. We lived there in the mansion. And it was pretty primitive, but we all gathered together in the kitchen to have either take-out food or we cooked outside or we cooked in the kitchen ... it was like a big family gathering. You know — a bunch of guys drinking beer and recording (laughs). But the good thing was that the work was very consistent and Ace was really focused. People think he was out of it and all that kind of stuff but he wasn't. We had our fun after we had finished

working. But when we were recording everybody was straight and cool because we all wanted to make sure we got the stuff down on tape right. But it was just such a joy. It was a big laugh; it was a laugh because Ace was always so funny. But more than that, he was very serious about his recordings. And he just played with such intensity. I have to say that this was an impressive record. Ace was so inventive and we came up with such cool sounds. That was the thing, it was such an inspiration. I think part of it came from the fact that I had recorded Led Zeppelin at Mick Jagger's house in England and that was part of the "Houses Of The Holy" and "Physical Graffiti" albums. I wanted that same kind of vibe, and [Ace's album] was very reminiscent of Zeppelin in that sense. We wanted to get that huge, fucking great big drum sound. And we did.

Eddie, Ace has mentioned that Paul and Gene were "partially responsible for him doing a great album." Do you recall Ace having a competitive streak in him during the recording of the album? In other words, did he want to prove something to Paul and Gene?
Oh, there's no question in my mind that the competition between Ace, Gene, Paul, and Peter was going to be huge. And certainly, they denigrated the possibilities that he would come up with a good album. And they all thought that they were going to have the top album. In fact, what happened was Ace trumped them all with a brilliant album. Most of it has to do with the fact that he played great and he sang great. Albeit though in the studio, which we'll talk about in a minute when we go to Plaza Sound for the overdubs. There were moments of anxiety in terms of trying to cut the vocals. But the idea of competition among the members of the band was a strong one. And Ace probably felt, "I'll show these bastards." I'm sure that was in his mind. And I have to say that I was so impressed with what he came up with, and the intricacy and the cleverness of some of the guitar parts. It was tremendous. Like I said, he's a much underrated guitar player. And I admired his tenacity to complete the album.

And Ace's album was very much a true solo album given he played a majority of the instruments on the album, drums aside. He played the guitars, 12-string guitar, double-neck guitar, bass, and synthesizer. Is it safe to say this album contains Ace's finest recorded moments?
There's no question this is probably the best album he made. The follow-up albums when he did his solo project with Frehley's Comet I thought were very good too. But I don't know if anything quite reaches the height of inventiveness that [the 1978] album had. Plus it had a bloody great big single, which is still being played today at Yankee Stadium.

Yes, indeed. Let's get into the vocals, Eddie. Ace has commented that you may have been surprised by how his vocals turned out, in hindsight. Given Ace only

had two recorded vocals under his belt at this point. Was this an area of concern going into the project?
Correct. And you know the fact of the matter is he was not known as a great singer. But once again, when one is pressed one comes up with the goods. And that's what he did. Now there was a specific technique that we learned worked very well for him. In Plaza Sound we would put him on the floor, on a nice rug, with a cushion behind his head. And he had a bottle of beer in one hand and he had a Shure 58 in the other hand, and he would lie down because he felt very insecure about standing up and singing. So we would start him completely down on the ground, with the "attachments" (laughs) and then we would do a verse or two, or a chorus or something. And then he started to feel better and he would be sitting up. And then gradually, as his confidence in his ability to be able to sing was regained, he was vertical by the time we got the vocal completed. And that was the process. I am not sure if we used that for every song but certainly I do remember it being used quite extensively (laughs).

That's a great mental picture (laughs).
Yeah, but that's the thing, we goofed off a lot. But in between the goofing off, we were very serious. And I think it's important that one must realize that rock and roll, for me, has always been this combination of crazy moments, silly moments and seriousness. You can't be serious all the time. You know, it's only rock and roll as somebody has once said. And the more fun you can make it in the studio, the better the music is I think.

On that note, Ace has said that there weren't any of the "negative vibes" that sometimes came with recording a KISS record. I'm not exactly sure what Ace was alluding to, but perhaps it speaks to the fact that he didn't feel confined on his solo album.
That's exactly the point. He's a very creative soul. You've seen his drawings. The public persona was (speaks like Ace), "Hey, Curly..." It's really a front, because underneath that is a very intelligent human being and a sensitive guy who really understood his music well and played it well. So this was the opportunity to do a solo album. The doors were kicked open and Ace was in and doing his thing. And he was great, man.

Well, it's hard to find an album where Ace played better guitar. His guitar solos, especially, are sterling throughout. Can you give us a snapshot of how you worked with Ace on his guitar parts? Did you bat ideas back and forth?
Oh yeah, all the time. The way I always work with guitar players, first of all, we have a sound. You've got to start with a sound first. "Okay, I'm going to do a rhythm part." "Fine, what are we looking for? Is it a Marshall? Is it a Fender? Is it a vintage amplifier? What the hell is it? What does the song need as a sound?" Once we have that nailed, then we pick the guitar. "Is it a Les Paul? Is it a Fender Strat? A

Telecaster? What is it?" And once we define that, then we figure it out ... [but] Ace was pretty quick. This sounds like a long-winded thing but essentially we go through the amps and say, "Okay, this song needs this for the rhythm. And the secondary rhythm needs to be a 12-string. And the third guitar needs to be something else." And then I'll suggest, "Well, how about if we play it backwards? Or how about we put the mic over here?" You know, it's a very fertile ground for improvisation. And lots of things sort of happen organically, whereby I would say, "Listen I heard something you just did there. Let's expand upon that idea." Or getting different ringing tones, like in that instrumental ...

"Fractured Mirror."
"Fractured Mirror" is just full of crazy stuff that we did that just adds to the tonal color.

Ace has said he used his Gibson double-neck and he put the Marshall stack on 10 and stood close enough to the amp so it wouldn't feedback, and he played the rhythm figure on the opposite neck, while the other neck's pickups were on. And the other neck was tuned to the open key of the song, which yielded this very clear and almost bell-like color.
That is absolutely correct.

That's such a cool composition, and it's a great atmospheric close to the album. Eddie, there are nine songs on the album. Do you recall Ace having more material to choose from?
You know, there may [have been]. We'd have to go into the vaults and ask them to look and see what's on those tapes (laughs). I don't know who owns them, whether Ace owns them or the KISS guys own them. Who knows?

Well, I believe there is an outtake from this album titled "All For Nothing." There are several instrumental takes that exist in fan circles, so it would seem Ace was working on vocals. Do you recall this track?
Oh, yeah, yeah. We did do that.

It's an instrumental, so it seems like it was in the works.
Correct. It was definitely a song that was not finished.

As you're aware, deluxe editions of rock albums have seemed to crop up more in the past few years. If the opportunity arose to oversee an "enhanced" or remixed edition of Ace's 1978 solo album would you be open to it?
Well, I mean remix the album, what is that going to achieve? The album is what it is. I mean, what would a remix do for anybody? It would just be a different interpretation. I am involved with two major companies with cutting-edge

technology, and I think Ace's album would definitely benefit from the expansion and aural excitement of this newfound technology.

Bob Ezrin oversaw a remixed version of "Destroyer" in 2012. He commented on how the technology of the time was limiting and how there were certain things that had irked him about the album sonically. He was able to revisit the album, with today's technology, and expand on the album's sonics.
I think Ace's album stands up extremely well by today's standards. Of course I could mix it differently with this new cutting-edge technology.

Very interesting, Eddie. And I was envisioning this would be a package deal, not just a remix. You know, if there was material in the vaults from the '78 solo sessions, demos and what not.
That's a whole different ballgame. Then it's worthwhile. Like what I do with the Hendrix estate. We just released an album called "People, Hell & Angels," you're probably aware of it?

Yes, indeed. I own the album.
That was a year's worth of very intense work to restore that and put that all together because that is the last of the studio albums. And that was remixed with the single purpose of trying to improve the sound that was there, which we can do now. And it makes sense because the stuff hadn't been heard before. And you can make the same comment about any tracks that are in the vault that Ace has. I would love to remix them, of course.

I definitely think fans would enjoy a deluxe edition of Ace's solo album. If we go past the 1978 solo albums, KISS ended up working with Vini Poncia, who produced Peter Criss' solo album, on their next two albums, "Dynasty" and "Unmasked," and then they charted into different territory. Given your track record with the group and the fact that Ace's album was a winner, I think some have questioned why you didn't come back onboard to produce KISS?
Well, you know (laughs), what can I say? I feel that my work with KISS stands the test of time. I think the albums I did with them are some of their better works. I think most fans and critics would probably agree, yes?

Absolutely, Eddie. When you think of KISS and Eddie Kramer, the one word that comes to mind is: classic.
But you know, Gene and Paul do their thing and they do it well. And that's ... that's them. I can't comment either way about how they do their records. I just know that what I did was certainly the core of what the fans love. But the KISS guys do their thing and they do it extremely well and they've been extremely successful, so you can't really knock that. I'm just very happy that the guys are still together — maybe

not with the original team — but that's life. The KISS saga goes on and they're still filling stadiums, which is incredible.

Eddie, do you remember the last time you spoke with Ace?
Oh, it was a few years ago. I think he moved to California and he was going to get re-married or something. And then I lost track with him.

KISS have recorded two studio albums in the last three years, with both being produced by Paul Stanley. There is a contingent of fans who would love it if KISS and Eddie Kramer took one last go around in the studio. If the phone rang and it was Gene and Paul asking you to come aboard for a new KISS album, would you be open to it?
Obviously I would. We have a long history. If, if they were open to it and they were really serious about it, I would be very seriously inclined to go in the studio with them again. I would love it. Nothing would please me more because I know I can make them sound like they were in the beginning with that raw sound that's in your face.

Well, Eddie a lot of fans think that you should have produced the first three albums, but that's another discussion, huh?
That's another discussion for another day.

"Peter Criss" Related Interviews

"To see people smile and move their feet and snap their fingers, and for everyone to have their own favorite cut, is a great, great feeling to me!" (PR)

Brendan Harkin

Guitarist recalls "one small credit" on Peter Criss' solo album, working with Sean Delaney and his tenure with Starz, and offers his perspective on how the solo albums affected Bill Aucoin.
Interview by Tim McPhate

Brendan, can you give us a snapshot of your musical career in 1978. What were you doing at the time?
Brendan Harkin: Well, I think it was right at the end of my time in Starz. I left the band after three albums, kind of burnt out from the road and everything. And that's when I just decided I was going to stay in New York — you know we were a New York City band — and just kind of try to make it as a workday guitar slinger, which I did. I did tons of recording sessions and all that stuff for years. The recording session scene started to dry up in New York around '82 or '83 and it was because of the advent of Linn drum machines. And so session work just kind of died. And what guys were doing was getting little 8-tracks and a couple of microphones and putting it in their apartment and [working that way]. So that's what I started doing. And that grew into a huge business for me and that's what I still do. I live in Nashville and I have a studio called Wildwood Recording. I still play all the time. I play on all the stuff I do. I do tons of mid-level records, lots of jazz stuff, lots of Southern gospel and contemporary Christian stuff, which is really big down here. I do very little country, although I do some. I used to do more when I first moved here 20 years ago but I don't do too much of that anymore.

Do you recall how you were offered the opportunity to play on Peter Criss' solo album?
This is interesting because I don't know if I've even listened to that record. This record was just one of many records I did at the time. You [mentioned] Vini Poncia [co-]produced it, and maybe he did, but my involvement was through Sean Delaney. And I just assumed that Sean was producing it. Maybe he just produced several tunes on it or maybe he was working with Vini, I don't know. But it was through Sean and he knew I could do the session [guitar] thing and put in what was needed on stuff. I actually played on a bunch of stuff on that record. I got credited with one song and Sean said, "Well, Peter wants stars, not Starz the band, but actual stars to play on the record. He doesn't want people who are not huge stars." And he said, "I can only credit you [with] one small credit on the record." But I went into Electric Lady with Sean numerous times to fill in lots of little parts, just kind of polishing stuff off. And to tell you the truth, I couldn't tell you what I played on and what I didn't. I can't even tell you what I got credited to play on.

Well, you are credited on the acoustic ballad "Easy Thing." Regarding the production, as I understand it, Sean had agreed to produce Gene Simmons' solo album. Peter was having difficulty securing a producer, and had apparently been turned down by Tom Dowd. And so Sean helped Peter get some material together for some demos that were designed to help Peter get a producer, and these are the sessions you were part of. Vini Poncia was then brought in to steward the ship from there.
I see. You know, that's a long time ago.

Yes, it's difficult to piece everything together.
That's almost 35 years ago and my memory of what happened is real thin. I mean, I used to do stuff with Sean in the studio all the time. He was a song guy who had visions of being an artist himself and we'd go in all the time and do demos on his tunes. So I was basically just a guy who was his buddy. I mean he was really involved with Starz; he was a total hands-on guy with Starz. So we know each other really well and he knew my playing really well. He used to call me all the time; he used to [do] jingles. In fact, the guys in Starz probably did a few jingles for him (laughs). There was a lot of recording going on and Sean was involved with a lot of it and I was involved with pretty much everything he did. I mean, I never played on Gene's record. Whatever he worked on for Peter, I was there for a lot of it.

Would you have played just rhythm guitar or leads too?
I have no clue. Maybe if I heard it I could recognize myself. But I have no idea (laughs). I remember numerous sessions at Electric Lady working on Peter's stuff and I can't tell you whether it was four songs, six songs, three songs. I just don't really remember, but it was all with Sean and it was all with me and Sean and an engineer. There may have been one tracking date — I think I did one tracking date with Neil Jason and Allan Schwartzberg.

Yes, on select tunes Neil is credited on bass and Allan is on drums.
Okay, I think it was one tracking session where those guys were there and I was [there]. Other than that, there was just a bunch of overdub sessions, afternoon, late at night, you know too many drugs kind of thing (laughs).

(Laughs) Did you know Peter and was he around when you were in the studio with Sean?
Well, I knew Peter from the whole association with Aucoin. But I can't say I was ever friends with Peter. I'm friendly with Lydia; she's a great gal. I'm still in touch with her and Richie Fontana, they live together in New York. She was always really nice and really friendly. They lived really close to me and my wife at the time, they lived on 2nd Avenue and 30th Street and I lived on 28th Street. Myself and my wife used to go over there, but never when Peter was there. I remember Peter as being kind of standoffish. The other guys were friendly. Ace, Gene and Paul were all real

friendly and all real kind and encouraging to the band, and I used to see them all the time. We did some gigs with them. But Peter, I don't ever remember having a conversation with Peter and he was not there for any of the sessions.

Did you think it was odd that Peter, as a drummer, wasn't playing drums on tracks for his own solo album?
Is he listed?

He is listed as playing on a majority of the tracks that were later produced by Vini Poncia.
Right, right. Well, I couldn't tell you any of that because, like I said, there was one tracking session that Allan was on. Other than that, I have no idea who played on what. Is Schwartzberg listed?

Yes, he's listed on a few tunes.
I might be wrong. Maybe I was there a couple of times when there were tracking sessions. But I definitely played on more than that one tune. But Sean said, "I can only give you a small credit because Peter wants big names on there." And I guess I wasn't a big name.

I have to be candid. I'm looking at the credit sheet and the only "big names" I see would be Steve Lukather and maybe Elliot Randall. Now, that's not to take anything away from the players on the album, they're all fantastic musicians. But in terms of star power, Gene was the one who turned that trick on his album.
Yeah, well that was Sean's story. And unfortunately, you can't ask Sean about it.

Yes, we lost Sean 10 years ago. Brendan, when Sean told you that, what was your reaction? Was that just standard procedure in terms of album credits?
Oh yeah, I didn't even think about it. You know, I had tons of credits on tons of different things. I don't think I even paid any attention to it. I got copies of the four solo records through the office, and they're probably still in cellophane up in my house right now. I doubt I ever opened hem up and listened to them. I did tons of records and three-quarters of them I got copies of and I listened to them so many times through the process of making them, that's it's kind of like the last thing I wanted to do. You don't get copies until months later and I'm on to tons of other stuff. So I never paid attention to it and it never bothered me. To tell you the truth, as a musician your name is spelled wrong more than it's spelled right. You're credited wrong more than you're credited right. In fact, I played on some Kool & The Gang records. And I just took it out and listened to some of it the other day and I looked at the credits and they're all wrong (laughs). I'm credited on a few tunes, I think maybe one tune I'm credited on I didn't play on and several that I played on I wasn't credited for. I know I played bass on a song — that's a pretty nice credential on a Kool & The Gang record because Kool is actually the bass player. So you get

used to it and it kind of evens itself out. Sometimes you get more credit than you deserve, and sometimes you get less. It never made any difference to me whatsoever; it didn't matter as far as being able to get more work. I don't really care about the credit part. I'm into the music part.

Of course, you would have been compensated for your work on Peter's album, yes?
Oh yeah. Sean paid me very well, probably better than he had to pay me just as a session guy. But since he was a buddy — I can't tell you how much — I remember it being better than it could have been.

The KISS solo albums were a major industry event in 1978. There was a huge marketing and publicity campaign surrounding the albums and they all shipped platinum. Did a sense of sensationalism trickle down to the musicians?
Well, KISS was big as I remember. And the solo records were going to be another big deal. But they didn't kind of turn out to be. That's my take on it. They spent a lot of money and they didn't sell like they thought they would. And I think it really hurt Aucoin. I don't pay too much attention to all that stuff and it's a long time ago, so anything I tell you could be wrong (laughs). But as I remember it, it was a major disappointment. Not necessarily to the guys because I think the guys were all fine. But I think Aucoin really needed the money and had banked on four records selling multi-millions and making tons of more money.

And 1978 was an insane time as far as spending money and having parties and doing drugs, and having dinners with two dozen people hanging out, drinking and partying. Money was going out like insane. I think Bill probably thought it was never going to end. And I think the solo albums were the beginning of the end. Shortly thereafter, I am pretty sure he moved out of his offices on Madison Avenue. He had like two floors of humongous offices, and a theater department and all kinds of people on payroll. God knows how much that must have cost to rent two floors at 645 Madison Avenue. But it couldn't have been cheap. I think he kind of went belly-up, financially, after those solo records. And as I remember, the solo records were part of the reason why.

Some interesting insight, Brendan. The fact is the solo albums did not perform up to expectations, as lofty as those expectations were. The albums were certified gold and platinum by the RIAA. Did you receive an RIAA award for your participation?
No I didn't.

I know Gene Simmons made arrangements to send RIAA awards to some of the people who played on his solo album.
Well, I'm pretty sure Richie [Ranno] got one. I think he plays one solo on one of Gene's tunes.

Correct. He played the solo on "Tunnel Of Love."
Right. I'm pretty sure I remember seeing one at Richie's house. But, you know, I never thought about it. I've got stuff on the wall that means things to me. I don't look at it as thinking, "Why didn't Peter look me up and get me a gold record or platinum record?" It wouldn't have made any difference in my life. Like I said, Tim, that's not what I'm into. I don't hold any grudge about it, that's for sure (laughs).

We've talked about Bill and Sean and both of them are unfortunately no longer with us. When you think about Bill Aucoin, what are the things that immediately come to mind?
Well, I loved Bill. He and Sean — and my guess is that Sean was probably the first one to suggest it — brought my band, what turned into Starz, kind of out of oblivion and into the big time. And he put up a lot of his own money and a lot of his own reputation. So I loved Bill. And I left the band before it all fell apart so I don't have any of the negative feelings about him that some of the other guys had at the time. I think maybe that's changed over the years. I know Richie had some pretty hard feelings and Michael [Lee Smith] had some pretty hard feelings about it. I don't know if they still do. I do remember there was a Starz gig about, I don't know, seven or eight years [ago] in New York and Bill showed up and Michael wouldn't talk to him. So I guess Michael still has some hard feelings toward him. I guess he thought maybe Bill should have worked harder for us and got us with a different record company or something.

But I think Bill did everything he could for us and I think he did a great job, given the band and [our] talent and our songs and records. I think we did about as good as we deserved to do. So I never had any negative feelings. I loved the guy. It was great to see him, seven or eight years ago. He looked great and he showed up and he held up a big Starz sign in the audience. He was dancing around. I thought that was pretty cool. I saw him once here in Nashville. He came to hear some artist and I don't know how I heard about it — whether he got in touch with me or somebody knew he was coming — but I showed up at the club and I saw him. That was maybe 15 years ago. So I only saw him those couple of times since the old days. He was the same old guy, sweet and smart. I only have the best things to say about him. And Sean also.

Of course, Bill and Sean were integral to KISS' success.
Oh yeah, absolutely. Well nobody would have made it without those guys. And my memory is Sean was the one who encouraged Bill to get involved. They got an

invitation or something to go to this show [KISS] put together. And I don't know if Bill was interested but Sean was interested. And they went and Sean said, "Man, you're crazy if you don't get involved with this band." So I think it was Sean who was really instrumental in pulling Bill into KISS. And it was a great combination: Bill and Sean. One was real heavy business and the other was real heavy creatively. And it worked great. They took something that could have fallen flat on its face, and never been remembered, and made it, at times, the biggest band in the world. They did great. I don't think without them, there wouldn't have been any KISS or any of the other artists that came through that management company.

Indeed. The band get a lot of credit, and deservedly so. But without the contributions of Bill Aucoin, Sean Delaney and Neil Bogart, I don't know that KISS comes to fruition.

Well, I don't see how. It was quite a go and it was a real interesting time. And it was interesting to be in the belly of the beast there. I got to kind of live my dreams and play to thousands and thousands of people and hear my songs on the radio and all that stuff. It was a great time. I don't have any regrets about it. I just got burnt out on it. Being on the road with a rock and roll band can be a real pressure cooker and a meat grinder. To tell you the truth, my heart wasn't into ... that kind of music (laughs). I did it because it was cool and it was fun. It wasn't bad music, but it wasn't my ideal [situation]. But being on stages where they were unbelievably loud — ringing in your ears all the time — too much travel, never sleeping in your own bed, and that kind of thing, I just got tired of it after a few years. And I said, "Guys, it's time for me to move on. I'm sure you can find somebody else."

Brendan, who do you cite as your guitar influences?

Well, early on it was guys like Stephen Stills and everyone was influenced by Clapton a bit. Now my influences are the greatest guys in the world, guys like Allan Holdsworth and Frank Gambale.

A couple of monster players.

Yeah, incredible players. I try to strive to be as much like those guys [with] the quality and professionalism of my playing. I think a lot of guys skate by on what they do. They look good and they sound pretty good — why spend all that time becoming great, you know? But I still work on it as hard as I ever did, probably harder. If I'm not working one day, I'll be playing for 10 hours. And I'll be on YouTube looking at Frank Gambale stuff.

Isn't that one of the great things about YouTube? The learning resources that are out there for musicians are unbelievable. Just think, that stuff wasn't available 10 years ago, let alone 35 years ago.

It's incredible, Tim. Young kids — like when I started at 10 — they can go and look at these guys and watch their fingers, anybody they want. I can only imagine what a

15-year-old kid who is highly motivated [is] going to sound like in 20 or 30 years, having all that information available to him. Because it's been a tremendous help to me, as a guy that's been playing guitars for 54 years now. It's a tremendous help for me and motivation to learn and to get better. I love it and I'm still doing it. I'm still doing it as hard as I ever did and I'm making as much music as I ever made.

As someone who has been in the music business for many years, what are your thoughts on the state of music and the industry, and general?
Well, other than the technology, I feel like it's a little bit more than it was in the early '50s before record companies got big and people starting selling humungous amounts of records. People have to kind of do it on their own. The major label thing is there but it's not by any means the only way you can get noticed and heard and make a living. It's like it used to be. People used to make records as a promotional tool, not as a way to sell a lot of records and make money, but as a way to get good gigs and stuff. And that's what [artists] are doing now; it's kind of a similar thing. So I think it's good. I really think that the music business got way out of control — way too much money, way too much drugs, way too much craziness, and way too little focus on music. And I think it's come back to more of a focus on music. There are more great musicians now than ever [and] more people making a living at it. Even if it's just somebody making $50,000 a year! That's great for a young musician or even a middle-aged musician to be able to promote their career on the Internet and go out and travel, even if it's in a van or whatever, with three or four guys, and go out and play clubs and people have already heard your music — not on the radio but on the Internet.

I think what's happened is healthy. And I think anybody that doesn't want to deal with it, they're better off not being in the business. I've seen the business change in major ways a few times, as a player and as a guy who's trying to keep trying to make a living. Every time you just got to adjust to it the same way that guys did when cars took over for horses and buggies. Guys who were making horse and buggy tires had to learn how to make rubber tires or they had to learn how to do something entirely different and get out of the business. Well, that's the same thing with music. If you want to have a lifelong career in music, you have to roll with the punches as far as how the business has changed and not get into saying, "Well, you can't get anywhere anymore. You can't do this and you can't do that." It's really not true. If you have initiative, you can make a success easily as well as you could at any time over the last 40 years. I have a studio now. I do all kinds of mid-level records. I don't do many huge records, although recently I did a record for Michael W. Smith. He's about as big as there [is] in the Christian world.

He's a Grammy-winning artist.
Yeah, I did his last record. It's called "Glory," it's an instrumental record. And I do some records for some other big Christian artists. I don't work with many of the big

country people; although I did a Jeff Foxworthy record back a ways. He did kind of a country music record and [told jokes] in the middle of it. And I work with a lot of the songwriters who write big stuff. But I'm doing very healthy business. Wildwood Recording [is my studio]. I've been here for 20 years and everyone knows about me. And I'm as busy as can be and it's all good.

John Tropea

Renowned jazz/R&B guitarist recalls his work on Peter Criss' 1978 solo album, meeting Gene Simmons and the New York session scene.
Interview by Tim McPhate

John, by the time 1978 rolled around, my understanding is that you had been a session musician for more than a decade and had launched a solo career. Can you give us a general outline as to the status of your musical career in 1978?
John Tropea: I guess by '78 I was just finishing up my third album with TK Records. And I was very busy doing record dates and jingles too. I'd started to work with Tommy LiPuma a lot and some of his associates. We did a lot of record dates out of House of Music in West Orange in [New] Jersey. Me and Tommy did [George] Benson's "Weekend in L.A." out there and stuff with my band and a bunch of other bands. And a lot of times we would do horn dates out there and rhythm sections, me and Steve Gadd out there with Will Lee, myself, Deodato, and the late Hugh McCracken.

You have a heavy jazz background. Who do you cite as some of your guitar influences?
In the early days, when I first started playing, I listened to Johnny Smith, Howard Roberts and a Brazilian guitarist named Louis Bonfá, a phenomenal Brazilian classical guitarist. In those days, I'd listen to Tal Farlow and a bunch of other guys. But mainly Johnny Smith. Until I went to college. I met George Benson when I was at Berklee in '64 with Jack McDuff. He was a big influence. Of course, I should mention Wes Montgomery.

Are there any rock players you admire?
Well, you know, it's funny, I wouldn't call myself a rock player but I loved Hendrix. I thought he was absolutely terrific and so cutting-edge in the beginning days. I didn't play like him because R&B and jazz was my niche. Also, at Berklee School of Music, I played R&B. I used to play with the Three Degrees and a bunch of other R&B bands up there, including my own. To me, if you play rock and roll, you've really got to play rock and roll. I've done rock and roll solos, absolutely. And without going into detail, I've fixed other people's solos — two or three times over the years — famous rock and roll guitar players. But that's just a craft, to fix a solo. They can't get a hold of them and stuff, you know, in those days they didn't have Pro Tools or anything. So I would go in and take whatever they played and fix it. But to get back to that, I'm not really a rock player. But you tell me what to play, and I'll play it.

So with your education and background, did you enjoy playing sessions outside of the jazz genre?
Oh, yes. First of all, I loved working with Bob Ezrin. We did one record for KISS, I believe, where I even did some of the horn charts too. I also did "Alice Cooper Goes To Hell" with Ezrin. So I don't mean to sound like I didn't play rock and roll. I wouldn't go onstage and play rock and roll, let me put it that way. I was good in the studio with it. But I wasn't really one of those dancing around rock players. But I love playing [with] overdrive, roots and fifth and stuff like that, and supporting the whole rock band syndrome.

How did you come to get the invitation to work on Peter Criss' solo album?
Well, I'm pretty sure that we all got the invitation — [Allan] Schwartzberg, Jimmy Maelen, myself, and Neil [Jason] — because we worked with Ezrin on other stuff. I mean that would be the reason why I would be on that record. I didn't know Peter Criss except for the stuff I did with Ezrin. That would be the connection.

I'm thinking it would have likely been Sean Delaney who oversaw the "Peter Criss" sessions you played on.
Honestly, it's been so long. I get those sessions mixed up with the "Alice Cooper Goes To Hell" record and whatever I did with the KISS record. So I'm a little mixed up with the three dates, the three projects.

It's interesting, I was aware of the Alice Cooper album and of course Peter's album. I don't know that I've seen your name tied to another KISS album.
You know, I could be wrong. I remember speaking a lot with the bass player.

Gene Simmons.
Gene. [It was] at the Record Plant. And we were there for about a week and I remember getting really friendly with him. We would talk for hours in the lobby, in the lounge. And I don't know exactly what the record was that I was doing at the time, maybe if you can dig around. I know I probably didn't play on all the cuts. In those days, that was the case a lot of times. They would call different guitar players in for different songs. And that was the case for Peter Criss' record.

You're credited on three tracks on Peter's album. The album was recorded at Electric Lady in New York and at Sunset Sound in Los Angeles. You probably would have been at the New York sessions, which I believe was headed by Sean?
Yeah, I was at Electric Lady.

Do you remember meeting Peter at all?
I know I met him. I don't remember too much about him. I remember more about Gene. I remember that Peter was a very nice guy, and so was Gene for that matter.

They were all very nice. You know, you have to understand, we were doing 10 to 15 record dates a week, working from 10 in the morning to 2 in the morning.

I totally understand. For the purposes of this retrospective, these albums are being put back in the spotlight. But for musicians such as yourself, it was just another session.

Well, you know, I don't mean to make it sound like it wasn't a big deal. It was a nice shot in the arm to say that you played with Gene Simmons or Alice Cooper or Ezrin and Peter Criss. Those are among the higher-level dates. And then there were a lot of dates when I wouldn't even meet the artist. I mean, when I played on "2001" I didn't even know it was me playing the solo when I heard the record on the radio, until I realized, "Wow, that's me." I only remember the rhythm section playing. Everything was done in pieces in those days.

Peter's solo album draws heavily upon R&B and traditional rock and roll flavors. And of course, KISS are very much straight-ahead hard rock. Do you recall that the material on this project reflecting a different direction than KISS' typical musical blueprint?

Oh, I absolutely was aware of that. I mean, playing acoustic guitar on Peter Criss' record definitely takes it out of a hard rock kind of thing. It was definitely understood that it was not the same thing as a KISS record. It was his solo album. Today, we would call it a vanity project, but not a vanity project that's vanity like, but for somebody who's a star.

You've mentioned some of the other musicians on the tracks you played on were drummer Allan Schwartzberg and bassist Neil Jason. At those sessions, I believe there was also guitarist Elliott Randall, and pianist Richard T. Bear. Do you recall tracking with the band live? Or were your parts an overdub situation?

As I remember, I think it was Elliott and myself together with the rhythm section. There may have been a day when we went in and either fixed guitars or did some acoustics on top of what we did. I'm sure there was a day like that because we usually did the rhythm section first with the percussion and then we would sweeten it with any additional guitar solos, doubling and whatever.

And of course, Peter Criss is a drummer but he didn't play on these particular songs. Do you remember that striking you as odd?

Nah, not really. I just viewed it as this big star group and everybody was doing their own solo record. And Peter had not only played great drums, he was a nice singer. I just thought it was the evolution of that kind of a situation, much like when I was with Deodato and I did my own solo album.

Generally speaking, can you give us a snapshot as to how you would have formulated your guitar parts? Did you have a free reign to play? Or was a direction discussed?
Most of the time, with a thing like that, there was nothing really written but chords. And it was discussed with the producer and if there was an arranger. When you worked with Bob Ezrin, Bob never really wrote anything down but he had a pretty clear idea of what he wanted. He'd say, "I want power chords over here. And Tropea I want you to do a solo over here." And that was the same with the Criss record. Nothing was written except for chords, but there was communication between the producer and the guitarist. And Elliott and I would work out parts. We always had a nice knack of working together. There were a few guitar players on the New York scene and we were really good at not overstepping each other's boundaries and really working together for the sake of the record.

Steve Lukather, one of L.A.'s top session players, is also on Peter's album. Obviously, there are some really talented players on this record.
Yeah, I love Steve. He's great.

You recalled playing some acoustic. In terms of your gear, would you remember the guitars and amp you were using for sessions in those days?
I think, if I remember correctly, I played a 12-string on it. I think I blew a high string. Other than that, I played a Fender Tele and I had my own pedal rack. Most of the times in the '70s, most of the gear I used was MXR, like an overdrive and a phaser and a compressor. Today, I pretty much use the same, except it's Boss.

Boss makes some great workmanlike pedals.
Yeah, they're really good.

John, I sent you the three tracks you played on: "I Can't Stop The Rain," "Easy Thing" and "Rock Me Baby." In listening back to these tracks 35 years later, what's your take?
My first impression is they're really good. I think going into digital recording today, they really had a nice production. Everything was good. I was proud to be on it.

Peter's album takes a lot of heat with KISS fans given it was outside the standard KISS fare. And to be candid, some fans simply think Peter's album is lackluster. In listening to these tracks, do you hear anything deficient from a musical perspective to your ears?
I really didn't get that far into it. I would have to listen to the whole album and evaluate it that way. But nothing jumped out at me that it was lacking. Is it the best album with the best choice songs in the world? I just thought it was a successful drummer with a successful group coming out and doing some of his songs and

some of the things he wanted to do as a solo artist. And it was his first record. I don't know how many records he did after that.

After he left the group in 1980, he did two. And in more recent years, he had an album in 2007. KISS releasing four simultaneous solo albums caused quite the stir in the music industry in 1978. You alluded to this earlier, but did playing on a KISS member's solo album seem like a big gig for you at the time?

I played on other sessions that were a bigger deal, absolutely. And when I say bigger deal, it's because I like their music better. Like when I played on Claus Ogerman's record with Michael Brecker, or when I overdubbed on Sanborn's record. That was more in line with what I did. But I was always proud of the fact that I worked with KISS, and Alice Cooper and Bob Ezrin. It was one of the compartments that I was proud of. I did a lot different things. I was playing on those rock and roll records; then I was playing on "Everybody Plays A Fool," which was R&B. Most of my records that I played on in those days, I would say 70 percent, was R&B. Then I'd find myself on jazz records — Ron Carter's record and Hubert Laws and Billy Cobham. It was kind of overwhelming to be able to get calls to play on so many different styles of music, with these guys that were heavyweights. So to answer your question, I'm very proud of the fact that I worked with Peter Criss, and KISS and Ezrin.

You started playing guitar at age 12 and went on to study at Berklee College of Music in Boston. With musicians, there is the age old debate of self-taught musicians vs. formally trained musicians. Are you a proponent of formal training and taking lessons?

Well, first of all, when I was 12 years old, I went to New York and took three [private] lessons a week from one teacher, Giovanni Vicari. I think it's a combination of everything. From the first week I was up at Berklee, I was playing seven nights a week with R&B groups and some jazz groups, but mostly R&B. So I don't think it's just one thing, unless you're just aspiring to be a classical guitarist. Just being self-taught is not the only way to go. Although, if you look at George Benson, he really is a phenomenal self-taught guitarist who doesn't read a note of music. But he's one in 10,000. So I think you need to study with a teacher, it's good to go to school and it's good to play out live — a combination of those three things is my way of thinking. And when I was 12 years old, I have to say, I always wanted to be the guy in the studio recording with the artist. I set out to do at 12 years old what I did my entire career.

Fantastic, you obviously made that happen. In terms of your recent solo activity, you released a studio album, "Take Me Back To The Ol' School," in 2007. This album contains a beautiful rendition of the Beatles' "The Long And Winding Road," featuring Lalah Hathaway on vocals. You play some beautiful guitar lines in this cover. How did you go about arranging this version?
Well that record was co-produced by me and Will Lee. Me and Will developed the arrangements together. The credit goes to both of us. I'm very proud of that record. I'm working on my 13th album right now. I did a video with Chris Palmaro called "Boulevard Strut."

That came out last year?
Yeah, in 2012. That's going to be on the new album and the title is "Got Your Rhythm Right Here." It's really heavily emphasizing rhythm playing, although I solo too.

Is there a tentative release date?
Hopefully it will be done by the end of the summer [2013]. [I've been] on the road with the Blues Brothers. [I'm hoping] to finish it up in August, depending on my schedule.

Aside from touring and your new album, do you still do a lot of session gigs?
Well, I'm not the 25-year-old hotshot session player anymore (laughs). The business has changed all around. People send me MP3 tracks to solo and I send them out. Like the last Deodato record, I did my solos out of my own studio. I never played with any other musicians. It's just changed. There [are] still dates that are going on, of course. But I don't do as many as I used to, none of us do.

So it's more of a virtual session scene.
Exactly, yes. Although, I'm doing this new record live. The new record is with a rhythm section. We actually have the whole thing simmarranged. As soon as we do the rhythm track, the horns come in, like the old days. Because it's a different thing when you sit next to an organ player and a drummer and a bass player; and you develop the recording that way.

Art Munson

Guitarist on Peter Criss' solo album checks in with a message, plus a brief Q&A.
By Tim McPhate

(Editor's Note: KISSFAQ caught up with guitarist Art Munson via email. After sending the tracks from Peter Criss' 1978 solo album on which he is featured, Munson responded with the following message. Subsequently, he agreed to answer a handful of questions.)

"I listened to the tracks and my first impression is that they are a lot better then I remembered them at the time. Vini [Poncia] was the producer on all the sessions I worked on. I believe that Peter had recently survived an automobile accident and this was one of his first gigs after the accident. It really was just another couple of days of session work for me so once they were over it was on to the next." — Art Munson, guitarist, "Peter Criss"

What was Vini Poncia like in the studio? A task master or more laid back?
Art Munson: I remember him as [being] easygoing.

Do you recall if you tracked your guitars live, or were they overdubbed?
I was working on the live tracks. No overdubs that I recall.

Did you play rhythm guitar or leads (or both)?
Pretty sure it was mostly rhythm.

You are correct in saying Peter recently had been in a car accident. Did you meet Peter at all? Any general impressions?
I did meet Peter as he was playing live with us. No distinct impression. I don't remember him having any kind of attitude because of who he was — pretty straight ahead. We were just a bunch of guys in a room playing together.

Neil Jason

Renowned studio musician discusses his bass double-duty on Peter Criss and Gene Simmons' solo albums.
Interview by Tim McPhate

Neil, going back to 1978, how did the opportunity to play on not one, but two of the KISS solo albums?
Neil Jason: Well, there were a lot of sessions going on back then. And one musician talks to another musician, et cetera, et cetera. A lot of the guys that were playing on Peter's record like Allan Schwartzberg and Elliott Randall were already really good friends of mine, so were the producers involved in all this stuff. I got called into Peter's sessions and I did [those] with Sean [Delaney] and that led to the sessions with Gene.

There were a couple of bass players on Peter's album. According to the lyric sheet, you played on the tracks "Easy Thing," "Rock Me, Baby" and "I Can't Stop The Rain."
Yeah, that sounds about right.

And Sean Delaney was overseeing these sessions?
Absolutely. Well, actually, now I can't remember who was in the booth producing, maybe it was Jack Ponti?

I don't believe so. Vini Poncia is credited as the album's co-producer with Peter.
Oh okay. [I think] Vini was in the booth. And I think, I can't remember some of the sessions, but a lot of these tunes were written and arranged by Sean for Peter to do.

Yes, two of the above tracks were Sean's.
Therefore, inside the studio, Sean took us through everything but Vini and the engineer were, as far as I remember, in the booth taking care of business and keeping us going forward. But Sean was like producing the band on a lot of the stuff. And it was basically like demos that Sean was looking to help Peter [with] and get this thing done. I don't remember how many tracks over how many days, but I definitely remember "I Can't Stop The Rain" ... it was very cool. They were great sessions [at] Electric Lady.

So you were part of the New York sessions only?
Yeah, it was a groove. It was a great time.

Do you recall Peter being around?
Yeah, I recall Peter being there a number of times. I think I remember a session where Peter wasn't there and Sean sang the vocal while we did the tracks so we could get them done. I remember another one with Peter from beginning to end. They were just getting tracks ready and done for Peter who I guess was busy on other stuff at the same time.

You all are obviously highly seasoned musicians. Generally, how many takes would it have taken to get a final?
It wasn't like a long and drawn-out affair. We'd rehearse it for a little while and then we'd do a couple takes. It was pretty straight ahead — they knew what they wanted. It wasn't like they were going into territory where it was like, "Holy cow, how do we play in 7/8 time over some jazz thing?" It was stuff they were in love with and were familiar with so it was us kind of catching up to them sometimes. So it moved very quickly.

As it turns out, Peter's album proved to be quite a departure from KISS' typical sound. There were some old-time rock and roll, R&B and soul influences sprinkled throughout. I'm curious if you recall any discussion that this material might be a little left-of-center for KISS' audience.
Well, obviously there's quite a few ways for us to look at it as sidemen and as musicians. But if your entire career is defined by the band and you want to do a "solo record" — which means you step away from the band — then maybe you do something that you wanted to do. Now if you didn't want to do anything else, like, "Well, I kind of just want to do that," then he would have done that. And as far as the production decisions, I think a lot of the tunes were chosen for Peter's voice and they sounded great and I didn't see it as a departure from KISS. It was Peter Criss, who is part of KISS. So some of the tunes are right there and some of them aren't. But that's how Peter sings. If you liked "Beth," then you'd like this.

Well said, Neil. There are certainly songs on the lighter side, a la "Beth," like "Easy Thing" and "I Can't Stop The Rain." I don't know, I just think the fans were expecting something different from Peter.
Well, I'm assuming that the fans that love them dearly and listen to every note wanted four KISS albums at the same time because that would just about be enough at the same time for them. But, they got, I don't know, two KISS albums — actually, they got four KISS albums. There are four personalities that make KISS and that's why those four guys have a sound. It's like if George Harrison does a record, it didn't necessarily sound like the Beatles. If Ringo did a record, it didn't sound like the Beatles. You know what I mean?

Sure.
But together, that was the Beatles.

As a fan, I've read quite a bit about these albums over the years. The late Stan Penridge, who was Peter's confidant and writing partner, described the New York sessions at Electric Ladyland as being chaotic and mentioned that Vini deserved some credit for salvaging the takes. Do you know what Stan was referring to?
Um (pauses), not really. I do remember working hard. I do remember us concentrating. Chaotic? As much as dealing with what they had to deal with schedule-wise — people not showing up, people running back and forth, people having things to do. I kind of remember not thinking about that or dealing with that very much. So I can't swear that it happened. It might have happened with other tracks they were recording. Like I said, I think "I Can't Stop The Rain" was a night where Peter couldn't make it. We didn't know why he didn't make it, et cetera, et cetera. But Vini made sure the stuff got recorded. And Sean ran the studio and had it perfect, in the right key, sang it for us, the whole thing, had it down for Peter so that he could overdub on it. He showed up the next day as I remember. Yeah, chaotic? It is a recording session. You're not going to a spa. So sometimes it gets chaotic, yeah.

Switching to Gene's album, sessions took place in L.A. at Cherokee Studios, Blue Rock Studio in New York, and at a couple of locations in England.
Right, I think I'm on the whole record.

Yes, I believe so.
I don't remember if there were just meetings in New York or there were actual sessions in New York. I pretty much almost remember every single track getting done in England and that New York and L.A. were for overdubs. I'm almost positive.

Did you find it odd to play bass on Gene Simmons' album since he was a bass player himself?
Well, first off, I actually was honored and thrilled that a bass player of his stature [asked me to play] — because in his band, this guy rules. He plays the right stuff, sings the right stuff. If [you] see them in concert, what they do is pretty amazing. Try putting on the gear and doing songs like that and playing for three hours and making people have a party — this is not easy. He played great on all the things he ever played on. So for him to want another bass player, because he wanted to concentrate on the songs and on singing and production and guitar playing, I appreciated that. I thought it was unbelievable. So I got an amazing chance to work with him. And on some tunes, yeah I tried to play like I was Gene Simmons. And on the other tunes I did stuff that Gene would not think to do, but it matched his song. It was cool. It was a lot of fun.

Did Gene give any suggestions for bass parts?
Oh, absolutely. All the time. And again, Sean and I think Gene together had already done a handful of [demos of] the songs, as far as I remember, that were pretty

convincing, even if it was piano and voice, that told you exactly what you needed to play. And of course, when we did it, Gene and Sean and Mike Stone behind the board all had great suggestions. I mean, come on, we were playing rock and roll.

Gene's album was highly eclectic. There were straight-ahead rock numbers like "Radioactive," Beatle-esque forays such as "See You Tonite" and songs featuring choirs and orchestras such as "Always Near You/Nowhere To Hide." Were you around for any of the orchestral recording?
I'm trying to remember where that happened. I was around for one of the sessions, yeah. And maybe Frangipane arranged it or something. It was very well done.

Yes, it was Ron Frangipane who did the arrangements, including the haunting introduction to the album.
Yeah, it's fantastic. He did amazing stuff.

It's such a left-field way to kick off the album. You have this swirling arrangement, Janis Ian singing in Latin and I believe Sean's voice is going through a harmonizer.
I met Janis — you got to remember, this thing is a snapshot of the times. And it's part of Gene's history. Again, you hear like half of the songs on the record — they're pretty close to pure KISS: it's Gene singing and it's his tune and we're rocking. And some of the tunes are departures — but not really, it's part of Gene's history. That's what the record's supposed to be. If he did more solo records, he would change with the times because his history would change. It's like KISS, you know, doing what they do together. So I really didn't see any of [the songs] as, "Wow, that's like the wrong thing to do." I think it was a very cool record.

Gene secured a cavalcade of stars. Aside from Janis Ian, there was Donna Summer, Cher, Joe Perry, Bob Seger, Helen Reddy, Rick Nielsen...
It was fantastic. Cher came out to the Manor in England and stayed with us and the band and Gene for — I don't know — we were there for a couple of months. Cher was there for a while with the family and she was fantastic. Some of the sessions were very intense, we'd stay there all night. I remember Allan Schwartzberg, the drummer, I'm pretty sure it happened on this session, [on] one of the tunes like "Radioactive," where Sean and Gene and Mike Stone wanted to get a really big drum sound. They sent the drums out into like the garage or something. Allan's drums were set up and we could only see him on the video camera. They got this amazing drum sound [with] natural echo. It was ridiculous. So the next morning we go down to record and if I remember correctly Allan goes around the drums one time. It was pretty early and he breaks like two or three skins and goes right through the bass drum because it got so cold in there overnight, but the heads, they were ready to pop! So they had to stack up heaters in the room and redo all

the heads. But it turned out sounding really amazing. It was part of a hysterical morning in recording history.

Neil, legend has it that Gene tried to secure the Beatles to guest on the album. Do you recall talk about the Beatles appearing on the album?
Actually, I don't recall. I don't doubt that it happened. But I don't recall any conversation about it.

He ended up securing Mitch Weismann and Joe Pecorino from Beatlemania to add Beatle-esque harmonies to some of the tunes.
Absolutely.

Sean and Gene are credited as co-producers. From your vantage point, was Gene as invested from a production standpoint as Sean?
Well, you got to figure the artist would be as invested as the producer. But I mean, Sean was a very intense producer. And Gene is a very intense artist and Mike Stone was a very intense engineer and he had a fairly intense all-star rhythm section. When we got down to business, it was good. We actually kind of sequestered ourselves and worked hard and came up with some nice stuff.

One rumor that I've heard is that Gene took to referring to the musicians by the name of their instruments during sessions. Does this ring a bell?
No, doesn't ring a bell to me. Even in a number of interviews that Gene has done, he was more than kind enough to me and a number of other guys on his solo record, which I thought was very kind. No, he remembered exactly who we were and he was a sweetheart. And if he called me, "Hey bass," it was probably an endearing funny moment. But no, I do remember my name being used (laughs).

And of course he ended his album with a major left-turn with his cover of "When You Wish Upon A Star."
Yeah, loved it.

Given your unique perspective, I'm wondering if you recall a dynamic of tacit competition during the tracking of these albums. In other words, did you get the sense that Gene and Peter wanted to "outdo" their bandmates?
No, you know what, I never actually heard that. And anybody making a CD wants to show everybody what they're made of. Just being in a band would make you want to show everybody, and everybody in the band, what you're made of. But it doesn't really change the objective of making your own album. So no, I never heard anything about it. But I wouldn't doubt it. You're in competition with everybody, including everybody in your band. It's not like you're just against them. It's a really big chart. You're against everybody (laughs).

Regarding your compensation, would this have been a union gig for you?
Actually, I don't remember.

But you did get fairly compensated?
Yes, of course.

You obviously met Gene and Peter. Ever come across the other two KISS members, Ace and Paul?
No, I don't remember meeting Ace and Paul at Peter's session at Electric Lady. But I thought I remembered meeting Paul, but I think we were playing at that time. So I would say I never met Paul or Ace and I wish I had. They had fantastic records too. I thought that everybody had a really good album.

Going back to the albums' release in September 1978, what do you recall regarding the publicity for the project?
I think back then it was a pretty good, not a stunt, but a pretty monumental thing. I don't think anybody with an actual band that was still together maybe had ever done that yet?

That's correct.
That everybody released one at the same time, as the band was still together, I would think as far as marketing goes that there's so many plusses to that it's like, "Hey, they have the time to do that because that is some kind of serious stuff." It's not like, "Okay, the four of us will go make records." That's four times as much KISS. They could have made one record with the four of them, or they could have made four KISS records. I mean, that's a lot of work. So somebody enjoyed the idea. And let's face it, I mean they'd been recording together for a long time. Sometimes, it's like, "You know what, I really want to play with those other kids down the block, just for like 10 minutes, and I'll be right back."

This April marked the 10th anniversary of the passing of Sean Delaney? Can you give us a snapshot of what it was like to work with Sean?
Sean was meticulously artistic, sometimes relentless. But otherwise he was a great influence. And he had a vision and the guys trusted his vision. And it was great to have somebody who had that much focus all the time.

A final question, Neil. What are you up to these days, musically?
I still write and arrange for a lot of different things. But right now I'm working with Brigitte Zarie. We're about to release her new CD and we're going to master it and have that out real soon.

Richard T. Bear

Pianist shares memories of playing on Gene Simmons and Peter Criss' solo albums, the New York scene, stories of his own career as a solo artist and songwriter, and offers perspective on working with the late Sean Delaney and being 30 years sober.
Interview by Tim McPhate

Richard, can you give us a snapshot of your career in 1978?
Richard T. Bear: Around 1978 I was signed to RCA. I had a solo album out. I was touring, before the album "Red, Hot & Blue" came out, with Billy Squier's band Piper, and the Babys, who had John Waite. The three of us were on tour together and we played free concerts for radio stations all over the West.

And how did you come into the KISS fold?
How I got to know KISS was playing in New York as a session player. I was hooked up with a couple of guys and we would play a lot of dates together. Then we would hang out at a place called Trax. I was also hanging out at Catch A Rising Star, The Improv, because I loved comedy, JP's, and Dr. Generosity's. And there was another place called Trudy Hellers and another called Reno Sweeney. But I was at Trax a lot because I lived close by. JP's was on the East Side, and had kind of a more folkie vibe, like James Taylor and Jackson Browne. JP, the owner of that club, opened Trax, which was a total rock and roll vibe. It was kind of like a Whisky or a Troubadour. Everybody would fall by there to play. I was over there playing and this guy kept walking in front of the stage, back and forth, in this whole leather outfit, with kind of a handle-bar mustache. He'd go back and forth and back and forth and glare at me (laughs). And during the break, he introduced himself as Sean Delaney. So that's how my involvement with KISS started, through Sean.

In 1978 KISS were arguably at the peak of their popularity. Did you have any impression of their music?
No, only because I didn't know much about them. I grew up working at Manny's Music on West 48th Street and getting free passes to the Fillmore [East]. I was 16 and I'd go down and see Iron Butterfly and Led Zeppelin would open for them. And then I'd see bands like the Who, Hendrix, Bowie and the Stones. I was like, "That's it, man." What I found out about KISS was that they were kind of a good rock and roll band that discovered that the kabuki makeup and the lasers and the fire, and the show — it was smoke and mirrors more than it was ability. Seeing them in the beginning, they were very raw, which was kind of cool. But it was more like cartoon characters coming to life. Now, I thought the show was the best visual spectacle I ever saw.

So you saw them live?
Oh yeah. In fact, I went out with them when they were doing their movie.

"KISS Meets The Phantom Of The Park," which was filmed in spring 1978. Did you go to the show at Magic Mountain?
I was at that show.

That's a legendary show among KISS fans.
It was great.

So you were impressed the spectacle of the KISS concert?
I was impressed and I'll tell you why. I learned a lot about live shows from being the opening act for Boston, the Outlaws, Doobie Brothers, and Peter Wolf. Peter used to tell me, "You've got to do this. You've got to do that. You've got to get the audience involved." And KISS were great at that. Sean was great at that. Sean got me so fucking high and drunk, and we carried on like you couldn't believe everywhere (laughs). We'd fly to lots of different places together a lot, places like L.A., and get in all kinds of situations. There was another guy who worked for them, was it Alan?

Alan Miller?
Alan Miller, who I liked a lot. There was another guy I didn't like so much. But anyway, I got to start knowing Paul a little bit, Gene a little bit, Peter a little bit. Ace, I never spoke to. We never really had a relationship. The one thing I do remember is Sean said to me, "I was kind of instrumental in putting a lot of this together," which he really was. He had the vision. And he said, "They all want to do solo albums. I'd like for you to work with me on their solo albums." So Sean and I started writing some songs together. Then he put me in touch with Gene. Gene liked me. We put a band together and I don't remember if I did Peter's album first or Gene's album first. But I do remember that we all went to London.

Yes, some of the sessions for Gene's album took place at the Manor in Oxford.
Right. We all went to the Manor. Now I went to the Manor a few times to record there. I was in the Manor with Sean with a band called Toby Beau. "My Angel Baby," I played on that. I had lived in London for a bit and knew the scene. I went to the Manor with the guys. We flew over in a Concorde, which was amazing (laughs).

Who would have been on that flight? People like Gene, Allan Schwartzberg, Neil Jason?
Yeah. Allan, Neil and I think Elliott Randall. That was like a little rhythm section I had. We all went over there. I think even Cher was with us.

I know you wrote a song on Cher's 1979 album, "Take Me Home."

It's all incestuous (laughs). I was in England for a long time and I remember just sitting around not doing a whole lot. And then they pretty much brought me in for some overdubs.

So on Gene's record, was it an overdub situation for your piano tracks?
Yeah. I think it wasn't anything else other than that.

Gene has a co-producer credit but was Sean running those sessions?
Yeah. Sean was basically running it. Actually, Peruvian marching dust was running those sessions (laughs).

(Laughs) What was the demeanor like in the studio?
I'll tell you what the demeanor was like going over on that Concorde (laughs). Everybody realized that it was only a three-and-a-half-hour flight instead of an eight-and-a-half-hour flight and everybody was in the bathroom most of the time. We had to finish everything we had before we got there. I remember Sean Delaney, may he rest in peace, went back to the bathroom because somebody was in there. He starts pounding on the bathroom door and it was like the president of Nigeria in there, literally the president of a country. And the guy comes out and Sean's going, "This ain't no R&B gig, let me in!" (Laughs)

(Laughs) Sean sounds like he liked to get in trouble.
Back in the day, cocaine and alcohol kind of ruled, although Gene was totally abstinent. And Cher did nothing. But the rhythm section and Sean, we were having some fun. I remember the techs at the Manor would fight to see who was going to go in there in the morning first and they would take the modules and scoop stuff up (laughs).

You ended up playing piano on two tracks. Why don't we take a listen to a sample of "True Confessions." (plays sample)
I didn't have much to do (laughs). A two-headed monkey could have come in and done that.

Those are pretty much straight triads.
Triads in straight eight-note rhythm.

Would they have played you the track and you came up with that part? Or did someone specifically suggest that idea?
I think that was Sean saying, "This is what I want. I just want eighths on this."

You probably banged that out in no time.
Probably. It was probably a late night when I overdubbed it. It was probably one or two takes.

Any thoughts on that track?
(Pauses) The backgrounds ... who's singing on that?

That's Helen Reddy.
Helen Reddy, really? Wow. I don't remember much about that track to be honest with you. I just played it. And I think when I played it, it had none of the sweetening. When I played it there were no background vocals.

And maybe Gene's vocal wasn't even done at that point?
Probably not. I think he did his vocals later.

How does a track like this hold up for you all these years later?
My opinion is it was a basic rock and roll track. Nothing special about it. You know, it's funny because a bunch of us went over, if I recall, a bunch of us went over to George Harrison's house.

No kidding? That's interesting because Gene was supposedly attempting to secure the Beatles. Ultimately, he couldn't secure them so he got the guys from Beatlemania. So you guys hung out with George Harrison?
Yeah, we went over to his house.

The next track you're featured on is "Always Near You/Nowhere To Hide." (plays sample)
It's funny because Sean always liked the Spector wall of sound. That was a big, big thing with him.

This track definitely has that flavor, and there are some other Spector-esque productions on this album.
There is. After listening to the whole record, when it was finished, I found it was a whole bunch of different things. It wasn't like one direction that this record went in.

Which is I think what KISS fans expected.
Yeah. It was a lot of different styles and ideas.

And he had the kitchen sink with the Disney cover of "When You Wish Upon A Star."
Yeah, it was Heinz 57 varieties. That's what I remember.

From what you observed, was Gene serious about the project?
Oh, Gene's really serious and really intense about things that he does. But I think what happened was there might have been distractions at the time.

Cher?
(Laughs) He was pulled into some different directions, doing different things. He was always a huge publicity hound so he was off doing things and kind of left Sean in charge.

Gene has admitted he had an "angle" for his album. Aside from the breadth of the material, he had a huge cast of special guests. There was Cher, Donna Summer, Joe Perry, Rick Nielsen, Helen Reddy. Getting into Peter's album, Sean was involved with that album in the beginning because Peter was having an issue securing a producer. He had approached Tom Dowd.
Interestingly enough, Tom Dowd was my mentor. I grew up in New York and Florida and I used to see Tom all the time. He was down in Miami. I got him to do a band for A&M around the same time, Pablo Cruise. I think I tried to get him for Peter.

So maybe you had a hand in helping with Peter's ask?
I might have had a hand in that. It sounds like I might have made a phone call. But Dowd was doing something else.

That's interesting. I'm not entirely sure of the exact chronology, but I believe Sean stepped in to help Peter. He got musicians like you, Allan Schwartzberg and Neil Jason and recorded some tracks, some of which he had written. And the goal was to put together a demo tape that would help get Peter a producer. Vini Poncia ended up coming onboard and he ultimately kept some of the tracks that Sean cut at Electric Lady. You played on "I Can't Stop The Rain," which is a lush ballad that closes the album. Do you recall being at Electric Lady?
Yeah, I had been in there a bunch of times. I used to go in there and do a lot of session work.

Do you recall Peter being around?
Yeah, I think he popped in a couple of times.

Did you get any vibe from him?
It's really interesting, the New York guys have a vibe all their own. Hand to God. Here's an example, I played on "Southern Cross" for Crosby, Stills & Nash. I lived with Stills for a while. Unlike that vibe — the Jackson Browne, West Coast vibe — the New York guys that made it were completely different. Everything about them was different. I was in an offshoot of the Rascals called Bulldog featuring Gene Cornish, Dino Danelli and John Turi. And they had this whole New York, New Jersey vibe. Peter was totally like that. He was totally like Dino in a lot of ways. He would come by and hang out for a little bit, not a long time, and then he'd be gone. And then three hours later, he'd stop by again. I think that was, in his mind, "I recorded today."

Interestingly, he didn't play drums on any of the New York tracks.
I always thought that was a bit strange, but then again he was a singer. He had "Beth." That was a big, big record.

Why don't we play a bit of "I Can't Stop The Rain." I'm not sure how you feel about ballads.
I love ballads.

(Plays sample)
That's a really good track.

Did you come up with the piano accompaniment? Or was that already written?
I think it was probably — and I'm going to be stretching here — from the demo where Sean and I had done a little lick that worked for him. He probably said, "Let's use that little figure." But I was always given a lot of free rein unless I was stepping on someone's dick or something. "No, there's going to a guitar part there. We don't need the piano there." It was kind of like, "Let's do a great ballad." Because of Peter's success with "Beth," you know. I think a lot of that had to do with "Beth."

Your piano is really center stage on that track. To be candid, Peter's solo album is perhaps the most maligned of the four, but this song is considered a favorite by a segment of fans.
(Laughs) Well, it was a Sean Delaney song. And that may be around the time that I wrote "Love & Pain (Pain In My Heart)," the Cher tune. It's got that same kind of vibe to it. But I think we did a demo of that for her. We did some demos — I wonder if I have any of Sean's demos.

You also played piano on the tune "Spotlights (And Lonely Nights)," which was featured on Sean's 1979 solo album, "Highway." This tune was reportedly demoed for Peter Criss' 1978 album. (Plays sample of Delaney's version.)
I remember doing the demo in a New York studio.

So this tune rings a bell?
Yes. It's fuzzy, but ... (pauses)

And who knows, it could be lying around on one of these tapes?
Could be.

When would have been the last time you saw any of the KISS members?
Interestingly enough, I ran into Paul at a Starbuck's one day and he was very kind and nice to me. And then I ran into Gene a few years back, he was having a book signing and I went to a Barnes & Noble. And maybe because he was with a lot of people, but he wasn't especially warm. I found that to be very weird. He was just

different. I don't remember him ever being like that. Maybe he was just busy at the time. Or since we hadn't talked for a few years, I may have caught him by surprise.

When was the last time you saw Sean?
The last time I saw Sean was in the late '90s. He was playing in a country band and he was at the Orange County Fair. Around the same time, I ran into Bill Aucoin, who was trying to get back into the industry.

Was it a good meeting with Sean?
Very much so. It was great. There were big hugs involved. He was so happy to see me. He was living in Utah and my biggest regret is I never got to see him again after that because I wanted to write more with him. At the time, I kind of took a hiatus from music. I put my last records out in Europe, because I got a record deal in Europe, into the late '80s, early '90s. Then I took a hiatus because I got married and started raising kids. Somehow Sean got a hold of me and I met him at the Orange County Fair. I wanted to write with him again because he had cleaned a lot of his act up. And I cleaned my act up. I got sober, believe it or not, February 8, 1983. I just celebrated 30 years of sobriety.

That's wonderful. Congratulations.
Thanks. I told Sean about an event that I had and we were talking about him coming and playing at it. I was on the board of directors for a thing called the Musicians Picnic. I used to get all kinds of people. I was playing with Mick Fleetwood and got him to come, [and] then I got Clapton to come and talk and play, and Chicago, and a bunch of people. We had that thing going for almost 25 years. It was a nonprofit organization that would put musicians who had no insurance into detox, and then into a sober living environment. Before there was MusiCares [Ed: The Recording Academy's nonprofit charitable organization], there was MAP — Musicians Assistance Program. I was at the start of MAP with a guy named Buddy Arnold. I got sober and Buddy invited me over to his house and we started the musicians meetings. There were like 12 of us — Paul Butterfield, Ray Sharkey, an actor, Dick Forest. A lot of those people died — there's only a few of us left. I remember saying to Sean, "I'm doing this thing called the Musicians Picnic. Maybe you come out?" And he never did it. I was really involved and invested in getting musicians sober. I think I stepped down the 21st or 22nd year, because I had enough (laughs). But that's kind of my legacy.

That's a great legacy to have. Do you know if Sean tried to get sober in his final years?
He tried a few times. For him, it was pretty good.

From your vantage point, just how talented was Sean Delaney?
Extremely talented. Maybe KISS would have eventually evolved but he was definitely a linchpin. Between Bill Aucoin, Sean Delaney and a few other people, I think they were the reasons that KISS happened. I will say that as far as intelligence and all that, Sean was kind of a tortured soul because he would envision himself as being like the fifth KISS member.

That's kind of his nickname, "the fifth KISS."
Right. As far as putting the show together, he was a genius. There's no question in my mind. If there was ever a KISS museum, they should have a statue for Sean Delaney.

Well said, Richard. There is a song called "All-American Man" from "Alive II" that was written by Paul Stanley and Sean Delaney. Sean once alleged that you helped co-write this song even though you were not credited.
(Laughs) I can't tell you how many times that happened.

(Laugh) Right. (Plays sample) Does this tune ring any bells?
Yeah. I think I was involved. The thing about when you get to be in rarified air, when you're there, you realize how much the publishing is worth. The writing is 100 percent and the publishing is 100 percent. None of those guys wanted to give up anything because that's where a lot of the money was. And unless they were taking your song or whatever, that was that. Look, I've played on a lot of demo dates where I have said, "How about go to this change? How about use this chord?" Or, "Here's a great phrase that might work." And it ended up on the record but my name never did. I have one which is sitting up there [points at his wall of platinum records] that I could have easily been given a piece. But I got paid for the sessions.

Speaking of which, I take it you got compensated fairly for your work on Gene and Peter's albums?
Absolutely, Sean took great care of me.

A few questions about yourself, if I may. What city were you born in?
New York City.

How long have you been in California?
I've been out here, on and off, for about 25 years.

Do you visit New York at all?
I do on occasion. I do miss it. I used to miss it terribly but I've become a Californian. I do have a family home there so I do go back. A year ago last summer, I got a call from Dino Danelli to join the Rascals and take Felix Cavaliere's spot and sing and play all the Rascals stuff. We had rehearsals here with a couple of the guys that he

chose for the band. It was going to be called Dino Danelli's Rascals, because they weren't all getting along. We were supposed to go out in the fall and we didn't because he didn't get the kind of money he wanted. And then what happened was Steve Van Zandt got them all to bury the hatchet and do a reunion, which happened last December at the Capitol Theatre in Port Chester. They sold out four nights and then they did a Broadway revival of the Rascals. Now they're doing limited dates and this and that. So we've put Dino Danelli's Rascals on the back burner. But that could come back. I was going to do it because I really like Dino and I love the Rascals songs. I was going to go back to New York for that stuff.

Your real name is Richard Gerstein. How did you get the stage name Richard T. Bear?
I played on lots of records under Gerstein. Interestingly enough, one of the first records that I played on that I remember was a Richie Havens record. He had just passed on. I played on that record, I was really young. They asked, "What name should we put on the credits?" I said, "Gerstein." And people had started calling me Bear. It was a nickname because I had a beard and long hair. When RCA wanted to sign me as a solo artist, I said "I'm Richard Gerstein." I had a big fight with my dad over this. He said, "That's your name. Be proud of it." And RCA went, "Jews don't sell in the South." And I said, "What about Springsteen?" (Laughs) They said, "No, we're going to use Richard T. Bear." Lots of stuff has Gerstein on it, lots of stuff has Bear. My Facebook page, I put Richard T. Bear in parentheses. With the sobriety thing, I was known as T. Bear for so long.

The "T" is your middle initial?
Yes, it's the middle initial. I think I had a contest once, "Guess what T stands for?" The one that I liked the most, I think Sean said. Sean said, "Trustworthy." (Laughs) So he named it and I kept Richard T. Bear.

Richard, who would you cite as your top musical influences?
(Pauses) The Beatles, the Who, the Stones, King Curtis, because he used to take me to shows. Richie Havens, I loved him. Odetta. Zeppelin. I loved Hendrix. Bowie. Stevie Ray Vaughan.

Do you listen to any current acts?
I listen to Mumford & Sons and the Lumineers. I like some of the Foo Fighters' stuff. And Gary Clark Jr. He's the real deal. My daughter is in love with My Chemical Romance. She's 14. My son is 16 and he's into rap. My 19-year-old is into country.

But when you want to unwind, you play the classics?
Yeah. I have an iPod. I just put it on shuffle because I've got 4,000, 5,000 songs on it.

Have plans for new music?

I got divorced a few years back and I remarried three years ago. My current wife Nina is an incredible muse and loves music. There's always music in my house. I started writing again — I have about 100 or 200 ideas. I think I'm going to end up doing another record. I had seven solo records in total, when you count the European releases, and now I'm going to do another one.

Good for you. Of course, you are known for "Sunshine Hotel," which became a hit in 1979. How does that song hold up for you some 30-plus years later?

I had a Top 5 hit with "Sunshine Hotel" in England. It was big over there at the time so I was riding the crest over there. By the way, that's the same rhythm section that's on Gene's record, Schwartzberg and Jason. My take on that is I still get residuals. It's been sampled about a dozen times and it's a big dance record still in house music. It's been at raves and all kinds of stuff (laughs).

Tom Saviano

Renowned L.A.-based session musician revisits his horn arrangements for Peter Criss' 1978 solo album and how he got his proper career start as an arranger and session musician, lends interesting insight into working with Vini Poncia, and provides his opinion on how Criss' album holds up 35 years later.
Interview by Tim McPhate

Tom, you have been described as a top session musician on the West Coast music scene. If we go back to 1978, what was your status as a musician?
Tom Saviano: In '78 I was back in town from Melissa Manchester's tour and had previously done some of her albums. Up to that point, I had done quite a few albums for Vini Poncia. Vini gave me my first big time opportunity in the studio realm as an arranger and saxophone player. I had recorded previous to that with a group called Churchill. I did all the arranging — as a matter of fact, I wasn't even the leader of the group. I was a horn player that was added to an existing rock group that had a previous album. I think they were called Churchill Downs. They were a power trio similar to Grand Funk Railroad. Rock bands with horns began to surface around the late '60s, early '70s. Tower Of Power, Blood, Sweat & Tears and Chicago were very popular. Churchill decided to add horns." So, I joined the band along with three other horn players.

The first three songs I ever wrote were recorded by this band. For some reason, the powers that be at the record company basically thought that I should be the leader of the band. That didn't sit well with the power trio because it was originally their record deal. I said, "I never asked for it." The record company said, "Well, he's the natural leader. He's writing all of the arrangements for the band and he's written a substantial amount of the songs on the new album." It never really got any further than that. The album got released but a big lawsuit followed. Frank Zappa's manager Herb Cohen got involved, which led us to three years of disappointment about the music business. I thought to myself, "Wow, here's what I really wanted to do and it turns out the first damn thing I do turns into a lawsuit." So I traveled around the country in various bands for about three or four years while residing in Orange County. Then, one evening I was playing at a club in Marina Del Rey with one of the bands I was in. It was a club band, but we were doing originals. It was a very good band. Vini Poncia was in the audience with a recording artist by the name of Gino Cunico, whom he happened to be producing.

Around what year was this?
Around 1973, '74. Vini called me over to his table and I was skeptical and laughing a little because my previous experience with the "big time" resulted in a lawsuit

(laughs). He asked me to sit down and he told me who he was. To be honest with you, at that time, I didn't know who he was. I didn't know he was Ringo's producer and that he had done Melissa's first album with her first hit, "Midnight Blue." He just said, "My name is Vini Poncia. I really like your group. We'd like you to be the backup group for Gino to support his new album. He's signed to Clive Davis." For me, none of this was ringing a bell. I just kind of laughed. He said, "If we can't get the whole group, we'd be happy just to have you." And I thought, "Well, I don't know." He said, "Do me a favor. Come on up to Fidelity Recording Studios in Studio City and we'll play some tracks for you and jam a little. You'll see that this is the real thing." And I said, "Okay."

So I started commuting up to L.A. and that's how our relationship started. From there he gave me an opportunity right away. The first thing he hired me for was David Pomeranz's album. He is an amazing writer. Vini called me and he said "I've got this song; it's called 'Home To Alaska.' Can you write a horn arrangement for it?" I said, "Sure." So it was myself and a trumpet player Rich Felts — we were a remnant of the Churchill horn section — the band went all different directions. A couple of the horn players went one direction and me and Rich went another. We ended up in Hollywood recording for Vini. It started out that way and Vini liked what I did. I still like that chart. That arrangement started a long and successful relationship and I think Vini was proud that he hired me. He said, "You did a great job." Not long after that, I got a call from Vini to do one of Melissa's records. I was thrilled!

So Vini Poncia is an important figure in your career?
Yes, he's was the launching point that gave me exposure as an arranger and studio musician.

Nice. Tom, in 1978 KISS were arguably at their zenith. Were they on your radar?
Oh yeah, I was aware of them. And I was aware of Vini working with them. I was aware that Gene was dating Cher. All the stories. There'd be a bunch of crazy stories (laughs). I had recently come off the road with Melissa, doing the Leo Sayer/Melissa Manchester tour. We did all the sheds, 10,000 to 15,000-seaters across the country. Possibly some of the same venues that KISS played in. I got my taste of touring and doing a whole summer tour on a bus. I saw what it was all about. It was great. Crazy too! I saw Leo Sayer fall off the stage and break his back while he was watching our segment of the show. It was at Alpine Meadows I think. We had to combine bands to finish the concert that night since Leo was taken to the hospital.

I remember Leo had asked me to tour with him because I had played on his album. I had done the sax solo's and some arrangements on the album "Leo Sayer." Richard Perry was the producer. Leo's management called me and said, "We'd like you to put together the horn section for Leo's tour." And I said, "I've already accepted the musical director position for Melissa Manchester. The two acts shared equal billing. So, Leo used to watch the band every night when we'd go on. We opened the show. Leo would stand off to the side and watch us play. Bill Bodine was in the band. Lenny Castro was playing congas. I put that band together.

How long were you the musical director for Melissa Manchester?
I did it for that tour and then maybe another half a year when we went to do Carnegie Hall. Around that time my wife Jean Marie was pregnant with my son. At that point, I wanted to stay in town. I started doing studio work for David Wolfert, Vini, Melissa, and a few others. The "Peter Criss" album happened soon after that.

Before we get into Peter's album, how would you describe Vini Poncia's production style in the studio?
He was fun to work for, different and quirky. I watched him during many different projects. It was usually the same. He would be tired from doing all the sessions, writing songs, cutting the tracks the way he did and maybe life in general. You know, Vini had his own way. He would sit in the middle of the rhythm section, "Hey, you play this. You play that." He was a hands-on guy. He wasn't going to leave until everything was what he thought it should be. He was very responsible that way. It was time consuming but well worth it. By the time the horn dates were happening, he had already gone through weeks of tracking the rhythm section, guitars, vocals, and all that stuff. So now it was time for the horns. He's like this on the console (puts head down on the table).

(Laughs)
(Laughs) You're out in the recording studio and he was in the control room. I would come in and say, "Hey, did you like it?" And he'd shake his head. When there was something he would like, he would actually lift his head up and he would smile at you. And I'd say, "Oh, he got up!" He would do that with many different artists when they were singing. He would be like (puts head down), "Again. Again. Do it again."

Was that his way of concentrating?
I don't know. If you knew him, you loved it because it was always entertaining and everybody would get a laugh out of it. The musicians would crack up. Vini would have his head down and you'd look into the control room after a take and you'd see a thumb up or down. You'd hear the talk back, (mumbles) "That was alright. Next take." (Laughs) It was humorous. You had to see the humor in it. It seemed like he was miserable but I knew he wasn't. If you were an insecure person you might crumble.

Humor goes a long way during a recording session.
Of course, and how could I not like it? This is the guy who gave me my start. At first, if you didn't know him, you'd have thought you did something wrong. But if you knew him, you knew that was his style. I miss it.

Tom, what are the elements of a Vini Poncia-produced track?
The elements are a strong rhythm section and nicely layered background vocals — sensible arrangements. I think the biggest factor with Vini is that it all starts with a great song.

Vini has been described as a "song guy."
Well, it comes from his background. He started out in New York and he had his own vocal group he was part of, Anders & Poncia. They were a singer/songwriter duo. They came from another group in Providence, a four piece that were like the Four Freshmen. They were writing their own songs. In those days, the songs had to have decent lyrics and maybe a few more chord changes than some of the simpler stuff that we're used to from that era of rock. Maybe it's got a couple of flatted sevenths and minor sevenths, where the rock tunes might not have that. That made him more of a song-oriented guy. He grew up in that era with Carole King and a lot of other great songwriters. Content was important. There's got to be more meat to the song. That's where it came from. I think him being a song guy, that's what attracted Peter. They were both Italian guys from back East too. Maybe that had an effect. They both liked the same kind of music. That's why this album ended up that way.

What do you remember about getting the invitation to play on Peter's album? Would Vini have called you?
That's not always how it went down. Usually it would be Annie Streer calling me and saying, "Vini needs you to do some horns." Annie was the production coordinator and worked for Vini. While Vini was in the studio, she took care of booking musicians. She was his right hand for everything. You know, every artist who got involved with Vini, including Patty Smyth with Scandal, they all liked him. Why not? What's not to like? He was the real deal. And on top of that, he worked with the Beatles. Ringo bought him all kinds of diamond rings. (Laughs) Ringo just loved Vini.

What was initially communicated to you in terms of your role on Peter's album?
When I talked with Vini, I asked, "What do you want on this?" He said, "Make it rock." I said, "Okay, I'll do my thing." Normally, before recording we would sit down and he'd say, "Let's talk about the arrangement." And I'd say, "Are you happy with everything?" "No, let's change this part. How about if you did this? How about if the trumpets don't play that high there?" But if I recall, we didn't do a lot of that with the "Peter Criss" album. I knew him well enough by then that I just wrote it

the way he liked it. He would give me free reign but if he didn't like it, he'd change it. I don't think there were many changes on that particular album.

In terms of location, where did you record the horns?
I seem to recall that we recorded the horn section at Sound Labs in Hollywood. Normally we would work at Sound Labs because that was our favorite room. It might have been Sunset Sound or the Sound Factory.

Would any other musicians have been present during the horn sessions?
No, the way those dates always went down was the rhythm section would do all their stuff first and we'd be done as an overdub. If somebody knew you were going to be there, they'd hang out. Peter was there in the control room with Vini. And I think Peter's girlfriend was there.

Any general impressions of Peter and his personality?
I don't specifically remember anything positive or negative about him. Only because I think it was more of a thing with me and Vini. When I went in to talk to Vini about the charts, he was sitting there. Vini introduced me to him and we shook hands and I said, "Nice to meet you." And then we got back down to business.

Peter has been quoted as saying he loved horns so that was surely an element he wanted to bring to his solo album.
I never knew that Peter was a horn fan. I didn't get close enough to him to know. You know, I get Facebook fans — people from Europe and all over the world — saying how much they like what I did on that album. And they like that album.

That's interesting. Because I think in 1978 a majority of KISS fans "didn't get it." Of course, there are some who really like it.
Yeah. I'll give you an example. I really don't expect someone who doesn't understand what a C7 with a flat five is to understand, if they only know a C, D and E chord and I throw this big chord at them. They might say, "What is that shit? That sounds wrong. Don't play all that crap." Sometimes Vini would say that if I threw in too much. Maybe he didn't care for it because he didn't like the dissonance and it seemed inappropriate. Looking back, he was right.

Was Vini a schooled musician?
Well, no I don't think he went to a music school or conservatory. He did it all by ear. He had a great ear. And if you threw something like that in, he'd hear it. "What is that you're putting in? Take that out." (Laughs) As an example, sometimes producers didn't want to hear the tension created by the way I voiced the Jimi Hendrix chord for horns.

The 7#9 chord.
Right. Some producers don't want to hear that clash between the major third and the sharp nine, which is the minor third. It's the dissonance, but that's what I liked about the chord. I liked the tension.

Who were the players in your horn section for Peter's album?
The horn section probably consisted of Steve Madaio, who did all the great Stevie Wonder albums. Steve is on "Superstition." He was originally with the Butterfield Blues Band and went on to Stevie Wonder and on to the Rolling Stones. He also recorded with Madonna and Earth, Wind & Fire. We're still working together. Chuck Findley probably played trumpet. He's one of the greatest studio trumpet players of all time. He's still very much at the top of his game.

You're credited on the album and so is Michael Carnahan. Any reason why the other horn players weren't?
A lot of times they would just list the arranger. I used to get mad about that too when I played on albums. Like with my Maroon 5 credit, the arranger is credited but I'm playing on the record. I've got the contract from the union to prove it. Luckily their manager acknowledged it and gave us a platinum record.

What do you remember about the Faragher brothers? They are credited with singing on a few tracks.
I did their first solo album.

David Wolfert was on that and Vini produced it.
They were fantastic R&B vocalists. Tommy Faragher is in New York today. He's a great keyboard player and producer in his own right. They were very good. I was very impressed with their vocal blend and their intonation. They were brothers that just blended perfectly.

Vini liked them enough to bring them in on Peter's album.
That's right. They would do a lot of vocals for him.

Back to the horn section. There was Steve Madaio, Chuck Findley and...
Let's see, there was Mike Carnahan. And there might have been a bari sax player, which could have been a guy named Vel Selvin. He ended up changing his name from David Luell. He was with the L.A. Express. He was another great sax player. Now, if it wasn't Vel, then it means that Vini rented a bari sax and I played it (laughs). Sometimes Vini would ask me to play the bari even though I didn't want to play it. He would rent it from S.I.R. so we wouldn't know what we were getting. It could have been a sax that some rocker guy threw off the stage. It might not even be working (laughs).

So there were four horn parts on these tracks?
Five. Probably two trumpets and three saxes.

In addition to arranging, you would have played on all of them?
Oh yeah. I played on all of them.

Tom, at this point why don't we fire up some tracks from Peter's album and get your perspective on the horn parts and your thoughts on the tracks in general.
Sure.

Let's start with "I'm Gonna Love You," which is the lead track on the album. (Plays song)
Right away that sounds like the Rolling Stones.

The horns don't come in right away on this tune.
Right, it's about the artist. It's not about the horn section. The horns are there to support, not steal the attention.

So you're picking up a strong Rolling Stones-style flavor?
Right from the top, the guitar and that drumbeat remind me of the Stones.

Putting your producer hat on, what do you think about Peter's vocal?
I like it. It's raw. It's powerful. And it fits the music.

He's got a kind of Rod Stewart gruff to his voice.
That's right. I like it. It works with that kind of music. Vini was good with vocalists. He probably made him sing it a few times. I don't even know, I wasn't there for the vocal sessions. But knowing Vini, he's very good with singers as a producer. He won't let it go until it's right. One thing Vini taught me about producing — I used to play him some of my early productions long before I became a well-known studio musician. I'd play him stuff, "What do you think of this?" He'd listen and say, "Well, this sounds good at the end but why did you wait until the end of the song? They've already changed the radio station." (Laughs) I'll never forget it because a light goes off in your head. You think, "Duh. Dummy, he's right." You've got all this great stuff going on at the end in the vamp, but what about the beginning of the song? Give it to them right away in a short song. That taught me something about pop music. We're dealing with ditties. David Foster said it, "These are not symphony pieces, these are ditties. They're two, three minute songs. Say it right away and get it over it. Get the hook in right away." There's a formula.

And what is the construction of the horn arrangement for "I'm Gonna Love You"?
I'd say it's two trumpets, maybe two tenors and a bari sax.

And what was your approach?
Well, the voicings are very simple. Notice when there's a minor chord, you don't really hear a seventh in the chord. The fifth's probably doubled in places and the root is probably in the bottom.

What's your thinking in doubling the fifth?
The hollowness of the sound of the fifth rubbed between the bari sax and the low tenor sounds raw. It sounds a little primitive because the song sounds a little primitive.

In hearing it some 35 years later, are you happy with your arrangement?
Yeah, I think I made the right call. I think I'd approach it the same way today. It sounds fat. It doesn't sound obtrusive. The song breathes but the horns add a little spice to it.

What about the rhythm section? Bill Bodine is playing bass on this track.
I thought it felt good. I like Peter's playing on it, especially the open hi-hat thing. Charlie Watts from the Stones played like that.

Let's take a listen to "Tossin' And Turnin'." (Plays Peter Criss' version and Bobby Lewis' original song) I think you took the horns in a slightly different direction compared to the original.
Yeah, I didn't even listen to the original. I basically let what Vini and what Peter did with the track influence where I was going to go.

So it was about putting a different stamp on it?
Yeah. I think those are some of my own licks that you're hearing there.

Do you think this is a good cover of the song?
It's a very good cover. I like the choices that they made as far as the rhythm section. That chord change that's in there (sings descending chord sequence at 2:20 on Criss' version), that's not on the original. Vini did some really cool stuff with the arrangement. And that wasn't written out. That was him in the room thinking about it with the rhythm section, "Hey, let's rehearse this. Let's change it to this." So they worked it out that way. Maybe he had Bill Bodine write out a chord chart. I don't know for sure because I wasn't there. I will go as far and say that Peter's version outdoes the original by a thousand miles. What do you think?

I think I'm biased because I grew up with Peter's version so I prefer his.
Well I think it's better all the way around. It's a better vocal. It's more powerful. The arrangement is better.

How about Michael Carnahan's sax solo?
I like it. Mike's my friend. We're buddies. He lives in San Diego these days.

When we chatted earlier, you mentioned he was a little intimidated playing on this track.
A little bit. He said, "Are you sure you want me to do it?" Michael's a high-level sax player. He's like a Michael Brecker. He could play anything. In this situation, I think it was a high-visibility record at the time and I threw him out there. That's what I remember. He may say, "I was never intimidated."

How many passes would he have taken for the solo?
A guy like him, usually you put the track up and it comes right away.

It's interesting to note that when KISS went on tour in 1979 they played "Tossin' And Turnin'" live.
It's funny. I thought after doing Peter's record, when Vini started producing KISS' albums, I thought, "Maybe I'm going to get a call to do horns on KISS." Maybe they voted on it?

No kidding? In giving it some thought, there might have been a track or two where I can hear horns working. There's a track that Peter sings called "Dirty Livin'" and I could hear horns working there.
How many albums did Vini produce for KISS?

There's two: 1979's "Dynasty" and 1980's "Unmasked." Essentially, he did three albums in a row for the KISS camp.
The KISS fans have to love Vini.

There's a segment of fans who love those records, but there's also a segment of purists who prefer the original KISS sound. Vini brought elements of pop and song-craft to the albums he produced, while the original KISS sound is very raw. With Vini, KISS became a bit more song-oriented.
See, maybe that is what KISS wanted from Vini. The fans should know that they may have asked him to do that.

Well, the funny thing is Peter's album is arguably the least well-received of the four solo albums. Paul Stanley and Gene Simmons have made some less than flattering remarks about the album. But that didn't stop them from working with the producer of Peter's album for the next two KISS studio albums. Paul has actually been on record as saying he can't give Peter's solo album any stars.
Maybe it's more because they don't like Peter. That's what I would say.

Some fans didn't like the results of Vini's work with KISS. Maybe they prefer the 1975 version of KISS, which was raw and in your face, compared to a more polished, song-oriented version of KISS.
There's fans like that in every segment of music. There's guys like that with Steely Dan. There's hardcore fans who won't change.

The next track we'll listen to is "Rock Me, Baby." (Plays song)
I like it. Cool tune.

I love your horn arrangement on this one.
So the KISS fans don't like this?

It's hard for me to speak for all the fans. There are some fans who like it. But generally speaking, this album wasn't well-received. ("KISS The Girl Goodbye" plays)
Now the KISS fans must have thrown up when they heard this.

(Laughs) ("Hooked On Rock 'N' Roll" plays)
I remember doing the horns for this one.

I don't believe you are credited on this track, for whatever reason.
35 years later, I have to say these tracks sound pretty good. I like the horn arrangement on this. I remember the chart. And I remember doing four tracks.

Why do you think you weren't credited on this one?
It was probably an oversight by the record company. Annie probably relayed the correct information to them and they forgot to put it on.

Generally speaking, what was your process for building your horn arrangements?
Well, in the old days, we didn't have digital so it was all done with cassettes. I'd get a cassette and cassettes could be problematic because the speed was never accurate on a cassette machine. You had to figure out, "Is that really the key?" (Laughs). In some instances, if the producer could read music or was classically trained or maybe had an arranger involved that wrote out the rhythm section chart, they would hand me a lead sheet. With Vini's projects, sometimes they had a chord chart, sometimes they didn't. Sometimes he'd just say, "You've got ears. You can hear it." I'd say, "Cool. Is it in this key because I don't know if the cassette is accurate?" The tracks on the cassette usually consisted of a basic rhythm section and a lead vocal — sometimes background vocals too. I would listen to what the vocals were doing and make sure that I didn't write on top of them too much. I tried to complement them. I would then write out the parts on regular score paper. When I finished, I would hand over the score to my copyist. That was the process.

Tom, how would you have gotten paid for a job like this?
Well, I have always been a member of the musicians union. Vini was always real cool about paying everyone. Everything went through the record company and I think Peter's album went through Aucoin Management. We filed the contracts through Annie and wrote down the price of the arrangements. I would always say, "Is it okay to charge this much?" With Vini, every time I did a new project for him, the price would go up a little more. He always took care of us. This was one of the later projects so this might have been one of the higher paying projects. It was good money for those days. It went through the union and payment was prompt.

So Tom, you think these tracks are well done?
I do. I like them. I think they're valid, which is a testament to Vini's production and Peter and Vini's choices.

And the arrangements?
Yes, the arrangements of the rhythm section and the horn section too.

And again, these aren't some hack musicians playing on this record. The quality of musicianship on this album is off the charts.
These are great guys. Fantastic musicians.

Obviously, it all comes down to the song. A great musician can't save a song if it's terrible. When you listen to these tracks, is there anything that stands out to you as "zero star" quality?
No, not at all. Especially considering there was no Auto-Tune. They couldn't cut and paste like they can do today in Pro Tools. As a matter of fact, synthesizers weren't really invented. They were just starting to come in.

And in "Hooked On Rock 'N' Roll," you mentioned you heard some Edgar Winter touches?
Yeah, I think I drew from some of my experience in listening to Edgar Winter's "White Trash." I thought they were one of the best rock groups to come along at that time. Rick Derringer was a great guitar player.

And in "Rock Me, Baby," you said you heard some James Brown-style elements?
Yeah. I borrowed a few chord voicings from "Cold Sweat" and fit it into the rock thing.

You were also talking about the high trumpet and how that was a sound Vini didn't prefer.
Generally, Vini didn't care for the sound of high trumpets. It was too brassy or thin sounding for him, no pun intended. He tends to like saxophone sounds and that comes from the old-school style of music that had a lot of saxophone players. That

was the traditional rock instrument. Trumpets were thought of as jazz instruments with players like Miles Davis. Although, the trumpet is a key element of a horn section, especially with groups like Tower Of Power. That's what I like more. I would try to put it in. I would try to throw it in on a Vini project sometimes and he might say, "That trumpet's playing too high. Lower it." (Laughs)

Why don't we go to another track? This is "You Matter To Me," which was a single and had a bit of a disco flavor. It was co-written by Vini, Michael Morgan and John Vastano. (Plays "You Matter To Me")
Yeah, I'm not really feeling this track. Love the song. I remember when it was written. This version is not my favorite.

I think this song sticks out as the one that perhaps doesn't fit with the rest of the bunch. This is "That's The Kind Of Sugar Papa Likes." (Plays song)
I could hear horns working on this song. It might have rocked it up a bit. Who knows?

Let's play one last track. This is the final song on the album, "I Can't Stop The Rain." (Plays song)
I like his singing on this right away. This is nicely arranged. I think it's the strongest ballad on the record.

Since you heard a cross-section of tracks, what sticks out to you in terms of Peter's vocal performances?
I like the comparison to Rod Stewart. I agree. It's a gruff voice.

And he's not a technically polished singer.
No, but you know what? The voice fits the music. It's like Dr. John. He has a funny voice but it works.

Overall, do you think "Peter Criss" is a good album?
Yes I do. You know, there are some things that could have been changed. If you play a track for a producer that he himself did not produce, he will usually identify things that he would do differently. There are always circumstances during the recording process that influence a project to go a certain direction. Like you said, it was the disco era, they might have tried to cop that feel for that one track. Looking back and becoming a Monday morning quarterback is easy for anyone to do. I do that with some of my own projects. Overall, excellent job by Vini and the crew!

"Paul Stanley" Related Interviews

"What I wanted to do was just do things I've always been able to do but never done on records, like do some more melodic singing. I think I've done a lot to broaden myself and I think that everybody who's ever been into us is going to enjoy it, and a whole new audience on top of that!" (PR)

Mikel Japp

The late song-writer discusses his work with KISS, and on Paul's solo album, in this interview originally conducted in 2005. Mikel passed away in January 2012.

Mikel Japp should be a name that most KISS fans recognize. Mikel co-wrote three songs that appeared on Paul Stanley's 1978 solo album. In 1982 he wrote with both Gene and Paul with a couple of songs appearing on the "Killers" and "Creatures Of The Night" albums.

Tell us a little of your background - i.e. where you grew up, your family, etc?
Mikel Japp: I was born in South Wales in the U.K. I am a Welsh man and have the same background as the likes of Anthony Hopkins, Shirley Bassey, Catherine Zeta Jones and of course we can't forget "The voice" Tom Jones. I was raised in a working class family in a working class town, with two brothers and two sisters. However, I did move to California many, many years ago and the States has definitely been home for me!

What artist would form your earliest memory of "music"?
As a young young boy my first memories were of Elvis and some crooners which my dad liked, such names as Frank Sinatra and Jim Reeves.

Who are your musical influences? Any all-time favorite band? Album?
Beatles were a big influence (and still are) in my early years, and I have been fortunate enough to meet both Ringo and Paul Mcartney. My other influences were Cream, but the artist that completely grabbed my attention as a musician and a performer was Jimi Hendrix. I was fortunate enough to see Jimi play, and even now when I see his videos I still see Jimi just loving what he is doing, with loads of sincerity and passion. That was, and is for me!

How did you get into music, as playing, rather than simply listening or enjoying?
I got into music through my cousin who had a guitar and who taught me a few chords. From there my dad bought me an electric guitar and I would jam with some guys who lived around the corner from me. We used to listen to Yard Birds, Kinks, John Mayall and the hit recording artist of the day, such as the Animals and the Who.

When did you make the transition from simply playing an instrument, to joining a band, and what was your first band?

I started playing in the local Y.M.C.A. with a band that I put together with some guys around the age of 10 years old with two guitar players and a drummer... We didn't have a bass player... Nobody around played one. From there I got better guitars, played with better musicians and was in some cool Welsh bands. I gigged out and then joined a famous British pop band called Marmalade (actually they were all Scots, and I was the only Welshman). I left that band and played with many other bands including a band with Matthew Fisher of Procol Harum fame. That band's name was Elephant. I also played guitar on Matthew's solo projects. You can find these records on the internet if you search. I also played guitar on all albums recorded by Roderick Falconer, who was produced by Matthew. I was still in the U.K. at this time but had moved from Wales to live in London where the music biz was happening. There I formed a band with Jimmy Bain called Harlot. When the band broke up Jimmy, as you know, joined Richie Blackmore's Rainbow and also played with Ronnie Dio for many years. Jimmy and I are still good friends.

What were you doing in your own musical career prior to meeting Paul Stanley in 1978?

I was persuaded to leave London and go Los Angeles California in 1976 by a writing partner friend by the name of Chas Sandford (Chas was one of the best friends and writing partners I have ever had). Together we wrote a song called "A Piece Of The Action" for the band The Babys, I was able to place that song with the Babys through a producer named Ron Nevison who was an old friend of mine. I went on to write another song for the Babys with John Waite (the singer) entitled "I Was One".

You met Paul through Barry Levine in 1978, how did that come about?

Funnily enough it was the version of the song "A Piece of The Action" that Chas and I had recorded with me singing lead vocal that Paul (Stanley) heard whilst staying in L.A. at a guy named Barry Levine's house. Barry was KISS's photographer at that time and played Paul that song, along with a few others on a cassette tape that was given to him by a girl named Ciri — she was a fashion designer and knew Barry.

Can you describe your first encounter with Paul?

I got a phone call from Paul saying how much he liked what I was doing and [he asked] whether I fancied getting together to do some writing. I was not aware of KISS at the time but said "Yes" as he sounded like a genuine guy on the phone. Paul came to my place, but before he did I got a KISS album to listen to. When he came to my house I held the album in one hand and pointed at it with my other and asked, "Which one are you?" He smiled and chuckled and we got off to a good start.

You're the only person to get a co-writing credit with Paul Stanley for his 1978 solo album. What can you tell us about the writing of "Move On," "Ain't Quite Right," and "Take Me Away (Together As One)?"
Paul then rented a room at S.I.R. (Studio Instrument Rentals) in L.A where we got a couple of guitars and started... Well, just playing. He asked me what ideas I was working on and if I had anything song wise that he could hear. I said "Yeah" and continued to play the beginnings of an idea which you now know as "Ain't Quite Right." That was the first song Paul and I completed. I carried on playing a few other ideas and Paul picked up on the song you now know as "Move On" we then continued to finish that.

We were on a roll that day and I proceeded to play him an idea that was later to become "Take me a Away" (Together as One). Paul then decided he loved it and finished it off. He wrote an amazing bridge section for it also. Paul was living in New York at that time and demoed up the songs in a studio there, he would play them to me over the phone as they were being recorded. His album sounded great and I was proud to have been a part of the writing and energy for his album.

I play "Ain't Quite Right" at my gigs with the band in the UK quite a bit, and it goes down very well! It is a special song for me and sounds great in naked form just with acoustic guitar as well!

What led to you writing with Paul and Gene in 1982?
A couple of years later Bill Aucoin came knocking on my door one day. Bill, as you know, managed KISS back then, and we still stay in touch. He asked me to go to a hotel where Paul was staying and go do some writing, I said "okay" and off I went to meet up with Paul. It was good to see him again and we started exchanging ideas. We worked for about 3 or 4 hours and I left there leaving behind a couple of ideas in completely naked form that have now become known as "Down on your Knees" and "Saint and Sinner".

Bryan Adams has recalled sitting in a hotel room in Los Angeles with Paul and working on "Down On Your Knees," what do you recall about the creation of the song and what do you consider your contributions?
KISS were then in rehearsal at S.I.R. playing ideas with different writers etc. Bryan Adams was there at that time and I got to meet him. He had some stuff he was working on with Paul and as you know Bryan became a writer along with Paul and myself on "Down On Your Knees". Bryan is a very quiet and nice person and is very talented. It was my pleasure to meet him.

How did writing with Gene differ from writing with Paul? What can you tell us about the creation of "Saint & Sinner?"

Gene and I met at S.I.R. for the first time and off we went on a writing spree at Diana Ross's house where Gene was staying for awhile. We wrote many things and had different titles every other day for the same song! We would change things inside out, to outside in, it was a lot of fun though. Paul and I had great fun also in different ways when writing. Gene and I ended up finishing off the idea that I had left with Paul at the hotel on the tape. That idea became "Saint and Sinner"(which of course had a least 3 titles before that). Gene and I also wrote a few other things such as "Eye of the Storm" and another "It's Gonna be Alright." Two real cool ideas I thought, that never really made an album. Apparently [these songs] are regarded as little gems by you KISS people who seem to not miss a trick... good for you!

Who else have you worked with?

Gene and Paul have written with many other outside writers from the band , and as I have said, I thoroughly enjoyed my time with them both. I did also write with Michael Des Barres and Steve Jones. They had a band called Chequered Past (and don't we all!) and we co-wrote a song called "Only the Strong Will Survive" This collaboration came about thru Michael Jackson who was KISS's producer at the time. He asked me to go meet up and hang out with them. A good bunch of guys and we had lots in common other that music. We were all getting and staying sober! Not to get into that too much but I want to thank Michael Des Barres for well... being there for me. I have been free of all substances for over 23 years!

You put out a self-titled solo album in 2000. How did that CD do, and what have you been doing since then?

I am living in the UK at this time and gig all over the place. I love gigging and as you know have a solo album out, entitled "Dreamer." The "Dreamer" CD is 13 songs penned by me with the exception of "A Piece of the Action" which was written by me and long time friend Chas Sanford. That was the song that started off KISS stuff for me. Also "Dead in the Water" that was written by myself and long time friend Joe Penny of "Jake and the Fatman" TV show fame. The songs are close to me and I am proud of each of them. I do show what I feel openly... and why not? I am told they are very relatable, so why not give them a listen?

Richie Fontana

Drummer recalls the comfortable creative environment during the sessions for "Paul Stanley," and provides insight on the tracks he played on, memories of Sean Delaney and more.
Interview by Tim McPhate

Richie, KISS fans will know you from Piper, a band that was also managed by Bill Aucoin. By the time KISS were working on their solo albums in 1978, had Piper disbanded?
Richie Fontana: Yeah, Piper had disbanded earlier that year. And right after that, after Piper broke up, I continued working for Billy Squier for the whole year that followed. Billy was working on his new material and so he kept me onboard with him. It was Billy and I and a couple of other guys. And we were recording demos of Billy's new material during that time. And right in the middle of all that, I got a call from the Aucoin office that Paul requested me to come down to Electric Lady to play.

Did Paul play you any of the material? How did you first hear the songs?
Actually, I first heard the songs — I think the other guys too, Bob Kulick and Steve Buslowe, probably also — when I walked into the studio to record them. I walked in; Paul was there [with] Bob Kulick [and] Steve Buslowe. We just sat around and Paul played the songs solo on guitar, just so we could hear them from top to bottom. And then we all plugged in, got on our instruments and we started to create the parts. And we just started running through some ideas of what to play where and all that. Everything was pretty much done on the spot. Once we had it together, we had a structure and an arrangement going for the basic track, they started rolling tape and we just started doing takes. And it was like bang! Just like that.

About how many takes do you think you did for each song?
Some more than others. Oh boy, that's a hard one to remember. I was there two or three days. The only song I remember doing the most takes off was "Wouldn't You Like To Know Me?" which was the most energetic song for me. And who knows, the best rhythm track for that song might have been left on the cutting-room floor (laughs). We did so many takes, I was drumming my brains out on each take. So who knows how the other ones came out. But this was the one Paul chose.

Did you play to a click track, Richie?
No click track. I was the metronome (laughs).

What kit did you play on these tunes? Was it your kit?
No, it wasn't. It was the Electric Lady house drums. I don't even remember what they were, they were probably Ludwigs.

As a drummer, did you find not playing on your own kit difficult?
I'll tell you, at the time it really didn't make a difference. Because the entire atmosphere was a whole new thing, just walking in and working with Paul, learning new songs. I said, "Yeah, okay, give me any drum kit." No, it really didn't matter.

It seems this quartet had a camaraderie from the get-go and that you all gelled together nicely. Is that what you remember?
Absolutely. Absolutely. It was really, really comfortable. I mean, the fact that Paul had each of us there, we knew we were all quite adequate to do the job, so that was understood from the beginning. The personalities — it was interesting because we had never met before. So here we are not previously knowing each other, walking into a room and learning new material from Paul Stanley and doing this. So our antennas were at a peak level. The work environment was really sharp and was really great. It was a nice vibe between us all.

You didn't make it out to L.A., correct?
Correct, I'm not on the L.A. tracks. That's Craig Krampf, a friend of mine.

And I understand that the chemistry wasn't like it was in New York. Since you were the missing link, maybe we can attribute the issue to you not being there?
Maybe, New York is just a different environment, a different atmosphere. I know Bob already knew Paul. I don't know if Steve had already known Paul. But I was like from in-house family with Aucoin and Piper and Sean Delaney and all this stuff. And plus Piper had opened for KISS in about eight cities, just before we disbanded. So that connection was there. New York is just different than L.A. That's all.

Is there a specific reason why you didn't come out to L.A.? Was it another commitment?
No, no. I don't remember anything, one way or another really. I was working with Billy Squier and I was getting calls from Sean Delaney — I was waiting on him to see what was going to happen with the project [the Skatt Brothers] with him. I think Bob made it out there [and Steve] — I don't even remember who played on the L.A. tracks.

Yes, it was Bob, Steve and, as you mentioned, Craig. There was also another bassist, Eric Nelson. Carmine Appice also played on a track.
Yeah, I think Steve played on one more track than I did. I don't know, it didn't make a difference either way.

Richie, you play on the album's first four tracks. I was hoping we could go track by track and you could provide some commentary. "Tonight You Belong To Me" is the lead track on the album.
That's one of my favorite songs. I thought Paul [made] a wise decision to have that as the opening track to the album because it has, what he even said, that epic feeling to it. It was ear-candy when I first heard that song because it was really melodic but at the same time it was really powerful.

It's very dynamic. There's the quiet acoustic intro and that electric guitar comes in and just punches you in the gut.
Right, it was really great. We did some cool stuff; we turned one of my cymbals into a gong. I did some overdubs where we didn't have a gong there so what we did was, I just took a crash cymbal and we sped up the tape really fast and I hit the crash and then we slowed the tape back down and it sounds just like a gong.

That's neat.
So I did some overdubs afterward, after we cut the basic track. But that one song, yeah [it's] one of my faves. Fantastic.

The second tune is "Move On."
"Move On," that's just good old rock and roll. You know, that was fun. It was pretty straight-ahead. There was not a lot of fancy drumming or anything.

Paul has described it as having a bit of a Bad Company feel.
Yeah, I'd agree.

A couple of the elements that really make the tune work are the dynamic swing with the piano during the bridge section and the background singers, the gals from Desmond Child & Rouge.
Oh yeah, that really made the song much wider. "Ain't Quite Right" is one of my favorites, because that's such a classy, great song.

That's one I feel gets overlooked on the album. It's a quiet tune and Paul's vocal is right on the money. And I think Bob adds some nice guitar work.
Oh yeah. That song has little Beatles elements in it that I love. It was my natural instinct to come up with the parts I came up with for that song. But thinking back, I'm really doing the Beatles' "In My Life" from "Rubber Soul." There's other things in there like some of the harmonies and things; there's an old Beatles B-side called "Yes It Is," and it was the B-side to "Ticket To Ride" way back in the day. I mean, little elements like that — it was so melodic and so classy [and] Paul's vocals were fantastic. That's one of my really favorite tracks even though I don't know if it's one of the more popular ones with the fans, because it is a quieter song. Very classy.

And "Wouldn't You Like To Know Me?" is one of the four on the floor, straight-ahead rockers on the album.
Yeah, "Wouldn't You Like To Know Me," I love that one too. It's like power pop, which is right up my alley. I mean the music I write is that way. It's just real melodic rock and roll — melodic, pop melodies with balls. Yeah, that was like a la Raspberries (laughs). It's a great track.

Yes, Paul has specifically referenced the Raspberries with that track.
Yeah, that influence is definitely there.

Though you didn't play on them, have you given a listen to the other tracks on the album?
Oh yeah. The production is fantastic. Some of the tracks on the other side — the B-side of the album. Yeah, it was really beautifully done. A lot of those tunes sound pretty sophisticated. "Hold Me, Touch Me," I mean I can see why they picked that as the single.

True confession time. I like that song because I enjoy ballads. But some KISS fans aren't particularly fond of that track and maybe would have preferred something else as the lead single.
Well, it's a very lush production. KISS fans, they don't go for those. Like they didn't like "Shandi."

There's something to be said for that sentiment. Personally, I like the diversity that adds up over the entire KISS catalog, including songs like "Shandi."
Yeah. With me, I have no problem with that. It's what we all come from. Paul and Gene and all the guys in KISS we were all influenced by the same things with the Beatles and things like that. That's in there. Paul's a great songwriter and that kind of stuff is gonna come out.

Richie, would you say that Paul had a "mission statement" going into the recording of this album?
Yeah, definitely. He wanted our input but he had the basic structure and everything together. He knew what he wanted to do. He had all his arrangements set in his head. I sat there with him when he was doing some of his overdubs, with the EBow guitars and things. So he had it mapped it out pretty good. He had a definite direction.

Paul's album is very strong throughout and it has been described by some as being the most KISS-like of the four albums. Do you think this album went a long way to prove that Paul really is the heart and soul of KISS?

Well, as far as the writing goes, he's one of the focal points. I think that's why, because first of all, the voice — it starts there. But he stretched a little. He did things that were unlike KISS in a way.

That's true. Paul has said the album broadened his scope as an artist. We were just talking about it, but take "Hold Me, Touch Me" — Paul hadn't recorded a ballad like that at that point.
Right. I've seen it written where if they say Paul's album was the most-KISS like, it was always mentioned as a compliment. I mean, he'll take it.

Are you familiar with some of the songs on the other KISS solo albums?
Oh yeah, definitely. Well, [I haven't listened] in a long time. Some of the things I remember. There's some really good stuff on Ace's album. Peter's got some good old rock and roll and R&B on his. There's a couple on Gene's that I really like, "Man Of 1,000 Faces," and the first track, "Radioactive." The opening to the album I think is fantastic how they did that.

I love that intro too. As a kid, one of my brother's friends was into KISS and one time when he was over he played that and it scared the living daylights out of me.
I'll bet it did.

And in living with it for all these years, I just think it was such a great way to start a Gene Simmons solo album.
Yeah, what I thought was great about it, is his character in KISS [is] the Demon, and he's up there singing rock and roll and all this stuff. And when he finally got a chance to do something solo for the first time, there was that thing, that sound. It was like, "Wow." It was really fantastic. I don't know who did the strings on that, it might have been Ron Frangipane?

That's exactly who it was.
Well, he scored an orchestra for one of the songs on the second Piper album. We had one song with strings. So he was like doing a lot the things for Aucoin's acts.

Obviously, there was a great deal of publicity surrounding the KISS solo albums when they were released in September 1978. Do you recall just how omnipresent KISS was during this period?
Yeah, it was very exciting, especially for the people in-house, at Aucoin. It was a little scary at first, I think for them, business-wise, because there was a lot for the public to swallow. I mean if you were a fan, you had to go out and buy four albums. So they didn't sell as fast as they thought they would, but eventually they did. It was like KISS times four, so it was asking a lot. But eventually they got it. They were criticized for that. It was like, "Ah, they didn't sell as well." But everybody had [the albums].

Following the KISS solo albums, the band reconvened for a new studio album, 1979's "Dynasty," which Peter Criss did not play on. After your successful stint on Paul's album, did you record any demos with Paul? Also, Richie, there is a rumor that you may have worked on some recordings that may have materialized on "Dynasty." Can you shed some light?
There's some truth to that and some not. That rumor, I don't know how that rumor ever got started that I played on "Dynasty" because I did not. It was Anton. As a matter of fact, some years ago I was at a party with Anton and I drove him home. And I said, "Anton, whenever I can, I try to correct that." (Laughs)

(Laughs)
He was in the back seat of my car, and I said, "I know you know that's going around." But yeah, I don't know how it got started but people thought that. I started demos with Paul. That did happen. After I worked with Paul on his solo album, he called me again because he was producing some demos not for himself, but for the Alessi Brothers — Billy and Bobby Alessi. And he got the same crew that he liked working with in New York. It was Bob Kulick, Steve Buslowe and myself. And I've said this before, I'm not 100 percent sure, but Bruce [Kulick] might have been in on one of those sessions. I'm not sure. So you know, Paul called me back again. We did some more stuff, it was all at Electric Lady. And we had a chemistry going. We just did his album and he was stretching a little bit, producing demos for somebody else. He said, "Let me get my guys." So we had a little studio clique going there for a little while. But as far as "Dynasty" goes, I did not play on that album.

Well, I'm glad we can put that to rest.
But the crazy thing that could be related to this, and it might be one of your questions, they may have considered me to replace Peter Criss at the time.

Yes, I was going to ask about that.
Well, I was in a band also handled by Aucoin, signed to Casablanca with Sean Delaney. It was this dance, power rock group called Skatt Brothers. I was living in L.A. and I got a call one day at the house from Bill Aucoin's West Coast secretary. She said, "Why don't you come down to the office. I want to talk to you." She goes, "Come down here alone." I went down there and she said, "Listen, I just want you to know that Bill called. He's with Gene and Paul and they're talking about you about possibly being in KISS." I just sat there like a deer in the headlights because my head started spinning. Like, first of all, "Oh my God." Then again, "I'm signed to Casablanca doing this with Sean." It was a mixed emotion. It was excitement mixed with paranoia (laughs).

And I harbored that secret for a while. I didn't talk about it with the band I was in or anything. But obviously it never came to be and we talked about it later on with Bill. It was obviously because, at that point, KISS had yet to be unmasked. You know, they needed someone who was unknown so they could preserve the mystique. And I had already been on two Piper album covers, I'd been in "Circus" magazines, all the rock magazines, with the Skatt Brothers, all kinds of things. I don't even know why they brought my name up. I think they liked me; I had already worked with Paul. Piper toured with them so they knew me, they knew I could sing. So they might have just said, "Richie Fontana might be good." But obviously, they couldn't. I think that and that alone may have been the only reason I never even got the shot at it. So that's the end of that.

That's all very interesting. Of course, KISS ultimately filled that position with a relative unknown in Eric Carr.
Yeah. And I met Eric once after he got the gig. I met him in Queens at a rock club. And I just walked over to him, he didn't know who I was. I walked up and said, "Congratulations." I told him who I was and he was very nice. That was the one and only time I ever met him. That was just when he first got the gig. There was a club in Queens called Camouflage and I was told that Eric used to like to wear camouflage clothes. I mean, he got out of that quickly once he was in KISS.

Richie, when is the last time you've chatted with Paul? Has it been a while?
Oh, a very long time. Well, let's see. It was the '80s because I was starting to really expand my musical horizons. I was doing a lot of songwriting, cutting demos and stuff. I would talk to Paul to get his opinion on some of the music I was writing. So one time, he told me to drop my tapes off at the hotel. He listened to them and he called me back and he gave me his critique. And that was like the early '80s, before I started working with Laura Branigan. That was the last time I spoke with Paul. Ace, I've seen more since than anybody. Oddly enough, because I really didn't know Ace or Peter very well back in the day.

I know some musicians got gold or platinum albums for their services. Did you get one Richie?
I got a platinum album, I'm looking at it right now. It's on my wall.

Who do you cite as your biggest drum influences?
Well, it's going to make me sound old, but I tell you, it started with Ringo Starr. I always rattle five names right off the top who are my drumming gods and there's Ringo, Keith Moon, B.J. Wilson from Procol Harum, Mitch Mitchell, and John Bonham. When I was a kid growing up in New York, those are the guys who influenced my playing the most. But I've never been much of a soloist as a drummer. I'm pretty much a band drummer but I try to be creative with my parts and try to play meaningful things. As I grew up, I practically lived at the Fillmore East as a teenager, and I saw a lot of great people. I saw every band you can think of in those days. Like when Jethro Tull came through town, Clive Bunker was a

great drummer. Jeff Beck had all these great guys, Cozy Powell. You know, it expanded later on, but those are my top five.

Switching gears, it's been three years since we lost Bill Aucoin. What do you think of when you think about Bill?

Oh my God, so many things. I mean, my career wouldn't have been what it was, for as much as it was, if it wasn't for Bill. Because he was a genius. He was more than just a rock and roll manager. He understood show business in general. He had a broad scan of the whole scene. For him to see KISS and see the potential in it, that was a brilliant move right there. With Sean with him, it's a fantastic story. And we all got educated from it, in a business sense. Then they signed Starz and they signed Piper — for a long time, we had just the three bands and then Toby Beau came along. Like I said, they were brilliant. They were very enthusiastic and very unique people. They created an incredible atmosphere, we were all part of it. A lot of us musicians stepped into the major leagues of the business via that. So that's all we knew when we first got in. Before everyone was dreaming about having a record deal and this and that, and worked hard for it. And we stepped into through it that way, under the umbrella of KISS and all the success that was going on. It was very, very interesting and I'm pretty sure it was unlike any other company. So I feel very fortunate to have met both those guys.

You released a solo album, "Steady On The Steel," in 2002. On this album you wrote all the songs and play all of the instruments and I've seen you describe it as "power pop." What is the back-story on this project?

Those are a bunch of songs, most of them I wrote in the '90s. I just decided to compile them and put them out like that. I got real serious about that. I made the commitment some years ago to step out and just go solo. And I would have been fronting my own band and this and that but ... yeah, all my influences are all in there. It's melodic music, it's rock and roll, and right now what I'm doing with those songs is, even though there's a very retro sound to them, I pitch those songs to other artists. And that's where I'm at nowadays. My performing days are behind me. I got that under my belt, I love it, it was great. But what I want to do now is just get my songs out there and get other artists to record my songs. And I have some that are more generic than others that would be good for some people. They could re-work them or do whatever they want with them. But that's what I do now.

Richie, I don't mean to get too personal, but I read on your website that you announced that you have multiple sclerosis. How are you feeling these days?

Oh, I'm happy to talk about that. That's okay. I'm doing great. Everyone that gets MS has their own version of it. People who don't know anything about it, they hear something like that, they probably think of the horror stories or the worse that they've seen, because there's some really bad cases. My clinical cause, I'm truly one of the lucky ones. I've had it for a long time, [but] I'm on my feet. I use a cane to get around, and I drive my car. And my version of it, I definitely can be considered lucky. I have my complaints but it hasn't got in my way too much. So thanks for asking but I'm doing fine.

Diana Grasselli

Desmond Child & Rouge vocalist recalls lending the group's signature sound to "Move On," working with Paul Stanley, the spark of the creative relationship between Stanley and Child, and details her current projects and signature vocal technique.
Interview by Tim McPhate

Diana, let's start with Desmond Child & Rouge. The group formed in 1973, correct?
Diana Grasselli: I think that's accurate.

And where did the group form?
We actually formed in Miami, Florida, and then we moved to New York together.

So if we back up, how did you initially meet Desmond Child?
We met in 1973 at Miami Dade College. We were in the theater and music departments together and we sort of just found each other (laughs), like soul mates, and started doing projects together right away, theater projects that we would write and produce ourselves and record projects.

Initially, the group formed as a trio with yourself, Desmond and Maria Vidal.
Yeah, we started working together in Miami as a trio. We were kind of an inseparable trio, doing all kinds of things together.

When did Myriam Valle come onboard?
Myriam was a friend of Desmond's that he met in upstate New York. She was a New Yorker. When we moved to New York, Desmond and Maria moved in 1974 and I moved at the beginning of '75. Then Myriam joined us at that point.

And the group proved to become quite a fixture on the local New York scene.
Yeah, we performed in every club in New York, let's just say that (laughs). We were really ambitious and really fired up about what we were doing and we did our own self-promotion and marketing. We just sort of barreled through New York City.

As it turns out, Paul Stanley frequented a few venues on the local New York music scene. Paul actually has gone on record with his praise for Desmond Child & Rouge as, and I quote, "one of the best live bands I ever saw in New York."
Yeah, that's amazing.

Do you remember meeting Paul at a Desmond Child & Rouge gig?
I can't say I know the date exactly, but I remember where. It was at Trax, a premiere rock showcase club on the Upper West Side, I believe it was on 72nd Street. We had quite a few gigs there. As a matter of fact when we did our national tour we ended it at Trax. And Paul was often in the audience and he would come backstage and we'd talk. We sort of became friends. He really loved the band and he loved Desmond's songs, and we just sort of kindled a relationship together.

And this would have been 1978 that you initially met Paul?
I think it might have been the end of '77, the beginning of '78. We got signed in the summer of '78 as I recall and I think we met before we got signed.

What was your general impression of Paul?
He was warm and sweet and respectful. He was a really grounded, upstanding guy.

KISS were quite popular at the time. Were they on your radar?
Oh yeah, sure. You weren't in New York without knowing who KISS was (laughs).

In 1978 each of the KISS members were busy working on their respective solo albums. What do you recall about the relationship between the band and Paul morphing into an offer to participate on his album?
It felt like a really natural, organic transition because we knew Desmond and Paul were kindling a songwriting relationship. We had a sound that we had developed together as a band and it was a sound that a lot of people hired us to add to their records. We were completely honored, of course, and excited. It was a really fun session. It went really well. It was fast and everything flowed the way it should. The working relationship was really easy and smooth. It was great.

The New York sessions for Paul's album took place at Electric Lady.
That's where we were.

Paul was wearing a few hats, creatively speaking. He was writing and performing and was quasi-producing at that point. Other than Paul and the band, do you recall any other people around the studio during your session?
I don't think I remember anybody else. Do you have some names?

Sure, Paul's solo album band at that point was Bob Kulick on guitar, Steve Buslowe on bass and Richie Fontana on drums. Then again, it's likely this was an overdub situation so maybe there was no one else around.
I think maybe Kulick was around. But like you said, most of these type of things were overdub sessions. And sometimes they were rather late at night (laughs).

Of course. You are featured on the track "Move On," which Paul has described as a straight-ahead Bad Company-style rocker. Do you recall Paul being specific in terms of what he was looking for or was it a matter of letting you guys just provide your "sound"?
You know, I think that he might have given us a little bit of direction that he might have wanted some kind of girly sound in the bridge. But I'm not sure about that because that was what we did. We had a really feminine sound. Yet, for most of the choruses we we're doing a straight-ahead Joan Jett kind of rock vocal. And we're adding that sweetness in the bridge. We were kind of known for doing that so I think that was why we were on the record.

My intervals are a bit rusty. In the song's fade-out, are you guys singing harmony or is it more of a stacked vocal?
I believe in the choruses we were singing chant style but we might have had a two-part at points because we also did that, which made it sound sort of modal.

I think the cool thing about the chorus is your voices provide the foundation for Paul to improvise some phrases in between. It gives the track a nice flavor.
Yeah, I think it was a really beautiful record.

And so we can get a mental picture, would you three have just gathered around one mic?
Yeah, we would often do that. Sometimes we would sing three-part harmony. Sometimes we would sing one harmony and triple it. I'm not sure what we did on that record, but it sounds like we did it in three-part. Or sometimes we would split off and two of us would do one part. We would experiment with what effect would work best for each song.

You mentioned that this went fairly quickly. So we're probably talking about one session?
Yeah, it was one session.

And I'm curious if you recall trying out any ideas other than what ended up on the final song? Maybe a different idea or two?
Yeah, that's always a possibility. There were four of us and we all had a lot of strong ideas (laughs). There were five of us with Paul there. We probably tried some things. But I think that what it ended up being was a pretty strong consensus that was the best way to go.

In terms of the credits, it's just the Rouge portion of the group who are credited with singing. Did Desmond sing at all?
I think that if he did, his name would have been on there. But he probably didn't sing on that. Paul probably wanted a girl sound.

But Desmond hung out during the session?
You know, he might have been there. I'm trying to think, did Desmond co-write the song?

He did not. He and Paul didn't collaborate on any songs for this particular album.
Okay, so that being the case, Desmond probably was not there.

Did Paul invite you to sing on any other tracks?
I don't believe so. I think he had an idea of what he wanted in his mind for this song and for the others. You know, he was really feeling his oats. I think that he wanted to do whatever he wanted to do from track to track. He wanted to indulge his whims (laughs). I think he got a lot of other people to work on the record that he maybe wanted to work with for a while.

In listening to "Move On" some 35 years later with fresh ears, what is your take on the track?
You know, I think it really stands the test of time. I think it's a classic rock and roll track. I think the song is strong, I think the production is strong. I think that the performances are strong. I think it really holds together.

It's interesting to hear your perspective. Paul's album seems to still resonate with fans to this day.
Yeah, that's great. Paul has really great taste. He listened to a lot of really, really exceptional music. People might have this thought of him as sort of a cartoon character rocker, but the guy is a serious musician. Even back then, he was a serious musician. One of his biggest influences was Laura Nyro. He was known to just play really artful music, and classical music too — he loved classical music. He had a lot of really good taste in music. I think that lasts. He was pretty well-educated as a musician and when you have those kind of roots, you can make music that lasts.

Given that you are a fantastic vocalist yourself and that you are a vocal teacher with your own voice method, what are your thoughts on Paul as a singer?
(Laughs)

I'm going to have to put you on the spot, Diana (laughs).
(Laughs) You know, Paul's a great singer. He's great. His voice has held up. He has a lot of control. He's taken his instrument seriously. I think he's taken good care of it. And yet he's got a lot of soul and a lot of really hip phrasing.

Getting back to Desmond Child & Rouge. From what I've read of some of the critics' reviews, your first LP was described as being "too soul-influenced and too

inner city-minded for rock stations." Do you think the group was ahead of its time?
I would say that they would even admit that. We were a little bit ahead of our time, we were about six years ahead of the trend. We were combining rock and R&B and nobody was doing that. You were either a black artist or you were a white artist. And we decided to fuse both together because we loved both and we loved the way it sounded, combining deep R&B grooves with rock guitar. So the label was absolutely perplexed because it was the end of the '70s and disco was very big. It was really dominating the music industry. Then there were the rockers and they were dominating the touring industry. And they really didn't have a clue about what to do with a band that was doing both.

I think the same year, or thereabouts, the Stones came out with "Miss You" and that was a milestone. I don't remember if we released our album just before that or after that, but still this was the Rolling Stones so they had a ready-made market and it wasn't going to hurt them to do something out of the box like that. But for a new band that needed to be branded, they just didn't know what to do. In their defense, radio was really segregated. It was going to be difficult to get black radio to play a white band or get white radio to play a black-sounding white band. Plus we had a completely different configuration. We had three women and a man.

That kind of lineup is unique, especially for the time.
There wasn't any such thing. If it was that way, It was one guy and three background singers. But the fact was the three women were a very powerful force in the live show as well as on the records because we all sang solo. It was very confusing for people. We were kind of like Culture Club, a few years prior.

All that said, the track "Our Love Is Insane," which features you on lead vocals, proved to be a hit, reaching the Top 50 on the Billboard Hot 100. I think my heart melts every time I listen to this track. What a vocal performance, Diana.
(Laughs) Thank you.

Your range is amazing and your pitch is spot on, and this is before the days of Auto-Tune. How many takes did you need to capture your vocal?
To be honest with you, it took one take to do the body of the song. And then I might have done two or three takes for the fade when all the other girls came in. It was a funny kind of situation because I was up all night the night before. I was very young and I was up the whole night without any sleep, partying and having fun. And I went into the studio the next day and it was like, "Okay, time for you guys to do your solos." It was like, "Okay, let's do it." And Desmond said, "Okay, I'll be right back. I'm going to the bathroom." And he came back from the bathroom and the track was done (laughs). And you're right there was no Auto-Tune in those days.

It's a superb lead vocal. The phrase you sing starting at 3:00 is astounding. I think you're hitting a high C there.
I think I just had a really good time that night (laughs).

I would say so (laughs). The group's debut album features a song co-written by Paul Stanley, "The Fight."
Oh yes, I remember that. And it sounds like it too.

I believe this might have been Paul and Desmond's first collaboration.
You know I really don't know the actual details of that happening. But I think it made sense that they would write a song together for that record.

The group's second album, "Runners In The Night," also was released in 1979.
Yes, I think the first one came out in January and the second one came out in like December (laughs).

That type of schedule was more common back then, but certainly these days would qualify as an anomaly. This album contained more of a streamlined pop/rock direction. In hindsight, what are your thoughts on "Runners In The Night"?
It was really a weird, interesting and fated occurrence. Because the label was so dumbfounded and confounded about what they were going to do with us as a group, we were kind of convinced by management and maybe the label to be more straight-ahead rock/pop, rather than combine all of the sort of theatrical elements and the colors and all the different stories. That first record had so many urban stories. And we already had procured G.E. Smith, we found him in a bar band in Connecticut and brought him on the road with us for the tour of our first record. So we had this jamming guitar player working with us. And Desmond was going through a big transition in his life so there was a lot of drama going on and a lot of angst and it just needed to come out in that way. A lot of elements came together at once. I'm not going to say it was easy, there was a lot of pressure on us because of how the business was having a hard time marketing us. And it was also a matter of respect at that point. I think that it was hard for them to really understand what this was, with three girls and a guy, and we felt a little bit like we weren't respected in the way that we wanted to be. So we just sort of said, "Okay, alright, here you go."

Staying in 1979, Desmond co-wrote a huge hit for KISS with Paul, the disco-influenced "I Was Made For Lovin' You." Do you recall how popular that track was?
Oh absolutely. It was a huge breakout and it was really, really good for Desmond.

That's the interesting thing, Diana. I think this track was really the catalyst for Desmond becoming Desmond Child, the songwriter.
That's right. And then it was through his relationship with Paul that he met Jon Bon Jovi and probably Steven Tyler too.

Yes, Desmond collaborated with Paul for songs on 1984's "Animalize" and 1985's "Asylum." Bon Jovi toured with KISS in 1984 and subsequently Desmond met Jon Bon Jovi and co-wrote songs on Bon Jovi's third album, "Slippery When Wet." And I don't think Desmond has looked back since.
Absolutely.

In knowing him in his formative musical years, do you recall sensing that Desmond had a special gift?
Oh God, yes. From the minute I heard his first song when I was 17 years old, I remember being at his mother's house and him sitting at the piano playing his songs. I would always just weep because he's known for these big, gigantic wide-stroke rock songs, but he actually started out with a really delicate sensitivity. And he wrote these heart-breaking, absolutely gutting, beautiful ballads. And we did a lot of those in our early days. We would just weep. We'd be sitting in rehearsal just weeping. He'd say, "Okay, I've got a new song. I'm going to play it for you." And all of us, we'd be crying our heads off. He really has a gift. He can write just about anything he wants to, it's just that he had early success with big rock songs so he kept doing that.

It's funny, Diana. There are some KISS fans who perhaps don't mind Paul working with outside writers like Desmond and seeing where it creatively leads for KISS. And then there are others who really don't like what a songwriter like Desmond interjects into the KISS formula. Personally speaking, I believe in the mantra that the song is king, and I don't really care who wrote it. That said, I certainly respect songwriters and their talents. I guess what I'm trying to say is that I think Desmond has been unfairly ridiculed by a certain segment of rock fans.
Well, I dare to say that most people who ridicule those kinds of things don't really understand music or the creative process. It was really only since the '60s that artists wrote their own songs. Before that, most people got songs from writers. You know, there were writers and they had really amazing writing skills. And there were singers who were the best singers in the world. They had the best writers and the best singers in the world and they put them together. This idea that you have to be a great writer and a great singer is new. I think it's not going to last. It's a limiting and a limited concept.

You performed with Desmond when he was inducted into the Songwriters Hall of Fame in 2008. As a matter of fact, the entire group reunited for that.
We sure did.

Did you enjoy the reunion?
It was ridiculous fun. It was unbelievable. We spent a week in New York together, which of course we love to do anyway because we adore each other. We're like family still. We just hunkered down and put together this great medley of all of Desmond's hits. Myriam sang the Joan Jett song "I Hate Myself For Loving You," we did "Our Love Is Insane," we did "You Give Love A Bad Name" and "Livin' On A Prayer," and "Dude (Looks Like A Lady)" (laughs). It was all his music, just 30 to 60 seconds of each song. It was totally fun.

So you still keep in touch with Desmond and the girls?
Oh yeah, I just talked to Maria today actually. And Myriam, I'm going to call her in the next day or two. We talk to each other every couple of months. The girls try to see each other once a year. And Desmond, we see him maybe every other year or something. He's really busy with so many projects. And sometimes we see each other more than once a year. We have multiple things going on. We do get together and do other things. We did a tribute for Laura Nyro in New York. Last summer we got together because she was inducted into the Rock and Roll Hall of Fame. And there was a big tribute put together for her at Damrosch Park at Lincoln Center and so we all converged on New York and rehearsed two gorgeous Laura Nyro songs and performed those there for a packed audience. There must have been 5,000 people there in Damrosch Park. Nona Hendryx and Sarah Dash sang, and so did Melissa Manchester and Felix Cavaliere. It was a beautiful day.

Diana, nowadays you are quite involved with teaching. Can you tell us more about that as well as your signature voice technique, "The Vertical Voice Method"?
Sure. I moved to Minneapolis in December '98. I was just really exhausted from living in giant cities and I had some friends who had some really lovely artist friends here. I came to visit them and fell in love with the gentleness of the city and the beauty of it and the vibrant music and arts scene here. It was shocking actually. There is some incredible world-class talent here. And I was fascinated with the extremes of the weather. I think my fascination with the winter is a little bit past its prime now (laughs). But it's been a really good town for me in that way. I went back to school. I quit school when I was 19 when I went to New York to work with Desmond, Maria and Myriam.

I just felt like going back and finishing my music degree because I didn't do that and I felt there were some holes in my education. I went back to do that here. And I started teaching here because it became obvious to me pretty soon that I wasn't really going to make a living as a singer like I had been doing in New York and L.A. And I thought, "Well, maybe I should teach? Let me see what that's like." It turned out I was quite good at it. I had a lot of real-world experience but all the time that I was working in New York and Los Angeles, I was studying classical singing. I just loved using my voice in that really optimal kind of way. To me, classical singing has been like a martial art because it takes every ounce of focus and every ounce of energy and you have to really train for it and stay in tip-top shape. I did that all along which was why I was able to do all those high-flying notes with the band with no problem. I never have had vocal fatigue or vocal damage or never had a day of hoarseness, because I really kept my voice in good shape. I was really lucky because I had such exceptionally good voice teachers all my life. I had one that worked at the New York City Opera, one that toured with Pavarotti, another one that worked with a lot of Broadway stars. I just had really good luck with that. I learned to love the human voice through all those experiences. I just started teaching and saw that I had a way of analyzing issues that people had and I was able to move them through it. Pretty soon, before I knew it, years would go by and I had these young students who started with me when they were 9 and 10 and they were going off to college. And at the same time, I've been working with really great artists here, doing fantastic shows and recordings and collaborations, really lovely work.

The concept of the "The Vertical Voice Method" came to me over my years of teaching. I had been thinking of writing this book for five years and last year decided, "Okay, now is the time." And I started writing it and little did I know it was going to take two years to write and produce, and all my savings (laughs) to make this beautiful, wonderful vocal method. I think it's really a very good product, if I do say so myself. I think it really works for people. I'm very happy with it. It was finished in January and I just need to find a publisher and get to marketing it.

So the book is finished. Is it available now?
It's finished and it's actually downloadable at this point. I have a website called theverticalvoicemethod.com and you can go on to that site and download it directly from there. It's 152 audio tracks and a 64-page PDF. It's a book, an audio book and 35 vocal exercises. It's a real vocal foundation textbook but it has beautifully designed photographs, diagrams and drawings. "The Vertical Voice Method" was written for both the contemporary singer and the classical singer. My largest niche as a voice coach has been helping contemporary singers build and maintain a healthy, balanced voice with which to sing contemporary styles like rock, country, theatrical, and R&B. I have been lucky enough to discover how to do this myself and I have found a really effective way to share it in "The Vertical Voice" technique.

And then I have also started a school. I had this vocal studio all these years and I just decided, "Well, I'm going to be here for a little while longer so let me just start a school." So I've got a full-fledged music school now called Chanson Voice & Music Academy and we've got 14 teachers. It's in St. Paul, and you can find us on Facebook. In the next few years I'd like to actually buy a really beautiful old building for the school and make a real academy of music in St. Paul.

You seem very passionate about music education.
I am. It's been really, really lovely. I still have a passion for performing and singing myself. I'm going to get back to that as soon as these projects get off the ground. But I have real relationships with my students that are lifelong because of how significant a mentorship is in one's life. And I've taken that role really seriously. I'm happy I've done it. I've taught probably over 5,000 people at this point. I want to add that out of so many of the students that I've worked with, there have been quite a few that have come to me because they're huge KISS fans.

No kidding? Imagine that (laughs). Diana, today, we've turned the clock back a bit. In just talking about the '70s, working with Paul Stanley, Desmond Child & Rouge and the great city of New York, is there any part of you misses those days and the scene?
Yes, I miss the high energy of the performing scene in New York a lot. I don't miss living in New York. That was always kind of difficult for me. The first five years, I had an absolute love affair with the city. After that, it got kind of hard for me because I'm a little bit more sensitive and kind of a delicate person. So New York was a little bit harsh for me. But I do miss those heady days of performing with the band and doing all those beautiful clubs and playing on Broadway with Gilda Radner and meeting lots of luminaries and working with them. I do miss that. But I do feel that I will get back to it on some level, in some way, at some point. But in a different kind of way.

Peppy Castro

Renowned artist/friend of the KISS family recalls collaborating with Paul Stanley on "Hold Me, Touch Me," working with Bob Kulick in Balance, teaching Ace Frehley barre chords, and details his creative process, current music projects and why he's "Just Beginning".
Interview by Tim McPhate

Peppy, how did you end up meeting Paul Stanley?
Peppy Castro: As you know, I was instrumental in teaching Ace Frehley how to play guitar. So I had known Ace for many years beforehand and was always aware of KISS. Back in the day, Bill Aucoin was very interested in this band I had called Barnaby Bye. So we would go up to his office at times and you could see the smoke stains on the sealing in the office from where Gene used to practice his fire (laughs). They used to practice it in Bill's office. This was in the early days when they were starting up. So I was aware of KISS through Bill Aucoin but it wasn't until a year or two later that I met Paul as a friend through a publicist, and one of my closest friends, Carol Kaye.

How did you meeting Paul turn into coming down to sing on one of the tracks on his solo album?
It's now 1978 and I had this musical "Zen Boogie" at the Solari Theater, which was in Beverly Hills. It's no longer there but it was a great little theater. So I'm living in L.A. It so happened that I was very friendly with Paul. Preceding that, we had done a lot of hanging out in New York. He would come over to my apartment all the time; I was over his apartment all the time. I had re-met Bob Kulick through Paul. I had known Bob Kulick from my early days in the Blues Magoos at the Night Owl Cafe in the Village in New York. I didn't know him well but we were in other bands. And then it wasn't until years later that I became very friendly with Paul that Paul reintroduced me to Bob Kulick. So I have a hit musical up in L.A. and KISS is out in L.A. doing the KISS movie at Magic Mountain. It turned out that I was sharing a house with Barry Levine, who was an iconic photographer at the time. He was doing a lot of KISS' conceptualizations and photos and stuff like that. The hangout was me, Barry Levine and Paul. So we were hanging out all the time and we were just having a lot of fun. That's really where it all kind of morphed out of. Since Paul was starting to do his solo album, he had asked me if I would sing on it with my friend Doug Katsaros, who later became my partner in Balance. Doug Katsaros was my musical director at the time for "Zen Boogie."

The track you sang on Paul's album, "Hold Me, Touch Me (Think Of Me When We're Apart)," was a radical departure for Paul at the time given it was a lushly orchestrated ballad. What do you recall about formulating the background vocal parts?
The studio was a lot of fun with Paul because Paul's a lot of fun (laughs). Paul's always been fun. He and Gene have always had a fabulous sense of themselves. They are very charming and they are very funny guys, and very witty. What I remember about the studio is it being a fun, creative environment. Paul was really happy to be able to stretch his wings a little bit. After years of being in KISS, you get typecast and popped in a little bit of a box there. Nobody ever wants to see you outside of just being KISS. And Paul really is very musical. He had a vast knowledge of songs. He always loved picking up his guitar and just singing songs, hit records from his childhood and different things like that. He was always very good at that. This was really a way for Paul to stretch and express himself and it was a great creative outlet for him. It was wall-to-wall singing. We put a lot of lush vocal parts on it and it was great. He was in total command. He had a good sense of what we wanted. "Hold Me, Touch Me" wasn't really something he could normally do in the framework of KISS.

As a trio, you, Paul and Doug formed a consonant vocal blend. Some 35 years later, what's your take on the track? Do you think it holds up?
Totally. It blew me away when I heard it because I hadn't heard it in decades. Listening to it, it kind of puts you back in the moment. I was like, "I remember being in the studio." It was a nice freeze-frame moment in time. I knew Paul very well back then in those days. And I kind of feel like I know who the song was written about.

I don't know that that story is out there.
It probably isn't. I don't know that it matters now in this day and age (laughs).

Some fans who are not into the lighter side of KISS are not particularly fond of the track. And some think maybe he should have went with one of his up-tempo rock tracks for the single. To someone who thinks the song is contrived or overly sensitive, what would you say?
My reaction is KISS purists don't want to see them be anything else other than KISS. It's something you have to expect because once you're typecast and put into a certain mold, it's very hard for those people to look outside of that mold if they are totally in love with you for the way they see you and with what they fell in love with in the first place. That's understandable. I think Paul probably understood that. But he was willing to take that risk because it was more important for him to stretch and do that. Where else was he ever going to get a chance to be that syrupy? And probably the only other chance he's ever had is when he asked to sing on the Balance record.

I want to touch on Balance in a minute. Bob Kulick has been praised for his lead work on Paul's solo album. Peppy, what are your thoughts on his guitar playing on the album?
Bob's guitar work is always stellar. He's a very dedicated guitarist. He lives and breathes it. He's 24/7 on that. You can't take his dedication and his playing away from him on any level. He's really a consummate rock guitarist. He's always had a good relationship with Paul musically. It was something Paul was very comfortable with. He knew by having Bob there that what he wanted to hear, the style of guitar playing and the finesse of it was going to be covered. He leaned on Bob for that.

Interestingly, Paul plays a very nice guitar solo himself on "Hold Me, Touch Me."
Yeah. Paul is very deceiving as a musician. Because KISS is so entrenched in image, a lot of that stuff gets side-tracked. People don't really get to see that or they don't even care about that because it's not the focus. Paul is a fabulous musician; he's got great feel. And now he's been around forever and he's just so seasoned. He's another one who just lives, eats and breathes music.

The solo albums made quite a bit of noise between the more than 5.3 million albums that were shipped and the multimillion dollar marketing campaign undertaken by Casablanca Records. What do you recall the talk being about the solo albums in your circle?
People love to pick you up and they love to tear you down. I think there was a lot of talk going on, people were saying, "This is the beginning of the end of KISS. It's the breakup of the band." I remember hearing a lot of pro and con about it. But they had a lot of power so they could do what they wanted and they did. They took their slams for it but at the end of the day I think they were all very happy to be doing it. It's the chance you take. I think at that point, I didn't see it so much as a risk, as much as it was causing a lot of attention. They knew they were going to slammed in certain corners.

Hanging around Paul during this time, you must have some great stories. How about it Peppy?
(Laughs) I did have a conversation with Barry Levine recently. Barry did "Detroit Rock City" with Gene and he's making movies now in L.A. He's got a company called Radical Comics and I know he's producing films out there. Barry's doing rather well for himself out there and still is very close with Gene and Paul. I haven't seen Gene and Paul for a few years. But Gene has also been very good to me. He was instrumental in me getting my covers with Cher and Diana Ross. But my story is "Zen Boogie" was up at the Solari Theater and Paul and Gene are doing the movie and Barry is their photographer. Barry and I are living up in a house in Laurel Canyon in the Hollywood Hills. So Paul is over every day and Barry had a few other guys hanging around — Barry Brandt, who was in [Angel], and Micki Free. It's at night and we're all running around the house and being complete A-holes and

having a ball (laughs). Either Paul or Barry throws the circuit breaker to the house so there are no lights on. And we're literally chasing each other around the house and smacking each other and catching each other in the dark and doing dumb, silly shit and laughing our asses off (laughs).

I'm standing around a corner in the house and I'm kind of getting a visual that Barry is around a wall and Paul is near him. So I'm standing behind this wall and when Barry comes out I'm thinking I'm going to scare the shit out of him or hit him with something and get one up on him. It's like playing paint ball in the dark (laughs). So Barry comes around from the wall and as he's coming around I just come out and scream, "Boo!" and scare the hell out of him. What I didn't realize was that Barry was in the kitchen and had picked up dishwashing liquid, you know the kind that's concentrated. And as I scare him, he squeezes the dishwashing liquid in the dark and it goes straight down my mouth (laughs). So now, I got this dishwashing liquid in my mouth. In a heartbeat, I just feel like I'm going to die. I can't breathe. I'm choking to death. The burn that's going up inside my nose and into my head and down my throat is excruciating. Paul yells out, "Peppy, wash your mouth out! Get that stuff out of your mouth!" So like a jerk I run over to the sink and try to wash this concentrated dishwashing liquid soap out, which didn't wash anything out (laughs). All it did was just mix this concentrated stuff into the most amazing amount of bubbles you've ever seen. And huge bubbles were coming out of my nose and my mouth and I'm literally choking to death. And Paul goes, "Hey Peppy, when you're done choking, do the dishes." (Laughs)

(Laughs)
(Laughs) I'm dying and I'm laughing still with this stuff coming out of my mouth. Paul was cracking up laughing and those guys were hysterical. Somebody turned the light on and they saw these bubbles coming out of my nose and my mouth. It was one of the funniest things you ever saw. It was like the movie "Jackass." (Laughs)

(Laughs) That's a riot. Of course, we can laugh about it now but it doesn't sound like it felt too good at the time.
Oh, it was everywhere. It took me a half an hour to get the shit out of my throat. There were bubbles all over the sink. The sink was full of suds and it was all coming out of my mouth! (Laughs) I mentioned this to Barry Levine the other day and he laughed his ass off. He said, "That was the greatest." (Laughs)

(Laughs) How about another one, Peppy?
Yeah, the cheesecake story (laughs)... Barry, Paul and I were hanging out all the time in 1978. It was like every day we were seeing each other. Paul would come down to the theater 20 minutes before the show would end because then we'd go out and hang out after that. Barry, Paul and I were out to dinner one night, there

was this Moroccan restaurant up on Sunset that was called Dar Maghreb. I doubt it's there anymore but it was like a big temple-style restaurant. You walked in there and took your shoes off, everything was kind of like finger food and you're sitting on mats. So we're eating, laughing and joking. And the dinner is over and the waiter said, "Do you want any dessert?" And Paul said, "I'll have a cheesecake." And Barry said, "Paul, you can't have cheesecake. You have a photo session with me in the morning. You have to watch what you're eating." Paul said, "I'm having cheesecake." So the cheesecake comes out and gets put on the table and just as Paul is getting ready to eat the cheesecake, Barry takes his fist and squashes the cheesecake. Splat! (Laughs) I'm cracking up and Paul's laughing but he's pissed. He wants his cheesecake and Barry just put his fist all over it and squashed it on the plate. Paul says, "Bring another cheesecake out." So now another cheesecake comes out and Barry squashes it again. And Barry goes, "I'll have a cheesecake." (Laughs) Barry was going to eat a cheesecake just to say "fuck you" to Paul. Barry's cheesecake comes out and before Barry can eat it, Paul smashes it. (Laughs). So this just went on and on. We were laughing our asses off. And I swear to you, within five minutes, there must have been a bucket brigade of waiters — like two or three waiters from the kitchen door to our table — and they were just passing the cheesecakes down. And we probably went though about 20 cheesecakes. And Paul finally ate his cheesecake (laughs).

(Laughs) He finally got his way.

(Laughs) Paul finally had his cheesecake. I don't know if he ate it all. We laughed our asses off. When we got out of that place, we were so fucking hysterical. It was like a game show when the three people are by the buzzer and whoever hits the buzzer first gets to answer the question. It was like, "How fast can we squash the next cheesecake?" (Laughs) That was the summer of '78. The funny thing, years later, I remember talking to Paul one time in the '80s and saying, "Wow, look at your six-pack." And Paul said, "Well, I do 500 sit-ups a day."

Moving ahead to Balance. Peppy, the self-titled debut album was released in 1981 and "In For The Count" followed in 1982. How did the band form?

What happened was after "Zen Boogie" I went back to New York with my managers in tow, Leber & Krebs. I was on their roster as an artist and they were shopping a solo record deal for me. We had just gotten a deal back in New York with Ron Luxemburg, who was an old record guy who used to be with Epic Records. Ron had a custom label and he was ready to sign me. And no sooner than I got signed to the label, he lost his financing. And the label never happened and the money folded. I got really pissed off because it was taking so long to put a record deal together. After that, I took my tail between my legs and said, "Alright, this is not that easy anymore." In order to facilitate a deal quicker, I decided that I wanted to package a band of real heavy hitters in New York. A kind of East Coast Toto, if you will. The band would be so good because of the talent and the caliber of musicianship that it would be hard for anybody to ignore. So I enlisted Andy Newark, Willie Weeks, Doug Katsaros, and Kulick on guitar. I came up with the name Balance because I remember looking at a stereo amp tuner and seeing the balance knob. I said, "Oh yeah, left and right stereo balance. Balance is the mix of the instruments. It's the final product of whatever the record is going to be." I thought it was a very cool name. I started the band in New York and we did a few showcases. And in no time, Leber & Krebs got us a deal and those two albums were the result of that deal.

Paul Stanley sang on the ballad "Falling In Love" on the first album. How did that come together?

Well, because of Paul's friendship and Paul knowing Bob, me and Dougie, Paul was very aware of the band. Anybody who came across the band, even if you didn't like the style of music, there's nobody who can find issue with the fact that it was an unbelievable, quality band. We were a musician's musician band. For the most part, even though it didn't see the kind of success it probably should have seen — you know, one of those woulda-shoulda-couldas — the band was excellent. Paul loved the band. And I had this song called "Falling In Love." He really loved the song. So Paul asked me one day if I would mind if he sang on it. And I was flabbergasted. It took me by surprise and I was totally blown away. I told him, "I would love nothing more than you to sing on it." Because he was like, "I can never do something like this with KISS and it would be really fun to be able to do that with you guys." I said, "Paul, I would love to have you on the record. My present guilt was such that I would never ask you." Because everyone was wanting something from him. You know, he's Paul Stanley of KISS. When you're in that kind of position, people are batting down your doors all day long, whether it's for an autograph, or for you to do something — show up here, do this, do that. You're being hounded and chased all the time. I never felt it was my place to even ask him to do something on it. When he offered, I was blown away. He even went anonymous because those guys were signed to [Casablanca] and when you're in that kind of an entity nobody could make a move or do anything without it getting signed off by the label, the management and the band. So he just did it for fun. It's classic, because when you hear "Falling In Love," you can hear Paul's falsetto sticking out right at the top. It's totally identifiable.

I think I shared with you that out of the first two albums, I tend to lean toward favoring the debut. What about you Peppy?

It comes down to a matter of taste. You lean toward it because you're more of a song person probably. I think the songs are more middle of the road and more power-pop on the first record where as on the second record Kulick was on a testosterone loop and wanted the band to be heavier and he wanted to compete more with acts like Journey. The second album became a little heavier and, unfortunately for us, the label didn't like the second record as much as the first. They weren't behind it at all. And on the release of the second record, there was a

Black Friday that went on at Epic/Portrait and I think they fired half of the staff of the label when the record came out. But then it becomes a can of worms because there are songs on the second record that I think are unbelievable, as there are on the first. I see the validity of both even though my heart probably leans more toward the first record as well. And it's probably the songs that are more akin to the first record on the second record that I like. I remember writing "On My Honor" [from "In For the Count"] and just loving that one. It was so funny, Andy Newark, who is such a great drummer, had a mental block when I was working with him in the studio. He had the hardest time grabbing it. Then he finally got it. When you're a songwriter, you don't think like a musician. You think more like a songwriter and sometimes you do certain things that are maybe a little unorthodox. There are definite things on the second record that have great melodics that I love. They're just a little heavier. "All The Way," when I listen to myself singing that thing, I go, "Wow, I was in my prime on those records." I sound like a Superman.

One of my favorites on "In For The Count" is "Slow Motion." What do you remember about the genesis of that tune?
Oh, "Slow Motion," I got to tell you, this girl from Detroit just found me within the last week on Facebook. She just discovered Balance within the last two or three weeks, by mistake or somebody led her to something on YouTube. She started sending me fan letters and she's like, "You don't understand. I'm immersed. I love this band. I'm listening to you in the stairwells, on the way to work, in my car. It's my complete steady diet — I'm listening to nothing else." The girl is head over heels over this and it's just now, it's coming out of the woodwork. She doesn't have the albums, she can't find them for the most part. She's grooving with little cuts she's found on YouTube, one was "Breaking Away" and the other was "It's So Strange." She was like, "Where can I find more stuff?" I said, "Well, if you like this kind of stuff, here's another one." And I sent her a link to "Slow Motion" on YouTube. It's now her favorite song (laughs). She said the guys at work in front of her are bouncing every time she puts it on and I can see that because of the way I wrote that intro (sings intro riff). It's got a bounce to it. I wrote "Slow Motion" when I came up with the intro. I said, "Boom. Done. I hit the nail on the head." The minute I hit that intro, I went, "Okay, I got one." It was undeniable.

I love the bridge in that song. It has a nice change of scenery, dynamically speaking.
(Sings) "And haven't you ever heard that nothing goes on forever?" It's typical of my writing. I'm a very melodic writer because I love to sing. I think that's all part of the melodics of my writing. I was very happy with "Slow Motion" as a song.

"Breaking Away" was a hit for the group. What do you recall about writing that one?

The writing process for "Breaking Away" was I wrote it in 20 minutes. I sat down and I had nothing in my head. I sat down at my keyboard, I started playing and in 20 minutes I had the song. I remember just pushing my chair back from the keyboard and looking up at the sky and saying, "Holy shit, where did that come from?" It was as if God channeled the song through me. I said, "Wow, 20 minutes ago this thing didn't even exist. It's here. It's born." I loved it and thought it was great. The process was so easy. There was no struggle; it just came right out. I said, "Wow, what a gift." I remember presenting it to the band. The band hated it. They hated it. They didn't even want to put it on the record. Fortunately, the label heard it and said, "This is far and away your single. This thing is great. We're putting it out." It went to No. 22, we did "Solid Gold" and I heard it on "American Bandstand" and it was really Top 10 most everywhere in the United States, just not in the New York market, which was kind of always a slap in the face since we were a New York band (laughs). New York is the toughest market. But I was glad the song got validated.

Someone has to upload that "Solid Gold" performance to YouTube.

Oh man, if I can find that, I'd be so happy. Someone's got to have it.

"Haunting" is a spectacular track. I love how the first chorus morphs into just voice and piano.

Thank you. Again, that's typical of my writing. I'm in search of the melodic. It's funny, after writing all these years, I found something out about myself. I found out that there was almost a little bit of a signature that would happen that I wouldn't think about. It was just something I would do naturally. Because I've always been a guitar player, I find that being in bands I always tried to pick up how to play drums, bass and keys, just by having access to those instruments. I found that my writing style on keyboards, because I write totally different on keyboards than I do on guitar — it just provokes a different mood — I found that lots of times if I'm singing something, I will leave the note of what I'm singing out of the chord. So when I'm playing keyboards sometimes, I notice in my writing that I'll look for the note that I'm singing in the chord and I'll go, "Holy shit, I'm not even playing it in the chord. It's not there. I'm not doing it in my phrasing. And I'm not doing it over here." And I see the spot where it's left out and I think what happens is it just naturally completes the chord for me when I sing because that's the note that's missing out of the chord. It's not intentional but it's just something that naturally started to happen. Now I'm aware of it and I look for it sometimes and I think it pleases me a little more when I play three notes instead of four or five in a chord. And I'm singing a note that would be in there, but I'm leaving it out. It kind of fits you into the music a little bit and it actually gives me a very harmonious feeling when I sing. But "Haunting," I always loved. Kulick rocked it up a little more than I wanted it to be from where I thought the style of the song was, which provoked me to do some falsetto screams in the song. As a rock song, it's very credible for what it is and obviously you still get the changes. The actual songwriting came through so I'm good with that.

I believe "American Dream" was a little bit more of a collaboration. How did that come about?
"American Dream" started with Bob. I think Bob originally had the intro on an acoustic guitar. When I heard that, I said, "Oh okay," which I loved because Bob was always coming up with heavy guitar riffs. Everything was like crunch, balls, testosterone rock guitar. When he came up with this intro, I went, "I love it." It definitely provoked the melody in me. Once he started playing that, we started working on it. It started off with me and Bob and then Dougie kicked in. Dougie did the string arrangements on it and conducted the strings. Dougie is just amazing and one of the most wonderful people and amazing musicians on the planet. It was a great collaboration and it got tons of airplay in New York. And you know what? The song still holds up. The subject matter of the song is such that America is always being scrutinized by the world.

More recently the band recorded the album "Equilibrium" in 2009. I know that you didn't have as pleasant an experience with this album.
Yeah, unfortunately "Equilibrium" is one of the things I'd do differently. We waited so long to do a reunion record. Bob approached me, he had spoken to a label in Italy that didn't have a lot of money but really wanted to hear a Balance reunion record because there's a fan base in Europe. Bob said, "If we're ever going to do it, this is the time to do it." It came down that we decided that if we were going to do it, we were going to do it over the Internet, which meant we weren't even going to see each other. There were no rehearsals or anything. And the label didn't want to bring anything new to the table. I was writing new stuff and I wanted to do what would be the Balance of 2009 with the progression and the writing. And Bob just wanted to take old used tracks he'd had in his head and stuff that really wasn't used for the last record, or maybe it was stuff he had lying around that we were going to do for another record — had we done another record [back in the 1980s].

That was a turn off for me, but I agreed to it because I agreed my only consideration with Bob was artistic. I just wanted to know because we weren't going to be working together and we were going to be sending files over the Internet, that if I wanted things changed artistically, he'd have an open mind. He reneged on that for the most part, which really pissed me off. It was not a pleasant experience. I was not a fan of the mixing or the sound of the drums. I made that known and when Bob refused to work with me or care about my feelings on that level, I requested that my name be taken off the record as a producer because I really didn't stand by the production. There was one song that I wrote with Bob called "Breathe," which I thought was rather special. I wrote it because my wife had passed away in 2007 and that was really about her. That was a special song for me. There's another song, "Liar," which I basically wrote in the style of Balance 1980-1981 just to send something new to Bob because he was coming up with all of this already canned music. Bob did the drums and guitars out in L.A. He'd send me files and I'd throw bass on it and write to those tracks. Dougie did the keys at his place. Then Dougie and I did do backgrounds in my studio. But I was really, really unhappy with the sound of the record and the mix and the fact that Bob was so difficult to deal with. In hindsight, I wasn't too thrilled about it.

Out of respect to Serafino, who owned Frontiers Records, I did not put a fly in the ointment when the record came out. But now that we're behind it, I'm letting my feelings be known. I towed "all the president's men" line just because I didn't think it was fair to the label to badmouth it. We took the hit for certain things. I saw a few comments that said, "Peppy Castro's vocals are nowhere near what they used to be." Well it's 25 years later, hello? And I wasn't happy with the way Bob laid up my vocals because he had to drop them in. Everything was sent over the Internet; we never spent one day together on the record. There wasn't any pre-production, but there wasn't any budget either. In hindsight, it was one of those things that I'm not thrilled that I did because I think it cheapened the name of the band, since the first two records were so amazingly wonderful. There are some things that I do like about the record. It's just not the record I would have put out. That's the footnote on that thing.

Peppy, going back to the beginning, if you could have a mulligan with Balance, what would it be?
When I looked at the knob on the stereo and I thought Balance and thought of the mix, I thought if I'm going to use the things Balance, I spiritually wanted it to connote all things in balance, you know, scales and the balance of nature. My original concept was to have the balance of nature in there as well. The first incarnation of the band, there was black, white and male and female in the band. That was my original concept because music has no color. It doesn't discriminate and so I wanted to know that we had a black guy in the band and I wanted a female in the band because I wanted to feel that balance of life, of male and female. There was a woman by the name of Bette Sussman, who is one of my dear friends and one of the most amazing musicians and women on the planet. She was Bette Midler and Whitney Houston's musical director, so Bette's no slouch. Having her and Dougie on two keyboards, I was like, "Oh my God, the orchestrations will be ridiculous. And the vocals will be ridiculous."

I allowed myself to be prostituted by Bob who pretty much put the fly in the ointment and said, "No, the band's got to be a real rock band. We shouldn't have a woman in the band. You can't be a heavy band with a woman in a band." And he kind of talked the others into it and I went along with it, against my nature. To this day, Bette Sussman will tell you that I've totally apologized to her and I've told her that it's really one of the reasons why the karma in the band didn't happen, because I allowed my original vision to be prostituted and I think I got penalized for it in some kind of karma way. Again, it's just the mistakes you make in life. I should have stood up for myself more when it happened. And I didn't. You live with those things. But that was the original concept of Balance.

Moving back to KISS, what do you remember about your contributions to "Naked City"? Was it lyrics or music?
Yeah, I think both. What happened was that Bob had the guitar riff — I think it initiated from Bob actually. I think Gene heard the lick from Bob. Bob and I had demoed up the song because Bob was looking to give stuff to Gene to see if there was anything he liked. Bob came over to my place and we demoed up the lick and the song. Gene heard it, embraced it and took it from there. I think he shared it with Vini Poncia and it kept ping-ponging back and forth. Once Gene liked it and decided he wanted to something with it, then it was pretty much everybody saying, "Okay, let's just give Gene whatever he needs." Gene would be sending back instructions, "Try this. I need this to be changed. I need this here. I need that." Gene is very good at directing traffic, that's for sure (laughs). We kept developing the song. It was a four-way effort, without a doubt.

Bob Kulick has said, and I quote, "KISS ruined 'Naked City.'" What's your take?
Well, Bob was a huge Balance fan and in Balance we were able to do things probably that KISS couldn't do just because of where we were at the time. The melodics, the songwriting and the caliber of musicianship was such that I think Bob, in hearing our demo, had no restrictions in his mind of how he saw the song. And Gene had to put it into the mold of KISS, so I can see Bob feeling that. I don't remember Bob necessarily saying that. He probably did voice his opinion back then to me, "Ah, they're fucking it up. They're butchering it." He's good at that (laughs). I can see that from Bob's expectation of the song. But KISS is KISS.

It would be interesting to hear your demo of the song. Maybe that's lying around in your vault?
Oh God, it probably was tossed because it was probably done on a four-track TEAC and I have changed formats over so many times. I'd love to find that somewhere but I don't even know where to begin. I spend all too many times changing things over from reel to reel to DAT, from DAT to CD, to dropping into digital recordings — the formats that have changed over the years, it's just been a friggin' nightmare. I've got a bunch of old two tracks lying around here of God knows what that I'll probably never get to because I'll have to go into a studio with 24-track two-inch tape and then drop that all into Pro Tools or Logic. Some of the stuff you just let go and leave behind.

In his book, "No Regrets," Ace reflected on how he met you and you showed him a few guitar tips. What do you recall about those early meetings with Ace?
Well, when Ace contacted me I was the rock and roll star out of the neighborhood and Ace was still a kid in the neighborhood. I was a total inspiration to Ace. Ace was looking at me like, "Holy shit, that guy made it. He's got a hit record." I'm just in the generation before him. I think that inspired him and it empowered him. To Ace's credit, he acted on it. How many people would act on it? I think he called my mother and said, "Where do I call him?" I knew who he was because Ace always had a drug nature, even when we were kids I remember him sniffing glue and being in this thing called the Ducky gang (laughs). But we were very young; I must have been 17 or 18 when Ace contacted me. He asked me if I would sit down and show him some stuff on guitar. So I said, "Sure." We got a guitar and an amp and we sat down in the basement and I showed him some stuff. He showed me what he knew already, he knew one or two chords. And then I showed him how to play a barre chord. That opened up the stratosphere for him. It's more about the inspiration more than anything. I think the fact that Ace was able to act on that, it changed his life for sure. He opened up and kept going. As fate would have it, he's probably 1,000 times more well-known than I am.

How gratifying is it that Ace acknowledged you as a positive influence?
That was nice. He said something in an interview on YouTube too. That always makes you feel good. It was very nice of him to do it. And it was the truth. I'm happy for Ace. He's a survivor. He's been through so much and his relationship with Gene and Paul has been so toxic over the years but at the end of the day, he's certainly a lot better off than he was being a kid coming out of the Bronx.

You spoke earlier about Paul and his ability to just pick up a guitar and sing a song. Do you think Paul and Gene get short-changed for their musical ability due to the KISS image?
Without a doubt. And probably rightfully so. I'm a guy who prides himself in being a jack of all trades, being able to do a lot of different things. And I do a lot of different things. I love the variety. It's not a boring existence; it keeps you fresh. I remember seeing onstage one night with Barnaby Bye years and years ago — Barnaby Bye is a fabulous band with amazing vocals and songwriting. The songwriting and the vocals are probably the most notable thing coming out of Barnaby Bye. I remember getting off stage one night and some guy coming up to me and saying, "Man, you're the fucking most amazing guitar player I have ever seen. I love your playing." I remember walking away from the guy and saying, "He didn't like my singing?" (Laughs) I'm thinking, "He didn't listen to me like that." It was like a natural reaction. Then I put it into perspective. So I think when you factor in what an amazing business guy Gene is and what an amazing business person Paul is — I mean their business is the most impressive thing, even more than the music. They are just so smart and cultivated at that, that they do so many different things

between the imaging, the stage production and the show. It's like, "Pick what is going to stick out first in your mind." A lot of purists are going to say, "Oh, it's a crutch because they can't play." And you know what, maybe it did overshadow their playing. Maybe Gene is not the greatest musician. And maybe Paul is not the greatest musician or the greatest singer. But show me who is. You're always going to find someone who's better. The bottom line is they are who they are and they are absolutely amazing. They multi-task and they've always been very focused and very loyal and very, very protective of their brand. Nobody has ever done what they've done. I think you've got to take that side stuff as incendiary chatter. Because if you can't even respect who they are and what they've done, that's probably your problem.

Peppy, I know you have a new solo album out, "Just Beginning." Can you fill us in about this project?
The project is something I've been waiting to do all my life. I have a few to do things and now that I'm in the second half of the movie, I'm methodically doing the things that I've always wanted to do. To me, it's all icing on the cake at this point. I put a solo record together of a collection of songs. It's self-engineered, it's self-written and self-performed, with the exception of just a handful of people. I do have Joey Kramer from Aerosmith playing on two cuts and Brad Whitford from Aerosmith playing on one cut. I love it and I'm getting great reviews. I've done something very unique that's never been done on a CD before because CDs are so small and there's not a lot of room for packaging. I made the credits to the record as little records, as audio files. You'll read some credits, but you won't read the credits of the record as to who is playing on it and how the song was written. I did those as separate audio files so the listener can hear in my own voice the story behind the song and how it was written. People seem to love it. I'm not affiliated with a label. Because of social media and the Internet, I decided it was a good time to put it out on my own and see if I could make lemons out of lemonade. It's where I am today. I think it's a good representation of my talent and my writing. I don't have to be locked into a box. I don't have to be KISS or Balance. I have different kinds of tunes on there, some ballads, some rockers, some softer stuff. I did it for myself and for anyone else that wants to come along for the ride and enjoy it. I'm very happy with it and I stand by it.

What else is going on in your world these days, Peppy?
I just got an offer to direct "Hair" at a theater in San Antonio, which has always been on the back burner of the to-do list but because I did the lead in "Hair" on Broadway it's something I want to do. I co-produce a show in New York called "The Gong Show Live," which is based and licensed from the iconic TV show "The Gong Show." The Blues Magoos have their first reunion record in 45 years, maybe in 50 years, coming out in late September, early October [2013]. I do have a musical that I've had in my head for 15-20 years called "X-Star," so I would tell people to keep

on the lookout for that. That's going to be something I'll hopefully get done in my lifetime (laughs). I'm just keeping myself busy.

Steve Buslowe

Bassist recalls laying down the bottom end on "Paul Stanley," the sterling guitar work of Bob Kulick, the atmosphere at the sessions in Los Angeles and New York, and working with Jeff Glixman, and provides his opinion on how the album holds up today and details on his current status as a music instructor.
By Tim McPhate

Steve, what do you recall about getting the offer to play on Paul Stanley's solo album?
Steve Buslowe: I was pretty excited about it. I got the introduction through Bob Kulick, with whom I had been working. We were touring with Meat Loaf at the time. Obviously Bob and Paul go back a long way and I guess Paul started doing some demos. And I can't remember if there was another bass player involved or not but somehow Bob recommended me to come and play for the original demos that we did at Electric Lady.

Had you met Paul prior to the solo album, or was this your first time meeting him?
First time meeting him.

What were your first impressions of Paul?
You know, my first impression and last impression was he was just a straight, normal kind of guy. Of course these were the days where nobody knew what they looked like because they all wore makeup all the time.

Yes indeed. Was your first time hearing Paul's material actually in the studio? Do you remember your first reaction to the songs?
Let me think this through for a second, when he played us the songs, as the session player as I was, I was writing out the chord charts to get a feeling for it. And I'm not really sure if I had a full impression of what the song was going to eventually be, I was just kind of learning the parts. I just know that when we all played together, it was just very natural and easy. And I know "Tonight You Belong To Me" might have been the first one we did — and I just loved playing that. I thought that was a great song.

Definitely. I believe the initial sessions took place in New York at Electric Lady in February 1978. One of the comments I've read from you is that upon entering the studio one day you heard Paul playing guitar through a Marshall amp and you described it as sounding majestic, almost like an orchestra. Do you recall this, and if so, can you re-paint the picture?

I do. I'll never forget it. As I said in that book you're referring to [Ed: "Behind The Mask"], I've heard guys play guitars before, of course, because I've played with them. And obviously Kulick is fabulous. But there was something about the way Paul struck the chord and the power of that Marshall amplifier and hearing it in a closed room. I've just never heard anything like it before. I know that sounds a little silly maybe. It's just interesting to know how musicians can play the same guitars or the same amps and they can sound different. There was something about the way he struck that guitar that was so powerful to me.

That's an interesting observation. Steve, the tracks recorded in New York were "Tonight You Belong To Me," "Ain't Quite Right," "Wouldn't You Like To Know Me," and "Move On." By all accounts, it seems that these sessions went fairly quickly — I believe something like 10 days. Is that your recollection?
You know, I don't think I was involved with it for 10 days. I actually thought we only got together maybe two times in the studio and maybe the rest were for overdubs.

And before the actual tracking, were there any rehearsals to refine the parts?
We really learned it in the studio. We didn't do like a week of rehearsing; we just kind of got together and we just played the songs and we recorded the songs. You have to remember that those initial sessions, I think, were being treated as demos. Paul was just trying to get us to play almost as if we were going to record a demo and then he would re-do it. I don't want to say we didn't put a lot of thought into it — but it was, "Let's just do it. Let's just get it down."

Paul ended up with a co-producer credit on the album. In Los Angeles Jeff Glixman came onboard and it seems that he was slated to produce the album. But I don't know he and Paul gelled. What's your recollection?
Yeah, I think it's what you were saying. If I got this right, Paul was producing the demo sessions that we did at Electric Lady. And I think the intention was once we all went to L.A., that he was going to try to re-record some of those tracks. And I believe that's where I met Jeff Glixman. And yeah, you know what, I could feel that the chemistry wasn't right. I don't want to say I didn't get on with Jeff Glixman, but I didn't have a great feeling about it. It was a lot more comfortable working with Paul and the guys back in New York. And I think what happened was, we did record — or at least I was a part of that one more song that we did in L.A. — and I think Paul somewhere along the way just decided to use the demos and probably had Kulick come in and do some overdubs and maybe repair some vocal parts.

Getting into some more of the tracks, the song "Ain't Quite Right," which is a quiet dynamic tune, contains a tricky bass slide that you've admitted was presenting an issue in terms of capturing it the way Paul wanted. Can you recount that story?

You know what's funny about it is I was listening to the CD ... and it was actually very interesting to hear it again. What's interesting is that overdub I'm referring to actually happened in Los Angeles. As I thought about it, there's a possibility that I didn't play on the track originally. And the only reason I say it is because there was another bass guitar track on there and I don't know if that was done afterward or if they recorded the song before I got involved. But Paul had asked me to replace it; he wanted me to just re-do the bass part. It was one section, I guess it was an area where the bass seemed to play by itself. And whoever played the part originally had a bit of a certain character to the part, with the slide. I couldn't capture it exactly the way he wanted me to do it. He actually picked up my bass and he played it just to kind of show me what he wanted. And he gave the bass back to me and I played it the best I could, but I don't think I actually got exactly what he wanted. But what I commented on in the book, what impressed me was he didn't try to humiliate me. He did his best to explain it and he could have played it himself if he wanted to or hired somebody else. But as a young guy — and I wasn't as skilled as a session player back in 1978 as I later became — I was just pleased that he didn't humiliate me. He kind of let me get through it. I was just impressed with him for behaving that way.

That story definitely stuck out to me when I first read "Behind The Mask." Perhaps because it's the type of story one wouldn't expect to read about someone of Paul's stature.

You know what, that's why I wanted to bring it up. Because a lot of times, I don't have to tell you, there are a lot of big egos in the music business. And some guys can be pretty condescending and pretty rude. Again, I admitted I was young and maybe not as experienced as I would have wanted to be in that situation, but just the idea that he behaved that way, I kind of wanted people to know that about him. It stayed with me. A lot of times you hear ugly stories about people, and I've had people be condescending to me who were a lot less important than Paul Stanley. So I just wanted people to know that about him.

In terms of your bass parts, you've also noted that Paul encouraged you to play more than what you would have normally played, and that he was accepting of your ideas.

Yeah, you know what, with "Move On" I know I [played] this kind of moving bass line that I seem to think he liked. Sometimes I'll work with an artist or a producer that really is so protective of the song that they don't want you to overplay, which is a common problem with bass players. They tend to play more than they should. So sometimes I walk into a session I'm not really sure what I should do. But I think he encouraged everybody to have fun, just to play with it. And it might have been "Move On" where he might have encouraged me to play a little bit more. And also I was playing a lot of lyrical things in the beginning of "Tonight You Belong To Me" and he might have encouraged me to do some of that.

"Move On" is one of my favorites. I love the feel and the girls from Desmond Child & Rouge add a nice element.
Yep.

According to my notes, sessions moved to Los Angeles in July at Village Recorder. I know KISS were filming "KISS Meets The Phantom Of The Park" that spring and they also briefly toured Japan in April. What do you recall about that time lapse?
I don't know what it was from Paul's end, but I will tell you that Bob Kulick and I had been on tour with Meat Loaf. And in the spring we were in Europe and then we went to Australia. So Bob and I flew directly from Australia to L.A. and we started [tracking] maybe the next day in L.A. So I'm not sure if it was also that Bob and I weren't available until that time.

That would seem to make sense.
I think I do remember Paul being involved with that movie but for whatever reason, again Bob and I would not have been available before that, maybe Paul said, "Hey, we've got this gap. Let's see if we can do it when you guys get back from Australia."

"Take Me Away (Together As One)" is really a centerpiece on this album and, to me, a true departure for Paul at the time. This track features a lot of acoustic guitar and dynamic twists and turns, topped off with some cinematic lyrics. What are your recollections of this tune?
That song, to me it always had a Led Zeppelin feel to it — something about the arpeggiated guitar part. I just remember playing with Carmine because that was kind of Carmine's powerful bit at the end. I enjoyed playing that song very much.

There were some tracks that you did not play on, "It's Alright," "Hold Me, Touch Me," "Love In Chains," and "Goodbye." A bassist named Eric Nelson played on these. Was there a specific reason why you didn't play on these tracks?
You know, I'm trying to think exactly what happened. Obviously Paul would know better than I would. But my memory is that when Carmine came in we were successful with "Take Me Away (Together As One)," but I think we tried to recreate some of the other ones we had done in New York and we may have actually tried to record one of the ones I didn't play on. And the same magic that we had in New York wasn't happening in Los Angeles and I think what happened was they found a drummer, Craig ... (pauses)

Craig Krampf.
Right. And it's possible that he was working with the other bass player so there was a team, a rhythm section. I guess Paul and Jeff Glixman must have decided, "Hey, you know what, these guys work together. Why don't we just have them come in and play?" That's certainly a common thing with bass players and drummers — it's important for them to have good rapport. It was a little disappointing for me

because obviously I was hoping to do the other tracks but somebody made the decision to use these other guys.

So perhaps you may have played on those tunes if Richie Fontana made it out to Los Angeles?
Yeah, it's funny you said that. I don't know why that happened because obviously Richie was around in New York. I don't know if he wasn't available or maybe it was just that Paul wanted to bring Carmine in to do the album. Again, I think the intention was to actually re-record all the things that we did in New York but they decided that they sounded so good they would keep them. But I think initially Paul may have wanted to re-record everything using Carmine and I guess when we did the one song that was successful, that was okay. I guess the other ones just didn't feel right. And I just don't know what happened with Richie. I don't know why he wasn't used [in Los Angeles].

Do you feel you and Richie had a good chemistry as a rhythm section?
I do. We just got in there, the four of us, and obviously Paul was the boss of the whole thing. I had worked with Bob before. I had never worked with Richie before — but we just got on as people and we were all just doing the right thing without a lot of effort.

Some fans consider Bob Kulick's guitar work to be superlative throughout the album. I personally think he brought a special energy to these tracks. What are your thoughts on Bob's guitar work on the album?
I'm glad you asked me that. First of all, I had met Bob when he and I worked together with a rock and roll Michael Bolton, believe it or not, a few years before. That's how I met Bob. And Bob was also the guy that got me involved with Meat Loaf when they were putting together the touring band. Bob and Bruce were the guitar players but they didn't have a bass player and I came in to audition, so I've always been appreciative of that. And I then I worked for many years with Bob in Meat Loaf. I gotta tell you, when I listened to Paul's album recently, the thing that shocked me — Okay, not shocked me — but I guess I had forgotten how well Bob played on it. I couldn't believe how good he sounded and, what you just said to me, I really never thought about how many people complimented Bob for his playing on that record. But it struck me immediately how great his guitar work was on that record.

Absolutely. I know he is very proud of his work on the album, and rightfully so. In KISS fan circles, I can tell you Paul's album is highly regarded. I think it's partly because Bob brought some great guitar work to the table.
He really did. It was really emotional. Some of the stuff — I don't want to sound surprised because I worked with Bob for so long and he was always a great player — but I really forgot how he brought that album to another level with his playing.

And Paul also played very well on that. I think he did a lot of that — what do you call that thing?

The EBow?
The EBow, the EBow stuff.

He had used it on a couple of tracks on KISS' 1977 "Love Gun" album. And he brought it back for his solo album and it added a nice layer of texture to some of the tracks.
I agree. He played great. It's funny, in listening to the album again, obviously the solo stuff, most of it I assume is Bob. But I'm not really sure if Bob kind of re-did a lot of the rhythm tracks as well. I really don't know — he might have doubled some of the stuff that Paul had done. That's another interesting thing because Paul, from what I remember, is a great guitar player. But he might have just thought, "Hey, you know, Bob might be a better guitar player and I have no problem having him play parts that I could play." And that's another sign of respect that I would have for Paul because a lot of times [someone's] ego would get in the way and say, "Hey, I'm going to play all this." So I really don't know who did what, but certainly Bob played most of the solos.

From what I understand, Bob did play some rhythm guitar, either doubling the parts or playing some complementary parts.
Right, okay.

How about gear, Steve? Do you remember the bass and amplification you used on these recordings?
Well, back then I was using a 1965 Precision bass. That was kind of my main bass. I'm pretty sure that's what I would have used on the sessions in New York and L.A. What's funny about bass amps, sometimes guys would record me using two tracks: like a direct sound and maybe record an amp sound. And a lot of times I found that they actually just used the direct sound with maybe a little bit of amp behind it. I don't remember what amplifier I used at either place — it was just a house amplifier or whatever the studio provided. I think for guitar players, that's a lot more important than for bass players.

Sure. I know Bob has recalled that there were lots of guitars around the studio.
Yeah, I recall that too. Even at the sessions at New York, I'm pretty sure they had a lot of guitars.

In terms of vibe, were these sessions pretty much all business, or do you recall having some fun?
Honestly, the ones in New York were fabulous. As I said, it just couldn't be more relaxed. I just don't remember one problem with any of us. The chemistry was

great. Having said that, I think in Los Angeles it was a little different from my perspective. It wasn't as comfortable, the chemistry wasn't there, whether it was a combination of Jeff or Carmine. The vibe wasn't there, which is why, frankly, I probably lost my gig for the rest of the album (laughs). It's always hard to say why it happened.

It's helpful that you've listened to the album recently, Steve. If pressed to pick a favorite stand-out track, what would it be?
It's got to be "Tonight You Belong To Me." There's just something that worked on that [song]. I probably liked my playing too because I got to be a little more melodic and lyrical with it. But there's just something about that song that works for me. And I actually like "Move On" very much too. It dawned on me that I went to see KISS in 1979 at Madison Square Garden and I think they played that song.

You're absolutely right. That was their tour in support of "Dynasty" and each member sang one track from their respective solo album. "Move On" was the song they played from Paul's album.
Okay, so I remember sitting in the audience, "Well, that's kind of cool. Here's Gene Simmons playing my bass part."

(Laughs) Absolutely.
Yeah, that was pretty cool (laughs). But something about "Tonight You Belong To Me" was really — I don't know, it all came together for me.

That's definitely an epic track. Paul played that on both of his solo tours. Steve, the KISS solo albums were heavily promoted by Casablanca Records with an unprecedented media campaign. Do you recall the heavy publicity surrounding the albums?
I do. It was a big deal and I felt very fortunate to be associated with it. It was a big deal back then because no band had really done that. It was a great promotion they had.

Ever take a listen to any of the other albums?
Yep, I did. I remember listening to all of them. I haven't listened to [the other three] in a very, very long time. I actually have the LPs. My memories are Peter's had kind of a more R&B vibe about it.

That's right.
It was okay but it was definitely a departure from the KISS thing. If I remember right, it seemed like Gene's was ... overproduced. But maybe — God, you know what, I should probably stop right there because I really don't remember (laughs). I know that he used some heavy session players on it. And it probably didn't have as

much of a rock and roll feel. But I do remember Ace's did have more of a rock feel to it.

Those comments are pretty close to some fan assessments, actually. Ace's was very much straight-ahead rock. He employed the services of Eddie Kramer and tapped Anton Fig for the drums.
Right.

It was very cohesive. And Gene's album was eclectic. He had a cast of special guests on his album, everyone from Joe Perry to Rick Nielsen and Cher. Allan Schwartzberg played drums ...
Yeah, I think Neil Jason played bass on it.

Correct. Helen Reddy, Donna Summer, Janis Ian — he just went to town with the guest stars. There are some Beatle-esque songs, songs with heavy orchestration and he also does a cover of "When You Wish Upon A Star." My personal belief is that Peter and Gene's albums confused many KISS fans at the time and Paul and Ace's were better received because they were more in alignment with what KISS sounded like.
Yeah. You know what's funny too, in listening to Paul's [album] again, it's very cool because I can hear there are some Beatles influences there, kind of poppy sounds. And again, the Led Zeppelin stuff. There was one track that I didn't play on but it had a real Stones vibe about it and even the ballad that he did — you know, it was great because it was rock but he seemed to say, "Okay, it's not KISS. It's my thing." And he allowed himself to have more of his personal influences in the solo album than he would on a proper KISS album.

That's right on target. Paul's commented that this album really allowed him to broaden his scope. And I personally feel it opened the door to some of his later KISS material.
Right. And there was one track that almost sounded like Kansas or Styx. And of course, Jeff Glixman was involved with that. I realized later that it was probably a little bit of his influence that made it sound that way.

Steve, if we fast-forward a bit, when was the last time you spoke with Paul?
(Pauses) I can't remember the last time I saw him. I think he came to see a Meat Loaf show that I was doing. It must have been about 20 years ago, we played at the Hudson Theatre in New York City — right before the "Bat Out Of Hell II" album came out. And I was told that he was at the show. Actually it might have been Bob Kulick that told me that Paul had gone to see the show but I didn't seen him then. So I haven't seen Paul in a very, very long time. I think there have been a couple of times where we've gotten messages to each other, like, "Tell Steve I said hello," or "Tell Paul I said hello."

Of course, your career includes work with Meat Loaf, Jim Steinman, Celine Dion, Southside Johnny, and Barbra Streisand, among others. Where does Paul's solo album rank in your career?
Boy, that's an interesting question. Obviously very high. It was obviously a big seller. It was a lot of fun to do, I'll tell you that. It might have been more relaxing than any of the other projects I've done (laughs), at least the New York sessions were. And, you know, I'm very proud to be part of that because it's 180 degrees away from Barbra Streisand or Celine Dion so the idea that I can play on all those kind of styles is important to me. In listening to the record recently, again I'm proud of my work and I'm proud to have been part of that project.

Steve, can you update the fans on what you're up to nowadays?
You know, Tim, I actually am out of the music business, as it were. My last tour was with Meat Loaf was in 1997.

No kidding.
Yeah, after doing all the touring, and I was considering doing some producing, I don't know, I think I had enough. So I came back to Connecticut and I've been teaching over the last 12 or 13 years. I primarily teach bass guitar but I'm a pretty good rock piano player and I give piano lessons to a lot of kids and I also give guitar lessons to people. I'm pretty good working on digital audio on computer — I've been doing that since the '80s with sequencers and things. I actually have a few students where I teach them how to use GarageBand and Pro Tools and all that stuff. So I'm kind of giving back that way. I really enjoy teaching kids how to play music but not [forcing them] to read music. I can't tell you how many piano students I have that love what I do because I explain music from a different point of view rather than just playing classical pieces. And it's more involved with pop music — whether it's Lady Gaga or Justin Bieber or whoever.

Is there a part of you that misses live performance or the studio environment?
The truth is very little. I always tell people that I think I did my first paying gig when I was like 11 years old. We all started so young. I always played in high school and college. When I was in college I was in a trio; we used to play five, six nights a week. So I just played and played and played. With all the years touring with Meat Loaf, I just kind of had enough with it. I have played locally with some people up here in Connecticut. But it just wasn't much fun for me anymore.

Well, that's certainly understandable.
Yeah, I think some people think, "Why don't you want to play?" I go, "I don't know, I think I'd rather stay home and watch a Yankee game on TV rather than go out and play 'Mustang Sally' in some bar." (Laughs)

(Laughs) Well, I think it's great that you're a teacher. I'm a big proponent of music education. A good music teacher can make so much of a difference in a young musician's life.

Yeah, I can tell you so many stories. To me, it's just about helping kids' self-esteem. I always say I'm not breeding potential professional musicians — you know, not everyone can be on the football team or in the chess club. It's just giving kids something to feel good about. I live in Newtown, Connecticut. As you know, we had a tragedy [in December 2012]. And some of my former students and current students wrote songs about how they felt. It's very moving to hear these things and know that I was part of their education. That's what it's all about.

Doug Katsaros

Multi-talented Emmy-winning musician recalls formulating the piano track for "Hold Me, Touch Me," constructing the lush string arrangement, and working out the background vocals with Paul Stanley and Peppy Castro, and shares his opinion on the album, information on his current projects and why there's always music to be made.

By Tim McPhate

When did you first meet Paul Stanley? Was it in '78?

Doug Katsaros: It was right around that time. I was working on a show out in Los Angeles called "Zen Boogie." The writer was Peppy Castro, who was an original member of the Blues Magoos back in the '60s. And he and Paul were friends and he was working with Paul. We sort of struck up a small acquaintance-type friendship just because we ended up hanging out at the same places. And Paul was working on his solo record and I said, "He's working on a solo record? I'd love to write a song for him." So I wrote him a song and I got a chance to play it for him. He said, "Well, that's a really nice song but I'm trying to do all my songs. But thanks for the song. I'll see where it takes me." And of course it was a ballad and I thought, "He's never going to go for it anyway cause it's a crazy ballad." He came back in a couple of days and he said, "I listened to your song and thought it would be cool to have a ballad. It inspired me and I wrote this." And he played me "Hold Me, Touch Me" on the guitar. And he said, "I would love for you to play piano on it." So it was soon after I met him that this all happened, all within a couple of weeks.

Do you remember your song that you played for him?

(Pauses) I don't. I may remember it eventually. It was somewhat disposable because I wrote it for a specific purpose and it wasn't used for that. It's on some cassette tape somewhere. (Laughs)

So you were in Los Angeles. You would have been at either the Record Plant or the Village?

Goodness now, was it the Village? I don't recall. It was certainly a world-class studio. I think I was driven over there, I think I went with Peppy. Gene was outside but he didn't come in. That was my first time meeting Gene and I've met him several times [since] and each time he just never has a clue that he ever met me before (laughs).

(Laughs)
But that's him, that's Gene. Paul, on the other hand — even though we're not hangout buds — he certainly has always been very gracious and nice for the couple of moments over the years that we've had to interact.

Getting to "Hold Me, Touch Me," you played piano on the track. Did you track piano live with the band, or was it overdubbed?
I believe I went in there and played the piano track down. There was no click or anything. We just played. He might have been singing a scratch vocal at the same time, so it was just me and [Paul]. And then I went in ... let's see, did he add drums and bass? It's a very quiet tune, I don't remember what else was put on it, but I know I was called in a couple of days later to add some strings and I used an ARP string synthesizer. At the time, it was state-of-the-art.

The ARP Omni string ensemble?
Exactly right. The ARP Omni. And I laid down, I don't know, four or five tracks and then we sat and mixed them down to a stereo pair because all those tracks for strings was not going to cut it (laughs). And then we went in and sang background vocals — me and Peppy and Paul, I guess it could have been just the three of us. It was great fun. It was nice, comfortable and we were all on an equal par. It was all very respectable, very cool.

With regard to your piano part, would you have played a few takes, or do you recall if it was a one-take job?
Oh yeah, I don't think it took very many takes. We may have done two tracks, you know, "The first one was great and the second one for safety." It's not a difficult song and I'm a pretty good piano player and Paul was very gracious and accepting of my interpretation of his playing guitar on the piano. I think we ran it down a time or two before we [recorded], but it's basically first or second take. It's either the original or the safety. I don't think we had to do it very many times.

You mentioned you played your "interpretation" of his guitar playing. Did Paul essentially give you free reign to construct the piano accompaniment?
He was very clear about the [accents], (sings) "Hold ... dun, dun." You know the upbeats and whatever. We sat around and I was at the piano and he was on his guitar, but no, as far as the notes I picked, I actually stretched it out harmonically, just a little bit. And he just seemed pleased. During his career, he hasn't run into a lot of piano players. So it was sort of new ground for him, and it went very smoothly. I remember it being mutual respect[ful] all around.

In terms of the arrangement, the rhythm section on the track featured Eric Nelson on bass and Craig Krampf on the drums. Do those names ring a bell?
(Pauses) I just cannot recall specifically. I was [in my] pre-Balance days, but I had done some recording. We always liked to play with a whole band. There could have been a band there, but I just don't recall. I remember the piano, I remember the room, I remember playing, [and] I remember Paul. I don't remember needing to think about if the other people were keeping up and stuff. I think they may have been added later.

And again, no click track?
No, no. I didn't start playing to click tracks until years later. It was rock and roll. Even if it was a ballad, you know, you feel it.

Doug, do you remember the piano you played?
It was a grand piano and it was either a Yamaha or a Steinway.

In terms of orchestrating the strings, can you outline the general process? Was it done in the studio on the spot, or did you take home a demo tape and work it out?
No, I did it on the spot, on the fly. The interesting thing was I came in and I asked for the synthesizer and they had it sitting there. I wasn't thinking of it as an orchestrator, I was thinking of it as a synthesist so it was just another keyboard part. Though I didn't feel I had to write anything out — no one else was going to play anything. At this point in my life I do a lot of writing out now. But at the time, the fact that I could actually read or write music never came up. It was like, "Come on in here and put the string part on." So I went in and the engineer was really wonderful and helpful and we got a nice sound for a high string line. I put on the top part and then I went back and we started again and I put in sort of middle chords. Then I went back in and put in sort of a bass line. And then we went back again and I think I doubled the high string part, and that was pretty much it. As I did it the first time, we just sort of played top to bottom and I said, "Look you can pick and choose whatever you want. You don't even need to bring the strings in until the second verse or the hook." But apparently they started right at the top and kept everything I played. But as I played, I sort of remembered what I did and each time it got more familiar so that doubling and tripling it was not such a big deal. As I said, it's a simple heartfelt song — not a country tune, but it is definitely not about making the changes difficult. It's very simple to listen to and therefore it wasn't difficult to play to.

The background vocals on this track are quite lush. There's you and Peppy Castro and Paul. Is there anyone else singing background vocals, perhaps a female?
Do they mention on the record who did it?

You and Peppy are listed background vocalists but not anyone else.
Here's the thing, Peppy and I both have really big ranges. You can hear that on all the Balance records, [and] there are a lot of great high harmonies. No women were necessary (laughs).

(Laughs)
Women were necessary, just not for singing (laughs). It's a different sound when you get guys singing up there (sings), "Hold me, baby won't you touch..." It's a different sound and Peppy and I had a great blend. It's one of the nice things that kept us working together. I'm still working with him — I just did something with him recently.

No kidding. And I know there was a Balance album a couple of years back.
Yeah, that's a whole other interesting story.

Well, I have a Balance question so perhaps we can get into that. With regard to the background vocals for "Hold Me, Touch Me," would you have helped arrange those?
Oh we also just did that on the spot. It was, "Start playing." And Peppy would start singing and I would start singing. We'd say, "Okay, that sounds good. Let's take that. Let's double that. Let's put another harmony on that. Okay, let's go to the next part. Let's repeat what we did. Let's do something else for the verse." It was inch by inch, carving the background vocals. Pretty much what we standardly [*sic*] do anyway. I mean it's different; it's not a Broadway show where you have to go in and teach people stuff. It's a record and you're creating the soundscape. I think Paul may have said, "I'd love some harmonies on the hook." But it was not pre-planned like, "This is what it's going to be." It was a bunch of guys getting together making a record.

Between the background vocals, strings and piano part, how many days would you have been in the studio?
Over the period of probably a couple of weeks. You know Paul had to do his lead vocal and he would do that on a day where he was comfortable, you know not the tracking day. I did the piano; like I said the bass and drums were added. I did the strings after that. And then Paul did his vocal sometime after that. And then we came in and did background vocals sometime after that.

And the cherry on the top of this track, as far as I'm concerned, is Paul's guitar solo. He really composed a melodically rich, expressive solo. Do you recall being around while he tracked his solo?
I was not there. But yes, he did a beautiful job.

It fits the song perfectly.
True, true. Yes, he was (pauses) very focused. He wasn't like a lot of rockers. I never knew him to get drunk. I mean he liked wine with dinner kind of drunk (laughs). I never knew him to get high. I never knew him to take the route of what you might expect a party band like KISS to go. It was business and it was pleasure all wrapped up enough that he was very straight and focused and when it came to the need to have melody or a beautiful song or something — even their rock songs have a bit of a melody. It isn't (sings monotone), "I want to rock and roll all nite." It's (sings melody), "I want to rock and roll all nite." They have little melodies. And (sings), "Hold me, baby won't you touch me" is very melodic and plaintive and there's no reason why his guitar playing would not have been the same.

I'm curious Doug, would you have played on any other tracks or is "Hold Me, Touch Me" the extent of your contributions on Paul's solo album?
Um, I don't believe they needed the piano on anything else. I think this was a "thanks for the inspiration for the song. Thanks for being a good piano player and in town at the right time. Come on in and we'll do this together and this will be our little dance." And I think, if I'm not mistaken, that was probably just it. Play one silly song on one silly KISS record and it goes on forever (laughs).

Yes indeed. In terms of the fans, Paul's album is held in high regard, as is Ace Frehley's solo effort...
The great thing about Ace's album is that everybody said, "Who's that drummer?"

Yeah, Mr. Anton Fig.
It totally turned everybody around that Ace got such a groove going for his record and a lot of that had to do with his spectacular drummer, who is now playing of course with the Letterman show.

Another interesting tidbit is that Anton would go on to drum on the next two KISS albums as a ghost musician.
Yeah. Anton is a warrior. And that was the brilliant thing — everything about Ace's album sounded so spectacular.

Paul's album is described as being the most KISS-like, though he also broadened his horizons. There's a ballad, which is actually the first ballad he ever performed on a KISS album, there are dynamic songs, mid-tempo songs, and straight-up rockers. What are your overall impressions of the album?
I thought it was a beautiful record. I thought it was well-crafted, well-written. It pays homage to his fans and also lets them know that there's something about the sensitive stuff. I mean, he's sort of the sensitive guy in KISS. He's the lead singer but he's got the star makeup. He's picking up chicks with beautiful songs (laughs). And he's honest and romantic. You can do that and also rock out. Do your dance and

play your guitar and hold stage in front of 30,000 people, and at the same time be intimate, write a song as if only one person is listening to it at a time. I thought he brought that to the record better than anybody. Kind of like putting on an entire series of concerts in [nine] songs.

You just paid some high compliments to Paul. Of course, with being in KISS sometimes the music tends to be overlooked. Given your perspective in working with Paul, do you think he's underrated as a songwriter and musician?
I'm not sure you could say underrated. I mean, Barbra Streisand might not be singing his tunes. But he spends a career doing what he does, you know. You know, KISS was, and still is, a party band. You feel good when you go to a KISS concert. They invented half of the stuff that most people do nowadays. I mean the only thing they didn't have is dancing girls. But the video, the fire and the pyrotechnics, and the costumes and the moving stages — and how to put on a performance — they created that stuff. So as you said, for the fans it may be about the music. But for everybody else, it's about the theatrics and the music as a vehicle for them to put on a show. I mean, Gene's bass solo when he would drip blood and fly across the stage was a lot of detuning and retuning his bass guitar. It was not really music, it was underscoring. It was musical but it's not something that he would release. But it was beautiful underscoring, very theatrical. And the same thing with Ace's guitar solos. They were meandering and just a lot of notes. But what it did was set up his exploding guitar and his motions onstage. And you know, Paul didn't have to take part in that. There was the drum solo, there was the guitar solo, there was the bass solo, and Paul was just the singer in the front. He played rhythm guitar and did his thing.

So as far as him not being well-thought of as a songwriter, I think it's the songs that he was writing were for a purpose other than living as standards in the standard library. I think he's rated perfectly fine. Certainly his Tiffany lamps and stuff will attest to the fact that he's written enough songs that make people happy (laughs). That they aren't in the American songbook — I'm not sure, you'd have to ask him. I don't know that would have been what he was going for.

That's some interesting insight, Doug. As a musician in 1978, how would you have been compensated for your work on Paul's record? Would this have been a union gig, a flat fee, or money under the table?
(Laughs) Well, here's the thing. Of course I would have done it just for the love of doing it. There are times when I have done that, just for the pleasure of working on an equal basis with someone you consider an icon. And if Paul asked me to play with him again, I would do it in a moment as a gift. If he asked me to go on the road with him, I might ask for a salary (laughs). It takes me away from my family and it takes me away from my home. But for a one-off, if he said, "Write a song with me." I'd say, "Sure, I will." And there are rules in the world — you know you split the

royalties. I don't recall if I was paid. I'm sure him being who he was, he probably offered. But I did not go in there flashing my union card. I went in there just grateful to be expanding the number of places where I could play in the studio. And indeed the engineer called me back up several years later, saying, "I remember what a great experience it was with you in the studio working with Paul. Would you come and work with another band?" Then through that, I met somebody who turned me on to the band Live, and I did some arrangements for them. And that's where I whipped out the union card (laughs).

(Laughs)

I think of things like this as not only an investment, but the right thing to do. If you're young and somebody gives you an opportunity to be on an album that's pretty much guaranteed to go platinum before it's even finished recording, you just kind of say, "Yes." And whatever it is for, you accept it. The fact that it's 35 years later and you're calling to ask me about this three minutes of someone's life is a testament enough.

Indeed. When the solo albums were released in 1978, KISS were arguably at their peak. Casablanca President Neil Bogart pulled out all the stops with a multi-million dollar publicity campaign for the solo albums. Do you recall the media coverage and hoopla surrounding the solo albums?

Well, I do. I didn't think of it as a circus so much as to be expected. Regardless of where KISS was in your level of, you know, "Is this a kid's band or an adult band or a show band or a music band or a rock band or a toy band or a merchandise band?" — They were definitely in the hierarchy of rock royalty. It's not like Paul pulled out to do a little solo project. They did four solo projects simultaneously as a band. And the stunning artwork on each of those covers was another testament to how it should be done — how it should always be done. Like when Steely Dan, the two artists from that [band] did little solo projects, perhaps there would have been a little more hoopla about that had they done them simultaneously, used the same cover art, you know that sort of thing. There are times when it's done right and this was done right. So I didn't think of it as a circus so much as the proper ad campaign. And there was the product to back it up. There was Ace's fantastic record, there was Paul's beautiful record, there was — well Gene put his thing out (laughs).

Gene's album was certainly eclectic. But fair play to him, I think that was his goal going into the project.

He wanted to show everybody everything. Paul, to me, feels like a team player. Even though he and Gene are at the top of the KISS, it's still his part to stand back and let the other people shine because he already knows how much he shines. Just like, as I keep saying, he was gracious to allow me to play. Any number of fantastic keyboard players could have done what I did. But it was a kindness and a team spirit that allowed me to be a part of this record, and I see that with what they did with all the marketing and everything as well. It was a team effort.

Of course, it just so happened that you were involved on the lone single from the album. "Hold Me Touch Me" managed to climb as high as No. 46.
Right.

Do you recall hearing the single on the radio?
I did hear it on the radio. To this day, I have the "they're playing our song" syndrome. When I hear a song — it's really rare I hear a Balance tune — but definitely back in the day when I was driving along in the street and all of the sudden "Hold Me, Touch Me" or "Breaking Away" or "American Dream" or even some commercial or something that I was a part of came on, I would roll down the window and scream. To this day I'm the same way. I'm sitting at a Wendy's or something and some commercial will come on the air and I'll go, "I did the string arrangement on that!" Or you know, Rod Stewart's "American Songbook" record, they'll play "The Nearness of You" or something and I'll go, "Wait a minute, that's my arrangement. I worked with on that!" I definitely will stop people and point out that I'm inside their ears at this very moment. I love it.

You just said something that reminded me that Paul has said that if "Hold Me, Touch Me" was recorded and interpreted by a contemporary artist, he thinks it could have the potential to be a hit.
Why not? Absolutely. Let's make it happen!

When is the last time you spoke to Paul?
I spoke to Paul a couple of years ago. I was collecting platinum records for my wall. And I said, "Hey, this is a platinum record." And I had a nice moment to be able to tell him how gracious he was for letting me play and what an honor it would be to put this record amongst my collection, since I have about two dozen gold and platinum records to my name. [I said,] "I would love this to be a centerpiece." And he, without hesitation, said, "Of course."

Very cool.
That was a couple of years ago.

So you have a "Paul Stanley" platinum album on your wall.
I have several of them, but his is definitely front and center.

Getting into Balance, the group featured not only Peppy Castro but Bob Kulick, who played guitar on Paul's album. Balance's debut album was released in 1981 and featured the ballad "Falling In Love," which Paul Stanley sang on.

Wow. Did Paul sing with us? I wouldn't put it past us that he did. I know that Peppy and I sang all of the background vocals on all of the Balance albums. It was just Peppy and me. Every now and then someone would come in and we'd bring them in and they'd do a little guest turn. And sometimes they were mentioned and sometimes they weren't. There's a definite possibility that Paul could have sung along. But if it's not mentioned on the record, I can't vouch for it for certain.

He's not credited.

I can't say it didn't happen, but I can't for sure say it did. I don't recall. Peppy and I used to sing our background vocals at 2 o'clock in the morning at Power Station in what they call "gobos"— those are giant 8-foot tall wooden sound baffles filled with foam. And we would lie the foam baffles down on the ground and lie down inside them and then hover a mic over our faces while we're lying down at 2 o'clock in the morning. And then we'd sing background harmony (laughs).

That was the secret to those fantastic Balance background vocals?

That was our trick (laughs).

Following the debut album, there was the more rock-edged "In For the Count." More recently, you reconvened for "Equilibrium" in 2009.

We didn't convene. That's the thing. There was no convening (laughs). All three of us were never in the same room.

So you emailed tracks back and forth and worked that way?

Exactly. I'm the tree hugger in the band (laughs). I'm the gentle soul who did not come into rock and roll through rock and roll. As rock and roll as I ever was, was the Beatles. But I was always a theater person and I was the guy who actually could read music and write out music and studied music and was a musician. I was a musician. So I was not just a songwriter. Apparently, in my life, my karma has been to make a lot of people sound better. I do a lot of arranging and a lot of taking elements of people's songs and turning it into something that they couldn't do themselves. Because of that, there's a lot more, I guess, generosity. And Peppy is a very kind and gentle person, but a definite rock star. Back in the day, he was the rock star, as a teenager. And Bob, of course, is a heavy metal guitar icon and deserving of every accolade that is sent his way — he's one of the great guitarists that I've ever worked with. He also has chops that nobody knows about. Every now and again he'll kick into a little jazz tune and then say, "You didn't know I had that, did ya?"

(Laughs)

He's an amazing guy with one of the most fluent vibratos and one of the most inventive ways to turn a guitar phrase. But personalities clashed in Balance from the beginning. Because Peppy is a frontman, Bobby is a frontman and I always thought that I was going to be a frontman. In my own little bands when I was in high school and growing up, I was always the leader of the band. I met Peppy because my girlfriend at the time was his old girlfriend, so we had that in common. And he came over and I spent more time with him than I did with her at times (laughs). But, in any case, when we put this band together we found that our personalities just conflicted so much that it led to the breakup of the band. I love Peppy and I love Bob. I think Bob and I get along and Peppy and I get along. But Peppy and Bob didn't always get along because Peppy has a way of critiquing and Bobby has a way of critiquing that each one of them doesn't want to listen to (laughs).

When the band was approached to put this record together, it was best that Peppy sang his vocals in upstate New York where he lived. I did the keyboard parts in Long Island where I lived. And Bobby was out in Los Angeles and he cut guitars and they did some bass and drumming where he lived. And then Peppy would put on some guitars where he lived and I would put on background vocals where I lived. And then Bobby would do some mixes where he lived. And then I flew out to Los Angeles and did some stuff with Bobby in the studio. And then Peppy and I got together and we wrote some words and did some vocals at his place. So I tied the band together — that's a lot of big words for I was the only one who visited everybody. But it was not a cohesive, filled with love, "Hey let's do it for the fans or for ourselves" recording. It was like labor. And I feel that on many of the tunes you can hear the work that's going into them. And I can hear the strain in Peppy's voice of trying to do what it is that Bobby keeps telling him to do. And I can hear the guitars trying to cover up what Bobby didn't like about the keyboards. I can hear the keyboards trying to kick through, and the drums sound different. To me, it was a nice gesture. But it was not making a great record. That said, I think there's some wonderful stuff on the record that snuck through. But the making of the record was not a pleasant experience. And I think it shows in the final product.

Interesting... I know some bands work that way. For example, Def Leppard, have recorded songs by sharing files. So you would have preferred to have gone into a studio with everyone and let the chips fall where they may?
Oh, absolutely. Look, I have no problem with working over the Internet. I'm happy to add my little touches and let them mix it [as they wish] for other people's projects. But when a project has my name on it, there is something about ... I keep going back to the word teamwork. Camaraderie. The energy that you get — even if it's bad energy. If you're all in the room, sometimes some really bad energy can turn out some really great results.

The proverbial creative friction.
Yeah, exactly. So what we had was not particularly great energy. But even so, as I said I'm the tree hugger, I wrote several of the songs that were on the record and

Peppy, as the singer — even when we were in Balance — always liked to say, "Look, I'm singing this. I would say different words here." And even as — you know, I was in my mid 50s at the time, I was like, "Okay, you do what you want with it" rather than [saying], "This is the way I wrote it. I think these lyrics are perfectly fine the way they are." Like "Old Friends," for example, it's virtually a different song than what I wrote. But in the spirit of collaboration and thinking, "Look, I've had this song for a couple of years. We're putting it together, no one has ever done it and no one will ever do it. Why not? Let Peppy have his way with it and we'll do what we do." In hindsight, I wish I hadn't. So I can't listen to the record because everything I did on it was pretty much changed and so it doesn't really reflect me.

I wanted to put on keyboard sounds that sounded vintage because I thought, "Well, it's Balance. Let's get some 1980s-sounding keyboards." And Peppy wanted me to get some really avant-garde "we can do new things with sound now" digital in the computer keyboard sounds. So even the keyboard parts, as much as I was playing them, were not particularly what I might have done. So I don't feel connected to this record. I love the cover art. I think the cover art nailed it on the head. But it's not a record that I am one with, unlike the first Balance album, which I think is actually one of the greatest records ever made. That [album] was definitely unsung. And here's the problem that I had with that, and I've told Peppy this and he disagrees with me, and I may have mentioned it to Bob: I've always been vocal about the fact that we put out "Breaking Away" and I think that was the beginning of the end for Balance.

Really? Right out of the gate?
"Breaking Away" was the song that we had finished recording the entire album. And if you're familiar with the first Balance album, it's got some phenomenal songs on it.

It's fantastic.
Between "No Getting Around My Love" and "American Dream," those two songs alone could have catapulted us [in with] Journey, Foreigner and Styx. What we put out was, "Let's make sure that there's a little pop tune that we can get out there so that we can follow it up with something." But we put out this little dance tune with a little electronic drum (mimics drum sound). As far as I was concerned, we were 1910 Fruitgum Company. And no matter how hard or heavy we tried to make the second album, there was no way to possibly follow it up. There was nothing we could do to salvage ourselves. That is my contention and will be that way until the day I die. Peppy 100 percent disagrees with me. He says, "Had we not released that song no one would have ever heard of us." And I'm like, "If we had put out 'No Getting Around My Love' as our first single" — that was like Toto's "Hold The Line." We could have just rocked our way into superstardom overnight.

At this point, would you be open to getting together proper to record another Balance album?

Yeah, it wouldn't happen (laughs). I'm working with Bobby. Bobby and I did Dee Snider's Broadway record [Ed. "Dee Does Broadway" released in 2012] together. And the "Sin-Atra" record that Bobby did, I did the orchestrations. We've been working a lot together. And Peppy and I have been doing a little work together ourselves. So split apart, we're actually continuing to be friends and co-workers and that's nice.

Doug, you've mentioned you write and read music. And you have formal musical training.

I do, indeed. You've probably seen my site, which is egotistically named "The Music of Your Dreams." There are examples of music that I have arranged for this symphony here and that artist here and records that I've played on. I do a lot of orchestrations. Right now, I'm working on a new Broadway show based on an old movie called "Somewhere in Time," [which starred] Christopher Reeve and Jane Seymour. It's a time-travel love story and it's coming to Broadway next year and I am the writer and the orchestrator. I've conducted Broadway shows. You know I'm a musician's musician, my friend. On the other hand, I love banging my head and hitting my fingers hard enough on the keys so that they bleed and my fingernails break. That is why I get called to music direct things like — there was an off-Broadway show called "The Toxic Avenger," written by David Bryan, the keyboard player for ...

Bon Jovi.

Bon Jovi, right. He just won a Tony Award for "Memphis" last year.

And you played on a Bon Jovi album, right?

I played on the first Bon Jovi album. I played and sang. I actually ghosted a couple of high notes for Jon (laughs). I was called the "stunt vocalist."

(Laughs) I like that. On a related note, your nickname on Paul's album is listed as "Gling." What is the origin of that nickname?

My girlfriend at the time — [Peppy and my] co-girlfriend — used to called me "Dougling," you know like, "Little Duckling." It was "Dougling" and that was her cute thing to call me, like "Boobie" or whatever. I was "Dougling." And Peppy walked in on her calling me that once and said, "The Gling?" And it just stuck. So I thought, "Well that will be cool. I'll be 'The Gling' and I'll have a little persona and people will call up 'The Gling.'" But it sounded worse and worse to me over the years. It was like something you do when something is stuck in your throat or something. So I just turned back into Doug. It still pops out. When I posted my latest Facebook picture from the late-'70s or something, half of the comments from all of my friends are like, "It's 'The Gling.'" (Laughs) There's been a lot of people who over the years never knew my name was Doug, they called me "Gling."

Other than the Broadway show, can you tell us about any other musical projects you're currently working on?

Let's see ... the thing I'm most excited about is the Broadway shows down the pike, and the one with the most cache at the moment is indeed "Somewhere in Time." That opened in Portland, Oregon, for it's out of town tryout in end of May, early June. And then we move to Broadway to open for next year's Tony Awards. So that's the most exciting thing. I have been working as an arranger and composer and [on] a lot of crazy things — I do underscores for scholastic books on tape for kids. Whatever it is, there's a lot of music to be made. I just did a Christmas arrangement for the Denver Symphony. I'm doing piano vocal charts for a friend of mine. I'm just trying to keep it busy. I've been playing keyboards and musical directing for a famous Argentinean pianist named Raúl di Blasio. And I've been doing that a few years, touring the world. This guy goes to Cairo and Beirut and Buenos Aires and Mexico — all over the world. I've been on the road with him. So it's varied and interesting and all creative.

Bob Kulick

Longtime member of the KISS family fondly remembers great music and great vibes during the "Paul Stanley" album sessions, the positive musical chemistry between himself and Stanley, and offers insight on his guitar tracks and his opinion on the album 35 years later.
Interview by Tim McPhate

Bob, when the calendar turned to 1978, in terms of your work with KISS, you had come off playing some guitar tracks on the studio recordings on "Alive II." When did you first learn about the KISS solo album project?
Bob Kulick: Well actually, I got a call from Paul and I got a call from Gene as well. Both asked me to play guitar on their solo albums. Paul was trying to do a more organic band-like approach, whereas Gene was trying to get a whole bunch of guests and piece it all together. You know, I would have liked to have played on both records. But the reality was if I played on Gene's record, as Gene pointed out to me, then there's two records with the same lead player on it, which I could understand his point. And also the fact that Paul was like, "Well, wait a minute. I'm using him so you can't use him." So I basically just said, "No problem. I totally understand." But [Paul's album] was a different project than the KISS "Alive II" thing in that Paul certainly gave me more latitude and longitude in terms of what I was able to play by virtue of me not trying to have to be somebody else.

Right. And I know that Gene was interested in you playing on his album but ultimately it didn't come to be since you were on Paul's album. Was this initially decided from the get-go then?
No, I wouldn't say it was from the get-go because we started Paul's record and then Gene went to England. And then it still went on from there. Gene actually sent me a letter, "I'm really sorry that it didn't work out. I feel bad." It was like, "No worries." I ended up writing a couple of things with Gene that saw the light of day. So you know, it kind of turned into like, "I write with Gene but I play with Paul." Although that changed when I got up and played with Gene at that beer fest they had here in downtown L.A. during Octoberfest [last year].

I saw some clips. That looked like a great time.
Yeah. It was very cool because Gene whispered in my ear, "You know with your brother and you up here with me, who could do any better?" And I was like, "Well, he didn't have to say that."

Yes, that's a nice compliment indeed. Bob, when you first got together with Paul regarding his solo album, did he play you some of the music he was working on? I'm curious what your first reaction was to hearing the material.
Well, by the time we got ready to do this, we basically went into the recording studio. And he would show us the song. "Here's what I wrote. Here's 'Move On.' "Okay." "Here's how it goes." And we'd play along, learn the song and come up with a vibe for the songs. The New York portion of the program was recorded at Electric Lady Studios, I believe with Dave Wittman as engineer. Paul conducted the sessions. You know, we really didn't have a producer. He asked me to suggest a bass player, which I did. Steve Buslowe, who was also the guy I suggested for the Meat Loaf gig. He is an amazingly creative bass player!!! And Paul wanted to use Richie Fontana, who I knew from Billy Squier's thing, Piper.

Yep.
The Aucoin connection! This was kind of a different band but the band had a vibe. Paul played and I played guitar — we played as a band until we got a good take, which didn't take very long to be honest. You know, they were simple, straight-ahead songs. His vocals and the lead guitar stuff — that's what really made them into what they were. It was my kind of opportunity to play with somebody who not only did I like on a musical level and who shared my taste in music — Zeppelin and that stuff — but was also somebody that I knew sounded good with. I sounded good with his vibe — it worked really good [*sic*].

"Tonight You Belong To Me" and "Wouldn't You Like To Know Me?" — Those songs were easy, because he was a fan of my playing and I played what was appropriate. You know, I was really into Dick Wagner at the time, who Paul was a big fan of as well. Dick Wagner, Steve Hunter — the guitar players that played on "Lou Reed Live" and the guitar players that played with Alice Cooper. I played with Dick Wagner when I did a tour with Alice Cooper in '77, filling in, in Australia and New Zealand, when Steve Hunter played with Peter Gabriel. So, here I am, "I'm playing with fucking Alice Cooper!"

(Laughs)
For Paul that was a big deal. And he was a big Balance fan, the band I had with Peppy [Castro]. The first time I met Doug [Katsaros] was [at] the "Paul Stanley" sessions in Los Angeles. Peppy and Doug were the other members in Balance. Half of Paul's record was done in New York and the other half was in sunny California where the car wrecks happened, where everybody was renting from Hertz. And the tour manager Chris Lendt was out here at the hotel, "What's going on?" Gene's crashing his car. Paul had the gate fall on his car. I wrapped my car around a pole. [And] Ace wrecked his car (laughs). We got very little done. It took forever to get anything done. And I guess Jeff Glixman was around at the time — not that any of that was his fault...

I was going to ask about Jeff Glixman. He ended up co-producing four tracks in L.A. but from what I have read it seems he and Paul didn't jell together. Do you remember what the issue was?
It was Paul's insecurity, "You know, maybe I need help?" And I said, "Help? What kind of help? It's just music. We know when it's right." So [Jeff Glixman] really had no effect on us whatsoever. I'm not saying anything bad about the guy. He was fine and he wasn't condescending in any way shape or form to me. He knew Paul loved my playing. To this day, "Larger Than Life," it stands on its own. "All-American Man" stands on its own. They might not do them [live] but that doesn't mean they don't exist and they're not great and people don't ask about them. But this was the opportunity to be me. So all that stuff — "Goodbye" and all those songs on Paul's record — I had a great time playing. And the added attraction was that I had become accustomed to: "Well, that's the last time you'll ever play on that. That's it. I played on the record and there ain't going to be no live band. You ain't gonna be touring." But in Paul's case, [nearly 10 years later], it was Paul asking, "What would you think about doing some shows?" "Excuse me?" "You know, like me and you and a few guys will go out and play." "Huh? You're kidding right?" "No, no, we'll play. We'll do a tour." Then it was like, "Wait a minute. Paul's serious!!!!!"

With Paul's record, I really got to play a lot of stuff that was me. "Tonight You Belong To Me," "Goodbye" and "Move On" — I was like, "Wow, this is really exciting." The [sings riff to "Tonight You Belong To Me"] — you know that riff. It's like a ball player; do they remember those games that were great games? You bet they do. You want to remember that. It's a good memory; those are good memories. Like yesterday I see the set-up. Paul had all those Gibson TV models, Les Pauls and a Flying V and all that. I was like, "Let me try that one." We just had a good time with it. And it sounded like it. And he sang his ass off. And that's what the Paul Stanley KISS would have sounded like, at least with me on lead guitar. Sort of like what KISS "Alive II" side four sounds like and "Nowhere To Run," because people ask me about that song too.

Getting deeper into some of the album's tracks, the solo in "Tonight You Belong To Me" is one of my favorites. It's very melodic, while maintaining an edge, and your fantastic vibrato really shines through.
I thought, "What should that be like? Maybe end on some high notes, start off with a definitive melody." Your mind and hand-eye coordination [take over] and you don't think about it and the idea just pops out and there it is. It just happens. I didn't work out any of those solos really; I just did them on the spot. Eventually we found what we were looking for. I say we, because Paul had to be happy and so did I.

Your leads do sound very spontaneous.

That's the way to make something special. It happened because the moment [was] right to have the kind of fun that one wants to have under those circumstances, which is [like] the batter batting in the bottom of the ninth with the winning run on base. A hit wins the game. You live for that. So this was one of those moments. I remember I had my old Les Paul, "Okay, here we go... 'Tonight You Belong To Me.'" And that's what came out, pretty much. I think I fixed a couple of notes maybe. That was it. It was like, "Fuck, that's great!" We tried a few other solos but they weren't as good.

So you tried a few takes and went with the one that felt the best?

Yeah. I recently heard a whole reel of outtakes (laughs) from "All-American Man" and "Larger Than Life." It was hilarious. I was just like, "Oh my God, there's part of it there." This must have been one of the attempts and then we used the good part in the comp. You comp together the best stuff.

Paul has described "Move On" as having a Bad Company-type feel. I think the girls from Desmond Child & Rouge really add a nice ingredient to this song.

Yes, that is correct. I don't think I was there for that. I don't recall that I was there, Paul just did that. He was good friends [with], and we were big fans of, Desmond Child & Rouge. That's how Paul became friendly with Desmond, that's how they ultimately wrote together, and that led Desmond to Jon Bon Jovi and on to fame and glory.

"Ain't Quite Right" is a moody song, a real departure for Paul at the time. To my ears, your solo is a clinic in dynamics. Your lines really fit perfectly with the music: they starts quietly and build momentum only to gently cascade into those final singable licks. What do you remember about this particular solo?

Well again, I hate to keep using the baseball analogy but baseball is my sport of choice. I play softball and hand-eye coordination — they are kind of linked together. The song and where it was — as you say, the vibe of the song — was in my wheelhouse. That's the pitch that I could hit out of the park. That groove, that feel, those licks ... they just [came] to me. You're able to just really play to this vibe. For me, it's an easy vibe to play with. That was the good thing about [the album] — the style of Paul's writing really fit the style of my playing. And it really easily married together, like, "Oh, that's seamless." "Yeah, exactly. It's the right vibe for what it is." It wasn't work, it was, "Let's just have some fun," which makes it 100 times better. We had fun doing it. And that's the thing; this was not a stressful situation. This was a really relaxed ... let's have some fun situation. We did.

"Take Me Away (Together As One)" is another departure. There is a lot of acoustic guitar and some dynamic swings. I don't know that I've heard a song from Paul like it before or after. Bob, did you play any acoustic on this track?

Yeah, some of the acoustics, I must have done. Some. But mainly the electrics and the solo. That was one of the L.A. songs. And that was when Carmine Appice came down to play.

One of the things I love about "Take Me Away" is your memorable fills in between Paul's vocal parts. I take it these were overdubbed after Paul sang his lead vocal?
Yes, that was a "wait until the vocal was on there and see if it needs anything else. You know what, let's see about putting some licks in here." See with guys that can really play — and I'm not saying that in an egotistical way — and that can fill a hole with something meaningful, then you try to [let them] find it. "Here's where the vocal ends. Stick something in there that will work with the vocal in the track that will help it." You know, [in the] second verse, something slightly different happens. Like "Goodbye," where we did the same thing — [we] stuck some stuff inside there, not just [the same thing], but also licks that definitely helped move the song along and answered Paul's vocals correctly. And it was definitely one of the things that Jimmy Page used to do. Paul's a huge Led Zeppelin fan, so he allowed me, "Yeah, yeah. Throw some shit in there. Go for it." If he didn't like it, he'd make that face, "Nah." "Can I try again?" "Sure." Eventually I'd find something and he'd say, "I like that!" "I like it too." Again, we were friends, we hung out together, we went to the same concerts together, we went out to eat together, we listened to music together — so was it so unusual that the guitar vibe was so really together on this [album]? No, it was the fact that we were in sync at that moment in our lives. We were very in sync. We were like best friends and I really cherish that time we spent together.

"It's Alright" is another straight-ahead rocker. It's interesting to note that Paul used a Gallien-Kreuger amp on this tune. Of course, that company is fairly known for its bass amps. Do you recall the Gallien-Kreuger being used?
I guess it's possible, I mean everything was in there but the kitchen sink (laughs). If you ever saw the picture of all the guitars, between his and mine, that were over at the Record Plant. There were like 20 guitars sitting there. It was pretty cool, including his flying V, and some acoustics and a Les Paul. Maybe that TV model I used, just a bunch of guitars.

Did you play any guitars on the ballad, "Hold Me, Touch Me"?
Paul just kind of tackled that himself. I was like, "That's good."

I know Paul is particularly fond of his solo in that song and I think he did a very nice job. "Love In Chains" features Steve Lacey on guitar.
Yeah, he played on some of it and I played on some of it.

Who was Steve Lacey?
He was somebody from L.A. that Paul was introduced to. It was just one of those, "Sure, he'll play. That's fine." And then ultimately it was like, "[You] play too." It was fun. "Hold Me, Touch Me" was [Paul's] thing so I thought it was appropriate, just like when he did "A World Without Heroes." I remember he played it for me and I said, "You know what, that's a pretty good solo Paul. You did that right?" He's like, "Yep." I said, "It's really good. It's very melodic." And I thought to myself, "It sounds like he's trying to play like me." And he said, "I was trying to play like you." I was like, "Wow, what a compliment. Thank you so much."

That's one of my favorite KISS guitar solos. Bob, your sound seems fairly straightforward on Paul's album. Aside from guitars, did you use any pedals or effects?
Mainly I just plugged directly into the Marshall. And they ran the effects through the board so if I had more delay — you know "[make it] a little bit wetter" — whatever it was, it went through the board. I may have used the wah-wah pedal on something. It's possible I just kind of set it in a setting — sometimes rather than "wah-wah-wah" you just set it somewhere and it kind of speaks in a cool way to what you're playing. But really, no, it was pretty much pure.

And Bob, how many guitar tracks would you guys have recorded on these songs? For instance, did you double some parts?
Easily, [there was] Paul's double, my double, my leads, auxiliary stuff [like] EBows — yeah, there was just tons of stuff.

I know Paul was quite fond of using the EBow around this period and that he used it on a few tracks. Did you use one as well?
No, he was the EBow king. He liked to play with the EBow. No, one did not infringe upon Paul's EBowing (laughs).

(Laughs) Bob, putting your studio hat on, what's your take on how Paul's album holds up, from a production standpoint?
Well, it's a great record. How could anybody fault it? It sounds like the people who were doing it were having a good time. And all the songs seem sincere. As a producer, that's all you could really ask for. Paul sang his ass off as he always does. Even live, he always gave 100 percent even if he didn't have it. He always went for it. [He never] chickened out. The record pretty much has that spontaneous vibe, especially the New York tracks. But all of it to me was special in that I enjoyed playing with him.

And sonically speaking?
I think it holds up. I do. Because the most important things are the songs and the performances. That's still the single most important thing. Paul's voice sounds great

and the guitars sound great. Those guitars are miked up really well in a recording studio. All of the sounds are organic. I like that. Everything fits.

Paul's album still resonates with fans to this day. If I had to ballpark it, I think either his album or Ace's album rank as the favorite among a majority of fans. Bob, did you ever give a listen to Ace's solo album?
"New York Groove" and all that stuff on his record? I thought it was great stuff. Very underrated, I mean "New York Groove" was the hit of all four of the records.

That's right.
He didn't write it, but so what? He was smart enough to whip it out and put his personality on it to make it work for him. And you can never say the guy didn't have his own personality because he did. And you know I wanted him to be on the Christmas record that I produced a few years ago with the late Ronnie Dio, may he rest in peace, and Lemmy, Billy Gibbons, Dave Grohl, Tony Iommi, and Geoff Tate and all the great artists who came in to work on it. But what can you say?

While working on Paul's album, you mentioned that was the first time you met Doug Katsaros. Was that also the first time you met Peppy Castro?
No, I knew Peppy from before. I knew Peppy back when he was in the Blues Magoos.

Which leads into my Balance question ... I love good melodic AOR rock and those first two Balance albums really fit the bill. The material is really in line with some of the great AOR of the period: Toto, Journey and Foreigner. If you could have one mulligan with Balance, what would it be?
I guess all I can say, and be politically correct, is the idea that we not tour until "something happened." Because the band did very few dates and that was Steve Leber's approach: "These songs are great. Let them just explode on radio. They'll be a hit, [and] the people that hear them will then want to see the band." If I could do it over again, David Krebs would have handled it and he would have sent us out on the road.

How many tour dates did Balance end up doing?
Not many. I mean we played a few. We did some shows in Japan, and that was it.

Bob, I know you've been working on a Michael Jackson tribute album. How is that coming along?
Yeah, the metal Michael Jackson tribute album is done and will be released on October 22 [Ed. 2013] through Cleopatra Records. You know I've played it for a few people — they've heard the songs and they were shitting their pants. The material is so great whether he wrote the songs or not. Like "Thriller," it's not [Michael Jackson's] composition. He's singing the song but it's not his composition. We have

a great version with [Testament's] Chuck Billy singing. How different can you get from that?

No kidding.

He did great. And some of the songs, "Man In The Mirror" and stuff like that, they're very emotional songs. I can't wait for people to hear them. They have some really great performances — Doug Aldrich, Bumblefoot, my brother, Billy Sheehan, Rudy Sarzo, Phil Campbell. Some of the playing on there is seriously really great. As far as the lead singers, they don't get better than these guys.

Speaking of your brother, have you guys kicked around the idea of doing an album together?

Yeah, we've been talking about it. We're talking about doing some shows, you know Europe, South America — wherever people are excited about seeing us play — and at least trying to do an EP so we have something out there. That is what we are discussing now, actually. I think it's going to happen; it will just take some time. But I assume it will be well worth it.

Jeff Glixman

The award-winning producer/engineer gives his first-ever in-depth interview about his involvement on Paul Stanley's 1978 solo album.
Interview by Tim McPhate

Jeff, let's rewind to summer 1978. What are your recollections of coming onboard for Paul Stanley's solo album?
Jeff Glixman: Well, they're pretty clear. We had some huge success with Kansas with our album in fall 1977, "Point Of Know Return." The band had done a big tour and a lot of things had gone on and they wanted to take a break for a little bit. So we all decided, "Let's take a little break and go to Hawaii and take a few months off." I returned from Hawaii and my attorney called me and said, "Paul Stanley is in the midst of an album. I know you've got another album coming up, but there's a little window of opportunity, would you like to work on it?" I was thinking, "Vacation or work with Paul Stanley? I'm going with Paul."

You came onboard for the album's sessions in Los Angeles. Do you recall being at the Village Recorder?
I remember working at the Village. We worked at the Record Plant too.

Legend has it that Paul visited a studio in the valley and decided it wasn't up to par. Does that ring a bell?
He might have taken a look at Sound City, I don't know. I had produced out of Sound City, which was funky to look at but an awesome-sounding studio. As you know, Dave Grohl just completed a documentary film about Sound City and the history of that place. It was a funky place but a really good studio. I just remember the studios being tossed around but I didn't handle the bookings.

Do you remember the type of consoles that were at the Record Plant and Village?
Sure, they were APIs at the Record Plant, either 550 or 500-A modules. And in Studio D at the Village there was a beautiful Neve 8078.

Can you describe what you remember about the first time you met Paul Stanley?
When I met Paul for the first time, I was sitting there waiting and this gentleman walked in, in makeup.

(Laughs)
No, just kidding (laughs). He walked in with like khaki slacks and a blue blazer with a little paper bag from a deli in his hand. I think he had just been to visit his mother. He was a very nice, refined gentleman.

Was this in L.A.?
We met in an office in New York. I was working basically out of New York at the time. It may have been Bill Aucoin's office.

And during your initial conversation, did Paul convey what he was looking to accomplish?
You know, he was far into this thing. I don't remember the reason, but he'd started cutting some of it in New York. I had a project coming up and I had only a certain amount of time I could spend on it. I believe Mike Stone mixed the record, if I'm correct.

That's right.
I had been on a couple of dates with Kansas recording some live stuff where they had done shows with KISS in the early days. It was pretty interesting to see them at that point. Obviously, they were a big band destined to become one of the greatest and most successful bands in the world. I was excited to meet him and see what he was up to. He had a very definite idea of what he wanted to accomplish.

When you were brought onboard, was it with the understanding you were going to produce the entire album?
(Pauses) Originally, I didn't have the time to produce the entire project. I had a time constraint because I had another record coming up that I had to get to that had a hard start date. As I said, I had planned to take some vacation time. It was my understanding that we'd certainly work on all the tracks — that there were certain things that either needed to be recut or worked on or that we'd recut parts of, or whatever. And I never intended to get to the mix unless we went really fast.

As you alluded to, the first four tracks on the album were recorded at Electric Lady Studios in New York, prior to your involvement: "Tonight You Belong To Me," "Move On," "Ain't Quite Right," and "Wouldn't You Like To Know Me?" Paul has stated that the recordings in New York were designed to be demos and that they originally were going to be recut. Do you remember giving these tracks another go in Los Angeles?
No, I don't believe we did. "Ain't Quite Right," we might have given a shot. But from the start, I don't recall re-cutting any of those New York tracks. I wasn't around for the New York tracks, but what's interesting is those were the four songs I first heard. Obviously, as evidenced from my later production with artists like Georgia Satellites, I've got a real rock and roll edge to me. Those were the most rock and rolly of the songs; they were kind of blues rock. "Ain't Quite Right," I love that song. But I don't recall that we recut those tracks.

So was there a decision made that the New York tracks were fine as is?

I think we recut bits and pieces on them. Basically, in my career I've never cut demos. I've cut songs that may have used part of a demo or something. I learned early on that it is hard to recapture stuff. Like "Keep Your Hands To Yourself" was part of a six-song Georgia Satellites demo. It was just a terrific cut that I did try to replicate because, in that case, two of the band members had left. It took three years to get the band signed and they wanted to recut it with the new band. But I never came close to topping the original demo, and that's the one on the album. It's hard to recreate something that you're excited about and when you first perform it. But I thought that those four Electric Lady songs sounded just terrific.

So you were impressed by the material Paul had come up with?
Oh yeah, I really liked the songwriting.

In listening to samples of those first four tracks, does anything stick out as being deficient?
You mean, would I like to go back and do them again?

In other words, given that there were tracks cut in New York that were designed to be demos alongside tracks cut separately in L.A., is there a lack of cohesion?
I don't think so. There's a different vibe to them. But are we talking engineering or are we talking production? You know, a great song performed well could be recorded in any condition and it can sound great, regardless of the technical aspects. A poor song poorly played, no matter how technically well you recorded it, it will still sound like crap. You just won't go on listening to it. So, I think from my standpoint as producer the question is: Do you get off listening to the song or do you not get off listening to the song? And that's about it. You know, I just listened to "Ain't Quite Right" and it still sounds great!

I should share with you that Paul's album is still highly regarded by fans even 35 years later. My question was coming more from an engineering perspective, as far as if there was anything glaring sonically.
You know, I'm not going to make that statement. Like I said, I try to look at the piece of work as a whole. I can look at every project I've ever worked on, and certain things were under duress. I've never had a project that was free from the limits and constraints of time and money so there's always compromises that are made and things that could be done differently. I think you can always look around and find things. But in my experience, I know it's highly regarded by fans and personally people have always said to me how much they enjoyed the record.

Jeff, I feel obligated to ask this next question. There have been a few things I've read over the years about your involvement on this album. One quote from Paul Stanley I want to bring up was published in the authorized KISS autobiography, "Behind The Mask." Paul said: "When I started recording with a co-producer it

wasn't what I hoped it to be and I went back to doing it myself." Jeff, you have the floor, how would you like to respond to that?

Okay, I want to say that there was a major misunderstanding going into this thing: Paul's idea of a producer and my idea of a producer. And this is something I'll share, I never worked in the studio as a studio engineer, I've never taken that role. For me as a producer, I've always been involved in determining the sonic landscape, the visual close-your-eyes aspects of how it was going to be done. I'm making this comment with all due respect to Paul. I believe what he really wanted was an engineer. What he needed was an engineer because he had very definite ways he wanted to do things. And that's not really the position I intended to be in. Paul said, "We're going to double-track every vocal." Well for me, when you double-track a vocal, your performance gets averaged out. He wanted to double things for effect and oversee how everything was going to be placed and everything was going to be done. So to be honest with you, Paul's really the producer of the record, regardless of what it says. I think his idea of producer was an organizational producer, what I might call an executive producer or a strong label person, not a creative person. And Paul had very definite ideas of what he wanted to do, how it was going to go. "This is going to go there. We're going to put this part on." I'm used to being more involved in the arrangement of the songs.

When I was very young, I spoke to Arif Mardin [Ed. Famed producer of numerous acts, including Aretha Franklin, the Bee Gees, and Phil Collins, who along with Tom Dowd and Jerry Wexler established the pop-soul style known as the Atlantic Sound in the late 1960's], who I was fortunate to meet because my manager was Jack Nelson, who was Queen's manager. Jack and Arif were friends. And I said, "What about songwriting?" He said, "Don't worry about taking a songwriting credit. You're going to get paid as a producer. And you'll find that if you assure your artist up front that you're not interested in taking a songwriting credit, they'll be very lenient in letting you get your ideas across." And so I'm used to co-writing a song, changing lyrics, moving melodies around, changing arrangements ... everything. For me, it was really odd to be in this situation, "I want this. I want more high-end on the guitar. I'm looking for this type of sound. We're going to double this track. We're going to do that." It was very much an engineering position. I don't know how Paul really looks at it. But to be honest with you, I've never been in the position where the artist, every single note that was played or sung, he said, "Let me hear it to approve it." I'm used to saying, "Okay, that was it. Let's move on." Do you know what I'm saying? It was a much different position. And I don't want this to come across negatively, because I just feel great about Paul's talents and abilities and what he does. But I was very young; I was only in my 20s. I come from playing in bands, writing songs and performing. So it was a very different situation for me. And going forward from that day, I never did another project without spending time in the studio with the artist before I accepted it.

Well, to be honest Jeff, it's refreshing to hear your side of things. I don't know that the fans have heard your perspective.

I don't mean it in a negative sense, but it wasn't what I hoped it would be either. It was very much Paul as the producer, and he is quite capable in that role. He wanted to give the instructions, the direction. There was a point in time, I suppose, when the producer was the guy who had the money, hired the musical director, hired a songwriter, and this, that and the other, but this was not role that I assumed. After that, I was very leery of working with any artist who was successful before I worked with them. I loved working with Gary Moore in his formative days and taking him to platinum status. Same thing with the Georgia Satellites. The next time I worked with a really big band that had already made it was Electric Light Orchestra because I find that English artists, in general, are just great about, "Hey, your job is on that side of the glass and mine is out here to play." I worked with these guys and you never heard: "Let me hear that" before we moved on. If I said it was right, it was right. We'd line up to do millions of tracks of vocals and start at 8 in morning. Never once did they want to play something back until it was completed and we could review the creative aspects of the performance. I worked with Ritchie Blackmore, same thing. He might say, "Let me hear what I played." But if I said we needed to do it again or it wasn't really what I was looking for, I would never get that conflict. It was very different working with Paul. It really changed my approach. I think he made a good, accurate statement there. That's why he continued on his own. To be honest, he wanted to be the producer, he deserved to be the producer and he should have been. You know, I would have done loads of things differently, sonically and musically, had I had the opportunity, but this was Paul's album and his prerogative.

That's all very interesting, Jeff. And I appreciate your honest thoughts.

Good. Because I'm very positive about the record. It was just different from what I anticipated. One of the records I did after that was with Gary Moore. He loved the first thing I said to him. He said, "What do you like? What's your approach toward recording?" I said, "Let's get the songs where we're happy with them. Once we're happy with the songs, I want to put you in a situation — a room or wherever it is — where you can perform at your best. I want to record this room. Paul's record was a much tighter approach, more recording parts to make up the whole. It's just a different approach. Mine's much more free-flowing. Mine is like, "Well, you didn't hit that tom-tom as hard in that place." "Well, that's because the drummer didn't hit it that hard. You don't even it out or work it over." I don't know how to explain technically what I'm trying to say any better than that. It's just a different concept all together.

So about the sonics of Paul's album, to me, the New York tracks sound better because they were done quickly in a demo fashion with the drums kind of loosely miked as opposed to all the care and attention that goes into, "Okay, we're in an expensive studio cutting the master, let's put a mic on everything and balance it out; we've got loads of tracks." To me, that's not the best decision-making process. Even when I record today in the day of 9 zillion tracks, I want to make the decisions upfront. We recently did a 40th anniversary reenactment of "Carry On My Wayward Son" for Kansas and I got a call from Sony. The guy was flipping out. He said, "I don't think these are the original tracks." I said, "Why?" He said, "Well, the drums are only on four tracks. They're premixed to four tracks." I said, "Yeah, Phil [Ehart] knew what he was going to play. I knew how it should sound. It's on four tracks, what's the problem?" So I think the demos, with all due respect, I think they're better. They just have a vibe, do you know what I mean? They're just, "Let's set up and play."

That's the sentiment some of the musicians have expressed in describing the New York tracks. Bassist Steve Buslowe said there was a "vibe" that was missing from the L.A. tracks.

Yeah, the L.A. tracks were, "We're going to put it down then we're going to replace everything. Okay, we've got the drum tracks. Now we're going to put on the bass, now we're going to put on this guitar, that guitar and the other." It just didn't have the vibe, even the ones I worked on. We did some vocal work and some solo work on the New York tracks, but I just like them better [than the L.A. tracks]. They've got the vibe.

In terms of the general process for the L.A. tracks, did the band play through the tracks and then specific instruments were replaced afterward?

Well, certainly reference guitar and bass and drums went down. But yeah, it was put back together. Paul was in the control room when we were cutting the drum tracks.

So your preference would have been the band would have played the tracks down and captured a great take and, hopefully, the "vibe" of the song?

Well, my way of doing it, and I'm pretty consistent about this, I would have done it with a band playing and working out the arrangement and getting it all together. But typically I'm going to go into rehearsal and pre-production and everyone is going to kind of know where we're going. We'll sort out the arrangement and 19 different things. With ["Take Me Away (Together As One)"], Carmine came in and learned a drum track and put down the drum track with the bass and guitar. Carmine's great, I still have a relationship with him to this day. We still see each other at NAMM [Ed. National Association of Music Merchants — mainly known for music related trade shows held in various locations]. But it's just a different approach that a lot of people have. You know, I've heard this argument where artists say to me, "I like the spontaneity of going into the studio." And I say, "I like the spontaneity of it too. But there's a big difference between getting down the hill without falling and doing some skiing. If you know how the skiing course runs, you're going to do some freestyle on the way down. If you understand the song and the arrangement instead of concentrating on how the song goes and where you're supposed to go to a chorus or verse, you're going to relax and you're going to do some playing. I like to go in having spent a good amount of time in rehearsal.

A great example of this is a record I cut with Saraya. I cut that record — basically 80 percent of it, vocals included — in a 10-day stretch at Bearsville where we would play most of the record before dinner. And then after dinner I would just pick the takes where they nailed it. In those 10 days, Sandi [Saraya] would sing it as it went down then we touched it up later. And the whole thing's got a tremendous vibe to it. So I prefer to be prepared and go in and get it. I think Paul, hearing the complexities of the music with Kansas, figured I was really used to doing this approach. But the odd thing is, and this is something that most people don't realize, the only Kansas track I ever cut to a click track was "Dust in the Wind" because there are no drums. Those songs were all played ensemble. The band played those songs; then we went back and added to it. So even with Kansas, the approach was still the same. So that's the real distinction.

Staying with "Take Me Away (Together As One")," this song is considered to be the epic track on the album. It's got a lot of acoustic guitar, cinematic lyrics and dynamics galore. As a matter of fact, this tune has a strong Kansas vibe. Did you have any influence on the direction of this song?
That's the one I had the most input on because it was a big complex song. And I think that's the kind of song Paul was less familiar with.

It was a departure for Paul at the time. He hadn't written a song like that, and I don't think he's written one like it since.
It was a departure. It was one of those songs that I liked. Of the songs I worked on, I was the most attached to it because I was very comfortable having a song that you could play on acoustic guitar or a piano that you expand into this bigger epic rock thing. That's always been my other stipulation, if you couldn't sit there and play the song on a guitar or a piano, and make it sound like a song, it really shouldn't be recorded. I was very comfortable in saying, "Okay, let's build this thing up and add various things to it." I think it came out well. I think that's the one where Paul was more open to suggestion because he wasn't used to working on a track like this.

It's a wonderful track. The interesting thing about Carmine Appice is that legend has it that his timing was off for the fills at the end of the song and the drum track had to be edited. Do you recall this?
First of all, he was on the spot because he was just learning the song and playing it and trying to get through it. Timing's a funny thing because you get back into that whole click track [versus] we're doing it straight ahead [argument]. You're talking to

me as a producer who is used to working across various time signatures with a band that really didn't even know that they were changing time signatures in the early days (laughs). I used to play with the guys in Kansas and we thought, "Well, that's great. Let's just drop a beat here." You have the song "Lonely Street" that had three bars of three and then one bar of two. It's (sings) 1-2-3, 1-2-3, 1-2-3, 1-2, 1-2-3, 1-2-3, 1-2-3, 1-2. We never thought about it. So I'm used to sliding across time but I'm also used to using tempo as a dynamic. I mean, Carmine was comfortable with it, too. I don't know if it was from his Vanilla Fudge days or whatever. But a lot of times people get caught up in the rigidity of that click track or being on time, do you know what I mean?

Absolutely.
When you listen to epic pieces or classical music, tempo is one of the dynamics. You know: loud, soft; fast, slow. Things are constantly moving. In Kansas, "Song For America," the thing speeds up and slows down all over the place. You know, one can get really sterile with these things as well.

For the rest of the L.A. tracks, there was a different rhythm section brought onboard. On bass was Eric Nelson and on drums was Craig Krampf. Do you recall why they were brought into the project?
These were all Paul's picks. Craig was great. I ended up keeping in touch with him after his move to Nashville. These guys were efficient. They were used to playing as hired help. But I want to go back to Carmine for a minute. One of the things I've also stayed away from in my career — although I was early in my career back then — I've stayed away from using studio musicians who had done lots of session work. Typically it's just the nature of the beast that people have a comfort zone. Anton Fig is a great drummer and a great friend of mine. He's very aware of this. When you approach a song and you have a huge repertoire of songs you've recorded, it's going to remind you of something you've previously recorded so you kind of tend to say, "I remember on this song, I did this." And you kind of fall into that routine. I always tried to look for unknowns that were taking their first real shot in the studio and work with them. A good example of how well this works is when I met Eric Singer, who plays in KISS. When I met Eric I was doing some pre-production work with Lita Ford. Although the label ended up dropping the project, I went on to work with Tony Iommi and I was so impressed with Eric that I said, "Eric, you've never been in a session? Come on; come work with Tony for me." He did Black Sabbath's albums for me. He went on to work with Gary Moore and tour with him. And he went on to join KISS.

I wasn't ever hampered working with Carmine. He was just the best. And I couldn't have been happier working with Craig. He was very proficient and professional. But Carmine was like a kid with the band recording his first song ... what enthusiasm!

Craig was awesome. His timing was great. He was very comfortable. But he had a different kind of feel.

Exactly. There are three different drummers on the album. I think if you listen closely, you can hear it. Switching gears to guitarists, Bob Kulick has been lauded by both fans and fellow musicians for his guitar work on the album. What are your thoughts on his guitar tracks in listening back to them with fresh ears?
Bob's a great guy. He's an A-plus guitar player. I don't care how many sessions he's been on, he was in his wheelhouse. He played some great stuff all the way around. He got the feel of the songs and the diversity. He's one of those all-star kind of players. I don't think he's known so much for being in any band but I thought he did an outstanding job all the way around. I've been fortunate to work with some absolutely killer guitar players and Bob is one of them.

Paul has described his rhythm guitar philosophy as owing a lot to Pete Townshend. What were your impressions of Paul's ability as a rhythm guitarist?
I would say that his description is accurate. He's kind of a conceptualizer and a facilitator. I don't care who was producing the Who, I imagine Pete Townshend was doing a hell of a lot of that production. I think they may have given Glyn Johns a production credit but Glyn's an engineer, and a fantastic one. He came up as an engineer. There's a real distinction. As I said, I didn't come up that way. I came up from the band side, writing and playing. That was really the main thing about me working on the record. With all due respect, Paul was expecting and deserved to have a killer engineer who would take his instructions. Instead, he got somebody who wanted to put in his opinion.

"Love In Chains" is one of the straight-ahead rockers on the album. A guitarist named Steve Lacey played on this tune. Do you recall why Steve was brought in?
That wasn't my call. But I like that track a lot. It's got that nice ascending riff. It's a good solid rock track.

Paul has recounted an interesting tale about the final song, "Goodbye." Apparently, the musicians came to the studio one day and Paul said he didn't have a song so he told them to go out and grab a bite and come back. When they returned, Paul presented them with "Goodbye." Do you have any memories of this song coming together in this fashion?
I do remember Paul had some ideas and it was an unfinished track and that it kind of came together in the studio. He's dead accurate on his recollection. But it wasn't like he said, "I'm starting from air." He had thoughts in mind. He had bits and pieces but it wasn't yet a song. It was more of a concept of a song that needed arrangement.

Given you said that you had a limited window for the project, would you recall how much time you spent in the studio with Paul?
I think we worked on it about a month. I had a project with EMI coming up — I had Mother's Finest for Atlantic that ended up being delayed. At that moment, I had a lot of work that I was involved in.

Jeff, what kind of interaction did you have with Paul regarding his lead vocals?
We did lots of vocals. But Paul said, "This is what I'm singing. We're doubling it." All of it was really his direction. I was recording the vocals.

What are your thoughts about Paul Stanley's vocal performance on the album?
I think Paul accomplished what he wanted to accomplish with the vocals. Some of it has really stood the test of time well. He was comfortable with all the keys he wanted to sing in and he knew what he wanted to sing.

Jeff, we've spoken about the difference in your definition of a producer compared to Paul's, but I feel I have to ask this question as well. I've heard that there was some tension between you and Paul during the sessions. Is that what you recall?
I don't know if tension is the right word. But yeah, there was definitely a conflict. Basically I wasn't prepared for it to be, "This is the way it is. Record it." I made a commitment and I wanted to fulfill my commitment. But as I said, I changed my whole interview process following that record. You know, Ritchie Blackmore was one of my heroes and I was hesitant to work with him. We had about six meetings and spent about four days in the studio and I told him I'd pay for it if we didn't continue just because I wanted to make sure that it was going to work. It worked beautifully but I've been very cautious. I've had at least three productions with Yngwie Malmsteen. I'm sure you've heard the rumors about Yngwie and how difficult he is. I don't find him so at all. I just think it is imperative to take the time to make sure there is a producer/artist match.

Paul knew exactly what he wanted and he was prepared for it. I was prepared to make a record where I had certain input. There was never, "Let's get together and you and I work over the songs. What do you think of these lyrics? What do you think about this for a melody line?" There was never, "Okay, but Paul, in that second verse, why don't you try going up to an A instead of down to the F#." It just didn't happen.

In hearing your side of the story, I guess my natural question is: Why did Paul even bring someone in, in a production capacity, if he already had such a clear vision of what he wanted from a production standpoint?
Well, I think it was about the definition of producer. Because a lot of producers out there are engineers — they are really fine engineers and they deliver. Not to sound immodest or anything, but in '76 and '77 the sound of Kansas was pretty strong on

the airwaves. George Marino at Sterling Sound told me that he's had people for 30 years use "Carry On My Wayward Son" as a reference, "Man, this sounds amazing." Maybe Paul thought my position as a producer was to engineer those records. But I played with the guys in Kansas prior to those productions. Recently we were inducted into the state of Kansas Hall of Fame, which was really weird because you've got Amelia Earhart and Eisenhower and people like that in there. I was really humbled by the speech the guys gave and Kerry talking about how I was the real seventh member of the band and was integral to them. That's where I came from. I came from a position of having that kind of input. Was mine always considered and did I dominate the room? No. I've never been put in a position in any of my productions, except for this project with Paul, where we couldn't find a place where we were both happy. I think, in retrospect, had I been more experienced and understood more at the time, I would have just said, "Paul, you need an engineer." But I thought, "Well, it's just me adapting." I didn't have a lot of projects under my belt. You ask a very good question. In retrospect, I think Paul and I would say, "Hey, let's shake hands and be buddies." And I'd say, "I want you to have a great record but call up Paul Grupp or Keith Olsen, or one of the killer engineers of the time and let them do the record."

Jeff, do you consider the "Paul Stanley" album a positive experience for you?
I'd say the result is a positive experience because whenever you can record something that does something for society that creates a positive social impact and pleases people, [then] yes it's a success. I would venture to say I do not think "Take Me Away" would have sounded like that had I not been involved. For me, there are two songs that are just classics on that record. One is "Take Me Away" and the other is "Ain't Quite Right." Those are my two favorite songs. I think they display the whole scope of the record. Yeah, it's positive. I was pleased to meet Paul. I have great respect for him personally and professionally. But I think we were both young and we both didn't have a ton of these situations under our belts. I think Paul's expectations were one thing and I my expectations were another. I think Carmine was outstanding and I'm very pleased to have worked with him and have maintained a lasting relationship with him. So yeah, it's positive.

In September 1978, KISS caused a stir with the simultaneous release of the four solo albums. Of course, the project was accompanied by a huge marketing and promotion campaign. What do you recall the dialog to be in the industry about the solo albums?
It was a huge deal. I had just come off a record that out of the box sold 4 million copies. I cut "Dust In The Wind" in Nashville. At the time, the biggest-selling record in Nashville was gold, 500,000 copies. So we had the Attorney General of the State make us honorary members of the Tennessee State legislature. But the solo albums were a big deal. I had just come off that 4 million seller and I remember the buzz around L.A. was KISS, "What are they doing? There is no way this is going to sell.

This is all overblown. They may ship a million but these are coming back." Everyone was talking about it. I recall Paul's album being well-received and I'm proud to have been part of it.

From the L.A. sessions, the only track you are not credited on is the ballad, "Hold Me, Touch Me (Think Of Me When We're Apart)." That song was actually released as the single from the album.

Which I was totally surprised by. Because I thought we'd go with "Ain't Quite Right" or one of the rockers, even "Love In Chains." I was totally surprised that was the single. I think the world was expecting Paul to come out and show that he could rock.

To be candid, that's probably the one blemish for a lot of fans who love the album. Some are not particularly fond of that track, let alone it being the single that represented the album.

That was the only other thing I remember at that time. "Why did he release that? He could have blown away 'New York Groove.' Paul really cut the rockin' album." It was like, "Why that?" But the buzz was huge on all the records.

Have you run into Paul at all since working with him on this album?

Oddly enough, we've never crossed paths. The closest I came is Eric Singer called me when they were on tour and said, "Why don't you come to the show?" I couldn't make it to the show. At the time, I was working out of the country in the Caribbean. Eric and I were going to connect but we never got a chance to. Of course, I've followed his career and they've done great. Paul is a wonderful person, so don't get me wrong, I hold him in the highest regard. I think that he has his own vision of who he is, as he is entitled and should. It's funny because I always thought if Paul and I sat down, we'd go, "Well, that was a mismatch," and we'd have a little laugh about it. I'd go, "I expected this." And he'd go, "I expected that." But you do what you can do. More than anything, I think the best way to put it is we each had different expectations. There was no animosity, at least not on my part. I didn't feel like there was friction.

An interesting aside is that KISS had just come off recording three studio albums, one with Bob Ezrin and two Eddie Kramer. As far as production style and philosophy, you'd be hard-pressed to find better polar opposites in terms of producers.

Yeah, Eddie's a straight engineer. At that time, Bob was coming into being a producer. But he has that same background. The guys in Kansas co-produced a record with Bob Ezrin [1988's "In The Spirit Of Things"]. So I have my own take about what that was like for them. But again, you're working with guys who were very open to input in the guys in Kansas. So maybe after that experience, Paul realized for his solo album that he knew exactly what he wanted.

Jeff, I understand you are now affiliated with a learning institution in Pennsylvania. Can you inform us about this endeavor and what else you are up to these days?
Well, we're in the process of putting together a media arts college with a gentleman who was with Full Sail [University] and Phil Ehart of Kansas. We have been working on a different concept, kind of a next-generation [institution] that works with the new technology that's available. I've watched the world change and music is no longer an end result as much as it is a component to a multimedia experience. We're taking an approach that incorporates music as such but looks at the aggregation of multimedia content in this world and the delivery mechanisms, and the opportunity to develop the skills to create while also being able to have a sustainable career when you come out of this school. There are a lot of opportunities and it's kind of readjustment of thinking. It's not, "Let's go in and this is how you make a hit record." It's a real multimedia arts school that we're putting together. Now, the process of this is also a way to enable high-quality audio and video production to be available to artists now that the labels aren't funding it and there aren't big studios to do this. We've figured out a way to make this whole package work together to continue the art form.

In the meantime, I still continue to do some production. Phil and I were involved with a band that we didn't end up doing the production for, but we did some consulting with them — a group called 21 Pilots that's just breaking out now. We're also consultants on a band in Trinidad. And Phil and I right now, we're working on a video book for Sony which is for the 40th anniversary for Kansas. It's a video book just as it sounds, deliverable online, that will have additional chapters as we go. We recently went down to the studio in New Orleans to do a reenactment of the mix of "Carry On My Wayward Son."

As we've discussed, you've worked with some gifted artists in Kansas, Gary Moore, Black Sabbath, Styx, Yngwie Malmsteen, and Georgia Satellites. How about a great studio story to take us out?
I remember I was mixing a record for Yngwie and it was late at night and he goes in the back of the room and smokes a cigarette and has a glass of wine. This kid walks in and taps me on the shoulder and he says, "Hi, I'm Chris Impellitteri and you're going to want to work with me. I can play every one of his solos." And he points at Yngwie. Yngwie looks up with the cigarette dangling from his mouth and says (mimics Swedish accent), "Yes, but can you play any of your own?" (Laughs)

Other Related Interviews

Victor
RECORDS & TAPES

キッス・ファンに急告！

いますぐいつものレコード店で
ばっちり予約しよう！
各￥2,500

4人の噂のソロ・アルバム10月下旬一挙発売決定！

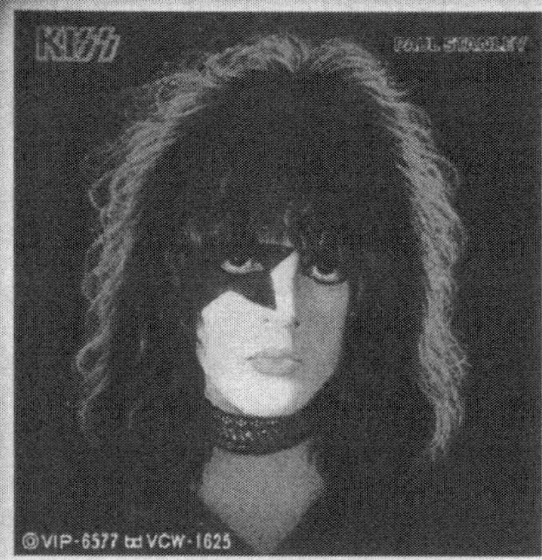

さあ大変だ、キッス・ファン諸君、待ちに待った噂のソロ・アルバムが一挙に出るぞ。メンバーが内容を極秘にしてるので、出るまでのお楽しみだが、問題はまずはお目当ての1枚だけにするか、1度にモノにしちまうか。キッスは映画もつくったし、当分新作はない、日本公演もない、となると、キッス・ファンたるもの、この4枚とじっくり付き合うことになりそうだ。さあ、4枚とも揃える作戦を立ててくれ。ともあれ、当座欲しいヤツは予約しとかないと手に入らんぞ!!

(Japan solo albums ad)

David Edward Byrd

Renowned graphic artist/illustrator details the "hellacious" experience of creating the interlocking solo album murals, plus other assorted KISS odds and ends
Interview by Tim McPhate

David, before we get into the solo album murals, you've mentioned that you were asked to design a logo for Neil Bogart for his new company at the time, Casablanca Records. And you also went to an early KISS photo shoot. Can you recount these stories for us?
David Edward Byrd: Yeah, let's see. At the time, I was a poster artist of the Fillmore East in New York. We opened in '68 and we didn't do a lot of posters in New York, unlike San Francisco. It's not that kind of theater situation. New Yorkers sit down and listen. So we didn't do a lot of posters because it wasn't like a poster scene. I think that's how Neil knew about me. He called me to his office, which was Buddah Records in the Brill Building as I recall. The Brill Building is very famous for songwriters as you know.

Yes indeed.
So he had this little office and I can see it now, [it had] kind of a cream-colored door. It was like just a room. I don't know if there was any more, but it didn't seem like it was very big. So we talked and I was aware of Buddah Records and I think we called it "bubble-gum." It was like bubble-gum music, like [1910 Fruitgum Company's] "Simon Says."

Yes, that was Neil's specialty.
Right. Teeny-bopper dance tunes that not-so sophisticated adults also liked. Let's see, I had been on a commune and we had done a lot of light shows and we also had sort of a high-class disco and I did the light show at the disco. I also alternated as DJ so I was used to playing a lot of those Buddah songs because it got the jet-setters up off their butts, for those silly songs. Anyway, he told me he was starting a new record company called Casablanca and he wanted him on the record as Humphrey Bogart. So it's not exactly a portrait, but it's kind of him as Humphrey Bogart and I did this neon lettering. We had talked about like Rick's [Café Américain in the film "Casablanca"], it would be neon lettering. And I did a little color version of that. And that's the last I heard of him for a while. I got involved with Broadway and he called to tell me that he was doing a photo shoot for his first new group on Casablanca Records, called KISS, and could I come to the photo shoot. And I said, "Sure." So I went to the photo shoot in this big photographer's loft. I can't remember where, I think it was like Chelsea, you know the photo district around 17th Street to 23rd Street. It was a big studio so it could have been uptown more

but that was a long time ago. Then I was sort of shocked because they were doing all this make-up. And I said, "Neil, what is this?" Because at the time, it was all about the return to chic and this was not — you know, the big Robert Redford movie of the F. Scott Fitzgerald novel was coming out [Ed: 1974's "The Great Gatsby] and so everything was about "the new elegance." And these guys were truly contrary to that. So I thought, "Well, Neil knows what he's doing. I guess this will do what it does."

David, that sounds like it might have been the first album photo session with Joel Brodsky.

Oh lord, I have no idea. We were all drunk. I mean, they had like a case of champagne and these little tootsies running around with hors d'oeuvres.

One of those types of deals. (Laughs)

Yeah, as I recall. And I had already had a hangover — I had been somewhere the night before. That was rock and roll at the time. But the mural thing [for the solo albums] was just hellacious. I think they called me on Friday and they had to have all four murals done by Monday.

No kidding. Wow.

Oh, it was horrendous. And fortunately, I had two assistants. One of them is a very famous artist now, Arthur K. Miller. And Rita [was the other]. And they both were students of mine at the School of Visual Arts. So we did this crash thing — I mean, I can't tell you how fast we had to do these big paintings. We did them in acrylic and you know, and we had to do these montages of everybody. And then they had to interlock. And, *oy gevalt*! It was like three days to do it. You know, they always call the artist, like, "Oh, he can do it."

Well, hopefully you got paid a rush fee on top of this project.

They must have, yeah. You know, I paid Arthur and Rita too. They got $10 an hour, but they were students. And they were good. Arthur could actually imitate me so I could do more work because he could do phony me and I would trick it up, which is an illustrator's secret, by the way. (Laughs)

What were you given in terms of the band members' likenesses to base the murals on?

They sent over a bunch of shit with a messenger, as I recall. Yeah, there was sort of a band press kit and I had to get poses — you know, I couldn't have them posing for me. They were nowhere in sight. You just had to do what you had to do with what you had.

Was there a definitive concept explained to you in terms of what was required for this job?

Well, they said it was like a mural for the kiddies. You know, that would encourage them to buy all four albums. It was really a [thing].

The first thing that comes to my mind is there is a very cartoonish flavor to them.
Yeah, oh yeah. I had no time to be arty. I mean I was amazed we got it fucking done!

I'm surprised to learn you only had a weekend to do these.
Oh, it was impossible. But I said, "Well, we've got to do it." And Arthur said, "Oh Dave, we'll do it." But he was much younger than I was. I was in my 30s and he was like 20. And Rita was 20. So they could do it. And they were good. Thank God for them, I just don't know what I would I have done.

So was it a situation where you took the lead on one mural and they would have taken the lead on some of the others?
Well, what we did was Arthur and I did pencils real fast. And then we ran out and blew them up and then we transferred them to boards. Rita was doing a lot of transferring. Then we all did painting and then we decided we got like, I don't know, 10 colors. And we did lots of stars. Rita would just cut out stars and we'd glue them on.

Ace Frehley was the lead guitarist and his persona was the Spaceman. So his mural contains the space theme with what looks like Saturn, and of course the stars.
Yeah, right.

So it would seem there was some direction in terms of capturing the personas of the band members?
Let me look at this. I have a file called "Murals" here. Yeah, Ace Frehley was officially "Space Ace." They each had a name. Gene Simmons was the "Demon." Paul Stanley was the "Starchild." And Peter Criss was the "Catman."

That's right. Gene's mural contains the fire and some blood, which are references to two of his stage routines.
That was part of his, you know, they did this incredible show. Grand Guignol is what I would call it.

The KISS show was certainly unique for the time.
Oh yeah. You know at the turn of the century, you could go and see people executed. It was all phony, but they were shows. So KISS was like doing that. They were recreating that whole European Grand Guignol [style of] theatre.

In looking at Paul's mural, there's a lot of purple, which was his theme color.
Well, I had to sort of differentiate each one from the other. We had to do this really fast and we kept it really flat because we couldn't spend a lot of time rendering or anything. It was, as you say, very cartoonish.

And given the interlocking component, some of the components run into each other. Like in Peter's mural, there are stars on his.
Yeah, the stars leap over there.

Peter, since he's a Catman, there's a jungle motif.
Right, we put him in the jungle.

When Peter performed the ballad "Beth" live there were roses that he would hand out.
Right, roses were his big thing. I didn't remember that point but yes he did. You're right, he gave out roses.

It seemed like a tough time crunch, but were there any other concepts that you came up with and ultimately discarded?
Well, we didn't have time to make many changes. When I look at [them], I forget how it was just so wacky how we were not even — you know, I used to stop and think about stuff and spend a lot of time. But I couldn't do that here. We just had to go for it. Actually, a collector bought all the original pencils.

When was that?
You know I have an art gallery in South Hampton. A friend Jim Ceravolo, he was the art director at the Beacon Theatre. So we knew each other and now he has the gallery and he sells my originals and sketches and stuff. And I think about 10 years ago we sold those to a bond trader on Wall Street, who was a KISS fan. You know, he grew up on KISS.

There are all sorts of us out there, David. We just can't shake KISS. (Laughs)
(Laughs) Well, that's good. I think that's a good thing.

David, would you have worked through Dennis Woloch on this job? Dennis oversaw the art direction on KISS' albums.
Yeah, that sounds familiar. Dennis.

In a perfect world, how long would you have liked to have for this type of project?
Oh, two weeks. Two weeks at least. But holy shit! And I think we were late. I think we didn't absolutely get it there on Monday.

But you got it finished. Under the circumstances, were you content with what you produced?
Well, at the time I was kind of embarrassed because I wasn't given the time I like to give to a project. But looking back it's kind of amazing that I got it done. I surely couldn't do that today. And they are kind of historical.

Sure, the KISS solo albums are a milestone in the band's history.
So now, I'm not embarrassed. I'm very glad I did it. You know, I was a perfectionist and I wanted them to be perfect and they weren't perfect. But you know, we were just smoking grass and laughing. I mean...

(Laughs)
I think we were drinking beer. What else could you do?

And the portrait of Gene Simmons you sent to me, I don't believe those were ever used?
Yes, I did four, one of each. No, I don't know if they were ever used.

They do look pretty similar in spirit to the KISS solo album covers. So maybe they were an initial concept or something else to accompany the project?
I think that may be the case, because those drawings were done fast. Those were just ink drawings and in those days we didn't have computers or anything.

That's a whole conversation unto itself. You did all this in 1978 before the days of all the tools and technology that are available today.
Oh yeah, this was all handwork.

Which makes it even more of a marvel considering the deadline involved.
Yeah, we had to cut all those fucking stars out. We painted paper yellow and then we spree-mounted them down. You know, we did all sorts of shortcuts. But still. ...

David, looking at your other music-related work, you've designed some remarkable posters for artists such as Elvis Presley, the Who, Jimi Hendrix, Iron Butterfly, Grateful Dead, and the commemorative poster for Woodstock. What are some of your favorite music-related pieces of art that you've done?
Well, my sort of Mt. Rushmore is my Jimi Hendrix poster, which I did for the Fillmore East. It was only the second poster I ever did. But it was chosen as one of the 125 icons of the 20th century, along with Lindbergh's plane and things like that. Also, "Billboard" named it No. 8 in the Top 10 rock posters of all time. So No. 8's not bad.

Definitely.
That's enough for me. You know, I didn't save any of those things. I just moved on and gave everything away all the time. Who knew? I didn't know this would become like a business.

The Hendrix poster was done in 1968?
Yeah, that was 1968. That was the second poster I ever did. I was a painter. I said, "Oh fuck, these things are so small. I can't do this." But I did. And I hand-inked the whole thing. Well, how else are you going to do it? So I hand-inked it and filled it in with water color. I'm also very [well] known for my follies poster for the Sundance Follies in 1971, which is in the Louvre [in Paris]. And the Jimi Hendrix is in about 20 museums, it's in the Museum of Modern Art, it's in the Museum of Rock, the Hendrix Museum, the Victorian Albert, it's all over the place. So I didn't do bad [sic] for not being famous.

In looking at your work, I'd say you've done quite well.
Well, thank you. It's always good to hear that.

Are you still active today in terms of creating art?
Oh yeah. Actually, right now I'm doing a poster for Prince. Yeah, the old hippie is still doing posters. (Laughs)

It seems poster art has enjoyed a bit of a renaissance in recent years. Would you agree?
Oh absolutely. It's very big. Fortunately I started using on the computer in 1990. I was at Warner Bros. for 11 years. I actually started their art department. And when I left, there were like 50 people, but there were just four of us when it started. I immediately said, "Well, we all have to get on the computer. This is the new thing." So I've been able to transition to the computer. You really appreciate it because it does a lot of work for you that we used to do tediously by hand. I mean, just to make a flat yellow you'd have to do five or six layers of paint to get it to be a flat yellow. Now you just fill with PMS 123 and you're done. It's a dream. (Laughs)

Stephanie Tudor

Former Aucoin Management director of production recalls working with the "genius" Bill Aucoin and the buzz and excitement surrounding the 1978 KISS solo albums
Interview by Tim McPhate

Stephanie, you were with Aucoin Management from 1977-1986. Can you outline what your responsibilities entailed?
Stephanie Tudor: Sure. I was actually the director of production from 1980 through '86. When I first started in 1977, I believe I was 23 years old and I was working under the director of production, Ken Anderson. We were handling everything that had to do with the groups under Aucoin Management [from] a touring aspect. Ken was hiring the set designers and the costume designers and I was working with the road crew, making sure that everything was going according to plan out on the road, meaning travel and equipment getting to all the different points at the right times and the right places. As you can imagine, a huge show involves many aspects. There are pyrotechnics, there's blood, there are costumes, [and] there are huge stage sets. And that company traveling around the world for a good part of the year, it was quite a big endeavor. So we used to handle all of that. After Ken left a few years after that, I then became director of production, although there was a little change in the job. I was not a set designer as Ken was, but I still handled all of the day-to-day production for the group, overseeing what was going out on the road as far as working with the road crews — again all the travel, taking on all the liner notes, booking all the studio time, and working with the producers and engineers for all of the Aucoin acts, other than KISS.

When you were first hired, what were your general impressions of Bill Aucoin?
Oh, he was a genius. He was a fireball, full of energy, full of creative ideas, and he loved what he did. He was a great businessman, a master at merchandising and marketing. And he was really just a joy to be around. He wore many, many hats. He was always considered, at the time, the fifth member of KISS. And he truly loved his artists and just did a fabulous job. I've never seen a manager quite like him, then or since. And he was my mentor. I was a young girl [though] I had worked at Columbia Records prior to working for Aucoin. I had never worked on a show or touring — I learned everything I know now basically from the 10 years I spent working under that man.

Do you recall meeting the members of KISS for the first time?
Of course! Aucoin Management and the artists were one big family. The artists — most of them were from the East Coast — that [lived there] were up in the office constantly. Everybody knew everyone. I also knew the group prior to working there. They used to play at a club in Queens called Coventry and it was two blocks away from where I grew up. And my parents used to manage a huge restaurant on Queens Boulevard, which was a block away. So they had their own relationships with all those groups that played there because they would come in there to eat. So I knew them from the neighborhood and as we all got older, I went into the music business.

What was the first big project you remembering working on at Aucoin Management?
If I can think clearly all the way back, I believe 1977 was the year that they went to Japan for the first time.

That is correct. They played dates in Japan in late March and into early April.
Yeah. And I think I started in February of '77 and they were gearing up to do this world tour and go to Japan. And if I'm not mistaken, they were working on "Alive II."

That's right.
So that's when I joined, at that point. We were just diving into making Japan work, and it was a huge year. And not only that, but Bill was also managing Toby Beau, Starz and Piper, which was Billy Squier's group. Everybody was out on the road.

That brings us to 1978, which was arguably the apex for KISS. There was not a lot of touring activity, primarily because of the solo albums and the film, "KISS Meets the Phantom of the Park." Did you have any responsibilities with the film?
I wasn't really all that involved with the film at all. Bill Aucoin, the group and the film company handled the film. But I did, of course, work alongside all of the producers and the group members while they were doing the solo albums. For instance, Paul was working with Jeff Glixman and they were in the studio and [I was] making sure the studio time was booked and all the arrangements [were handled], whatever they needed — paying the bills, booking the time, hiring musicians, putting together the liner notes for them, making sure the records got mastered on time. I handled all of the album production stuff.

Basically, all the important stuff. (Laughs)
Yes, absolutely (laughs). I mean, everything is important. Everyone has their specific job. Publicity is important. Marketing is important. Wardrobe's important. Production is certainly important.

You were essentially one year on, and the solo albums were KISS' biggest project to that point. Did it feel like an immense undertaking at the time?
Oh absolutely. It was the most important thing that we were doing. It was extremely exciting because no other group in their genre had done this before. And you know, it was also an emotional thing because they were very much a group, and here they were spreading apart, being creative on their own. And I'm sure that they felt, at times, torn. Like, "Oh, this is exciting and great. But at the same time, will it help the group or will it hurt the group?" You never really know what the outcome is going to be. It was an extremely exciting time; they all supported each other immensely during that time. And I don't really know anyone that doesn't remember when those albums came out and what a big deal it was.

Artist Eraldo Carugati was contracted to paint portraits of the band members for the solo albums. It was an interesting direction to go with portraits, but they have emerged as iconic pieces of art for KISS.
Yes they have. They are so beautiful and they were tastefully done. They were separate works, but one cohesive work when they were all put together. It was very impressive.

Getting into the albums, you mentioned Paul and Jeff Glixman. Paul is credited as co-producer on the album and Jeff only worked on four of the songs. From what I understand, they didn't really hit it off. Does anything ring a bell with you?
I honestly don't recall. I don't remember anything negative happening. I don't remember them not hitting it off. It could very well be but I just don't recall that.

If you look at Gene's album, he secured a big group of guest stars. Donna Summer, Joe Perry, Rick Nielsen, Janis Ian, Helen Reddy. It seems like that would have been a logistical nightmare.
You know, he pursued all of those artists on his own, to his credit. And he personally went out and spoke to everyone and gathered everyone. Michele Slater at the time was assisting Sean Delaney. And she probably was the one, because it was not me, who handled the coordinating all of those celebrity schedules and the studio time.

Meanwhile, Ace Frehley secured the services of Eddie Kramer to produce his album.
They quietly worked together. I think they worked most of the time in Connecticut on that. They were used to working together so it was a very easy fit. And they quietly just did their thing.

And Ace took people by surprise in scoring the lone hit out of the four solo albums.
Yeah, he did. "New York Groove." That was such a great song.

Peter Criss worked with Sean Delaney initially and later Vini Poncia came onboard to produce. Rumor has it that Peter was hoping to work with Tom Dowd. Does that sound familiar?
Well, the name rings a bell. I certainly know Tom Dowd. But I honestly do not remember the details leading up to Vini being hired. You know, if you hadn't brought that up, I probably wouldn't have even remembered that (laughs). I remember Vini being onboard, working with [Peter] on his record. And that's all I really remember. And Vini also worked on [KISS] records.

That's an interesting tidbit, I think. Paul and Gene have been very forthcoming regarding their feelings about Peter's solo album but yet they chose to work on two subsequent KISS albums with the man who produced Peter's album.
That's right.

In terms of results, Stephanie, do you quantify the KISS solo albums as a success?
Oh, absolutely. I think the project was received very well. I think there was such a buzz about it, and everyone was so excited. And I don't think there was ever a moment when anyone thought, "Oh, this could really not work." I think everybody was extremely positive about it. The group was psyched about it. You know, as a project moves along, of course the manager hears bits and pieces of it and Bill was always super positive about what the outcome was going to be. And he was right. And I don't think it ever took away any of the mystery of the group at all. It stayed intact. KISS went on after the solo albums as a unit and it was just a creative outlet. I mean, there was a huge buzz back then.

From some of the people I've talked to in the industry, when you say the KISS solo albums, they joke that those are the albums that "shipped platinum and came back double platinum." This of course speaks to the fact that Neil Bogart shipped more than 5 million of the KISS solo albums to record stores. Do you think there is an unfair stigma attached to the albums?
I think so. To be honest, I remember a little bit about that but that doesn't stick out in my mind. Again, I was very involved in it and I was all caught up in the excitement of it all, [but] not so much on the business and financial end of it. So I think that those albums, whether they sold the exact numbers that everyone predicted isn't really the importance of them. I think it's the stamp that they made at the time, for the group and the fans. I think it made a significant stamp and I don't think anything negative sticks out or is attached to it, at least not on my level, knowing that group during that time and being involved in the industry during that time. I don't know, to me it isn't relevant how many records were sold.

I'd like to play a word association game with the KISS members. I'll say their names and anything you say the first words that come to mind. Let's start with Paul Stanley.

Affectionate, intelligent and creative.

Gene Simmons.
Confident, loyal and creative.

An interesting aside, you are actually credited in the "thank you" list on Gene's album.
Yep, I do remember that.

Peter Criss.
Peter Criss. Peter was a fireball. He was sensitive. And creative.

And that leaves us with the Spaceman, Ace Frehley.
Okay, Ace Frehley. (pauses) Self-assured, creative, and ... flamboyant.

And perhaps one who liked to have a good time back in the day?
He was definitely the life of the party. No doubt about it.

Moving ahead just a bit, Bill and KISS ultimately severed ties in 1982. Do you recall that being a difficult situation?
Extremely. It was extremely difficult for everyone. It was difficult for me to watch them because they were all kind of suffering through it, like a divorce. As I said earlier, I came in, in 1977, and they were pretty much peaking then. It was a difficult time. And they held it together as best they could and they tried to keep the separation as private as they possibly could. And I respected them for that — all five of them.

And KISS moved into new territory in taking off the makeup for a 13-year period. And they reunited the original band in 1996, and have been going since.
Right.

Unfortunately, Bill passed away in 2010. Did you stay in touch with Bill at all through the years?
I did. I did. I still worked with Aucoin Management after KISS left and I was there until 1986 and it was well after the success of Billy Idol. And then I moved on to other things and Aucoin Management dissolved. And I did stay in touch with Bill. We would try and speak a few times a year. And unfortunately the last few years of his life, I hadn't spoken to him. He was living down in Florida, and he was running his new company, Aucoin Global, from the East Coast, in Florida and in New York. And I really wasn't in touch with him at that time, the last few years. You know, you just drift apart [and] years go by. But he was always in my mind; he'll always be my mentor. I learned so much from that man. He was just a terrific person.

Do you think Bill gets enough credit when it comes to his contributions to KISS?
You know, I think the group does give him a lot of credit. I've read many, many articles over the years and whenever they mention Bill they always mention how important he was in their career. He signed them, he got them their first record deal, he worked with them and nurtured them for years. They have a whole life after Bill as well, and that needs to be respected absolutely. But I really don't feel he isn't given the credit that is due.

Stephanie, can you update fans about what you are up to nowadays, professionally?
More recently, I spent 18 years as the VP of A&R and administration for Jive Records. And as you may know, Jive Records was dissolved in the last few years into RCA. And now I've reinvented myself. I'm a personal manager; I manage Grammy mixer Stephen George. He is mostly known as the mixer for the R. Kelly hit "I Believe I Can Fly." He's worked on many genres of music. I am also a realtor and I specialize in artist and executive relocation. So I took my skills from touring and working with artists all over the country and reinvented myself and am using that in my real estate career.

Carol Kaye

Publicist recalls KISS being on top of the world in 1978, the promotional strategy for the solo albums and "a very special time" working at the Press Office.
Interview by Tim McPhate

Carol, let's go back to 1978. You were on staff at Aucoin Management's publicity subsidiary the Press Office, correct?
Carol Kaye: That is correct.

How long had you been on board at that point?
Well, I started working directly at Aucoin Management in June 1977. I was just this young kid who didn't even know there was a music industry. When Bill hired me I remember he said "I have a feeling about you." You know, Bill continued to be my mentor and my inspiration and my very, very dear friend. And I always viewed Bill, in a way, like a big brother. As a matter of fact, I'm looking at a picture of him right now! There are so many times I go to pick up the phone to call him and get his advice on something that I'm working on. I still cannot bring myself to erase his phone number from my phone. But anyway, it was '77 when I started working at Aucoin Management. In January 1978, I believe the Press Office launched and I moved over to the Press Office representing all of the Aucoin-managed bands, which were KISS, Starz, Toby Beau, and Piper (Billy Squier's) band. And then of course, the Press Office, being an independent PR company, represented many other artists such as Paul McCartney, Uriah Heep, Triumph, Blondie, the Ramones and many others.

How did you come across the job opportunity?
I had just graduated high school. I decided I was going to take some time and work for a while. You know how it is, you want money, you just want to chill out for a while before heading off to college. I was working for Otto Preminger, the film director; I [had] worked with OP, as I called him, for about six months. A friend of mine called me one day and she said, "Carol, Bill Aucoin is looking for a publicist. You should go in and interview for the job." And I said, "Who's Bill Aucoin and what's a publicist?" (Laughs) It was that foreign to me! She said, "Well he manages KISS." And I was like, "Okay." I really didn't know much about KISS. I was not like a rock chick (laughs). I know it's funny now; I had heard of them but I didn't know a lot about the band. I went and I interviewed. I first interviewed with Bill's assistant, Linda West. When I walked into the office, it was like nothing I had ever witnessed before. There was music coming out of every room, people running around, phones ringing off the hook, there were gold and platinum records all over. I never saw

anything like this — it was like walking onto a movie set. Linda interviewed me and I thanked her very much for her time. And I really didn't think very much about it.

The next day, she called me and said, "Mr. Aucoin would like to meet with you." So I said, "All right. I can come over on my lunch hour." What was supposed to be a 10-minute interview turned into an hour and a half. I was sitting in his office and behind me were these huge puppets, bigger than me. It was crazy! That's when Bill said to me, "I just have a feeling about you and I really would like you to start working here. I asked if I could answer the phones because I needed to familiarize myself with everything he had been discussing. And he started laughing and said, "Just start in two weeks." I had to tell OP that I would be leaving him. And of course he was like, "Is it more money? Do you need more money?" I said, "No, no, no. I think this would be a really fun opportunity for me." Little did I know I was stepping into a hurricane. And that's how it started. I was part of Al Ross' team on the publicity end at Aucoin Management. And I just took to it like, pardon the stupid phrase, but like a fish to water. I really did. I never looked back.

And what was the staff configuration of the Press Office in 1978? How many people were on staff?
There was Carol Ross who headed the company. Her husband was Al Ross, myself, Julie Steigman, Harriet Vidal, Julie Harrison and two others. We each had our own artists that we worked. KISS were my babies, so to speak, with Carol Ross, of course.

Of course, the KISS solo albums weren't just any KISS project, but four solo albums released simultaneously on the same day. What do you recall about initially learning about the project and what were your thoughts?
[With] the solo albums, there was a lot of buzz — there was a lot of excitement. And of course, we would have creative meetings with Bill all the time about how we were going to put this out to the media. And as you know, Bill was very, very hands on about the image of the band. It was a lot of fun to sit around and hash out ideas and throw ideas around. You know, it's very different today, the way things are done. But we were all very instrumental in the process. We were a family. We lived and breathed and worked KISS. As a matter of fact, my home was pretty much destroyed in October from the Superstorm Sandy.

I'm really sorry to hear that Carol.
I lost two floors in my house and more memorabilia and memories than I care to discuss. I lost a lot of KISS memorabilia and things that I had been offered so much money for over the years to purchase, which I would never even consider doing. I mean, this is my life and these are my memories. I had tour books with my notations about who was doing what interview at what time — you know, a really detailed and amazing history. But one of the reasons I mention this is I did happen

to save the press kit that I found [from] the KISS solo records. It was one press kit that had all four photos on it and inside we had individual bios of each band member and individual photos of each band member. We also had shopping bags that were made [with the] same images and we put all four albums, along with the press kit, in the shopping bag and had them hand-delivered to all the New York media. Now you have to understand Tim, at that time there was X amount of publications. It wasn't obviously like it is today. And we had a great relationship with all of the editors. I'd say we had maybe 25 packages that we sent out. It was a very big deal. I mean it was Christmas all over again.

Can you please expand on that, Carol? In the context of the 1978 record industry, just how big of an event was the KISS solo albums?
It was huge. It was huge: The buzz, the momentum and the excitement leading up to the releases — and then the actual releases. And of course, people were like, "Is Gene selling more than Paul? Is Peter pissed off? What about Ace?" It was really crazy. But that wasn't coming from the band; they were happy for each other. It wasn't an internal "let's see who sells more" [competition]. It wasn't that way at all. But it was an amazing thing. They were on top of the world and being part of it, we were just thrown into this with them. From the minute we got into the office in the morning, the phones were ringing off the hook. We did crazy, crazy things. We did fun things. I remember doing events like the one where there was a painted Volkswagen on display at Sotheby's with all of the KISS faces on it and we had a big press event about that and [wrote] press releases about it. It was so creative and that's how I still think of my business. I try to be an extremely creative publicist, which I learned from the greatest band in the world.

The press kits for the solo albums have been described as comparable to those put together by major Hollywood studios to promote movies. Just how atypical were they for a music release at the time?
The press kits were beautiful. They were chock full of photos and press clippings. It wasn't printed out on a Xerox machine (laughs). It was beautiful, heavyweight [paper]. Bill always did everything the best that it could be. They were beautifully copied, they were glossy. Everything about it was first-class.

According to Chris Lendt's book, the advertising campaign orchestrated by Casablanca totaled $2.5 million across TV and radio spots, print and in-store displays. One item from the campaign is what is known today as the "KISS Bible," or "black box." The black box features a KISS logo on the front and contains a cassette of pre-recorded answers from each member of KISS discussing their respective solo album, along with a set of questions and some postcards of the band members. Do you recall how this idea came about?
Well that probably occurred between Bill Aucoin and the radio promotion team. But if you think about it, that was the pre-cursor to today's EPKs.

You know, I think you're right.
They were so innovative and so ahead of their time to think about sending that out to radio programmers. They would have their questions and here are the answers on cassette. Nobody else was doing that at the time.

Indeed. Generally speaking, what do you recall the feedback being from the press in terms of their reaction to the KISS solo albums? For example, I believe I've read that some press might have been confused upon hearing Peter's album.
Well, I think that people were very surprised when they heard Peter's record because they didn't expect that from Peter. I think they were really thinking that all of the solo albums would be much more in line with KISS music. So when they heard it with his jazz influences, they were confused. They didn't expect that. I thought it was amazing because each solo album just showed the strength of each artist. Paul and I were very close during that time and I spent a lot of time in the studio with him at Electric Ladyland Studios while he was recording this record. And he had these lush background vocals, you know [the girls in] Desmond Child & Rouge. His record is the iconic straight-ahead rock and roll record. There are songs on there that just stand the test of time. Gene's record was fantastic. Ace's record, obviously [he had] "New York Groove." And then Peter's [album] — it just showed the strength of each as songwriters. And then you were able to say, "Okay, I see how each part of this created and made up the sound of KISS."

I agree. The four solo albums show the diversity of the band at the time and display each member's unique personality, which, I think, at the end of the day is the goal of solo album.
As a matter of fact, I had introduced my best friend Peppy Castro to Paul and they ended up writing a couple of songs together. Peppy sings background vocals on "Hold Me, Touch Me." As I said, we were all family. It was just an amazing time.

Gene, Paul and, to a lesser extent, Ace participated in promo tours across the country, doing assorted radio interviews or in-stores. But I don't know that Peter participated in any similar kind of press efforts. Do you recall why, Carol?
No, I don't recall. I know that when we set up interviews, we set them up for each and every member of the band. We didn't just set them up for Gene or Paul. We had interviews for every band member. But I don't recall Peter not participating.

In terms of performance, the albums performed relatively well. However, Casablanca shipped more than one million copies of each album, totally upwards of 5.3 million albums. Ace's album was the best-selling of the four, but the others did not perform as well. Larry Harris has said that the KISS solo albums were a fiasco for the label. Was this a case of Casablanca biting off more than they could chew?

That's a great question. And I think the only one who could really answer that would be Bill. And unfortunately he can't. Talking about Casablanca and their involvement and Aucoin Management and the Press Office, we had such a big machine going. Yet there weren't that many of us. It's very interesting. At Casablanca, we used to deal all the time with Irv Biegel who was heading the sales and distribution, and Larry Harris and Neil [Bogart]. And at the Press Office, it was Carol Ross and myself and the team there. And then we had Aucoin Management with the innovative, amazing, brilliant Bill Aucoin. It was really the first management company that had everything in house. They had a radio promotion department in-house, production department with Stephanie Tudor and Ken, the publicity department. The tour managers used to come up to the office where they were booking the travel for the tours. We had the production team up there working on the stage show. I'm telling you, it was magical. And the band would come up and they were very much a part of what was going on. It was an unbelievable experience. And for me, that's how I learned. We had an opportunity to learn every aspect of the business. It wasn't just segmented or, "Okay, you just do publicity. Go sit in the corner." It wasn't like that at all. We were all very much a part of everything. But as I said, there weren't that many of us and when you think back at how all of this was accomplished and how they've stood the test of time is just awesome. Great, great memories!

Depending on who you talk to, the KISS solo albums were either a success or failure, in terms of results. But how would you gauge the success of the solo albums' promotional campaign? Did you accomplish what you set out to accomplish?
Absolutely we did. I mean, they were the greatest band to do publicity for. Can you imagine — what better speakers are there than Gene Simmons and Paul Stanley and Ace Frehley and Peter Criss? They each had such distinct personalities. I remember one of the first television bookings I did was "The Tom Snyder Show," which is now infamous.

Yes it is.
The talent booker for the show was Donald Berman, who now is very much a part of "The View." But I will never forget standing on the side of the stage when they were being interviewed and Ace was ... a little tipsy (laughs).

(Laughs)
And there was that back and forth going on with Tom and Ace and the bear. But you didn't really see a lot of it — you know they broke to commercial. I was convinced that I was getting fired. I was like, "I'm getting fired. This is crazy." (Laughs) But you know, these became iconic moments in rock and roll history. It was like that all the time. It was on 10 — or 100 — all the time. Full steam ahead.

A month after the solo albums, "KISS Meets the Phantom of the Park" aired on NBC. Rewinding to April 1978, "Double Platinum" was released. Various retailers were littered with KISS' merchandise, from lunch boxes to makeup kits and dolls. Do you think 1978 was the zenith of KISS' popularity?
Oh, I think '77, '78, '79 — it's all kind of melded into one because, as I said, it was just continuous momentum. We were going, going, going. There was "Love Gun;" there was "Double Platinum;" there were the solo records; there was "KISS Meets the Phantom of the Park;" there were tours! It was non-stop. Yeah, it was absolute insanity. And it didn't stop. They were number one on the Gallup Poll. Remember "Knights In Satanic Service"? Somebody called me one day and said, "Carol, you're on the front page of 'The Wall Street Journal.'" I'm like, "What are you talking about?"And there it was, "KISS publicist Carol Kaye can't seem to squash the rumors that KISS does not stand for 'Knights In Satanic Service.'" You never knew what you were going to walk into. For me, it was baptism by fire. It was sink or swim. Because, as I said, I entered this business not even knowing there was a music business. I did not set out to work for a rock and roll band in the music business. That was not my goal. I was a very, very lucky girl.

And how long did you end up staying onboard at the Press Office, Carol?
I stayed with KISS through, this is where it gets foggy, I think 1980. And then I went on to record companies and working in management with Aerosmith, AC/DC, Def Leppard, Rex Smith [and] Ted Nugent with Leber/Krebs. I've had an amazing career. I worked at a label doing publicity and traveling with Queen, the Cars, Linda Ronstadt, Carly Simon, the Eagles [and] Roy Orbison. I've been blessed.

You've worked with an impressive group of artists, and continue to do so through your own company today. Do KISS hold a special place in your heart?
Absolutely. They are the best. They always will be. If not for KISS and Bill Aucoin, I don't know ... I'm sure I would have had a good life, but it would not have been this life. So I will always hold a special place in my heart for KISS. I try to see them every time they are in town. But because of the experience that I had with KISS, I was able to apply that to everything else that I do in my career. When I first started Kayos Productions, after doing music supervision for a number of films, the first clients I had — funny enough — were [both] KISS and Ace separately.

That's nice how things came full circle.
So that's another conversation! And I continued to work with Ace for over 20 years on his career. But it's been an amazing ride. Just getting back to what you and I talked about at the beginning of our conversation, I've been around. I know all the players. I would never ever ever think about writing a book or telling "my story." There's a lot that will stay quiet and that's the way it should be. But when I hear about these people that spend five minutes with KISS, literally, and they're writing

books about their experience, it freaks me out a bit. I can't imagine how the band feels about it. But I just say, "I can't believe they're doing this."

I think I know exactly what you're talking about.
Really, it's crazy. But there will always be those trying to piggy-back on somebody else's fame and you've got to feel sorry for them, you really do. But I have to tell you it was a wonderful experience in my life. Writing a book is just not in my makeup. But I thank them for giving me the opportunity and I miss Bill. I truly do. The last time I saw Bill actually was when we went to a KISS concert at Madison Square Garden just a couple of months before he passed. Bill passed on a Monday — Paul called me on Saturday while they were in Europe and we spent quiet time on the phone talking. We knew the end was near. They're great guys. And all I can say is I just hate to hear people bashing them.

Final question, Carol. I don't need to tell you that the music industry has undergone quite the transformation. Today, the industry is constantly evolving. There are MP3 files, YouTube and social media. In thinking back to the '70s and people like Neil Bogart, Bill Aucoin and bands like KISS, is there a part of you that misses the traditional record industry and the days of working in an environment such as the Press Office?
Absolutely! Without a doubt! You know, it's funny because talking about all the various things we just mentioned, imagine doing all of this the way we did it, without email, without faxes — I mean we had Telex machines and we used to sit there and wait for the Telex to come in (laughs). It was a completely different world and look at what we were able to accomplish. It was also quite a feat at that time to keep all the band's images without makeup from being published. That in itself was a trip. I remember photos in the daily newspapers, "Paul Stanley was spotted at Studio 54." And it wasn't even Paul, it was like, "Who is this guy?" It was really funny. But look at what they accomplished — world domination, without the tools that we have today. I have that mentality still when I do publicity: "Let's create. Let's see what we can do. Let's try to really make this special." That's how I was trained so I have that sort of mindset. I do miss the camaraderie and the excitement of this group of people who come in to work every day with the same focus and the same goal. You're a team and you're a part of the family. It's all for one... And that was a very special time.

Carol Ross-Durborow

Head of the Press Office discusses the promotional campaign for the 1978 solo albums, working with Bill Aucoin from the beginning, the challenges in representing KISS, and why Cadillac, Michigan, was the major turning point in KISStory.
Interview by Tim McPhate

Carol, I believe you've mentioned that KISS were the first client you brought into Rogers & Cowan. But can we back up and talk about how you came into the KISS fold?
Carol Ross-Durborow: Yes, I first was introduced to the band through a friend of mine, Alan Miller, who knew Bill Aucoin. At that time I was just doing some freelancing, I had been working at a radio production company doing syndicated radio shows. And I was doing some freelance on the side. Alan said, "My friend has this band he's just started working with. They're going to be performing at a place down in the Village, and I'd really like you to come. He wants to get an opinion from you." So I said, "Sure." So I go down to 14th Street and the Academy of Music and I'm standing in the back, which I like to do. I don't like to sit because I like to get a sense of audience and reaction. And I'm standing in the back with Bill Aucoin and this strange-looking group comes out with this big backdrop sign that said KISS on it, and some of the lights were working and some weren't (laughs). And these guys come out in leather and these platforms and this makeup and my mouth dropped. Because in 1974 you just didn't see anything like that. The closest to anything unusual was David Bowie but this was four guys and they really came right in your face. And there was the blood and the fire and it was crazy and the music was loud. It was an attitude and it just blew me away.

Bill looks at me and says, "So, what do you think?" And I said, "Well, wow! What can I say?" He said, "I just sense something with these guys. They're hungry; they want it. And I just feel that there is something here." I said, "You may be right. There's no one doing this." Ultimately what they were doing that night is that they were opening for a band called Argent who was very big at the time. And ironically of course, down the road, Argent then opened for KISS (laughs) and the tables were turned. Anyway, I said [to Bill], "It certainly is a PR dream, but let's talk about it." In the interim, I was approached by MCA Records to run their New York publicity office. I accepted the position and so Bill was kind of down in the dumps because I couldn't work on KISS at the time. But I told him that I certainly would be there for him to give him any suggestions or whatever that I could. I wanted to stay close to that band. I was at MCA Records and after two years I was asked to join Rogers & Cowan. And I called Bill and I said, "I think I'm going to make the move. It was an offer I couldn't refuse." And I said, "Now would be the time. I can bring KISS into the PR company with me." And he got so excited. That's ultimately how it evolved for me to start working with KISS formally, although I had been kind of moonlighting on the side with him during my tenure at MCA just to give him some things to think about, publicity wise.

And how did you segue into the Press Office?
After some years at Rogers & Cowan, people kept saying to me, "Carol, you should open your own office. You have all these great accolades." And I thought to myself, "That could be a dangerous move or it could be an interesting one." Bill Aucoin, as we had become very close friends, said, "Carol, you should do it." So that's when I finally decided to make another move and open up my own company, the Press Office. And of course at that point Bill was thrilled because he knew KISS would be in good hands, so to speak (laughs). So that's what happened. And at that time, Carol Kaye was working at Bill's office and I was hiring people so she asked if she could come and work for me. So that's how Carol Kaye came over to my company and worked for me along with several other people I had hired.

And to get a sense of time, what year did you open the Press Office?
It was '78.

That's right in the time frame we're primarily discussing, so it's a perfect segue into the solo albums. When I think of the classic era of KISS, the solo albums stand out as perhaps the band's biggest milestone, if not the biggest KISS project from a publicity standpoint. Would you agree?
Yes, I agree with you. Let me tell you something, deciding to do the solo albums was a long process. There were a lot of meetings with Casablanca. But Neil Bogart — in spite of what other people in the industry thought — he was so committed to this band. Neil was going to spend the money. He was told, "This is crazy. You shouldn't be doing this. This is taking a big risk. It's a lot of money involved." But he was just so into it. And beside the fact, he enjoyed working with Bill Aucoin and thought that Bill was one of the great managers in the business, which we all agreed. But it was a real labor of love. And it was a long process. It was a turning point for wonderful, incredible projects. We thought, "Wow, this is going to be wonderful because this has not happened before." I wanted to really make it very special. And so with what Casablanca was doing, and what we had planned to do for the media, it was great. I had suggested from the individual albums that we do special posters and have a gallery showing, which we did for the press. And then of course each member of the band signed their specific poster and we gave them away as collectibles. We made it very, very special. And it was only a limited edition. So that added to what Casablanca Records was doing promotion-wise. It was interesting because people were taking bets on which album and poster was going to get the most play. It became, "Is it going to be Gene? Is it going to be Paul?"

And which posters are these specifically? Are these posters of the album covers?
Yes, but what we did is we took them and did lithographs of the posters and that's what made them special and a limited edition as a collectible item. We sent them to special press people that had been very supportive of us, and to radio and to VIPs in the business. So it wasn't going to be blanketed. Those lithographs were going to be a really special item, so anyone who got one, it wasn't like a mass-produced thing.

In addition to yourself, who else had input into generating ideas and executing the solo album publicity campaign?
Well, it was myself, obviously Bill Aucoin, Alan Miller, who worked for him, and Neil Bogart and his staff. It was a labor of love with everyone involved. I would be the one to go to the conference meetings and then I would come back with my notes and I would sit with my staff and determine who was going to work on this and what this person would focus on. And that's how we would do it. Because of the enormity of the project, it needed several hands to do certain things.

And did the band have any input regarding the campaign?
Oh absolutely. The band had input from the very beginning. That was the great thing about it. They were there at every meeting. Nothing was done without their 100 percent consent. Gene is a marketing genius. Their input was so valuable and we gave them the respect. And not every artist would get that kind of acceptance in decisions made by the record company.

Of course, the campaign was a huge effort across print, TV and radio, totaling expenses of $2.5 million. Carol, in hindsight, was this figure excessive or ultimately was the dollar figure necessary to publicize this project?
For everything that they were doing, and for all of the promotions — because I was setting up promotions at radio and big giveaways and stuff — yes [it was necessary]. And that's why I was saying, people were telling Neil this was going to be an expensive package. And he said, "Yes, but what we're going to get out of it promotion-wise is going to be amazing. And we're going to do it the right way." The great thing about Bill Aucoin was everything had to be first class with him. He would not skimp on anything. It was either going to be a massive, really first-class presentation or it wasn't going to get done. And Neil Bogart understood that because he felt the same way. That was very important.

Well, when you say first class, as it pertains to the solo albums the first thing I think of is the artwork. Eraldo Carugati painted a set of beautiful portraits of the band members.
Yes, and that's exactly what we wanted to do. Because when we were in the initial meeting I had thrown my two cents in to say, "If you're going to do these, they really need to be done to look like pieces of art." And that's why I decided that we

should do the lithographs afterwards because to me they were individual works of art.

One interesting component of the solo album publicity campaign that comes to mind is what's known today as the "KISS Black Box," which contained pre-recorded interview answers from the band and some suggested questions for the press. I believe these were sent to radio stations. Carol Kaye and I chatted about this and she made a great point about how this idea was ahead of its time in some ways and a pre-cursor to today's EPK (Electronic Press Kit). Those were sent exclusively to radio stations, correct?
Yes. And that initially came from the record company so we didn't have too much to do with that, although we sent out releases about that being done. And this was the other great thing, when we sat in meetings there was no resistance to doing unusual things or creating crazy things as far as marketing and promotion went. And that was where the fun came in because you could come out with the most outrageous piece of product and everyone would look and say, "Yeah! That could work. Let's do this."

It was very hard in the beginning to get the media interested in KISS. They did not take them seriously. So we had to come up with unusual things to get their attention and it was the same with radio. That's why doing all of these innovative ideas, events and utilizing different products to generate excitement and attention had to be done. The creative situation in a meeting was amazing because we would get hysterical. Somebody would say, "Why don't we do this? And why don't we top with something else?" It was a necessary evil, so to speak, because Bill knew that the band was not yet taken seriously as musicians so we had to market them for their visual appeal and for the innovative things that were being done in conjunction with what they were doing. And no one can dispute that. I think the KISS marketing machine is probably a lesson for anyone, then and today, to pay attention to.

Another example of going outside the box is the press kit that was put together for the solo albums. This wasn't just a simple bio sheet and a photo, it was very elaborate and colorful.
Yes, they were. And of course that is the ideal situation for a publicity firm because so many times people think, "Okay, you put in a bio and picture in the press kit, and that's it." And they allowed us to create whatever we wanted to do.

There was also a shopping bag sent out to the press containing the albums and a press kit, which was hand-delivered to certain press outlets in some cases.
Yes, we did that. As I said before, anything to generate the interest, [we did it]. We had unusual product, we had unusual ways of delivering it and we wanted to do it. And that was a great creative PR dream.

One of the ads issued for the solo albums was featured in the Sept. 9, 1978, issue of "Billboard," and it had the four album covers and the headline "4 Million Sold The First Week!" It seems this ad was designed to grab some attention right out of the box?
Right. With KISS everything had to be bigger than life. That was the standard line. Any time we'd go into a meeting that was what was first said by Bill: "Remember, everything with KISS has to be bigger than life." And it was. What was interesting, and what I had fun with, is the guys were hungry and they were eager. So they would do anything. I was able to take them all over the city. I don't know if you have a copy of Waring Abbott's book called "KISS: The Early Years"...

Yes I do. It's fantastic.
Well, those pictures, I was with him. He became our exclusive photographer and I had these guys walking everywhere. I put them on top of the Empire State Building, hanging over the sides, we walked up and down Broadway — and people would see these four guys and it was so amazing. They were so easy to work with and were so cooperative and knew the value of doing what they were doing was going to be. We had a lot of fun with that because ultimately — I didn't say this to them at the time — but when I would be calling the press, I'd say, "I'm calling about KISS," and a lot of these journalists laughed at me. "Oh come on, Carol, you've got to be kidding me." I got a lot of that for a long time. And I used to hang up the phone and say, "Someday, someday, you're going to be calling me." And I said, "When I get them on the cover of 'People' magazine, when I get them in 'Rolling Stone' magazine, you guys are all going to turn your heads." And sure enough it happened because that gave me more determination than anything else (laughs). But it was actually the Cadillac, Michigan, event that really turned the tide for mainstream publicity.

I want to get to Cadillac in a minute. Carol, I believe you have said that the press would ask primarily to interview Gene and Paul. Was it a challenge to get Ace and Peter equal time?
It was to some degree because Gene's personality was so out there. And he was so accessible and easy to talk to, and intelligent. Ultimately, a lot of the journalists kind of gravitated to him. Paul was terrific but he was a little shy. He didn't throw himself out there. It seemed in the beginning that Gene was the one that they were kind of focusing on. So I had to work a little harder for Paul and then it came around for Paul. And it was the same thing for Peter and Ace. They really didn't have the finesse to do interviews and be as outgoing or gregarious as Paul and Gene. We'd have to work a little harder and create a little harder. The best thing about [the solo album for] Ace was finally he got validated for his musicianship, because it was hard. When I could get a guitar magazine to do a piece on his music, rather than on just this flashy, flamboyant member of KISS, it became a little bit more credible. People then started wanting to talk to him a little bit more. So we

utilized what we felt were there inlaying talents to bring them out more. We had to think like that because at first I didn't think there was going to be a problem, but when I would talk to press or press called me, they would ask for Gene or Paul most of the time. But when we started talking about musicianship, then they started looking at Ace a little bit closer. And the same with Peter: we drummed up his drumming! (Laughs) Then it became a little bit easier.

Carol, did you get a pulse on which albums seemed to be received best by the press?
Well, I would say again, it was Gene and Paul's that stood out, to some degree, a little bit more than the others.

Of course, Ace literally pulled an ace from his sleeve in scoring the big hit of the four albums with "New York Groove."
Yes, that was very good for us because we could then play that up. That's what was happening. Again, Ace was able to talk about the music from his album. It was great. It kind of came out of left-field and we were thrilled about it.

And it probably took Gene and Paul by surprise?
Right.

From some of the people I've talked to in the industry, when you say the KISS solo albums, they joke about the albums. It seems there's a stigma attached...
Big stigma! That's why I said to you, that was one of my biggest problems. It was a stigma, because nobody took them seriously. It was difficult to break through and that's why the publicity came from all of the marketing and promotions that were done — the innovativeness and creative marketing so people were talking about it. You know what I always said, "If you're not making it through the front door, there's always a back door." And that's what we utilized in the beginning.

I think part of the stigma with this particular project is that Neil Bogart shipped more than 5 million of the KISS solo albums to record stores. And not all of them sold, and there were a lot of returns.
Yep. Well, people were looking for anything they could to downgrade the band's growing popularity. And look, eventually [the publicity] worked because even at the time [they sold], and they still sell. People are still looking for those albums.

It's also been intimated that some label executives perceived this solo album marketing campaign as over-excessive and that other artists from other labels subsequently questioned why their label couldn't promote them like Casablanca did with the KISS albums.
Exactly. And what's interesting is that my company, the clients that came to me were the biggest in the world. I had McCartney, Billy Joel, Cher, Van Halen, it was

amazing. And that's because they knew that we could do the job publicity-wise for them.

Van Halen?
Well, what's interesting is that Gene found Van Halen. Fortunately, they stood on their own and were able to make it big too. I loved working with them as well. The thing is [the solo albums] gave us the opportunity to show what can be done when you work closely with a record company in marketing, radio promotion, advertising, and public relations. Every one of those entities is important to the success of what you're trying to get across.

Aside from the solo albums, in 1978 for KISS there was also "Double Platinum" and "KISS Meets the Phantom of the Park." Do you think 1978 was KISS' peak year?
It was a peak. But it didn't come down after that. I think that was probably the busiest year for them. At that point they became a staple. Once they started touring, especially in Japan, it was such an enormous turnaround. '78 was the busiest year with many things happening.

KISS and "Rolling Stone" have always seemed to have a tenuous relationship. Given your unique perspective, can you shed some light on the rub between KISS and that particular publication?
"Rolling Stone" saw itself as a valid, credible "music" publication and ultimately did not want to bring a show band [like KISS] into the fold. So it was just a bit of snobbery.

Well, when I look at the magazine and see some of the acts who have made the cover, especially in recent years, I think it's surprising that KISS never made the cover, especially in the '70s.
I know. And believe me, it wasn't for not trying. Then you get to a point where there was an arrogance about them. And you say, "I'm not begging for this. This band doesn't need to beg." Then you understand where they're coming from and you say, "Okay," and that's it. With every other national, regional, local, and international publications around the world, I wasn't going to worry about "Rolling Stone."

Bill Aucoin passed away in 2010. Can you talk about what Bill meant to you and how important he was to the success of KISS?
Yes. Bill and I hit it off right from the beginning. He was such a gentleman. He wasn't your typical music manager. He was brilliant. He could get his point across without being crass. He had such insight. He had such determination. I mean, he spent all of his own money with this band, who had nothing when he picked them up. He invested every bit of his money because he believed, he saw something and

he was determined to make it happen. And he did. He was diligent. He was honest. He was forthright. He was so creative. All without ever raising his voice or hurting anyone. He could get what he wanted; he had that finesse. He included the band in every decision. He showed them respect. He showed everyone respect. He demanded your attention and 100 percent commitment because that's what he gave. I was asked when he passed away to be the emcee at his memorials so I went to the one in Florida and then Carol Kaye and I worked together to put together the one in New York.

And Ace and Peter came to the memorial in Florida?
Yes. Gene and Paul were down there but they didn't come to the big event. But they did go down. They showed their respect to him. As far as my point of view, Bill was just an amazing human being. And we stayed close all these years. I'd been with him just a couple of months before when he was sick and he was brushing it off that it was nothing. And I said to him, "Bill, you need to take care of yourself." I adored this man. He should go down in music history as one of the greatest managers of all time.

If you think to some of the major publicity coups during your tenure with the band, I would guess that Cadillac, Michigan, would be right up at the top. Carol, take us back to Cadillac.
Well, I'll tell you, that was my project, which I'm very proud of because I had received the letter from the football coach at Cadillac High School saying that his team had been losing. And he decided that during practice he was going to put on some music that he thought might generate some energy and get his guys on track. He was a KISS fan himself and he said he put on KISS albums and he said the transition was amazing and he wanted to let me know and to please tell KISS that their music got this high school football team to start winning games. And I thought to myself, "What a lovely story!" And I said, "And what better place, the heartland of America, to give credibility to this band." So I called Bill and Alan, and I said, "Is there a possibility KISS would go to Cadillac, Michigan, and meet the football team?" And of course, they were always up for something, and they said, "Sure, sure! That sounds great." I got back to the coach and told him that we were going to be coming, and we figured out a time when the band was off. He almost flipped; he could not believe it. We planned a time where we would bring the band in and meet the football team and the guys would talk to them. It was really going to be that kind of a situation.

Well, it evolved into a major, major event. When the coach called me back, he said he told the president of the school and the principal that KISS was coming! Everybody got so excited so not only did the school get involved, but the town got involved. And what they were planning for KISS was this major event whereby the town officials — the mayor and all of the politicians, the councilmen and teachers

— everybody was going to have a "KISS Day." When the band came in, they were going to have floats and a marching band. And I thought to myself, "My goodness. What better thing could we have done?!" And so I coordinated with everybody there, we sent the teachers makeup kits and they were putting the makeup on the students. And mothers and fathers were putting makeup on the kids. The town mayor and the councilmen had makeup on. The football team put makeup on. When everybody came to greet us when they arrived, they were all in KISS makeup. It was the wildest thing. We got on to the football field and then we went through the town and they had floats. I brought Waring Abbott along with about 20 key press people there. Of course, Waring was our official photographer so he was able to document everything. It was spectacular and that was the major turning point for me. I knew if we could get middle America to believe in this band and do what they did — with little kids, teachers, political figures and the school principal and everybody there with makeup on — then nothing is wrong. Because before that I used to get threatening letters and phone calls from people down South who said the band "were the demons and the devil and we're all going to hell." I tried to explain to them that this was not the case; that the KISS makeup [designs] were cartoon figures and I explained what each member's makeup was. But it didn't help. The Cadillac, Michigan, event absolutely gave credibility to them as a "wholesome" band (laughs). That was the crossroads.

It's just such an unlikely, but amazing, chapter in the band's history.
I didn't even anticipate it to be as huge as it became. We were basically going to surprise the football team and do a good deed and show up. And it just evolved. So we said, "Okay, if this is evolving like this, then we're going to make it work well." And the guys were wonderful. It was so amazing and, as I said, it was a turning point as far as the acceptance and credibility the band could have with Middle America on a national level, and not just as a cult band.

Though you've worked with many other great artists, do KISS hold a special place in your heart?
Absolutely, they were the one band from the very beginning and they will always hold that first place in my heart. I've talked to Gene and I'm so proud of what they've done. I sat with Peter and Ace at Bill's memorial down in Florida and they seem to be in a decent place for themselves. And I'm glad to see that. I always feel like the sister who is looking out for the brothers. And I'm happy when I see all the good things that happened to them because I remember that first night when they were wearing the costumes they made themselves, and one of them was a little torn (laughs). And to see what they became and know that I was a part of it from the very beginning is just a wonderful thing for me.

Dennis Woloch

Art director details the creative process for the iconic solo album portraits, his goal to make them look "classic and timeless," working with artist Eraldo Carugati, and more.
Interview by Tim McPhate

Dennis, 1978 was a big year for KISS. There was "Double Platinum" in April, the KISS solo albums in September, followed by "KISS Meets the Phantom of the Park" in October. When do you first remember learning that KISS were doing solo albums?
Dennis Woloch: Well, I don't remember any details or specifics about it. It probably just happened the way everything else happened. Somebody walked into the art department or they summoned me into Howard Marks' office and they let me in on what the latest project is. As soon as they knew they were going to do the solo albums, they were planning the marketing deal that they came up with. They would all be released on exactly the same day, which was an unusual thing for any group. No group had ever done that before, or since.

That's right.
It was just a one-time thing. Pretty ingenious marketing really. They even went so far as to come up with a little shopping bag. Remember that shopping bag?

I do. I have one (laughs).
Right, right. So if you went to Sam Goody and bought all four of them at the same time, they'd put them all in there. That was the idea. The bag had all four of the albums printed on it. It was a pretty cool marketing deal.

It was certainly an unprecedented campaign. As you alluded to, no one had ever done something like this before. Do you remember thinking that the ante for the artwork needed to be upped accordingly?
There's no question about it. I thought that this was the most important KISS-related project to date. My immediate goal that I set for myself was to try to make them as classic and timeless as possible. I didn't want these things to look dated. I actually never want anything I do to wind up looking dated. I try to avoid anything trendy because if you do something trendy, it looks great now and it looks terrible tomorrow. It's just always like that. You go back and look at something that was done years ago and it was obviously designed for the times, but it doesn't hold up. But I think most of the KISS stuff does hold up still.

I agree, Dennis.

Yeah, you know, I really had that in the back of my mind. "Let's not be too trendy with type styles that come and go [and] colors that come and go, [and] silly ideas that come and go." So for these solo albums, I said, "Okay, timeless and classic." And I sort of right away knew that they would have to be portraits of each guy. I just couldn't imagine any other image on there even though I tried. Because portraits was one of the first ideas that came into my head, I said, "Well, it's got to be their face." I mean now it seems so obvious, in retrospect, to say, "Well, yeah. What else would you have done?" Well you could have done a lot of things. I mean, they could have all looked different — one from the other. You could have tried to maybe capture each guy's individual personality on it. Or talk to each guy and say, "What do you like? What are your favorite colors?" But that would have been wrong because it really is KISS. KISS is an entity, as a whole. So I kept it that way. Then I said, "Okay, portraits. That's a given. But let me keep thinking." I kept thinking and I said, "Maybe it should be their whole body standing there? Their whole figure? Hmmm ... No!" (Laughs) Because then you have costumes and that comes and goes and that becomes dated where you could point at it and say, "Oh, 1978." So I didn't do that. And so I went back to portraits. I think this was a key decision — when I decided not to do a photograph.

I've always wondered if photos of the band members were ever a consideration.

Yeah, I don't know why, because of the "classic" feeling that I was trying to put across, I thought it would be better served by illustration. You know, a photo is just not the same as art.

And even though a photo can be classic, maybe it doesn't have that timeless appeal that, say, a piece of art does.

Yep, there's no question about it. I said, "Okay, art." And so then the task became to find the artist. And we found him in the usual way that we searched for artists back in the day. We had these art director's annuals that came out once a year, the best in advertising. There were the illustrator annuals put out by the Society of Illustrators — the best in illustration that year. Grafische had an annual that [contained] everything illustration, graphic design, photography. There's another one, Communication Arts (CA) that came out and had all the best of that year in advertising, illustration and photography. In one of those annuals we saw Eraldo Carugati's work. It was something he did for "Playboy." It was very realistic. But could he do likenesses of somebody? He obviously had the chops to paint realistically, but I didn't know if he could pull off a mood, a likeness, [and] all these other things that he would have to do.

I've looked at his credits and he did do the painting for the album cover for Rush's 1975 album "Fly By Night."

I had no idea. I don't think he ever said anything to us about it either.

So when you came across his work, Eraldo Carugati was a new name to you?
Absolutely. I had never heard of him.

Was there ever another artist in contention?
I think there was another artist that we asked to do a rough. And I cannot for the life of me ever remember who that was. I just can't remember. And that rough was floating around somewhere too. I actually saw it somewhere, but I don't know where. It was a long time ago.

I don't think I remember seeing that.
Well, you know, it's neither here or there really. But Eraldo did a layout.

You would have gotten in touch with Eraldo?
Yeah. He didn't have an agent, I don't think. So I didn't have to go through an agency.

And was he receptive about doing the project from the outset?
Totally. He was a good guy. He was in his late 50s when he did that. He had an Italian accent. He was from Italy.

Apparently, he spoke multiple languages, including Italian, English, French, and German.
I didn't know that. He was a really good guy. He told me that he refereed soccer games on the weekend. I couldn't get over that, because he was about 57 at the time. He was in great shape, good health, and he ran around refereeing soccer games. But he was in Chicago. So we had to fly out to Chicago and talk to him out there. He worked at a big company — the name of which also escapes me. I don't know what his relationship was there. [Editor's Note: Carugati worked for Stephens, Biondi and DeCicco, a Chicago-based commercial art and photography studio.] I think he may have rented space in the company and also did work for them when need be. It was an old-fashioned set up, the kind of thing they used to have in the '40s or '50s where you have a graphic design company and under the same roof there would be a little photography studio, there would be guys who could do very realistic renderings of products — you know cars and a can of beans, whatever they were selling. Then down the hall would be the retoucher and the airbrush guy. Then around the corner would be the guy that did pastel mockups and renderings. They had to use pastels before they used magic markers — it was unbelievable work. I used to see this when I was first coming into the business. That's the kind of place it was. And it was huge; it had a couple of floors. And he sat there; he had this space in there where he did the KISS work. And like I said, I don't know if Eraldo got all the money or if he had to split that with them because he was working with them or for them, or if he just rented space from them. I really never got that straight.

I have to be candid; it seems information on Eraldo Carugati is pretty scarce.
Yeah, I know. You can find some of his paintings that he did. He did sort of realistic landscapes, which I understand they were all destroyed in a fire.

That's too bad.
Yeah, I read that somewhere. So anyway, we went out there to [Chicago to] look at the work in progress. And it was coming along beautifully. It wasn't done or anything. He didn't know what to do with the bottom, like the neck area. He was just kind of ending it sharply and abruptly. I said, "Oh no Eraldo, we've got to do something about that. That's got to fade it to black. Fade to black." And he couldn't do that with the technique that he was using, he was just using little paint brushes. So he took it down the hall — I went with him (laughs) — and he talked it over with the airbrush guy and the airbrush guy probably did a little bit on there while I was watching, just to see if it would work. And I said, "Yeah, that's going to be it. That's going to be beautiful. They'll just fade into the background from the neck down." Because it would have ended abruptly, it would have looked horrible. So he did that. And it really was classy and beautiful.

Was Eraldo given anything as a guide? I think lore has it that the solo album images were inspired by either the embossed gatefold images in "Double Platinum" or the images on the cover of the 1977-78 tour book.
I tell you, you're going to know about as much as I know. I don't remember exactly — now obviously we had to give him something to look at. You can't do this out of your head. Now what exact pictures I gave him? Your guess is as good as mine. If you look around and see something that looked just like those pictures, that's the one we gave them (laughs). I think you're right about the "Double Platinum" ones. That's probably the best pictures we had of them, full face, lying around.

Would you recall about how long it took Eraldo to finish the job?
I would only be guessing if I told you, and I'd rather not. I mean, it wasn't an inordinate long amount of time. He was a professional. He really knew how to approach these things. He didn't have to doodle around and scratch his head and say, "Hmm, what do I do next?" He knew. He knew how to approach these things. And he was excellent.

What type of paint did he use?
It was like a gouache. It's a water-color. It comes in little tubes and it's water soluble. That's what he used. So if you took the original and spilled something on them, it'd be all over.

And about how large were each of the paintings?
24 inches square, give or take. About twice the size of an album.

And on a canvas?
No, on a kind of illustration board.

Of course, the colors are very striking and help given each painting a unique feel. Were the different "aura" colors part of the original instructions?
Yeah. Early on, I think this is even before I did the "Alive!" album, which was the first one I did. Bill Aucoin said, "Dennis, we're going to put out these little trinkets for the fans. It's going to be each guy's signature done in metal. And it will be a pin and fans could wear it." It was just made out of crappy, silver-colored metal. It came out in a little cardboard card, and the cards hang on a hook in the store, that sort of thing. And maybe blister-packed, I don't know. And he said, "Can you design those for us? Like a Gene Simmons signature pin [with] KISS logo?" I said, "Sure." And he said, "It's one color because it's a cheap job." I said, "Okay. Just a simple one-color [job] with some simple typography on there." And so I'm starting to lay it out, put the KISS logo on it and the signature. And I said, "Well, it's one color but there's four separate ones. Do they all have to be the same color? Or could each one be a different color?"

So I go back and said, "Look, I don't think it's going to make any difference, cost-wise, because maybe they'll be run at different times. Let's make each guy one color." He said, "Yeah, that's Okay." I went back and had to think, "What guy gets what color?" That was the very first time where I assigned colors to each guy. So I said, "Okay, Gene's going to be red because he splits blood and he has fire. So he's red." He was easy. And I said, "Ace? Blue." Space, the sky — I don't know, Ace and blue made sense. And then I said, "Okay, green for the jungle cat." And I did not know what to do for Paul (laughs). I scratched my head for a while on that one. I said, "Actually, we don't know what Paul is. (Laughs) We know who everybody else is, but we don't know what he is. He's got a star on his face, what the fuck is that? (Laughs) "Oh, he's the lover. Oh, I see." I said, "What the hell is that?" I said, "Purple. Purple is passion."

Right.
So there we go. We got that. They became the little colors on these cardboard cards that held their signature pins. And that was it. I didn't have to think about that for years until we did the solo albums and I'm standing with Eraldo, and I said, "You know, they have black backgrounds that they're on, and their hair is black. So they're going to be back-lit. So the hair picks up a fringe of color like a halo." He was going to originally just do them all with a yellow-ish light, as though it was really back-lit, like in a photograph. And I said, "No, no, no. Gene is going to have a red glow," and it came back to me, the colors that I had assigned to them. So I told him, and that's how that happened on the solo albums. And it's all these little things that pop into your head at the right time that really make it work. Because I could have forgotten that, it was four years ago. We never talked about each guy

having his own color since that time I did those little pins. But I'm standing there and I'm talking to him and we're talking about back-lighting, and I said, "Oh, wait a minute..."

It's just the perfect icing on the cake. I can't even imagine the album covers without the colors.
There's no question, yeah.

How many times did you go out to meet with Eraldo Carugati? Was it a series of meetings?
I went out there one time to see the work in progress, to make sure it was coming along okay, because I was worried. I was worried all the way to the end because to me this was a huge job. It had to be right. And I was happy with what I saw, very happy. So I came back to New York and he said, "I'll deliver them in two weeks." Eraldo came to New York with all the art and blew us away. They were so wonderful.

The first time you laid eyes on them, was it a "wow" moment?
Yes, because he had enough of it rendered realistically that I knew that we really had something great here. Although it wasn't done yet. So I was, let's say, very optimistic. When he delivered them, that was the end of the story. I was over the moon. I said, "This stuff is fantastic." I walked into Howard Marks' office and I showed it to him. Everybody was just floored. Even if you look at those things — you can probably see them on the reproductions, if you get a good reproduction — their eyes look wet. They're just rendered so beautifully.

They feel very alive.
I tell you, it's a feeling you can't get with a photograph.

There is just something about these images that is indescribable.
It's hard to put it into words. It's a special quality that comes out. And the thing is, when you look at them now, like we both said, it's hard to imagine it any other way. But it came out of nothing. It came out of zero. All these decisions had to be made. "It's going to be a portrait." "Oh, well that's obvious." No it isn't. It's not obvious. I could have had Gene standing on a mountain top, howling at the moon. We could have put Paul in a harem full of girls, you know. And he's had that picture before. We could have done all those sorts of fantasy things, but that would have been ... not so great.

Of course, the story I always tell about Eraldo is Gene didn't always have the dribble of blood when he first brought it in. Now, I'll be perfectly honest, I don't remember who or how that suggestion came out, that Gene needed a little something extra. Maybe it was Bill Aucoin, who was standing there looking at them. I don't think it was me, but it was a long time ago (laughs). [Someone] said, "Well, Gene needs a little something extra. He spits blood onstage." And so Eraldo actually had, in his pocket, a little piece of cardboard. It was a palette where he had dried up globs of paint on it. You know, they were dry. They come alive when you add water. And he had a tiny skinny brush in his pocket. And Eraldo always wore a jacket and a tie. He was a real gentleman. Even when he worked, I think he just rolled up his sleeves, and he had a tie on. Old-school, very European in a way. And he takes out the brush and he said, "Can I have a little water?" We gave him a little thing full of water and he dips it in. He had some red on the palette he brought that back to life with the water. And he just starts painting right on the painting. I mean, he doesn't do like a little pencil outline.

He went right at it?
Oh my God. I'm walking away, looking out the window. I'm saying, "Oh, fuck me. He's going to screw it up now." And I kept walking back and taking a peek at it. And like a magician, out of nowhere, boom, this beautiful little drop of blood with the shadow and the highlight on it. I said, "Oh, man. This is too good!"

That little nuance really makes Gene's portrait. It's absolutely perfect.
Yep. And it was. He didn't make it big, he didn't overdo it. It was just right. I then said, "Hey Eraldo, you want some coffee?" He says, "Yeah." I said, "How do you take it?" He said, "Black like my soul." (Laughs)

(Laughs)
That was the first time I ever heard that phrase (laughs). Eraldo was a great man and I really, really enjoyed working with him. I wish I could see him again, just to hug him or something. You know, he was so good.

So you all are blown away at the final product. Did the band come in and see them at that point?
You know, I don't remember that meeting. You think I would. But I just don't quite remember that specifically. So anything I told you would be like conjecture. Like, "Yeah, we showed it to them and they loved it."

I would think that they would have been floored as well. Plus, the solo album art have been used on so many pieces of KISS merchandise over the years.
Because they hold up. And they look just like them. They're great likenesses. The other thing that's unique about them is the logo, which I changed for just that project.

With the portraits out of the way, how did you approach the logo and the typography?
I wanted to make the solo albums a little bit unique, a little different from a KISS album because they weren't; they were just each individual guy. And so I just turned it into the skeletal basics of the logo, to put it that way: the double outline with no solid filled in letter. And I also thought that would give it a sophisticated look.

To me, the logo feels subtle on these album covers.
Yeah, that's good.

The likenesses are really the focus, and the logo is just hanging there in the top-left corner. When you consider the context, it's a brilliant combination.
We didn't want to draw too much attention to it. It has to be there. I wanted to make it different because this was a different project — it wasn't a KISS album. It was one-quarter of a KISS album, so one-quarter of a KISS album maybe (laughs).

How about the font that was used on the back cover?
It's extended. It's an extended font. There are two fonts that are almost identical and it's one or the other. But I think it's Euro style. But it could be Mircogramma (laughs). But Euro style is easier to find. It's probably Euro style. Some guy called me up and he did a tribute to Eric [Carr] or somebody, and he had an illustration done of his own face. Some KISS fan made the album. And I remember he called me up and he asked me that, "What was that font?" And that was the first time I had to go back and remember.

Aside from Gene, did any of the others have any other last-minute modifications?
Really he was the only one. The other ones were done man. It was such an easy job, really. I guess we went through the proper steps along the way to make sure everything was going to come out the way we thought it should. So there were no surprises: "Oh, I didn't think you were going to have that that way," or anything like that. None of that happened. Because we talked about it all the way through, step by step. Visiting him in Chicago helped because we solved the fading thing, on the spotlight there, because that was not something you could anticipate until you saw the artwork. And you say, "Wait a minute, that can't end abruptly like that." We had no surprises. He did such an excellent job. Everybody looked at it; they loved what they looked like. And they were done. There was no going back and saying, "Can you fix my eye? My nose looks funny..." None of that. Anytime you try and do a portrait of somebody, you know that's going to happen — it happened on "Rock And Roll Over." But those changes were good changes that we made on "Rock And Roll Over." They were right. Paul was right, "My nose looks funny. This looks funny. That looks funny." He made good suggestions.

I've always wanted to ask this question: In looking close at Ace's face, it seems one eye is lower than the other. Have you ever noticed this?
I don't think I ever noticed that, no.

Paul's face is tilted slightly, so one is naturally lower. But Ace seems to be looking straight ahead, and it just looks like one eye is slightly lower.
Let me try and find this on my computer (laughs). Here it is. Oh yeah, [it's] really lower. I never paid much attention to that. Yeah, that's funny. Huh, maybe his eye is lower in real life, who knows? (Laughs) I've always loved the way he rendered that silver. Oh my God. You can see the flesh through the silver, you know.

Yeah, Ace's is tremendous. Dennis, are you even able to pick a favorite out of the four?
You know, I like Ace. I think Peter looks fantastic too.

You can see more of Peter's costume compared to the others.
Maybe it's that silver nose that gets me. And I like that pose, Peter's pose, looking down a little bit. That looks pretty good. Let me look at the others real quick. (Pauses) They're all remarkable in their own way.

It's a tough question. I think I'd be hard-pressed to pick a favorite.
Paul has a lot of hair going on there. That's all done a stroke at a time with a little brush. One at a time, hair by hair.

Amazing.
Yep. Beautiful!

So once you had the final album art, what was the process of getting these onto album covers?
The printing process back then — some of it is still the same; a little bit of it is different now with computers. You would take artwork like that and you would send it out for somebody to shoot photographs of [them]. And we used an 8x10 camera, a large film camera. So the film would actually be one piece of film, which was 8x10 inches. So it's a large transparency, just like a slide, but huge. So it was a positive image on film, and you really got beautiful, vibrant colors. They would just shoot it and they would bracket their exposures to make sure that they got it exactly right, and you'd get the exact right one. You'd look at it with a magnifying glass when you got it back to make sure it was all sharp and perfectly exposed, the colors were just exactly right, and that they didn't shift or change. And once you picked out the best photo of each one, we had to make a mechanical. A mechanical is a piece of cardboard, illustration board, [on which] you would lay out the album cover. So it was 12 inches square, then there was a little eighth-inch spine on it, then there was the back cover. And that was printed on the same piece of paper at

the same time. So when you laid it out, you had yourself a 24-inch wide thing, with an eighth-inch spine and then various for bleed so the ink can go off the edge. And you sent out that photograph of the guy's face. You sent it out to size; you sized it up to be what size it was going to be on the album cover. It came back black-and-white Photostat.

Photostat is not even a good photograph, it's very down-and-dirty — it's only for position. And you'd put rubber cement on the back, cut it out, [and] stick it down in the exact position on the 12x12. Then you'd send out your KISS logo and get that sized exactly the size you want it. And you'd stick that down sometimes right on the Photostat, sometimes on an acetate overlay. And you'd get the typography for the back. You'd send out and get all the type set because you couldn't do that in house, they had type shops that did that. And they would send back the type in a reproduction quality print of the type. You'd put glue on the back, cut it out, [and] stick it down where you wanted it. Every little piece of type had to be done that way. And then with a tracing paper — or vellum overlay — you would give the printer instructions: "The logo drops out of the four-color photo in white. The name drops out white out of all four plates." You would make a big X on the photograph, and you'd say, "This is four-color art A." Then you'd mark the transparency A. And on the back you would say, "This is 100-percent black. Type drops out white. This is red made out of 100 percent magenta and 100 percent yellow. This is blue made out of 50 percent cyan and 10 percent black." And so on. All these handwritten instructions... And you had to know about printing — you had to know the process so you could give instructions, and I did. And that's how it was done. It was a big pasted up, what we called a mechanical. Everything that ever got printed had to be done that way. Ads for magazine, anything!

That sounds like quite a process.
Razor blades, rubber cement, T squares, triangles, rulers, erasers — all kinds of graphic equipment. There were ruling pens so you could make straight lines with black India ink. All sorts of equipment — we kept the art stores in money.

I bet.
We had big drawers full of these illustration boards, which were high-quality boards. They were expensive. Tracing pads and vellum pads and acetate pads and on and on and on — we had a room full of equipment.

Would Eraldo have been paid a flat fee for this work?
Yeah, sure. Whatever it was. He got paid. We bought the art outright and that was the end of the story.

Typically a painter signs his name at the bottom of a piece of art. But there's no signature on these. Was that not considered?

That's a good question. I've never thought of that. That's a good one. I think Eraldo was an ego-less guy. He did not have a big ego. He knew he was good and that was all. He didn't need to go any further than that. And he also, I think, felt "this is a commercial product. You don't sign that. I'm just an artisan. I'm a craftsman here, providing a service." No more, no less. I just think that's the way he approached it.

Of course, the solo albums kept up the tradition of featuring KISS goodies inside, with the interlocking posters.
Oh yeah, the posters were done by David Byrd. Actually the work he did for us on that KISS job is not his best work. He's done other work that was so beautiful. I think David was sick when he was doing that. I think he was not feeling well at all. And he had assistants helping him and everything. I think he was struggling with that.

Those posters were designed specifically to be interlocking, so when you put them all together, it forms a mural.
Well, it's another marketing ploy. In other words, if you buy one, obviously there are parts missing to your poster because of the interlocking deal, so you have to go out and buy all the rest to make one complete poster. It was just another way to get you to buy all four records.

There were also some promo materials that were sent to record stores.
I do remember some kind of mobile or hanging posters.

How about the actual original paintings? Where would those be?
Yeah, probably each guy has their own.

I would hope that they would.
Right. Then of course we eventually did one for Eric when he joined the band. Just for no reason really, just to make Eric happy, I guess.

I've seen the Eric one. There's also a solo album-esque rendering of Vinnie Vincent that I've seen out there. Have you seen that one?
I guess ... I vaguely remember that. You know, I had nothing to do with that. I had nothing to do with that. And I had very little to do with Eric's. Very little. What happened very often is I find these artists, I supervise the jobs from zero, get it going and then Bill Aucoin would just like make a phone call to Eraldo later because he figures he could do that and he'll go and have something done. And he didn't feel like he had to come back through me again.

So Eraldo did paint the Eric Carr portrait?
Oh yeah.

That would have been 1980, maybe 1981.
Right. But Vinnie Vincent, I have no idea what happened there. I don't know where that came from.

That could be a fan creation.
Maybe, I just don't know.

Not ringing a bell?
I don't know why — maybe they were just trying to make each band member happy by doing that. But it seems a little silly. It doesn't have any reason to exist really.

As we discussed, KISS were breaking new ground by releasing four simultaneous, cohesive solo albums. Do you recall about the huge amount of publicity surrounding the solo albums?
Just only in general, I remember. And really starting in 1976 from "Destroyer," when they really got huge, and on for the next two or three years. You know, KISS was big. They were always mentioned on TV. They were here, there and everywhere. I remember "Saturday Night Live" doing a little [skit with] Dan Aykroyd.

John Belushi too.
Yeah, yeah. So they were just everywhere. And we were working for the most famous band in the world. It was pretty cool. I'll tell you, I walked out of the office one day on Madison Avenue, I was going to lunch. I had long hair and a big mustache — it was the '70s, you know what I mean?

(Laughs)
And I was walking out of the office and there are two young boys, I don't know 12, 13 years old maybe. And they're both wearing KISS T-shirts so I said, "Nice shirts, where'd you get 'em?" They told me where they got them. And they were nice. I hadn't designed them, I guess the marketing people did [or] the merchandising people. So I said, "Nice shirts." And I was going to continue walking. And they said, "Hey stop, who are you? Who are you?" I said, "I'm nobody." (Laughs) He said, "No come on, who are you?" I said, "Well, sometimes I design these guys' album covers." He said, "You're Dennis Woloch." I said, "Wow!" That's when I knew KISS was famous. (Laughs) And they made me sign an autograph and that sort of made my day. I said, "Holy shit, I'm an art director and I'm signing an autograph."

(Laughs) Dennis, Casablanca's costs for the solo albums were very high, with the recording and advertising campaign estimated at $4 million. Do you remember anyone thinking that the entire project was a bit overboard?

(Laughs) Yeah, I really don't know what to say about that. We were, if nothing, about excess.

When the smoke cleared, KISS fans liked some of the albums, others not as much. Paul and Ace's albums seemed to have more traction with fans, musically speaking, while Peter and Gene's were considered radical departures.
Peter always saw himself as a different kind of an artist, rather than a pure rock guy.

In hindsight, the solo albums sold fairly well, but expectations were so high that "fairly well" wasn't good enough. Neil Bogart essentially shipped them all platinum and when all the albums didn't sell initially, it attached a stigma of failure to the project.
(Pauses) Yeah, I guess they overshot. But what are you going to do? They were kind of on top of the world at that point, and maybe that was the beginning of not being on top of the world. I think shortly after that a lot of their popularity started to go down the tubes.

That's true.
They were really only huge for three years, I guess. And then it sort of faded away a little bit, and then it came back, et cetera. Gene has a lot of thank yous, doesn't he? (Laughs)

Yeah he sure does. He has everyone on his album and it seemed he wanted to thank the world.
Well I know when I made the thank you list that he was overdoing it.

He even thanks Lassie.
Yeah, whoever he liked as a kid.

Dennis, you've recounted a positive experience with Eraldo Carugati and have been highly complementary of the solo album art. Does this project hold a special place in your career?
I would say so. It was a big deal at the time. I think I did the exact right job for those guys when I did that. I really do. So I feel very confident in saying that they really couldn't have been much better. I think they really solved, if you want to call it a problem, and met the expectations. I think they did what they really had to do, in a very beautiful way, thanks to Eraldo. Thank our lucky stars that we found the right guy. He just did a miracle job. I'm sure Eraldo never heard of KISS. I loved using these artists or illustrators that never did an album cover before. That was always fun for me. Like I don't think Michael Doret ever did an album cover and he certainly didn't know who the hell KISS was when he did that. He never heard of them.

Are the solo album portraits the most iconic images in KISStory?

(Pauses) That or "Destroyer." "Destroyer" because it shows them in their full figure glory, you know the vision of their whole bodies. And then the solos because they're classic, they're really strong images and they're never going to look old. They're just always going to look just the way they look. They're really, really cool. I'm proud of them.

Larry Harris

Former Casablanca Records executive VP goes on record about the internal friction within the band, Neil Bogart's gambling mentality and why the KISS solo albums were a "death knell" for the label.
Interview by Tim McPhate

The KISS solo albums were released in September 1978. Prior to their release, how would you describe the overall health of Casablanca Records?
Larry Harris: (Pauses) Interesting question. Really good. Lot of hits, tons of hits.

In doing some research, I came across an article in a May 1977 issue of "Billboard" in which Bill Aucoin mentioned the idea of the KISS members doing solo albums. And I also understand there was a proviso regarding solo albums in KISS' record contract that was signed in late 1976. Larry, when do you recall the solo albums becoming a topic of conversation around the office?
To be honest, I don't remember the date, it was so long ago. It probably initially came up in typical conversation about when the next album would be. What I do remember, which I talk about in the book [Ed."And Party Every Day: The Inside Story Of Casablanca Records" written with Curt Gooch & Jeff Suhs, published in 2009], was Howard Marks coming in — and Aucoin may have been there too — and telling us that the guys weren't getting along very well. And possibly one way to get more product out in the street and stop them from breaking up would be solo albums.

Yes, you mention that Bill Aucoin implied that the band would break up if the label refused to release four solo albums. Were the label's hands essentially tied into going forward with the project?
Well, it was either that or taking our only big rock act — because everybody else we had was either R&B, disco or comedy — that we started the label with and having them disintegrate. So we really had no choice in the matter if we wanted them or hoped that they would stay together.

You mention that the label "hated" the idea of the solo albums and that you did your best to "stonewall" Aucoin.
Well, the contract called for any album that came out as KISS, whether it was [a] regular [studio album] or solo [album], first of all we had to pay $500,000 up front for it and we had to also guarantee that we would ship 500,000 copies of an album. And we had to spend $500,000 in advertising. So that meant a lot of money. Aside from the fact, although each band member was pretty well-known to their fans,

they weren't the greatest musicians in the world, even though we made people believe they were.

Well, I'll go one further. In 1978, were KISS fans really pining for a Peter Criss or Paul Stanley solo album?
I don't think any fans cared about the solo albums from any of them. The whole magic of KISS was this cartoon group that we built up through "Circus" and "Creem" magazine. "Rolling Stone" hated them. But we had built this image of this group, of Ace being a great guitar player. He wound up on "Circus" magazine's poll. I talk about it in the book how we filled out all the forms at the office to get them to be considered great musicians. But I don't think there was one critic out there that thought that at the time. And the other thing with KISS was it was the magic of the show. And where was the show related to these four solo albums? I mean, what was going to happen? Was Peter going to go out and just do drum solos somewhere? Or would Ace stomp around the stage and fall over by himself?

According to your book, Neil Bogart initially thought to release a total of 2 million solo albums, which equated to half a million for each album. But Howard Marks balked by quoting that KISS' contract stipulated 1 million of each album needed to be pressed. I'm no lawyer, but if one solo album counted as half an album in the record contract, wouldn't it be possible that pressing half the normal total would have been permissible?
I have no idea. I don't remember that saying that in the contract, nor do I remember memorizing the contract 40 years ago (laughs). Neil was a gambler. And Neil felt if he was going to do this kind of investment — which was all that advertising per album — he was going to go for the throat. He wasn't about to say, "I'm afraid to do it." That wasn't his style.

Understood. But did Neil ever show any hesitance, maybe at the beginning?
Howard Marks had a large influence on our company because he was a very smart guy and he helped Neil negotiate with KISS on a few levels when we were having some difficulties with them. Howard also made a fortune from KISS. From the $500,000 for each album in advertising, Howard wound up with 15 percent of that, aside from whatever else he was making with the band. So it behooved Howard for this to happen. I remember there was initially some reluctance about putting out four albums at one time and the cost involved but I think once Neil realized that it was either the group breaking up or this happening, he embraced it.

No band had ever done a project of this scope before. Was there an appeal in terms of Casablanca boldly going somewhere no label had gone before?
Yes. That was fascinating for Neil. He loved doing shit like that.

For your part, you mention that the specter of the four KISS solo albums was "very troubling" to you. Larry, why did you have such a strong premonition from the get-go? Did you think the project was doomed from the start?
No, I thought it was doomed once I heard the albums. I mean, I embraced it because Neil embraced it. What was I going to do, was I going to fight him on it? That made no sense. You know, [KISS] normally did sell a million or 2 million albums on each release, so there was a little comfort there.

In your book, you mention that Neil "eventually embraced" the idea of shipping 1 million copies of each album. Ultimately, more than 5.3 million KISS solo albums were shipped. Did the label actually believe that all of these units could be sold?
Well, with the amount of advertising we were spending on television and radio and newspapers and everything, yes. We actually shipped more than we planned to. But that's the way the orders came in when we went to some of the big distributors and told them about the advertising that we were doing and how we were backing it up. And we wanted to make a lot of noise on the level of "this is the biggest initial shipment of records ever."

Was there a general targeted timeframe to move all of the units of the initial shipment?
No. We weren't that scientific.

The solo album advertising campaign was equally unprecedented, totaling some $2.5 million. There was $1.2 million spent on ad buys in various media. There were bus and subway ads, and billboards in New York and L.A. There were digital ads for Times Square. There were sampler LPs and pre-recorded interviews sent to radio. There were elaborate press kits and a 4-pack plastic bag. In hindsight, did the campaign border on over-saturation?
If we could have pulled a hit out of each album — which would be hard to do — then it would have worked. But it shocked us all that the only hit out of any album was Ace's.

So that was a definite surprise when the lone hit from the four albums came from Ace Frehley?
Yeah, it wasn't a huge hit, but it was a hit.

Gene and Paul's singles stalled in the 40s. In your book, you recount some shenanigans in terms of how the "Billboard" charts were formulated. Were any "schemes" considered to help push their solo singles?
The schemes got them to go to No. 40.

And from there, they were on their own?
They weren't selling. Nobody wanted to play them, they sounded terrible. None of them had a great song on it. Since "Beth" was so big, we were at least hoping that Peter's album would do better.

Interestingly, each album was backed by one single each, except for "Peter Criss." There were two singles from Peter's album, with the second being "You Matter To Me," a song with a definite disco flavor. Neither of these singles charted. Do you recall why there were two singles released from Peter's album?
(Pauses) I don't remember why.

It just seems odd that there would have been two singles from Peter's album, because his is considered to be the poorest selling of the four.
You could be right. I honestly don't remember which one sold the best. None of them sold well. I mean, if we sold 200,000 of each, it would have been a lot.

As you mentioned in your book, the promotion of the KISS solo albums really got the attention of the music industry. Was Casablanca on the receiving end of any sort of formal backlash?
No, the backlash, if there was any, came from radio. In those days, there wasn't any MTV. It was radio, you didn't have other outlets.

Were there any considerations to put out a second set of singles from the other three albums to continue the promotion of the albums into 1979?
No. At that point, it was kind of like a death knell. We had blown our wad on advertising and there were displays in every store, huge displays and stand-ups and all that crap you mentioned we made, and the record stores weren't going to keep them in there forever. It has a certain life.

KISS had filmed promotional videos for songs as early as 1975. Were promotional videos for the solo album singles ever considered?
Well, the problem would have been, this is KISS. So that would have meant taking their makeup off, and that wasn't happening yet. It would have been very hard to put a video out and they wouldn't be wearing their makeup. It wouldn't make any sense if Peter did a video with him in his cat makeup. And in a lot of cases, it was a different kind of music too.

I don't mean to propose a glib question, but why didn't these albums sell? Is it as simple as the music contained within the grooves just didn't appeal to the masses?
Absolutely. Their fans didn't even like them.

And here's another angle to the previous question: In reconsidering the idea of solo albums, was it really practical to expect fans to buy four KISS solo albums?
Well, we never thought that every fan would buy every album. I don't think that ever entered our consciousness. We really thought out of the four there'd be a couple of songs that would generate some sales. But the music just wasn't there. And Ace's hit, it wasn't even written by Ace.

That's right. It was written by Russ Ballard. Larry, is it possible to approximate how much money the label lost on the KISS solo albums?
The KISS solo albums brought the label down. PolyGram, who was our distributor, and owned half the company at that point, were totally pissed off at us. And it started PolyGram looking at us much more carefully than they were and checking our books closer than they used to. It was just a drain of so much money and what they considered to be a major mistake — because we also had to take the records back — so besides all the money on advertizing and production and whatever, we had to take all this stuff back, which cost money.

You mention in your book that PolyGram eventually sold the lion's share of album returns to discount retailers and flea markets. But this was this accomplished unbeknownst to Casablanca or the band?
Yeah, I also have a feeling, if I'm not mistaken, that their contract called for the fact that we couldn't sell [their albums] that way.

Of course, that would be the subject of a lawsuit brought on by KISS against the label. Larry, in 1979 there was a serious downturn in the U.S. economy, which affected the entire industry, let alone Casablanca. That year, the $4 billion a year record industry experienced an 11 percent drop in sales. In an alternate universe, say the initial shipment of 5.3 million KISS solo albums sells out. If this happened, would prospects for Casablanca have been different?
Well, disco was huge. And the Village People and Donna Summer and Parliament were still selling well. We had the Studio 54 album then, which did well. We had Robin Williams' first album and Rodney Dangerfield, which did very well. We were still selling a lot of records. But we took a huge hit with KISS. Where previously we would have all the disco stuff selling well and KISS selling well, KISS was taken out of the equation and we just had a big hole there from all the money we had committed. And it also made everybody believe that KISS was probably over. It really did backfire on that level. Where at one point, this band could do no wrong, all of a sudden it was, "Woah!"

KISS moved on with 1979's "Dynasty." That album spawned the hit "I Was Made For Lovin' You," which had a strong disco influence.
Which caused a backlash as well.

Yes, that didn't seem to agree with hardcore KISS fans. So it seems the solo albums really started a snowball effect for the band, because from that point they inched downward until they finally took off the makeup in 1983.
Yes, the originals eventually did break up.

Say you were allowed to have a mulligan with the solo albums, and you could go back and change some things, what would you do differently to make the project successful?
I don't know that anything could be done differently. At that point in time, we had no say in what their albums sounded like. Initially, the first two or three years we were working with them, we could make them do stuff. You know, like we made them do "Kissin' Time," or [we'd] kick it back in the studio and say, "No, change this." But at that point, they were so big they had their own industry going. They were selling KISS dolls by that point and all that merchandise — they had the KISS pinball machine and all that stuff. So I don't know that anything could have changed. Looking back on it and guessing, we couldn't have put out only 200,000 or 300,000 of each album, that wasn't an option. The only option would have been that we held the line at 4 million albums or held the line at only spending $2 million on advertising. Again, Neil was a gambler and if he was going to gamble on something, he went in full force. He didn't back off. It's like when PolyGram bought half the company, the deal was that they would buy the other half of the company for five times his earnings after five years so Neil's attitude was, "Okay, we're going to spend their money to try and make the earnings as big as possible." Instead of playing it safe and saying, "Oh okay, so we'll only make X millions of dollars profit and we'll get this much money after five years," Neil said, "No, we're going to make X, Y and Z profit so we really get some huge money out of PolyGram after five years." He wasn't conservative on that level, at all.

Whenever I talk to people who worked in the industry at the time about the solo albums, it's seems they are something of a punchline to a bad joke. You know, kind of like the "they shipped platinum and returned double-platinum" line.
That started with us with the Johnny Carson album. When we left Warner Bros. and went independent, we shipped 750,000 copies of Carson's album supposedly and got back a million. But that's the way the industry worked, if you bought two albums, you got one for free. That's how they did the discounting and sales report. On KISS, it wasn't shipped gold and got back platinum. We shipped platinum and got back platinum.

Years later, there are KISS fans who love the music contained on the four solo albums. In your view, what is the ultimate legacy of the solo albums?
I think the legacy is that this was the shining example of the excess that Casablanca had in various areas.

A couple of final questions. According to a report in May [2013], a financier has been secured for "Spinning Gold," a film in which Justin Timberlake is set to portray Neil Bogart. Larry, are you involved with the film in any capacity?
I worked with them a little bit on the script. And they're using some of the background from the book in the movie. But aside from that, I'm not involved in any major way.

Do you know anything about KISS' involvement at this point?
Well, they'll be involved somehow, I don't know exactly how. But you have to keep in mind that the movie is a Neil Bogart bio pic and it starts at Buddah Records. It doesn't start at Casablanca Records. While they'll be involved and have KISS in it, there's also going to be a lot of stuff about Gladys Knight, Curtis Mayfield and the old song "Put Your Hand In The Hand" from the Buddah days, because Casablanca was really an outgrowth of the four people who ran Buddah Records. KISS will be a part of the movie but again so will Donna Summer and Parliament. Neil became famous initially because of bubble-gum at Buddah and all the hits we had in the R&B field, you know Bill Withers, Curtis Mayfield, the Isley Brothers, and Gladys Knight. We had so many hits on that level. And Casablanca got its biggest fame because of the disco stuff. We put out so much disco [music]. So we'll see how it all winds up. With movies, even if the script is written, it changes if the director wants to do something different. But at this point, does KISS get 10 minutes of the film, or six minutes of the film, or 15 minutes? I have no idea.

With the star power of Timberlake, do you think this film stands a chance at making some noise?
Well, Timberlake, from everything I've seen, everybody really thinks he's a good actor. And he's embracing this because it's a serious role. Most of his [previous] parts were light and funnyish, with relationship stuff with women. This is going to be a serious role for him. He's not singing and dancing in this. He's being an actor. And I think he's so big right now, a lot of people are going to be curious to see if he can pull it off.

Christopher K. Lendt

Former vice president of Glickman/Marks Management takes us inside the business of the solo albums from his perspective, details his responsibilities for the project and lends insight into one of the more fascinating chapters in Super KISStory.
Interview by Tim McPhate

Chris, by the time the calendar turned to 1978, KISS had just come off a huge year in 1977, with a gross income of $10.2 million according to your book. In other words, business was good.
Christopher K. Lendt: Very good.

Would you describe 1978 as the definitive starting point for the "Super KISS" era?
I think the Super KISS era started to take shape after the high-water mark of the '77-'78 tour. I think that gave them a tremendous impetus to want to become more ambitious and more extraordinary in terms of how they presented themselves to the public.

I'm curious, is Super KISS a phrase that you coined?
Yes. It's entirely my own invention and no one else should take credit or blame for it.

(Laughs) Maybe you should look into trade-marking that.
(Laughs)

I recently read an article from a May 1977 issue of "Billboard" in which Bill Aucoin mentioned the idea of the KISS members doing solo albums. And I believe there was a proviso regarding solo albums in KISS' record contract that was signed in late 1976. In advance of 1978, do you recall discussions at Glickman/Marks about the KISS members doing solo albums?
(Pauses) I don't recall any specific discussions. Since the albums came out in the fall of 1978, they obviously were starting to gel by the end of the '78 tour, which I believe was in February. You know, a lot of things were discussed primarily with Bill Aucoin and we caught wind of it after the band had their discussions with him. I didn't really become aware of it until late winter of '78, which is not to say they weren't talking about it prior to that. There are many things that they were talking more on a one-to-one basis with Bill about the next creative project they were going to embark on, as opposed to somebody like myself who was at the time primarily concerned with the mechanics and the administration of how the project would get done and what the timetable was.

While Bill Aucoin was certainly in his element in orchestrating a grand KISS assault in 1978 with four solo albums and a film, it seems there was more to the story. Certain parties have described tension between the band members during this time and implied that KISS would break up if Casablanca Records refused to release four solo albums. Was your company privy to the internal tensions during the time of the solo albums?
There was always tension between Bill Aucoin and Neil Bogart and it ebbed and flowed. I wasn't directly connected to that relationship, but I knew through Howard Marks, because he was a little closer to it than I was, that they were always looking to try and get the edge on Casablanca because they felt that in many cases Casablanca shortchanged them financially. So any opportunity they would have to better their contract or improve their payout from Casablanca, they would try and take advantage of. That was something that Bill was trying to manipulate behind the scenes.

What was Howard Marks' reaction to the solo albums? Was this a project he was behind 100 percent?
I don't recall anybody opposing it. The only problem with the project was it was extremely ambitious. Nobody in KISS had ever made a solo record before. And now you're talking about making four of them [simultaneously] and they were all going to be released at the same time, and they all had to be ready at the same time. In each case, they required a producer and somebody had to be available immediately. We couldn't wait six months for a better producer or a better match to be had. We had to work with [whoever] was ready, willing and available at that time. And it had to be four at the same time.

In contrast to the typical KISS studio album, can you outline the financial implications of the solo album project for Glickman/Marks?
Well, I honestly don't recall all of the contractual details. I don't know that we got four times the advance of a studio album, but there were substantial advantages to doing the [solo] albums and Glickman/Marks, I guess, got at least as much if not more of a commission on the four albums as opposed to one. But I don't know that it was four times. I just don't recall.

So we can get a sense of your whereabouts during this time, I believe you arrived in L.A. in May 1978. Were you out in L.A. for an extended period?
Yes, I was in Los Angeles for the entire filming of the movie. And then as soon as Peter had his auto accident, I stayed out in Los Angeles through August until his album was completed, along with Paul Stanley's and Gene Simmons'.

Chris, can you outline your responsibilities for the solo album project?
Well, my job was to be the administrator or the business manager; to make sure that everybody who was working on the album, including the band members, had

accommodations; that whatever contracts were required with studios and producers were administered with me within a certain budget. I also monitored things on a day-to-day basis since Bill Aucoin couldn't relocate to California for that period of time. I also had to make sure that we were on schedule and to provide whatever organizational expertise I could to make sure that everything was coalescing to meet that deadline.

In your book, you mention that a lot of money was spent between booking studios, living expenses and securing musicians...
Right, it was really being a coordinator and the organizational manager for those three productions and to make sure that everybody was in the right place at the right time. I had to report to Howard Marks and Bill Aucoin to troubleshoot anything that came up that might have interrupted our schedule.

If you had to ballpark it, how much did all of the costs add up across all four albums?
Ace Frehley's was the least expensive. I think that Gene Simmons' was the most. I don't remember exactly what all four cost but, now that I think about, they couldn't possibly have cost much less than a million dollars.

Eraldo Carugati was commissioned to create four paintings for the albums' artwork. Would you recall what Carugati would have been paid for his work?
I don't recall exactly. It wasn't in six figures, I can tell you that. It was probably in the four or five figures. But it wasn't anything out of sight.

What were your impressions of the work Carugati produced?
I thought he did a splendid job. He was a very good artist and in terms of rendering KISS the way they wanted to look or how they wanted to appear at that time, I thought he did excellent work. That was part of what people like Bill Aucoin, Howard Marks and Dennis Woloch were responsible for — finding these artists and finding these designers to create images for KISS that would be entirely compatible with how they wanted to present themselves creatively. That's something that managers, and in this case the advertising agency, really don't get enough credit for because those people just don't come out of a phone book. They have to be researched. People have to look at their work. And they have to be at a level of professionalism that they could do a job like this — four individual paintings on a deadline — and at the same time they couldn't charge Andy Warhol prices (laughs).

(Laughs) Right.
That is to the enduring credit of Bill Aucoin's legacy, and also the roles of Howard Marks and Dennis Woloch and what they were contracted to do by KISS, which was to create all their advertising and images and find the people to render them in a way that was commercially viable.

Well said, Chris. If we get into the music, Peter's album was reflective of his diverse influences and the music he grew up with. And of course, Peter was older than the other members of the band. In hindsight, doesn't it seem unlikely that KISS fans were going to embrace the music on Peter's album?
The music on Peter's album, as you mentioned, reflected the music that he grew up playing since he was a teenager. It was more of a rhythm and blues-influenced kind of pop music. I think the fans at that time expected all the albums to be somewhat different. I don't think Peter was expected to produce more of a stripped-down hard rock album like Ace Frehley did. I think the whole idea was for them to make an album that would be an album for their creative energies and everybody knew going into it that Peter was not going to be unfaithful to the style of music that he grew up with, even though perhaps that was a difficult pill for some to swallow.

Generally speaking, you have two albums that are more in alignment with KISS' sound in Ace and Paul's albums.
Yes.

And then you have two albums that maybe threw KISS fans for a bit of a loop in Gene and Peter's albums.
Well, the idea behind the solo albums, which Bill Aucoin was instigating, was that everybody in the band should have the opportunity to make an album of the music that they're closest to, as opposed to having to make a KISS-sounding album. So it was designed to be a creative outlet that would actually make the band stronger because you didn't put them in a straight jacket and say, "Well, you have to go out and make another KISS record now. It has to sound a certain way; it has to be disciplined in a certain way. You can go and now have freedom to create new music in the way that you want and connect with your fans." With freedom comes certain risks, but I don't know that any of Peter's fans were disappointed that he produced an album that was his thing as opposed to Gene's thing.

Pardon my pun, but Ace's album was a bit of a wild card given he had only two lead vocals to that point in his KISS career. Do you remember a sense of surprise when Ace scored the lone hit of the solo albums with "New York Groove"?
Yeah, I think there was. It was unexpected, which is one of the reasons you do creative projects that hopefully stake out some new territory. Because with that sometimes comes a surprise in a positive way. I don't know who identified the Russ Ballard song for Ace Frehley — I never really looked into it or asked — but obviously that was a brilliant choice and the way it was produced was perfect for Ace.

In your book, you describe Paul arriving to a recording studio in the San Fernando Valley and him ending up being dissatisfied. Do you remember why Paul did not like the studio?

I recall that he didn't like the sound or the feel of the studio. And he just didn't feel comfortable in it and he wanted to walk away from the whole situation.

And a deposit was forfeited?
To the best of my knowledge, yes.

That's a costly decision then.
Yes it was.

Apparently Jeff Glixman and Paul didn't hit it off. And from what I can gather, all signs point to Paul wanting creative control of his album. Do you recall if there was a contract stipulation that stated each member needed to work with a producer? In other words, why didn't Paul produce his album himself?
Well, I think Bill Aucoin insisted that everybody have a producer because nobody in the band had ever produced before and we were all working on a very tight deadline. There's got to be somebody who can take responsibility for seeing that the project is completed and is expedited, if necessary. So I think it was probably reaching too far to expect that Paul would be producing his own album. And if he produced his own album, why wouldn't Gene want to do the same?

That's a fair point. One interesting thing to note is that each solo album had one single, except for one. Peter Criss actually had two single releases: "Don't You Let Me Down" and "You Matter To Me." In hindsight, this didn't amount to much for Peter's album in terms of sales. But would a properly promoted second single for each album have done anything to help stimulate sales?
Well, the answer is, in theory what you say makes sense, but in practice, record companies — if they can — identify a second single on the album. Or if there is competition that's getting in the way of them coming up with the second single to promote, it's not going to happen. In other words, Casablanca is like any other record company. They had a full slate of other releases, in addition to KISS, and once the initial singles came out from the KISS albums, they obviously had other releases to promote at that time. You know, those are the business judgments that they make. "Is there a second single on this album? Does this album justify us bringing a second single into the market and promoting it? Is it going to take away from the success that perhaps some of the other KISS albums were having with their singles?" And then they have to assess, "How does that affect the other releases that we have for other artists going on at the time?" Every record company has a finite degree of resources available. And to promote four solo albums at one time and do them justice and come out with an initial single requires marshaling a tremendous amount of resources. To come out with subsequent singles — unless that album has been a clear, over-the-top chart-busting success — requires some strategic thinking as to whether or not that effort will be rewarded and be sensible.

I just find it odd that Peter's album was chosen as the one that would be given a push with a second single, especially since his album charted the lowest out of the four. When we spoke with Larry Harris, he couldn't recall why Peter's album had a second single.
A lot of things happen because somebody at one particular moment in time makes a decision, perhaps instinctively. But it isn't necessarily indicative of a master plan that something happened with Peter's album, so why didn't it happen with the other three. It probably was just a decision made at the time out of what they felt was opportunism, and so be it.

Speaking of Harris, he has described the solo albums as a "death knell" for Casablanca Records, given the returns of more than 2 million albums. Neil Bogart was a gambler, but by pressing more than 5.3 million albums maybe he gambled a little too much.
Well, Larry would know better than anyone. If you manufacture 5-plus million albums and 2 million come back, like you said it was a "death knell." Bogart was a real promoter, he was a big risk taker [and] he had very good creative instincts. But that doesn't mean he's infallible. A lot of times people who are very successful at gambling, they keep upping the ante and by making the gambles bigger and bigger they think that automatically the payouts will be bigger and bigger. It doesn't happen that way. He made a big error in over-promoting and over-selling the albums. And this is a business, like the movie business, of expectations. If he printed a million solo albums and they sold out right away, that would have been considered a huge success. If he printed 5 million and half of them came back, it looks like a fiasco. And obviously, financially it was.

Harris also said in his book that Neil Bogart initially thought to release a total of 2 million solo albums, which equated to half a million for each album. But apparently Howard Marks balked by quoting that KISS' contract stipulated 1 million of each album needed to be pressed...
Well, I can't say what Howard Marks did or didn't say. He was very much a close confidant of Neil Bogart. I don't recall anything in the contract saying a certain amount of copies had to be printed. That's news to me. If you're saying that maybe Howard Marks egged on Bogart to take on more risk and print more albums, I'd say it could have happened like that. It's not out of character. I can't say it did because I don't know. But I can't say it's unthinkable that he would say something like that.

In searching for answers as to why there were more than 2 million returns and why the albums didn't sell, one of the theories I have is the simple fact that there were four albums. Taking into account the average age of a KISS fan in 1978, was it logical to think fans would be able to spend in the neighborhood of $40 on four albums, versus $10 for a regular KISS studio album?

Yes, it's clear that if they had sold 2 million albums, that would have been what a very successful KISS record would have sold at that time and everybody would have been very satisfied. I don't remember what the thinking was in terms of the fans having to spend four times what they normally would spend to buy a KISS album. Assuming that the kids have so much disposable income that they can just go out and buy four records as opposed to one, you're right, in retrospect it's a mystery to me why that thought didn't sink in. But that's the music business. People just push ahead with creative ideas that are bold and provocative and sometimes very risky, thinking that the positives will outweigh the negatives.

Given the returns of the albums, there is a stigma attached to entire project. Whenever I talk to people who worked in the industry at the time, it's seems the KISS solo albums are something of a punchline to a bad joke. In the grand scheme of KISS' career, do you view the solo albums as a success or a failure?
Well, I don't think it could be considered a failure because it was something unique in the history of the music industry that a rock and roll band would be able to produce four solo albums and release them simultaneously. It certainly did something to promote the KISS mystique and the fact that they were four separate characters with their own identities. I don't think it was a failure from that standpoint. Obviously financially it was a failure for Casablanca because they made some grievous business decisions and over-extended themselves in manufacturing so many albums. But I think that that's part of the legacy of KISS — that they did these creatively ambitious undertakings and they helped to burnish their reputation at that time for being a band that does big things and was always looking to push the envelope.

KISS were very fluid at the time in moving from one project to the next. Do you recall a true sense of disappointment in the KISS camp given what materialized with the solo albums? Or did everyone just move on to 1979 and what would amount to the "Dynasty" album and tour?
Nobody was thrilled that the albums were considered a failure by the standards of the industry, notwithstanding what I just said. Actually, they all thought they would sell a million or more each. That didn't happen. So they were a little bit chastened by it. They didn't get the claim or the commercial success that they anticipated. So we decided once that was over that we had to move on and make a new record as a band the following year.

Paul, in particular, has not held anything back in terms of his feelings for Peter's album. As a matter of fact, he has said he can't give it "any stars" on a five-star scale. That's all well and good, but what I've always found a bit peculiar is that the producer of said album ultimately was brought onboard for the next two KISS studio albums. What is your sense as to why Vini Poncia's services were retained for two consecutive KISS albums?

Well, because Vini Poncia was an experienced producer. Vini Poncia was a very good musical arranger and he also had experience and professional credits as a songwriter. He apparently jelled with the members of KISS and felt that he could create an album that would be musically respectable and in more of a pop direction, which KISS felt at that time that they wanted to pursue because that was a way of broadening their appeal to the public. In that sense, he was an ideal choice. They wouldn't have brought in Vini Poncia if they wanted to make a basic hard rock record — they could have worked with Eddie Kramer who could do that very well or probably a number of other producers from that era who were very well-known for producing hard rock albums. The fact that they chose Vini Poncia suggests to me that they were looking to go with a more pop sound. They certainly heard the "Peter Criss" album so they knew the kind of music that he created in the studio. They obviously felt that he was the right person at the right time to create a more commercially mainstream sound that would be a little bit more distant from the hard rock sound but put them more in the middle of a pop rock sound, which again is what they wanted. Believe me, it was their decision. Nobody had to give them a sales job. And I guess that Vini got along very well with the band members professionally and they found him very reliable and rewarding to work with, which is important. Because if you don't get along with the producer — he may be extremely talented, but he might not be the right person for you.

You've described the solo album campaign as being overreaching and "too much" KISS. Fans have long ruminated about possible alternative scenarios if the KISS solo albums never came to be. If here was an opportunity to go back to the start of 1978, do you think there could have been a better strategy for the band for that particular year?

The best way I can answer that is that, according to what I remember Bill Aucoin telling me at the time, the group was getting kind of ragged from the extensive amount of touring they were doing and the very tightly controlled release schedule they had for their group albums in recent years. You know, they did a live album and they did several studio albums — they had as many as two albums being produced over a single year. So he felt that it was time to let off a little steam and have them do something different. That's what managers do. They're very close to the artist. You can't just put them in a cookie-cutter, which we had been doing for many years very successfully. We'd do a new album in the fall, and then we'd tour in the spring and we'd start another album six months later. That becomes like a machine. And it can wear people down. Apparently that's what he felt. And this would be a way to, first of all, satisfy the importance of producing new KISS recordings for the public and, at the same time, give every member a chance to do something individually and not have to work in the studio together and give each of them some space to create their own music. But it would still conform to the KISS strategy for developing their career for the next phase.

In terms of actual results, as we've discussed, the KISS solo albums fell short. KISS soldiered on, though ultimately the original lineup disintegrated and popularity began to waver to the point where KISS ultimately unmasked by 1983. Chris, in looking back, do you think the solo albums the snowball that sent the original KISS lineup in a downward spiral?

I think that's kind of a stretch. The solo albums — with the exception of "Ace Frehley," [since] he did have a hit single — weren't commercial milestones in terms of sales. That's clear. But I don't see how they hurt the band. The following year they did "Dynasty." That was, I believe, their biggest album worldwide at the time. It did very well in a number of countries. They did a tour to promote the record beginning in the summer of 1979, and I don't want to get ahead of myself but the problem with that tour was not that KISS couldn't play big shows; they just couldn't play multiple big shows. That was a business decision made with some degree of creative chutzpah. It really brought them down a notch because they bit off more than they could chew. The "Dynasty" album did reasonably well; it certainly had one big hit single. So I don't think the solo albums hurt them. I think they helped solidify the fact that there were four individuals in this group called KISS and they got a tremendous amount of promotional value from it.

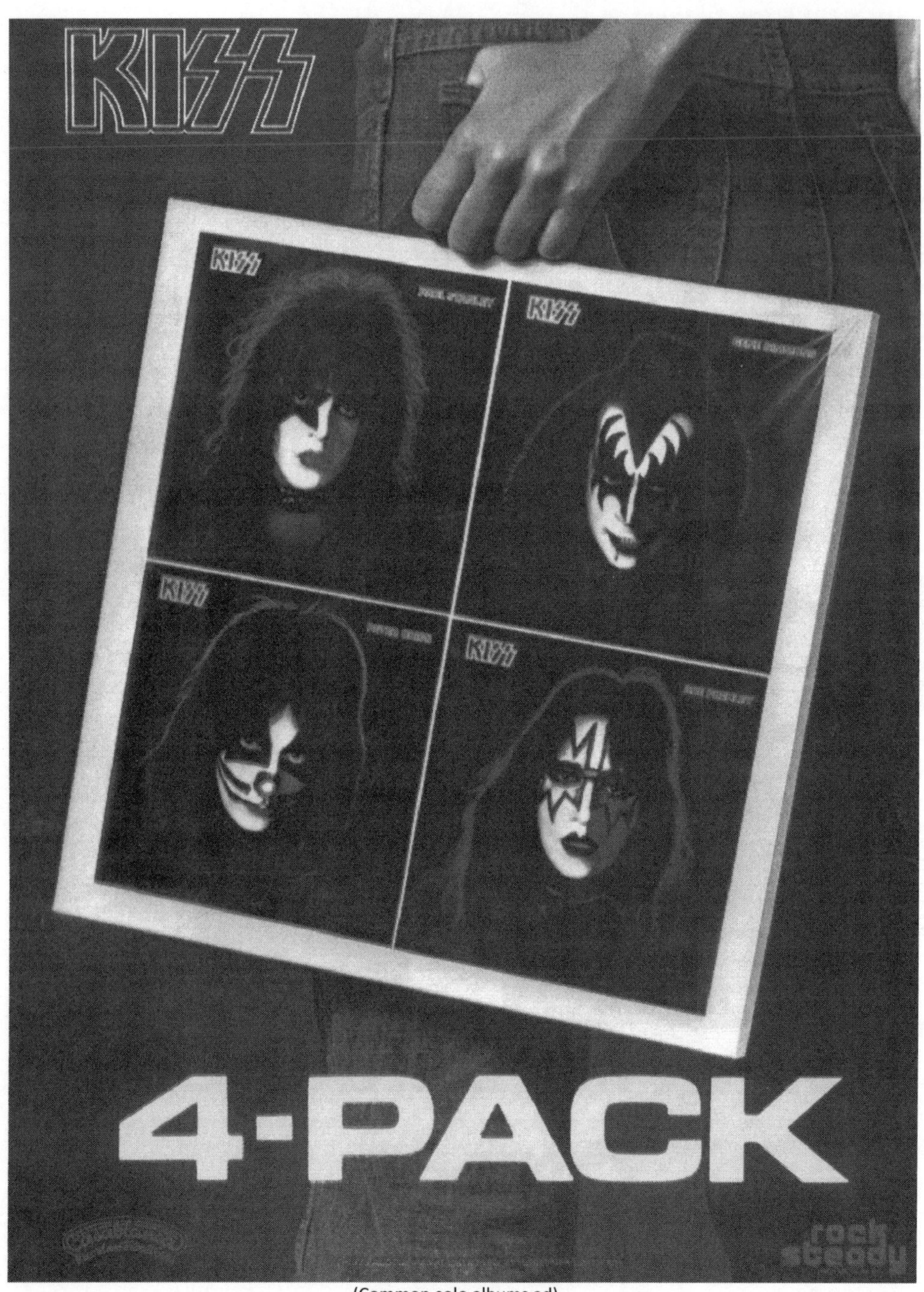

(Common solo albums ad)

1978, The Year And More

"Double Platinum," Front and Center

1978 wasn't all about the KISS solo albums... KISS also released their first proper international "greatest hits" package. In this piece we put "Double Platinum" under the microscope...

As 1978 opened, Rolling Stone Magazine writers continued their obdurate ignorance regarding the success of a band that the so-called pop-culture wizards simply couldn't understand. In their belated review of "Alive II" they pompously opined, "One of the perennial saving graces of rock & roll is its accessibility to the true believer. In a sort of Horatio Alger formula, if you need it badly enough and have the right attitude, eventually you'll become an adequate rocker. KISS, a band built almost entirely around an image, offers the latest proof of this maxim" (RS #256, Jan. 1978, John Swenson). Perhaps it was an attempt at intellectual humor, perceived to be over the heads of many KISS fans who may or not have cared (or even known) about the stories of the 19th century author referenced, but it wasn't without a hint of truth. The following month the magazine provided a platform for Charles M. Young to suggest that the band was becoming both boring and safe: "The thrill is gone. Much as I enjoy watching Gene Simmons puke blood; he's been doing it every night for three years... Their demographics are changing. Through overexposure, KISS seems no longer Forbidden Fruit. They are losing their traditional support among proletarian teenage boys and picking up children impressed by costumes. A third of the crowd appeared to be parents with little kids. KISS records are selling phenomenally well, but maybe to Shaun Cassidy weenie bops" (RS #258, Feb. 1978, Charles M. Young). In retrospect, the crux of Young's superficial analysis was undoubtedly true - KISS' core demographic was indeed changing (again). As it had changed in 1976 when "Destroyer" was released, moving the band away from their leather and flame glitter beginnings, the high-point of "Alive II" had set the stage for the next progression: Vegas-like flash in a safe and family-friendly manner. But that was a step the band had yet to take, even if the groundwork was being laid...

Between 1973 and 1978 both KISS and their label had shared a mirrored incredible trajectory of growth. KISS had gone from the clubs, a band struggling to find placement on the national touring circuit, to a merchandising powerhouse with ever broadening scope of commercial activities: Comic books, action figures, trading cards, clothing, and just about any licensing idea imaginable. The merchandise sold better than the records or the live shows. KISS had become a highly visible consumer goods provider. Casablanca had gone from a new label with 11 dedicated employees, struggling with distribution via Warner Bros., to an independent $100 million music and film behemoth employing 175. It ingested numerous labels as the need arose and grew a large artist roster with few acts, outside of a highly successful core, finding any real levels of success. As Casablanca hit $55 million revenue in 1977 the push was on to scale even greater heights, particularly as disco was taking off. The expansion of the "Filmworks" side of the business was envisaged and was going to pay dividends leveraging a five movie deal that Peter Guber had negotiated with Columbia prior to the merger. As a business no break was allowed - it was push on, push hard, or fall behind, though label President Neil Bogart did take the opportunity to cash in, selling a majority stake in the label to PolyGram (Casablanca's distribution partner) for a sum reportedly in the range of $10-15 million. For the core team that had bought into Casablanca in 1973, they were finally to see some dividends for their efforts. For KISS, on the other hand, they had toured extensively and recorded non-stop for four years by 1978 and a break was needed while the band member's executed their solo and film projects.

KISS' U.S. "Alive II" touring cycle had concluded at the Civic Center in Providence, Rhode Island, on February 3. The band took six-weeks off before embarking on their visit to Japan for a 5-night stand at Tokyo's Budokan. The first KISS Army Newsletter of the year hyped the forthcoming release: "The boys are busy right now remixing an array of their double platinum hits, plus some re-recorded, all time favorites for this dynamic two-record set" (Volume 3, Number 1). Casablanca had arranged in their late-1976 contract with the band that if they did not present them with new studio material, or the equivalent thereof, that they would have the right to issue a compilation "Best Of" album without the band's consent. Because of the studio side on "Alive II" being not considered enough to equal the requisite minimum 25 minutes for a studio album, the latest KISS had to deliver a new studio album was the end of May 1978. It was clear, with the planned projects throughout 1978 that the band was not going to meet such a schedule. As a result Casablanca executed their contractual option to issue a compilation, collecting material from KISS albums that had all sold "Double Platinum," though in the United States KISS wouldn't officially have a "double platinum" album until 1996 (regardless of any of the legend or hype that surrounds their catalog)...

KISS' involvement in the project was minimal, other than recording a new version of "Strutter" at Electric Lady Studios in February 1978. The re-recording of this song had been considered to be a mistake by Sean Delaney, though Neil Bogart reportedly wanted the song redone with a more "disco" flavor. Ace also didn't see the point in messing with a song that had turned out fine the first time. There are few real changes to the song other than it having an additional solo, making the song sound closer to the 1973 demo version, than the version recorded for the debut album. The production values were even smoother than the original KISS album version. According to Paul, "We once re-recorded a song, it was 'Strutter.' And I thought it sucked. It was bullshit. There was no reason to do it, it was pointless because we had no new point of view and no reason to re-cut something that came out so good the first time" (Jeff Schaller, Late Night Magazine). There have also been allegations that Sean or Bun E. Carlos drummed on the track in place of Peter Criss, though these rumors have never been substantiated. Whatever the case, as far as the contract is concerned, the band played ball with the album, even though it didn't reduce their contractual obligation to the label — it simply bought them time to attend to other matters.

Executive producer for the project was Jimmy Ienner. As producer of the Raspberries he had appeared on Bill Aucoin's "Flip Side" TV show, with the band, in 1973. By 1977 he was head of Millennium Records which was acquired by Casablanca (initially a custom label distributed by Casablanca, the artists on the roster were transferred to Casablanca) - the label's "Star Wars" score performed by Meco provided Casablanca with their first #1 single. It was probably a result of this merger that the Godz were given an opening slot on tour with KISS in 1977. Jimmy's involvement with Casablanca would only last through the end of 1978, due to a conflict in philosophies between Ienner & Bogart (Billboard, July 11, 1981). Mike Stone and Sean Delaney remixed 22 tracks for the album at Trident Studios in England, in less than two weeks. Sean recalled, "Mike and I were so burned out, and then they told us that we had to do twenty-two titles in nine days. Because of the way they were recorded we actually had to remix to make everything sound like Bob Ezrin mixing... When he produces, he records the way he actually puts it down. For example, if there's an echo on a guitar, it's recorded that way, so you can't change anything Bob Ezrin does. So all the other songs had to be mixed in a way to sound like Bob Ezrin. Otherwise, you would have an album that would have a weak-sounding song, a big-sounding song, a thin-sounding song, a good-sounding song, song that had drums in mono as opposed to a song that had drums on stereo. If you had these things so you could compare them, it's not a good thing. Eddie Kramer had a strange habit of doing all of his drums in mono. So if you had mono drums in one song and the next song has drums in stereo, it's so different that it doesn't sound good to you... So we had to redo a whole bunch of things" (Steve Stierwalt Jr., Interview with Sean Delaney). The remixing was required to provide a sonic equilibrium across the original material created by a disparate group of producers. As a result of the process many subtle changes resulted, though it is also possible that the individual master tapes sources varied slightly from the versions originally released. The amount of work done on the tracks, within the timeframe Sean mentions is quite staggering, with nearly half of the tracks undergoing alterations of some description.

If making the album's tracks sound sonically similar was the goal, then it's not surprising that "Do You Love Me," "God of Thunder," and "Beth" are nearly identical to the original Ezrin versions. Understandably, "Detroit Rock City," with the cinematographic introduction and segue into "King of the Night Time World," required some editing. Rather than utilizing the heavily butchered 1976 single version, which only took out the radio introduction "scene," whole break sections are removed while some additional effects, perhaps buried in the original final mix, are allowed to surface. These changes result in the song being reduced from 5:13 to a more manageable 3:35. Songs from "Rock And Roll Over" provide an interesting contrast in approaches. "I Want You" and "Makin' Love" are negligibly adulterated. For "Hard Luck Woman," the drums on the introduction are removed to place more emphasis on the acoustic guitars. Instead of starting at 0:16 the drums start at 0:31 and the song is shortened, with the ending fade out starting earlier, at 2:55 instead of 3:04. There is also an enhanced echo on some guitar components. "Calling Dr. Love" was given an alternative effect and the beginning of the song making it more demonic. The song loses nearly half a minute of its duration, notably the drum break section following the second chorus on the original recording. At 1:45 this originally continued into a break into the second verse. Instead, on the remix, the song heads straight into the solo rather than repeating the chorus prior to the solo and then heads into another break before continuing the chorus with a completely different drum fill for the transition.

Four of the five debut album songs have modifications of note. "Firehouse" has a slightly increased tempo compared with the somewhat plodding original. With the tempo increase, the track length is maintained as the same as the original by adding an additional repetition of "Get the firehouse / Whoo-hoo, yeah!" at the end of the song. Additionally, the pitch of the of song was raised one-half step compared to the original recording. Finally, instead of ending with the famed fire siren of the original the track fades out over a repetition of the introduction riff. "Deuce" has the chorus that follows the guitar solo changed slightly: The original line of "And baby, if you're feeling good" is replaced with "Baby, if you're feeling good." Likewise "100,000 Years" where the original version of the recording timed in at 3:22. On "Double Platinum" the song remains essentially faithful to the original, with only the production equalization bringing up the clarity of the guitars and cymbals. One minor difference is the change to "For a hundred thousand years" in the third verse rather than "in a" on the original recording. There is also a minor change in the drum pattern at the end of the guitar solo. Noticeable changes were also made to "Black Diamond," in addition to the general remixing and sound equalization. The song starts off with a pure acoustic guitar introduction rather than beginning immediately with vocals as on the original version. This adds some 9 seconds to the beginning of the song before Paul yells "Hit it!" In the second verse Peter's "no, no" is removed from the end of the "There's nothin' that you can do" lyric. The most noticeable change removes the extended outro section of the original version and replaces it with a further repetition of the acoustic/vocal section that started the song. Following Paul singing the introduction, the fade out begins after Paul yells "Hit it!" As a result the song is reduced in length by nearly a minute. "Cold Gin" is essentially left alone.

It may seem strange, considering the sonic issues that plague the production values on the "Hotter Than Hell" album, that little seems to have been done to the two songs, "Let Me Go, Rock 'N Roll" and "Hotter Than Hell," included. Perhaps little could be done with the master tapes? Three of the songs featured are from "Dressed to Kill." The strange hatchet job of tacking the acoustic "Rock Bottom Intro" section onto the beginning of "She" is perplexing. More so, in that the full introduction is not used, with only the last 52 seconds of the piece being pasted creating an odd hybrid. The fade-in masks the odd starting point of the piece. "She" is expanded, further from the original, instead of fading out over the third chorus and guitar work, the core riff and first two lines of the first verse are added on for the fade out. As a result the song is some 25 seconds longer than the "Dressed to Kill" version. "C'mon And Love Me" simply features a slightly longer fade-out while "Rock And Roll All Nite" is left unchanged. Only one song is included from "Love Gun," the title-track, and nothing is changed. The twenty-second remixed track was either the B-side of the "Strutter '78" single, "Shock Me," or the unreleased "Queen for a Day" (as suggested in the "Black Diamond" book). If the former then the B-side is identical to that used on the "Christine Sixteen" single the year prior and doesn't appear to have been changed in any way. As for the latter, that's obviously not made it into circulation. Yet.

For all of the minor changes, the track-listing of "Double Platinum" seems odd, particularly with "hit" singles or B-sides being excluded in favor of what could be described as obscure tracks. Notable missing songs could be considered to include "Rocket Ride," "Shout It Out Loud," and "Christine Sixteen," though no doubt every fan would have their own list. In the United States "Double Platinum" was released on cassette (MC5), 8-track, reel, and vinyl formats. The LP album cover was an impressive mylar-laminated and embossed affair. However, the manufacturing technique has resulted in many copies losing the definition of the embossing. Some copies also seem to turn up with the foil removed (an increasing trend) to mirror the valuable Australian "white" cover version. When Astor records, in Australia, ran out of copies of the imported foil covers (made in the US) for their domestically pressed vinyl, they resorted to printing their own covers which reproduced the originals in black and white, with a red logo, and line art for the inner gatefold. Casablanca was apparently not amused and few of these covers ever made it into circulation. The US album package included a "platinum" award and mandatory merchandise order form. The lavish packaging might be seen as symptomatic of the same sort of situation that had taken hold at Casablanca: Extravagance, often unnecessary, permeated every level of the business process with the business reportedly spending PolyGram's money at an incredible clip. Mercedes and Porsches littered the parking lot and cocaine allegedly found its way up many an executive's nose. Successes with films such as "Thank God, It's Friday" and "Midnight Express" fueled the culture.

One error creeps up with the packaging of the album. On the track listing in the inner cover of the original release of the record, "Rock Bottom (Intro)" is listed as the first song on side three. On the cassette the inclusion of the piece is not even noted on the packaging or actual cassettes. The piece is actually the fourth track on side three and precedes "She." Unfortunately the mix of this piece is so low that it is barely audible. This wasn't fixed with the release of the remastered version of the album in 1997. Most copies include the track-listing printed in red on a clear sticker on the back cover. "Double Platinum" was released on April 24, 1978 and debuted on the Billboard Top-200 album charts at #75 on May 20. The album peaked at #22 on July 1, ultimately charting for 24 weeks. Internationally the album charted at #15 in Canada, #17 in Australia and #19 in Japan and New Zealand. "Double Platinum" was certified gold and platinum by the RIAA on 5/16/78. It has sold over 510,000 copies since the SoundScan™ era commenced in 1991. The album was certified gold by the CRIA (Canada) for sales of 50,000 copies on 6/1/78 and was awarded in in-house gold award by Astor Records (Australia) for sales of 20,000 copies in October 1978. "Strutter '78" didn't chart in any country, other than Australia where it scrapped to #89.

A promotional "Taste of Platinum" 12" EP was released in the United States (NBD-20128DJ) featuring "Strutter '78," "Do You Love Me," "Love Gun," and "Firehouse" in a die-cut sleeve. What is interesting from a collector's point of view is that there are several highly notable versions of the "Double Platinum" album. On some copies the inner gate-fold prints, repeating Paul and Gene's, or Ace and Peter's, images on both sides of the cover. The 1982 British reissue version (PRID-8) includes photo-pictures in a non-metallic gate-fold. In the UK there was question over whether the album was released domestically in 1978. It was (CALD-5005). Some copies of the regular version of the album are simply US import albums with a cover sticker added that uses British spelling and Pye's (Casablanca's distributors in the UK) call letters. This seems to have led to some believing that the album was never domestically issued there. In turn this indicates that like the Australian market, the UK release used US-produced covers over domestically pressed vinyl. The UK also released the single with the ugliest cover ever to grace a KISS release. Featuring dreadful line art, the "Rock And Roll All Nite" b/w "C'mon and Love Me" single (CAN-126) is highly collectible even if it will curdle milk! The alternative mix of "Strutter '78" is also a desirable single to collect and was recently reissued as part of the Casablanca Singles box set. In Japan, some original copies of the Victor version include a highly collectible poster.

Solo Era Timeline

As the "Alive II" era came to a close, 1978 opened with several major projects on the horizon that would ultimately change the trajectory of the "Hottest Band in the World..." This timeline runs January 1978 to April 1979.

June 1977

21 - During a KISS financial meeting, Bill Aucoin asks the band members to start thinking about who they would like to produce their solo albums.

July

24 - While in town for the Vancouver, BC "Love Gun" concert (the two days either side of this date) Gene was reported by the local Georgia Straight magazine as working on solo material with Doucette drummer Duris Maxwell at Pinewood Studios. Duris also rents Gene his Leslie speaker for the session.

September

10 - Bill Aucoin in Billboard Magazine: "You have to think of your acts visually as well as audibly. But TV or movie cameras are brutal. And if you're going to be able to bring your acts through to that medium, you really had better start thinking about it now. There's a lot of guidance and direction that must be given before an act is ready because TV can destroy an act overnight. It's very personal and hard on any performer." The feature also mentioned that the band planned movie of-the-week, but that they'd yet to receive a satisfactory script.

December

31 - Shipments of KISS "Alive!" stand at 2,113,933 units. U.S. catalog shipments stand at 9,113,359 units.

January 1978

7 - KISS "Alive II" hits its high position of #7 on the US Billboard Top 200 album charts...

7 - Carl Glickman hosts a party in Cleveland inviting sponsors of KISS' show there.

8 - The band are invited to WMMS in Cleveland, on the day of their show there, to be guest disc jockeys in the afternoon.

10 - NBC's "Land of Hype and Glory" airs exploring hype in media and popular culture, using KISS as a primary example.

16 - KISS appear on the American Music Awards via satellite from Largo, MD.

21 - "KISS Alive II" sheet music, published by Almo, becomes their biggest seller at one point reaching 30,000 units per week.

21 - KISS donate $4,000, from their Ampex Gold Reel awards for 4 gold records, to cancer and diabetes research.

21 - "Shout It Out Loud" (Live) debuts on the US Billboard singles charts at #85.

February

1 - Contract signed between Hanna-Barbera Productions, Inc., KISS-Aucoin Productions, and KISS for the then tentatively titled "KISS Meets The Phantom" TV movie of the week project.

3 - Final date of the U.S. "Alive II" tour in Providence, RI. The tour grossed over $2 million from 46 shows.

11 - The "Shout It Out Loud" single reaches its high position of #54 on the US Billboard singles charts. It charts for two weeks at that position and then drops off the charts completely.

14 - The "Treasures of Tutankhamen" exhibit opens at the Los Angeles County Museum of Art. Running through June 15, Ace recounted in "No Regrets" attending the exhibit during the filming of the TV movie, after being given a ticket by a kindly woman — tickets had sold out within 36 hours of going on sale on January 3.

22 - Recording sessions at Electric Lady Studios for Paul Stanley's solo album.

25 - Recording sessions at Electric Lady Studios for Paul Stanley's solo album.

25 - "Rocket Ride" debuts on the US Billboard singles charts at #89.

27 - Paul Stanley's friend, actress and singer, Victoria Medlin dies. Paul dedicates his solo album in her memory.

March

11 - Saturday Night Live season 3, episode 13, broadcast with special guests Art Garfunkel and Steven Bishop. Art participates in the "KISS Concert" skit playing Paul Stanley's "brother" Angus who's trying to gain access to the show. This show marked the first appearance of Bill Murray's music agent character, Jerry Eldini, while John Belushi plays the security guard trying to prevent a variety of people gaining backstage access.

24 - KISS arrive in Japan via PAN-AM flight #801.

25 - "The Originals II" released in Japan. The album compiles the second trio of the band's studio albums, including "Destroyer," "Rock And Roll Over," and "Love Gun," in deluxe packaging with poster book and reproduction make-up masks.

28 - Japanese concert stand commences at the Budokan Hall in Tokyo.

April

2 - Japanese tour ends after five purportedly sold-out dates at the Budokan Hall in Tokyo.

5 - Boots from each of KISS member's costumes are provided to the touring "The Great American Foot" touring show. Paul and Gene's are rejected and returned to the band on April 24, but Peter and Ace's tour until April 1981.
6 - At an internal Aucoin Management meeting, challenges finding a producer for Peter's album are discussed with second choice Tom Dowd having not responded to scheduling requests. Jack Richardson is suggested as an alternative. Paul's initial choice of Ron Nevison is mentioned as also being unavailable for the project. Also at the meeting the decision is made to hold "Any Way You Want It" as the third single off "Alive II" in favor of "Strutter '78" as the first from "Double Platinum."
8 - Ace Frehley completes mixes of the instrumental backing tracks of "All for Nothing" and "I'm in Need of Love" at Soundmixer Studios.
11 - Former tour truck driver JB Fields dies in a crash on tour with BOC. Paul dedicates his solo album in his memory.
22 - The "Rocket Ride" single reaches its high position of #39 on the US Billboard singles charts. It only charts for one additional week.
24 - "Double Platinum," the band's first domestic US compilation collection, is released in the United States. Also, Michelle Slagter reports, in a memo to Marvin Mann, that other than Elliott Randall's work, the musicians have completed recording work on Gene's album.
XX - Gene appears on BBC Radio 1, during the recording of his solo album, and is self-effacing and out of character: "KISS doesn't really mean anything in England and I'm not fooling myself into thinking we're huge or anything... I figured I could communicate a little bit more if I talked straight-ahead instead of coming across affected [Ed. pretentious]."

May

1 - The planned first filming day at one of the "KISS Meets the Phantom of the Park" locations, Kings Dominion Park in Doswell, VA, near Richmond. The film was being promoted in the trade magazines as the "first rock gothic mystery filmed for TV." Filming also took place at Culver City Studios, Magic Mountain, and as Ace puts it, "at some mansion up on top of some hill" (in the Hollywood Hills - Ed.).
16 - "Double Platinum" certified Gold & Platinum by the RIAA in the USA.
18 - KISS perform a free concert for around 8,000 at Magic Mountain in Valencia, CA parts are filmed for use in the "KISS Meet the Phantom of the Park" TV Movie. The concert sequences are on a stage in the parking lot near the Colossus roller coaster, which at the time was still under construction. Peter embellished the shoot for the press: "We played for 60,000 people... It was real live music" (The Nashua Telegraph, 10/21/78). Neither was true.
19 - "Double Platinum" debuts on the US Billboard Top 200 album charts at #75.
20 - The Citrus College Singers (who would work with Gene on his solo album) sing Bread's "If" to Cher, on the lawn in front of one of the bungalows at the Sunset Marquis in Los Angeles, to celebrate her birthday.

25 - Members of the band, except Peter, meet with their management and financial advisors, at Culver City Studios, for their regular meeting. One item reviewed is the solo album recording budget, of which Gene's has already incurred expenses of nearly $90,000 on a $300,000 project estimate. Howard Marks suggests that each album should be limited to a cost of $150,000. Bill Aucoin also recommends a completion date of August 5, so that the release date would not be missed. The band members agree to separate the royalties from their solo albums from the rest of the catalog. Paul also suggests splitting songwriting and publishing royalties for future KISS albums too, though that topic is tabled for future discussion. The band also holds a press conference concerning the movie.
26 - Final day of filming for the KISS movie.
27 - Fritz Postlethwaite and Peter Criss are involved in a car accident following the wrapping of filming the KISS movie. According to Rolling Stone magazine, "KISS drummer Peter Criss got a concussion, plus rib and finger injuries... Fritz suffered serious burns but said he would recover quickly, while Criss was healthy enough to start work on his solo album."

June

X - "Alive II" certified Gold by the ARIA for sales in Australia in excess of 20,000 copies.
1 - "Double Platinum" certified Gold by the CRIA.
6 - An acoustic version of "Beth" is recorded at Electric Lady Studios with Dave Wittman engineering.
17 - Final initial charting date of "Alive II" on the US Billboard Top 200 album charts at #160.
21 - Casablanca's executive VP Larry Harris' son born.
25 - Cancelled recording session for Ace at The Estate.
27 - Start of a recording session by Ace at Plaza Sound Studios in New York City. Alessi Brother's album "Driftin'" is released. Paul Stanley plays guitar and sings background vocals on "You're Out Of Love" on the album, becoming the first member of KISS to make a credited guest appearance on another artist's album outside of the band.
29 - Song-writing agreement between Peter Criss and Sean Delaney for the Delaney written tracks used on Peter's solo album, plus the unused "Spotlights (And Lonely Nights)" which would have been shared 50/50.
30 - "Double Platinum" hits its high position of #22 on the US Billboard Top 200 album charts...

July

X - Bally Corporation announces the KISS pinball machine model. It would eventually be made available on June 1, 1979, nearly 18 months after

representatives of the company had been invited to KISS' Chicago Stadium show to pitch the idea. Some 17,000 units would be sold.
11 - Ken Anderson details in a memo that the KISS Tokyo Special, filmed by NHK during the band's March 1977 visit to Japan, is being re-edited to replace the Japanese titles with American versions for the KISS 60 minute special. The show is eventually licensed to HBO for broadcast.

August

2 - Comedienne Totie Fields dies. She'd infamously sparred with Gene on the Mike Douglas Show in 1974. He mentions her on his album liner notes.
14 - "Ace Frehley" 8-track sequence finalized.
17 - Test pressings of "Ace Frehley" ordered from Columbia Record Productions by PolyGram for Eddie Kramer.
19 - "Alive II" returns to the US Billboard Top 200 album charts at #175.
22 - At a "Face The Music" panel in Chicago, Clive Davis (Arista) and Joe Davis (Elektra) advise Neil Bogart to cut back the shipments of the KISS solo albums to 750,000 per album. Bogart insists that with the low (6%) return rate of KISS product that he expects to ship 8 million copies by Christmas. The others felt that major band individual members sold poorly and that over-shipments created an illusion of the artist's success (Billboard, 9/2/78). Prophetic...
26 - "Alive II" on the US Billboard Top 200 album charts at #175.
28 - The second Marvel "KISS" comic goes on sale. Peter's album mastered at Allen Zentz in Hollywood, CA.

September

3 - Final "Alive II" charting on the US Billboard Top 200 album charts at #180.
5 - "Assembled Especially for Radio" promotional 12" distributed to select reviews and account managers.
8 - KISS' merchandise company, Boutwell Inc., and Topco Sales finalize the contract for the AM KISS Radio.
18 - The "KISS" solo albums are released in the United States backed with a $2.5 million marketing support. 500,000 special plastic bags are printed and sent to retailers for purchasers of the four albums. 5.3 million copies of the albums are shipped. Ace Frehley's "New York Groove" and Paul Stanley's "Hold Me, Touch Me" singles, respectively, are released.
30 - PolyGram distribution changes the return policy on Casablanca product preventing returns until 180 days after release in an effort to keep product in stores longer and prevent over-ordering.

October

X - "Double Platinum" certified Gold by the ARIA for sales in Australia in excess of 20,000 copies.

2 - The solo albums simultaneously certified Gold & Platinum by the RIAA in the USA.
14 - Ace Frehley's "New York Groove" debuts on the US Billboard singles charts at #87. The "Peter Criss" album debuts on the US Billboard Top 200 album charts at #85. "Ace Frehley" debuts at #87, "Gene Simmons" at #88 and "Paul Stanley" at #89.
21 - Final "Double Platinum" charting on the US Billboard Top 200 album charts at #177.
25 - The solo albums are released in Japan.
28 - "KISS Meets the Phantom of the Park" broadcast on NBC television.
28 - Neil Bogart honored as "Man of the Year" by the United Jewish Appeal's Federation of Jewish Philanthropies at the New York Hilton, the youngest recipient (at that time) of the award.

November

X - Tour manager Fritz Postlethwaite gets married in New York. Band members attend.
4 - "Hold Me, Touch Me" debuts on the US Billboard singles charts at #85.
8 - Ace makes a promotional appearance at WGCL in Cleveland, OH (KAF).
15 - Eddie Kramer pays Greg Raffa $4,575 to cover the balance of the bill for Ace's recording and mixing sessions at Plaza Sound.
18 - Gene makes an in-store appearance at Tape City in Metairie, LA (near New Orleans).
25 - "Peter Criss" hits its high position of #43 on the US Billboard Top 200 album charts.
28 - Gene interviewed at Cosmic Comics in Cleveland, OH by WMMS' Denny Sanders. Broadcast on the "Afternoon Exchange" show. During the day Gene was also interviewed by Jane Scott for the Cleveland Plain Dealer.

December

X - Returns of the solo albums reach a reported 2 million copies...
1 - Paul in-store appearance at the Record Theatre in Cincinnati, OH reportedly attended by 4,000 fans.
1 - "Gene Simmons," "Ace Frehley," and "Paul Stanley" certified Gold by the CRIA.
1 - "New York Groove" (CAN-135) released as a single in the UK backed with "Snow Blind." Special colored-vinyl versions include a paper mask.
2 - An edit of "Radioactive," removing the Ron Frangipane/Janis Ian "Demonic" intro section, debuts on the US Billboard singles charts at #84.
4 - Paul in-store appearance at Oasis Records in Pittsburgh, PA.
5 - Paul interviewed live on KJR-Seattle radio station promoting his solo album and local in-store appearance.
6 - Paul in-store appearance at Peaches in Seattle, WA.

12 - Partnering Disney to celebrate the re-release of the movie "Pinocchio," Gene hosts a KISSmas party at Fiorucci's in Beverly Hills. The movie is aired along with his recording of "When You Wish Upon A Star."
16 - "Paul Stanley" hits its high position of #40 on the US Billboard Top 200 album charts.
21 - Ken Anderson memos KISS about plans for KISS' 1979 world tour: "Most spectacular show ever to go on the road."
23 - "Hold Me, Touch me" reaches its high position of #46 on the US Billboard singles charts.
30 - Ace guests live on 99X WOR-FM, WXLO NY, with his pet dogs Blondie & Seamus also in the studio. Tracks are played from the solo albums and he talks about the new show/tour.

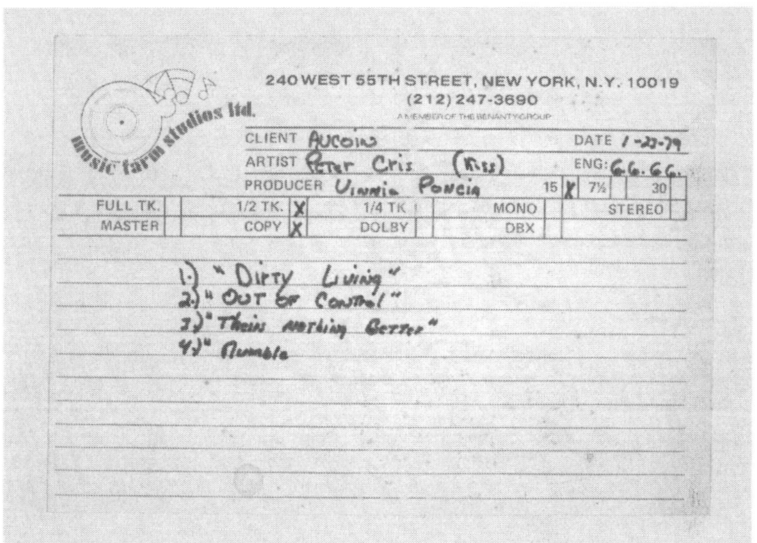

music farm studios ltd.
240 WEST 55TH STREET, NEW YORK, N.Y. 10019
(212) 247-3690

CLIENT Aucoin — DATE 1-23-79
ARTIST Peter Cris (Kiss) — ENG: G.G.G.G.
PRODUCER Vinnie Poncia — 15 X | 7½ | 30

FULL TK.		1/2 TK.	X	1/4 TK		MONO		STEREO	
MASTER		COPY	X	DOLBY		DBX			

1.) "Dirty Living"
2.) "Out of Control"
3.) "Theirs nothing Better"
4.) "Rumble

January 1979

3 - Lydia Criss served with divorce papers...
6 - "Gene Simmons" hits its high position of #22 on the US Billboard Top 200 album charts. Paul Stanley serves as a guest panel judge at the Manhattan Music Playoffs, held at Hunter College Auditorium, along with Art Garfunkel, Billy and Bobby Alessi, Eddie Kramer and others. Winners, a band named Roc, were awarded a singles contract with Infinity Records and broadcast on King Biscuit Flower Hour.
9 - Sean Delaney's "Highway" album (Casablanca NBLP-7130) released. He dedicated his album, along the lines of the KISS solo albums. To: Gui, Gene, Paul, Ace & Peter.
13 - "Ace Frehley" hits its high position of #26 on the US Billboard Top 200 album charts.

13 - "Radioactive" reaches its high position of #47 on the US Billboard singles charts. It only charts for one additional week.
23 - Completion of Peter's demo sessions at Music Farm Studios in New York City with Vini Poncia. The four songs recorded with Stan Penridge were later presented for use on KISS' "Dynasty" and include "Dirty Livin'," "Out of Control," "There's Nothing Better" and "Rumble."
25 - Japanese V1 & V2 Gene/Peter and Paul/Ace singles issued promotionally in Japan.
27 - UK single "Radioactive" (CAN 134) reaches its highest position of #41 on the official British Market Research Bureau/Music Week 'Top 75' singles' chart.

February

3 - "New York Groove" reaches its high position of #13 on the US Billboard singles charts. It charts at that position for two weeks.
10 - Final US charting week of "Paul Stanley" at #162.
24 - Final US charting week of "Peter Criss" at #195.
24 - Planned KISS appearance as Grand Marshalls at the Endymion Parade during Mardi Gras celebrations in New Orleans. KISS had to cancel due to a police strike in the city, though management had felt that it was quite a PR coup at the time the event was being organized.

March

2 - Gene makes a guest appearance in make-up on the "Mike Douglas Show," as part of a Cher skit (working in a Jack in the Box fast food restaurant) during her co-hosting week.
11 - Final US charting week of "Gene Simmons" at #179.
18 - Final US charting week of "Ace Frehley" at #176.
26 - Gene, along with Cher and Neil Bogart, present the NARM "Best Selling Album By A New Artist" awards to Meat Loaf, The Cars, Toto, and Gerry Rafferty at the NARM closing banquet at the Diplomat Hotel in Miami Beach, FL. Bill Aucoin and Larry Harris also attend.
28 - The band along with Bill Aucoin, Ken Anderson, Chris Lendt, Howard Marks, Fritz Postlethwaite, Rosanne Shelnutt, Jack Tessler and Dennis Woloch conduct a production meeting concerning the staging for the "Return of KISS" tour. The "straightjacket" cover is rejected for the album since Ted Nugent had used similar for trade ad previously. The title for the album was discussed with several possibilities being considered: "KISS Together," "KISS 1980," "Dirty Loving," "United," and the then-current favorite, "Fourplay." Most shockingly, perhaps, the band had considered only touring June through September and then recording another studio album!

April

12 - Taping of the "Robert Klein Radio Hour" show at RCA Studios in New York City with Gene and Ace appearing in make-up. This is the last known appearance of band member's wearing their "Love Gun/Alive II" costumes. Robert had been one of the guests on the Mike Douglas Show on which KISS appeared in 1974.

25 - A solo album box set is released in Japan containing the four albums.

May

3 - The "Robert Klein Hour" broadcast, with guests Robin Williams, Ace and Gene, airs. This appearance features the debut of several songs from the "Dynasty" album, and effectively bookends the solo album era.

5 - New England's "Don't Ever Wanna Lose Ya" single debuts on the Billboard Hot-100 charts at #83, ultimately rising to #40 (June 16). Paul Stanley co-produced the band's eponymous album with Mike Stone and sang backing vocals on the track.

14 - A trade publication reports, "Rumors are flying that Ace Frehley may be the next man behind the greasepaint to exit KISS," one of the earliest suggestions of Ace's exit from the group (other than his obvious missing events).

19 - The New England album debuts on the Billboard Top-200 charts at #116. It eventually climbs to #50 (June 23). Members of the band, Jimmy Waldo, Hirsh Gardner and Gary Shea, later work with one Vincent Cusano...

June

29 - An internal Casablanca audit details the numbers of solo albums (LP, cassette tape, and picture disk) shipped to that point: A staggering 5,397,466. Returns are not noted. U.S. catalog shipments stand at 20,760,219 units, more than double what they'd been at the end of December 1977.

The Year in Rock: 1978

KISS go solo and the rock genre erupts with a banner year.
By Tim McPhate

"When I woke up/Mom and Dad were rolling on the couch/Rolling numbers, rock and rollin', got my KISS records out." — Cheap Trick, "Surrender"

With the release of a greatest hits set and four band member solo albums, plenty of fans had their KISS records out in 1978. But it just so happens that 1978 wasn't just a big year for the Hottest Band in the World, it was a robust year for the entire rock genre. Following is a brief overview of 15 other notable rock albums released in 1978, followed by a condensed timeline culling notable news happenings in music. What are some of your favorite albums and notable moments from 1978?

Journey, "Infinity"

Producer: Roy Thomas Baker
Released: Jan. 20. 1978
Peak position: No. 21

Journey emerged from the Bay Area in 1973 under the direction of former Santana manager Herbie Herbert. The group's early output was closely aligned with elements of progressive rock and jazz fusion. Marking a definitive change in direction, "Infinity" is the first Journey album to feature soaring tenor lead vocalist Steve Perry. "Patiently," a quite ballad penned by Perry and fiery guitarist Neal Schon, marked the duo's first collaboration and a harbinger of a successful partnership that would bear fruit on later albums such as "Departure" (1980) and "Escape" (1981). Keyboardist Gregg Rollie adds a classic rock feel and lead vocals to "Anytime," while "Winds Of March" is a deep album gem. The opening track "Lights," an ode to the "city by the Bay," has emerged as one of the band's live staples. Fun fact: The Journey classic "Wheel In The Sky" was co-written by Robert Fleischman, who was briefly in the group in 1977. Fleischman would later provide lead vocals on the debut album for Vinnie Vincent's post-KISS group, the Vinnie Vincent Invasion.

Judas Priest, "Stained Class"

Producers: Dennis MacKay, Judas Priest and James Guthrie
Released: Feb. 10, 1978

Peak position: No. 104

The British metal band's fourth studio album, "Stained Class" spans nine tracks reflective of a more streamlined songwriting style, discarding the traces of blues and progressive rock elements found on previous Judas Priest albums. Lead vocalist Rob Halford explores a range of dark themes from the horror-influenced "Saints In Hell" to "Heroes End," a song lamenting the premature death of heroic figures. "Beyond The Realms Of Death" contains a shining lead vocal from Halford and soaring dual leads from guitarists K.K. Downing and Glenn Tipton. The album's third track, "Better By You, Better For Me," is notoriously linked to a 1990 civil suit brought against the band by the family of teenager James Vance, who committed suicide after listening to the track on Dec. 23, 1985. The suit was eventually dismissed. "Stained Class" was the first Judas Priest album to enter the Billboard 200 and eventually earned gold status. The album is also notable for being the lone Judas Priest album to contain songwriting credits from each band member — Halford, Downing, Tipton, bassist Ian Hill, and drummer Les Binks.

Van Halen, "Van Halen"

Producer: Ted Templeman
Released: Feb. 10. 1978
Peak position: No. 19

Arguably the most impressive rock debut of album of the decade, let alone 1978, "Van Halen" erupted on the scene with an explosive sound combining the powerful backbeat of drummer Alex Van Halen, the thundering bass (and high harmony vocals) of Michael Anthony and the street-minded jive of frontman David Lee Roth. As for guitarist Eddie Van Halen? Quite simply, he single-handedly changed the course of guitar history with his stellar rhythm work and fret-board pyrotechnics throughout "Van Halen." Interestingly, the band's debut single was a cover of the Kinks' "You Really Got Me," which broke into the Top 40. Fun fact: Simmons produced a 1976 demo tape for the group, which featured the album's first and final tracks, "Runnin' With The Devil" and "On Fire," respectively. Around that time, the Van Halen brothers also played on select Simmons-recorded demos, including "Christine Sixteen."

Wings, "London Town"

Producer: Paul McCartney
Released: Mach 31, 1978
Peak position: No. 2

The release of Wings' sixth studio album was preceded one week by the single "With A Little Luck," which hit No. 1 on the Billboard Hot 100. "London Town" spans 14 tracks, with a majority written by songwriter par excellence Paul McCartney. The album's seventh track, "Girlfriend," was subsequently recorded by Michael Jackson on his 1979 album "Off The Wall." (The duo would go on to record a pair of duets, 1982's "The Girl Is Mine" and 1983's "Say Say Say.") During the recording of the album, McCartney and wife Linda gave birth to son James. "London Town" is said to represent the peak of Wings' commercial output. The album has been certified platinum in the United States.

AC/DC, "Powerage"

Producers: Harry Vanda and George Young
Released: May 25, 1978
Peak position: No. 133

The fourth international studio album and fifth studio album overall from Australia's finest rock export, "Powerage" features nine tracks written by sibling guitarists Malcolm and Angus Young and lead vocalist Bon Scott. (The European release contained a 10th track, "Cold Hearted Man.") Two of the album's tracks, "Riff Raff" and "Rock 'N' Roll Damnation," would be featured on the live album, "If You Want Blood You've Got It," which was released later in 1978. Joe Perry has cited "Sin City" as his favorite AC/DC song. Initial editions of the European album featured a different mix. The album was later remixed for the U.S. market, with the new mix becoming the global standard. Despite its low chart position, the album has been certified platinum in the United States. "Powerage" marked the debut of bassist Cliff Williams. AC/DC would follow-up with 1979's "Highway To Hell," their last studio album recorded with Scott before his passing on Feb. 19, 1980.

The Cars, "The Cars"

Producer: Roy Thomas Baker
Released: June 6, 1978
Peak position: No. 18

With their self-titled debut album, the Cars revved a sonic engine melding '70s guitar-oriented rock with elements of contemporary synth-oriented pop. Described as a "genuine rock masterpiece" by AllMusic.com, "The Cars" features nine songs, with eight solely penned by rhythm guitarist/lead vocalist Ric Ocasek, including the hits "Just What I Needed" and "My Best Friend's Girl." The former track is a shining example of not only the group's compact ensemble playing, but guitarist Elliot Easton's complementary rhythm guitar and lyrical lead style. Film buffs will recognize track eight, "Moving In Stereo," from the "fantasy sequence" featuring Phoebe Cates and Judge Reinhold in the 1982 film "Fast Times At Ridgemont High." Original Cars bassist/vocalist Benjamin Orr passed away in 2000. The remaining members of the Cars reunited for an album in 2011, "Move Like This." Fun fact: The late Russian-born model Natalya Medvedeva is the girl featured on the debut album's cover.

The Rolling Stones, "Some Girls"

Producers: The Glimmer Twins
Released: June 9, 1978
Peak position: No. 1

Hailed as a classic return to form, "Some Girls" topped the Billboard 200 and became one of the Rolling Stones' best-selling albums in the United States, with sales in excess of 6 million copies. Frontman Mick Jagger claimed to be under the influence of dance music, notably disco, during the recording of the album, while citing New York City as a lyrical inspiration throughout. The album's signature song, the Jagger/Keith Richards-penned "Miss You," mixed subtle disco elements with the classic Stones swagger, yielding a No. 1 hit. (An extended version of the song was released as a special dance remix on a 12-inch single.) "Beast Of Burden," another golden Jagger/Richards composition, cracked the Top 10. "Some Girls" was re-released in 2011 as a two-disc deluxe edition including a bonus disc of 12 songs recording during the album's sessions.

Foreigner, "Double Vision"

Producer: Keith Olsen
Released: June 20, 1978
Peak position: No. 3

Proving their multi-platinum debut was no fluke, Foreigner's "Double Vision" spawned three signature hits for the band, "Hot Blooded," which reached No. 3 on the Billboard Hot 100, the title track (No. 2) and "Blue Morning, Blue Day" (No. 15). All three were written by the formidable songwriting duo of lead vocalist Lou Gramm and guitarist/keyboardist Mick Jones. The album features the only instrumental to ever appear on a Foreigner album, the progressive-minded "Tramontane." Jones and Gramm were inducted into the Songwriters Hall of Fame in 2013. Meanwhile, Foreigner continue today with a renovated lineup fronted by lead vocalist Kelly Hansen.

Boston, "Don't Look Back"

Producer: Tom Scholz
Released: Aug. 2, 1978
Peak position: No. 1

Faced with the daunting task of following up his mega-selling debut album, 1976's "Boston," group founder Tom Scholz retreated to his home studio in 1977 to begin work on "Don't Look Back." The multitasking Scholz not only served as producer, but composed a majority of the songs and engineered and mastered the album, in addition to playing guitar, bass, piano, and percussion. The album's title track — featuring Scholz's patented guitar layering and Brad Delp's distinctive vocals — reached No. 4 on the singles chart. Scholz has gone on record saying that the band's label, Epic Records, pushed him into releasing the album before he felt it was ready. Despite his reticence, the album topped the Billboard 200 and sold more than 7 million copies in the United States. Boston would not resurface with another studio album until 1986's "Third Stage."

Black Sabbath, "Never Say Die!"

Producers: Black Sabbath
Released: Sept. 28, 1978
Peak position: No. 69

Black Sabbath's eighth studio album proved to be the final recording featuring the band's original lineup. While recording "Never Say Die!" the members of Black Sabbath were all heavily abusing drugs and alcohol. Osborne said in 1981 that the album "was the worst piece of work that I've ever had anything to do with." The title track was a hit in the UK, reaching No. 21 and earning the band an appearance on "Top Of The Pops." While scoring a modest charting position in the United States, the album reached No. 12 in the UK. Osbourne and Sabbath parted ways in 1979, with the Prince of Darkness forging ahead with a solo career. Meanwhile, Sabbath recruited powerful lead vocalist Ronnie James Dio and resurfaced with 1980's "Heaven And Hell." The original Sabbath lineup, sans drummer Bill Ward, reunited for 2013's "13," which debuted at No. 1 on the Billboard 200.

Heart, "Dog & Butterfly"

Producer: Mike Flicker
Released: Oct. 7, 1978
Peak position: No. 17

The musical duality of Heart is arguably best reflected on "Dog & Butterfly," an LP containing two disparate sides. The "Dog" section contains up-tempo numbers such as the slinky "Hijinx" and infectious hit "Straight On" — a tune powered by the tight rhythm section of drummer Michael Derosier and bassist Steve Fossen — while the "Butterfly" portion spans quieter numbers propelled by acoustic guitars, such as the hit title track. Lead vocalist Ann Wilson soars on songs such as "Cook With Fire" and the moody epic "Mistral Wind" and brings the dynamics to a whisper on the lilting ballad "Lighter Touch." Sister Nancy Wilson adds her own dreamy number to the mix with "Nada One," in addition to providing acoustic rhythm guitar and harmony vocals throughout. The complementary fretwork of guitarists Howard Leese and Roger Fisher adds additional sonic color to the proceedings. Heart were inducted into the Rock and Roll Hall of Fame in 2013.

Toto, "Toto"

Producers: Toto
Released: Oct. 15, 1978
Peak position: No. 9

While Van Halen broke out in 1978, fellow Southern California collective Toto quietly scored a Top 10 spot with their debut album. Formed in 1977, the group's lineup comprised all-star-caliber musicians Steve Lukather (guitar), brothers Steve and Jeff Porcaro (keyboards and drums), and David Paich (keyboards/songwriter), and vocalist Bobby Kimball. The Top 5 single "Hold The Line" showcased the masterful groove of Jeff Porcaro and the melodic, explosive nature of Lukather's guitar style. Other charting songs on the debut were "I'll Supply The Love" and "Georgy Porgy." "Toto" earned the group national acclaim as well as a Grammy nomination for Best New Artist in 1979. Fun fact: A seasoned studio musician, Lukather contributed guitar solos to two tracks on Peter Criss' 1978 solo album.

Rush, "Hemispheres"

Producers: Rush and Terry Brown
Released: Oct. 29, 1978
Peak position: No. 47

Rush's sixth studio album marked the finale of four consecutive studio albums containing conceptual-based pieces, dating back to 1975's "Caress Of Steel." For "Hemispheres"' epic lead track, "Cygnus X-1 Book II" — a continuation of the final song on the prior year's "A Farewell To Kings" — drummer/lyricist Neil Peart played on the album title in presenting a lyrical theme exploring the two different ways in which the human mind thinks (logic and emotion are separated by separate sides, or "Hemispheres," of the brain). The Canadian rock trio are arguably at their finest during the album's closer, the instrumental "La Villa Strangiato," with Peart laying down complex rhythm foundations underneath driving bass lines from frontman Geddy Lee and stunning guitar flourishes from Alex Lifeson. Following "Hemispheres," Rush would chart a different (and highly successful) course on albums such as "Permanent Waves" (1980) and "Moving Pictures" (1981). The group was inducted into the Rock and Roll Hall of Fame in 2013. Fun fact: "Cygnus X-1 Book II" contains six separate sections and collectively clocks in at 18:08.

Cheap Trick, "At Budokan"

Producers: Cheap Trick
Released: October 1978
Peak position: No. 4

Considered one of rock's all-time classic live albums, "At Budokan" captured a two-night run by Cheap Trick at Budokan (a venue familiar to KISS) in Tokyo in April 1978. Tracks such as "I Want You To Want Me," which reached No. 7 on the Billboard Hot 100, and deep cut "Big Eyes" codify the group's power-pop sound, featuring drummer Bun E. Carlos and bassist Tom Petersson and the combustible combination of vocalist Robin Zander's wail and guitarist Rick Nielsen's riffing. "Surrender" is a proverbial rock classic, and continues to receive airplay at rock radio stations today. Certified triple-platinum, "At Budokan" is Cheap Trick's best-selling recording. A 30th anniversary four-disc set was released in 2008. Fun fact: Cheap Trick opened select dates for KISS in 1977.

The Police, "Outlandos d'Amour"

Producers: The Police
Released: Nov. 2, 1978
Peak position: No. 23

Hailing from London, the Police stormed the music scene with an impressive debut that embodied the trio's punk blueprint while also showcasing progressive pop and reggae leanings. "Roxanne," a song about a man falling in love with a prostitute penned by bassist/lead vocalist Sting, peaked within the Top 40. (Miles Copeland III, the band's manager and brother of drummer Stewart Copeland, utilized the song to secure the band a deal with A&M Records.) Eight of the album's 10 songs were written solely by Sting. On subsequent albums such as "Regatta De Blanc" (1979) and "Zenyatta Mondatta" (1980), the group would further mine elements of rock, pop, reggae, and jazz. Fun fact: Guitarist Andy Summers replaced original

Police guitarist Henri Padovani in 1977. Summers' slick chordal work and heavily chorused sound ultimately added a distinct depth to the group's sound.

The Year in Music: 1978

A listing culling some of the more notable events in music of the year...

January 1978

14- The Sex Pistols play their final show (until their 1996 reunion) at San Francisco's Winterland Ballroom
21 - The "Saturday Night Fever" soundtrack hits No. 1 on the Billboard 200 as the film becomes a cultural phenomenon
23 - Chicago guitarist Terry Kath dies

February

10 - Van Halen's self-titled debut album released
23 - Fleetwood Mac's "Rumours" takes home Album Of The Year and the Eagles "Hotel California" wins Record Of The Year at the 20th Annual Grammy Awards

March

18 - Aerosmith, Ted Nugent, Santana, Foreigner, and Heart are among the acts to perform at California Jam II in Ontario, Calif., for more than 300,000 fans
25 - "Mamas Don't Let Your Babies Grow Up To Be Cowboys" by Waylon Jennings and Willie Nelson spends four weeks at No. 1 on Billboard's Hot Country Singles chart

April

3 - The score from "Star Wars" by John Williams earns Best Original Score honors at the 50th Annual Academy Awards
22 - The Blues Brothers, featuring John Belushi and Dan Aykroyd, make their final appearance on "Saturday Night Live"
25 - KISS' "Double Platinum" is released

May

13 - The Bee Gees' Barry Gibb becomes the only songwriter in history to have written four consecutive No. 1 singles on the Billboard Hot 100 with "Stayin' Alive," "Love Is Thicker Than Water," "Night Fever," and "If I Can't Have You"

June

10 - The Rolling Stones launch a 25-date U.S. tour
11 - The movie musical "Grease," starring John Travolta and Olivia Newton-John, opens in theaters and emerges as a box office hit

July

24 - "Sgt. Pepper's Lonely Hearts Band," a film featuring the Bee Gees, Peter Frampton, Sandy Farina, and Aerosmith, premieres in New York

August

2 - Comedienne Totie Fields dies. (KISS fans will remember Fields' playful discourse with Gene Simmons on "The Mike Douglas Show" in 1974.)
7 - Death of The Who's drummer Keith Moon

September

18 - The KISS solo albums are released

October

10 - Aerosmith's Steven Tyler and Joe Perry are injured by a cherry bomb thrown onstage in Philadelphia
12 - Nancy Spungeon, the girlfriend of Sex Pistols bassist Sid Vicious, found stabbed to death in her room at the Hotel Chelsea in New York City. While Sid was charged with her murder, he died of a heroin overdose before any trial could be conducted
24 - The Rolling Stones' Keith Richards convicted of heroin possession in Toronto
28 - "KISS Meets The Phantom Of The Park" airs on NBC

November

21 - Alice Cooper emerges clean from rehab and releases "From The Inside," a concept album about Cooper's stay in a New York sanitarium where he had battled alcoholism. Many of the album's song's lyrics were written with Elton John's lyricist Bernie Taupin
27 - 15-year-old drummer Rick Allen joins Def Leppard

December

23 - Andy Gibb's "Shadow Dancing" is the No. 1 song of 1978 according to "Billboard" magazine
31 - In its seventh year, Dick Clark's "New Year's Rockin' Eve" special airs on ABC, featuring performances by Rick James, Barry Manilow, the Village People, and Tanya Tucker, among others

Solo Albums in The Press

Some were, but not everyone was, excited about the release of the KISS solo albums. Here we track some contemporary reviews of the albums and other press surrounding the release...
By Julian Gill

The KISS solo albums

(Billboard, Sept. 30 1978, no author credited)
Geared to the KISS Army, Casablanca intends on merchandising these four solo albums as a set. Choosing which one to buy might prove tough as each album sounds awfully similar, sparked by the hard driving primitive riffs and banal lyrics. Yet each LP contains enough high points to justify its release. The Gene Simmons LP boasts an impressive cast of "special guests" pace by the relentless bass riffs of Simmons. Lead guitarist Ace Frehley, drummer Peter Criss and guitarist Paul Stanley all shine on a couple of cuts, but in each case, it's the more subdued rockers and ballads which are most effective. And not surprisingly, since it's been the KISS ballads which have been the group's biggest successes. There are ample enough hooks, lyrically and musicality to keep listener attention. However, the notion of each LP shipping platinum remains mind boggling. And the packaging is ultra-commercialized. Each LP is grooved with identically tailored jackets, merchandise accessory forms inside, color posters that piece together to form a KISS mural and respectful dedications to each member of the group.

Best Cuts: KISS fans will probably like them all.
Dealers: The KISS television movie slated for next month should help spur sales.

The four greatest solo albums of all time (Not that we believe a word of it)

(Sounds, Oct. 14, 1978, Geoff Barton)
Peter Criss ***1/2
Gene Simmons ****
Paul Stanley ****1/2
Ace Frehley *****

Strictly no surprises? Well, it certainly seemed that way for a while. First spins revealed that Gene Simmons' solo LP sounded almost exactly like a KISS platter, that Ace Frehley's independent attempt sounded well night indistinguishable from a KISS original, that Paul Stanley's individual album sounded too close to a KISS disc to be true... but that Peter Criss' package was another jar of make up entirely. See, despite past assertions by the four KISS members that their single-handed efforts were going to be 'radically different' from their collective work as a band, in the final reckoning only drummer Criss has had the bottle (or maybe the ability?) to go out on a limb and - ahem - do his own thing.

But that's not to say that he succeeds all that well. Truth is, as you've probably noticed from the star ratings, in straying so far away from the KISS scheme of things, Criss' own LP has ended up sounding too diverse and ambitious for its own good. Proving that you should really stick to doing what you do best. In the past, the merest idea of a 'solo album' has been enough to drive critics and punters alike to the brink of insanity. But for the moment try to forget about such disasters as Ken Hensley's 'Proud Words On A Dusty Shelf' (thank God Mick Box has never released an album of his own) and Jon Anderson's overblown 'Olias Of Sunhillow'. Instead, translate the whole 'solo album' ethic into the context of the KISS career. Now, doesn't it all seem just kind of ... natural? These four albums have just been released on the same day throughout the States, each shipping platinum (or something) almost instantaneously - but so what? Since KISS's inception just four years ago, it's been a case of overkill all the way down the line. You just have to get used to it.

But down the brass tacks - and to begin with the least spectacular of the quartet, the 'Peter Criss'. On previous band albums, Criss has hardly impressed with his his songwriting expertise (except for 'Beth', and that was co-written with Bob Ezrin I believe). For example, his track 'Hooligan' (from the 'Love Gun' album) contained the immortal lines 'I'm a hooligan / Won't go to school again'... see what I mean? However, for his solo LP, the drummer's largely abandoned one-chord basics and instead has made an excursion into the field of gospel-tinged white soul, with diversions into 'Beth'-type sensitive balladry along the way. Admirable attempts to be sure, but unfortunately the playing of the various (and mostly nondescript) session musicians is so polite, the production of the album so restrained and uneventful, that the most complimentary word I can find for the LP is 'pleasant'. That said, and despite numbers with such awe-inspiring titles as 'Rock Me Baby' and 'Hooked On Rock 'N' Roll', there were some confoundedly memorable tunes on this album, tunes that could do well in Eagles, MoR-slanted territory, notably 'You Matter To Me' and 'Don't You Let Me Down', both graceful, gentle ballads with Criss excelling on 'emotional' vocals.

Bassist Gene Simmons has also tried with his LP... he's tried to inject some of his own (onstage) eccentricity and menace on to the record, but he really doesn't take it far enough. Despite superb, expensive-sounding production, off-the-wall between-track snippets and the odd untypical instance ('Man Of A Thousand Faces' being a distinctly different tune, a tribute to Lon Chaney/horror movies with lyrics that may or may not be personal: 'For years I've lived inside my dreams / Somehow I've made them real it seems'), the bare fact is that this still sounds like a KISS album, pure and simple. So, while it's undeniably enjoyable (especially the tracks 'Radioactive', 'Burning Up With Fever' and 'Tunnel Of love'), solo disc it is not. Simmons even reworking the old KISS standard 'See You In Your Dreams' just to prove the point. The LP closes oddly with 'When You Wish Upon A Star' from 'The Wizard Of Oz' [Actually 'Pinocchio' - Ed]. It has sweeping strings and endearing gruff, out-of-place vocals, but ends up sounding just plain silly. Never mind.

Moving up in (he ratings, we have Paul Stanley's platter which, again, sounds just like KISS with a few exceptions. It's a whole lot more dynamic than Simmons' however, and is therefore rather more successful. Balladic interludes merge neatly with moments of HM mayhem. Stanley sings well and goes 'Oooh-yeah! ' and 'Woooa-no!' quite a lot throughout. But whatever, this is a fine record and would be the best of the bunch if not for the remarkable efforts of Ace 'The Space' Frehley. The KISS axe hero's LP has no pretensions to be anything other than a wild, total, no-holds-barred heavy rock guitar extravaganza. The song titles tell the tale: 'Rip It Out', 'Wiped-Out', 'Snow Blind'... metallic madness from a booze-crazed, drug-addled mind. Frehley's and Eddie Kramer's production makes the album sound one long, raw, cranked-up grind. No subtleties in evidence. Frehley's no vocalist (he shouts rather than sings, lying on his back on the studio floor most of the time, if an interview in Circus is to be believed) but it doesn't matter a jot, it's all perfectly in keeping with the LPs unrefined nature.

'Speeding Back To My Baby' contains the entirely predictable line 'And I don't mean maybe, the cocaine craziness of 'Snow Blind' has Frehley bellowing 'I can't see a thing / I don't wanna sing / Think I'm lost in space' most effectively and 'Wiped-Out' rips off (he Surfaries' original of (almost) the same title before becoming too titanic for words, Frehley telling the tale of how he was approached by a girl in a bar but was so drunk he couldn't take up her offer. In other words, he says, 'I was wiped out / Had my lights out / Falling right out / 'Cos I was wiped out'. All this, plus a marvelous version of that old Hello (or was it Kenny?) pop single 'New York Groove.'

Although in some ways these four may only give added weight to the old adage 'the whole is greater than the sum of the parts', I still have no hesitation in saying that they are undoubtedly 'the greatest solo albums of all time'. But of course.

"Four Ways To KISS"

(RS #279, Nov. 1978, John Swenson)

"The worst thing is that the kids think we are breaking up," frets bassist and KISS spokesman Gene Simmons about the recent joint release of the four members' solo albums. While not in the running for album of the year, each is miles beyond the recording standards applied to any one KISS LP. But the group is worried that its audience will consider the move betrayal. "We're asking everyone not to refer to these as solo albums," prods KISS publicist Julie Harrison about the identically packaged, self-titled LPs. "We want them to be called KISS albums."

In fact, the albums by Simmons and guitarists Ace Frehley and Paul Stanley won't seem too foreign to kids raised on the KISS brand of recycled heavy metal. But drummer Peter Criss' solo album has absolutely nothing to do with KISS, a fact which makes Criss very proud. "I've always been different," he explains, "because Gene, Paul and Ace are more into Zeppelin, Humble Pie and Hendrix, while I was always into the Stones, Beatles and R&B performers like Sam Cooke. When I'm home I listen to the Eagles, old Beatles, Sinatra, Tony Bennett, Dionne Warwick."

This is not the first time Criss has created a stylistic dilemma within the band. Though his song "Beth" became a big KISS hit, the ballad didn't fit the band's image, he explains. "KISS is a strange group, a lot of voting. They didn't want to do the song, the kids aren't gonna accept it, they said. Gene was against it because he said it didn't fit the concept. But our public is gonna dig it. KISS never made good albums, our shows always outsold our albums, but it's time that changed."

The drummer chose Vini Poncia (Nilsson, Ringo) to produce his album, and Poncia's star-maker production provided Criss with the slickest support of any of the solo efforts. There are several pleasant surprises, notably an energetic remake of "Tossin' and Turnin'" and an autobiographical tune called "Hooked on Rock and Roll." Criss feels that his album is the first step toward separating his career from KISS. "I see myself eventually on my own without the make-up and the bombs, without theatrics. I could dig getting up there with a white suit and three chick-singers. I don't know if this is it for the band - nothing lasts forever. I've made it. At least now it's a steppingstone for each of us. If the band split up I really wouldn't mind."

Unlike Criss, the other members of the group had strong ideas about how their solo albums should sound and sought help only during the engineering and mixing stages. As a result the three albums have marked similarities to KISS' music. "I've never had more fun doing an album," says Ace Frehley. "It was more exciting than KISS because I had more freedom. I didn't have to listen to three other guys telling me what to do." Frehley played most of the instruments himself on his LP and experimented a lot musically. "Ozone," "I'm in Need of Love," and "New York Groove" employed innovative guitar and recording techniques. His favorite track is "Fractured Mirror." "It means a lot to me he says, "because it's an advanced instrumental that holds up to 'Tubular Bells.'"

It's no surprise to find that KISS mastermind Gene Simmons' solo album is a roughly conceptual treatise on stardom which features a celebrity line up including Cher, Helen Reddy, Bob Seger and Cheap Trick's Rick Nielson. "Paul McCartney Wanted to sing on those songs," he says with a straight face, "but he wasn't available so I got the guys from Beatlemania [Mitch Weissman and Joe Pecorino]."

It is somewhat surprising, however, that the record comes across with the macabre humor more characteristic of Who bassist John Entwistle. But it's downright astonishing to hear Simmons do softly lyrical Beatles influenced pop songs like "See You Tonite," "Always Near You/Nowhere to Hide" and "Mr. Make Believe." Simmons is proud of the shock value. Many of the songs on the album were written before his involvement with KISS, which explains many of the stylistic differences. However, Simmons maintains that KISS will be able to assimilate this material into future stage shows. "We're breaking down every preconceived notion people have about us," he says, "and showing everybody that we can be the biggest and not be dictated to by our own confines. It's KISS just because we play it."

Paul Stanley's album comes the closest to sounding like KISS, except that his songs have more dynamic range than the group's work. But it's his album that provides a blueprint of how KISS might expand its scope without retreating too much from the band's old image. "I tried not to contradict what I did before," he explains. "There's nothing wrong with progressing. I never said anything in KISS that I didn't believe. If you want to do something different it shouldn't be mislabeled.

"These albums are an introduction to another KISS, another level," he concludes "The next KISS album will sound a lot closer to the solo albums than the last KISS album. People forget how uncompromising we are. They see the chrome, not the engine."

Solo Ace Finds His Own Space

(The Village Voice, 11/13/78, Billy Altman)

In the fall of '76, I accompanied Robert Duncan – world's leading authority on KISS and author of an unauthorized biography of said band, one of the most imaginative and witty "quickie" rock books you could ever read – on a visit to temporary KISS headquarters in Nanuet, New York, where the band was recording Rock and Roll Over. They were working on "Calling Dr. Love," and guitarist Frehley, apparently off in the stratosphere somewhere, spent half an hour and 15 takes looking for a solo. Finally, producer Eddie Kramer stopped the tapes, stared Ace right in the eye and barked, "You're Ace FREHLEY, Ace. Now let's hear a great guitar solo." Then, as if in a new kind of trance, Frehley proceeded to unleash one monstrously fierce scorcher of a break. And you'd figure, all that trouble for one short solo, how on earth could this guy do a whole album?

Well, Kramer produced, along with the space kid himself, the Ace Frehley solo album, and damned if it isn't not only the best of the four KISS solo LPs, but a rather fine hard-rock album on its own. I can't honestly say that I was expecting any of these records to be any good. The recession following Rock and Roll Over's now-or-never victory in the aftermath of Destroyer (KISS's Vietnam; Alive was their WWII) has been severe; I myself went AWOL during Love Gun (easily their worst) and avoided all but the studio side of Alive II as a conscientious objector – no one except James Brown should ever be permitted more than one in-concert album. Since KISS was barely functioning as a unit, hopes for anything decent from the four members separately were minimal indeed.

The big question in my mind was just how much of the makeup would wear off with each Kissie given his own space to operate in. Other than Ace, each one has proven to be fairly predictable. Peter Criss's album is an almost totally transparent, innocuous blend of not-too-soul-deep R'n'B, medium-tempo rockers, and "big" ballads. It does, however, feature one exquisite track, "Don't You Let Me Down," a Drifters-esque tune with a melancholy edge that does not, as do the other slow numbers here, smack of capital-S sentimentality. Gene Simmons's affair is one the greater portion of the Western world was apparently invited to participate in, and if you think the bat-lizard and Ms. Cher make strange bedfellows, how about Helen Reddy and Rick Nielsen, Donna Summer and Bob Seger, Janis Ian and Joe Perry, all of whom do cameos? Simmons just can't help bringing in obnoxiously ridiculous (sample lyric: "Let me visit your tunnel of love"; sample waste of time: Jiminy Cricket's "When You Wish Upon a Star," done completely straight – *tres charmant, non*? Evil blood-spitting man makes nice-nice for 2:40); his idea of hilarity is using two of the Beatlemania clones to sing backup vocals. Then there's the Oriental prelude and the phone call from the groupies on "Living in Sin"—"at the Holiday Inn," of course. You could say this guy's just a bit taken with himself. Oh, yeah, one good song here, too – "Radioactive" — quite hummable if you forget that the lyrics are so sexist and make no sense to boot. As for Paul Stanley's LP, I didn't really expect it to be the worst one of the lot. Stanley sings half of KISS's songs and contributes much of their aural personality, so it's not surprising that this one is reminiscent of KISS throughout. Very bad KISS. No memorable vocals, no memorable songs, and plenty of used riffs. The highlight is "Hold Me, Touch Me (Think of Me When We're Apart)," a mellow tune that deserves someone like Joey Travolta to do it justice.

But Ace, bless his smoldering little guitar, has plenty to be proud of. A good-natured, freewheeling personality that has never even been hinted at on KISS albums, at voice that is more than passable, and songwriting that exudes all the sledgehammer, turn-me-loose madness of great metalloid hard rock. The entire record zooms by in a swirl of power chords and frenzied fills. Sonic guitar worshippers (and there are obviously plenty of them, for Frehley is outselling his three mates) must revel in the Black Sabbath ploddings of "Snow Blind," but the extraterrestrial squeals of "Wiped-Out" are the key. Frehley makes no bones about operating on some kind of chemically stimulated level; Gene may boast about his "Larger Than Life" organ, Paul may decide that he's too good-looking to settle with anyone for more than a one-night stand, and Kitty Kat may search for "true love," but Ace, like most of KISS's audience, inst wants to get off, anyway he can. Personally, though I find "Rip it Out" and "What's on Your Mind"—plenty of neat pre-Utopian Todd Rundgren moves on this one—the most infectious and impressive tracks. In general, there's an unassuming, unpretentious force at work here that puts the other KISS boys to shame. I dunno, maybe Kramer used hypnosis. I'm sending away for my Ace necklace today.

Keeping Up... With Youth

(Cedar Rapids Gazette, Nov. 26, 1978, Pamela Swift)
Almost every musician who plays with a rock group yearns to make it as a soloist, to cut his or her own album, to rake in the mounting royalties that accompany a solid hit. For the first time in modern musical history, all the members of a group have released solo albums simultaneously. They are Gene Simmons, Peter Criss, Paul Stanley and Ace Frehley, who together form the rock group KISS.

Their individual .albums, released recently by Casablanca Records, are backed by an incredible advertising and sales promotion budget of $2.5 million. Neil Bogart, 35, maverick president of Casablanca, says: "People in this business think I've flipped my lid. But we've already received more than a million orders for each album, and that should easily double or triple by Christmas. "What happened is that we began to note that each member of KISS was developing his own fan following. We could tell from the fan mail - also from the newspapers and magazines that featured stories on [each member]. From that came the concept of individual albums."

Solo albums by group members frequently provide record producers with a stiff pain in their vital organs. "If you do it for one member of a group," explains one record company executive, "how do you turn down another? And if the solo album bombs, how do you explain to an ego-ridden guitarist that he's great in a group but lousy as a soloist? Maybe Neil Bogart can pull it off, but I have my doubts. "Most of the KISS fans are in the 11-16 age group. How many can afford to buy all four of the albums at, say, $5 or $6 a throw? Not too many. But in this business, the way things have been going, who knows."

If the KISS solo albums do well, other record labels will probably follow suit; but experience seems to prove that when members of a successful rock group abandon it for the solo spotlight, their records do poorly. A few years ago the big boys in the

Rolling Stones and the Who tried the solo route and failed. Maybe the KISS boys with super promotion can prove the exception.

Review of the Solo albums

(RS #281/2, Dec. 1978, Robert Duncan)

Good taste is murder to rock & roll. Just take a look around. Fact is, from Elm to the Sex Pistols, the best rock & roll has always been strictly in bad taste. But time and again rock & rollers refuse to remember this, and as they get older and richer, sure enough, they start worrying about which fork is for the salad.

Except for a brief and regretted lapse on the oily Destroyer, KISS has stood for nothing if not bad taste. And it's the utter vulgarity of the blood spitting, the platform shoes, the makeup and the under-produced songs about grimy sex and dumb partying that's made these guys one of the only genuine rock and roll bands in this benighted decade. But now, having constructed a most magnificently meretricious commercial empire from a consummate sense of grossness and stupidity the members of KISS have decided, so it seems, to remove the camouflage and reveal themselves on these solo albums for what they really are: four tuna with good taste. Alas, fellas, KISS don't need tuna with good taste. KISS needs tuna that taste good. Don't they ever learn?

But wait. What's that word? What's that sound? Miracle of miracles, good taste behind KISS' bad taste is even worse than what passed before! Whole new realms of revulsion from rock & roll's supreme Awful Majesties! That said, it'd be difficult and not a little unfair to single out any one of the four KISS-ers for worst bad-taste honors. But when drummer Peter Criss, a guy who made a million bucks wearing a silver button nose and kitty whiskers, tells me in his "Hooked on Rock 'n Roll " that it's been a rough road to the top, I wince with him. I also hasten to add that the further soul posturing in "Tossin' and Turnin'" and Criss' kitsch classic, "That's the Kind of Sugar Papa Likes," isn't going to make the road back down any smoother. Of course, the name of the game is: get bad.

In between the funk on Criss' record are several ballads, a form that almost everyone in the group apparently be1ieves is the true hallmark of a rocker's good taste. The Catman (who wrote and sang the tear-jerker hit, "Beth," on Destroyer) is in his element here and almost scores again with die grandiose "I Can't Stop The Rain." Beyond that my note say: "Out-of-tune acoustic playing. One note is good." Which just about sums up this LP. Criss couldn't be worse.

Then again, he could be Ace Frehley, who reveals in tunes such as "Snow Blind," "Ozone," and "Wiped-Out" that he's got booze and drugs on (in?) his mind much of the time. Musically, Frehley illustrates this fact with a lot of pre-washed Jimi

Hendrix-style guitar playing and some oddly appealing Todd Rundgren-like teenage-spacester singing. In his particular bid for respectability, KISS' lead guitarist eschews ballads, preferring instead to crank up long instrumentals like a veritable Sheepshead Bay Beethoven. One result, "Fractured Mirror," has a duh-hey simplicity that in other quarters might make it Eno-esque. Only on "Rip It Out," a fast rocker with great nasty lyrics that urge the girl to actually rip her heart out, does Frehley get it all together. Whatever it is.

True to his KISS persona as the Lover (he wears red lipstick), rhythm guitarist/lead vocalist Paul Stanley concentrates on love songs. Presumably because he's one of the band's two chief song-writers and thus gets more practice at the craft, Stanley's no stranger to a nice melody and airy harmonies. (His "Ain't Quite Right" is nearly Brooklynese Crosby, Stills and Nash.) Fortunately, good taste falters when Stanley's singing ventures too close to the Art Garfunkel threshold of high-pitched sensitivity and is finally brought low by his lyrics, especially in the two bittersweet parenthetical moister works, "Hold Me, Touch Me (Think of Me When We're Apart)" and "Take Me Away (Together as One)?" Bad. And wondrously so!

Gene Simmons, singing bassist Bay-Lizard and gross-out king of KISS is probably the brains behind the group. But his album begs the question: how much brains does it really take to be the brains behind KISS? Less than Einstein, more than sweet potatoes would be my ballpark answer. While he definitely understands bad taste and its effective, applications, Simmons here appears torn between the diligent grudge that's been his specialty and the True Self he no doubt displays privately to girlfriend Cher (who, incidentally, appears on "Living in Sin" as the telephone groupie, if my ears don't deceive me).

Perhaps more than anything else, Simmons seeks respect for his notable wit. In his wittiest move, he's used two of the Beatlemania cast for backup vocals on a couple of Rubber Soul-type numbers. Gene Simmons also knocks off the best rock & roll song on any of these records with the extremely catchy "Radioactive?" For the hat trick, he executes a brilliant defense of his gross-out ride in "Tunnel of Love." "'Tunnel of love / Tunnel of love / I've got to visit your tunnel of love" Simmons growl-sings like a guy who has to pee really bad after a long car ride. In another line, he tells a would-be lover: "You'll jump off the roof if I say." Now if that isn't a rock & roll sentiment, I don't know what is.

All's well until Simmons breaks out the "close to my heart" stuff - ballads again - such as his Lon Chaney tribute, "Man of 1000 Faces," the autobiographical(?) "Mr. Make Believe" and the Emerson, Lake and Palmer-like "Always Near You/Nowhere to Hide" (sung in his most painfully normal vocal style ever). I'll admit the old Bat-Lizard almost moves me with these, but in the end, they're just too slick and too disconcertingly out of character. On the other hand, what exactly is this whimpering rendition of "When You Wish Upon a Star?" A bad joke? Gong!

If you ever worried that these bozos were going to ditch you for the mainstream just like all the others, their solo LPs will put your mind to ease. As long as KISS is on the job, rock & roll is here to stay and Charlie Tuna is king.

How to listen to KISS and not suffer permanent injury.

(Summit Press, Jan. 6, 79, Joel McNally)
Danger is my business. Hah! I laugh in the face of it. If the world as we know it is to remain secure, there always must be those of us who are willing to lake risks. Still, I must admit that I underestimated the chances of death and disfigurement. I know now that I narrowly escaped permanent injury. Children, do not attempt this without proper training and equipment.

Yes. I listened to all four of the KISS solo albums. I was about three fourths of the way through that I started losing my already tenuous touch with reality. I might still be catatonic if it were not for my loved ones. They walked me around the block, fed me with a spoon and played Little Golden Records until I came around. Not that I blame any of the fine musicians who make up the group KISS, mind you. They were only doing what they thought was right. Namely putting out a product that they could sock little kids more than $20 for.

Then someone came up with the ingenious idea of simultaneously releasing four albums, one by each member of that group. If the Mormon Tabernacle Choir had thought of that, they could have cleaned up. So far, all four albums are bunched together on the charts, indicating that the plan worked. Apparently, most parents are forking over enough money for a complete set. To do anything less would be interpreted as a lack of love. As an added incentive to buy all four, each album contains one piece of a KISS poster puzzle. Now a four-piece puzzle may not seem like much of a challenge, but you would be surprised how many KISS fans spend hours trying to figure it out.

So what do the albums sound like? Before everything went blank, I was able to make a professional judgment. I can honestly say that each individual member was able to maintain the same level of quality that has been produced by the group as a whole. Gene Simmons, lead tongue of KISS, is joined on his album by a host of legitimate and illegitimate entertainers including Helen Reddy, Bob Seger, Janis Ian, Donna Summer and Cher somebody. Cher and Gene sing a sweet romantic duet called 'Living in Sin.' Even old Helen, of Walt Disney movie fame, sleazes around a song with Simmons called 'True Confessions.' Possibly the highlight of all four records is Gene Simmons' inclusion of one of the most important songs in the history of our popular culture: 'When You Wish Upon a Star.' There is a lot of irony in the fact that it is probably the only song that young KISS fans will think is dumb.

Ace Frehley's album is probably the most aggressive. It includes songs with titles like 'Wiped-Out,' 'Snow Blind' and 'Fractured Mirror.' You might detect a certain theme of destruction there. Paul Stanley is supposedly the sex-symbol of KISS. He sings songs like 'Hold Me, Touch Me,' which are the musical equivalent of the love parts that we used to hate m the cowboy movies. But like any self-respecting member of KISS, Paul can be real peppy, too.

Peter Criss, KISS drummer and balladeer, actually has one song, 'I Can't Stop the Rain,' which could even be on a grown-up album someday. But he makes a puny attempt at the old rock classic 'Tossin' and Turnin'.' Criss has a song about tearing somebody's heart out, too. Kids used to get hurt trying to imitate the fire breathing of KISS. I sure hope not too many of them try this heart surgery stuff.

Now that the threat to my personal well-being has passed, I can even feel a certain admiration for the price which KISS was able to achieve. But I am sure that we haven't seen the end of this thing yet. After all, records are made to be broken. Especially KISS records.

Collecting the KISS Solo Albums

Some of the interesting solo album related collectibles are detailed in this feature.

Collecting material from the solo albums encompasses a broad range of media. Obtaining mint condition, still shrink-wrapped albums (rather than modern re-seals), or finding original U.S. issues without cut corners can be quite a challenge to the collector. Simply put, the numbers of solo albums that ended up in cut-out bins means that those "cut-outs" often appear more prevalent in modern commercial channels (By March 1982, overstock companies, such as Great Atlantic & Pacific Music Co. if St. Louis were offloading excess copies of the "Peter Criss" and "Paul Stanley" solo albums for $0.50 each — so there certainly exists a glut of excess copies, with condition being the key). Each of the original U.S. issues came with a folded poster segment, member specific merchandise order form, and printed inner dust-sleeve. These dust-sleeves have been notoriously flimsy, often suffering seam splits (even in sealed product). Of the four albums, only Peter's has any major difference with the inclusion of the separate printed performance credits insert sheet, green text printed on white paper stock. It should also be noted that not all of the poster segments include the interlocking notches — some are simply rectangular and fully trimmed of the notches. If the collector obtains four near-perfect copies of the albums, then they might as well add the $20-40 required to purchase an original 1978 Aucoin "Solo Albums" bag which were used by many original points of sale for purchasers of all four LPs. There are certainly enough of these around in the collector's market.

Casablanca also hopped on the picture disk (or picture LP, as they were referred as at the time) band-wagon that was reaching its peak in late-1978/early-1979. However, in general Casablanca, somewhat surprisingly, did not fully embrace the fad of picture disks that most labels were over-saturating the market with during the period 1977 - 1979. That simply means they didn't press picture disks for every release, even those for mid-level artists, but released product for a limited number of releases: The Village People's self-titled 12", "Macho Man" and "Cruisin'" (1978); Donna Summer's "Best of Live & More" (condensed to a single disk, 1978); the four KISS solo albums (1978); Parliament's "Motor-Booty Affair" (1978); and Cher's "Take Me Home" (1979). There were multiple challenges for labels, not least limited pressing capacity for production which often added to delays in product availability and quantity. There was certainly popularity of the format with many of the standard 50-100,000 copy limited production runs being snapped up by consumers with the intent to hoard the item in hopes of it becoming a valuable commodity in the future. Cut-out bins ultimately prove that many releases never attained any market value. By late-1978 there was a fear that what had started out with major successes, such as the "Rocky Horror Show" and Beatles picture disk releases, would lead to an over-saturation in the market killing the format (Billboard, 9/30/78). From Casablanca's playbook, anything worth doing was worth over-doing! And by early 1979 PolyGram distributed label picture disks were among the worst performing in the industry for retailers. Many retailers "Indicated that they don't plan on purchasing any of the disks by the individual members of KISS. Lampshire [Ed. Bob; a regional PolyGram sales rep] says by the first week in February he had sold only 400 to 500 each of the picture disks by the four superstars" (Billboard, 2/24/79).

Using the NBPIX matrix prefix, the U.S. versions were housed in die-cut sleeves with vinyl inner sleeves. The backing behind the die-cut features an ad for the four solo albums. The discs feature the respective solo album cover art on both sides. An article in Billboard described the early production technique: "the technology surrounding the picture disks is still costly and time consuming. They are actually a record sandwich, with a black plastic center covered by photographic paper containing the image. This is laminated with clear plastic and the grooves are then cut on the plastic" (Billboard, 7/29/78). Check out US patent #4,267,001 to read all about the process. Disclaimers on many releases appeared warning the purchaser of the visual appeal and sonic sacrifice: That the "sound quality may not be comparable to the conventional edition" warning certainly didn't seem to hinder the format! Whatever the case, late-1978 marked a peak in the popularity of the format, and by the following year production numbers dropped backed to the pre-fad novelty levels due to "high prices, no returns, poor audio quality, and oversaturation of product" (Billboard, 1/13/79). As is the case with the regular LPs, many copies come with cut corners due to the market disappearing. An internal Casablanca shipment audit of the picture disks indicated that less than 19,000 copies of each had been shipped by June 1979. For those who care, Ace had the most (18,739) followed by Gene (18,646); Peter (18,052) again beat Paul into last place, though only by a total of 25 units. By "SuperKISS" standards it was less than impressive.

In the U.S. no reel-to-reels were issued for the solo albums. However, variant collectors can dig into the nightmare landscape of cassette and 8-track formats. Original cassette issues come with ubiquitous "white spine" J-card (that's the folded picture insert inside the cassette case). Since there were various plants manufacturing the tapes, or printing the J-cards, there are plenty of variants to be found. Some tapes have printed cassettes; others have the pasted paper labels. Some J-cards are printed with the cover art oriented on the right hand-side, others seemingly backwards on the left. To hazard a guess, other than some simply being errors not deemed worthy of removal from retail, there is the possibility that there may have been the intention to package two different titles in a double-cassette holder — a concept that would make the "opposites" design make sense. That, however, may simply be a matter of overanalyzing the irrelevant and trying to fit a square peg into a round hole! Later U.S. issues of the tapes, through 1982–3 can be found with black J-card spines. PolyGram cassette media stock becomes apparent for those tapes manufactured in the 1982–1983 period with almost translucent or "PolyGram" profiled media. There are reissues on white and clear media in the late-1980s and finally the 1997 remaster versions. And add large or small tape window to the mix, or PolyGram logo either with stars under it or a simple underline! As is the case with vinyl production there were multiple manufacturing plants responsible for tape duplication and screen-printing. One also has to consider that cassettes were issued in most markets, so many of the same factors apply to those releases/reissues too!

The solo albums have been reissued on multiple occasions in the U.S., in addition to the inherent variations in PolyGram and Casablanca produced 1978 versions. The 1982–3 vinyl editions had the standard PolyGram "Filmworks" center-ring (name and address on lower circumference of center label). The individual solo album artwork is not reproduced, and the album still carries the original NBLP matrix, on the center-ring, cover, and etched in the vinyl run-out. Usually, a generic Casablanca dust sleeve was used. Covers can be identified by the lack of UPC barcode and presence of the "501" designation to identify the Shorewood Packaging printing plant. PolyGram had only agreed (albeit in principle) in mid-1981 to adopt the UPC standard, but gave no indication of when they would start implementing barcodes on packaging. By the summer of 1982 U.S. PolyGram had started to introduce the UPC on packaging, in many cases post-1985 through the application of UPC stickers (that include the new 1985 release codes) onto existing product sleeves as existing stocks were used up or product recycled back into the market. Copies of the album reissues from 1984–5 include a printed UPC on the cover, and a cheaper translucent dust sleeve is used. SuperSaver copies were again issued during 1988 marking the final batch of vinyl issues for many years.

The solo albums were reissued by Universal, as part of the "Back to Black" campaign in 2010, though there were complaints of a lack of quality with the product even though it purportedly included remastered audio and a MP3 download card. A reissue series, under license in Russia in 2006, made better looking product, though with some modifications in design that strayed from the originals. Both of these reissue series are easily available and can often be found, at modern premium prices, in collector stores. In 2014, as part of the band's "KISS 40th Anniversary" catalog refresh, the solo albums were reissued digitally and on 180g LPs in the U.S. and Europe. Among other international LP issues, Australian Astor pressings include a modified printed inner dust sleeve that includes all of the solo album track listings in quarter panels on one side and the usual cover arrangement on the other. German Bellaphon issues uses a unique dust sleeve showing the interlocking solo posters and advertizing all four of the albums.

However, to utterly break both bank and soul, one can attempt the laborious task of assembling a set of El Salvadorian colored vinyl issues issued by local Casablanca distributor Boni Discos (Ace: BONI-33092; Peter: BONI-33093; Paul: BONI-33094; And Gene, presumably BONI-33091 or 33095!). These issues are some of the rarest, and yet most exquisite, KISS related vinyl, and a concept so seemingly obviously overlooked by others for so many years!

Picture discs were also released in Japan in April 1979. These are, by far, the highest quality versions issued, each featuring B-side artwork created from elements of the original poster inserts. Complete and mint sets of the four sell for in excess of $1,000, which has long played a role in the discs having been pirated (some unofficial issues are easily spotted with the spines having the member's names listed last, first) on multiple occasions. The discs included the 4-page black-and-white booklet insert in Japanese and obi, though apparently not the poster (which makes sense with it being integrated into the disc art - a point sometimes debated). The regular LP versions were also distributed in a special Victor box. The LPs contained all of the premiums expected in the regular individual versions. The black box simply featured a KISS logo on the top with the album art from each member on the back (or bottom side). A separate top-opening version was used promotionally. These boxes can often be found individually meaning that many hybrid sets with varying contents have been assembled over the years resulting in mismatched albums, some with obis or posters, and some not. The original intent of such a box remains unclear. Japanese versions of the solo album singles have always sold for a premium, along with the white-label promotional counterparts. However, of exceeding rarity are the two V-1 & V-2 promotional singles that combined "New York Groove" backed with "Hold Me, Touch Me;" and "Don't You Let Me Down" and "Radioactive" respectively. These have gone for well over $500 individually at auction leading to the appearance of fakes.

In recent years fakes have permeated all areas of higher-valued KISS collecting. These include the unofficial releases of pseudo-UK singles such as "Don't You Let Me Down" backed with "Hooked on Rock 'N Roll" (Casablanca/Pye CAN-142) and "Rip It Out" backed with "What's On Your Mind?" (Casablanca/Pye CAN-149). Both of these abominations are also available in varying vinyl colors (a dead giveaway really). While they may look good they are nearly as pointless as the so-called Vinnie Vincent Brazilian "Creatures of the Night" cover, but less expensive mistakes for the uninformed collector or impulse buyer to make. And, to be honest, some people simply don't care. Solo singles were officially released in many countries, so collecting all of the picture sleeves can be a particularly enjoyable (and expensive) challenge. In the UK, the singles were the only official releases of material from the albums with the full albums only being available as UK-priced imports for many years (one way of unloading the excess stock of U.S. LPs, directly into the cut-out bins of another country!).

Casablanca's distributor, Pye, went all out offering promo versions, black vinyl in picture covers, and the famed colored vinyl versions that came with member make-up design masks. Paul's single offers an interesting "extra" version with some copies coming with a mis-press: While Side-B states that "Goodbye" is included on the vinyl; it actually plays "Love in Chains". This mis-pressed version seems to be as common as the correctly pressed version, but it is interesting nonetheless. It is also possible that this applies to other versions of the single. Solo single sets from France (Vogue) and Germany (Bellaphon) can be a challenge to assemble, while Italy rounds out the European countries to have issued picture sleeves. In terms of pure rarity, some of the South African or Zimbabwean issues end up being the most expensive. A Mexican "Radioactive" EP featuring the four primary songs (Casablanca/PolyGram EP-2463) is also well worth tracking down with its attractive picture sleeve. By August 1981 the EP had sold an impressive 141,595 copies making it readily available, though a challenge in better condition... The United States remains the only country to have issued two singles for Peter's album, though neither is an expensive addition to one's collection. Most copies of the "You Matter to Me" single seem to have been misprinted, with the title appearing as "You Still Matter to Me." The issuing of the second single seems to indicate that Casablanca were at least attempting to kick-start sales of the album. Both are also easily available as promos.

Promotional items include the "Assembled Especially for Radio from the KISS Albums" sampler (Casablanca NBD-20137DJ). This 12" single in die-cut sleeve featured two tracks from each of the albums. On Side-A: "Don't You Let Me Down," "You Matter To Me," "New York Groove," and "Fractured Mirror; and Side-B: "See You Tonite," "Radioactive," "Hold Me, Touch Me," and "Take Me Away (Together As One)." All of these tracks had been included on special "Presentation Tapes" used for the album listening parties. In addition to those songs, the finalized presentation tapes also included "Move On," "I Can't Stop The Rain," "Burning Up With Fever," and "Snow Blind." One earlier version that surfaced at auction included "When You Wish Upon A Star" and "Man of 1,000 Faces" in place of "Burning Up with fever for Gene's selections. Probably the most interesting promotional item is the "Black Box" open-ended interview cassette box. Originally, the black box housed a cassette tape (that included interview question answers from the band members allowing radio stations to conduct pseudo-interviews), postcard, interview sheet with suggestion "questions," housed in a further white slip-sleeve. The cassette also included each of the solo single A-sides. A stack of these sets were sold at auction making them much less rare than they had been. Cassette issues from many countries are available with Japan again winning the rarity contest. For collectors outside of the musical realm items such as spiral-bound notebooks (The Stuart Hall Company) and the JC Penny LP storage unit were made featuring the solo album artwork.

KISS
BEST OF SOLO ALBUMS
THE BEST OF...
ACE FREHLEY
PAUL STANLEY
PETER CRISS
GENE SIMMONS
The Best Of The Solo Albums

The Best of Solo Albums

A look into the murky world of the 1979 non-USA solo album compilation.

As if collecting the solo albums individually wasn't enough, there is also a plethora of international variants of "The Best of Solo Albums" that compile tracks from the four albums on to a single volume release. Ostensibly, the album is based on "Assembled Especially for Radio from the KISS Albums" featuring the same core cuts. The album was issued in numerous markets outside of the U.S. and Japan; and in some cases was issued instead of separate individual albums. All told, some 27 songs from the albums with nine songs featuring from Peter's album. By far, the most common issue to be found will be the German 1980 Phonogram reissue. Often available in North America as a PSI issue (PolyGram Special Import) versions for those markets either have a gold "PSI" emboss stamp on the cover (usually rear), or a sticker on the cassette case. The album was among the first batch of titles available in North America under the PSI program, which started as a mainly classical music program under the PolyGram Classics division in February 1982 ("KISS Killers" was added when issued later that year). The program's intent was to allow the record labels to go head-to-head against record importing companies such as JEM. The purpose of the PSI marking was not only to indicate the source of the physical product, but for "inventory control and as a guard against returns of product purchased from other than PolyGram sources... restraints on returns are far more than domestic product" (Billboard, 2/13/82). The 1980 reissue retained the German discography, updated with the new release codes, but changed the song text to plain white. For all intents the equally common Dutch (also available with censored logo) and Nordic Phonogram (NCB present on center ring label) issue share the same track listing (see below). Only the latter of these has any particular collector's value having been pressed in lesser numbers for the Scandinavian markets. These three issues are the most "generic" of the release.

The 1980 German reissue completely changed the track-listing (see below) in comparison with the original Bellaphon version. Also changed was the iconic KISS logo with the banned Nazi Schutzstaffel-style "SS" once and for all being replaced with the "ZZ" version for the domestic market. The Bellaphon version had been released around the same time as the reissue of the "Sure Know Something" single (Bellaphon BF-18684), in October/November 1979, with cover art that changed the song focus to "Dirty Livin'." The album was advertised on the rear cover of the "Double Hit Special" version of that single's picture sleeve. The Bellaphon release is impressive with complete German Phonogram discography (including 7" and 12" singles) on rear, with the song titles printed in the respective band member's "aura" color. "New York Groove" and "Radioactive" lead off either side. Just remember, "Complete Your KISS collection!"

The Australian Astor version of "Best of the Solo Albums" (NBLP2) is grammatically correct on the cover (in neon-esque flowing font), but still billed as "Best of Solo Albums" on the center-ring. Like Germany, it represents one of the fullest embodiments of Casablanca's sell-sell-sell smart attitudes. The rear cover advertises the seven studio albums released through 1979 (including "Dynasty") plus "Alive!" The album somewhat amusingly omits any advertizing for the actual solo albums. This was hardly a new practice in Australia where albums such as "Love Gun" had integrated ads for other albums on the cover artwork. Initially issued by Astor Records, with a particularly flimsy cover, the album was the final release of their distribution deal with Casablanca. Premiums that invariably turn up (in both the original and reissue) included a sticker panel featuring the solo album art and KISS logos, along with a flyer advertisement for the "Attack of the Phantoms" movie. Many of the original Antipodean copies have the minor downside of a stand-out circular red (AUZ) or white (NZD) cover sticker that noted the inclusion of the premium "6 full colour stickers."

The erroneous grammar of the album title was eventually corrected by PolyGram when the album was reissued in April 1980 with the same matrix number. The track-listing wasn't adjusted and the sticker was included in some copies, but not noted via cover sticker. The PolyGram reissue had proved a popular seller, shifting some 36,149 copies between April 1, 1980 through Jan. 15, 1980 (in fact, the "Unmasked" visit to Australia contributed to the sales of some 492,736 album and 95,284 singles in that period). That made it the third most popular KISS album in Australia during that period, behind only "Unmasked" and "Dynasty," understandably as "fresh" albums rather than back-catalog. The album was also advertised on the rear cover text-only discography on the "Star Trax" EP. The album, along with sticker, was also issued in New Zealand via PolyGram records. It has the same mismatched album titles akin to the Aussie Astor issue.

Heading into the more collectible and obscure realm, one of the most visually appealing, and therefore unique, versions is "Paul, Peter, Ace Y Gene" issued in Argentina (6399 079). Issued in 1980, the cover combines the four album portraits onto a single black field with the glowing "KISS" logo from the "Alive!" album booklet. The album's track-listing is unique including songs such as "Wouldn't You Like To Know Me," "It's Alright," "That's The Kind Of Sugar Papa Likes" and "What's On Your Mind?" The rear cover features a prominent large "KISS" logo, and song-titles in Spanish and English. A similar version was distributed by Lauro & Cia in Bolivia with a slightly different rear cover. The version issued in Chile (Casablanca/Quatro LPCAS-8022) in 1980 used the 1976 "Casbah" (aka Camel) label stock, and therefore appears visually incongruous with the period (where the "Filmworks" label should have been used). It features a front cover with the four solo covers arranged in a 2x2 square with white background and no album title.

The rear cover is simply white text on black background, again with no title. Only 10 songs from the albums are featured, with Gene and Paul having two, and Ace and Peter three songs, each. Score one for the bad boys of KISS! Even the center-ring has no album title, simply noting "KISS." Completing the South American trinity, the Peruvian version, issued in 1981 by distributer El Virrey (6302060.2), is notable for using the German "ZZ" logo on the cover art. It is essentially a facsimile of the 1980 German Phonogram reissue. However, the plain white rear cover simply lists the songs titles in black text. The center-ring title for the album is simply, "The Best of ..."

Featuring cover artwork totally at odds with the era, the French Vogue issue (571059), shares the same track-listing as the later standard Phonogram release. Studio photo-shoot pictures of the band members from the "Destroyer" era are used both front and rear. On the front the photos are combined with the solo album member name font encased with a yellow border. Above, in large text, is simple "The Best of ..." Saving the rarest for last, both African issues feature the same track-listing as the European Phonogram issue, albeit in a different running order (see below). Both albums are simply titled "KISS, KISS, KISS, KISS" and use small versions of the individual album covers arranged 2x2 on a white background. The South African issue plain black cover, with white text, noting distribution by the Teal Record Company Ltd. indicates a release date of 1979. Uniquely, the album (NAC-7066) uses U.S. "Dynasty" styled center-rings, making it highly desirable in addition to the fact that most African issues are incredible difficult to obtain, and even more so in a condition worth the effort. The Zimbabwean (technically Zimbabwe Rhodesia at the time) issue used plain white center-ring labels with light blue text. Even with the cut & paste appearance of the front cover, both of these albums have sold in excess of $300 on the rare occasions that they have surfaced.

Best of the Solo Albums															
Song/Country	USA	ARG	AUZ	AUZ	BOL	CHI	FRA	GER	GER	HOL	NZD	NOR	PER	RSA	ZBW
Label	Casablanca	Casablanca	Astor	PolyGram	Lauro & Cia	Quatro	Vogue	Bellaphon	Phonogram	Phonogram	PolyGram	Phonogram	El Virrey	Teal	
Release Code	NBD-20137DJ	6399-075	NBLP2	NBLP2	6399-075	LPCAS-8022	571059	NB-7060	6302-060	6302-060	NBLP2	6302-060	6302060.2	NAC-7066	NAC-7066
Hold Me, Touch Me	B3	A3	A1	A1	A3	A1	B6	B6	B6	B6	A1	B6	B6	B3	B3
Tonight You Belong To Me			A2	A2		B4	B4	B2	B4	B4	A2	B4	B4	A3	A3
Move On			A3	A3			B5		B5	B5	A3	B5	B5	B2	B2
Don't You Let Me Down	A1		A4	A4		B1		A6			A4				
Hooked On Rock 'N' Roll			A5	A5			A6		A6	A6	A5	A6	A6	A6	A6
I Can't Stop The Rain		A6	A6	A6	A6			B5			A6				
New York Groove	A3	B1	B1	B1	B1	A2	A1	A1	A1	A1	B1	A1	A1	A1	A1
Speedin' Back To My Baby			B2	B2			A3		A3	A3	B2	A3	A3	B6	B6
Rip It Out		B2	B3	B3	B2		A2	A4	A2	A2	B3	A2	A2	A5	A5
Radioactive	B2	B6	B4	B4	B6	A3	B1	B1	B1	B1	B4	B1	B1	B1	B1
Mr. Make Believe			B5	B5			B2		B2	B2	B5	B2	B2	B4	B4
Living In Sin			B6	B6				A2			B6				
I'm Gonna Love You						A4									
Burning Up With Fever						A5									
Snow Blind						B2									
Easy Thing						B5									
You Matter To Me	A2	A4			A4		A4		A4	A4		A4	A4	A4	A4
Tossin' And Turnin'							A5		A5	A5		A5	A5	B5	B5
See You Tonite	B1	B4			B4	B3		A3							
Fractured Mirror	A4							A5							
Take Me Away (Together As One)	B4							B3							
Rock Me, Baby								B4							
See You In Your Dreams		B5			B5		B3		B3	B3		B3	B3	A2	A2
Wouldn't You Like To Know Me		A1			A1										
It's Alright		A2			A2										
That's The Kind Of Sugar Papa Likes		A5			A5										
What's On Your Mind		B3			B3										

Solo Album Song Stories

A reboot of the "Song Stories" behind the material released on the solo albums.

Radioactive

"Radioactive" originally started out as a song called "Penny Arcade" that Gene had written at The Record Plant studios (Sharp, Ken - Goldmine). His initial idea was revamped and developed into a pulsating rocker and lead-off track for the album. "Radioactive" was a song, like Paul's "Hard Luck Woman," that had originally been considered to be offered to another artist. In this case Gene had the legendary Jerry Lee Lewis in mind, since he'd been offered the chance to produce him, though Bill Aucoin ultimately nixed the idea, though Lewis was invited to perform on the song, arriving too late to the session to do so.

The introduction to "Radioactive" was written by composer/arranger Ron Frangipane, who had also worked on the Lyn Christopher album in 1972. According to Gene the introduction was, "Based on some things that he's heard on the album, mainly 'Radioactive,' and the piece sounds kind of like the themes from Jaws, the Exorcist. It's basically strings, lots of brass, and uh, Janis Ian... Singing in Latin... The Latin says something like, 'I see no evil, I hear no evil, it's not around me at all,' but underneath her is Sean (Delaney) doing a kind of deep voice growl" (Rock Magazine). Pure Bob Ezrin.

Released as the single from Gene's solo album, "Radioactive" only managed to reach #47 on the Billboard Hot-100 singles charts in early 1979 during a short 8-week run. At 2:54 the radio edit simply removed the extended "demonic" introduction from the song. According to Gene, Joe Perry, from Aerosmith, only plays guitar on the choruses with Steve Lacey playing the solo. Other guests on the piece included Eric Troyer (piano) and Bob Seger (backing vocals).

Burning Up With Fever

Originally demoed in early 1975 by KISS, and again in 1975/6 with the vocal assistance from "The Group With No Name." Donna Summer provided the backing vocals on the studio recording. Donna , according to Gene, "Blew the roof right off" (KISS & Make-up) with her vocal performance. Sean recalled the session: "A funny thing that happened with Donna Summer (because I had used her on 'Tunnel Of Love') when I first walked in, she tried to fool me by suddenly speaking to her manager in German. Well, I had just been living in Germany for about a year and a half, so as she was sitting there thinking she was speaking behind my back, I just jumped in with German and said, 'Excuse me, but if you're going to have to speak German then it's cool, but a lot of people here don't really understand what you're saying so you might as well just speak English.' I thought she was going to die. Because she was saying rude things" (Special Delivery #13).

See You Tonite

Of all of the songs released during the original era of KISS, this piece was the most representative of the sort of material Gene wrote during his early years. In fact, this song was originally dates from that period and was used on the album to show a different side of the "Demon." It clearly demonstrates his Lennon/McCartney roots. It was hardly surprising that the song was eventually dug out of the catalog for the band's "Unplugged" era and resulting "MTV Unplugged" album.

Tunnel Of Love

Gene had recycled parts of the original lyrics for "Man of 1,000 Faces" on "Got Love For Sale," which was recorded for the "Love Gun" album the previous year. He'd use additional remnants of that song on "Tunnel Of Love." This song had been mentioned in the KISS Army Newsletter in early 1977 as a prospective candidate for release on the "Love Gun" album. Gene had initially written it and "Got Love For Sale," while the band were in Japan in March/April 1977.

Interestingly, this song had been included in the batch of song that had originally been demoed by Gene with the Van Halen brothers in 1977. "You're a victimless crime / It happens all the time / You'll jump off the roof if I say / I'm gonna take your love away, gonna force you to stay / You wouldn't have it any other way" were the lyrics for the original bridge in "Man Of 1,000 Faces." Parts of this bridge would be used in the second and third verses, respectively. Interestingly, for the track's recording, Joe Perry, Jeff "Skunk" Baxter, and Richie Ranno are all credited as playing guitar on the track. However, only Richie's guitar work was used on the final track when the other two efforts were deemed unsuitable.

True Confessions

Ironically, this song featured the feminist icon Helen Reddy on backing vocals. According to Gene, "Helen Reddy was incredibly straight. She was like, 'I am woman, glorified.' She had a song called 'I Am Woman' and that was her big hit and I think she was offended by all this male 'cock rock' type of music, but she was willing to do it" (Special Delivery #13). She and Gene played ping-pong while in the studio working on the recording. The message of the song was based in part on Gene's life at the time, "When you get to be famous, and people aren't so anxious to know you as *you*" (Circus, 10/17/78).

Living In Sin

Originally fully titled "Living In Sin At The Holiday Inn," the song's title was shortened rather than possibly offend one of America's largest hotel chains. This song featured an offbeat appearance of Cher, Gene's then girlfriend, as the hysterical female telephone voice with some assistance from her daughter Chastity. Gene recalled, "He [Neil] was having a party at his house, and I was there and Cher was there, Marilyn McCoo and Billy Davis, and people like that were there. So it was kind of a special affair. I didn't care so much for Cher, she just happened to be there. And Neil went over and asked her to sing on my album because she had just signed with Casablanca Records. And I walked over and I apologized. You know, he shouldn't have done that. 'If anybody's going to ask you to sing on the album it's going to be me,' I said. And then the next day I played her the stuff, from the material and then within a week or so we were friendlier" (Grooves, 1978). Most of Cher and Chastity's contribution is unintelligible, though Gene does answer the phone with a "Hello... Baby," very similar to the Big Bopper's classic telephone conversation start of "Chantilly Lace" (1958) — though he sounded to some like he was imitating Popeye. Cher later performed KISS' "I Was Made For Lovin' You" on her television show.

Always Near You/Nowhere To Hide

Jeff "Skunk" Baxter guests on guitar, while Mitch Weissman and Joe Pecorino (both of Beatlemania fame) provide backing vocals with Richard T. Bear on piano. This "song" had originally been two separate pieces, one of which probably dated back to 1975, since it was a song-title that had appeared on one of Gene's song lists.

"Always Near You" runs some 2:33 before transitioning into the vastly different "Nowhere To Hide." The introduction of Mitch Weissman into the KISS camp didn't have an immediate impact, though during the 1980s he co-wrote copious quantities of material with Gene, Paul, and Eric Carr. Beatlemania was a tribute stage-show, and later movie, to the Beatles, and it is perhaps because of Gene's inability to get any of the real "Beatles" to appear on his album that he recruited the cast members representing Paul McCartney and John Lennon, respectively, who were enjoying popularity at the time.

Man Of 1,000 Faces

This song was written as a tribute to one of Gene's Hollywood horror film heroes, Lon Chaney, though by the time it was recorded, it had already been through the recycling machine. Parts of its original lyrics were used for "Got Love For Sale" and "Tunnel Of Love." The remaining parts, with lyrics which went: "I've got to tear your heart apart / I've got to finish anything I start / Because I haven't got a heart" and "I'm gonna take your love away / Gonna force you to stay / You wouldn't have it any other way" were simply discarded.

The only part of the original version to remain was the essence of the chorus. The 1978 form of the song became almost autobiographical in nature. When asked about whether this was the case by Kris DeLorenzo, Gene responded, "I think so. I think for the first time... although nobody's going to see behind the mask, what I'm trying to tell everybody is that it really isn't a mask. It's just one of the different faces, and everybody's got many, many different faces. And people are not the same with any two people. You always change the way you are with your parents which is not the way you are with your friends, which is not the way you are with your enemies... Everybody's got problems with different faces. With the face on stage everybody knows me, and it's just one of the faces. I think this album will be another" (Grooves, 1978).

Gene purportedly used the L.A. Philharmonic Orchestra on the track. He recalled, "One morning they [the orchestra] had arrived and were seated inside the recording studio ready to do their parts on a song I had written called 'Man of 1,000 Faces.' Sean had arranged to have them all wear Gene Simmons face masks, the ones that were for sale in stores. It was certainly one of the most bizarre moments in my life: to open the door and see a roomful of violin players all looking like me" (KISS & Make-Up).

Mr. Make Believe

Written while KISS were on tour in Detroit, Gene headed into a local studio to record the demo of this song. Like other songs on his solo album, this piece follows something of a theme in exploring his character while stylistically remaining acoustically flavored.

See You In Your Dreams

Gene re-recorded "See You In Your Dreams" because he was apparently not happy with the way KISS' version had turned out on "Rock And Roll Over." According to Gene: "I didn't like the way KISS did it" (Firehouse #58), and as a result he wanted to re-record it to make the recording "more powerful." Unfortunately, Gene wasn't particularly happy with this second version either: "In my head I heard much more a Humble Pie thing, but it came off sounding much poppier than that" (Firehouse #58).

Michael Des Barres sang backing vocals on the new version with Rick Nielsen of Cheap Trick making a guest appearance on lead guitar. KISS had already taken Cheap Trick out on the road with them during the "Love Gun" tour of 1977. Cheap Trick had also by then mentioned KISS in their classic song "Surrender" which had been released on their "Heaven Tonight" album in 1978.

When You Wish Upon A Star

This song was a sentimental tip of the hat to the Disney cartoons that helped Gene learn English soon after moving to America in 1958. According to Gene, "'Pinocchio' is everybody's story. If you can believe hard enough, your dreams can come true. Mine did" (Billboard, 1/20/79). Additionally, Gene's belief in the underlying message of the song — that all things are possible if you are willing to work on them and that opportunities are endless — embody the American dream, something that Gene certainly is an embodiment of. He recalled, "The lyrics are the heaviest lyrics that have ever been written because they can apply to anybody. Anybody who's got a dream can relate to them... But I think it's universal at the same time. It can be personal to everybody. It doesn't have anything to do with age or sex or anything" (Grooves, 1978). The Disney Corporation liked Gene's rendition commenting that they found it to be a "faithful and sensitive version" (Billboard, 1/20/79). With Gene hosting the re-launch of the movie at Fiorucci's in December 1978, one must wonder whether there was an arranged commercial tie-in...

The song was written by Ned Washington and Leigh Harline and was performed in the movie "Pinocchio" (first released in 1940) by Cliff Edwards, the voice of Jiminy Cricket. This song has also been covered by Louis Armstrong and Linda Rondstadt. When recording the song Gene was overcome with the emotion. Sean recalled, "If you listen (to Gene's version), you'll hear his voice crack, because at that point he was crying. I wouldn't let him re-record the vocal" (KISSaholics #16).

Rip It Out

The opening track on Ace's album is credited to Ace, Larry and Sue Kelly. Larry had been the lead vocalist in some of Ace's pre-KISS bands such as the Magic People and Cathedral. Larry also came in to the studio to sing backing vocals on the track.

So-called promotional copies of a single backed with "What's On Your Mind?" (Casablanca/Pye CAN-149) are modern pirate releases, since there was never any release of the single or any second single from Ace's album anywhere. Because "New York Groove" was still active on the charts, while the band were in the studio already recording "Dynasty," a second single wouldn't have made much sense with the next project and tour already well advanced. A second single, were it issued (and successful), could have been very problematic.

Speedin' Back To My Baby

Ace gave a song-writing credit on this song to his wife Jeanette. According to Ace's friend Bobby McAdams, "Ace would write a song (like 'Speedin' Back To My Baby') and would let her write a line and give her a song writing credit just to appease her" (KISS & Tell, p.102). Ace also experimented with backwards masking on the track. Ace recalled, "I'll tell you the story behind that. I cut a solo and I said to Eddie, 'Eddie, maybe we should try a backwards part here'? I thought that it would go with the sounds of the cars on the choruses and towards the end of the song. They are Ferraris, by the way — we had to wait a week to get tapes of them. Specifically, we needed Ferraris because Eddie is a racing car bug and so am I. So anyway, we tried playing a mediocre solo backwards and [engineer] Rob Freeman transferred it to a half-track. On unused tracks, when the part came up, he started up the other machine backwards to sync it up, and he hit it the first time. The parts fit perfectly, and that's what came out. Then we re-edited certain sections of it. The intro came in just fabulous, which was the end of the original solo. I was really happy with the way it came out — it just rips at the intro. It's funny, because it was the end of the solo and I was all out of ideas, but you turn it around and there is new life to it" (Guitar Player, 1979).

Backing vocalists David Lasley and Susan Collins were brought in to work on this song, "New York Groove" and "What's On Your Mind." David, in particular was an in-demand backing vocalist, songwriter, and singer who was working with the legendary James Taylor.

Snow Blind

While Ace's album was full of musical independence, much of the subject matter drew on what had become his life experience by that point: Dependence. In an interview on WPIX-FM's "Sunday Magazine," in October 1978, Ace amusingly suggested the song was about a snow storm.

Ozone

Ace didn't play bass on this track, one of only three songs that instead feature session player Will Lee. Ace played 12-string guitar on this track which again alludes to his recreational pursuits of a chemical kind. Also utilized was the ARP Avatar synthesizer. Ace recalled, "I called them [ARP] up and told them that I wanted to use their synthesizer and said that I would endorse it for them, and they said, ah, well, you know, they'd take $150 off the price, $200 maybe, and I said, Oh, I won't bother then. If they want to take a few hundred dollars off, big deal. [Ed. Note: An ARP spokesman responded that company personnel were pleased when they learned that Ace was interested in using their products, and they recognized that KISS could introduce synthesizers to a new, younger market; however, as a matter of policy ARP does not trade equipment for endorsements.]" (Guitar Player Magazine, Dec. 1978)It is interesting to note that both Will Lee and Anton Fig would in later years become members of "The CBS Orchestra / The World's Most Dangerous Band" led by bandleader Paul Schaffer for the David Letterman show. Will has also played on numerous other KISS-related albums including Felix Cavaliere's "Castles In The Air," Cher's "Take Me Home," Anton Fig's "Figments," Laura Nyro's "Nested" and Ronnie Spector's "Unfinished Business," to name a few.

What's On Your Mind?

Ace played 12-string guitar on this track. It was the third song to utilizing the background vocals of David Lasley and Susan Collins & Co.

New York Groove

This song had been originally recorded by the British band Hello in 1975. The members of this band included Bob Bradbury (Guitar & Lead Vocals), Keith Marshall (Guitar & Vocals), Jeff Allen (Drums and Vocals), and Vic Faulkner (Bass). The song was a Russ Ballard composition, inspired by his return to New York in 1975. However, the song wasn't written until Russ was in the studio working with the band. Produced by Mike Leander, the Hello version was released as a single and was a hit in Germany, spending 19 weeks on the charts and reaching #7. The song was included on the 1976 album "Keeps Us Off The Streets."

Ace's version barely differs from the original recording, in terms of arrangement, and stands as the only hit from the five singles released from the KISS solo albums. Minor lyrical changes were applied to the original song's first verse: "It's been a year since I was here / On the street I'm just passin' my time away / To the left and to the right / A town of stone grows to the sky / And it's outta sight, in the dead of night / Here I am again in this city / With a fistful of dollars / And baby, you'd better believe." It reached #13 during early 1979 during a 21 week run on the charts, the longest charting of any of the KISS solo singles. A disco mix of the song was completed, but never issued, since the band were originally unwilling to enter into the 12" singles market tightly associated with the "Disco" movement.

I'm In Need Of Love

The second of three tracks on which Ace would not play bass, with Will Lee providing that instrumentation. The demo was recorded in April 1978.

Wiped-Out

This song was written by Ace and Anton Fig. According to Anton, Ace had come up with the riff while the two were in the studio and added a verse to the growing song. Anton would write the rest of the words to the song to which Ace then made some additional changes. Interestingly, another song with a similar title, a classic surfing song from the 1960s, would be one of the songs Ace played in one of his earliest bands. This, the Surfaris recording of "Wipe Out," was originally released (London HLD-9751) in 1963.

The Surfaris instrumental version of the song reached #2 on the US Billboard charts in June 1963 and #16 in July 1966. Ace imitated the beginning of that classic hit on his introduction to his song, which certainly had little to do with surfing. With lyrics such as "I was gettin' drunk / the next thing I knew I looked at you / I was blind as a skunk, I was..." the source of inspiration is obvious! The recording of this song also features Will Lee on bass, and for the guitar solo Ace would use an old pawn shop Vox to attain the wah-wah effect. While Ace wasn't a big fan of using the effect for his guitar solos, he had first used it on "Rocket Ride."

Fractured Mirror

Ace's magnificent instrumental, setting the standard for his releasing one on each successive solo release. This track was the only one on the album to not feature Anton Fig on drums, with those duties being handled by Carl Tallarico. Bill Scheiniman performed the ominous atmospheric "bell" that appears at the beginning of the recording. According to Ace, "I used an old Gibson electric double-neck for that, a very rare one with a 6-string guitar neck and a mandolin neck. I don't think they make them anymore. On that intro I tuned the mandolin neck to open E and let it drone and resonate while I was picking the figure on the other neck. I don't think I've ever heard it on record before, that sound. We really got excited about that when I came up with it. I was also going through a Marshall stack that we were micing, so that's how we got a lot of the ambience" (Guitar Player Magazine, 1979).

Ace expanded on the natural effect: "I had a Marshall stack on 10; I stood just close enough to the amp so it wouldn't feedback, and I played the figure on the opposite neck, with the other neck's pickups on. And I had the strings on the other neck tuned to an open whatever key the song was in. What ended up happening is that the resonance of what I was playing was going through the wood and making certain harmonic sounds come out through the Marshall amp. I've never heard it anywhere else. It was just one of those flukes I just said, 'let me try this fucking idea'" (Fuzz, 1997).

All For Nothing (Demo)

This song is currently the only known out-take from Ace's solo album recording sessions dating from April 1978. Quite simply, the sound quality on the circulating 3:34 vocal version is atrocious, and it is near impossible to decipher what the lyrics may have been; other than the chorus sounding like it's repetitions of "All for nothing..." While there is lead guitar it's not clear whether this piece is a rehearsal or actual demo.

Two instrumental takes of the full track were mixed at Soundmixers Studio in New York. It is clear from the length of the song that the piece was a work in progress and that it is stylistically different to the other tracks that appeared on the final album. No lead work was over-dubbed on these bed tracks. The riffs and general structure marry up with the rehearsal piece validating its legitimacy. Bassist Larry Russell, who had been a close friend of Ace's from the 1960's, has recounted that he played bass on one track that wasn't used on the album, a blues jam recorded soon after Anton auditioned for Ace. While that track remains a mystery, this recording was certainly recorded early in the year, prior to the proper album sessions. Larry had been responsible for Ace's connection with Anton Fig, having auditioned for a band Anton was a member of, Siren. While he hadn't joined the band he took their demo to Ace having been impressed by Anton. Ace liked the drummer and had Larry bring Anton to an audition at Eddie Solan's studio.

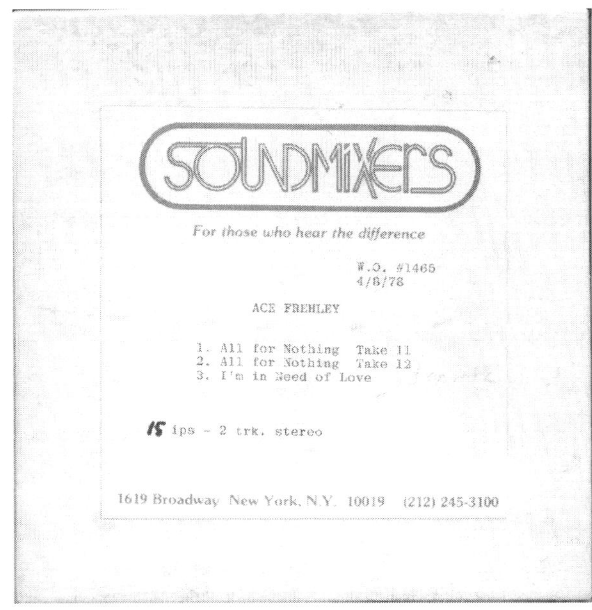

SOUNDMIXERS

For those who hear the difference

W.O. #1465
4/8/78

ACE FREHLEY

1. All for Nothing Take 11
2. All for Nothing Take 12
3. I'm in Need of Love

15 ips - 2 trk. stereo

1619 Broadway New York, N.Y. 10019 (212) 245-3100

Ozone (Demo)

The alleged demo that circulates in collector's circles is actually a recording of the song by another band... The Foo Fighters (actually Dave Grohl) used the recording as a B-side for their "Big Me" single off their debut album in 1995. Dave had not been a member of Nirvana at the time that band covered another KISS related song, "Do You Love Me?"

I'm Gonna Love You

"I'm Gonna Love You" was a slight reworking of a song that had originally started out during Peter's partnership with Stan Penridge and Michael Benvenga in Peter's pre-KISS band Lips. While there were minor changes between the 1970/1 demo and the version Peter used on his solo album, the basic essence of the piece remained. Stan performed some guitars, along with session player Art Munson, on the 1978 recording.

Noticeably, a new second verse was written for the song, with the original second verse becoming the third verse with slight lyrical changes: "Sayin' that you need me / Around you all the time (time)" would be changed to, "You know you're gonna find me (gonna find me) / Around you all the time (time)." Naturally, while the original version featured Stan on lead vocals, its folk feel would become more of a Bob Seger-styled song with Peter singing. The new arrangement added some 30 seconds to the song, resulting in a 3:18 piece.

Additional musicians on the recording included Bill Bodine on bass, Bill Cuomo on keyboards, and Tom Saviano arranging the horns. Tom later had then pre-KISS member Vinnie Vincent perform guitar during the sessions for on one of his "Heat" albums (the work wasn't released at the time). Backing vocals were provided by the Faragher brothers — Davey, Tommy, Danny, and Jimmy — and Maxine Dixon. The Faragher brothers, considered part of the "Blue-eyed Soul" movement, had recorded their 1978 album with Vini Poncia producing and had provided backing vocals for artists such as Melissa Manchester and Ringo Starr. Additionally, Art Munson had been the guitarist (along with one David Wolfert) on that album. One of the band's previous albums had been produced by Kenny Kerner and Richie Wise.

You Matter To Me

Written by John Vastano, Michael Morgan, and Vini Poncia. John Vastano had been a member of the Blue Jays, a Poncia produced band that had plenty of R&B horns and a rasping singer, almost a cliché, but fused soul and funk. The band were signed to Vini Poncia's record label, Map City, for an album release in 1971 before becoming White Water and releasing an album on RCA in 1973. This song was also recorded, with a stronger disco flavor, by Joey Travolta, who was the younger brother of the more famous John. His version was recorded in its original form — solely credited to Vastano and Morgan — on his Casablanca-distributed album earlier in 1978. While there are quite a few minor changes throughout, it is likely that Vini's writing credit was a result of re-writing the final two lines of both the second and third verses: "It has been said I'm a ladies' man / But there's only one way I understand" and "See how it feels to be missing you / I swear that's all it would take" respectively. Elliott Randall, who performed on Peter's album, also did session work on Joey's!

If any project draws together many of the participants on Peter's 1978 solo album, then one strong piece of evidence would be the 1976 Gino Cunico album released on Arista. The cast of characters appearing on that album, who also would work on Peter's album, makes it clear where many connections originate: The Faragher Brothers (backing vocals), Lenny Castro (percussion), Brie Howard (backing vocals), Vini Poncia (backing vocals & producer), Tom Saviano (horns arranger & saxophone), John Vastano (guitar), and David Wolfert (guitar). Invariably, this song is incorrectly titled "You Still Matter To Me" due to the lyrics.

Tossin' And Turnin'

"Tossin' And Turnin'" was the only cover included on Peter's album, having been written by Richard Adams and Malou Rene. The song was originally recorded by Bobby Lewis in late 1960 and hit #1 on the singles in April 1961. The song was performed by KISS live during the "Return of KISS" tour of 1979, even though it hadn't been featured on either of Peter's solo singles.

Peter was faithful to the original arrangement of the song, though he would change one lyric: "The clock downstairs was striking' four / Couldn't get you off my mind / I heard the milkman at the door" became "The clock downstairs was striking' three / Couldn't get you off my mind / I heard the milkman on the street." Naturally, this incorporated Peter's lucky number into the song. Musicians on the track were the same as the first two songs. Allen Toussaint and backing vocalists Maxine Willard and Julia Tillman enhance the feel of the song.

Don't You Let Me Down

According to Peter, "For anything on that album and for all the songs I wrote there was a lot of meaning behind 'em from 'Don't You Let Me Down' and all that type of stuff. I was showing my Beatles roots and my R&B roots" (KISS Hell, 1997). The song was credited to Peter and Stan Penridge, and arrangement changes were negligible from the 1972 demo recorded by Lips. That version had no harmonies on the first chorus which begins the song. The end of the Lips version also had fewer repetitions of the "fallin' down, down, down" lyric, with two additional repetitions of the chorus. Another of Vini's first-call session players, Lenny Castro made a guest

appearance on percussion on the recording. This song was released as a slightly edited single. The 3:20 edit simply started the fade-out earlier during the repetitions of "fallin' down, down, down."
While the song was written eight years before being recorded for Peter's album, he saw it as being about how he felt about his then second-wife-to-be, Debbie Svensk. Peter recalled, "She was absolutely gorgeous, you know, Playmate of the year, popular, absolutely gorgeous, but I always had this insecurity, and I really think that that's one thing I love about song writing is that you can really put it down, and no matter how many people maybe don't get to hear it or do get to hear it, somebody's got to relate to it somewhere" (Steve Gerlach, Cat Club, 1997). She was apparently present in the studio during the recording of the song.

That's The Kind Of Sugar Papa Likes

Another of the Lips-era remakes, with Peter replacing the vocal that had originally been sung by Stan. Minor changes to the song included the first verse being changed from "But now I love you, thinking of you / I sure do wish you'd come around" to "You know I love you, I really love you / Sure do wish you'd come around." A third repetition of the verse was added before the outro vocalization section. While both Art Munson and Stan played guitar on the track, Steve Lukather performed the solo. Steve ultimately performed on all three of Peter's Casablanca solo albums. One of Peter's choices for a producer for his album, disco guru Giorgio Moroder, rejected him after hearing several of the demos he and Stan had recorded for the album.

Easy Thing

The first of three songs on the album were credited as being produced by Vini Poncia, Peter and Sean. That credit is indicative of the original source of the material: Sean Delaney. While the song was written by Peter Criss and Stan Penridge, Sean recorded the original demo for Peter. The situation itself was not entirely happy according to Sean, who recalled, "So I'd go into the studio with all my friends, who were Paul Shaffer from Late Night [with David] Letterman, Elliot Randall (lead guitar player for Steely Dan), and Jeff "Skunk" Baxter (lead guitar player in the Doobie Brothers). So I had all of these hot musicians go out to the studio with me to record because I had to have the best to record (quickly) demos for Peter. So I recorded a bunch of demos for Peter, then he and Vini Poncia just used them! It caused a big stink between Peter and myself" (Steve Stierwalt, Jr.).

Rock Me, Baby

Sean Delaney recorded several demos of material for Peter by using studio session players he knew. Sean recalled that when he agreed to be Gene's solo album producer, Peter was upset at having already been rejected (Steve Stierwalt, Jr.) by one prospective producer, Tom Dowd. According to Sean, "Gene, knowing that all four albums had to do well and this type of publicity would not be good for the band, said that I could go into the studio with Peter and do some demo tapes for him so he could get a producer. We ended up doing my songs, and with that, he got himself a producer" (Otaku). According to an Aucoin memorandum to Peter, Sean agreed to split the royalties 50/50 while retaining his writing credit and ownership of copyright. Sean registered the copyright for his contributions in August 1978.

KISS The Girl Goodbye

Written by Peter and Stan Penridge, "KISS The Girl Goodbye" is not all sweet and niceness, as Peter explained in a Cat Club interview: "'KISS The Girl Goodbye' was about my first wife which I was really leaving to see my second wife" (Steve Gerlach). So unlike "Beth," this song really was about Lydia! On the Electric Lady recording for the solo album, Peter and Stan performed in a stripped-back manner similar to their Lips roots, with Peter playing percussion and Stan playing guitar and providing harmonies.

Hooked On Rock 'N Roll

Credited to Stan Penridge, Peter, and Vini Poncia, this was the final of the pre-KISS tracks recycled for the album. The differences from the older demo are quite noticeable. While the tense of the song would be changed to first person, the lyrical arrangement was also different. The first verse was changed to "The boy could play before he learned to grow / Worked in a band who had no name at all / Every mornin' at the break of dawn / You could see him draggin' home his drums / I was vaccinated with a Victrolla needle / And I'm hooked on rock and roll" from "Well now the boy could play like no one you'd ever saw (yeah) / Played in a band that practiced all day long / He told his mama that schoolin's gotta go / I've seen cases like this before / Your boy's been vaccinated with a Victrolla needle / He's hooked on rock and roll / Oh yeah, yeah, right."

I Can't Stop The Rain

According to Peter, "I get a lot of compliments on that song man and it really is funny through all the years that have gone by, that's the tune that people still say 'Jesus that is one great ballad'" (KISS Hell, 1997). The song was written by Sean Delaney and was one of the pieces that Sean had demoed with his well-known cast of session players. Richard T. Bear would guest on keyboards on the recording. This was also the first classic KISS era song to include a swear word, in the "It takes a witch to curse that goddamn sky" line. This is New York, yo!

Spotlights (And Lonely Nights)

"Spotlights (And Lonely Nights)" is the only known out-take from Peter Criss' solo album recording sessions (though various demos and alternate versions of the released tracks do exist). According to Peter, "It never got released. Sean Delaney is the only person I know who has it. What a great song that was, but people thought it was too depressing so the Company never released it" (KISS Army International via LF#80). But with lyrics like "Spotlights, and lonely nights / It's just a game I'm in / Wake up, in the morning / And I wonder, when will I see you again / And those rock and roll bars / And limousine cars / Just want somebody to hold / I don't need no friend with a helpin' hand / I don't need no drink, to help me pretend I'm alone," over a manic monotone piano key, it's not too surprising it was left off.

Simply put, the song was too graphical in a dark way for what KISS' audience were becoming. Even Peter admitted, "It was about how unglorified this life is. It was getting into this world, into this business, and then becoming a hopeless alcoholic or a drug addict, because it makes you that way, it turns you into an animal. The song had deep, deep lyrics" (Curt Gooch w/ Peter Criss, Firehouse #71). Perhaps, considering where Peter was heading in 1978 it was too ironic, regardless of what the record label thought.

Ultimately, Sean released the song on his 1979 album "Highway" (recorded in the latter half of 1978 while Sean was helping record demos for Peter's album). As a matter of discussion concerning the writing of the song in a June 29, 1978 memo from Bill Aucoin to Peter Criss, Sean had apparently agreed, "Spotlights (And Lonely Nights) - to be shared equally (50/50) for writers credit, copyright and royalties" (Aucoin). The version of the song recorded by Sean credits Richard T. Bear on piano, making it likely that Richard also plays on the demo with Peter's vocals. For release the song reverted to its sole writing credit by Sean, since the agreement with Peter was only applicable if the song appeared on Peter's album.

Tonight You Belong To Me

The majority of the first side of his solo album was recorded at Electric Lady Studios in New York, Paul's favored location for recording his demos. In discussions in Guitar Player magazine, Paul comments about some of this technical experimentation and the creation of the album: "I used the E Bow on quite a few [tracks]. I really found it incredibly useful. I don't know how practical it is for live performing, because you can only utilize it on one string at a time, which really makes it a little difficult. Most of the time on [the album] when there was an E Bow there was really between three and six of them over-dubbed. They were on 'Tonight You Belong To Me'; on the melodic line from the front of the heavy section, it's not a keyboard, it's the E Bows" (GPM, 1978). Steve Buslowe played bass on this and the first five tracks. Richie Fontana drummed on this and the first four album tracks. These tracks were nearly completely recorded in late-February 1978 (Sharp, Ken — BtM).

An alternative, perhaps rough mix, of the song circulates though it's known Paul remixed some tracks not being happy with the original efforts. The most noticeable difference on this version of the song is the acoustic guitar intro which is more basic (rough) and lacks the variable speed overlay (VSO) of the album version. Apart from that the two are essentially the same track with different production qualities.

Move On

Written by Paul Stanley and Mikel Japp. Mikel was the only co-writer credited on Paul's album, working on three songs with him. Mikel had been introduced to Paul by hearing some of his material via photographer Barry Levine, who suggested that the two get together to write. This song also featured the E-bow. According to Paul, "They come in around halfway through the solo; there's about six of them there" (Guitar Player Magazine, 1978). The backing vocalists on the recording were Diana Graselli, Miriam Naomi Valle, and Maria Vidal, in other words the "Rouge" part of "Desmond Child & Rouge." Rouge was a band that had been formed while the members was in college and were starting to build a following when they met Paul Stanley in New York.

Ain't Quite Right

Written by Paul Stanley and Mikel Japp. The third track to utilize an E-bow. According to Paul the purpose was a result of the tool providing "a certain kind of mood, like a haunting kind of sound. To me it's something like an oboe, or a synthesizer crossed with an oboe, and I've been fascinated with sounds like that ever since I can remember" (GPM, 1978). Interestingly, there are some similarities between the chorus of this song and Peter Frampton's "I'm In You" which has lyrics that go: "Cause you gave me the love, love that I never had / Yes, she gave me the love, love that I never had" (1977).

Wouldn't You Like To Know Me

Paul has admitted that this song paid homage to one of his favorite bands: The Raspberries. It contains elements that had defined their musical style, combining touches of their songs "Tonight" and "Ecstasy" (Sharp, Ken - Goldmine). Like the other so-called "Alternative Mixes," a second version of the song varies mostly by production qualities. However, it is some 20 seconds longer than the album version, having a third repetition of the chorus at the end of the song during the fade out, versus the album version, which starts fading on the second chorus repetition.

Take Me Away (Together As One)

Written by Paul Stanley and Mikel Japp. The song was recorded in Los Angeles with Carmine Appice on drums. Notably, Carmine had been in the band Cactus, which, for a short period, included session guitarist Ron Leejack who had also been a member of Wicked Lester. Carmine recalled, "I used to hang out with Paul. When they were doing the solo albums Paul asked me to play on his - so I did" (Metal-exiles.com). Peppy Castro sang backing vocals on this song.

An "Alternate Mix" of this song, in collector's circles, is some 16 seconds longer than the album version. Of the three so-called "Alternative Mixes," the differences between this and the album version of the song are most noticeable. Immediately, in the 25-second introduction there are multiple cymbal fills, rather than the single fill prior to the lead guitar and vocals beginning on the album version. Instead of ending with a simple fade out, as does the album version, this song continues the instrumental section before ending with an amp feedback section culminating in a single struck chord (tada). Like the other two "Alternate Mixes," there are no lyrical or other arrangement changes on this track.

It's Alright

Craig Kampf drummed and Eric Nelson played bass on this track and the rest of the album. This song was one of the last completed for the album. Paul used a D, B, G, D, G tuning with a Gallien-Krueger amp for the song, in an attempt to get a "Stonesy, ballsy rhythm sound" (Guitar Magazine, 1978).

Hold Me, Touch Me

"Hold Me, Touch Me (Think Of Me When We're Apart)" was the single released from Paul's solo album, backed with "Goodbye." Released in October 1978, the song didn't storm the charts and would falter at #46 during a 12-week stay. An interesting oddity would be available in the form of a miss pressed UK single, which accidentally included "Love In Chains" as the B-side. While being one of Paul's favorite guitar solos (Sharp, Ken - Goldmine), he also played all of the guitars on this track. According to Paul, "I wanted a very glassy sound, so I used an acoustic guitar strung with the high strings, and I capoed it at about the 9th fret. It's very, very tinkly" (Guitar Magazine, 1978). This was the second track on the album to include Peppy Castro on backing vocals.

Love In Chains

Produced by Paul Stanley and Jeff Glixman, this track featured a guest appearance by Steve Lacey on rhythm guitar. Steve also did some session work with Gene Simmons on his solo album.

Goodbye

Produced by Paul Stanley and Jeff Glixman. The song was supposed to be the B-side on the UK "Hold Me, Touch Me" single, but "Love In Chains" plays while the label details the former song. "Goodbye" was performed live during Paul's 1989 and 2006/7 solo tours, along with "Tonight You Belong To Me." Bob Kulick, who had played guitar on the original recording, was a member of Paul's 1989 solo band along with then future KISS drummer Eric Singer.

(U.K. Paul solo single sleeve)

Casablanca
Record and FilmWorks
BF 18636
(BZ 2409)
3'40
Kiss
℗ 1978 Casablanca Record & FilmWorks, Inc.
Side 1
IC 3272
GEMA
45 UpM
STEREO
Hold Me, Touch Me
(Paul Stanley)
Paul Stanley
From The Casablanca LP "Paul Stanley — KISS"
Produced by Paul Stanley

50 Fun Facts Relating To The 1978 Solo Albums

A list of random factoids pertaining to the KISS solo albums.
By Tim McPhate

Has your well of KISS knowledge run dry? Need some factoids to impress fellow friends and KISS fans? Here's a list of 50 completely random facts relating to the solo albums and the participants who played on the recordings.

1. "Gene Simmons" is the only album to feature one drummer throughout the entire recording. Allan Schwartzberg played drums on all of the songs (excluding "When You Wish Upon A Star").

2. "Paul Stanley" is the only 1978 solo album not to contain a cover song.

3. Richard T. Bear, Neil Jason, Steve Lacey, Elliott Randall, and Allan Schwartzberg are session musicians who performed on two of the KISS solo albums.

4. "Peter Criss" producer Vini Poncia is the only KISS producer to win a Grammy award. Poncia, along with Leo Sayer, won a Grammy for Best Rhythm & Blues Recording for Sayer's "You Make Me Feel Like Dancing" in 1977.

5. Casablanca Records spent $2.5 million on marketing support and collateral merchandising.

6. "Peter Criss" is the only solo album to spawn two singles: "Don't You Let Me Down" and "You Matter To Me."

7. "Ace Frehley" has sold the most copies since the implementation of Nielsen SoundScan in 1991. Frehley's album has sold more than 142,000 copies since 1991, followed by "Gene Simmons" (more than 93,000), Paul Stanley (more than 89,000), and Peter Criss (more than 71,000).

8. The KISS solo albums simultaneously shipped platinum upon their release in 1978 but did not reach the Top 20 of the Billboard 200 album chart. The following year, the RIAA began requiring 120 days from the release date elapse before recordings were eligible for certification, although that requirement has since been reduced and currently stands at 30 days.

9. "You Still Matter To Me" was covered by Joey Travolta, younger brother of John Travolta, on his 1978 self-titled debut album.

10. Guitarist (and KISS fan) John 5 covered "Fractured Mirror" on his 2010 album "The Art Of Malice."

11. "When You Wish Upon A Star" was originally written by Leigh Harline and Ned Washington for Disney's 1940 film "Pinocchio."

12. The Azusa Citrus College Singers participated on Gene Simmons solo album after Simmons approached Director Ben D. Bollinger to sing for Cher for her birthday in May 1978 at the Beverly Hills Hotel. The ensemble serenaded Cher with the Bread hit "If."

13. "Ace Frehley" held the longest stay on the Billboard 200 with 23 weeks. "Paul Stanley" was the solo album with the shortest stay on the chart (18 weeks). "Gene Simmons" spent 22 weeks on the chart; "Peter Criss" was charted for 20 weeks.

14. "Peter Criss" album participant Bill Cuomo co-wrote Steve Perry's solo hit "Oh Sherrie," which reached No. 3 on the Billboard Hot 100 in 1984. ("Paul Stanley" drummer Craig Krampf is also a co-writer on the song.)

15. "Tossin' And Turnin'" was first recorded in 1961 by Bobby Lewis. The song was authored by Ritchie Adams and Malou Rene. Lewis' recording spent seven weeks at No. 1 on the Billboard Hot 100 and was named the single of the year. Other artists who have covered "Tossin' ..." include Joan Jett and polka star Jimmy Sturr.

16. "Paul Stanley" features participation from Peppy Castro, Doug Katsaros and Bob Kulick. The trio would form the melodic AOR band Balance, releasing two albums "Balance" (1981) and "In For The Count" (1982). Paul Stanley sang (uncredited) background vocals on the charting 1981 single "Falling In Love," authored by Castro.

17. Michael Des Barres sings background vocals on Gene Simmons' "See You In Your Dreams." Des Barres was the frontman for the group Detective, a four-piece that opened select concerts for KISS in 1977. His previous band Silverhead played on the bill with KISS at the Academy of Music on Jan. 26, 1974.

18. "Hold Me, Touch Me (Think Of Me When We're Apart)" is the first ballad to be written and actually performed on record by Paul Stanley. Stanley also plays the guitar solo. "Hold Me ..." was inspired by a song authored by Doug Katsaros, who contributed background vocals, piano and strings to "Hold Me ..."

19. Tom Saviano arranged horns on four tracks on "Peter Criss": "I'm Gonna Love You," "Tossin' And Turnin'," "Rock Me, Baby." and "Hooked On Rock 'N' Roll." While with his own group, Heat, Saviano would later come into contact with future KISS guitarist Vinnie Cusano, who played a guitar solo on "What Does It Take," which was released in 2013 on "Heat Revisited."

20. Carl Tallarico plays drums on "Fractured Mirror," the only track on "Ace Frehley" not to feature drums by Anton Fig.

21. Michael Carnahan plays the saxophone solo on "Tossin' And Turnin'." Carnahan has played on recordings for such artists as Melissa Manchester, Leo Sayer and Dusty Springfield.

22. Members of the Azusa Citrus College Singers are featured on three tracks on "Gene Simmons": "True Confessions," "Always Near You/Nowhere To Hide" and "When You Wish Upon A Star."

23. "Peter Criss" contains four Stan Penridge-authored songs that date back to the group Lips: "I'm Gonna Love You," "Don't You Let Me Down," "That's The Kind Of Sugar Papa Likes," and "Hooked On Rock 'N' Roll."

24. Prior to painting the KISS solo album portraits, Eraldo Carugati painted one album cover: Rush's 1975 album "Fly By Night."

25. Plaza Sound Studios, the facility utilized for select recording, overdubs and mixing for Ace Frehley's solo album, was located on the seventh floor of Radio City Music Hall.

26. Out of the KISS members, Ace Frehley plays the most instruments on his album. Frehley played electric guitar, acoustic guitar, bass and synthesizer.

27. Guitarists Richie Ranno and Brendan Harkin played on Gene Simmons and Peter Criss' solo albums, respectively. The duo was in the group Starz, another Aucoin Management act.

28. Ace Frehley's solo album features the least amount of instrumentalists. There were four individuals who played instruments on the album: Frehley, Anton Fig, Will Lee, and Carl Tallarico.

29. Gene Simmons' solo album features the most instrumentalists. Including Simmons, there are 14 instrumentalists credited.

30. "New York Groove," written by Russ Ballard, was originally a hit for UK pop/rock band Hello in 1975, reaching No. 9 on the UK singles chart.

31. Curt Cuomo, co-writer of "Psycho Circus," among other KISS tracks, is the son of Bill Cuomo, who played keyboards and arranged and conducted strings on "Peter Criss."

32. Also in 1978, Vini Poncia produced actress Lynda Carter's debut album, "Portrait." Several musicians/professionals credited on Peter Criss' album also appear on this album, including Bill Cuomo, the Faragher Brothers, Art Munson, and Tom Saviano, as well as engineer Bob Schaper. Carter portrayed the lead role in the "Wonder Woman" TV series from 1975-1979,

33. Gene Simmons' cast of "special guests" on his album totaled 12, ranging from Cher and Janis Ian to Joe Perry and Bob Seger.

34. Steve Lukather, who plays two guitar solos on Peter Criss' album ("That's The Kind Of Sugar Papa Likes" and "Hooked On Rock 'N Roll"), is a co-founder of the group Toto. Toto released their debut solo album in October 1978.

35. "Ace Frehley" musicians Will Lee and Anton Fig are longtime veterans of the CBS Orchestra, the house band for the "Late Show With David Letterman." Lee joined the band in 1982; Fig joined in 1986.

36. Mike Stone, the executive engineer for "Gene Simmons" album, also mixed Paul Stanley's album and engineered select tracks on Peter Criss' album. Stone is best known for his work with Queen on such albums as "Sheer Heart Attack" and "A Night At The Opera." Stone died in 2002.

37. David Lasley, a background vocalist on "Ace Frehley," scored one Top 40 hit as a recording artist. The ballad "If I Had My Wish Tonight" reached No. 36 on the Billboard Hot 100 in 1982.

38. David Edward Byrd was commissioned to create the interlocking solo album murals. Byrd is best known for his work as the exclusive poster and program designer for the Fillmore East. Between 1968 and 1973, he created posters for artists such as Jimi Hendrix, Jefferson Airplane, the Who, Traffic, and the Grateful Dead.

39. Solo album portrait artist Eraldo Carugati was born in Italy in 1921. In 1996 Carugati suffered an aneurysm and was bedridden for 20 months before passing away at age 76 in 1997.

40. "New York Groove," the lone hit from the solo albums, was actually cut three times during the sessions for "Ace Frehley." One recording was cut at the Colgate Mansion in Sharon, Conn., and two additional recordings were captured at Plaza Sound Studios. The third recording proved to be the proverbial charm.

41. "That's The Kind Of Sugar Papa Likes" is a phrase originally used by Humphrey Bogart in the 1948 film The Treasure Of The Sierra Madre.

42. Anton Fig was referred to play on Ace Frehley's album by a bass player named Larry Russell. A friend of Frehley's, Russell met Fig during an audition for Fig's group at the time, Siren.

43. John Vastano, co-writer of Peter Criss' single "You Matter To Me," was previously in a Vini Poncia-produced band White Water.

44. "Paul Stanley" co-producer Jeff Glixman produced Kansas' classic "Dust In The Wind."

45. Rob Freeman, engineer for "Ace Frehley," once designed and installed a home recording system in Paul Stanley's uptown New York City condo.

46. The working model for the EBow, which Paul Stanley utilized on select tracks on his solo album, was officially debuted at NAMM in Chicago in 1976. The device produces a powerful infinite sustain, rich in harmonics that yield a keyboard-like sound.

47. Desmond Child is the sole member of Desmond Child & Rouge not to be featured on "Move On" on Paul Stanley's album. Child and Stanley would go on to develop a songwriting partnership, co-writing "I Was Made For Lovin' You" with Vini Poncia on 1979's "Dynasty." Stanley later introduced Child to Jon Bon Jovi, which led to Child's breakout success as a songwriter.

48. "Paul Stanley" drummer Craig Krampf played drums Kim Carnes' "Bette Davis Eyes." The song spent nine weeks at No. 1 on the Billboard Hot 100 in 1981 and won Grammys for Record and Song of the Year in 1982.

49. Ron Frangipane wrote and conducted the symphonic arrangements on "Gene Simmons." Frangipane arranged and conducted strings on the track "Dreams" on Sean Delaney's 1979 solo album, "Highway." He also arranged and conducted strings for Grace Slick's 1980 cover of the song.

50. Susan Collins is the female voice on "Speedin' Back To My Baby" on Ace Frehley's solo album. Collins also sings backgrounds on "What's On Your Mind?" and "New York Groove."

The 1978 Solo Albums Impact

The solo albums were illustrative of a bigger problem in the music business in late-1978...

September 18, 1978, a day that will live on in ignominy... Well, kind of. Few bands have a construct that results in each of the members becoming iconic enough, in their own right, to release solo albums. Usually, a band is dependent on the visibility or talent of one or two primary members. The Beatles were one such band. The closest that band came to releasing solo albums at the same time was the period September 25, 1970 through May 1971 when the former band members released "Beaucoups of Blues," "All Things Must Pass," "John Lennon/Plastic Ono Band," and "Ram," following the band's disbandment on April, 10 1970. However, by then the Beatles were obviously no longer an active band. Perhaps the Monkees were another such band, to a far lesser degree, certainly capable of such a feat. Some might add the Jacksons or Osmond family too. Yet, whatever the band or group, none had ever taken the unprecedented step of releasing four solo albums on the same day. Or three. Or two... But then again, none of those bands had Neil Bogart and Bill Aucoin behind them!

"The history of the world is but the biography of great men" (Carlyle) may be a theory of leadership long since superseded in the realms of leadership studies, but there does seem to be a certain amount of "divine inspiration" embedded within the story's foundation. Those two transformational leaders were imbued with incredible vision, determination, ethos of determination and no small amount of balls to gamble it all — even with a losing hand and just a poker face. *Cojones*, yes, but there was also no small matter of delusion. KISS were a band of incredible arrogance, but also a band of incredible determination and persistence. They had taken advantage of every little bit of luck that had taken them from a dingy little pub in Queens, New York, to the world-class stages of the Budokan or Madison Square Garden. They had also made their own luck rather than wait for it to arrive. Yet, there was a price to be paid for the Faustian-like deal with the Devil. While the roots of the band's decline, both musically and interpersonally, stretched back to their formation and development, the little man with the "End is nigh" sign was getting ready to make an appearance with the fat lady when the solo albums were included in the band's 1976 contract with Casablanca.

Neil Bogart was a wheeler-dealer par excellence. His track-record is mixed with an incredible run of successes: His moderate #58 chart hit with "Bobby" for Portrait Records in 1961, as a solo artist, or his coup in 1966 of snagging the distribution deal for the Tex-Mex garage band from Question Mark & The Mysterians' #1 single

"96 Tears" for Cameo Parkway Records (which was followed by the Bogart "directed" #22 hit "I Need Somebody"). He'd come to Cameo from MGM where he'd been a regional promotion manager who'd worked with Bobby Sherman; His role in the establishment of the Bubblegum pop movement while an executive at Buddah Records in 1967 with the 2-man production team: The so-called "Super K" guys, Jeff Katz and Jerry Kasenetz. Where Katz and Kasenetz came up with the term and produced the music Bogart was the one who seized on it and promoted it to death. Hits included The Lemon Pipers' "Green Tambourine" (written/produced by Colgate Mansion owner CRS Studio owner Paul Leka), 1910 Fruitgum Company's "Simon Says," The Ohio Express' "Yummy Yummy Yummy," and others that provide the signature to a brief musical movement. Outside of fads, Bogart had the pull to bring stars such as Curtis Mayfield and Gladys Knight & The Pips to Buddah. Neil had an ear for "big things," be they singles or new sounds like disco which he saw as "the new wave in the music business" (Billboard, 7/22/78). This probably goes some way to explaining KISS' flirtation with that sound in 1978/9. While not his ultimate gamble striking out on his own in 1973, with backing from Warner Brothers, was a major step in challenging the established mainstream record labels.

Bogart had gambled from the outset at Casablanca with his scattershot approach of signing anyone and anything with half a chance or less at success. He had survived the near catastrophe of the release of the Johnny Carson "Tonight" album long enough for roster artists such as KISS, Donna Summer, and Parliament build stability at the label through their rising popularity. Yet one need only look at the label's roster to see the amount of release fodder that never amounted to much in terms of either sales or popularity. Neil was aware of the paper thin foundations the perceived success of the label was built on. It was tenuous at best. The 1977 deal between Casablanca and PolyGram injected a large amount of cash into Bogart's hands, perhaps increasing a sense of infallibility at a label that seemed to operate under the standard of "spend, spend, spend!" The Jeff Franklin (ATI, who had been a major player in the establishment of Casablanca in 1973) deal was supposed to be a marriage of well-suited partners: According to Jeff, "They (PolyGram) understand how to spend money. And Neil understands how to take an aggressive approach to marketing" (Billboard, 12/10/77). And spend money doing so — with the deal he had other people's money to burn!

Unfortunately, that aggressive approach had to pay dividends, not just burn through cash. That Bogart could score an even larger payoff if profits rose in time for a full PolyGram buyout simply fueled what almost appears to be a decision to bluff at every opportunity, whatever the losing hand held, to bolster the label's profitability in the short term. As such, Bogart bullishly foresaw a record-breaking 1978, expecting some $75 million in sales (Billboard, 12/24/77), no doubt including a major contribution from his prime acts. Mixed in with all of the failures were the successful acts such as the Village People, Parliament, Donna Summer, and projects such as collaborations with Studio 54. Mac Davis, Lipps Inc., Santa Esmeralda, Cher, Captain & Tennille and Robin Williams were some of the small percentage of Casablanca's acts to score RIAA "Gold" awards (for whatever that accounts for when it isn't in the label's interest to accurately account for sales). KISS had also grown into a monster for the label. The costs involved in marketing the band's releases and turning them to profit were massive: "Casablanca now has to sell 750,000 copies before it breaks even on a new KISS album. The company's biggest expense goes for what can make or break a new record: promotion" (New West Magazine, 10/10/77). This, in part, may help explain why the risks were taken, and indeed deemed absolutely necessary.

By June 1979 Casablanca had shipped some 5,397,466 copies of the solo albums, including picture disks (accounting for nearly 75,000 of that number). It was a massive number that far exceeded the shipments of "Rock And Roll Over" and "Love Gun" combined to that point and even though they were backed by a $1.5 million promotion campaign, it was the last hurrah for Bogart at Casablanca. Other industry figures had publicly warned against such blatant *chutzpah*, "Bogart further explained that there are four KISS albums being released together and each is shipping one million. Each will feature a different member of the KISS group. Bogart said that from the four albums he expected to ship eight million by Christmas. Both Davis [Ed. Clive - Arista Records president] and Elektra/Asylum chairman Joe Smith advised Bogart to cut back his shipments to 750,000 per album" (Billboard, 9/2/78). Bogart could not be swayed, and record distributers fueled the false sense of market interest with large orders knowing that there was zero risk from their over-ordering when they were protected by returns policies. Combined with the economic downturn in the United States, PolyGram had enough invested in the company to later impose a more reasonable operating structure that resulted in cut backs to the many existing levels of excess including returns.

Immediately following the release of the albums PolyGram distribution changed their return policy on Casablanca product preventing returns until 180 days after release in an effort to keep product in stores longer and prevent over-ordering and over-pressing. The industry was, in general, at the end of the 1970s, were over-saturating channels with singles and other product of every description with albums rapidly appearing in bargain bins. Pressing vinyl had almost taken on the perception of minting coins, though like many pyramid schemes the reality was quite different. Mixed in with the pressing frenzy was a decline in the quality of the product with 1978/9 being many releases being marred by huge amounts of poorly pressed albums, affecting a number of popular artists. The transition between 1960 and 1978 from a 10% return to 100% return/exchange policy had changed the dynamic in favor of retailers who could easily over-stock with no risks other than their natural overhead for product storage. This was something that Bogart had leveraged in order to over-inflate the success of Casablanca's titles, and Casablanca had always been careful to protect their independent distribution channels. Bogart's (no doubt other labels operated in a similar manner) manipulation of a system that had initially benefitted him was in essence about to turn on him.

As part of PolyGram's machine Casablanca left that arrangement and had to play by another set of rules as PolyGram as started to build its own distribution network (by the early 1980s PolyGram had reduced the number of pressing plants from 20 to 4). Where Larry Harris alluded to Neil's "If I'm seen with famous people, I will be famous" (And Party Every Day: The Inside Story of Casablanca Records) attitude, the same could be said of his business attitude: Perhaps if Casablanca shipped enough copies product it will be successful. However, wishing it so wouldn't make it so; hence the phrase "shipping gold, returning platinum" that had described the 1974 Johnny Carson "Magic Moments From The Tonight Show" LP fiasco that had nearly torpedoed Casablanca in its infancy! Such a phrase seemed far more apt to describe the ultimate impact of the solo albums.

While 1978 was a turning point for the label, and industry, Casablanca's demise can't be solely blamed on KISS' solo albums. The decline of disco played a part, which the famed "Disco Demolition" night at Chicago's Comiskey Park on July 12, 1979, was symptomatic of a public shift against a style of music that was by that time five years-old. Casablanca had loaded its roster with disco acts, novelties, or generally unsustainable acts (Angel). The over-saturation of product in channels that PolyGram had wanted to prevent the return of included the "Grease" and "Saturday Night Fever" soundtracks and failures such as Robert Stigwood's "Sgt. Peppers" soundtrack on RSO. As had been the case with other fads, disco was dying out and Casablanca was already looking to Nashville with Casablanca West for their next big thing. That "Big Thing" was something that had been keenly on Bogart's radar, dating back to bubblegum where he could milk something for all it was worth before hopping on the next bandwagon. Coupled with the glut of albums, illustrated by the late-1978 production challenges for many pressing plants that were running at capacity, the period also saw the beginnings of the move to $8.98 product pricing.

In conjunction with oil price increases cutting into the bottom line for labels, plus production numbers, this presented a major challenge. A direct result of Casablanca's operating strategy, in 1979 the RIAA started modifying its certification requirements resulting in alums only being eligible for certification following a 120-day delay from July 1 (modified to 60-days in 1980). 1978 had seen 102 platinum albums (which 5 titles from KISS certified represented 4.9% of that total) up from a total of 68 in 1977. The changes were seen as a reaction to the gaming of the system with product such as the RSO "Sgt. Pepper's Lonely Hearts Club Band" soundtrack and KISS solo albums shipping platinum with massive return numbers.

Where do the solo albums fall in this messy industry period? They are often perceived as unnecessary product that permeated a perception of failure, which in turn further tarnished the image of both the band and label. That a solo album could have been considered as selling half as well as the then more recent KISS studio albums was probably pure delusion — as was the expectation that the fan demographic could necessarily afford four simultaneous releases. If nothing else it may have been wiser to have simply have staggered the releases or have pursued a format similar to that done in many markets with the "Best of the Solo Albums" compilations. The over-hyping of KISS was certainly nothing new, before or since, but the extremely poor performance would have brought many crashing back down to earth. The albums could be found in cut-out bins for nearly a decade following release even though they were soon being heavily discounted or exported en masse to markets that had not bothered to press domestic copies (UK). It could be argued that such a business impact also changed the corporate perception of the band. In the case of Ace Frehley, the solo albums certainly did more to make the case for his external success outside of KISS. He had fully trumped the members who were the visual focus of the band, those who were responsible for the majority of the material recorded by the band. While Peter's album should have reinforced that he was better off in the band. For further answers we perhaps need to look into the contract KISS signed with Casablanca Records...

The Solo Albums & the KISS Contracts

As many KISS fans know, the KISS solo albums were defined in various contracts the band signed with Casablanca in the years prior to them becoming an active project for the individual members. In this terse feature, we dig into the legal ramifications of the various contracts KISS signed in the years leading up to the solo albums.

There is a long-standing myth that the KISS solo albums were the result of the band's deteriorating interpersonal relationships following the "KISS Meets the Phantom of the Park" TV movie. As with many things KISS, the party line or historical myth blends truth with a heavy dose of fiction. Without doubt there had been a steady decline in the band's interpersonal relationships. The band had fractured into two ("Fractured Too"?) disparate factions: Gene and Paul, business oriented and focused; Ace and Peter, chemically affected, unstable, and marginalized from the business side of the band. The why the band was in decline interpersonally is pretty clear cut: The grind. The band had been maintaining a highly scheduled record and tour cycle for several years, and each contract sequentially adding to the overall demands on the signatories. While the TV movie may certainly have irreparably damaged the band's relationships, the groundwork for the solo albums went much further back than the tenuous timeline often provided for fairytale purposes. In fact, with the end of filming in late-May 1978 there was barely any time for the band members to then record solo albums in time for the August 5 deadline required for September 1978 release.

The wheels of business were in motion, advertizing campaigns budgeted, eating money, and progressing towards that date, well before any shooting had commenced for the movie. Simply, changing the scheduled release date for the albums would have resulted in an incredible financial hit to all parties, on top of the staggering amounts that had already been spent. The reality was that the majority of the solo album recordings were in well advanced states by that time, and in Gene's case had been completed, before filming commenced in May 1978. Only Peter's album was one of concern for meeting the deadline. Whatever the case in May/June 1978, the solo albums, themselves, had been considered and planned for years in advance of their eventual release date. They were explicitly defined in the band's legally binding contracts with Casablanca Records — then most recently negotiated in late-1976 and signed by the band in January 1977. They were certainly not a spur of the moment attempt to save the band.

Taking a step back to the beginning to set the stage, starting with the band's earliest contract, dated November 1, 1973, it should be noted that KISS were not a direct signatory with Casablanca Records, Inc. (then based out of Neil Bogart's 116

Central Park South penthouse apartments). Instead, that contract was between the label and Rock Steady Productions, Inc., signed by the band's co-managers Joyce Biawitz and Bill Aucoin. The band, instead, had entered into individual formal contracts with Rock Steady on October 15, 1973. These were modified with the evolution of Rock Steady into Aucoin Management, Inc., in May 1975. The initial contract period, spanning November 1, 1973 through October 31, 1974, called for the delivery of "one long playing album or 10 45r.p.m. record sides or their equivalent" — nothing particularly onerous or unreasonable. The original contract had specified in paragraph 21 to extend the contract by 1 year extensions for 4 years after the original period. The one major gotcha present in that contract, "additional recordings shall be performed by Artist and recorded by Company at Company's election," likely didn't become a concern until Neil Bogart requested the recording of "Kissin' Time" the following year. While having nothing to do with the solo albums at this point, the relationship between the label and band was tightly defined from day one. However, like many contracts, the November 1 agreement was not a suicide pact and the band and label renegotiated and modified on several occasions, as required.

A renegotiated contract dated May 1, 1975, directly between the band members and Casablanca Records, was for 1 year term with three additional separate 1 year extension options. It changed the language of the master delivery requirements, "of new material not previously recorded by Artist for two 12-inch, 33-1/3 rpm recordings having a playing time each of not less than 25 minutes nor more than 50 minutes." This remained standard language in the next contract. Interestingly, the penalty for failure to deliver the minimum number of masters was an automatic 120 day extension of the contract period after the delivery of the final master required to meet that contract's terms. Double albums only counted as a single album, and had to have the express prior written consent of the label before being delivered to the label. A slight carrot for the band, perhaps, was that if they managed to deliver two albums during each of the first two option periods, in the third they'd only have to deliver one — something that almost sounds like a vacation! The label also agreed to pay up to $40,000 in production costs, charged against royalties, for the creation of each album. In essence, contrasting the amount of material that KISS delivered to Casablanca between November 1, 1973 and April 30, 1975, the rate was simply unsustainable — even if a similar amount of new music was expected between May 1, 1975 and that contract's end during 1977. Casablanca exercised the first extension option in September 1975, binding the band through October 31, 1976. The option to extend drew attention to the 1973 contract exhibit "A" section 2 that stated the somewhat ominous, "the company may enforce Producer's rights directly against Artists if in the event Producer fails to enforce Producer's rights against Artist."

Running times of the first three studio albums had been and 35:15, 33:12 and 30:15 minutes respectively, creeping downwards towards the absolute minimum required even with the tricks of longer in-between song gaps. So, if fans have any complaints about the length of KISS' studio albums during that time, the guidelines had been explicitly defined since mid-1975 and were standard for the industry at the time. Perhaps that 1975 planned schedule could have worked, with the original intention having been to issue a Bob Ezrin produced studio album in November 1975. However, as soon as the next contract was negotiated Casablanca vice-president Larry Harris recalled, "As far back as mid-1976, when Glickman/Marks had arrived on the KISS scene, solo albums had been mentioned in their contract. Under the terms of their agreement... but releasing four solos at once, they would eliminate two full albums from their contractual obligations. For a long while, very little had been said about doing solo records, and the idea was largely forgotten, at least around our offices. Then, probably in the summer of 1977, the idea began to heat up and take shape, and by the beginning of 1978, Aucoin was pressing it hard. This may have been an attempt on his part to appease Peter and Ace, to soothe egos and repair the band mates' relationships. We hated the idea and did our best to stonewall Aucoin" (Harris, Larry - And Party Every Day: The Inside Story of Casablanca Records).

The late-1976 contract, immediately prior to the execution of the solo album option included the staggering requirement that he band had to deliver five albums during the contract period. The contract term was somewhat flexible, ranging from 2 years and 6 months to 3 years and 9 months depending upon the actual delivery of the albums, from June 1977. Album masters were supposed to be delivered either every six months or alternatively, if "Artist has given Company reasonable notice thereof, in writing" (Contract, 1/1/77). Failure to deliver the albums as required on the defined schedule would result in the automatic extension of the contract by a period of two months. Casablanca was also given an option to extend the contract for a period of 30 months once the fourth album of the contract was delivered. The contract also defined that multiple album sets would only count as one album against the contract, and that "'Best Of' albums shall not be deemed to reduce Artist's album recording and delivery commitment" (Contract, 1/1/77). Casablanca, however, retained the right to issue a "Best Of" album if the release schedule interval of the album requirements exceeded 9 months. Hence following the release of "Alive II," and the known gap that was required until the solo albums were released in September 1978, Casablanca was within its rights to release "Double Platinum." The first album delivered under this contract was "Love Gun," released June 30.

Section five of the January 1, 1977 contract specifically deals with "Individual Recordings," in other words, the solo albums. The contract defined the label's right to request a solo album from each of the members during the contract lifespan.

Importantly, the albums weren't valued against the five album minimum requirements of the contract in the same way a "KISS" recording would be. Instead, "such Solo Albums shall not be deemed compliance with part of the recording commitment... except upon delivery of every second Solo Album, in which case each series of two Solo Albums shall then count as one (1) delivered albums" (Contract, 1/1/77). However, the label did not consider the non-delivery of solo albums as a breach of contract, in other words they could request solo albums, but the band did not have to comply, or the band could push the label to request the albums, as Larry Harris as suggested was the case. Interestingly, the solo albums were governed by the same advances as the studio albums: Recoupable against royalty payment of $500,000 on delivery, "inclusive of all recording costs, payable at the rate of $15,000 per week" towards the next album commitment. The band was responsible for paying producers, and all costs in the creation of the product. The label was only responsible for mastering and the costs required for the manufacture of the product. In relation to the solo albums there was no specific requirement that the member's use Casablanca approved producers. A general catch-all was provided for the overall contract: "At each recording session, Artist agrees to render services hereunder to the best of Artist's ability, and Artist will make proper preparations for such sessions and will rehearse, record and rerecord the selected musical compositions and will comply with such instructions under the general direction of Company, or its duly authorized agent, until a master technically acceptable to Company is obtained" (Contract, 1/1/77). Whatever the case, four solo albums per the contract resulted in advances of some $2 million to the band, so there was without a doubt definitely more than just economic reason for the band to pursue the option: Striking off two albums off the contract requirements while appeasing interpersonal issues within the band. The money would be useful in feeding the ever-growing KISS machine too. Again, Larry Harris: "Solo albums were a lose-lose proposition for a record company. They rarely did well, so financially they made little sense, but by saying no to your artists you ran the risk of fracturing the always-fragile act-label relationship. KISS wanted to do four at once? No thanks. It wasn't until Bill implied that the band would break up if we refused that we finally agreed to it, but we were skeptical about their motives. We thought that they might be attempting to fulfill their contract with us quickly so they could find a new record company or that they were trying to force us into offering them a sweeter deal" (Harris, Larry - And Party Every Day: The Inside Story of Casablanca Records).

The financial horror of the 1/1/1977 KISS contract, for the record label at least, went further than simply amounting to the advances. The label had agreed to "provide an advertizing agency designated by Artist and approved by Company a budget of $350,000 for each Album delivered herein for advertizing and promotion of each Album recorded hereunder." Furthermore, "Company shall additionally expend the sum of $150,000 for each such Album for advertising and promotion (e.g. distributor advertising, trade publication advertising, etc.) Such sums shall not be deemed to be advances chargeable against royalties earned under this agreement." Howard Marks was an obvious beneficiary of section 25 of the contract, as no doubt was Bill Aucoin who received a cut as manager. Perhaps that was the plan. In one sense the solo albums were a pay off, that played against Neil Bogart's nature as a gambler. He had rarely folded in the face of pressure and had never been risk-adverse. The band's business had an insatiable financial appetite and simply had to keep being fed, regardless of the long-term damage that such a short-term escapade may have caused. There certainly is truth in the question, "who really wanted a solo album from any of the band members?" The magic about KISS was in the whole, rather than the parts, even if each of the members had highly identifiable personas through their make-up. Delusion meant that the grandiose ego-driven idea of four simultaneous releases was more important than the advice of close confidents such as Sean Delaney, who was soon on the outs with the band anyway. He'd suggested, according to Peter, that the other members each back each other on an album allowing each member the solo spotlight, but still presenting a unified band. Avoiding competition in the face of growing personal tensions couldn't be written into any contract, and the band had gone the path of "Alive II" to limit their studio time together as the relationships degenerated. Regardless, rock and roll lifestyles required money.

One clause would come back and bite the label in the post-solo albums aftermath when there were masses of returns to dispose of: "Records given away or sold by the Company at $1.00 or less, which shall not take place prior to one year after initial release of the applicable album master" (Contract, 1/1/77). This clause formed part of the band's case against PolyGram in 1982. According to Larry Harris, "PolyGram, unbeknownst to us or to KISS, sold the lion's share of the returns to discount retailers and flea markets, contravening the terms of our contract with KISS. If your albums landed in the cutout bin, it usually meant that you were finished. This certainly didn't help KISS's career... Years later, KISS would sure PolyGram" (Harris, Larry - And Party Every Day: The Inside Story of Casablanca Records). However, judging by the number of cut-out KISS albums, the over-shipping problem wasn't limited solely to the solo albums, even though the contract demanded no minimum number of albums pressed per title. KISS were awarded a whopping $520,000 by a jury on December 13, 1982 for PolyGram and their "predecessors in interest [Casablanca] engaging in massive and unwarranted over-shipments ... at distress of 'schlock' prices" (Billboard, 12/25/82). By then, such a paltry award was too little to undo the damage already done to the band.

Who's Who & What's What on the KISS solo albums!

By Julian Gill & Tim McPhate

The 1978 KISS Solo Album Roll Call: From the obvious to the obscure, learn more about the diverse cast of talented musicians, studio wizards, and various industry locations and professionals who contributed to one of biggest milestones in KISStory...

0 – 9

10 East 23rd Street

Noted on Gene's album liner notes. Better known as the address of the loft Gene and Paul rented to use for rehearsal space for the new incarnation of Wicked Lester they were planning in mid-1972. The auditions for a lead guitarist were held there in December 1972.

A

A Moveable Feast

Catering company (and also the title of a Fairport Convention album) thanked by Ace Frehley on his solo album liner notes.

Adamany, Ken

Cheap Trick's manager, thanked by Gene on his album notes.

Adams, Richard

Co-writer (with Malou Rene) of "Tossin' and Turnin'" on "Peter Criss." Better known as Richie, he wrote for numerous artists including Engelbert Humperdinck and Tom Jones.

Aliberte, Ric

Thanked on Gene's solo album liner notes, Ric was an Eastern Regional promotions executive at Aucoin Management involved in some of the crazier gimmicks such as staging an "accident scene" outside of A&M's Los Angeles HQ to promote Piper's "Can't Wait" album. He became an independent artist manager and was later Vice President of Pop & Rock Entertainment division of Skeleton Key Entertainment.

Allman, Elijah Blue

Cher's son with Greg Allman thanked on Gene's album liner notes.

Angie
Thanked on Gene's album notes.

Anderson, Ken
Thanked on Gene's liner notes. Aucoin Management executive who had worked with Bill Aucoin prior to KISS. Ken was responsible for the financial magic that kept the band afloat throughout the 1970s and was also their production manager, 1976 – 82. Anderson died December 15, 2013 in Florida.

Andrews, Punch
Thanked on Gene's liner notes, Punch was Bob Seger's manager who had been in Bob's early 1960's band The Decibels.

Annie's Tea
Thanked on the liner notes of Peter Criss' solo album.

Appice, Carmine
Carmine drummed on "Take Me Away (Together as One)" and had been working with Rod Stewart and was friendly with Paul. Carmine had been a member of Cactus, a band that briefly included guitarist Ronnie Lee Jack, prior to his involvement in Wicked Lester in 1971. He also worked with Vinnie Vincent prior to his recruitment by KISS (Carmine Appice's Rockers, 1980/1). During the 1980s Carmine was a member of King Kobra, for whom Peter Criss made a guest appearance on their "King Kobra III" album in 1988 on backing-vocals.

Aucoin Management, Inc.
(AMI) KISS' management company headed by Bill Aucoin.

Aucoin William, M. (Bill)
KISS' co-manager (with Joyce Biawitz, later Bogart) 1973 – 75, and sole manager 1975 – 82. Bill managed other acts such as Spider, Piper (who were signed instead of prospects Van Halen), Starz, and Bill Idol. Bill started out his career at public broadcaster WGBH in Boston. As director for Teletape Productions, Bill had won 6 Clio Awards, three Art Direction Awards, and a Hollywood Reporter Award by 1970 (Billboard, 10/31/70). By 1972 he'd teamed with Joyce Biawitz and formed the production company Direction Plus. They won a bronze award at the 16th International Film & TV Festival for a music promo for Tony Orlando & Dawn (with Bill as director and Joyce as co-producer). The team also produced a 13-episode TV program called "Flipside" through Direction Plus subsidiary Marks-Aucoin Productions. Thanked by Peter Criss and Gene Simmons on the liner notes of their albums. Bill had been responsible for getting the band a recording deal with the then new Casablanca records.

Azusa Citrus College Choir

Choir used on "True Confessions," "When You Wish Upon A Star" and "Always Near You/Nowhere To Hide" on Gene Simmons' solo album. Directed by Ben Bollinger.

B

B.O.C.

Blue Oyster Cult, for whom KISS had opened in 1974 and who were opening for KISS the following year thanked on Gene's album liner notes.

Balandas, Eddie

Thanked on Gene's album liners, Eddie was the "voice" who announced the KISS introduction at shows after JR Smalling left. He also served as a personal assistant of sorts to Gene (and Ace's bodyguard) outside of his role as security chief for the band. He continued in that role for other bands, but died in 2011.

Ballard, Russ

Born in Waltham Cross, Hertfordshire, England, Russ Ballard rose to prominence as the lead singer/guitarist for the English rock band Argent, with whom he wrote the hit "God Gave Rock And Roll To You" and sang such gems as "Hold Your Head Up." After leaving the band in 1974, Ballard turned his interests to songwriting and a solo career, with the former endeavor yielding hits such as Three Dog Night's "Liar" and Hot Chocolate's "So You Win Again." In 1975 Ballard teamed with pop/rock band Hello to record "New York Groove," which became a Top 10 hit in the UK. Three years later, in 1978, Ace Frehley scored the lone hit of the KISS solo albums with the song, which reached No. 13 in the United States. "New York Groove" became a signature staple for Frehley, who performed it live on subsequent tours with KISS and as a solo artist. Frehley covered another Ballard composition, "Into The Night," for his first post-KISS solo album, 1987's "Frehley's Comet."

Aside from Frehley, Peter Criss recorded two Ballard songs on his second post-KISS solo album, 1982's "Let Me Rock You": "Some Kinda' Hurricane" and the title track. KISS rebooted Argent's "God Gave Rock And Roll To You II" for "Bill & Ted's Bogus Journey" in 1991, with the song subsequently appearing on 1992's "Revenge." KISS' version became their highest charting single ever in the UK, reaching No. 4. Ballard's songs have been recorded by other artists such as Bay City Rollers, Roger Daltrey, Uriah Heep, Graham Bonnet, America, Santana, and Rainbow, among others. As a solo artist, Ballard's albums include "At the Third Stroke" (1979), "Barnet Dogs" (1980), "Into the Fire" (1981), "Russ Ballard" (1984), and "The Fire Still Burns" (1985). In the United States, he scored a Billboard Hot 100 entry as a solo artist with "On The Rebound," which hit No. 58 in 1980. His most recent solo album, "Book Of Love," was released in 2006. In 2012 Ballard earned Classic Rock Magazine's Classic Songwriter Award in recognition of his acclaimed body of work.

Ballou, Phillip

Background vocalist, and member of the gospel group Revelation (he also sang with Luther Vandross, Aretha Franklin, James Taylor and many others), who recorded parts for Ace's solo album which weren't used.

Barreto, Ines

Security helper for Ace Frehley for his solo album. Ines had worked security at the Capital Theatre in Passaic, NJ (along with John Harte and Rosie Licata).

Barth, Jim

2nd engineer at Sunset Sound Studio in Hollywood, CA for Peter Criss' recording sessions.

Baxter, Jeff "Skunk"

Guitarist on "Burning Up With Fever," "See You Tonite," "Tunnel of Love" (contribution not used), and "Mr. Make Believe." Jeff was a member of Steely Dan and the Doobie Brothers and also did numerous sessions.

Bear, Richard T.

In music circles, New York-born Richard Gerstein (aka Richard T. Bear) is known for being a fixture on the New York session scene and his work as a solo artist. His 1979 album "Red Hot & Blue" spawned the disco-flavored rock hit "Sunshine Hotel," which climbed the charts not only in the United States but overseas. Bear performed the song on the popular German TV show "Rock Pop." Bear recorded several additional albums, including 1980's "Bear" and 1984's "The Bear Truth." For Gene Simmons' solo album, Bear played piano on "True Confessions" and "Always Near You/Nowhere To Hide." On "Peter Criss," he played piano on the album's closing ballad "I Can't Stop The Rain." He also contributed piano to Sean Delaney's 1979 solo album "Highway." Other artists Bear has collaborated with include Cher, Billy Squier, Rick Moses, and Crosby, Stills & Nash. Fun fact: Bear made his acting debut in 1985 as Tim Stewart, a pilot who James "Sonny" Crockett busted for smuggling. Bear was on the board of directors for the Musicians Picnic, a clean and sober backyard barbecue that grew into an annual event that generated nearly $1 million in contributions.

Belkin, Jules

Concert promoter thanked by Gene on his album notes.

Benvenga, Michael

Added to the official dedication line of Peter's solo album following Ace, Paul & Gene. Born September 22, 1949, Michael had been the bass player in Chelsea and Lips, and the Brooklyn band The Wall, but had died in March 1977. He'd left the music to settle down and raise a family. Peter had once promised Michael that if he ever made his own album he'd have him play on it.

Bingenheimer, Rodney

DJ at Los Angeles KROQ who had booked Van Halen into the gig at the Starwood where Gene "discovered" them. Rodney, as part of the industry (or in his role as a rock socialite, the mayor of the Sunset Strip), had attended KISS' Mann's Chinese Theatre event in Hollywood in 1976.

Bishop, Steven

Recording artist connected with Chaka Khan thanked on Gene's liner notes. Steven was a guest on Saturday Night Live Season 3 #13 in March 1978 which included the famous "KISS Concert" skit with Art Garfunkel.

Block, Eric

Assistant engineer on Ace Frehley's solo album. Block is a professional sound engineer based in Chicago. He has recorded hundreds of records for independent artists and labels covering a wide musical range. Always sensitive to the unique needs of each project he works on, he would be glad to talk to you about yours. In addition to studio work, Block is a seasoned live sound vet and has mixed thousands of bands over the years.

Blue Rock Studio

Recording location of Gene Simmons' solo album in New York City, NY. Located on 29 Greene Street, in the area that became Soho, this studio was founded by Eddie Korvin in 1970 and operated until 1986. The New York Dolls, with original drummer Billy Murcia, cut some of their earliest demos at this facility in June 1972 with Marty Thau producing.

Bodine, Bill

Bill was the primary bassist on Peter's album, performing on all but three of the songs. A session player, Bill had also been a member of the LA country-rock act Funky Kings.

Bogart, Neil

Casablanca Records' President, thanked by both Gene and Peter on the liner notes of their respective albums. Neil, then head of Buddah Records appeared on Bill Aucoin's "Flipside" TV show in the spring of 1973, well before KISS came into his life. With the birth of KISS, Neil gave them unprecedented support and scope to develop their act and exposure. A flamboyant and fearless personality, Neil drove Casablanca to incredible heights in a relatively short period of time and had massive success with musical acts such as KISS, Donna Summer and Parliament. After leaving Casablanca Neil founded Boardwalk Records and signed Joan Jett whose #1 hit with "I Love Rock & Roll" book-ended a career that included #1s at Cameo (? & The Mysterians' "96 Tears"), Buddah (Lemon Pipers' "Green Tambourine" and others), Kama Sutra (Stories' "Brother Louie"), and the four Donna Summer #1s.

Born Neil Bogatz, Neil pursued a recording career with a minor label release in 1959. He scored a minor hit for Portrait Records, "Bobby," in 1961. Singles followed for other labels before Neil concentrated on music from the other side of the desk. His ear for music led to the emergence of "bubble gum" rock music fad, with acts like 1910 Fruitgum Co. and Ohio Express in the late 1960s. He died on May 8, 1982, aged 39, following a long battle with cancer (he'd had a kidney removed in the summer of 1981). Gene and Paul attended his funeral and sang as part of an all-star choir performing "Gonna Keep an Eye on Us," a song from Neil's first attempt at producing a Broadway show, "The First," a musical based on the life of ground-breaking baseball player Jackie Robinson.

Bogart, Joyce
Neil's wife, and originally KISS co-manager with Bill Aucoin (as Joyce Biawitz), thanked on Gene's liner notes. Joyce was a co-producer partnered with Bill for Direction Plus production company prior to her involvement with KISS.

Bollinger, Ben
Director of the Azusa Citrus College Choir who appeared on Gene Simmons' solo album. Internationally renowned and universally admired, the Citrus Singers program was founded in 1968 by Ben D. Bollinger. The mission of the Citrus Singers is "to cultivate, refine, and develop talent, preparing students to ascend to the highest ranks of the music industry." Bollinger, who was also the school's dean of fine and performing arts, retired from Citrus College in 2005. In 1985 he founded the Candlelight Pavilion Dinner Theater, which offers an array of entertainment from musical productions and children's workshops to a summer concert series. Situated in Claremont, Calif., the pavilion is a family business. Staff members include Bollinger's wife Lois, who is CFO, and his daughter Mindy and son Michael, who serve as assistant producer and general manager/vice president, respectively.

Bono, Chastity
Cher's daughter with Sonny Bono thanked on Gene's album liner notes.

Boutwell, Ron
From 1976 Boutwell Enterprises were responsible for KISS' tour merchandise producing the band's first tour book. Thanked on Gene's album liner notes.

Boyle, Jack
Concert promoter (founder of Cellar Door) thanked by Gene on his album notes. He became CEO of SFX Music Group.

Brand, John
Assistant engineer on Gene Simmons' solo album.

Brats, The
Thanked in Gene's album liner notes, The Brats were a New York band for whom KISS opened during the club days of '73. Fronted by Keith West, the band's guitarist was the former New York Dolls co-founder Rick Rivets. The line-up was completed by drummer Sparky Donovan and bassist Andy Doback. They released a single, "Be A Man" backed with "Quaalude Queen" in 1974. Following several line-up changes the band split in 1977.

Burbank Studios
Studio in Burbank, CA, the location of additional recording for Peter Criss' solo album.

Buslowe, Steve
On 1978's "Paul Stanley," Buslowe played bass on the first five tracks. After playing bass guitar in every corner of the globe and participating in enough New York and Los Angeles recording sessions to put 40 gold and platinum records on his walls, Steve Buslowe is happy to pass on his love of music to others. He recorded and toured with Meat Loaf from 1977-1997 - playing major venues in the UK, Europe, Australia, New Zealand, Iceland, Africa, the Middle East, and Japan - becoming musical director in 1988. He has songwriting, production, and background vocal credits on many Meat Loaf recordings, including 1977's multi-platinum "Bat Out Of Hell." He also performed live with such artists as Bonnie Tyler, Flo & Eddie, Luciano Pavarotti, Simon Le Bon of Duran Duran, and Dolores O'Riordan from the Cranberries. As a session player, he can be heard on No. 1 hits with Meat Loaf, Celine Dion, Bonnie Tyler, and Air Supply, and recordings with Barbra Streisand, Aldo Nova, Southside Johnny & The Asbury Jukes, and Blackjack (a project featuring Michael Bolton and Bruce Kulick), among others. A multi-instrumentalist, the Connecticut-based Buslowe puts his years of touring and recording experience to good use today as a music instructor, working with students of all ages and abilities on bass, guitar, rock piano, improvisation, music theory, and computer-based recording and songwriting technique.

Byrd, David Edward
Graphic artist/illustrator who created the solo album mural posters. In early 1968, Tennessee native David Edward Byrd signed on as the exclusive poster and program designer the Bill Graham's new Fillmore East. Between 1968 and 1973, he

created posters for artists such as Jimi Hendrix, Jefferson Airplane, the Who, Traffic, and the Grateful Dead. In 1969 Byrd created the commemorative poster for the legendary Woodstock festival. That same year he designed the graphic for the legendary Rolling Stones 1969 tour that tragically ended at Altamont. In 1970 he began his career as a Broadway poster designer and over the next 20 years would do many Broadway & Off-Broadway shows, including Sondheim's "Follies," "Godspell" and "Jesus Christ Superstar." In 1978 Byrd was commissioned by Howard Marks Advertising to create the interlocking mural posters that were included in each of the four KISS solo albums. From 1970 to 1979 Byrd taught at both Pratt Institute and the School of Visual Arts. In 1991 Byrd took the position of senior illustrator at Warner Bros. Creative Services, which he held for exactly 11 years. Besides creating illustrations, backgrounds and style guides for all the Looney Tunes and Hanna-Barbera characters, Byrd created commemorative plates for the Franklin Mint, souvenir posters for the "Batman" franchise of films, and style guides for feature films such as "Space Jam" and "The Wizard of Oz," television shows such as "Friends" and "Scooby Doo," and the Cartoon Network. Today, Byrd resides in Silver Lake, a suburb of Los Angeles.

C

Cafe Geiger
German New York café, once located at 206 East 86th Street known best for its cakes for which Gene was well known to have a propensity for, thanked by him on his album notes.

Camp Surprise Lake
Properly Surprise Lake Camp, a Jewish camping & youth program in Cold Spring, NY that Gene attended during the summers as a youth. He thanked the program on his album liner notes. It had been at this camp, in 1956, that Neil Diamond meets folk singer Pete Seeger who inspires him to start writing songs. Other notable alumni of the camp include Walter Matthau, Neil Simon, Jerry Stiller, and Larry King. Gene recounts his experiences at the camp in "KISS & Make-up."

Carlson, Rich
Security helper for Ace Frehley for his solo album.

Carnahan, Michael
Player of the baritone sax solo on "Tossin' And Turnin'." Michael had also played with Melissa Manchester who Vini Poncia had produced throughout the mid-1970s.

Carugati, Eraldo
Artist responsible for the KISS solo album cover paintings. Eraldo was an Italian artist imprisoned by the Nazi's during the Second World War. He immigrated to the US in 1949 plying his artistic trade out of Oklahoma City before moving to Chicago

as a commercial illustrator. With work published in Playboy, Newsweek, Time, The New Yorker, and other magazines Eraldo found success across both sides of the Atlantic. He also created the cover of Rush's "Fly by Night."

Casablanca Records & Filmworks

KISS' record label, 1973 – 82. Founded by Neil Bogart with Bucky Reingold, Larry Harris, and Cecil Holmes in 1973 as "Casablanca Records" with distribution via Warner Bros. records, the label was independent by late summer of 1974 (though rumors of Neil splitting from Warner were published in December 1973 before the label had even released any product). The "Filmworks" moniker was added in late-1976 when Casablanca merged with Peter Guber's Filmworks production company. The new company scored a hit with the movie, "The Deep," the follow-up to the original "Jaws" movie. In 1977 Neil sold part of Casablanca to PolyGram for a reported $10 million, resulting in the label being absorbed by the German/Dutch conglomerate in 1979. The label has shuttered in 1983 as PolyGram moved the remaining artist to other subsidiary labels such as Mercury Records.

Cassidy, Shaun

Thanked on Gene's album notes. One of the bands Gene was working with in 1978 was Virgin which included Dirk Etienne (vocals), Tom Moody (guitar), and Chuck Billings (drums). They were managed by Aucoin and Gene utilized Chuck as a drummer on some of his demos at the time. The band had toured with Shaun, who may have been a prospective guest due to his "heart-throb" status at the time.

Castro, Lenny

Lenny is a session percussionist who performed on "Tossin' And Turnin'" and "Don't You Let Me Down" on Peter's album. Born in Puerto Rico and raised in NY, Lenny moved to LA in the late 70's "and started to break-through the studio scene together with the guys from Toto, Neil Stubenhaus, John JR Robinson, Vinnie Colaiuta, Nathan East and other studio legends. Some of first high-profile jobs were touring with Stevie Wonder, Diana Ross and Boz Scaggs (at the time where he had a huge hit with 'Silk Degrees'). In the early 80's, and throughout his career, Lenny played on many hits from Toto, most notably 'Rosanna' and 'Africa.' Over the years, he has recorded and/or toured with Karizma and Los Lobotomys (his pet projects with David Garfield), Fleetwood Mac, Stevie Nicks, George Duke, George Benson, Oasis, The Crusaders or Mick Hucknall. Most recently he worked with Maroon 5, Noel Gallagher, Adele (on her smash hit '21') and Joe Bonnamassa."

Castro, Peppy

Peppy Castro has done it all and is a successful seasoned professional with great variety in his music. His fame and first hit record began at age 17 as one of the founding fathers of the legendary rock group, the Blues Magoos. His rock and roll status led him to a starring role in the original Broadway production of "Hair." He is also Emmy-nominated and an award-winning playwright and multi-instrumentalist, having penned and/or performed hundreds of well-known jingles for decades for Budweiser, Chevy, Bounty, Nestlé's Crunch, and Kodak, among others. His songs have been recorded by the likes of Diana Ross and Cher, among others. On "Paul Stanley," Castro contributes background vocals to the single "Hold Me, Touch Me (Think Of Me When We're Apart)" and "Ain't Quite Right." He'd met Paul through a mutual female acquaintance (Carol Kaye), though he'd also known Ace Frehley well before KISS and had given him guitar lessons! He was later a member of Balance with Bob Kulick and Doug Kasatoros and made a guest appearance on Ace's "Trouble Walkin'" album. He was also the co-writer of "Naked City" from KISS' "Unmasked" album. Castro has also collaborated with artists such as Laura Branigan, Michael Bolton, Liza Minnelli, Ronnie Spector, Joan Jett, Richie Havens, John Denver, Aldo Nova, David Johansen, and Darlene Love, among others. Castro has enjoyed years of diverse music as an original member of the bands the Blues Magoos, Balance, Wiggy Bits, and Barnaby Bye, who is newly inducted Long Island Music Hall of Fame. Castro is also an associate producer for the new off-Broadway show "The Gong Show Live." He recently released his latest solo album titled "Just Beginning." The album features longtime friend Joey Kramer from Aerosmith on two tracks and Aerosmith guitarist Brad Whitford on one track. In an interesting twist, Castro recorded audio liner notes for the album, allowing listeners to gain first-hand perspective regarding the creative process for the songs while listening to the album.

Catherine
Thanked on Gene's album notes.

Cavazos, John
Known as John Caleb in theatrical circles, John is a well-known voice teacher, vocal coach and session singer in the Orlando, Fla., area. A trained dancer and singer, Cavazos made his Broadway debut in the 25th anniversary production of "My Fair Lady" with Rex Harrison. He was chosen by Stephen Sondheim to appear in a leading role in "Pacific Overtures," in which he received unanimous rave reviews from critics including Frank Rich of "The New York Times." He made his debut at Carnegie Hall with Marilyn Horne in the opera "Tancredi." In addition to performing with Seven, Cavazos also performs with the gospel group ReGeneration and has appeared in concert with the Orlando Philharmonic as well as the West Coast Symphony. Originally from Los Angeles, he is an alumnus of the renowned Citrus College Singers ensemble and attended Brooklyn College Conservatory of Music in New York as an opera and vocal performance major. He is also currently an adjunct music professor at Rollins College in Winter Park, Fla. He was a member of the Azusa Citrus College Choir appearing on Gene Simmons' solo album.

Chavarria, Paul
Early KISS roadie/guitar tech (1974 – 79) who stayed with the band long after they became successful. Thanked on both Peter and Gene's album liner notes. In recent years Paul has worked as Production Director for tours for artists such as Alice in Chains.

Checker, Chubby
Famed recording artist of the 1960's thanked on Gene's liner notes. Chubby had provided Gene his first introduction to Rock 'N' Roll in 1962 with his hit "The Twist."

Cher
Gene's girlfriend at the time, and guest vocalist, providing the screeching telephone voice on "Living In Sin."

Cherokee Studios
Recording location of Gene Simmons' solo album in Los Angeles, CA. Opened by the Robb brothers in 1973 the studio was a 16-track facility that had a highly modified Trident "A" board.

Clarice
Thanked on Gene's liner notes.

Clark, Dick
Legendary US music industry/TV figure (America's oldest teenager) who gave KISS their first national broadcast on his "In Concert" on ABC TV show in 1975. Gene thanked him on his album liner notes. Dick would continue to support the band throughout their career, and after his passing in 2006 Gene recalled, "He made it a point to come up to our small, cluttered dressing room, stretch out his arm, and say - 'If there's anything you need, just let me know. It's a pleasure to have you here'. And he smiled. And I never forgot the kind gesture. Since that day, because of him, I have tried to always offer a kind word to young talent starting out in their career. Dick Clark made the world a better place."

Collins, Susan
Backing vocalist on "Speedin' Back to My Baby," "What's On Your Mind," and "New York Groove," with David Lasley. Collins is a singer/songwriter who started out a cappella on the streets of Brooklyn in the '60s and went on to work with Jimi Hendrix, Joe Cocker, Ace Frehley, Todd Rundgren, NRPS, Electric Light Orchestra, John Lennon, SNL, and more. In "You Can Take The Girl Out Brooklyn," Collins tells her remarkable true life musical story: emerging from singing a cappella on the street corner of her Brooklyn housing project in the 1960s to an insider's career as a singer songwriter, working with the likes of Jimi Hendrix, Todd Rundgren, Brian Wilson, KISS, ELO, John Lennon, and more. Featuring three stellar background

singers and piano accompaniment, the audience gets an up close and personal view of pop culture history through her alternately humorous and touching experiences: in a landmark Greenwich Village coffeehouse, flying in and out of Woodstock, singing comedy with NBC's Not Ready for Prime Time Players, arena rock shenanigans on the road with the Electric Light Orchestra, minting gold records as a session singer, show biz heartache at the hands of a vengeful record company executive, and ultimately, happiness in a fulfilling personal life as a wife and mother, still singing at the top of her game. Collins was the voice of NFL image advertising in the 2011 – 12 season and gives master classes with students on TV, Broadway, and, beyond.

Columbia Record Productions (CRP)
Test pressing manufacturer for Ace Frehley's album.

Contessa, Maria
KISS costume designer thanked on Gene's liner notes. Maria owned a costume store in New York City and was approached by the band to help with the costumes in 1973. She even toured with the band during the 1979 "Return of KISS" tour to maintain the complex designs, notably Gene's.

Coronel, Steve
Thanked on Gene's liner notes, Steve was one of Gene's childhood friends. He would be the responsible party for introducing Gene to Paul Stanley and was the first guitarist in Wicked Lester having played in bands with both, separately. Later, songs which had been co-written with Steve ultimately appeared on "Hotter Than Hell" and "Dressed To Kill."

Coventry
Thanked on Gene's album liner notes, the location of the first KISS concert on Jan. 30, 1973. The Coventry, also known as the Popcorn Pub prior to January 1973, was located at 47-03 Queens Boulevard near 47th Street. A home for the early New York glam movement, many bands cut their teeth at the venue including the New York Dolls, Blondie, the Dictators and Ramones. The club became a disco in May 1976.

Criscoula, Joseph
Peter's father, thanked on the liner notes of his album.

Criscoula, Loretta
Peter's mom, thanked on the liner notes of his album.

Criss, Lydia
Peter's wife (1970 – 79) thanked on the liner notes of his album. Gene Simmons also thanked her on his album notes.

Criss, Peter
KISS drummer and vocalist.

Cuomo, Bill
Bill was the primary keyboard player (on six tracks) on Peter's album having worked with Vini on Lynda Carter's debut album earlier in the year. He also arranged the strings on "I Can't Stop The Rain" and "Easy Thing," and played synthesizer on "You Matter To Me" and "Don't You Let Me Down." His session work had included Buffy Sainte-Marie, Walter Egan, and Rick Springfield. He later co-wrote Steve Perry's "Oh Sherrie."

D

D'Amico, Frank "Cheech"
Assistant engineer on Gene Simmons' solo album. Frank worked at Cherokee Studios in Hollywood, CA in the late 1970s.

Daisy
Thanked on Gene's album liner notes, club venue in Amityville, Long Island, where KISS performed in 1973.

Davis Jr., Sammy
Famed entertainer and member of the "rat pack" with Frank Sinatra, Dean Martin, Peter Lawford, and Joey Bishop. Gene had wanted him as a guest on his album and thanked him on his album notes.

DeCarlo, Joe
Cher's manager, thanked by Gene on his album notes. Joe had also managed Sonny & Cher and had been Gregg Allman's best man at his and Cher's wedding in 1975.

Delaney, Melanie
Production coordinator for Gene Simmons' solo album.

Delaney, Sean
KISS choreographer, guru, and co-writer. Sean produced Gene Simmons' album and received a co-producer credit on three songs on Peter Criss' album, two of which he had composed. Sean's material recorded with Peter was supposed to be demos to solicit a new producer, but were used for the album anyway. Sean also sang backing vocals on Gene's album. Peter had wanted Sean to produce his album, after being rejected by Tom Dowd, but in the interim Gene had recruited him.

Delsener, Ron

Concert promoter who was to the East Coast what Bill Graham was on the West. Thanked on Gene's album liner notes, Ron had promoted many of KISS' most notable concerts, to that point, including their home-coming to New York City at Madison Square Garden on February 18, 1977. With 19,600 attending the sold-out show grossed $145,000.

Des Barres, Michael

Background vocalist on "See You in Your Dreams." Michael Des Barres has been on the rock and roll scene for more than four decades. A European Marquis, Des Barres was raised in England and now lives in Los Angeles. His enduring love of delta blues and the rock and soul of the mid-'60s beat boom, carries forth from his days as the front man for such seminal '70s bands as Silverhead (with whom KISS shared bills, opening for Savoy Brown, in 1974) and Detective, a band personally signed by Jimmy Page to Led Zeppelin's Swan Song label in 1975 and who opened for KISS in 1977. He recorded the demo for "Mongoloid Man" with Gene and Joe Perry. Des Barres was also the touring singer for the Duran Duran spin-off group, the Power Station, which performed at Live Aid in 1985. Meanwhile, Des Barres has been ever-present on screens large and small for more than five decades. From plum roles in the beginning with "To Sir With Love," he has guest-starred in countless TV shows such as "WKRP In Cincinnati," "Melrose Place," "Seinfeld," "Ellen," and as beloved, long-running characters on "Roseanne" and "MacGyver." He continues to delight fans with his recent roles on "NCIS," Bones" and "Nip/Tuck."

Recorded and mixed in only 10 days, Des Barres recent studio album, "Carnaby Street," is pure, unadulterated rock and roll, inspired by his experiences in the late-'60s/early-'70s. Steven Van Zandt of SiriusXM's Underground Garage and the right-hand man of "The Boss" himself has been a very vocal champion of the album. The album is available at Amazon and iTunes. He also has a weekly radio show, "Roots & Branches with Michael Des Barres," which explores the origins of rock and roll, soul, jazz, and hip-hop and their influences on popular music. Des Barres keeps in close touch with his fans via his extremely active Facebook and Twitter accounts.

Di Carlo, Yvonne

Actress who famously played the role of "Mrs. Munster" in the famed U.S. television series, "The Munsters." Thanked by Gene on his album notes.

Diggs, Benny

Background vocalist, and member of the gospel group Revelation (he also sang with Luther Vandross, Aretha Franklin, James Taylor and many others), who recorded parts for Ace's solo album which weren't used.

DiMarzio, Larry
Musical instrument pick-up designer thanked by Gene on his album notes.

Dixon, Maxine
Backing vocalist on "Tossin' And Turnin'" and "I Can't Stop The Rain" who had worked with Julia Tillman (her sister) on the "Elliot Lurie" album in 1975, and Looking Glass and DC Larue.

Doobie
Thanked on Gene's album notes.

Dogramajin, Seth
Thanked on Gene's liner notes, Seth was childhood friend of Gene's who had been involved in Gene's sci-fi fanzines. He was also a member of the Long Island Sounds with Gene and Stephen Coronel. Seth died in 1998.

Douglas, Allen
Assistant engineer on Gene Simmons' solo album.

Dowd, Tom
While Tom died on October 27, 2002 he was already a legend by 1978 when he was first choice as producer of Peter Criss' solo album. He'd produced Ray Charles, Aretha Franklin, Young Rascals, Rod Stewart, and numerous artists in Peter's preferred genres, following his start in the industry for Atlantic in 1947. He declined to participate.

Duncan, Robert
Music journalist for Creem Magazine thanked on Gene's liner notes. Robert was later author of "KISS," a 172-page book about the band published in 1978.

E

Eisenberg, Franny
Backing vocalist on Gene Simmons' album Franny was a member of the "Group With No Name" and later Bette Midler's Staggering Harlettes (with Linda Hart and Paulette McWilliams).

Elayne
Thanked on Gene's album notes.

Electric Lady Studios
Studio in New York City, the location of the recording of four basic tracks each for both Peter Criss' and Paul Stanley's solo albums. Electric Lady Studio was the location where Peter Criss had first met Paul and Gene in 1972, and the location of

the band's first recording session in March 1973 - their demo. Gene thanked the studio on his album liner notes.

Eli
Gene's step-father thanked on his album notes. Gene's mother had remarried after Gene left home and went to college. Gene discusses Eli in his "KISS & Make-up" book.

Elias, Chuck
Thanked on Peter Criss' liner notes, Chuck was a KISS tour drum technician who also fulfilled a handyman role living with Peter. Chuck worked with KISS from 1974 – 79 and left with Peter to become his stage manager. Ultimately that role wasn't required. Chuck has since appeared on the KISS Expo circuit.

Ezrin, Bob
Producer of "Destroyer" thanked by Gene on his album notes.

F

Famous Monsters of Filmland
Horror fanzine first published in 1958 that Gene had enjoyed in his youth. He thanked them on his album.

Farragher, Danny
Backing vocalist on Peter Criss' album. The Farragher Brothers were a blue-eyed soul band whose debut album had been produced by Vini. He considered the vocalists his studio songbirds and had used them in other sessions such as Lynda Carter's debut. Interestingly, KISS producers Kenny Kerner and Ritchie Wise were recruited to produce the second Farragher Brothers album...

Farragher, Davey
Backing vocalist on Peter Criss' album.

Farragher, Jimmy
Backing vocalist on Peter Criss' album.

Farragher, Tommy
Backing vocalist on Peter Criss' album.

Fedco Audio Labs
Fain Electronic Devices Company. Remote recording equipment providers for Ace Frehley's sessions in CT. The company was based out of Providence, RI, and was founded by Lyle Fain in 1969. The company was soon providing recording services

throughout New England, notably at the Fillmore East in New York City. Fedco did several live recordings for Led Zeppelin via Eddie Kramer. And KISS' "Alive!"

Fields, J.B. (Joel Barry)
A former KISS tour truck driver who died in a head-on collision, with a car on the Oglethorpe Bridge, on April 11, 1978 while on tour with Blue Oyster Cult. The effort to avoid a slowed vehicle resulted in the rig plunging off into the Chattahoochee River, near the Columbus Municipal Auditorium in Georgia. He had driven with band's lighting equipment on a 2-day 550 mile drive from Little Rock, Arkansas. Paul dedicated his solo album to his memory.

Fields, Totie
Comedienne, who famously sparred with Gene on the Mike Douglas show in 1974, thanked on his solo album liner notes. Where Gene had attempted to come across as demonic and intimidating ("I am evil incarnate"), middle-aged Totie had put him in his place with the line, "Wouldn't it be funny, if underneath all this (makeup) he was just a nice Jewish boy?" The coup de grace, in response to Gene's weak, "You should only know," was "I do, you can't hide the hook!" Totie died on August 2, 1978.

Fig, Anton
Born in Cape Town, South Africa, Anton Fig — "The Thunder from Down Under" — began playing drums at age 4. After moving to Boston to further pursue his musical interests, Fig attended the New England Conservatory of Music in Boston, studying both jazz and classical disciplines and graduating with honors in 1975. In 1976 he moved to New York where he began to establish a career as a freelance musician. In 1978 Fig was recruited to play drums on Ace Frehley's solo album, adding a key element that helped shape the album's hard-edged soundscape. Fig was subsequently brought into the KISS fold to play "ghost" drums on 1979's "Dynasty" and 1980's "Unmasked," though his participation was kept a secret for many years. Fig is also credited as the co-writer of "Dark Light" on 1981's "Music From 'The Elder.'" Around this time, Fig was a member of the New York-based pop-rock outfit Spider, which featured songwriter Holly Knight (who would later collaborate with Paul Stanley). The group recorded two studio albums, scoring a Top 40 hit with "New Romance (It's A Mystery)." He later hooked up with Frehley, taking the drum stool in Frehley's Comet from 1984 – 1987. Since 1986, Fig has been the drummer in the CBS Orchestra, the house band for "Late Show with David Letterman." During this tenure he has played with scores of great artists, including Miles Davis, James Brown, Bruce Springsteen, Stevie Winwood, Bonnie Raitt, and Tony Bennett, among others. The CBS Orchestra is also the house band for the Rock and Roll Hall of Fame induction ceremonies, playing with some of music's most influential personalities.

Fig's discography as a studio musician is both extensive and impressive, including work with artists such as Bob Dylan, Mick Jagger, Cyndi Lauper, Madonna, Gary Moore, Joan Armatrading, Rosanne Cash, Joe Cocker, John Phillips, Warren Zevon, Sebastian Bach, and Paul Butterfield. In 1996 Fig released a drum instructional video and book titled "In the Groove" and "Late Night Drumming," respectively. In 2002 Fig released his debut solo album, "Figments." Produced and co-written by Fig, the album represents three years of work and features collaborations with, among others, Richie Havens, Brian Wilson, Ivan Neville, Sebastian Bach, Ace Frehley, Al Kooper, Chris Spedding, Donald 'Duck' Dunn, Blondie Chaplin, Paul Shaffer, Chris Botti, Randy Brecker, and Richard Bona. More recently, Fig played drums on albums by guitarists Oz Noy and Joe Bonamassa. He also played on Frehley's 2009 solo album, "Anomaly." Today, Fig continues to be an in-demand studio and live musician and is currently recording and composing for numerous projects.

Flo & Eddie

(Mark Volman, Flo, and Howard Kaylan, Eddie) Founding members of The Turtles (a 60s band) who had become radio personalities in the 1970s. They introduced KISS (completed in their own make-up designs) at their major stadium appearance at Anaheim on August 20, 1976, a show that 43,000 attended grossing an impressive (at the time) $437,653. Thanked on Gene's album notes.

Fontana, Richie

Native New Yorker Richie Fontana was the drummer for Piper, a five-piece power pop group that was managed by Bill Aucoin. Fronted by Billy Squier, the group released two studio albums, "Piper" (1976) and "Can't Wait" (1977), and opened select dates for KISS in 1977. As a member of the Aucoin Management family, Fontana was selected by Paul Stanley to play drums on the first four songs on his 1978 solo album. Fontana subsequently joined forces with KISS creative guru Sean Delaney in the Skatt Brothers, a pop-rock/dance group that issued 1979's "Strange Spirits" via Casablanca Records and scored a hit, "Life at the Outpost," in Australia in 1980. He also worked on Paul's first production project, the Alessi Brothers, and was considered as a replacement for Peter Criss. Fontana subsequently played drums for platinum-selling solo artist Laura Branigan from 1983 – 1985. Branigan was best known for Top 10 hits such as "Self Control," "Solitaire" and "Gloria." In 2002 Fontana issued his debut solo album, "Steady on the Steel." Produced and arranged by Fontana, he also performs nearly all the instruments and vocals. Despite rumors to the contrary, he never recorded with KISS for the "Dynasty" album.

Foxe, Cyrinda

Thanked by Gene on his album notes. Wife of David Johansen, of New York Dolls fame, with whom Steven Tyler had an affair in 1978. They married later that year.

Frangiapane, Ron

Symphonic arrangements and conductor of the members of the New York and Los Angeles Philharmonic Orchestras on Gene Simmons' solo album. Ron was responsible for the creation of the demonic introduction section to "Radioactive." Ron had also worked on the Lyn Christopher album in 1972, Gene and Paul's first professional recording credit.

Franklin, Jeff

Thanked on Gene's liner notes, Jeff was the head of ATI who expanded the company beyond the scope of talent booking. Jeff had worked with Neil Bogart, dating back to his Buddah days in 1968, and had helped with financing the formation of Casablanca Records in 1973. He later arranged the deal selling a share of Casablanca to PolyGram.

Freeman, Rob

Engineer on Ace Frehley's solo album recording sessions at Plaza Sound Studios. Rob also mixed the album with Eddie Kramer. From 1974 until 1979, Rob was head engineer and part owner of Plaza Sound Studios, a classic recording facility situated atop Radio City Music Hall. His years at Plaza Sound coincided with the advent of New York's punk rock and New Wave scenes and Rob was uniquely positioned in the middle of it all as recording engineer on such seminal albums as the Ramones' debut album Ramones, Blondie's Blondie and Plastic Letters, and Richard Hell and the Voidoids' Blank Generation. Throughout his Plaza Sound years, Rob made records with an array of artists including KISS, Ace Frehley, Rupert Holmes, Twisted Sister, Salsoul Orchestra, Robert Gordon, Link Wray, Martha Velez, Sunny Fortune, Genya Ravan, John Miles, The Laughing Dogs, and many more. In 1979 Rob began the free-lance chapter of his career that continues to this day. Early free-lance projects had him recording albums with KISS, Julie Brown, and The Elektrics and mixing a Top 40 single for Agnetha Faltskog of Abba.

In time, Rob made the jump from engineer to producer, and, over the decade that ensued, produced singles, EPs, and/or albums for Twisted Sister, Lawrence Gowan (currently of STYX), Tim Moore, Jailbait, Single Bullet Theory, Regina Richards, The Go, Surgin', and Queen City Kids, among others. Notably, Rob co-produced, engineered and mixed Beauty and the Beat, the debut album by the Go-Go's that went multi-platinum, topped the US Billboard album charts at #1 for six weeks, spawned two hit singles, was the first #1 album by an all-girl group who wrote their own songs and played their own instruments, and, incredibly, was crowned the CMJ (College Music Journal) Top Album of the Decade 1980-1990. Rob's efforts over those busy years garnered him a variety of acclamations and awards such as Billboard's Top 15 Producer of the Year (1982), Pro Sound News' Engineer of the Year (1983), Pro Sound News' 2nd Runner-up Producer of the Year (1983), one RIAA Gold Single, two RIAA Gold Albums, two RIAA Platinum Albums, two BPI Gold

Albums, one CRIA Gold Album, one CRIA Platinum Album, and eight Ampex Golden Reels. Today Rob resides in Florida with his wife Teresa, Broker/Owner of Florida Realty Elite. Though still taking on occasional music projects, Rob has refocused his sound recording skills to include production sound for feature films, documentaries, commercials, and broadcast television shows.

Frehley, Ace
KISS’ lead guitarist and vocalist. Ace is credited with lead and background vocals; lead, rhythm and acoustic guitars; guitar synthesizer; bass; and co-producer on his album.

Frehley, Jeanette
Ace's wife, given a co-writing credit on "Speedin' Back to My Baby." Ace also thanked her for her "love and understanding" on the rear cover of the album. Gene Simmons also thanked her on his liner notes.

Fresca
Thanked on Gene's album notes.

Friedman, Lee
Thanked on Gene's album notes. Management operations for Boutwell/Niocua, KISS' merchandising partner from 1977 after Bill bought into the ownership of the company. According to Ingo Floren in his "The Official Price Guide to KISS Collectibles" book it was Lee's concept to marry KISS & Bally for a KISS-themed pinball in January 1978 though the company's initial response was not positive.

Frondelli, Michael
Assistant engineer to Dave Wittman on "Tonight You Belong To Me," "Move On," "Ain't Quite Right," and "Wouldn't You Like To Know Me." Michael, who had worked with Paul Stanley's pre-KISS drummer Neal Teeman as engineers on Johnny's Dance Band album in 1977, became head of operations at Electric Lady by 1980 and was later a VP at Capitol Studios and Mastering in Hollywood. He also worked with acts such as Oingo Boingo and Joe Jackson.

G

Gallin, Sandy
Thanked on Gene's liner notes, Sandy became Michael Jackson's manager in 1990. Sandy also managed other artists such as Mariah Carrey and Dolly Parton. He had been an executive producer on NBC's "The Paul Lynde Halloween Special" featuring KISS in 1976.

Gatza, Dolores

Thanked by Gene on his album notes, Dolores worked for Glickman/Marks Management.

Gerstein, Richard

See Richard T. Bear.

Gibson Guitars

Endorsed by Gene Simmons on his solo album. Gibson had been among the first group of musical businesses endorsed by the band in 1975, on the rear cover of "Dressed to Kill." The band, the company's only direct purchasing act, had even visited the factory in Kalamazoo in March 1975 and received custom guitars and basses (including a custom EBO bass that had been discontinued in 1959 for Gene). Naturally, Paul also broke plenty of Marauder guitars on tour...

Glickman, Carl

Thanked on the liner notes of Gene and Peter's albums, Carl became one of KISS's business managers (Glickman/Marks) in May 1976, managing the band's money and finances, a role he'd fill until 1988. The two had been associates dating back to a common past in Cleveland, OH. Carl died in early 2013 at age 86.

Glixman, Jeff

Jeff Glixman has produced and mixed albums for artists such as Kansas, Gary Moore, Yngwie Malmsteen, the Georgia Satellites, and Black Sabbath, among others. Combined sales for his projects have exceeded 30 million units. Glixman was a vocalist/keyboard player in White Clover, a band that evolved into Kansas. His first production was the 1975 Kansas album "Song For America." Glixman would go on to be a key creative contributor to Kansas, producing subsequent albums such as "Masque," "Leftoverture" and the quadruple-platinum "Point Of Know Return." Glixman helmed Kansas' classic chestnut "Dust In The Wind," which is one of the most played songs in rock radio history. His discography also includes Gary Moore, "Victims of the Future"; Georgia Satellites, "Georgia Satellites"; Black Sabbath, "Seventh Star"; Yngwie Malmsteen, "Odyssey"; and Blackmore's Night, "Under a Violet Moon," among others. Glixman has also worked on projects for artists such as Allman Brothers, Eric Clapton, Ludacris, Marvin Gaye and Bob Marley & the Wailers. In addition to his production career, Glixman's love "of all things studio" led him to play an integral role in the development, operation and ownership of professional recording studios throughout the world, from Axis Sound Studios in Atlanta to Caribbean Sound Basin in Trinidad and Star City Recording in Bethlehem, Pa. In 2013 Glixman and Kansas were inducted into the Kansas Hall of Fame, an honor coinciding with the group's 40th anniversary. Glixman is the co-founder of Pennsylvania-based Producers Institute of Technology, "the new standard in next-generation media arts colleges."

Goldberg, Danny

Thanked in Gene Simmons liner notes, Danny had done PR for KISS' "Rock And Roll Over" album (as Danny Goldberg, Inc.), prior to Aucoin Management taking over that function in the mid-1970s. He came back to the band in the early 1980s as a creative consultant and later became President of Mercury Records during the Reunion era. In recent years he has moved on to artist management as president of Gold Village Entertainment.

Goldsmith, Lynn

Celebrity photographer thanked by Gene on his album notes.

Grasselli, Diana

A talented recording artist and vocal producer, and a budding screenwriter and film and stage actress, Diana Grasselli recorded two albums for Capitol Records in 1979 with the popular East Coast group Desmond Child & Rouge. Their Top 50 single, "Our Love Is Insane," with its funky bass, infectious beat and Grasselli's soaring lead vocal, rocked airwaves and dance floors throughout the United States. For Paul Stanley's 1978 solo album, the female component of the band — Grasselli, Maria Vidal and Myriam Valle — sprinkled their talent on the album's second track, "Move On." After a successful national tour and appearances on several contemporary television shows, including "Saturday Night Live," Grasselli appeared with Vidal and Valle in the hit Broadway show, "Gilda Radner - Live from New York at the Wintergarden Theatre." Grasselli has also lent her shimmery vocal sound to artists such as Dionne Warwick, Luther Vandross, Cher, Belinda Carlisle, Alice Cooper, Chynna Phillips, and Ronnie Spector. Uniting with Desmond Child & Rouge, she performed at the opening event for the 2008 Songwriters Hall of Fame induction ceremony, where Child was presented with his induction into the organization. Now based in Minneapolis, Grasselli has owned, directed and been the primary instructor for Chanson Voice & Music Academy since 1999, and has instructed, directed, counseled, mentored, and produced performances and recordings for thousands of young vocal and theater artists and teachers. She recently debuted her signature vocal technique, "The Vertical Voice Vocal Method Series."

Gray, Diva

Backing vocalist on Gene Simmons' album who had also worked with Doug Katsaros, Aretha Franklin, Bette Midler, and BB King.

Greenan, Laurie

KISS wardrobe designer thanked in Gene's album notes. Laurie worked with Maria Contessa.

Grimaldi, Rick
Executive in Charge of Production on the "KISS Meets the Phantom of the Park" TV movie. Rick, who had worked in TV from the early 70s, worked for Aucoin Management and was enlisted to help the band and script writers to improve the movie script dialogue (CK Lendt).

Grody, Gordon
Backing vocalist on "Rock Me, Baby" and "Easy Thing." Gordon was an aspiring disco/funk artist who did session work with Sean Delaney, John Blair, and Vicki Sue Robinson. He also appeared on Gene Simmons' album.

Gruen, Bob
Photographer who had been responsible for the "Hotter Than Hell" album cover photographs thanked on Gene's liner notes.

Grupp, Paul
Engineer, with Jeff Glixman, of "Love in Chains" and "Hold Me, Touch Me" on Paul Stanley's solo album. Throughout his career Paul often worked with producer John Boylan recording artists such as Charlie Daniels and Air Supply.

H

Haber, Danny
Guitarist in Gene's first band, Lynx/The Missing Links, who is thanked on Gene's album liner notes.

Hap, Syd
Thanked on Gene's album notes. Syd was a renowned sculptor, doll maker and created the KISS (and Cher) marionettes.

Harkin, Brendan
Brendan Harkin was a guitarist for New Jersey-based rock band Starz, an act Bill Aucoin managed from 1975-1977. Signed to Capitol Records in 1976, the group scored their lone Top 40 hit, "Cherry Baby," from 1977's "Violation," which was produced by Jack Douglas. Aside from Starz, Harkin has worked as a session musician on recordings for artists such as Kool & the Gang, among others. Also adept in the recording studio, Harkin has engineered recordings for artists such as Crystal Gayle, Beegie Adair and Grammy winner Michael W. Smith. In 2003 Harkin and guitarist Richie Ranno joined drummer Joe X. Dube and vocalist Michael Lee Smith for select Starz reunion concerts on the East Coast. The reunion was documented via the concert DVD "Back in Action: Live 2003." Today, Harkin owns and operates Wildwood Recording, a private music studio located on 13 acres of Franklin, TN, farmland. Recruited through Sean Delaney, Brendan provided guitar sweetening throughout Peter's album, but was only credited on "Easy Thing."

Harline, Leigh
Co-writer, with Ned Washington, of "When You Wish Upon A Star," from the 1940 movie "Pinocchio" recorded by Gene Simmons.

Harpoon Man
Thanked on Peter Criss' liner notes.

Harris, Larry
Thanked on Gene's liner notes, Brooklyn-born Larry Harris began working for Buddah/Karma Sutra Records in 1971 as the local New York promotions representative. In 1973 he joined his cousin Neil Bogart in founding Casablanca Records, ultimately ascending to executive vice president and managing director in 1976. Harris left the label in 1979. In 2009 he published "And Party Every Day: The Inside Story of Casablanca Records" (Backbeat Books, 2009), the definitive, first-hand look at the label's remarkable story. Today, Harris resides in Seattle.

Harrison, Julie
Thanked by Gene on his album notes.

Harte, "Big" John
Head of KISS' security, 1975-88, and Ace's production coordinator thanked on his solo album. John returned to work with KISS, during the 2003 tour with Aerosmith, and later did security with Peter Criss. Gene also thanked him on his album's liner notes.

Heidi
Thanked on Gene's liner notes.

Hemingway, Margeaux
Daughter of the writer Ernest Hemingway, and actress, thanked on Gene's liner notes.

Hope
Thanked on Gene's liner notes.

Howard Marks Advertising, Inc.
Howard Mark's company responsible for the design of the packaging of the solo albums.

Howell, John Shane
John plays the classical guitar segue between "Radioactive" and "Burning up with Fever."

Hunerberg, Don
Assistant engineer on Ace Frehley's solo album. He is now a veteran recording engineer, whose extensive list of credits included working at Radio City Music Hall and recording the music for the Macy's Thanksgiving Day Parade since 1976.

I

Ian, Janis
Vocalist singing the Latin section of the "Radioactive" introduction. Janis, another graduate of Paul's Manhattan High School of Music and Art, had a penchant as a solo artist for dealing with taboo subject matter, had several critically acclaimed hits and performed on the first ever broadcast of Saturday Night Live in 1975.

Ienner, Jimmy
Executive producer of KISS' "Double Platinum" thanked by Gene on his album notes. Jimmy ran C.A.M. Productions U.S.A., a publishing, management and production company in addition to being a producer. He had appeared, along with the Raspberries (who he was producing), on Bill Aucoin's "Flipside" syndicated TV show in mid-1973. His record label, Millennium, partnered with Casablanca in 1977, though he had left the partnership in late 1978 to team with RCA.

Interlaken Inn
Hotel in Sharon, CT where Ace, Eddie, and John Harte stayed during sessions at The Mansion.

Iovine, Jimmy
Jimmy was a producer who was one of Peter Criss' first choices for his solo album. In 1978, still relatively new in the industry, Jimmy had already worked with John Lennon, Meat Loaf and Bruce Springsteen.

Issak, Barbara
Assistant engineer on "Love In Chains," "It's Alright," "Goodbye," and "Take Me Away (Together As One)" on Paul Stanley's solo album. Barbara is an award winning sound engineer who was one of the early female engineers to break into the industry in the mid-1970s starting out at the Village Recorders in Los Angeles. She'd work with Frank Zappa during the recording of Sheik Yerbouti, Joe's Garage Act I, Joe's Garage Acts II & III and was a part of "The Utility Muffin Research Kitchen Chorus" (KillUglyRadio).

J

Japp, Mikel
Welsh musician who wrote material for The Baby's (featuring John Waite) produced by Ron Nevison. Mikel was introduced to Paul by photographer Barry Levine. Mikel co-wrote "Move On," "Ain't Quite Right," and "Take Me Away

(Together as One)" with Paul and returned as a co-writer, with both Paul and Gene separately, in 1982. Mikel also worked with Michael Des Barres and Steve Jones for their Chequered Past project and continued to write material for other artists, and perform solo, until his death in January 2012.

Jason, Neil
An Electric Lady Studios session player, Neil plays bass on "I Can't Stop the Rain," "Rock Me, Baby," and "Easy Thing" on Peter Criss' solo album. He also played bass throughout Gene Simmons' solo album. Born and raised in New York City, Neil Jason is a professional bassist, producer and composer. He played bass throughout Gene Simmons' 1978 solo album and on select tracks on Peter Criss' album. His resume includes work with artists such as John Lennon, Yoko Ono, Billy Joel, Roxy Music, Bryan Ferry, Hall & Oates, Mick Jagger, Pete Townshend, Charlie Watts, Carly Simon, Paul Simon, Janis Ian, Harry Chapin, Debbie Harry, Joe Jackson, Michael Jackson, Diana Ross, Gladys Night, the Brecker Brothers, Bob James, David Sanborn, Celine Dion, John McLaughlin, Michael Franks, Cyndi Lauper, Dire Straits, Eddie Van Halen and Luciano Pavorotti, among others. Jason was a member of the "Saturday Night Live" house band from 1983-1985 and has made more than 100 appearances with Paul Shaffer's band on "The Late Show with David Letterman." Jason currently plays bass with jazz artist Brigitte Zarie and produced her 2013 studio album, "L'Amour."

Jill
Thanked on Gene's liner notes.

Johnsen, Ron
Thanked on Gene's liner notes. Ron had produced the Wicked Lester album. He also got Gene and Paul work on the Lyn Christopher album singing backing vocals on three tracks. He was also the engineer on the Peter Criss involved Chelsea album and was manager of Wicked Lester and later KISS until supplanted by Bill Aucoin.

Johnson, Skip & China
Husband of Grace Slick (1976 – 94) and Grace's daughter (with Jefferson Airplane's Paul Kanter) respectively, thanked on Gene's album liner notes. Skip was a well known lighting director who had worked with KISS on their "Alive II" and "Dynasty" tours. Gene recalled in "KISS and Make-Up" that Grace was going to record with him on his album.

K

Karanauskas, Elli
Thanked on Gene's liner notes.

Katsaros, Doug

A musician's musician, Doug Katsaros is an Emmy Award-winning composer, arranger, orchestrator, vocalist, conductor, and keyboardist. He has collaborated with artists such as Donny Osmond, Rod Stewart, Sir Elton John, Bon Jovi, Peter, Paul & Mary, and Cher, among others. Katsaros played piano and arranged the strings for "Hold Me, Touch Me (Think Of Me When We're Apart)," which was the single from Paul Stanley's 1978 solo album. He has composed, arranged, conducted and/or orchestrated for a host of Broadway and Off-Broadway productions such as "Laughing Room Only," "The Life," "Footloose," "The Rocky Horror Show," "Diamonds," the Outer Critics Circle Award-winning "A ... My Name Is Alice," and "The Toxic Avenger." For his contribution to Off-Broadway's "Altar Boyz," Katsaros was nominated for a Drama Desk Award. His television credits include "The Tick," "Macuso FBI" and ABC's "Afterschool Specials," all three of which earned Emmy nominations, "The Jim Henson Hour," "Larry King Live," the "By Mennen" jingle, and films such as "If Lucy Fell" and "Me And The Mob." In 2012 he won an Emmy for Outstanding Original Song for his special piece, "(Won't You) Join Our Parade," written for the 85th Annual Macy's Thanksgiving Day Parade. More recently, he composed music for the production "Somewhere In Time," a musical based on the classic novel by author Richard Matheson.

Kaye, Carol

Thanked by Gene on his album's liner notes. Carol Kaye came into the KISS fold in 1977, working directly for Bill Aucoin at Aucoin Management, before segueing to work in the subsidiary press arm, the Press Office. There she represented all of the Aucoin-managed bands: KISS, Starz, Toby Beau, and Piper. As the owner of her own company, the New York-based Kayos Productions, Kaye has overseen successful PR campaigns for such iconic artists as KISS, Ace Frehley, Aerosmith, Ted Nugent, Paul McCartney, Queen, AC/DC, Alice Cooper, the Eagles, the Ramones, Blondie, and many others. The company represents bands of all genres, from classic rock, indie, and punk to blues, instrumentalists and jazz.

Kelly, Larry

Co-writer of "Rip It Out" on Ace Frehley's solo album. Larry had been a member of Ace's pre-KISS bands, Cathedral and the Magic People, and sang backing-vocals on the track.

Kelly, Sue

Co-writer of "Rip It Out" on Ace Frehley's solo album. Sue was the wife of Larry Kelly.

Kerner, Kenny

Thanked on Gene's liner notes, Casablanca house producer who had co-produced "KISS" and "Hotter Than Hell" with Richie Wise.

Khan, Chaka
Former member of Rufus who was in the process of going solo in 1978 and who would become a soul Diva. Thanked on Gene's album liner notes.

King, Casey
Belkin Productions (concert promoter) executive thanked by Gene on his album notes.

Kirby, Fred
Thanked on Gene's liner notes, Fred was an early supporter reviewing KISS shows in the clubs in Variety Magazine in 1973.

Kirby, Jack
Comic book artist thanked by Gene on his album notes.

KISS Army, the fans, the club, etc.
Thanked by Gene on his album notes.

Klein, Florence
Gene's aunt, George's wife, thanked on his album liner notes.

Klein, George
Gene's uncle, thanked on his album liner notes.

Klein, Larry
Gene's uncle, thanked on his album liner notes.

Klein, Linda
Gene's cousin, thanked on his album liner notes.

Klein, Eva
Gene's cousin, thanked on his album liner notes.

Klein, Magda
Gene's aunt, and Larry's wife, thanked on his album liner notes.

Koppleman, Charlie
Thanked on Gene's album liner notes. President of The Entertainment Company, who would later be the executive producer of Cher's 1979 album "Take Me Home" released on Casablanca Records. Charlie had worked for Don Kirshner in the 70s.

Kramer, Eddie

Producer of Ace Frehley's solo album. By any standard, Eddie Kramer is regarded as a music industry icon. Born in South Africa, Kramer studied classical piano at the prestigious South African College of Music. At a young age his interest switched from classical to jazz. He moved to England at 19, where he recorded local jazz groups in a home-based studio and installed hi-fi equipment as a hobby. He started his career at Advision Sound Studios in 1962. He joined Pye Studios in 1963 where he recorded a variety of artists, including Sammy Davis Jr., Petula Clark, the Kinks, and the Searchers. Over the course of his five-decade production and engineering career, Kramer has been behind the boards for the biggest names in music: The Rolling Stones, Traffic, Peter Frampton, Carly Simon, Joe Cocker, Johnny Winter, David Bowie, the Beatles, and Bad Company, just to name a few. But he is perhaps best known for three long-term associations in which he not only helped create some of the most important music of the rock era, but also set standards for rock production that set him aside as a true innovator. His work with Jimi Hendrix, Led Zeppelin and KISS produced music that continues to influence rock musicians and producers today.

Kramer is an integral figure in KISStory. He produced the group's 1973 demo tape recorded at Electric Lady Studios and went on to helm classic albums such as "Alive!" (1975), "Rock And Roll Over" (1976), "Love Gun" (1977), and "Alive II" (1977). Kramer was the producer/engineer for Ace Frehley's 1978 solo album, the lone set to spawn a hit single in "New York Groove." Kramer would subsequently team with Frehley on solo recordings such as "Frehley's Comet" (1987) and "Trouble Walkin'" (1989). Kramer reconvened with KISS in 1993 for "Alive III."

In 2003 Kramer received a Lifetime Achievement Award at the AES convention. In 2009 Kramer and Waves released the Eddie Kramer Collection of audio software plug-ins, five application-specific plug-ins targeting guitar, drums, vocals, bass and special effects. In 2012 Kramer celebrated his 50th year in the music business and his 70th birthday. In conjunction with the Hendrix Estate, Kramer oversaw the 2013 release of "People, Hell & Angels," a collection of 12 previously unreleased studio recordings from guitar legend Jimi Hendrix. Also in 2013, Kramer launched F-Pedals, a brand new line of mind-blowing guitar pedals that are incredibly compact and fantastic sounding. Gene thanked Eddie on his album liner notes.

Krampf, Craig

Drummer on the final four tracks on Paul Stanley's solo album. Craig worked with Leon Rusell, Steve Perry, Alice Cooper, Dolly Parton, Nick Glider, the Robbs, Flo & Eddy's band and many others. He later co-wrote Steve Perry's "Oh Sherrie" with Bill Cuomo. He'd also been a drummer in the Skatt Bros. with Sean Delaney.

Krupa, Gene
Thanked on Peter's liner notes. Gene, a jazz drumming legend, had inspired Peter during his youth and had given him some drum technique pointers at the Metrople Club in New York City in the early 1960s.

Kuchner, Cedric
Thanked on Gene's liner notes.

Kulick, Bob
Brooklyn-born Bob Kulick is a longtime member of the "KISS family," dating back to his late-1972 audition with the band. He subsequently landed live gigs in Meat Loaf's touring band and with Alice Cooper. Kulick was brought back into the KISS fold to play "ghost" guitar on tracks on side four of 1977's "Alive II," including "All-American Man" and "Larger Than Life." A year later, he was recruited by Paul Stanley to play guitar on his 1978 solo album. Kulick's guitar work on "Paul Stanley" proved an integral ingredient to the platinum-certified album. In 1980 Kulick earned a co-writing credit on "Naked City," a song featured on "Unmasked." Kulick joined forces with Peppy Castro and Doug Katsaros to form the AOR band Balance. The group issued two albums, 1981's "Balance" and 1982's "In For The Count." (Balance convened for a reunion album in 2009 with "Equilibrium.") Kulick later played on select cuts on KISS' 1982 compilation "Killers," including the solos for "Partners In Crime" and "Nowhere To Run." He later joined Stanley for his first ever solo tour in 1989, playing cuts from Stanley's 1978 album along with hits from the KISS catalog.

Kulick's studio credits include playing guitar on albums for artists such as Lou Reed, Diana Ross, Meat Loaf, Michael Bolton, W.A.S.P. and Doro. More recently, Kulick has produced several tribute albums featuring all-star casts of hard rock and metal musicians, including "Spin The Bottle: An All-Star Tribute To KISS" (2004), "Butchering The Beatles: A Headbashing Tribute" (2006), "We Wish You A Metal X-Mas And A Headbanging New Year" (2008), and "SIN-atra: An All-Star Metal Tribute To Frank Sinatra" (2011). In 2004 Kulick won a Grammy for Best Metal Performance as the producer for Motörhead's cover of Metallica's "Whiplash." Kulick's latest tribute project, "Thriller: A Metal Tribute to Michael Jackson," is set for release Oct. 22 via Cleopatra Records. The album features performances by his brother Bruce Kulick, Chuck Billy (Testament), Billy Sheehan (Mr. Big, The Winery Dogs), Lajon Witherspoon (Sevendust), Chris Jericho (Fozzy), Elias Soriano (Nonpoint), and Doug Pinnick (King's X), among others. Today, Kulick works out of his Los Angeles-based studio, Office Studios, with his business partner Brett Chassen.

L

Lacey, Steve
Steve played guitar on Gene's "Radioactive" (solo) and Paul's "Love in Chains."

Lasley, David

Provided background vocals on "Speedin' Back to My Baby," "New York Groove" and "What's On Your Mind?" Born in Sault Ste. Marie, MI, Lasley has contributed background vocals to recordings by such artists as Bonnie Raitt, James Taylor and Luther Vandross. Lasley started his music career in his teens, forming a singing group with his sister and achieving some success in the Detroit area. In 1970 he joined the cast of "Hair," performing first in Detroit and then on tour. Lasley started his career as a back-up singer at this time. Along with Vandross, he performed on many of Chic's and Sister Sledge's recordings. In 1977 he began touring and recording with James Taylor. Other performers that he has worked with include Todd Rundgren, Melissa Manchester and Bonnie Raitt, who has recorded a number of Lasley's compositions. Lasley's lone hit song as a solo artist, "If I Had My Wish Tonight," reached No. 36 on the Billboard Hot 100 in 1982.

Lassie

Gene even wanted the legendary iteration (the then current one anyway) of the television canine heroine to appear on his album and went so far as to send a mobile truck to her residence to record her bark.

Leber-Krebs

Artist Management company thanked by Gene on his album notes.

Lee, Stan

The Marvel Comics guru whose comics inspired Gene in his youth, and who KISS would issue their own comics throughout the 1970s. Thanked on Gene's album notes.

Lee, Will

Bassist on "Ozone," "I'm In Need of Love," and "Wiped-Out," the only songs on Ace's album on when he doesn't perform bass himself. Along with Anton Fig, Lee was also a member of the CBS Orchestra, joining in 1993. His resume includes work with artists such as Burt Bacharach, Ray Charles, Cyndi Lauper, Diana Ross, and Ray Charles, among many others. Lee is no stranger to high-profile gigs, lending his bottom end to notable events such as the recent Rock and Roll Hall of Fame induction ceremony. An inductee into the Musicians Hall of Fame in Nashville, Lee also has the enviable position of having performed or recorded with all of the Beatles, which is thrilling for a guy who is a founding member of the world's premier Beatles band, the Fab Faux. He released a studio album, "Love, Gratitude and Other Distractions," in 2013.

Lendt, Chris

KISS' tour business manager, for Glickman/Marks 1976 – 88 (an employee for Glickman/Marks Management from 1976-1990, ultimately ascending to the level of vice president), who was thanked on Peter Criss' and Gene Simmons' album liner notes. He served as business manager for KISS, managing their concert tours and overseeing the band's growing business affairs. Lendt also was the business manager for legendary artist Diana Ross. Since 1992, Lendt has been an adjunct professor of marketing at New York University. He also currently acts as a consultant for artists and entertainment companies. In 1997 Lendt published "KISS & Sell: The Making of a Supergroup" (Billboard Books, 1997), a riveting account of his tenure with KISS that is considered by many fans to be one of the best first-hand accounts about the band's history. A graduate of the University of Southern California, Lendt today resides in the New York area.

Lerner, Karen
NBC executive producer thanked by Gene on his album notes..

Lettang, Bill
Not thanked on Gene's album notes. Session drummer who recorded numerous demos with Gene that were ultimately recorded for his solo album, including "Man of 1,000 Faces," "True Confessions," "Burning Up With Fever," and "Radioactive" (Sharp, Ken - Behind The Mask).

Levine, Barry
Famed rock photographer thanked on Gene's liner notes..

Lewis, Jerry Lee
Legendary Rock 'N' Roller who was invited to perform piano on Gene's "Radioactive." Gene had been the offered the opportunity to produce Jerry, but schedules for both didn't work out. Gene thanked him on his album notes..

Lewis, Peter
Assistant engineer on "Love in Chains," "Hold Me, Touch Me," and "Goodbye" on Paul Stanley's solo album at the Record Plant. He also worked with Bad Brains and Bonnie Pointer.

Licata, Ross "Rosie"
Ross was Peter's bodyguard, handler, and assistant who pretty much took care of all of his needs and whims, and in many cases served as a partner in crime. Also thanked on Gene's liner notes.

Linet, Lew
Wicked Lester's manager, thanked by Gene on his album liner notes. Lew, head of Infinity Management Corp., was nominally managing KISS in early 1973, even though he simply didn't "get" the direction the band were taking. He did, however, get the band gigs at the Daisy in Amityville, Long Island (another band he managed,

J.F. Murphy and Salt, played there), before Ron Johnsen took over. Lew later moved his management business to Hollywood.

Linett, Mark
2nd engineer at Sunset Sound in Hollywood, CA for Peter Criss' album.

Lott, Jim
Thanked on Gene's album liner notes. Member of the "Group With No Name" with whom Gene had gone to school. Jimmy's band had helped Gene with demos and backing vocals.

Lukather, Steve
Guitar solo provider for "That's The Kind of Sugar Papa Likes" and "Hooked on Rock 'N' Roll." A session player for his early career he had been a founding member of Toto who released their debut album in late-1978.

M

"Man of 1,000 Faces"
Not just a song-title, this would have been the album's title, according to Gene, prior to the unified commercial campaign plan being solidified.

Manor, The
Recording location of Gene Simmons' solo album in Shipton-on-Cherwell, Oxfordshire, England. The studio was owned by Virgin Records' Richard Branson. Other notable albums recorded there include "Tubular Bells," Black Sabbath's "Born Again," and backing tracks for Queen's "A Day at the Races."

Mansion, The
Filston House (The Estate aka The Colgate Mansion), located on 106 acres of land in Sharon, CT, was a rented house used for the recording of the basic tracks on Ace Frehley's solo album. Built for Romulus Riggs Colgate between 1901 and 1906 the house was desiged by award-winning architect J. William Cromwell, Jr. Soon after the recording of Ace's album the house was bought by singer, songwriter and producer Paul Leka (died October 2011) who had co-written Steams' 1969 #1 hit, "Na Na Hey Hey Kiss Him Goodbye." Paul gave guitarist Vinnie Vincent several of his early session opportunities at Connecticut Recording Studios in Bridgeport during the early 1970s. It is currently for sale for an asking price of $9 million.

Mansky, Dr.
Thanked on Gene's album notes.

Marino, George

Legendary mastering engineer responsible for mastering both Gene Simmons' and Ace Frehley's solo albums. George joined Sterling Sound in the summer of 1973. Here he worked on many of the industry's most influential albums. These include recent Billboard chart toppers like Coldplay's "Parachutes", Bon Jovi's "Lost Highway", and The Offspring's "Rise & Fall, Rage & Grace." George also worked on Three Doors Down's eponymous release and Arctic Monkey's "Favourite Worst Nightmare." He worked on Billboard classics including Journey's "Frontiers", Cyndi Lauper's "She's So Unusual", eponymous releases by both KISS and The Cars, Mötley Crüe's "Dr. Feelgood" and Guns N' Roses "Appetite for Destruction". George started as a musician playing rock n' roll guitar in New York City bands. His first job in the industry was as a librarian and assistant at Capitol Studios in 1967. He then apprenticed in the mastering department, helping cut rock, pop, jazz and classical albums. When Capitol shut down its New York studio, and before heading to Sterling Sound, George joined the fledgling Record Plant, eventually becoming a partner in the recording- mastering studio. There he quickly established his reputation with projects such as Don McLean's "American Pie" and classic albums by the Allman Brothers Band and Stevie Wonder. As is clear in his discography, George has always been sought out for his versatility and dead-on instincts on how music should sound. He won a Grammy in 2011 for Album of the Year for Arcade Fire's "Suburbs." Marino died in 2012 following a bout with lung cancer.

Marks, Howard

Head of KISS' advertising agency. Howard had become one of KISS's business managers (Glickman/Marks) in 1976, a role he'd fill until 1988. Paul, at one point, described him as an "administrator." He and Sean Delany had been partners in a company, "Music Dept," prior to KISS, and he also served as an Executive Producer on Bill Aucoin's "Flipside" 13-episode TV series as part of Marks-Aucoin Productions in early 1973. In August 1973 Howard left his post as promotion manager at April to join Chevron Music (York Records). Howard came up with the line, "Living in Sin at the Holiday Inn" and was given a co-writing credit (and thanks) on Gene's album. He was also thanked on the liner notes of Peter's album.

Marshall, Paul

Thanked on Gene's liner notes, KISS' lawyer who was responsible for the renegotiation of Bill Aucoin's percentage down from 25 to 20%.

Martin, Nickey

Thanked by Gene on his album notes. Nickey had been guitarist in the band Street Punk who played gigs with KISS in the clubs in 1973. Nickey wrote most of the band's songs with lead vocalist Jon Montgomery. Gene had (unsuccessfully) tried to get the band signed through Aucoin.

Mason, Dave
Member of the rock band Traffic who had performed with the likes of Joe Walsh, Stephen Stills, and Paul McCartney. Gene thanked him on his album's liner notes.

Mastering Lab
Mastering company in Hollywood, CA responsible for Peter Criss' solo album.

McAdams, Bobby
A close (former) friend of Ace Frehley's since 1963, McAdams was the Spaceman's guitar/amp technician. He contributed the "power mouth" vocals to Frehley's hit "New York Groove" (the "wah-wah" talk-box effect on the song that Ace couldn't get while playing guitar at the same time). McAdams remained friends with Frehley through KISS and into adulthood where each served as Best Man at each other's weddings. Along with Gordon G.G. Gebert, McAdams authored "KISS & Tell," their personal account of what it was "like to be best friends with a rock and roll legend." Gene also thanked Bobby on his album liner notes.

McCartney, Paul & Linda
Former Beatles and Wings members who Gene had hoped to have on his solo album. Regardless, it was the Beatles on Ed Sullivan who had been a great influence to Gene in the early 1960's. He thanked them on his liner notes, regardless of their non-involvement.

Medlin, Victoria
An actress and musician with whom Paul was friendly. She died in early 1978 and he dedicated his solo album to her memory.

Meyrowitz, Wally
Thanked on Gene's liner notes. Wally was KISS' ATI (American Talent International) booking agent who had become a VP at the company in 1974 in charge of the East Coast concert department. He left ATI for ICM in 1981.

Miller, Alan
Thanked on Peter and Gene's liner notes. "Little Bill" was Bill Aucoin's Vice-President for promotions who was part of the team that created the "KISS Army" in 1975. Alan's involvement with KISS pre-dated Peter Criss', with him having introduced Gene and Paul to Wicked Lester and early KISS manager Lew Linet in 1971.

Miller, Billy
Thanked on Gene's liner notes, Billy took over from Frank Scinlara as the band's tour manager during the "Rock And Roll Over" tour.

Minakami, Haruko

Thanked on Gene's liner notes. Editor and music critic for the Japanese magazine Rokh Show for Shinko Music Publishing Co. She had also been involved in the KISS "Music Life" specials published in 1977 & 1978.

Mom

Thanked by Gene on his album notes. Naturally, Gene's relationship with his mother has been extensively explored in his books and TV program, "Gene Simmons' Family Jewels."

Monier, Richard

Assistant tour manager during 1977 who travelled with the band to Japan in 1977. Thanked by Gene on his album notes.

Morgan, Michael

Co-writer of "You Matter to Me" with John Vastano and Vini Poncia.

Moroder, Giorgio

Another of Peter's choices for producer. The Italian producer would need several chapters in the Casablanca "book," having produced numerous artists on their roster, most notably Donna Summer, along with releasing several solo titles and band projects (Einzelgänger and Music Machine) on Oasis/Casablanca.

Myers, Michele

Thanked by Gene on his album notes.

Mr. Udo & Tats

Japanese concert promoter for KISS' 1977 and 1978 tours, thanked on Gene's album liner notes.

Munao, Susan

Thanked by Gene on his album liner notes. Susan was Donna Summer's personal manager.

Munson, Art

For several decades, Art Munson has been involved in many facets of the music business as a guitarist, recording engineer, songwriter and record producer. He has worked with artists as varied as John Lennon, Barbra Streisand, Cher, Billy Joel, the Righteous Brothers, Paul Williams, Kris Kristofferson, Vonda Shepard, Brenda Russell, David Sanborn, Bill Medley, and many more. Munson has also been involved in scoring for numerous TV shows, jingles and films. His numerous TV credits include the "Today" show, "Oprah," and "ABC World News," among other shows. On "Peter Criss," Munson participated in the sessions in Los Angeles helmed by Vini Poncia. He played guitar on the tracks "I'm Gonna Love You," "You Matter To Me," "Tossin' And Turnin'," "Don't You Let Me Down," "That's The Kind Of Sugar Papa Likes," and "Hooked On Rock 'N' Roll."

N

Nanny
Peter's nickname for his grandmother, thanked on the liner notes of his album.

Nelson, Eric
Bass player on the final four tracks on Paul Stanley's solo album. Eric had worked with Chip Taylor and Nick Glider and met Paul in L.A.

New York City
Gene's adopted, and the band's, home town thanked in his album liner notes.

Nicks, Stevie
Member of Fleetwood Mac, and highly successful solo artist, thanked by Gene on his album notes.

Nielson, Rick
Rick, guitarist in Cheap Trick, plays the guitar solo on "See You in Your Dreams." KISS had toured with Cheap Trick in 1977.

Nugent, Ted
The "Motor City Madman," a regular opening on KISS tours thanked on Gene's album notes.

O

One Dollar Magazine
Baltimore horror fanzine Gene thanked in his album notes.

Oreckinto, Peter
A.k.a. "Moose," one of the very early KISS roadies thanked on Gene's album notes. Peter was responsible for many of KISS' early pyro-techniques, almost losing a hand with Peter Criss' rocket-firing drum sticks.

Osmand, Donnie & Marie
Entertainment partners in the 1970s, and prospective guests, who were thanked on Gene's album notes. In "Behind the Mask" Gene recounts how he wanted Marie to duet on "Living in Sin."

Ostrander, Brooke

Thanked on Gene's liner notes, keyboardist and flute player in Wicked Lester. Brooke had recording equipment at his house where Gene would go to work on demos before Wicked Lester was even an idea. Brooke died on September 3, 2011.

P

Pearl Drums

Endorsed by Gene Simmons on his solo album.

Pecorino, Joe

Member of Beatlemania (as John Lennon) who provided background-vocals for "Mr. Make Believe," "See You Tonite," and "Always Near You/Nowhere To Hide."

Penridge, Stan

Guitarist in Peter's pre-KISS bands Chelsea and Lips, Stan's unused songs for those bands were revisited for Peter solo album. Stan also played guitar on seven of the songs and sang backing-vocals on "Hooked on Rock 'N' Roll." Following his departure from KISS Peter worked with Stan on his "Out of Control" album (1980) and made his first post-KISS live performance debut with Stan in April 1983. The two also toured, briefly, the following year as part of the short-lived Alliance project. Born January 9, 1951, Stan died on May 11, 2001.

Perry, Joe

Lead guitarist from Aerosmith who played guitar on "Radioactive" (chorus) and "Living in Sin" at Cherokee Studios. KISS had opened for Aerosmith a couple of times in 1976 and Gene had written the unreleased "Mongoloid Man" with Joe in 1976 in addition to socializing with him.

Philips, Binky

A New York musician thanked on Gene's album liner notes. Binky knew Paul Stanley from school (The High School of Music and Art), prior to Wicked Lester, and met Gene while that band was attempting to record their album for Epic. He and Gene became friends and Gene would use his services to record demos (you can hear Binky playing on the 1975/6 demo of "Rotten to the Core"). Binky regularly attended rehearsals of Gene, Peter, and Paul as they tried to develop their act. In 1976, Ace was asked to record a "Binky" solo when tracking "Calling Dr. Love." Binky's band, The Planets, played with KISS in the clubs in 1973.

Phillips, Michelle

Former singer in the Mamas and Papas thanked on Gene's liner notes.

Plaza Sound Studios
Studio located atop Radio City Music Hall in New York City used for the recording of Ace Frehley's solo album, particularly over-dubs and remixing. See more under Freeman, Rob.

Plimpton, George
Broadcast journalist/critic, who in the early 1970s was involved at CBC/ITV in Edmonton, Canada. Thanked on Gene's album notes.

Poncia, Vini
Producer of Peter Criss' solo album, Vini was third choice after Tom Dowd declined and Sean Delaney had already committed to Gene Simmons (Sean has also mentioned that Glyn Johns was approached). Bill Aucoin suggested Vini, due to his work with Beatles' drummer Ringo Starr. Vini had also produced one of the earliest Casablanca releases, Fanny, in 1974. Vini would produce the two KISS studio albums that followed the solo albums.

Postlewaite, Fritz
Thanked on Peter and Gene's liner notes. Driver of the Porsche 928 that was wrecked, in Marina del Rey, following a party at L'Ermitage celebrating the wrapping of filming "KISS Meets the Phantom of the Park" (5/27/78). Both were seriously injured. Fritz started out as a roadie with the band eventually becoming their tour manager.

Price, Vincent
Vincent is thanked on Peter's liner notes. Peter had rented Vincent's 37-room estate in Holmby Hills (between Bel Air and Beverly Hills) during the recording of his album in the Los Angeles area. He hosted extravagant parties there and apparently wrote a love song which he was saving for future use...

Q

Q, Johnny
Thanked on Peter Criss' liner notes.

R

Randall, Elliot
Session guitarist on "I Can't Stop The Rain" and "Easy Thing" from Peter Criss' album. Also played guitar on select tracks on Gene Simmons' album (might be the "Randy" on the thanks list). Elliot had recorded with Steely Dan, Felix Cavaliere, Vicki Sue Robinson, and numerous others.

Randy
Thanked on Gene's liner notes.

Ranno, Richie
Guest guitarist on "Tunnel of Love," Richie was a friend of Sean's and a member of the band Starz who were also managed by Bill Aucoin. Richie recorded his solo at Blue Rock Studios.

Ray, Carolyn
Backing vocalist on Gene Simmons' album.

Record Plant Studios
Location in Los Angeles of recording sessions for Paul Stanley's solo album engineered and co-produced by Jeff Glixman and Paul Grupp. The studio had been opened by Gary Kellgren and Chris Stone in 1972 (with companion studios in New York City and Sausalito, CA). Studio C, which had been destroyed in a fire in January 1978, wouldn't have been available for use. KISS used the studio for recordings for "KISS Killers" and "Creatures of the Night" in 1982.

Reddy, Helen
Feminist singer of "I Am Woman" fame who played ping-pong in the studio with Gene during her session work during which she sang on "True Confessions." Not to pigeon-hole Helen, she had starred in Disney's "Pete's Dragon" movie and appeared as part of the all-star chorale in the "Sgt. Pepper's Lonely Hearts Club Band" film.

Reese, Mike
Mastered Peter Criss' album at The Mastering Lab in Hollywood, CA.

Reingold, Bucky
Thanked on Gene's album liner notes, Bucky had been one of the original partners in the formation of Casablanca Records in 1973 along with Neil Bogart, Larry Harris, and Cecil Holmes. Like Neil he came from Buddah Records and attended the band's showcase at La Tang Studios prior to their signing with the label.

Remarkable Productions
Eddie Kramer's production company.

Rene, Malou
Co-writer (with Richie Adams) of "Tossin And Turnin'" on "Peter Criss." Malou wrote for numerous artists including Bobby Rydell, Bill Haley, The Supremes, and The Guess Who.

Reno
Thanked on Gene's album notes. Bob Reno?

Robb Bros.
Thanked by Gene on his album notes. The Robb brothers included Dee (chief engineer), Joe, and Bruce (engineers). They owned Cherokee Studios where Gene recorded part of his solo album.

Robinson, Richard
Music journalist for the "Pop Wire Service" thanked on Gene's album liner notes. Richard later wrote for music magazines such as Rock Scene and Hit Parader (editor). Richard wrote the text used in the booklet insert for "The Originals."

Ross, Alvin
Head of ASR Enterprises, a publicity and management company, who became president of the Press Office, Ltd. on its formation in early 1977. He became a vice-president at Aucoin Management, Inc. in early 1978. He became President of Virgin Music Merchandising in 1985. Thanked by Gene on his album notes.

Ross-Durborow, Carol
Take a look through the top music, entertainment and news journals and, in large part, the images and the stars (and even more important - the persons behind the images) will have fallen under the aegis and direction of Carol Ross-Durborow, one of the industry's premier, reputable image-builders. She's done it all: from introducing the group KISS to the world to representing Elton John, Paul McCartney, Billy Joel, Cher, Bette Midler, Diana Ross, David Bowie, Hall & Oates, Burt Bacharach to Blondie, to Van Halen and the list goes on. During her tenure at MCA Records, Ross-Durborow was responsible for such legendary performers as Elton John, Olivia Newton-John, the Who, and other artists on the roster. At Rogers & Cowan, the esteemed international public relations firm, she began as director of their music division representing the biggest names in the business, Paul & Linda McCartney, Dolly Parton, the Beach Boys, and a host of others. This eventually paved the way for her to go on to open her own agency, the Press Office, a subsidiary of Aucoin Management.

The same philosophy that had served her so well in the arts was equally successful in the corporate arena. Her client list had grown to include not only the super-stars of music and entertainment, but corporate power-houses as well. England's entrepreneurial man Richard Branson chose Ross-Durborow and her company to launch his new airline, Virgin Atlantic Airways, in the United States and to handle the Virgin Group of Companies. More recently, her former client, the legendary Tommy James, enticed her out of retirement to become his manager and direct all publicity and media for his burgeoning multimedia company, Aura Entertainment Group. Back in her element, she quickly stepped in to encourage James to finish writing his autobiography and with a publishing deal with Scribner/Simon & Schuster in place, the next step was to bring his compelling story to the silver screen, which is now in development. Ross-Durborow will be an associate producer on this project. Carol was thanked on Gene Simmons' liner notes.

Rothberg, Gerry
Publisher of Circus Magazine thanked by Gene on his album notes.

Russell, Larry
Friend of Ace's, from his youth, who suggested Anton Fig when asked about prospective drummer candidates for his solo album.

S

Sagal, Katey
Background vocalist on Gene Simmons' album and a member of the "Group With No Name" who had been signed to Casablanca and released their debut self-titled album in August 1976. She went on work with Bette Midler and Bob Dylan, but is better known as Al Bundy's wife on the popular "Married With Children" television show.

Saviano, Tom
The son of a Chicago big band conductor and arranger, Tom Saviano's appreciation for jazz, classical music and arrangements was born of a constant exposure to sophisticated musicians and music. Saviano's career began as one of Los Angeles' most talented session players, a reputation that landed him a stint as Melissa Manchester's musical director. Saviano arranged and played saxophone on three of Manchester's albums: "Help Is On The Way," "Singin'," and "Don't Cry Out Loud," with the former two produced by Vini Poncia, who Saviano cites as giving him his career start as an arranger and session musician. Saviano would go on to work on several projects with Poncia, including Peter Criss' 1978 solo album, on which he arranged the horns for four tracks: "I'm Gonna Love You," "Tossin' And Turnin'," "Rock Me, Baby," and "Hooked On Rock 'N' Roll."

Saviano subsequently formed the group Heat with whom he released two critically acclaimed albums ("Heat" and "Still Waitin'"), generating the Top 40 R&B hits "Just Like You" and "This Love That We Found." On both albums, Saviano produced and arranged all of the music, played sax and keyboards and wrote and/or co-wrote all of the songs. In July 2013 Saviano oversaw the release of "Heat Revisited," a collection featuring 16 tracks, including 11 tracks from the first two Heat studio albums, plus five previously unreleased songs originally recorded during the same period. The set was re-recorded, remixed and remastered by Saviano with the goal of adding more fidelity and sonic impact. The band is made up of Saviano and vocalists Jean Marie Arnold, Joe Pizzulo and Ed Whiting. Contributing session musician talent includes all-stars such as Bill Champlin, Michael O'Neill, Bruce Gaitsch, Neil Stubenhaus, Vinnie Colaiuta, Nathan East, Paul Jackson Jr., Carmen

Grillo, Bill Bodine, and Harvey Mason, among others. Vinnie Cusano (Vinnie Vincent) plays guitar on the unreleased track "What Does It Take."

Saviano has played with a host of high-profile musicians such as Brenda Russell; Earth, Wind & Fire with whom he played sax for the Grammy-winning hit "I Wanna Be With You"; and Sheena Easton for whom he wrote the hit single "It's Hard to Say It's Over." Saviano's more recent work includes recording sessions on Muse's "The 2nd Law," Maroon 5's "It Won't Be Soon Before Long," Meat Loaf's "Bat Out Of Hell III," Neil Diamond's "12 Songs," and Ray Charles' Grammy-winning "Genius Loves Company." Saviano played saxophone on the Grammy-winning Dolly Parton single, "9 To 5," and contributed to Michael Nesmith's "Elephant Parts," the first music video to ever win a Grammy. He was a featured soloist and permanent member of "The Late Show With Joan Rivers," the show that launched the Fox Television Network. Saviano released his first solo album, "Making Up Lost Time," in 1998, followed by 2000's "Crossings."

Schaffer, Ken
Inventor of the wireless microphone and guitar system adopted by KISS following the electrocution of Ace Frehley in 1976. Thanked on Gene's album notes.

Schaper, Bob
Overall engineer of Peter Criss' solo album.

Scheniman, William
A musician/studio engineer, Bill "Bear" Scheniman is credited with playing the "bell" on the epic "Ace Frehley" instrumental closing track, "Fractured Mirror." He was also Eddie Kramer's technical assistant and remote recording coordinator for Ace Frehley's solo album. His engineering credits include work with Bon Jovi ("7800 Degrees Fahrenheit"), Mick Jagger ("She's The Boss"), Bruce Springsteen, "Born In The U.S.A."), Chic ("Real People"), Luther Vandross ("Love, Luther"), and Diana Ross ("Diana"), among others. Scheniman also has done some TV work as a music producer and engineer, including "The George Carlin Show" and "Frontline."

Schwartzberg, Allan
Session drummer on three tracks ("I Can't Stop The Rain," "Rock Me, Baby" and "Easy Thing") on Peter's and all of Gene's solo albums.

Scinlara, Frankie
Thanked on Gene's liner notes, KISS' tour manager 1976 – 77.

Seger, Bob
Backing vocalist on "Radioactive" and "Living in Sin." Bob was a friend of Sean Delaney's whose Silver Bullet Band had toured with KISS in 1976.

Shannon, Scott
Casablanca director of promotions thanked by Gene on his album credits. Scott played a key role in turning around the failure of the "Detroit Rock City" single and breaking "Beth" on radio. It had also been his idea, as a DJ at WMAK in Nashville in 1974, for KISS' "Kissin' Time" promotion. He left Casablanca at the end of 1977.

Shore, Dinah
Thanked on Gene's liner notes. Gene had apparently wanted her as a guest on his album. Dinah had a successful recording career in the 1940s and 50s, before moving into television in the 1960s. Her "Dinah Shore Show" competed with the likes of Mike Douglas and Merv Griffin. While her show featured musical performances, KISS never appeared as guests. She'd also dated Gene Krupa.

Silfen, Stu
One of KISS' lawyers, specializing in record deal negotiations, thanked by Gene on his album notes.

Simmons, Gene
Lead vocalist and bass player from KISS.

Skopp, Roberta
Casablanca's East Coast director of press and creative projects thanked by Gene on his album notes. She worked as an account executive for the Press Office, Ltd., prior to joining Casablanca in the summer of 1978, and had been director of publicity for Kirshner Entertainment.

Slater, Michele
Michele Slater started her career in the entertainment industry in music production with high-profile artists such as Billy Joel, Paul Simon, KISS, Chicago, Barbra Streisand and industry icons Phil Ramone, Jerry Wexler, Elliot Scheiner, Garland Jefferies, and Bob Clearmountain. As an employee for Aucoin Management, Slater worked as a production coordinator for Gene Simmons' solo album. Setting up shop in Los Angeles, Slater's responsibilities included coordinating logistical details in the studio for co-producer Sean Delaney as well as coordinating the communication, booking and travel for the cast of "special guests" on the album. Later, Slater worked as the production assistant for Grammy-winning producer Ramone and subsequently continued her career as the music talent coordinator for "Saturday Night Live." Her public relations background includes work with record companies, boutique advertising agencies and global corporations. Today, Slater works with as an independent public relations and social media specialist, lending her expertise to artists such as Jana Mashonee. Her surname was incorrectly spelt "Slagter" on the album credits.

Sluts of Oxford
Thanked on Gene's liner notes. Apparently Gene's "needs" were taken care of while recording his solo album...

Smalling, J.R.
Early road manager thanked on Gene's album notes. J.R. was the stage announcer who introduced the band on stage and can be heard on the "Alive!" album.

Solan, Eddie
Early KISS soundboard operator who is thanked by Ace on his album's liner notes for "inspiration." Eddie's studio, Backstreet Studios in the Bronx is also plugged one Ace's album, it being the location where Ace and Anton first jammed after meeting. Eddie had often driven Ace to rehearsals in 1973 and helped the band build a PA for their first shows. He was their very first roadie running the early soundboard. Gene also thanked Eddie on his liner notes.

Sound Labs, Inc.
Studio opened by engineer Armen Steiner on Argyle Avenue in Hollywood, CA, where additional recording for Peter's solo album was conducted. Artists such as Bread, Dolly Parton, and Waylon Jennings ("Are You Ready for the Country") had used the facility.

Soundmixers
Studio in New York used for mixes for Ace Frehley demos/recordings in April 1978. The studio was a new facility on the second floor of the famed Brill Building at 1619 Broadway that had opened in 1977. Construction of the four studio facility had been supervised by John Storyk who was later recruited by Ace to design and build his home studio in Connecticut.

Stanley, Paul
Lead singer and rhythm guitarist from KISS.

Starr, Ringo
Former Beatle drummer, whose albums of the 70s had often been produced by Vini Poncia. Ringo was invited to appear on Gene's solo album, but was the only Beatle to decline.

Stasiak, Corky
Thanked on Gene's liner notes. Recording engineer, most notably on KISS' "Destroyer" album in 1976.

Sterling Sound Studios
Mastering studio in New York City used for Ace Frehley's album.

Stone, Mike
Engineer at Electric Lady Studios, New York City, for recording of tracks for Peter Criss' album. Mike had also engineered KISS' re-recording of "Strutter" earlier in the year. Mike was the executive producer of Gene Simmons' solo album and mixed Paul's album with him at Trident Studios in London. Paul and Mike would produce New England's debut album in 1979.

Stowe, Ellen Louise "Star"
Playboy's playmate of the month, February 1977, who had done photo-shoots with the band in 1976. She dated Gene for a while and was thanked on his album notes.

Streer, Anne
Peter Criss album project manager and Vini Poncia assistant.

Stunts Unlimited
Stunt company used for the "KISS Meets the Phantom of the Park" movie and thanked by Gene on his album notes.

Summer, Donna
Casablanca's queen of disco and guest backing vocalist on "Burning up with Fever."

Sunset Sound Studios
Studio in Hollywood, CA, the primary location for the recording of Peter Criss' solo album. Opened by Salvador "Tutti" Camarata in 1958 as a personal use studio doing contract work for Disney, this studio had seen the likes of Buffalo Springfield, Doors, Mamas and the Papas, and Harry James recording as it expanded in the 1960s. It was also where industry legend Jim Messina started making a name for himself as staff engineer. By the time of recording Peter's album, Vini had worked at the studio with Lynda Carter and Melissa Manchester.

Sutton, Annie
Backing vocalist on "Rock Me, Baby" and "Easy Thing." Annie was a sought after session artist who had worked with Bette Midler and DC LaRue.

Sutton, Bernie
Thanked on Gene's liner notes.

T

Tallarico, Carl
Drummer on "Fractured Mirror." This is his only known session work. He is credited as the founder of Factory Sound.

The Girl with Purple & Green Hair from Edmonton
Gene's first groupie, on the Canadian tour of February 1974, as noted on his album liner notes.

The Kitchen Sink
The only thing not thanked or noted on Gene's album liner notes.

Tilman, Julia
Backing vocalist, with Maxine Willard (her sister) and Marian Dixon, on "Tossin' And Turnin'" and "I Can't Stop The Rain." She had done session work with Al Kooper, Masekela, and Donovan.

Tiny, Mr.
Michael McGurl. Thanked on Gene's album notes. KISS' road manager 1977 – 78.

Trident Studios
Studio located in the Soho area of London, England where Gene Simmons' and Paul Stanley's solo albums were mixed. Built in 1967 artists such as the Beatles, David Bowie, Queen, the Rolling Stones, and Genesis had utilized the facility with their custom Trident 'A' Range console. The studio was one of the UK industry innovators and first adopters of Dolby noise reduction. The Trident 'A' range console was sold in 1983 to Cherokee Studios in Los Angeles.

Tropea, John
A musician's musician, John Tropea is one of the most admired and highly regarded guitar players of his generation. With the ability to play in a variety of styles, Tropea has written for and collaborated with major recording artists from around the world. His resume includes his own solo career and work with Deodato, Laura Nyro, Harry Chapin, Paul Simon, Alice Cooper Eric Clapton, Dr. John, and many others. His credits on Peter Criss' 1978 solo album are guitar on the tracks "Easy Thing," "Rock Me, Baby" and "I Can't Stop The Rain." Tropea began his guitar studies at age 12 and went on to Berklee School of Music in Boston, where he studied jazz guitar, harmony, composition, and big band arranging. He is currently working on his latest solo album, "Got Your Rhythm Right Here," which is set for release in 2013.

Troyer, Eric
Plays piano on "Radioactive" and "Living in Sin" on Gene Simmons' album. In 1978 Eric was a session player who had written a song for Cher (which wasn't used). He made a guest appearance on Bruce Kulick's Blackjack "Worlds Apart" album in 1980. Indiana native Eric Troyer's professional resume reads like a who's who of rock history. His voice can be heard on mega hits such as "Woman" by John Lennon, "Uptown Girl" by Billy Joel, "Total Eclipse Of The Heart" by Bonnie Tyler and on songs by Aerosmith, James Taylor, Meat Loaf, Lou Reed, and many others. A

founding member of ELO Part II, Troyer's distinctive voice and keyboards — not to mention his tireless work ethic — have been a staple of the band for more than 20 years. Troyer has managed to survive years of exposure to the highest levels of rock and roll insanity with his good humor intact. And for good measure, he is a health nut and history buff.

Tudor, Stephanie

Thanked on Gene's liner notes. Aucoin Management employee who was assistant to Ken Anderson (1977 – 80), and later director of production (1980 – 86). Stephanie Tudor began her tenure at Aucoin Management in 1977, working with Aucoin acts such as KISS, Piper, Starz, Toby Beau, and Billy Idol, among others. She subsequently spent nearly two decades as the vice president of A&R and administration for Jive Records. Today, Tudor is an artist manager and specializes in artist and executive relocation in the real estate field.

Tyler, Steven

Lead singer of Aerosmith thanked by Gene on his album notes. KISS had opened a couple of shows for the Boston band during 1974.

U

Uhelszki, Jan

Thanked on Gene's liner notes. Music journalist and early supporter of KISS, Jan was given her own make-up design and appeared on stage with the band for four-minutes in Johnstown, PA on May 17, 1975! She wore the combined make-up design from the back cover of "Hotter Than Hell" (KISS Alive Forever) and was the only person to share the stage with the made-up band until Joe Perry in 2003. She recalled the event in the legendary "I Dreamed I Was Onstage with KISS in my Maidenform Bra" piece for Creem Magazine in August 1975.

V

Valle, Miriam Naomi

A member of the band Rouge, formed by Desmond Child in 1974, and background vocalist on "Move On" on Paul's album. Miriam went on to work with John Waite, Jennifer Rush, Cher, Bonnie Tyler, Alice Cooper, Michael Bolton, Ratt, and many others.

Van Halen

Thanked on Gene's liner notes, the band that Gene had discovered in Los Angeles in 1976. Gene produced their demo tape, and they served as his backing band for his 1977 "Love Gun" demos. By 1978 they were on a trajectory for fame, with Warner Bros., far exceeding KISS'. Bill Aucoin turned down Van Halen in favor of Piper, fronted by Billy Squier, who'd sign with A&M Records.

Vastano, John
Co-writer, with Michael Morgan and Vini Poncia, of "You Matter To Me." John had been the lead singer/guitarist in the band White Water that Vini had produced in 1973. They performed blue-eyed soul/R&B that was a perfect fit for Peter's voice and style.

Vidal, Maria
A member of the band Rouge, formed by Desmond Child in 1974, and background vocalist on "Move On" on Paul's album. While the band played the clubs of New York City hoping for a break Paul Stanley became aware of them and formed a friendship with Desmond, resulting in them co-writing a song for the Rouge album, and the first disco-rock hybrid for KISS "Dynasty" album. While Rouge went nowhere, Paul liked their sound and recruited the female vocalist trio for background duties on his solo album. Maria went on to have a #48 hit single with "Body Rock," the theme to the movie of the same title in 1984 and recorded her debut solo album in 1987, "Do Me Right" which included contributions by Bruce Kulick, Desmond Child, Diana Grasselli, and Neil Jason.

The Village Recorder Studios
Location in Los Angeles of recording sessions for Paul Stanley's solo album engineered and co-produced by Jeff Glixman. KISS had recorded "Hotter Than Hell" at the legendary studio in 1974 and Gene had taken the unsigned Van Halen into the studio in 1976 to record demos. "Goodbye," "Take Me Away (Together as One)," and "Love In Chains" were recorded at this studio which prided itself on having several females (including Barbara Issak) on the staff.

Voorhees, Scott
Thanked on Gene's liner notes. Scott worked security with the band.

W

Wald, Jeff
Janis Ian's manager thanked by Gene on his album notes.

Walsh, Jan
Thanked on Gene's liner notes. Gene's girlfriend in the period 1972 – 75, who introduced him to the music of Slade, and was present at the first ever KISS show on January 30, 1973. She sued Gene in 2005 "based on the use of her photograph, without her knowledge or consent, in a documentary" in conjunction with comments he made (allegedly making her sound like a "sex-addicted nymphomaniac"). The case was settled in June 2006 with an "amicable resolution" after Gene won the first phase of the case having the motion concerning use of the photograph dismissed in November 2005. Gene commented, "I value my early

relationship with [X] and wish her well... My quotes in the documentary that [X] took issue with were solely about me, not Ms. Ward or anyone else."

Washington, Ned

Co-writer, with Leigh Harline, of "When You Wish upon a Star," from the 1940 movie "Pinocchio" recorded by Gene Simmons. This song was a sentimental tip of the hat to the Disney cartoons that had helped Gene to learn English soon after moving to America in 1958.

Wassen, Nancy

Thanked on Gene's album notes.

Weissman, Mitch

A native New Yorker, Mitch Weissman debuted in the original New York case of "Beatlemania." He was chosen for not only his musical ability but his uncanny resemblance to Paul McCartney. Originally conceived and produced by Steve Leber and David Krebs, "Beatlemania" premiered on Broadway in May 1977 and ran until October 1979, with more than 1,000 performances. Weissman and fellow "Beatlemania" cast member Joe Pecorino were brought in by Gene Simmons to provide Beatle-esque vocals on "See You Tonite," "Always Near You/Nowhere To Hide" and "Mr. Make Believe." Weissman would go on to become a key KISS contributor, writing songs with Simmons and Stanley in the early '80s. His writing credits include songs such as "Get All You Can Take," "While The City Sleeps," "Murder In High Heels," and "Thief In The Night." Weismann also collaborated on several demos with Stanley and Simmons, in addition to co-writing songs that appeared on Simmons-produced albums for Keel and Wendy O. Williams. Mitch had seen one of Gene's pre-KISS bands perform at a Bat Mitzvah. Today, Weissman resides in Los Angeles.

Weisman, Toni

Thanked on Gene's album notes.

West, Linda

Bill's executive assistant at Aucoin Management. Thanked on Gene's liner notes.

Whitmore, Stewart

2nd engineer at Sound Labs, Inc. for Peter Criss' album recording sessions.

Willard, Maxine

Backing vocalist, with Julia Tillman (her sister) and Marian Dixon, on "Tossin' And Turnin'" and "I Can't Stop The Rain." She had done session work with Al Kooper, Dave Mason, Rita Coolidge, and others.

Wittman, Dave

Engineer at Electric Lady Studios, New York City, for recording of tracks for Peter Criss' album and "Tonight You Belong to Me," "Move On," and "Ain't Quite Right" on Paul Stanley's album. Dave had engineered the original KISS demo in 1973 and many KISS recordings since.

Wise, Richie

Thanked on Gene's liner notes, Casablanca house producer who had co-produced "KISS" and "Hotter Than Hell" in 1974 with Kenny Kerner.

Woloch, Dennis

Thanked by Gene on his album notes. An employee of Glickman/Marks Management Corp., Woloch served as the art director for KISS from 1975-1987. Woloch oversaw art direction for several graphically iconic KISS albums, including "Alive!," "Destroyer," "Rock And Roll Over," the 1978 solo albums, and "Creatures Of The Night." For the solo albums, Woloch secured the services of artist Eraldo Carugati and worked closely with him to see the artwork come to fruition. Aside from KISS, Woloch has also designed albums for artists such as Diana Ross, Starz and Peter Gallway. Today, Woloch designs albums, logos, advertising campaigns, books, and more under the auspices of his own company, Dennis Woloch Design.

X

Y

Z

Zarella, Tony

Thanked on Gene's liner notes, drummer in Wicked Lester who was hired because he apparently looked like Geezer Butler of Black Sabbath.

A Look at "KISS Meets the Phantom of the Park"

"Easy, Catman, they are serious." In this feature we look back at the movie that started it all, an expensive and critically successful..., well maybe not. Here's an exploration of KISS' made for television movie — and we'll leave the description there...

The movie, according to Peter Criss was "Gonna blow minds cuz we're the first rock group to do a feature movie" (Bluefield Daily Telegraph, 10/22/78). Well... Yes, it certainly did blow minds, but depending on your definition of "rock," no, KISS weren't the first band to do so — not that a bit of hyperbole ever did the slightest bit of harm. Whatever the case, no exploration of KISS in 1978 would be complete without a look at the band's first full-length foray into acting — though perhaps a lose application of the definition of the word "acting" might assuage the horror of thespians of higher order. The idea KISS would attempt such a project was hardly top-secret: At a Billboard/UCLA seminar in May 1977 Bill Aucoin had commented, "Marvel comics is putting out a KISS comic book in June and there might be a TV movie of the week. There will also be a major flick assuming the group is willing and can rise to it. There is also the idea of the group doing solo LPs" (Billboard, 5/21/77). By early as November 1977 press sources were reporting on the plans for "KISS Meets the Phantom." Even the fall 1977 edition of the KISS Army Newsletter had mentioned the prospects of a "movie-of-the-week." Suggesting, "If it really happens, and the wheels are already in motion, television ain't never gonna be the same," may well have been prophetic!

While the "of the Park" title appendage had yet to make its appearance, there were few other concrete facts about the project other than it being a Hanna-Barbara production. The first location suggested for the filming of the movie was King Island near Cincinnati, OH, a location having already been featured in episodes of television shows such as The Partridge Family and The Brady Bunch. Hanna-Barbera operated a section of the park, known as The Happy Land of Hanna-Barbera that featured a wooden roller coaster named Scooby Doo (who also makes a brief appearance in Phantom - see if you can spot him). That location may simply have been too skewed towards the younger demographic, too family friendly. By early 1978, press reports indicated that the two-hour television movie would instead be filmed at Kings Dominion Park in Doswell, near Richmond, VA — where much of the 1977 movie, "Rollercoaster" (starring George Segal, Richard Widmark, and Henry Fonda) had been filmed. Billed as the "first rock gothic mystery filmed for TV," ultimately the Virginia location was changed due to the near-clichéd "scheduling conflict" excuse, though that suggestion certainly alludes to some of the know solo album recording work that was being done by three of the members on the West Coast. According to the contract signed February 1, KISS were to receive $40,000 for appearing in the movie. Aucoin received a production fee of $52,000 and a 50% share of the "Producer's net profits."

During May, filming of the movie commenced in California based on a screenplay written by Jan-Michael Sherman and Don Buday. Jan's previous work had included the spy thriller "Too Hot to Handle," also written with Don. Magic Mountain amusement park, outside of Los Angeles in nearby Valencia was ultimately chosen. Also utilized was the former "Gone with the Wind" set at Culver City Studios, on the outskirts of Los Angeles, and as Ace described it, "some mansion up on top of some hill," in the Hollywood Hills. Gene was more helpful: "A person, whose name I don't know, but he's said to have invented the altimeter, has a lot of land up on top of the Hollywood Hills, so we did a lot of the film up there" (KISS Meets The Phantom Official Magazine). The mansion was likely Paul Kollsman's "The Enchanted Hill" estate formerly located on North Angelo Drive in Beverly Hills. Kollsman was an engineer and inventor who had the altimeter setting window named after him. He'd bought the estate in 1945. The location had been used in various Colombo, Charlie's Angels, and Dynasty episodes (the estate no longer exists). Tightly scheduled, the filming of the project was scheduled to take around five weeks and the non-post-production work was completed in June. The basic premise of the movie was simple: Theme park facing financial ruin turns to KISS to perform concerts that will financially save the park. Formerly key park employee is seen as old-school and out-of-date and pushed to the side. He plots his revenge... That antagonist, straight out of the Frankenstein evil genius mould, is one Abner Devereaux, creator of the parks once popular animatronics characters and displays. The movie alludes to earlier disappearances of people from the park, and of course Abner is seen to be responsible for them during the movie though the context is never actually explained.

Played by Emmy Award winning actor Anthony Zerbe, who had starred in the cult film, "The Omega Man" (an adaptation of Richard Matheson's "I Am Legend" novel), Devereaux is almost a mousy caricature of a cookie-cutter creep, subtle rather than overt — laughably so at times, with his delivery of serious lines, "Best, best for whom Calvin. What about my work?" Or, "There's nothing for my outside this park" and "You will regret this day!" — Or his overly melodramatic swooning in the scene after being fired. Quality of the scene was, as Paul Stanley suggested in "Face The Music," was not as important as simply getting a scene cut. Director Gordon Hessler had directed Vincent Price in several movies would no doubt have appealed to the horror fan in Gene Simmons! The movie was produced by Terry Morse, Jr. with Joseph Barbera in executive producer role. While KISS were the movie's main protagonists, imbued with supernatural powers, the other main characters in the movie included park owner Calvin Richards (Carmine Caridi, who had played the role of Carmine Rosato in the Godfather, Part II — He was also apparently Francis Ford Coppola's first choice for the role of Sonny Corleone), Melissa (Deborah Ryan), and her boyfriend and park employee Sam Farrell (played by Terry Lester who'd later play the role of Jack Abbott on the soap opera The Young And The Restless). Calvin almost seems a poor facsimile of Moe Greene from the Godfather movie with his dialogue, "He [Abner] built this part and *I* run it," but he's struggling under the decline of the park's fortunes and desperate to turn it around. Famed disc jockey Don Steele also made a brief cameo appearance as a KISS make-up contest announcer. One secondary character Brion James, who played one of Snede's security guards, went on to play roles in many other movies including Blade Runner, Red Heat, and The Fifth Element. Richard Hein plays the second guard (without mustache).

With KISS scheduled to play three concerts at the park, Melissa turns to the band to help her find her missing boyfriend, who unbeknown to her has been turned into a cybernetic zombie controlled by Devereaux for becoming too curious about what is going on in his underground workshop/control center. Paul summed up the film in an interview in Grooves Magazine: "You're used to seeing KISS with guitars singing into microphones. The story is about KISS, a park and a mad inventor who winds up kidnapping us and having our powers taken away 'cause we have superpowers. And he sends out a phony KISS (cybernetic KISS), to go onstage and all kinds of havoc ensues and we finally escape and do battle with our robots. It's a wonderful, wonderful movie. Very deep,' Paul jokes with a grin" (Groove Magazine). Deep enough with lines such as, "Chopper don't hurt nobody unless he wants to" delivered by Lisa Jane Persky who plays Dirty Dee, one of members of a teen gang. Her troublesome (or mildly annoying perhaps) companions included Chopper (John Dennis Johnston) and Slime (John Lisbon Wood). Lisa has kept active in the industry and made a podcast appearance to discuss her memories of the filming. She did her own make-up and wardrobe on the movie.

Ultimately, following the malfunction of a ride due to vandalism by the gang, Calvin fires Abner, who proceeds to descend into full insanity blaming KISS for his downfall. He plots his revenge planning to have a cybernetic band rile up the concert crowd to destroy the park. Perhaps world domination was a little bit too much for Abner. The plot may seem somewhat lowbrow and corny decades on, but in terms of the audience the movie was being created for, pure PG, it was likely deemed safe enough even with the innuendo and suggestiveness that does sneak in throughout — "Remember who you cum with Chopper" (in the Simon the Gorilla scene). One highlight of the film is the acoustic version of "Beth," that had likely been recorded at Electric Lady Studios in early June. Peter had no memory of being involved in the song so it is likely that his original 1976 vocal was simply mixed with the new instrumental track. While ghost-guitarist Dick Wagner has asserted that he recorded acoustic guitars for the original song in 1976, those parts were designed to augment the orchestration and were not "picked" as required for an acoustic performance in the movie. Additionally, Peter has commented, "Paul didn't really play [the acoustic guitar in the scene where 'Beth' is played in the film] — it was done by a studio musician. I was supposed to fake playing the guitar but I was so sloppy with the finger work that Paul jumped right in and said, 'I'll do it,' where Ace really should have done it" (Behind The Mask). As a result, KISS fans have the mystery of yet another ghost musician in the band's recorded history... Musically though, further highlights of the movie are the live performance sequences of songs such as "Shout It Out Loud," "I Stole Your Love," "Rip & Destroy" and "Rock And Roll All Nite." They give a tantalizing glimpse at what a proper multi-cam professionally filmed concert of KISS at their height could have looked like. And, perhaps, leave tears at the prospect of the unused footage that might simply have been discarded as part of the film making process. Whatever the case, the camera angles, some shot from behind Peter, offer a fascinating look at the band during the period.

While characters and plot weren't particularly strong, the dialogue of the film was also particularly lacking. Ace was reduced to saying dumb lines like "Ack!" or "Insufficient data to compute, Starchild," making him sound more like a moronic Vulcan than the loveable Space Ace! Part of this, according to Gene, was the result of Ace being uncooperative with the screenwriters who were trying to get some idea of the band member's characters to write material into the script for them. In his autobiography Ace defended the movie, and perhaps his attitude towards it, suggesting, "It wasn't the greatest movie, but that never bothered me because I wasn't under the impression that anyone expected it to be anything other than a ridiculous farce — including the people who wrote, directed and produced it" (No Regrets). Gene too was left more in character growling responses rather than actually saying much. Paul, who had the most dialogue, was left with poorly delivered lines. However, he can't be blamed completely with the scene lines apparently having been shouted out (loud) to him immediately before the scene was filmed. Some KISS-related teasers are spread throughout the movie, such as Peter's "Destroyer" stage cat statues being present in the "Chamber of Thrills."

Special effects, which were particularly important in the aftermath of the release of "Star Wars" in 1977, were supposed to play a large role in the $2 million movie. Paul got a laser that shone from his eye, almost an early prototype Borg implant. He'd hoped to use the effect on the next KISS tour until he realized how dangerous it was to have a laser so close to his eye. Gene got to growl demonically and breathe fire. Ironically, at times he seems to be the most uncomfortable of the band members in front of the cameras. Ace had powers of teleportation. For Peter, no special effects would have made up for his spoken parts being overdubbed during post-production by voice actor Norman Alden. Peter's lines are reported to have been muttered and sometimes incomprehensible with his strong Brooklyn accent. Peter's attitude towards the movie had been made clear earlier in the year: "I want to go into acting. I always wanted to act. Even though KISS is doing a movie, it's not what I want. I want to go out solo and do some really serious shit. I think I'd be really good at it because I don't mind crying" (Circus, 4/13/78). Chris Lendt recalled that Peter was having other issues: "Peter was battling his own personal demons during the movie's filming. The shooting schedule was constantly being re-jiggered to accommodate him. Toward the end of the filming, Peter exploded in anger in his suite at the L'Ermatage, smashing a guitar while in a fight with a girl he was seeing in LA. At 4:00 am he phoned Fritz Postlethwaite, KISS' tour manager who was on location for the movie production telling him to 'call my lawyer — I just killed someone.' Luckily, he hadn't. Peter's girlfriend eventually became his second wife despite her close call with a guitar" (KISS And Sell). For Peter this period of turmoil would culminate in the collapse of his marriage to Lydia.

Paul was later very embarrassed about how the film turned out, with the concept rapidly deviating from the course it was originally to take and becoming, if anything, too unintentionally comic for the band. Ace's unpredictable nature resulted in him becoming highly frustrated with the whole process of film-making, particularly the tedium of filming. Ace remembers: "The most difficult thing for me was the waiting between scenes when they were doing other people's close-ups and things like that. Sometimes we'd have to wait around three or four hours to get in front of the camera again because they were filming something else" (KISS Meets the Phantom Official Magazine). However, Ace enjoyed the live music sequences: "After weeks of doing still shots and sitting around the pool or inside a house, the concert sequence was, in a way, getting back to our roots... the concert sequence at Magic Mountain was probably the most enjoyable because we could really let loose and do the thing we do best, which is playing live" (KISS Meets The Phantom Official Magazine).

Paul remembers that the project wasn't easy, even if the result made it look like a no-brainer: "We could be outdoors from 6 at night 'til 6 in the morning. To run around in a jumpsuit when its 30 degrees out and try to look like you're comfortable, that alone could get me an Oscar. Between takes we'd be literally shaking and they'd yell Action! And we'd just be cool, calm, and collected and as soon as the take was finished they would run on with cloaks or robes 'cause it was bitter outside. We've always been good at torturing ourselves" (Grooves). In recent years Paul expanded on the whole film situation: "Accomplishing something that's out of the norm for most bands is always a feather in your cap. But that film was an abomination of what was sold to us – we were told we were going to make 'A Hard Day's Night' meets 'Star Wars.' There were so many elements against us. We had no concept of what acting entailed, and by that time the band weren't on speaking terms any more. People wouldn't show up or would show up and leave. The entire band didn't know their lines and were being fed them off camera. It was certainly the beginning of things going awry" (Classic Rock Magazine, 11/01).

On May 19 KISS played a concert for around 8,000 fans (mainly local radio contest winners) at Magic Mountain to provide the live concert sequences for the film. "Hotter Than Hell" was not performed at the show, even though it was transformed into the evil-KISS song, "Rip & Destroy," designed to drive the audience to destroy the park. Paul took fifteen minutes in his trailer on the movie set to rewrite the lyrics to "Hotter Than Hell" (Sharp, Ken – Goldmine). Paul has also recounted the use of doubles during the concert scenes: "We had to play a fake concert at Magic Mountain amusement park for another scene. When we were onstage, I turned around and saw some random old man in cat makeup and a wig playing the drums and chewing gum. Peter had taken off, and they threw this guy up there" (Face The Music). Perhaps he shouldn't have been particularly surprised since Ace's absence for certain scenes had to be rectified by the use of his African-American stunt double who really looked nothing like him! Ace recalled, "My double was a black man. [He Was] a terrific guy. Hell of a stunt double, too, but he didn't look anything like me facially, and even with all the makeup on it was painfully obvious. I mean, you can see it clearly if you watch the movie" (No Regrets).

The band had originally intended to include new material in the movie, but didn't having the time, or perhaps inclination, to write or record anything for it while struggling to complete their solo albums and have a break from one another. With the condition that the band was in at the time there was little choice but to take the easy road. One chorus, one verse, both would be repeated *ad nauseum*. The verse: "It's time for everyone to listen good / We've taken all we can stand / You've got the power to rip down these walls / It's in the palm of your hand." The chorus: "Rip, rip, rip and destroy / You know the hour's getting late / Rip, rip, rip and destroy / Break it down and seal your fate (whoa)." The only other "new" music in the movie would be the live version of "I Stole Your Love." This concert was KISS' last live show for over a year, until the "Return of KISS" tour kicked off the following June.

While Paul was embarrassed about the movie, Gene saw the whole project as a learning experience and his first step into Hollywood proper. Some who have seen his body of work since 1978 might disagree that he actually learned much from the experience. According to Gene, "In retrospect it was like looking at my childhood pictures — what was once embarrassing is now kinda cute. Other bands may look at the 'Phantom' and say it was awful, but what was the last movie they made" (Classic Rock Magazine, 11/01)? At the time he sang a similar line, "KISS in front of a camera... just one of our m any faces. We're playing out a story. We never took an acting lesson. It's a science fiction fantasy, a genuinely fine film, like Disney for the whole family... When we do anything it's as a band. We're going down in history like Elvis and the Beatles" (Bluefield Daily Telegraph, 10/22/78). Though in promoting product it's understandable that he wouldn't be critical or self-loathing.

During August 1978 the second Marvel Comic went on sale while members finalized their solo albums. "KISS Meets the Phantom of the Park" premiered on US television channel NBC's "Saturday Night at the Movies" on October 28 with masses of viewers. The movie purportedly did very well in the TV ratings despite its failure as a serious theatrical project. That only the TV adaptation of James Clavel's "Shōgun" did better is another KISS urban legend — it wasn't broadcast until 1980! The scheduling of the film for TV rather than at the cinemas was a result of KISS' plan to do a proper full-length theatrical release (with soundtrack) the following year, depending on the reception the initial project received. Musically, the original TV version included a mix of 70's porn-esque incidental music with parts of several KISS songs including "Christine Sixteen," "Shock Me," "Black Diamond," and "God of Thunder." Also used (in both versions) was a bit of award-winning barbershop quartet Golden Staters' "It Must Be That Look In Her Eye." Paul explained the plan, "By doing a 'Movie of the Week' we get such a huge and varied audience that when we do our film for the theater (next year, folks) we're pretty well insured of those same people coming to see us. If a 15-year-old or a 20-year-old is watching it, chances are his parents are gonna walk in and see it. And once they see how much fun it is and that it's really not anything to look down upon, really just entertainment, they'll probably come to see the film in the theaters. The idea of appealing to my grandmother and my sister is very appealing to me. Some people think, well, 'who wants to be commercial?' We do! To me, there was never any glamour in being a starving artist" (Grooves).

close up

MOVIE
8:00 4 20 22 30

KISS MEETS THE PHANTOM

Anthony Zerbe and KISS (Gene Simmons, Peter Criss, Paul Stanley and Ace Frehley)

A musical adventure starring the rock group KISS.

The four KISSes are known for their garish get-ups, outlandish theatrics and rather unflattering makeup, which doesn't come off in this 1978 TV-movie. The story is set at a financially floundering amusement park, where the four have been hired to boost the take. But their chores don't stop at performing.

A mechanical wizard named Abner Devereaux (Anthony Zerbe), the brains behind the rides and attractions, has been fired by the park owner, and now he wants to get back—at KISS. The result: a battle between good and evil pitting the quartet against Abner's army of robots.

KISS performs "Rock & Roll All Night," "Love Gun" and "Black Diamond." KISS: Gene Simmons (bass), Paul Stanley and Ace Frehley (guitars), Peter Criss (drums).

Other Cast . . . Melissa: Deborah Ryan. Sam: Terry Lester. Calvin: Carmine Caridi. Chopper: John Dennis Johnston. (2 hrs.)

In another Grooves interview, Gene expanded on this plan, "Our first feature movie... is going to start in February, and so far it's up to $8 million. So I think in the next couple of years people are going to see the kind of movies that they always thought should exist... I think it's going to be in the same kind of league as 'Superman' and 'Star Wars,' that kind of taste. But I think it's going to be on a huge scale. You're going to be talking about millions upon millions of people going to see these movies. And more importantly, I don't think they're going to be the kind of movies that are going to make you believe they have anything to say other than enjoy the movie. Not try to tell you something about life, because that's the most boring thing." However, those plans fell through, and "Phantom" was distributed theatrically to some markets the following year. There would also be plenty of repeats on late-night television throughout the 1980s. It wasn't the only television role considered for the band: "In 1978, KISS was the first band offered the role of FVB (Future Villain Band) in the movie 'Sgt. Pepper's Lonely Hearts Club Band' that starred Peter Frampton and the Bee Gees. KISS turned down the role in fear of hurting their 'super hero' image, and it was then given to Aerosmith" (Lynn's KISS Dominion Facts). The role hardly did that band any favors either and it is probably just as well that KISS passed on it. It is ironic that this Robert Stigwood film was panned as badly, if not more, than the KISS film; though going for a full cinema release made it a more damaging situation for those involved — KISS had been fortunate to avoid on their own project!

During 1979 a re-edited and modified version of the movie was released internationally, AVCO/Embassy Pictures, as "Attack of the Phantoms." Using some alternate footage, and differing sequences in part, the most striking difference was the replacement of much of the incidental music with additional songs, notably songs from the member's solo albums ("Hold Me, Touch Me," "Fractured Mirror," "Easy Thing," "Radioactive," "New York Groove" and "Love In Chains," among others). These give the movie scenes a different feel from the original even if the choice of song used in certain scenes is questionable: For example, the samurai fight scene is backed with Peter's " That's The Kind of Sugar Papa Likes," utterly mind-boggling. A good example of the changes between the two versions can be found at the beginning of the movie, which in "Attack" starts with the rollercoaster sequence with Sam and Melissa, followed by the opening credits, and then further rollercoaster footage and transitional ride footage including the out-of-control ride scene. Some of the changes in these scene sequences cut out key parts of the plot for non-U.S. viewers (the ride going haywire contributes to Abner's firing). Another obvious difference is present at the end of the film when Sam is rescued by Paul simply pulling off the mind-control diode with his fingers. In "Attack" he destroys it by zapping it with his eye laser. Many parts of the plot are simply not explained in either version of the movie: In "Phantom," when did Snede become a zombie, for instance (the scene with the Revolutionary War soldiers gassing the security guards is missing) and the "Monorail" scene that helps explain the park, and Abner, is missing. In "Attack" the talismen are never explained, the dialogue about protecting their power is missing (it's inexplicable that Sam is searching for them before their purpose is explained), and the great "insufficient data Star Child dialogue" sequence is omitted. But in both versions what on earth happens to Devereaux at the end? "Attack of the Phantoms," as issued on "Kissology, Volume 2" in 2007 is 9 minutes shorter than the video version of "KISS Meets the Phantom of the Park." As a result both versions exhibit unique overall character.

When reissued as part of "Kissology" actors Carmine Caridi, Deborah Ryan and Don Lewis (a classical mime who played various robots) provided a commentary track for the movie. Hanna-Barbera had signed a long-term distribution agreement with Worldvision Enterprises, Inc., which resulted in the domestic and foreign rights being transferred to the company. This deal also resulted in the TV movie being released on VHS from 1985 in numerous markets including the U.S., Europe, and Japan. An unofficial pressed DVD of the TV broadcast, through Cheezy Flicks, was issued October 25, 2005 and rapidly sold out, prior to a purported Cease & Desist being issued against the company and remaining copies being pulled from distribution. As a result it has become something of a collectible despite its low quality. While campy and typical of 1978 the movie has become something of a cult favorite in the years since it first aired. As a first foray into acting for untrained participants it was never going to be high art, but for many of those involved, and those viewing, it was fun. The approach of the four members to the project is somewhat typical. Paul took a very theatrical approach while Gene delved into his horror background. Ace and Peter certainly can't be seen as being any worse or better, given what their contributions were limited to. Of those involved, Carmine Caridi garnered the greatest press in later years (2004) becoming the first member of the Academy of Motion Picture Arts and Sciences to be expelled from the body under its then new anti-piracy policy. He had allegedly provided copies of Oscar screener DVDs to an alleged pirater, Russell Sprague, who died in jail the following year.

Main characters (in order of appearance):

Snede - John Chappell
Calvin Richards - Carmine Caridi
Guard 1 - Richard Hein
Guard 2 - Brion James

Canyon High School Band

Melissa - Deborah Ryan
Sam Farrell - Terry Lester

Chopper - John Dennis Johnston
Dirty Dee - Lisa Jane Persky
Slime - John Lisbon Wood

Abner Devereaux - Anthony Zerbe

KISS Soldier - Marc Winters
Man in KISS Booth - Bill Hudson
Don Steele - himself

Peter Criss - Cat Man
Paul Stanley - Star Child
Gene Simmons - The Demon
Ace Frehley - Space Ace

Girl atop Human Pyramid - Mary Kay Morse
Robots (Gorilla and others) - Don Lewis
Robots (Chamber of Thrills axe-man and others) - Richmond Shepherd
Robots (Samurai and others - Peter Kwong
Robots - Jan Sturridge

Chamber of Thrills father - Leon Delaney
Chamber of Thrills mother - Sandra Pann

KISS Continuity

This continuity sheet is built from an original production notes on the timings used for the TV broadcast of the movie. Added in are the time-markers from the Cheezy Flicks DVD version. "dial" simply refers to "dialogue."

		Setting	Scene	Time	Cheezy DVD
R-1	EXT	MAIN TITLE	"Rock And Roll All Nite" with intro credits	2:16	2:42
		PARK	Band - Crowd Calvin dial. to Snede	1:16	4:14
			Roller Coaster Sequence	0:51	5:17
			Sam - Melissa exit - Lowriders in		6:05
			Abner and Lowriders dial - Calvin & Abner dial.	2:27	6:54
	INT	LAB	Sam disappears	0:58	7:47
R-2	EXT	PARK	Rides	0:17	8:22
			Melissa at refreshment stand - boys - Melissa exit	0:33	8:48
			Melissa Souvenir - Wrong Sam	0:24	9:23
			Abner & Calvin dial. - sign in air - Abner exits	1:10	9:52
			Gorilla sequence	1:27	11:02
			Don Steele - KISS Look-A-Like - Pan to Melissa & Snede dial	1:13	12:26
			Ride out of control sequence	1:08	13:32
			Transitional rides	0:14	14:42
			Melissa to Abner's tower - dial. - Enter elevator	1:11	15:02

1ST COMMERCIAL

R-3	INT	LAB	Melissa & Abner - Barber shop Quartet - Melissa exit - Abner to Sam	3:55	15:56
	INT	CHAMBER OF THRILLS	Lowrider sequence	5:50	19:45
R-4	EXT	PARK	Calvin to Abner's tower - both exit	0:14	25:07
			Calvin fires Abner	2:43	26:07
			Abner walking - going crazy	0:36	27:42
			Dusk - crowd gathering	0:29	28:47
	INT	LAB-NITE	Abner viewing monitor - "I will destroy you"	0:33	29:13
	EXT	PARK-NITE	KISS arrival	1:01	29:45
	EXT	PARK-NITE	1st concert "Shout It Out Loud"	2:11	30:54
	INT	LAB-NITE	Abner - mechanical man - to restored Lowriders	1:24	33:23

2ND COMMERCIAL

R-5	EXT	PARK-NITE	Instrumental concert - Stage up	1:44	34:41
	INT	LAB-NITE	Abner - "Start shooting now"	0:36	36:55
	EXT	PARK-NITE	KISS backstage - acknowledge crowd - Sam takes pictures - Melissa in, gets zapped - dial. with KISS	2:13	37:21
	INT	LAB-NITE	Abner with KISS pictures	0:24	38:50
	EXT	PARK-NITE	Guards walking - rides start - demon fight	2:23	39:16

3RD COMMERCIAL

R-6	EXT	MANSION DAY	Calvin & guards exit to pool	0:40	41:38
	EXT	POOL	Pool sequence	0:28	42:25

	INT	LAB	Melissa in - dial. with Abner	0:40	42:57
	EXT	POOL	Continuation of sequence - Gene in	3:30	43:39
			Melissa in - dial.	0:21	47:00
	INT	MANSION	KISS & Melissa dial. about talismen	0:51	47:21
	INT	LAB	Abner with fake Gene	0:58	48:28
R-7	EXT	PARK-NITE	Concert - "I Stole Your Love"	3:07	49:03

4TH COMMERCIAL

R-7	INT	LAB	Abner - sprays ape head		52:38
	INT	MANSION	Sam in - looks for talismen	1:16	52:49
	EXT	MANSION	KISS sings "Beth" - Melissa exits group	1:54	53:35
	INT	MANSION	Sam finds talismen - sparks	1:00	54:54
	EXT	MANSION	KISS reacts - Sam exits - confrontation with Melissa - KISS to Melissa	1:52	55:51
R-8	INT	MANSION	KISS & Melissa in - dial. around talismen box	0:50	57:44
	INT	LAB	Abner "Come ahead KISS"	0:11	58:42
	EXT	PARK	KISS over fence - lured through colossus - ape fight	4:42	58:53
	INT	LAB	Abner "Let the dance begin"	0:27	1:03:48
R-9	EXT	PARK	KISS walking - ride starts with no people - KISS exit	0:44	1:04:10
	EXT	PARK	Samurai fight	2:48	1:04:48
	INT	LAB	Abner shows Sam gun "Get talismen"	1:06	1:07:43

5TH COMMERCIAL

R-9	INT	MANSION	Sam shoots talismen	0:54	1:08:48
	EXT	PARK	Merry-go-round sequence	0:53	1:09:37

R-10	EXT	PARK	KISS spots Sam - Sam exits across bridge - KISS follow	1:38	1:10:44
	INT	LAB	Abner views KISS on monitor	0:12	1:11:19
	INT	CHAMBER OF THRILLS	KISS fight - captured	6:31	1:11:31
R-11	EXT	PARK	Crowds at concert - backstage - Melissa dial. with Calvin as guards pull her back - Calvin reacts to crowd "KISS, where are you"	0:43	1:17:37
	INT	LAB	KISS in jail - Abner in dial. Abner exits	1:56	1:18:24
	EXT	PARK	Crowd at concert - backstage - fake KISS exit trailer - Melissa spots fake KISS - Melissa see's Snede transformed - concert crowd	1:16	1:20:17
	EXT	PARK	Concert - "Rip & Destroy"		1:21:39
	INT	LAB	KISS in jail - reacts to "Rip & Destroy" - concentrates on talismen box	2:07	1:23:17

6TH COMMERCIAL

R-11	EXT	PARK	Concert "Rip & Destroy" continued		1:23:49
	INT	LAB	KISS concentrating on talismen		1:25:47
	EXT	PARK	Concert continued		1:25:57
	INT	LAB	KISS still concentrating - talismen into jail - KISS opens box	2:37	1:26:07
R-12	EXT	PARK	"Rip & Destroy" continued - KISS fly - in - KISS fights fake KISS	2:00	1:26:37
	EXT	PARK	Paul dial. to crowd - concert "Rock And Roll All Nite"	2:52	1:28:55

7TH COMMERCIAL

R-12	INT	LAB	Melissa dial. to Abner "Give him back to me" KISS enter - Calvin dial. about Abner -	1:43	1:31:55

			C.U. Abner's face		
			End credit concert "God of Thunder" and logo	1:46	1:32:50
					1:34:32

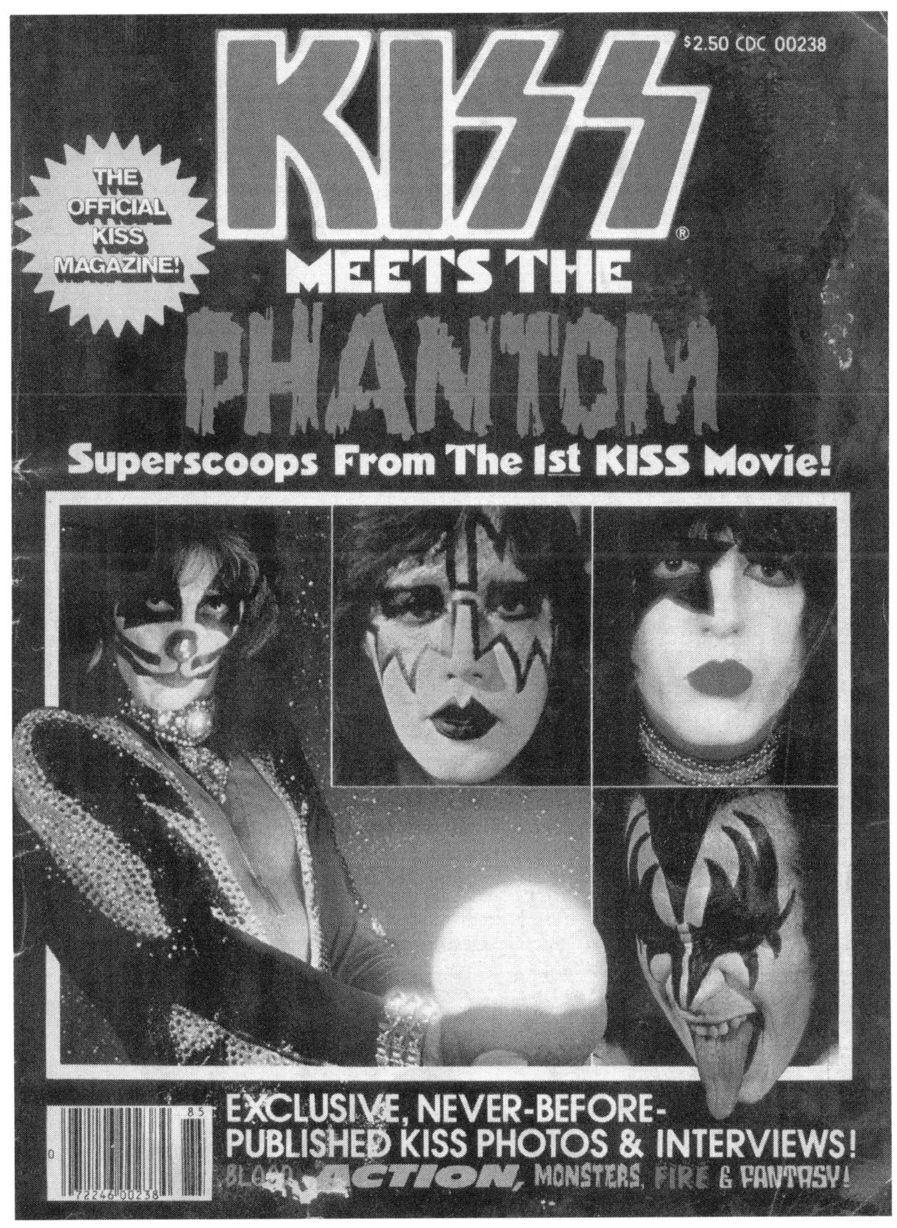

"KISS Meets the Phantom" versus "Attack of the Phantoms"

Built off the KISS Continuity sequence above, this is a side comparison between the two main versions of the movie. A further edited version of the TV movie was broadcast, mainly on late night TV in the U.S. during the 1980s, though the deletions aren't really worth cataloging.

Scene (Phantom)	Scene (Attack)
Spinning "Rock And Roll Over" movie title	Roller Coaster Sequence
"Rock And Roll All Nite" with intro credits	"Rock And Roll All Nite" with intro credits
Marching band	Roller Coaster Sequence
KISS in concert announcement scene	KISS in concert announcement scene
Crowd Calvin dial. to Snead	Transitional rides
Roller Coaster Sequence	Ride out of control sequence
Marching band	Rides (blue boat down the right water slide)
Sam & Melissa exit ride	Crowd Calvin dial. to Snead (additional dial. At human pyramid)
Sam - Melissa exit - Lowriders in	Marching band
Calvin and Snede dial. - "you and your boys are going to start earning your badges"	Sam & Melissa exit ride
"Come and see the fireworks"	"Uh-oh, there's Mr. Devereaux (Not in Phantom)
Human pyramid - Abner and Lowriders dial. - Calvin & Abner dial. "What's so important"	Sam - Melissa exit - Lowriders in (the lowriders cutting line scene is omitted)
Samurai automatons	Abner and Lowriders dial. - Calvin & Abner dial.
Sam disappears (shorter sequence looking on wall, and screams)	Monorail scene (not present in Phantom)

Rides (red boat down left water slide)

Melissa at refreshment stand - boys staring - Melissa exit

Melissa Souvenir - Wrong Sam

Astronaut automaton

Abner & Calvin dial - sign in air - Abner exits

Astronaut automaton

Gorilla automaton sequence

Free passes to Chamber of Thrills

Don Steele - KISS Look-A-Like - Pan to Melissa & Snede dial

"I thought we had another disappearance on our hands"

Ride out of control sequence - Lowriders flee ride engine room (missing from Attack)

Transitional rides

Melissa to Abner's tower - dial - Enter elevator

Melissa & Abner - Barber shop Quartet - Melissa exit - Abner to Sam

Lowrider sequence

Calvin to Abner's tower - both exit

Where are KISS signing autographs? - "Major breakthrough" - sign in air

Gorilla automaton sequence

Sam disappears (longer sequence, but no scream)

Melissa at refreshment stand - boys staring - Melissa exit

Don Steele - KISS Look-A-Like - Pan to Melissa & Snede dial.

Melissa Souvenir - Wrong Sam

Melissa to Abner's tower - dial - Enter elevator

Melissa & Abner - Barber shop Quartet - Melissa exit ("I'll send you up more slowly, my dear" - Abner to Sam

Chamber of Thrills sequence - Chopper and Slime's trip down the slide are cut

Calvin to Abner's tower - both exit

Abner & Calvin dial - Abner exits

Calvin fires Abner

Abner walking - going crazy

Dusk - crowd gathering

Abner viewing monitor - "I will destroy you"

KISS arrival

Calvin fires Abner	1st concert "Black Diamond" ending (shorter than Phantom)
Abner walking - going crazy	2nd concert "Shout It Out Loud"
Dusk - crowd gathering	Abner - mechanical man - to restored Lowriders
Abner viewing monitor - "I will destroy you"	Instrumental concert - Stage up
KISS arrival	Abner - "Start shooting now"
1st concert "Shout It Out Loud"	KISS backstage - acknowledge crowd - Sam takes pictures - Melissa in, gets zapped - dial. with KISS
Abner - mechanical man - to restored Lowriders	Park closing scene (not in Phantom) - Melissa sees Sam's VW bug
Instrumental concert - Stage up	Abner gives Melissa security badge
Abner - "Start shooting now"	Sam brings Abner pictures (not in Phantom) - Abner with KISS photos (shortened)
KISS backstage - acknowledge crowd - Sam takes pictures - Melissa in, gets zapped - dial with KISS	KISS sings "Beth" - Melissa exits group
Abner with KISS pictures	Sam in - looks for talismen (earlier than Phantom, before what talismen are is explained)
Guards walking - rides start - demon fight	Sam finds talismen - sparks
Calvin & guards exit to pool	KISS reacts - Sam exits - confrontation with Melissa - KISS to Melissa
Pool sequence	Melissa in - Dial
Melissa in - dial with Abner	KISS & Melissa dial about talismen (no "Beethoven's Fifth quip)
Continuation of sequence - Gene in	Continuation of sequence - Gene in
Melissa in - Dial	Abner with fake Gene

KISS & Melissa dial about talismen

Abner with fake Gene

Concert - "I Stole Your Love"

Abner - sprays ape head

Sam in - looks for talismen

KISS sings "Beth" - Melissa exits group

Sam finds talismen - sparks

KISS reacts - Sam exits - confrontation with Melissa - KISS to Melissa

KISS & Melissa in dial around talismen box

Abner "Come ahead KISS"

KISS over fence - lured through colossus - ape fight

Abner "Let the dance begin"

KISS walking - rides starts with no people - KISS exit

Samurai fight

Abner shows Sam gun "Get talismen"

Sam shoots talismen

Merry-go-round sequence

KISS spots Sam - Sam exits across bridge - KISS follow

Guards walking - rides start - demon fight

Calvin & guards exit to pool

Pool sequence (shortened) - No Melissa at end. No "insufficient data Star Child dialogue! No Melissa asking for help finding Sam!

Concert - "I Stole Your Love"

Abner shows Sam gun "Get talismen"

Concert - "I Stole Your Love"

Sam shoots talismen

Abner - sprays ape head

Security guards immobilized by Revolutionary War soldiers (not in Phantom)

It all adds up to Devereaux

Abner "Let the dance begin"

KISS walking - Merry-go-round sequence

Rides starts with no people - KISS exit

KISS over fence (no jump sequence) - lured through colossus

Abner "Come ahead KISS"

Ape fight - No "Ack! Ack!" from Space Ace

Samurai fight

KISS spots Sam (Ace's "Rocket Ride" removed) - Sam exits across bridge - KISS follow

Abner views KISS on monitor	Abner views KISS on monitor
KISS fight – captured	KISS fight - captured
Crowds at concert - backstage - Melissa dial. with Calvin as guards pull her back - Calvin reacts to crowd "KISS, where are you"	Crowds at concert - backstage - Melissa dial. with Calvin as guards pull her back - Calvin reacts to crowd "KISS, where are you"
KISS in jail - Abner in dial. Abner exits	KISS in jail - Abner in dial. Abner exits
Crowd at concert - backstage - fake KISS exit trailer - Melissa spots fake KISS - Melissa see's Snede transformed - concert crowd	Crowd at concert - backstage - fake KISS exit trailer - Melissa spots fake KISS - Melissa sees Snead transformed (Missing) - concert crowd
Concert - "Rip & Destroy"	Concert - "Rip & Destroy"
KISS in jail - reacts to "Rip & Destroy" - concentrates on talismen box	KISS in jail - reacts to "Rip & Destroy" - concentrates on talismen box
Concert "Rip & Destroy" continued	Concert "Rip & Destroy" continued
KISS concentrating on talismen	KISS concentrating on talismen
Concert continued	Concert continued
KISS still concentrating - talismen into jail - KISS opens box	KISS still concentrating - talismen into jail - KISS opens box
"Rip & Destroy" continued - KISS fly - in - KISS fights fake KISS	"Rip & Destroy" continued - KISS fly - in - KISS fights fake KISS
Paul dial. to crowd - concert "Rock And Roll All Nite"	Paul dial. to crowd - concert "Rock And Roll All Nite"
Melissa dial. to Abner "Give him back to me" KISS enter - Paul removes Sam's diode with hand - Calvin dial. about Abner - C.U. Abner's face	Melissa dial. to Abner "Give him back to me" KISS enter - Paul zaps Sam's diode - Calvin dial. about Abner - C.U. Abner's face
End credit concert "God of Thunder" and logo	End credit "Mr. Make Believe" with scene montage
1:34:32	**1:25:51**

KISS on the Cards

What merchandise represents KISS '78 for you? A look at one of the core KISS collectibles of 1978 — the Donruss bubble gum trading cards!

Providing a keystone to many a fan's youth in the late-1970s, trading cards of many types provided school lunchtime trading entertainment and a challenge to empty one's pockets of any remaining money in search of an elusive card (and for some causing a lifetime affliction). During 1978 the marketing of KISS' image became a blitz, with radios, AM radios, lunch boxes and many more products being manufactured emblazoned with the band's image and logo. One of the iconic KISS collectibles from the solo era, if not the whole of the "originals" era, was the release of the Donruss bubble gum card sets. Two KISS series were issued starting in the summer of 1978 culminating in a third issued only in Australia in 1980 (a reissue of series 1 with 19 changed cards that essentially replaced the images of Peter or the band with new photos of Eric Carr). The second series coincided with promotion for the "KISS Meets the Phantom of the Park" television movie. According to Ron Boutwell, "There was an article that came out in 1978, which said KISS had generated over $111 million in the retail sale of KISS merchandise in 1978 alone. Probably the most popular item that people bought was the Donruss chewing gum cards. We got incredible royalties on that" (Sharp, Ken - Behind the Mask). The cards were essentially a cash cow.

The partnership came at a time when the bubble gum industry was doubling its market, generating approximately $300 million in 1978 alone! Quality, however, was not of tantamount importance to these products. Card stock was spongy and many cards are miss-cut or off-center. With so many having been handled by younger fans, a premium can be expected for those seeking excellent quality graded examples. Quality can be noted on the back of the cards that comprise the series 1 image - a crop of the band posed on the cubes is reversed! Questionable, though not necessarily related to quality, is the duplication of images between the two series, exceeding 10%! For series 2 there is also duplication within the set with cards #75 & 79 and #84 & 86 featuring the same image in differing orientation (vertical versus horizontal)! Cards #119 and 121 are very similar, as are the "stage bow" shots comprising cards #7, 51, and 107. Yet for what they were, essentially cheap disposable product, the photos covered the band with what were then reasonably current images. The majority of cards from either set primarily featured photos from the "Love Gun/Alive II" era — either with the band/members in posed or live concert settings. The few exceptions include a blurred shot of the band live on stage from the "Alive" era (#115) or the individual band members in their "Destroyer/Rock And Roll Over" costumes (#5, 13, 49, 124, 126 and 131).

In early 1979 Donruss issued a 66 card "Rock Stars" set that included a 14 card subset of KISS cards along with artists such as Queen, the Babys and the Village People. That set is of less interest to the original two KISS-centric collections which were distributed in cases of 16 boxes each containing 36 packs (or 576 packs per case). The packs were somewhat more variable, containing 6 – 8 cards and the obligatory stick of gum. Interestingly, an auction of a case of each series sold for $3,939 in April 2002, even with some moisture damage! At .15c the card packs were easy targets for the youth demographic.

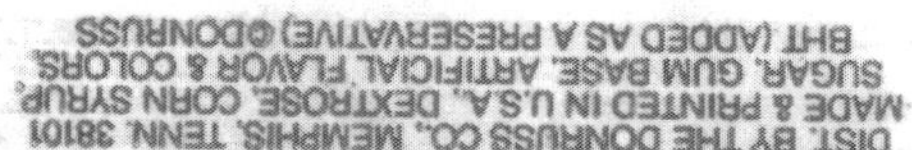

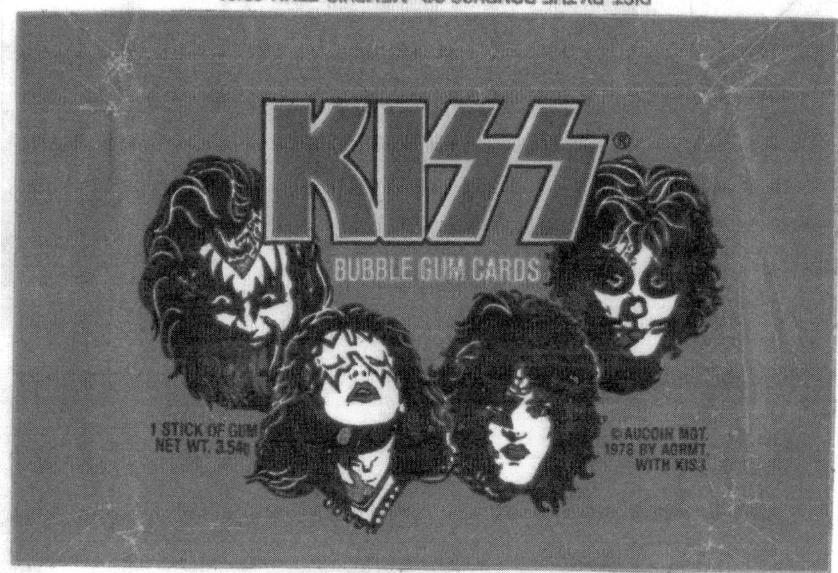

(Series 1 wrapper)

Donruss Series I

Card	Description
1	Paul with Iceman on "Love Gun/Alive II" stage
2	Peter Criss behind drum kit
3	Peter Criss close-up
4	Gene Simmons on stage
5	Ace Frehley "smokin' guitar" close-up
6	Paul Stanley "cubes" photo shoot
7	Band "Love Gun/Alive II" stage, taking bow
8	Gene Simmons stalks the stage
9	Ace Frehley with other band members in background
10	Paul Stanley on cherry-picker
11	Gene Simmons "shimmering tie-die" background photo shoot
12	Gene Simmons with Sam the Serpent in background
13	Peter Criss sings "Beth"
14	Paul Stanley under spotlight
15	Ace Frehley on knees, Gene, Paul and Peter full flight live
16	Paul Stanley close-up raising arm
17	Peter Criss behind drum kit close-up
18	Ace Frehley on stage
19	Ace Frehley under blue light strikes classic pose
20	Ace Frehley "shimmering tie-die" background photo shoot
21	Ace Frehley gyrates on stage
22	Ace Frehley under spotlight
23	Gene Simmons pumps fist, oooh-yeah!
24	Paul Stanley and Ace Frehley on "Love Gun/Alive II" stage
25	Peter Criss points drum-sticks
26	Bloody Gene Simmons points at audience
27	Gene Simmons sings
28	Paul Stanley hails audience
29	Gene Simmons, Paul Stanley, Ace Frehley looking down
30	Paul Stanley on "Love Gun/Alive II" stage with white garter
31	Paul Stanley on "Love Gun/Alive II" stage stairs
32	Gene Simmons with mini coffin
33	Peter Criss plays drums
34	Paul Stanley pouts
35	Paul Stanley wrings guitar neck

36 Peter Criss behind drums under red light
37 Ace Frehley and Paul Stanley live on "Love Gun/Alive II" stage
38 Gene Simmons and Paul Stanley live on "Love Gun/Alive II" stage
39 Peter Criss behind drums
40 Gene Simmons with leg on stage monitor
41 Gene Simmons growls and Paul Stanley pouts on stage
42 Gene Simmons breathes fire
43 Gene Simmons on stage
44 Band "Love Gun/Alive II" stage, taking bow
45 Paul Stanley on cherry-picker
46 Gene, Ace, and Paul frontline choreography
47 Gene Simmons on stage
48 Gene Simmons on stage
49 Paul Stanley with flying-V
50 Gene Simmons on stage
51 Band "Love Gun/Alive II" stage, taking bow
52 Paul Stanley close-up
53 Gene Simmons obscured by smoke
54 Paul Stanley studio photo shoot holding rose
55 Ace Frehley "Alive II" album cover out-take
56 Peter Criss behind drums with sparks flying
57 Peter Criss behind drums side view
58 Gene, Ace, and Paul frontline choreography ("Star Trax" cover)
59 Peter Criss pensive close-up
60 Paul Stanley humps guitar
61 Peter Criss behind drums side view
62 Larger Than Life Gene Simmons on "Alive II/Love Gun" stage
63 Ace Frehley and his guitar
64 Ace Frehley at work on stage
65 Ace Frehley and his guitar
66 Band "Love Gun/Alive II" stage

Donruss Series 2

Card	Description
67	Gene Simmons with leg on stage monitor and serpent in background
68	Gene Simmons bloody face
69	Paul Stanley receives adulation
70	Gene Simmons with leg on stage monitor besides serpent
71	Gene Simmons sings
72	Gene Simmons in concert
73	Paul Stanley pouts in concert
74	Paul Stanley squats and thrusts his guitar
75	Gene Simmons and Ace Frehley live in concert (cropped version of #79)
76	Looking up at Paul Stanley with Ace in background
77	Gene Simmons bass solo under red light
78	Gene Simmons with tongue and eyes rolled back; and Ace
79	KISS "Love Gun/Alive II" live on stage
80	KISS "Love Gun/Alive II" live on stage
81	Peter Criss behind drums
82	Paul Stanley raises arm
83	KISS "Love Gun/Alive II" live on stage
84	Gene Simmons faces right
85	Peter Criss behind drums
86	Horizontal alignment of #84
87	Gene Simmons sings
88	Paul Stanley points to audience
89	Same as series 1 #19
90	Paul Stanley with flying V and arm raised
91	Peter Criss behind drums
92	Gene and Ace back-to-back
93	Paul Stanley in action (cropped version of #76)
94	KISS "Love Gun/Alive II" live on stage
95	KISS "Love Gun/Alive II" live on stage
96	Paul Stanley close-up
97	Peter Criss behind drums
98	Peter Criss behind drums
99	Same as series 1 #1
100	KISS "Love Gun/Alive II" live on stage
101	Paul Stanley and Ace Frehley at microphone

102	Same as series 1 #21
103	Peter Criss close-up
104	Paul Stanley thrusts his guitar
105	Same as series 1 #12
106	Same as series 1 #48
107	Same live stage bow sequence as series 1 #7 & 51
108	Paul Stanley and Ace Frehley at microphone
109	Same as series 1 #64
110	Peter Criss behind drums
111	Ace Frehley at work on stage
112	Ace Frehley with smoking guitar
113	Same as series 1 #33
114	Demonic looking Gene Simmons
115	KISS "Alive" era on stage
116	Same as series 1 #65
117	Alive II album gatefold picture
118	Paul Stanley jumps by stage stairs
119	Looking up at Gene Simmons
120	Ace Frehley sings
121	Gene Simmons deploys devil's horn sign
122	Similar picture to series 1 #61
123	Peter Criss with vertical strip vest
124	Peter Criss sings "Beth"
125	Close-up of Paul Stanley's face
126	Same as series 1 #49
127	Ace Frehley enveloped by smoke
128	Paul Stanley teases with cherry
129	Looking up at Paul Stanley
130	Peter Criss sings behind drums
131	"Destroyer" era Gene Simmons
132	Gene Simmons bass solo in full glory

Acknowledgements

Julian Gill would like to thank **Tim McPhate** for the dedication and passion that he brought to the KISSFAQ during his tenure as co-admin of the site, not only represented by the vast majority of this work, both the interviewing and transcribing! I also thank all of the people who welcomed the "Back In The Solo Album Groove" interview inquiries and so graciously gave their time: Russ Ballard, Richard T. Bear, Ben D. Bollinger, Steve Buslowe, David Edward Byrd, Peppy Castro, John Cavazos, Susan Collins, Anton Fig, Richie Fontana, Rob Freeman, Jeff Glixman, Diana Grasselli, Brendan Harkin, Larry Harris, Christopher K. Lendt, Mikel Japp, Neil Jason, Doug Katsaros, Carol Kaye, Eddie Kramer, Bob Kulick, Will Lee, Art Munson, Richie Ranno, Carol Ross-Durborow, Tom Saviano, Michele Slater, John Tropea, Eric Troyer, Mitch Weissman, Dennis Woloch. Special thanks to Paul Stanley, Gene Simmons, Ace Frehley, Peter Criss and the vast cast of individuals who worked on the 1978 KISS solo albums projects.

Certainly not least, I'd like to thank Nils Brekke Svensson for the creation of the incredible cover for this work.

And my family for their unwavering support for me and tolerance this affliction I suffer!

DIST. BY THE DONRUSS CO., MEMPHIS, TENN. 38101
MADE & PRINTED IN U.S.A., DEXTROSE, CORN SYRUP,
SUGAR, GUM BASE, ARTIFICIAL FLAVOR & COLORS,
BHT (ADDED AS A PRESERVATIVE) ©DONRUSS

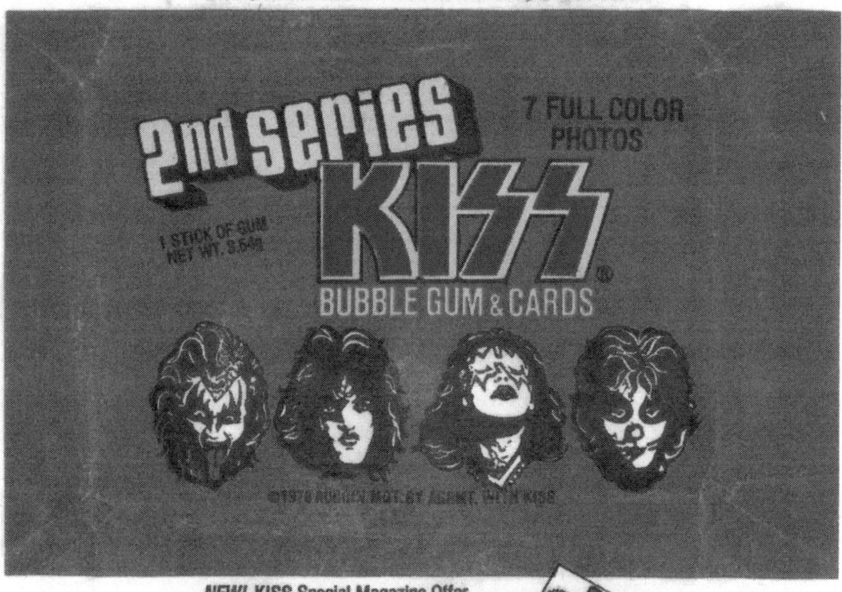

NEW! KISS Special Magazine Offer
"KISS MEETS THE PHANTOM OF THE PARK"
Only $1.00 (Regular Price $2.50)...send 5 KISS wrappers,
your name, address, city, state & zip and $1.00 plus 50¢
per order for handling to:
KISS MAGAZINE OFFER
7949 Deering Ave.
Canoga Park, Calif. 91304
California residents add 6% Sales Tax
KISS Army Fan Club information
7949 Deering Ave., Canoga Park, Calif. 91304

WATCH
NBC-TV
OCT. 28

14769809R00301

Printed in Great Britain
by Amazon.co.uk, Ltd.,
Marston Gate.